# PLAYFAIR
# CRICKET ANNUAL
# 1993

*All statist*

# PLAYFAIR CRICKET COMPETITION 1993
## TEST CRICKET QUIZ
### £1500 TO BE WON

#### PLUS NATWEST FINAL TICKETS AND HOSPITALITY
#### PLUS 25 CONSOLATION PRIZES

**First Prize**   £500 + overnight accommodation (B and B) at the Regents Park
Hilton Hotel (opposite Lord's) on 3 and 4 September +
TWO tickets to the 1993 NatWest Trophy Final + NatWest
hospitality

**Second Prize** £400 + TWO tickets to the 1993 NatWest Trophy Final

**Third Prize**   £300 + TWO tickets to the 1993 NatWest Trophy Final

**Fourth Prize** £200

**Fifth Prize**   £100

**Consolation prizes**

Senders of the next 25 correct entries will
each receive a copy of HITTING ACROSS
THE LINE by Viv Richards and published
by Headline at £14.95

**Closing date for entries
is 12.00 noon on 27 July 1993**

Winning entries will be drawn by the Man of the Match Adjudicator at one of the
NatWest semi-finals on Tuesday 10 August.

# PLAYFAIR CRICKET COMPETITION 1993

## ASHES TEST CRICKET QUIZ

### ENTRY FORM

## Please PRINT your answers in the spaces provided and answer every question.

1  Who, at The Oval in 1948, bowled Don Bradman for nought in his final innings in Tests? ..........

2  In which year did 27 wickets fall in a single day at an Ashes Test match? ..........

3  Who was the first England captain to regain and then successfully defend the Ashes? ..........

4  Which Australian Test cricketer changed his surname from Durtanovich? ..........

5  Who, at 50 years and 327 days, was the oldest Australian to appear in an Ashes Test? ..........

6  On which English ground was an Ashes Test completed in just six hours 34 minutes? ..........

7  Who, during an Ashes Test, became the first wicket-keeper to complete the Test 'double'? ..........

8  How many century opening partnerships did Hobbs and Sutcliffe share against Australia? ..........

9  Who, during an Ashes Test, became the first cricketer to appear in 100 Test matches? ..........

10  Which famous Australian fast bowler was known as 'Nugget'? ..........

Your name and address:

..........................................................................................

..........................................................................................

..........................................................................................

Your daytime telephone number: ..........................................

Post to: PLAYFAIR CRICKET COMPETITION, Special Events, Corporate Affairs Department, National Westminster Bank PLC, 1st Floor, 2 Broadgate, London EC2M 2AD.

Entries must be received before noon on 27 July 1993. All-correct entries will go into the prize-winning draw on 10 August and an announcement detailing all prize-winners will appear in the October edition of *The Cricketer* magazine. A list of winners is available on request by writing to Mrs B.J.Quinn at the above address and enclosing a stamped addressed envelope.

**Rules:** All entries must be on this official form. Proof of posting is not proof of entry. The decision of the editor regarding the answers to this quiz shall be final and binding; no correspondence may be entered into.

# 1992 PLAYFAIR CRICKET COMPETITION

## TEST CRICKET QUIZ ANSWERS

1. Who was the first batsman to score a hundred in each innings of a Test match? — **Warren BARDSLEY**
2. In which season did Bramall Lane stage a Test match? — **1902**
3. Who was the first wicket-keeper to make 200 dismissals in Test cricket? — **T.G. (Godfrey) EVANS**
4. Who first scored a hundred and took six wickets in an innings of the same Test? — **J.H. (Jimmy) SINCLAIR**
5. Who was knighted for his services to cricket in the 1992 New Year's Honours? — **M.C. (Colin) COWDREY**
6. Who was the first bowler to take 300 Test wickets? — **F.S. (Fred) TRUEMAN**
7. Against which country did South Africa last play a Test match? — **AUSTRALIA**
8. In which year did Dr W.G. Grace first play Test cricket? — **1880**
9. Who is the only man to captain England in his only Test match? — **C.A. (Aubrey) SMITH**
10. Who was the first cricketer to represent more than one country at Test level? — **W.E. (Billy) MIDWINTER**

There were 893 sets of correct answers out of a total of 1103 entries. The winners were drawn by Philip Sharpe (Yorkshire, Derbyshire and England) at the 1992 NatWest Trophy semi-final between Warwickshire and Northamptonshire at Edgbaston.

| | | |
|---|---|---|
| **First Prize:** | £500 + two nights accommodation + two tickets to include hospitality at the 1992 NatWest Trophy Final | I.McKIE (Wallasey) |
| **Second Prize:** | £400 + two tickets to the 1992 NatWest Trophy Final | S.BOWER (Melton Constable) |
| **Third Prize:** | £300 + two tickets to the 1992 NatWest Trophy Final | J.C.BLANSHARD (Clevedon) |
| **Fourth Prize:** | £200 | R.STARK (Sutton Coldfield) |
| **Fifth Prize:** | £100 | J.W.SMITH (Melton Constable) |

**25 Runners-up** each received a copy of *Jack in the Box* by Jack Bannister:

R.Appleby (Worcester)
I.P.Atkinson (Barnsley)
P.D.Bartlett (Bracknell)
D.P.Brewitt (Doncaster)
M.T.Davison (Keighley)
H.M.Draper (Reading)
Mrs S.P.Francis (Taynton)
A.D.Green (Solihull)
Ms B.Hazeldine (Northallerton)
J.T.Heslop (Leeds)
S.Higley (Bournemouth)
D.Kay (Cranfield)
M.G.Konstant (Bristol)
V.E.Lewis (Newton-le-Willows)
D.Millard (Sutton)
K.Morris (Dukinfield)
M.Porter (Swindon)
C.B.Pring (Bristol)
B.Redding (Putney, London)
D.W.Slater (Ramsbottom)
J.B.Smithson (Shipley)
D.Stephens (Wigan)
P.Stone (Bath)
T.L.Wiggett (Crayford)
M.Woolley (Barry)

# EDITORIAL PREFACE

Although an Australian summer is always special, the coming season must assume particular significance on several counts. Top of the agenda is the six-match battle for the Ashes and we bid Allan Border's new campaigners a warm welcome and look forward eagerly to a vintage Ashes series.

Inevitably, after their charges' humiliating 'spinwash' in India, the selections of the England committee will come under the closest scrutiny. While elementary foresight dictated that the omissions of Russell and Gower were monumental blunders, it was also regrettable that both the captain and cricket manager had experienced traumatic previous tours of India. Perhaps we should congratulate them on choosing a side which not only provided Indian cricket with a desperately needed boost but also diverted that nation's attention from potential civil war. From the carnage of a mission which highlighted England's technical and mental shortcomings, Hick, Lewis, Smith, Jarvis and Fairbrother will have returned as more confident and mature international cricketers and, hopefully, many lessons will have been painfully learned.

Alec Stewart's selection as the subject of our cover is intended as a tribute to a batsman who played a sequence of outstanding innings for England against New Zealand and Pakistan last year.

Almost as significant as the Ashes campaign will be the drastically revised domestic scene involving the much-debated four-day County Championship. Whatever its shortcomings, the new format should remove those banal third-day contrivances with gratis runs acquired against farcical bowling. Regrettably the chance to reduce the number of limited-overs thrashes by jettisoning the Sunday League has been missed. Instead it has been extended to 50 overs and will be paraded in coloured shell-suits of the most gaudy hue. Scarlet should have been the uniform colour as never has there been a clearer case of cricket prostitution.

The ICC's inane decision regarding the status of 'rebel' tours of South Africa so clearly flouts their own definition of a first-class match that it is likely to be ignored by the majority of statisticians and publications. As far as *Playfair* is concerned, Graham Gooch has already scored his hundredth first-class hundred.

Once again the compilation of *Playfair* has been greatly assisted by the county secretariats and scorers, by Tony Brown, Tim Lamb and Kate Jenkins of the TCCB, by John Jameson of MCC, and by David Armstrong of the MCCA. We are delighted to report that NatWest have extended their sponsorship of this annual to include the 1995 edition and thank Barbara Quinn and her Special Events team for their continuing support.

Headline, our new publishers, sensibly acquired Ian Marshall when they took over *Playfair* and his expertise has again seen the manuscript safely to publication via our conscientious typesetters, J&L Composition Ltd.

**BILL FRINDALL**
Urchfont

# WEST INDIES v SOUTH AFRICA
## (Only Test)

Played at Kensington Oval, Bridgetown, on 18, 19, 20, 22, 23 April 1992.
Toss: South Africa.  Result: WEST INDIES won by 52 runs.
Debuts: West Indies – J.C.Adams, K.C.G.Benjamin, D.Williams; South Africa
– All except K.C.Wessels.

### WEST INDIES

| | | | |
|---|---|---|---|
| D.L.Haynes c Wessels b Snell | 58 | c Richardson b Snell | 23 |
| P.V.Simmons c Kirsten b Snell | 35 | c Kirsten b Bosch | 3 |
| B.C.Lara c Richardson b Bosch | 17 | c Richardson b Donald | 64 |
| *R.B.Richardson c Richardson b Snell | 44 | lbw b Snell | 2 |
| K.L.T.Arthurton c Kuiper b Pringle | 59 | b Donald | 22 |
| J.C.Adams b Donald | 11 | not out | 79 |
| †D.Williams c Hudson b Donald | 1 | lbw b Snell | 5 |
| C.E.L.Ambrose not out | 6 | c Richardson b Donald | 6 |
| K.C.G.Benjamin b Snell | 1 | lbw b Donald | 7 |
| C.A.Walsh b Pringle | 6 | c Richardson b Snell | 13 |
| B.P.Patterson run out | 0 | b Bosch | 11 |
| Extras (LB7, NB17) | 24 | (B17, LB11, NB20) | 48 |
| **Total** | **262** | | **283** |

### SOUTH AFRICA

| | | | | |
|---|---|---|---|---|
| M.W.Rushmere c Lara b Ambrose | 3 | (2) | b Ambrose | 3 |
| A.C.Hudson b Benjamin | 163 | (1) | c Lara b Ambrose | 0 |
| *K.C.Wessels c Adams b Ambrose | 59 | | c Lara b Walsh | 74 |
| P.N.Kirsten c Lara b Benjamin | 11 | | b Walsh | 52 |
| W.J.Cronje c Lara b Adams | 5 | | c Williams b Ambrose | 2 |
| A.P.Kuiper c Williams b Patterson | 34 | | c Williams b Walsh | 0 |
| †D.J.Richardson c Ambrose b Adams | 8 | | c Williams b Ambrose | 2 |
| R.P.Snell run out | 6 | | c Adams b Walsh | 0 |
| M.W.Pringle c Walsh b Adams | 15 | | b Ambrose | 4 |
| A.A.Donald st Williams b Adams | 0 | (11) | b Ambrose | 0 |
| T.Bosch not out | 5 | (10) | not out | 0 |
| Extras (B4, LB6, W1, NB25) | 36 | | (B4, LB3, NB4) | 11 |
| **Total** | **345** | | | **148** |

| SOUTH AFRICA | O | M | R | W | O | M | R | W | FALL OF WICKETS | | | | |
|---|---|---|---|---|---|---|---|---|---|---|---|---|---|
| | | | | | | | | | | WI | SA | WI | SA |
| Donald | 20 | 1 | 67 | 2 | 25 | 3 | 77 | 4 | Wkt | 1st | 1st | 2nd | 2nd |
| Bosch | 15 | 2 | 43 | 1 | 24.3 | 7 | 61 | 2 | 1st | 99 | 14 | 10 | 0 |
| Pringle | 18.4 | 2 | 61 | 2 | 16 | 0 | 43 | 0 | 2nd | 106 | 139 | 66 | 27 |
| Snell | 18 | 3 | 84 | 4 | 16 | 1 | 74 | 4 | 3rd | 137 | 168 | 68 | 123 |
| **WEST INDIES** | | | | | | | | | 4th | 219 | 187 | 120 | 130 |
| Ambrose | 36 | 19 | 47 | 2 | 24.4 | 7 | 34 | 6 | 5th | 240 | 279 | 139 | 131 |
| Patterson | 23 | 4 | 79 | 1 | 7 | 1 | 26 | 0 | 6th | 241 | 293 | 164 | 142 |
| Walsh | 27 | 7 | 71 | 0 | 22 | 10 | 31 | 4 | 7th | 250 | 312 | 174 | 142 |
| Benjamin | 25 | 3 | 87 | 2 | 9 | 2 | 21 | 0 | 8th | 255 | 316 | 196 | 147 |
| Arthurton | 3 | 0 | 8 | 0 | | | | | 9th | 262 | 336 | 221 | 148 |
| Adams | 21.4 | 5 | 43 | 4 | 5 | 0 | 16 | 0 | 10th | 262 | 345 | 283 | 148 |
| Simmons | | | | | 5 | 1 | 13 | 0 | | | | | |

Umpires: D.M.Archer (28) and S.U.Bucknor (5).       Test No. 1188/1

# ENGLAND v PAKISTAN (1st Test)

**Played at Edgbaston, Birmingham, on 4‡, 5, 6, 7, 8 June 1992.**
**Toss: England.   Result: MATCH DRAWN.**
**Debuts: Pakistan – Aamir Sohail, Ata-ur-Rehman, Inzamam-ul-Haq.**     (‡ no play)

### PAKISTAN

| | |
|---|---|
| Aamir Sohail c Stewart b DeFreitas | 18 |
| Ramiz Raja lbw b DeFreitas | 47 |
| Asif Mujtaba c Russell b DeFreitas | 29 |
| *Javed Miandad not out | 153 |
| Salim Malik lbw b DeFreitas | 165 |
| Inzamam-ul-Haq not out | 8 |
| †Moin Khan | |
| Mushtaq Ahmed | |
| Waqar Younis ⎫ did not bat | |
| Aqib Javed | |
| Ata-ur-Rehman ⎭ | |
| Extras (B2, LB5, NB19) | 26 |
| | |
| **Total** (137 overs; 542 minutes) | 446-4 dec |

### ENGLAND

| | |
|---|---|
| *G.A.Gooch c Asif b Aqib | 8 |
| A.J.Stewart c Salim b Rehman | 190 |
| G.A.Hick c Miandad b Waqar | 51 |
| R.A.Smith lbw b Mushtaq | 127 |
| M.R.Ramprakash c Moin b Rehman | 0 |
| A.J.Lamb c Miandad b Rehman | 12 |
| C.C.Lewis b Mushtaq | 24 |
| †R.C.Russell not out | 29 |
| D.R.Pringle not out | 0 |
| I.T.Botham ⎫ did not bat | |
| P.A.J.DeFreitas ⎭ | |
| Extras (B5, LB5, W1, NB7) | 18 |
| | |
| **Total** (119 overs; 472 minutes) | 459-7 dec |

| ENGLAND | O | M | R | W |
|---|---|---|---|---|
| DeFreitas | 33 | 6 | 121 | 4 |
| Lewis | 33 | 3 | 116 | 0 |
| Pringle | 28 | 2 | 92 | 0 |
| Botham | 19 | 6 | 52 | 0 |
| Hick | 13 | 1 | 46 | 0 |
| Gooch | 10 | 5 | 9 | 0 |
| Ramprakash | 1 | 0 | 3 | 0 |

| PAKISTAN | O | M | R | W |
|---|---|---|---|---|
| Waqar | 24 | 2 | 96 | 1 |
| Aqib | 16 | 3 | 86 | 1 |
| Mushtaq | 50 | 8 | 156 | 2 |
| Rehman | 18 | 5 | 69 | 3 |
| Asif | 8 | 1 | 29 | 0 |
| Sohail | 2 | 0 | 8 | 0 |
| Salim | 1 | 0 | 5 | 0 |

### FALL OF WICKETS

| | P | E |
|---|---|---|
| Wkt | 1st | 1st |
| 1st | 33 | 28 |
| 2nd | 96 | 121 |
| 3rd | 110 | 348 |
| 4th | 432 | 348 |
| 5th | – | 378 |
| 6th | – | 415 |
| 7th | – | 446 |
| 8th | – | – |
| 9th | – | – |
| 10th | – | – |

**Umpires: M.J.Kitchen (4) and B.J.Meyer (24).**          Test No. 1189/48

# ENGLAND v PAKISTAN (2nd Test)

Played at Lord's, London, on 18, 19, 20, 21 June 1992.
Toss: England.   Result: PAKISTAN won by 2 wickets.
Debuts: England – I.D.K.Salisbury.

‡ (Malcolm/Russell/Lewis)

## ENGLAND

| | | | | |
|---|---|---|---|---|
| *G.A.Gooch b Wasim | 69 | lbw b Aqib | | 13 |
| A.J.Stewart c Miandad b Asif | 74 | not out | | 69 |
| G.A.Hick c Miandad b Waqar | 13 | (4) c Moin b Mushtaq | | 11 |
| R.A.Smith c sub (Rashid Latif) b Wasim | 9 | (5) b Mushtaq | | 8 |
| A.J.Lamb b Waqar | 30 | (6) lbw b Mushtaq | | 12 |
| I.T.Botham b Waqar | 2 | (7) lbw b Waqar | | 6 |
| C.C.Lewis lbw b Waqar | 2 | (8) b Waqar | | 15 |
| †R.C.Russell not out | 22 | (9) b Wasim | | 1 |
| P.A.J.DeFreitas c Inzamam b Waqar | 3 | (10) c Inzamam b Wasim | | 0 |
| I.D.K.Salisbury hit wkt b Mushtaq | 4 | (3) lbw b Wasim | | 12 |
| D.E.Malcolm lbw b Mushtaq | 0 | b Wasim | | 0 |
| Extras (B6, LB12, NB9) | 27 | (B5, LB8, NB15) | | 28 |
| **Total** (76.1 overs; 320 minutes) | 255 | (52.4 overs; 250 minutes) | | 175 |

## PAKISTAN

| | | | | |
|---|---|---|---|---|
| Aamir Sohail c Russell b DeFreitas | 73 | b Salisbury | | 39 |
| Ramiz Raja b Lewis | 24 | c Hick b Lewis | | 0 |
| Asif Mujtaba c Smith b Malcolm | 59 | c Russell b Lewis | | 0 |
| *Javed Miandad c Botham b Salisbury | 9 | c Russell b Lewis | | 0 |
| Salim Malik c Smith b Malcolm | 55 | c Lewis b Salisbury | | 12 |
| Inzamam-ul-Haq c and b Malcolm | 0 | run out (‡) | | 8 |
| Wasim Akram b Salisbury | 24 | not out | | 45 |
| †Moin Khan c Botham b DeFreitas | 12 | c Smith b Salisbury | | 3 |
| Mushtaq Ahmed c Russell b DeFreitas | 4 | c Hick b Malcolm | | 5 |
| Waqar Younis b Malcolm | 14 | not out | | 20 |
| Aqib Javed not out | 5 | | | |
| Extras (B4, LB3, NB7) | 14 | (B2, LB5, W1, NB1) | | 9 |
| **Total** (98.5 overs; 431 minutes) | 293 | (45.1 overs; 222 minutes) | | 141-8 |

| PAKISTAN | O | M | R | W | O | M | R | W | FALL OF WICKETS | | | | |
|---|---|---|---|---|---|---|---|---|---|---|---|---|---|
| Wasim | 19 | 5 | 49 | 2 | 17.4 | 2 | 66 | 4 | | E | P | E | P |
| Aqib | 14 | 3 | 40 | 0 | 12 | 3 | 23 | 1 | Wkt | 1st | 1st | 2nd | 2nd |
| Waqar | 21 | 4 | 91 | 5 | 13 | 3 | 40 | 2 | 1st | 123 | 43 | 40 | 6 |
| Mushtaq | 19.1 | 5 | 57 | 2 | 9 | 1 | 32 | 3 | 2nd | 153 | 123 | 73 | 10 |
| Asif | 3 | 3 | 0 | 1 | 1 | 0 | 1 | 0 | 3rd | 172 | 143 | 108 | 18 |
| | | | | | | | | | 4th | 197 | 228 | 120 | 41 |
| ENGLAND | | | | | | | | | 5th | 213 | 228 | 137 | 62 |
| DeFreitas | 26 | 8 | 58 | 3 | | | | | 6th | 221 | 235 | 148 | 68 |
| Malcolm | 15.5 | 1 | 70 | 4 | 15 | 2 | 42 | 1 | 7th | 232 | 263 | 174 | 81 |
| Lewis | 29 | 7 | 76 | 1 | 16 | 3 | 43 | 3 | 8th | 242 | 271 | 175 | 95 |
| Salisbury | 23 | 3 | 73 | 2 | 14.1 | 0 | 49 | 3 | 9th | 247 | 276 | 175 | – |
| Botham | 5 | 2 | 9 | 0 | | | | | 10th | 255 | 293 | 175 | – |

**Umpires:** B.Dudleston (2) and J.H.Hampshire (10).

Test No. 1190/49

# ENGLAND v PAKISTAN (3rd Test)

**Played at Old Trafford, Manchester, on 2, 3‡, 4, 6, 7 July 1992.**
**Toss: Pakistan.   Result: MATCH DRAWN.**
**Debuts: England – T.A.Munton.**                                      (‡ no play)

## PAKISTAN

| | | | | |
|---|---|---|---|---|
| Aamir Sohail b Lewis | 205 | c Smith b Lewis | | 1 |
| Ramiz Raja c Russell b Malcolm | 54 | c Hick b Lewis | | 88 |
| Asif Mujtaba c Atherton b Lewis | 57 | c Atherton b Lewis | | 40 |
| *Javed Miandad c Hick b Munton | 88 | not out | | 45 |
| †Moin Khan c Gower b Malcolm | 15 | (7) | not out | 11 |
| Salim Malik b Gooch | 34 | (5) | b Gooch | 16 |
| Inzamam-ul-Haq c Gooch b Malcolm | 26 | | | |
| Wasim Akram st Russell b Gooch | 0 | (6) | c Atherton b Gooch | 13 |
| Waqar Younis not out | 2 | | | |
| Mushtaq Ahmed c Lewis b Gooch | 6 | | | |
| Aqib Javed did not bat | | | | |
| Extras (B9, LB4, W2, NB3) | 18 | (B8, LB5, W5, NB7) | | 25 |
| | | | | |
| **Total** (126 overs; 519 minutes) | **505-9 dec** | (77 overs; 301 minutes) | | **239-5d** |

## ENGLAND

| | |
|---|---|
| *G.A.Gooch c Moin b Waqar | 78 |
| A.J.Stewart c Inzamam b Wasim | 15 |
| M.A.Atherton c Moin b Wasim | 0 |
| R.A.Smith lbw b Aqib | 11 |
| D.I.Gower c Moin b Wasim | 73 |
| G.A.Hick b Aqib | 22 |
| C.C.Lewis c Moin b Wasim | 55 |
| †R.C.Russell c Aamir b Aqib | 4 |
| I.D.K.Salisbury c Aamir b Wasim | 50 |
| T.A.Munton not out | 25 |
| D.E.Malcolm b Aqib | 4 |
| Extras (B8, LB8, W2, NB35) | 53 |
| | |
| **Total** (100.4 overs; 485 minutes) | **390** |

| ENGLAND | O | M | R | W | O | M | R | W | FALL OF WICKETS | | | |
|---|---|---|---|---|---|---|---|---|---|---|---|---|
| | | | | | | | | | | P | E | P |
| Malcolm | 31 | 3 | 117 | 3 | 12 | 2 | 57 | 0 | Wkt | 1st | 1st | 2nd |
| Lewis | 24 | 5 | 90 | 2 | 17 | 5 | 46 | 3 | 1st | 115 | 41 | 1 |
| Munton | 30 | 6 | 112 | 1 | 17 | 6 | 26 | 0 | 2nd | 241 | 42 | 143 |
| Salisbury | 20 | 0 | 117 | 0 | 13 | 0 | 67 | 0 | 3rd | 378 | 93 | 148 |
| Gooch | 18 | 2 | 39 | 3 | 16 | 5 | 30 | 2 | 4th | 428 | 186 | 195 |
| Hick | 3 | 0 | 17 | 0 | 2 | 2 | 0 | 0 | 5th | 432 | 200 | 217 |
| | | | | | | | | | 6th | 492 | 252 | – |
| PAKISTAN | | | | | | | | | 7th | 497 | 256 | – |
| Wasim | 36 | 4 | 128 | 5 | | | | | 8th | 497 | 315 | – |
| Waqar | 32 | 6 | 96 | 1 | | | | | 9th | 505 | 379 | – |
| Aqib | 21.4 | 1 | 100 | 4 | | | | | 10th | – | 390 | – |
| Asif | 1 | 1 | 0 | 0 | | | | | | | | |
| Mushtaq | 10 | 1 | 50 | 0 | | | | | | | | |

**Umpires: R.Palmer (1) and D.R.Shepherd (14).**                    Test No. 1191/50

# AAMIR SOHAIL'S 205

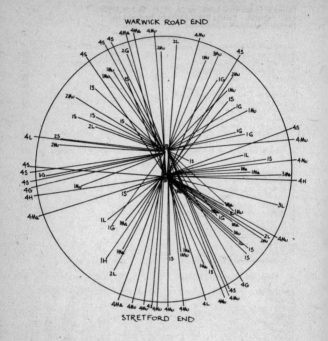

WARWICK ROAD END

STRETFORD END

| BOWLER | SYMBOL | BALLS | R U N S | | | | |
|---|---|---|---|---|---|---|---|
| | | | 1 | 2 | 3 | 4 | TOTAL |
| GOOCH | G | 35 | 6 | 1 | 1 | 2 | 19 |
| HICK | H | 9 | 1 | - | - | 2 | 9 |
| LEWIS | L | 42 | 4 | 4 | 1 | 2 | 23 |
| MALCOLM | Ma | 43 | 9 | - | 1 | 4 | 28 |
| MUNTON | Mu | 94 | 10 | 5 | 1 | 12 | 71 |
| SALISBURY | S | 61 | 13 | 1 | - | 10 | 55 |
| TOTALS | | 284 | 43 | 11 | 4 | 32 | 205 |

ENGLAND v PAKISTAN

Third Test at OLD TRAFFORD

All scored on the first day

(2nd JULY 1992)

In 342 minutes, out of 378-3

© BILL FRINDALL 1992

10

# ENGLAND v PAKISTAN (4th Test)

**Played at Headingley, Leeds, on 23, 24, 25, 26 July 1992.**
**Toss: Pakistan.  Result: ENGLAND won by 6 wickets.**
**Debuts: England – N.A.Mallender.**

## PAKISTAN

| | | | | | |
|---|---|--:|---|---|--:|
| Aamir Sohail | c Atherton b Mallender | 23 | c Stewart b Mallender | | 1 |
| Ramiz Raja | b Pringle | 17 | c Atherton b Munton | | 63 |
| Asif Mujtaba | b Mallender | 7 | c Hick b Mallender | | 11 |
| *Javed Miandad | c Smith b Pringle | 6 | c Stewart b Mallender | | 4 |
| Salim Malik | not out | 82 | not out | | 84 |
| Inzamam-ul-Haq | c Hick b Munton | 5 | c Smith b Pringle | | 19 |
| Wasim Akram | run out (Gooch/Lewis) | 12 | c Ramprakash b Pringle | | 17 |
| †Moin Khan | c Hick b Lewis | 2 | c Hick b Mallender | | 3 |
| Waqar Younis | c Hick b Mallender | 6 | (10) b Mallender | | 3 |
| Mushtaq Ahmed | b Lewis | 11 | (9) lbw b Pringle | | 0 |
| Aqib Javed | c Hick b Munton | 0 | run out (Hick) | | 0 |
| Extras | (B1, LB2, W7, NB16) | 26 | (B4, LB1, W2, NB9) | | 16 |
| **Total** | (79.3 overs; 341 minutes) | **197** | (69 overs; 304 minutes) | | **221** |

## ENGLAND

| | | | | | |
|---|---|--:|---|---|--:|
| *G.A.Gooch | b Mushtaq | 135 | c Asif b Mushtaq | | 37 |
| M.A.Atherton | b Wasim | 76 | lbw b Waqar | | 5 |
| R.A.Smith | c Miandad b Aqib | 42 | c sub (Zahid Fazal) b Waqar | | 0 |
| †A.J.Stewart | lbw b Waqar | 8 | (5) c Moin b Mushtaq | | 2 |
| D.I.Gower | not out | 18 | (4) not out | | 31 |
| M.R.Ramprakash | lbw b Mushtaq | 0 | not out | | 12 |
| G.A.Hick | b Waqar | 1 | | | |
| C.C.Lewis | lbw b Waqar | 0 | | | |
| D.R.Pringle | b Waqar | 0 | | | |
| N.A.Mallender | b Waqar | 1 | | | |
| T.A.Munton | c Inzamam b Mushtaq | 0 | | | |
| Extras | (B1, LB14, W1, NB23) | 39 | (B5, LB3, NB4) | | 12 |
| **Total** | (113.5 overs; 467 minutes) | **320** | (42.4 overs; 175 minutes) | | **99-4** |

| ENGLAND | O | M | R | W | O | M | R | W | FALL OF WICKETS | | | | |
|---|--:|--:|--:|--:|--:|--:|--:|--:|---|--:|--:|--:|--:|
| | | | | | | | | | | P | E | P | E |
| Lewis | 23 | 6 | 48 | 2 | 16 | 3 | 55 | 0 | | 1st | 1st | 2nd | 2nd |
| Mallender | 23 | 7 | 72 | 3 | 23 | 7 | 50 | 5 | *Wkt* | *1st* | *1st* | *2nd* | *2nd* |
| Pringle | 17 | 6 | 41 | 2 | 19 | 2 | 66 | 3 | 1st | 34 | 168 | 11 | 27 |
| Munton | 10.3 | 3 | 22 | 2 | 10 | 0 | 40 | 1 | 2nd | 54 | 270 | 53 | 27 |
| Gooch | 6 | 3 | 11 | 0 | 1 | 0 | 5 | 0 | 3rd | 60 | 292 | 64 | 61 |
| | | | | | | | | | 4th | 68 | 298 | 96 | 65 |
| PAKISTAN | | | | | | | | | 5th | 80 | 298 | 147 | — |
| Wasim | 36 | 12 | 80 | 1 | 17 | 4 | 36 | 0 | 6th | 111 | 303 | 177 | — |
| Aqib | 16 | 3 | 48 | 1 | | | | | 7th | 117 | 305 | 205 | — |
| Waqar | 30 | 3 | 117 | 5 | 12 | 2 | 28 | 2 | 8th | 128 | 305 | 206 | — |
| Mushtaq | 29.5 | 6 | 60 | 3 | 13.4 | 3 | 27 | 2 | 9th | 192 | 313 | 213 | — |
| Aamir | 2 | 2 | 0 | 0 | | | | | 10th | 197 | 320 | 221 | — |

**Umpires: M.J.Kitchen (5) and K.E.Palmer (20).**                    Test No. 1192/51

# ENGLAND v PAKISTAN (5th Test)

**Played at Kennington Oval, London, on 6, 7, 8, 9 August 1992.**
**Toss: England.   Result: PAKISTAN won by 10 wickets.**
**Debuts: Pakistan – Rashid Latif.**

## ENGLAND

| | | | | |
|---|---:|---|---:|
| *G.A.Gooch c Asif b Aqib | 20 | c Aamir b Waqar | 24 |
| †A.J.Stewart c Ramiz b Wasim | 31 | lbw b Waqar | 8 |
| M.A.Atherton c Rashid b Waqar | 60 | c Rashid b Waqar | 4 |
| R.A.Smith b Mushtaq | 33 | not out | 84 |
| D.I.Gower b Aqib | 27 | b Waqar | 1 |
| M.R.Ramprakash lbw b Wasim | 2 | c Asif b Mushtaq | 17 |
| C.C.Lewis lbw b Wasim | 4 | st Rashid b Mushtaq | 14 |
| D.R.Pringle b Wasim | 1 | b Wasim | 1 |
| N.A.Mallender b Wasim | 4 | c Mushtaq b Wasim | 3 |
| P.C.R.Tufnell not out | 0 | b Wasim | 0 |
| D.E.Malcolm b Wasim | 2 | b Waqar | 0 |
| Extras (B4, LB8, W1, NB10) | 23 | (B1, LB8, NB9) | 18 |
| **Total (78.1 overs; 328 minutes)** | **207** | **(72 overs; 307 minutes)** | **174** |

## PAKISTAN

| | | | |
|---|---:|---|---:|
| Aamir Sohail c Stewart b Malcolm | 49 | not out | 4 |
| Ramiz Raja b Malcolm | 19 | not out | 0 |
| Shoaib Mohammad c and b Tufnell | 55 | | |
| *Javed Miandad c and b Lewis | 59 | | |
| Salim Malik b Malcolm | 40 | | |
| Asif Mujtaba run out (Smith) | 50 | | |
| Wasim Akram c Stewart b Malcolm | 7 | | |
| †Rashid Latif c Smith b Mallender | 50 | | |
| Waqar Younis c Gooch b Malcolm | 6 | | |
| Mushtaq Ahmed c Lewis b Mallender | 9 | | |
| Aqib Javed not out | 0 | | |
| Extras (B2, LB6, W4, NB24) | 36 | (W1) | 1 |
| **Total (127.5 overs; 540 minutes)** | **380** | **(0.1 overs; 1 minute)** | **5-0** |

| PAKISTAN | O | M | R | W | O | M | R | W | FALL OF WICKETS | | | | |
|---|---|---|---|---|---|---|---|---|---|---|---|---|---|
| | | | | | | | | | | E | P | E | P |
| Wasim | 22.1 | 3 | 67 | 6 | 21 | 6 | 36 | 3 | | *1st* | *1st* | *2nd* | *2nd* |
| Waqar | 16 | 4 | 37 | 1 | 18 | 5 | 52 | 5 | *Wkt* | 1st | 1st | 2nd | 2nd |
| Aqib | 16 | 6 | 44 | 2 | 9 | 2 | 25 | 0 | 1st | 39 | 64 | 29 | – |
| Mushtaq | 24 | 7 | 47 | 1 | 23 | 6 | 46 | 2 | 2nd | 57 | 86 | 47 | – |
| Aamir | | | | | 1 | 0 | 6 | 0 | 3rd | 138 | 197 | 55 | – |
| | | | | | | | | | 4th | 182 | 214 | 59 | – |
| ENGLAND | | | | | | | | | 5th | 190 | 278 | 92 | – |
| Mallender | 28.5 | 6 | 93 | 2 | | | | | 6th | 196 | 292 | 153 | – |
| Malcolm | 29 | 6 | 94 | 5 | | | | | 7th | 199 | 332 | 159 | – |
| Lewis | 30 | 8 | 70 | 1 | | | | | 8th | 203 | 342 | 173 | – |
| Tufnell | 34 | 9 | 87 | 1 | | | | | 9th | 205 | 359 | 173 | – |
| Pringle | 6 | 0 | 28 | 0 | | | | | 10th | 207 | 380 | 174 | – |
| Ramprakash | | | | | 0.1 | 0 | 5 | 0 | | | | | |

**Umpires: H.D.Bird (47) and D.R.Shepherd (15).**                    Test No. 1193/52

# ENGLAND v PAKISTAN 1992

## ENGLAND – BATTING AND FIELDING

| | M | I | NO | HS | Runs | Avge | 100 | 50 | Ct/St |
|---|---|---|---|---|---|---|---|---|---|
| A.J.Stewart | 5 | 8 | 1 | 190 | 397 | 56.71 | 1 | 2 | 5 |
| D.I.Gower | 3 | 5 | 2 | 73 | 150 | 50.00 | – | 1 | 1 |
| G.A.Gooch | 5 | 8 | – | 135 | 384 | 48.00 | 1 | 2 | 2 |
| R.A.Smith | 5 | 8 | 1 | 127 | 314 | 44.85 | 1 | 1 | 7 |
| M.A.Atherton | 3 | 5 | – | 76 | 145 | 29.00 | – | 2 | 5 |
| R.C.Russell | 3 | 4 | 2 | 29* | 56 | 28.00 | – | – | 6/1 |
| T.A.Munton | 2 | 2 | 1 | 25* | 25 | 25.00 | – | – | – |
| I.D.K.Salisbury | 2 | 3 | – | 50 | 66 | 22.00 | – | 1 | – |
| G.A.Hick | 4 | 5 | – | 51 | 98 | 19.60 | – | 1 | 10 |
| A.J.Lamb | 2 | 3 | – | 30 | 54 | 18.00 | – | – | – |
| C.C.Lewis | 5 | 7 | – | 55 | 114 | 16.28 | – | 1 | 4 |
| M.R.Ramprakash | 3 | 5 | 1 | 17 | 31 | 7.75 | – | – | 1 |
| I.T.Botham | 2 | 2 | – | 6 | 8 | 4.00 | – | – | 2 |
| N.A.Mallender | 2 | 3 | – | 4 | 8 | 2.66 | – | – | – |
| P.A.J.DeFreitas | 2 | 2 | – | 3 | 3 | 1.50 | – | – | – |
| D.E.Malcolm | 3 | 5 | – | 4 | 6 | 1.20 | – | – | 1 |
| D.R.Pringle | 2 | 2 | 1 | 1 | 2 | 0.66 | – | – | – |

*Played in one Test:* P.C.R.Tufnell 0*, 0 (1 ct).

## ENGLAND – BOWLING

| | O | M | R | W | Avge | Best | 5wI | 10wM |
|---|---|---|---|---|---|---|---|---|
| G.A.Gooch | 51 | 15 | 94 | 5 | 18.80 | 3-39 | – | – |
| N.A.Mallender | 74.5 | 20 | 215 | 10 | 21.50 | 5-50 | 1 | – |
| P.A.J.DeFreitas | 59 | 14 | 179 | 7 | 25.57 | 4-121 | – | – |
| D.E.Malcolm | 102.5 | 14 | 380 | 13 | 29.23 | 5-94 | 1 | – |
| C.C.Lewis | 188 | 40 | 544 | 12 | 45.33 | 3-43 | – | – |
| D.R.Pringle | 70 | 10 | 227 | 5 | 45.40 | 3-66 | – | – |
| I.D.K.Salisbury | 70.1 | 3 | 306 | 5 | 61.20 | 3-49 | – | – |

*Also bowled:* I.T.Botham 24-8-61-0; G.A.Hick 18-3-63-0; T.A.Munton 67.3-15-200-4; M.R.Ramprakash 1.1-0-8-0; P.C.R.Tufnell 34-9-87-1.

## PAKISTAN – BATTING AND FIELDING

| | M | I | NO | HS | Runs | Avge | 100 | 50 | Ct/St |
|---|---|---|---|---|---|---|---|---|---|
| Salim Malik | 5 | 8 | 2 | 165 | 488 | 81.33 | 1 | 3 | 1 |
| Javed Miandad | 5 | 8 | 2 | 153* | 364 | 60.66 | 1 | 2 | 5 |
| Aamir Sohail | 5 | 9 | 1 | 205 | 413 | 51.62 | 1 | 1 | 3 |
| Ramiz Raja | 5 | 9 | 1 | 88 | 312 | 39.00 | – | 3 | 1 |
| Asif Mujtaba | 5 | 8 | – | 59 | 253 | 31.62 | – | 3 | 4 |
| Wasim Akram | 4 | 7 | 1 | 45* | 118 | 19.66 | – | – | – |
| Inzamam-ul-Haq | 4 | 6 | 1 | 26 | 66 | 13.20 | – | – | 4 |
| Waqar Younis | 5 | 6 | 2 | 20* | 51 | 12.75 | – | – | – |
| Moin Khan | 2 | 4 | 1 | 16 | 46 | 9.20 | – | – | 7 |
| Mushtaq Ahmed | 5 | 6 | – | 11 | 35 | 5.83 | – | – | 1 |
| Aqib Javed | 5 | 4 | 2 | 5* | 5 | 2.50 | – | – | – |

*Played in one Test:* Ata-ur-Rehman did not bat; Rashid Latif 50 (2 ct, 1 st); Shoaib Mohammad 55.

## PAKISTAN – BOWLING

| | O | M | R | W | Avge | Best | 5wI | 10wM |
|---|---|---|---|---|---|---|---|---|
| Wasim Akram | 168.5 | 36 | 462 | 21 | 22.00 | 6-67 | 2 | – |
| Waqar Younis | 166 | 29 | 557 | 22 | 25.31 | 5-52 | 3 | – |
| Mushtaq Ahmed | 178.4 | 37 | 475 | 15 | 31.66 | 3-32 | – | – |
| Aqib Javed | 104.4 | 21 | 366 | 9 | 40.66 | 4-100 | – | – |

*Also bowled:* Aamir Sohail 5-2-14-0; Asif Mujtaba 13-5-30-1; Ata-ur-Rehman 18-5-69-3; Salim Malik 1-0-5-0.

# SRI LANKA v AUSTRALIA (1st Test)

**Played at Sinhalese Sports Club, Colombo, on 17, 18, 19, 21, 22 August 1992.**
**Toss: Sri Lanka.   Result: AUSTRALIA won by 16 runs.**
**Debuts: Sri Lanka – R.S.Kaluwitharana.**

## AUSTRALIA

| Batsman | Dismissal | R | | Dismissal | R |
|---|---|---|---|---|---|
| M.A.Taylor | lbw b Wickremasinghe | 42 | (2) | c Gurusinha b Anurasiri | 43 |
| T.M.Moody | lbw b Ramanayake | 1 | (1) | b Ramanayake | 13 |
| D.C.Boon | c Ramanayake b Hathurusinghe | 32 | | c Ranatunga b Anurasiri | 68 |
| D.M.Jones | lbw b Hathurusinghe | 10 | | run out (Gurusinha) | 57 |
| M.E.Waugh | c Kaluwitharana b Hathurusinghe | 5 | | c Kaluwitharana b Wickremasinghe | 56 |
| *A.R.Border | b Hathurusinghe | 3 | | c Gurusinha b Anurasiri | 15 |
| G.R.J.Matthews | lbw b Ramanayake | 6 | | c Kaluwitharana b Ramanayake | 64 |
| †I.A.Healy | not out | 66 | | lbw b Hathurusinghe | 12 |
| C.J.McDermott | c Ranatunga b Ramanayake | 22 | | lbw b Ramanayake | 40 |
| S.K.Warne | c and b Anurasiri | 24 | | b Anurasiri | 35 |
| M.R.Whitney | c and b Wickremasinghe | 13 | | not out | 10 |
| Extras | (LB10, W3, NB19) | 32 | | (LB23, W1, NB34) | 58 |
| **Total** | | **256** | | | **471** |

## SRI LANKA

| Batsman | Dismissal | R | | Dismissal | R |
|---|---|---|---|---|---|
| R.S.Mahanama | c Healy b Waugh | 78 | | c Boon b Matthews | 39 |
| U.C.Hathurusinghe | c Taylor b Waugh | 18 | | run out (Moody) | 36 |
| A.P.Gurusinha | c Jones b Whitney | 137 | | not out | 31 |
| P.A.De Silva | lbw b Matthews | 6 | | c Border b McDermott | 37 |
| *A.Ranatunga | c Waugh b Matthews | 127 | | c Border b McDermott | 1 |
| M.S.Atapattu | b Matthews | 0 | | b Matthews | 0 |
| †R.S.Kaluwitharana | not out | 132 | | b Matthews | 4 |
| C.P.H.Ramanayake | c Healy b McDermott | 0 | | lbw b Matthews | 6 |
| G.P.Wickremasinghe | c Matthews b McDermott | 21 | | c Waugh b Warne | 2 |
| A.W.R.Madurasinghe | not out | 5 | (11) | c Matthews b Warne | 0 |
| S.D.Anurasiri | did not bat | | (10) | c Waugh b Warne | 1 |
| Extras | (B2, LB7, W1, NB13) | 23 | | (B2, LB3, NB2) | 7 |
| **Total** | (8 wickets declared) | **547** | | | **164** |

| SRI LANKA | O | M | R | W | O | M | R | W |
|---|---|---|---|---|---|---|---|---|
| Ramanayake | 20 | 4 | 51 | 3 | 37 | 10 | 113 | 3 |
| Wickremasinghe | 18 | 4 | 69 | 2 | 19 | 0 | 79 | 1 |
| Hathurusinghe | 22 | 5 | 66 | 4 | 27 | 7 | 79 | 1 |
| Madurasinghe | 10 | 1 | 21 | 0 | 14 | 1 | 50 | 0 |
| Gurusinha | 2 | 0 | 17 | 0 | | | | |
| Anurasiri | 12 | 2 | 22 | 1 | 35 | 3 | 127 | 4 |

| AUSTRALIA | O | M | R | W | O | M | R | W |
|---|---|---|---|---|---|---|---|---|
| McDermott | 40 | 9 | 125 | 2 | 14 | 4 | 43 | 2 |
| Whitney | 32 | 10 | 84 | 1 | 5 | 2 | 13 | 0 |
| Moody | 17 | 3 | 44 | 0 | 5 | 0 | 10 | 0 |
| Waugh | 17 | .3 | 77 | 2 | 2 | 0 | 6 | 0 |
| Warne | 22 | 2 | 107 | 0 | 5.1 | 3 | 11 | 3 |
| Matthews | 38 | 11 | 93 | 3 | 20 | 2 | 76 | 4 |
| Border | 4 | 1 | 8 | 0 | | | | |

### FALL OF WICKETS

| | A | SL | A | SL |
|---|---|---|---|---|
| Wkt | 1st | 1st | 2nd | 2nd |
| 1st | 8 | 36 | 41 | 76 |
| 2nd | 84 | 128 | 107 | 79 |
| 3rd | 94 | 137 | 195 | 127 |
| 4th | 96 | 367 | 233 | 132 |
| 5th | 109 | 367 | 269 | 133 |
| 6th | 118 | 463 | 319 | 137 |
| 7th | 124 | 472 | 361 | 147 |
| 8th | 162 | 503 | 417 | 150 |
| 9th | 207 | – | 431 | 156 |
| 10th | 256 | – | 471 | 164 |

**Umpires: K.T.Francis (5) and T.M.Samarasinghe (1).**

Test No. 1194/5

# SRI LANKA v AUSTRALIA (2nd Test)

**Played at Khettarama Stadium, Colombo, on 28, 29, 30 August, 1, 2 September 1992.**
**Toss: Sri Lanka.   Result: MATCH DRAWN.**
**Debuts: Sri Lanka – D.K.Liyanage, M.Muralitharan.**                    ‡(D.R.Martyn)

## AUSTRALIA

| | | | | |
|---|---|---|---|---|
| T.M.Moody c Kaluwitharana b Liyanage | 1 | (2) | b Muralitharan | 54 |
| M.A.Taylor c Jayasuriya b Hathurusinghe | 15 | (1) | lbw b Hathurusinghe | 26 |
| D.C.Boon c Jayasuriya b Liyanage | 28 | | c Mahanama b Anurasiri | 15 |
| D.M.Jones lbw b Gurusinha | 77 | | not out | 100 |
| M.E.Waugh c Jayasuriya b Ramanayake | 0 | | lbw b Muralitharan | 0 |
| *A.R.Border b Liyanage | 13 | | lbw b Anurasiri | 28 |
| G.R.J.Matthews c Muralitharan b Ramanayake | 55 | | c Mahanama b Anurasiri | 51 |
| †I.A.Healy lbw b Gurusinha | 0 | | not out | 4 |
| C.J.McDermott lbw b Muralitharan | 9 | | | |
| A.I.C.Dodemaide not out | 16 | | | |
| M.R.Whitney b Ramanayake | 1 | | | |
| Extras (B10, LB14, W2, NB6) | 32 | | (B4, LB9, NB5) | 18 |
| **Total** | **247** | | **(6 wickets declared)** | **296** |

## SRI LANKA

| | | | | |
|---|---|---|---|---|
| R.S.Mahanama c Moody b Dodemaide | 14 | | lbw b McDermott | 69 |
| U.C.Hathurusinghe b Moody | 67 | | c Moody b McDermott | 49 |
| A.P.Gurusinha c Healy b Whitney | 29 | | not out | 8 |
| P.A.De Silva c Healy b McDermott | 85 | | | |
| *A.Ranatunga c sub‡ b Dodemaide | 18 | | | |
| S.T.Jayasuriya c Healy b McDermott | 19 | (4) | not out | 1 |
| †R.S.Kaluwitharana c sub‡ b Border | 1 | | | |
| C.P.H.Ramanayake b McDermott | 8 | | | |
| D.K.Liyanage c Healy b McDermott | 4 | | | |
| S.D.Anurasiri not out | 2 | | | |
| M.Muralitharan not out | 0 | | | |
| Extras (LB6, NB5) | 11 | | (LB6, NB3) | 9 |
| **Total  (9 wickets declared)** | **258** | | **(2 wickets)** | **136** |

| SRI LANKA | O | M | R | W | O | M | R | W | FALL OF WICKETS | | | | |
|---|---|---|---|---|---|---|---|---|---|---|---|---|---|
| | | | | | | | | | | A | SL | A | SL |
| Ramanayake | 23.3 | 7 | 64 | 3 | 12 | 0 | 49 | 0 | Wkt | 1st | 1st | 2nd | 2nd |
| Liyanage | 30 | 10 | 66 | 3 | 13 | 1 | 47 | 0 | 1st | 1 | 26 | 61 | 110 |
| Hathurusinghe | 9 | 1 | 26 | 1 | 12 | 4 | 12 | 1 | 2nd | 34 | 67 | 102 | 129 |
| Gurusinha | 9 | 2 | 18 | 2 | | | | | 3rd | 69 | 174 | 104 | – |
| Anurasiri | 8 | 0 | 17 | 0 | 44 | 11 | 66 | 3 | 4th | 72 | 211 | 104 | – |
| Muralitharan | 17 | 2 | 32 | 1 | 34 | 7 | 109 | 2 | 5th | 109 | 240 | 149 | – |
| | | | | | | | | | 6th | 181 | 243 | 280 | – |
| AUSTRALIA | | | | | | | | | 7th | 183 | 243 | – | – |
| McDermott | 20 | 4 | 53 | 4 | 19 | 7 | 32 | 2 | 8th | 200 | 255 | – | – |
| Whitney | 16 | 1 | 49 | 1 | 5 | 2 | 13 | 0 | 9th | 239 | 258 | – | – |
| Dodemaide | 25 | 4 | 74 | 2 | 5 | 2 | 11 | 0 | 10th | 247 | | – | – |
| Matthews | 10 | 2 | 20 | 0 | 21 | 5 | 59 | 0 | | | | | |
| Waugh | 4 | 0 | 11 | 0 | | | | | | | | | |
| Moody | 6 | 1 | 17 | 1 | | | | | | | | | |
| Border | 11 | 3 | 28 | 1 | 4 | 0 | 15 | 0 | | | | | |

**Umpires: I.Anandappa (1) and W.A.U.Wickremasinghe (2).**          Test No. 1195/6

# SRI LANKA v AUSTRALIA (3rd Test)

**Played at Tyronne Fernando Stadium, Moratuwa, on 8, 9, 10, 12, 13 September 1992.**
**Toss: Australia.   Result: MATCH DRAWN.**
**Debuts: Nil.**

## AUSTRALIA

| | | | | |
|---|---|---|---|---|
| T.M.Moody b Ramanayake | 0 | (2) | c Tillekeratne b Ramanayake | 2 |
| M.A.Taylor c Ranatunga b Anurasiri | 19 | (1) | c Mahanama b Liyange | 3 |
| D.C.Boon c De Silva b Ramanayake | 18 | | lbw b Liyange | 0 |
| D.M.Jones lbw b Liyange | 11 | | b Anurasiri | 21 |
| M.E.Waugh b Ramanayake | 0 | | c Tillekeratne b Liyange | 0 |
| *A.R.Border b Ramanayake | 106 | | lbw b Ramanayake | 78 |
| G.R.J.Matthews run out (Mahanama) | 57 | | b Ramanayake | 96 |
| †I.A.Healy c Jayasuriya b Muralitharan | 71 | | c Jayasuriya b Liyange | 49 |
| C.J.McDermott c Tillekeratne b Hathurusinghe | 10 | | | |
| S.K.Warne c Gurusinha b Ramanayake | 7 | | | |
| A.I.C.Dodemaide not out | 13 | (9) | not out | 2 |
| Extras (B3, LB9, W3, NB10) | 25 | | (LB4, W1, NB15) | 20 |
| **Total** | **337** | | **(8 wickets)** | **271** |

## SRI LANKA

| | |
|---|---|
| R.S.Mahanama lbw b Matthews | 50 |
| U.C.Hathurusinghe c Boon b McDermott | 4 |
| A.P.Gurusinha c Healy b McDermott | 0 |
| P.A.De Silva b Dodemaide | 58 |
| †H.P.Tillekeratne c Waugh b Dodemaide | 82 |
| *A.Ranatunga c Jones b McDermott | 48 |
| S.T.Jayasuriya c Boon b McDermott | 2 |
| C.P.H.Ramanayake not out | 15 |
| D.K.Liyange c Moody b Dodemaide | 1 |
| S.D.Anurasiri b Dodemaide | 0 |
| M.Muralitharan did not bat | |
| Extras (LB8, W3, NB5) | 16 |
| **Total (9 wickets declared)** | **274** |

| SRI LANKA | O | M | R | W | O | M | R | W |
|---|---|---|---|---|---|---|---|---|
| Ramanayake | 31 | 3 | 82 | 5 | 22.1 | 4 | 75 | 3 |
| Liyange | 17 | 0 | 54 | 1 | 16 | 3 | 56 | 4 |
| Hathurusinghe | 21 | 8 | 50 | 1 | 4 | 2 | 3 | 0 |
| Anurasiri | 22 | 2 | 57 | 1 | 29 | 5 | 49 | 1 |
| Muralitharan | 15.1 | 2 | 58 | 1 | 7 | 1 | 26 | 0 |
| Jayasuriya | 2 | 0 | 9 | 0 | 7 | 1 | 17 | 0 |
| Gurusinha | 3 | 0 | 15 | 0 | 1 | 0 | 5 | 0 |
| Ranatunga | | | | | 1 | 0 | 9 | 0 |
| Mahanama | | | | | 5 | 0 | 27 | 0 |

| AUSTRALIA | O | M | R | W |
|---|---|---|---|---|
| McDermott | 31 | 6 | 89 | 4 |
| Dodemaide | 23.5 | 9 | 65 | 4 |
| Moody | 3 | 0 | 8 | 0 |
| Matthews | 31 | 8 | 64 | 1 |
| Warne | 11 | 3 | 40 | 0 |

### FALL OF WICKETS

| Wkt | A 1st | SL 1st | A 2nd |
|---|---|---|---|
| 1st | 0 | 4 | 6 |
| 2nd | 42 | 4 | 6 |
| 3rd | 46 | 111 | 6 |
| 4th | 57 | 116 | 9 |
| 5th | 58 | 232 | 60 |
| 6th | 185 | 234 | 132 |
| 7th | 252 | 262 | 261 |
| 8th | 283 | 274 | 271 |
| 9th | 302 | 274 | — |
| 10th | 337 | — | — |

**Umpires: B.C.Cooray (1) and K.T.Francis (6).**

Test No. 1196/7

# SRI LANKA v AUSTRALIA 1992-93

## SRI LANKA – BATTING AND FIELDING

|                      | M | I | NO | HS   | Runs | Avge  | 100 | 50 | Ct/St |
|----------------------|---|---|----|------|------|-------|-----|----|-------|
| R.S.Kaluwitharana    | 2 | 3 | 1  | 132* | 137  | 68.50 | 1   | –  | 4     |
| A.P.Gurusinha        | 3 | 5 | 2  | 137  | 205  | 68.33 | 1   | –  | 3     |
| R.S.Mahanama         | 3 | 5 | –  | 78   | 250  | 50.00 | –   | 3  | 3     |
| A.Ranatunga          | 3 | 4 | –  | 127  | 193  | 48.25 | 1   | –  | 3     |
| P.A.De Silva         | 3 | 4 | –  | 85   | 186  | 46.50 | –   | 2  | 1     |
| U.C.Hathurusinghe    | 3 | 5 | –  | 67   | 172  | 34.40 | –   | 1  | –     |
| S.T.Jayasuriya       | 2 | 3 | 1  | 19   | 22   | 11.00 | –   | –  | 5     |
| C.P.H.Ramanayake     | 3 | 4 | 1  | 15*  | 29   | 9.66  | –   | –  | 1     |
| S.D.Anurasiri        | 3 | 3 | 1  | 2*   | 3    | 1.50  | –   | –  | 1     |

*Also played* (2 matches): D.K.Liyanage 4, 1; M.Muralitharan 0* (1 ct); (1 match): M.S.Atapattu 0, 1; A.W.R.Madurasinghe 5*, 0; H.P.Tillekeratne 82 (3 ct); G.P.Wickremasinghe 21, 2 (1 ct).

## SRI LANKA – BOWLING

|                     | O     | M  | R   | W  | Avge  | Best  | 5wI | 10wM |
|---------------------|-------|----|-----|----|-------|-------|-----|------|
| C.P.H.Ramanayake    | 145.4 | 28 | 434 | 17 | 25.52 | 5-82  | 1   | –    |
| D.K.Liyanage        | 76    | 14 | 223 | 8  | 27.87 | 4-56  | –   | –    |
| U.C.Hathurusinghe   | 95    | 27 | 236 | 8  | 29.50 | 4-66  | –   | –    |
| S.D.Anurasiri       | 150   | 23 | 338 | 10 | 33.80 | 4-127 | –   | –    |

*Also bowled:* A.P.Gurusinha 5-2-55-2; S.T.Jayasuriya 9-1-26-0; A.W.R.Madurasinghe 24-2-71-0; R.S.Mahanama 5-0-27-0; M.Muralitharan 73.1-12-225-4; A.Ranatunga 1-0-9-0; G.P.Wickremasinghe 37-4-148-3.

## AUSTRALIA – BATTING AND FIELDING

|                  | M | I | NO | HS   | Runs | Avge  | 100 | 50 | Ct/St |
|------------------|---|---|----|------|------|-------|-----|----|-------|
| D.M.Jones        | 3 | 6 | 1  | 100* | 276  | 55.20 | 1   | 2  | 2     |
| G.R.J.Matthews   | 3 | 6 | –  | 96   | 329  | 54.83 | –   | 5  | 2     |
| I.A.Healy        | 3 | 6 | 2  | 71   | 202  | 50.50 | –   | 2  | 7     |
| A.R.Border       | 3 | 6 | –  | 106  | 243  | 40.50 | 1   | 1  | 2     |
| D.C.Boon         | 3 | 6 | –  | 68   | 161  | 26.83 | –   | 1  | 3     |
| M.A.Taylor       | 3 | 6 | –  | 43   | 148  | 24.66 | –   | –  | 1     |
| S.K.Warne        | 2 | 3 | –  | 35   | 66   | 22.00 | –   | –  | 1     |
| C.J.McDermott    | 3 | 4 | –  | 40   | 81   | 20.25 | –   | –  | –     |
| M.R.Whitney      | 2 | 3 | 1  | 13   | 24   | 12.00 | –   | –  | –     |
| T.M.Moody        | 3 | 6 | –  | 54   | 71   | 11.83 | –   | 1  | 3     |
| M.E.Waugh        | 3 | 6 | –  | 56   | 61   | 10.16 | –   | 1  | 3     |
| A.I.C.Dodemaide  | 2 | 3 | 3  | 16*  | 31   |       | –   | –  | –     |

## AUSTRALIA – BOWLING

|                 | O   | M  | R   | W  | Avge  | Best | 5wI | 10wM |
|-----------------|-----|----|-----|----|-------|------|-----|------|
| C.J.McDermott   | 124 | 30 | 342 | 14 | 24.42 | 4-53 | –   | –    |
| A.I.C.Dodemaide | 53.5| 15 | 150 | 6  | 25.00 | 4-65 | –   | –    |
| G.R.J.Matthews  | 120 | 28 | 312 | 8  | 39.00 | 4-76 | –   | –    |

*Also bowled:* A.R.Border 19-4-51-1; T.M.Moody 31-4-79-1; S.K.Warne 38.1-8-158-3; M.E.Waugh 23-3-94-2; M.R.Whitney 58-15-159-2.

# ZIMBABWE v INDIA (Only Test)

**Played at Harare Sports Club, on 18, 19, 20, 21, 22 October 1992.**
**Toss: Zimbabwe. Result: MATCH DRAWN.**
**Debuts: Zimbabwe – All except A.J.Traicos who had previously appeared for South Africa.**

## ZIMBABWE

| | | | | | |
|---|---|--:|---|---|--:|
| K.J.Arnott c Raman b Kumble | | 40 | b Prabhakar | | 32 |
| G.W.Flower c More b Srinath | | 82 | c More b Kapil Dev | | 6 |
| A.D.R.Campbell lbw b Kapil Dev | | 45 | b Kapil Dev | | 0 |
| A.J.Pycroft c Azharuddin b Prabhakar | | 39 | lbw b Shastri | | 46 |
| M.G.Burmester c Azharuddin b Prabhakar | | 7 | | | |
| *D.L.Houghton c More b Srinath | | 121 | (5) not out | | 41 |
| †A.Flower b Prabhakar | | 59 | (6) not out | | 1 |
| G.J.Crocker not out | | 23 | | | |
| E.A.Brandes lbw b Srinath | | 0 | | | |
| A.J.Traicos b Kumble | | 5 | | | |
| M.P.Jarvis c Raman b Kumble | | 0 | | | |
| Extras (B1, LB19, NB15) | | 35 | (B13, LB2, NB5) | | 20 |
| **Total** | | **456** | (4 wickets declared) | | **146** |

## INDIA

| | |
|---|--:|
| R.J.Shastri c Pycroft b Burmester | 11 |
| W.V.Raman b Crocker | 43 |
| S.V.Manjrekar c sub (S.G.Davies) b Jarvis | 104 |
| S.R.Tendulkar c and b Traicos | 0 |
| *M.Azharuddin c G.W.Flower b Traicos | 9 |
| S.L.V.Raju c Arnott b Traicos | 7 |
| Kapil Dev b Traicos | 60 |
| M.Prabhakar c Arnott b Traicos | 14 |
| †K.S.More c Traicos b Burmester | 41 |
| A.Kumble c A.Flower b Burmester | 0 |
| J.Srinath not out | 6 |
| Extras (B2, LB9, NB1) | 12 |
| **Total** | **307** |

| INDIA | O | M | R | W | O | M | R | W | FALL OF WICKETS | | | |
|---|--:|--:|--:|--:|--:|--:|--:|--:|---|--:|--:|--:|
| | | | | | | | | | | Z | I | Z |
| Kapil Dev | 39 | 13 | 71 | 1 | 15 | 4 | 22 | 2 | Wkt | 1st | 1st | 2nd |
| Prabhakar | 45 | 15 | 66 | 3 | 14 | 4 | 22 | 1 | 1st | 100 | 29 | 16 |
| Srinath | 39 | 12 | 89 | 3 | 5 | 1 | 15 | 0 | 2nd | 175 | 77 | 16 |
| Raju | 39 | 15 | 79 | 0 | 7 | 2 | 15 | 0 | 3rd | 186 | 78 | 93 |
| Kumble | 35.2 | 11 | 79 | 3 | 9 | 1 | 17 | 0 | 4th | 199 | 93 | 119 |
| Shastri | 17 | 3 | 52 | 0 | 12 | 4 | 32 | 1 | 5th | 252 | 101 | – |
| Tendulkar | | | | | 4 | 3 | 8 | 0 | 6th | 417 | 197 | – |
| | | | | | | | | | 7th | 445 | 219 | – |
| ZIMBABWE | | | | | | | | | 8th | 445 | 287 | – |
| Brandes | 2 | 0 | 3 | 0 | | | | | 9th | 454 | 294 | – |
| Burmester | 39.4 | 18 | 78 | 3 | | | | | 10th | 456 | 307 | – |
| Jarvis | 38 | 17 | 73 | 1 | | | | | | | | |
| Crocker | 35 | 18 | 41 | 1 | | | | | | | | |
| Traicos | 50 | 16 | 86 | 5 | | | | | | | | |
| G.W.Flower | | | | | | | | | | | | |

**Umpires: H.D.Bird (48), K.Kanjee (1) and I.D.Robinson (1)‡.**   Test No. 1197/1
**‡Kanjee 1st and 3rd days; Robinson 2nd, 4th and 5th days.**

# ZIMBABWE v NEW ZEALAND (1st Test)

**Played at Bulawayo Athletic Club, on 1, 2, 3, 4, 5 November 1992.**
**Toss: New Zealand. Result: MATCH DRAWN.**
**Debuts: Zimbabwe – A.H.Omarshah (known as A.H.Shah); New Zealand – S.B.Doull, M.J.Haslam.**

## NEW ZEALAND

| | | | | |
|---|---|---|---|---|
| M.J.Greatbatch c Campbell b Shah | 87 | | c Houghton b Jarvis | 88 |
| R.T.Latham run out | 119 | | c Houghton b G.W.Flower | 48 |
| A.H.Jones not out | 67 | | retired hurt | 39 |
| *M.D.Crowe c Jarvis b Traicos | 42 | (5) | c A.Flower b Jarvis | 6 |
| K.R.Rutherford not out | 7 | (7) | not out | 11 |
| †A.C.Parore | | (4) | c Houghton b Jarvis | 12 |
| S.B.Doull | | (6) | b Traicos | 2 |
| D.N.Patel | did not bat | | not out | 11 |
| M.L.Su'a | | | | |
| W.Watson | | | | |
| M.J.Haslam | | | | |
| Extras (LB3) | 3 | | (B1, LB3, NB1) | 5 |
| **Total** (3 wickets declared) | 325 | | (5 wickets declared) | 222 |

## ZIMBABWE

| | | | | |
|---|---|---|---|---|
| K.J.Arnott c Haslam b Patel | 30 | | not out | 101 |
| G.W.Flower c Latham b Patel | 29 | | c Latham b Patel | 45 |
| M.G.Burmester c Haslam b Patel | 0 | | | |
| A.D.R.Campbell run out | 0 | (3) | not out | 48 |
| A.J.Pycroft b Doull | 2 | | | |
| *D.L.Houghton b Patel | 36 | | | |
| †A.Flower c Haslam b Su'a | 81 | | | |
| A.H.Shah c Parore b Su'a | 28 | | | |
| G.J.Crocker b Patel | 1 | | | |
| A.J.Traicos b Patel | 4 | | | |
| M.P.Jarvis not out | 2 | | | |
| Extras (LB4, NB2) | 6 | | (LB2, W1) | 3 |
| **Total** | 219 | | (1 wicket) | 197 |

| ZIMBABWE | O | M | R | W | O | M | R | W | FALL OF WICKETS | | | | |
|---|---|---|---|---|---|---|---|---|---|---|---|---|---|
| | | | | | | | | | | NZ | Z | NZ | Z |
| Jarvis | 26.1 | 4 | 87 | 0 | 11 | 0 | 38 | 3 | | 1st | 1st | 2nd | 2nd |
| Burmester | 14 | 1 | 71 | 0 | | | | | Wkt | 116 | 54 | 102 | 92 |
| Shah | 14 | 6 | 46 | 1 | 7 | 0 | 36 | 0 | 1st | 116 | 54 | 102 | 92 |
| Traicos | 23.1 | 4 | 56 | 1 | 17 | 1 | 82 | 1 | 2nd | 243 | 56 | 181 | – |
| Crocker | 14 | 1 | 57 | 0 | 5 | 0 | 30 | 0 | 3rd | 314 | 59 | 193 | – |
| Houghton | 0.5 | 0 | 9 | 0 | | | | | 4th | – | 62 | 196 | – |
| G.W.Flower | 4 | 2 | 5 | 0 | 8 | 0 | 32 | 1 | 5th | – | 64 | 204 | – |
| | | | | | | | | | 6th | – | 134 | – | – |
| **NEW ZEALAND** | | | | | | | | | 7th | – | 194 | – | – |
| Su'a | 9 | 3 | 18 | 2 | 6.1 | 2 | 9 | 0 | 8th | – | 213 | – | – |
| Patel | 40.4 | 12 | 113 | 6 | 28 | 7 | 60 | 1 | 9th | – | 213 | – | – |
| Doull | 15 | 6 | 29 | 1 | 4 | 1 | 8 | 0 | 10th | – | 219 | – | – |
| Watson | 7 | 3 | 10 | 0 | 7 | 2 | 21 | 0 | | | | | |
| Haslam | 21 | 8 | 44 | 0 | 19 | 4 | 76 | 0 | | | | | |
| Jones | 1 | 0 | 1 | 0 | | | | | | | | | |
| Latham | | | | | 3 | 2 | 6 | 0 | | | | | |
| Crowe | | | | | 4 | 0 | 15 | 0 | | | | | |

**Umpires:** H.D.Bird (49), K.Kanjee (2) and I.D.Robinson (2).          Test No. 1198/1

19

# ZIMBABWE v NEW ZEALAND (2nd Test)

Played at Harare Sports Club, on 7, 9, 10, 11, 12 November 1992.
Toss: New Zealand. Result: NEW ZEALAND won by 177 runs.
Debuts: Zimbabwe – D.H.Brain; New Zealand – D.J.Nash.

## NEW ZEALAND

| | | | |
|---|---:|---|---:|
| M.J.Greatbatch c A.Flower b Brain | 55 | c Brandes b Brain | 13 |
| R.T.Latham c A.Flower b Crocker | 15 | c Houghton b Brandes | 10 |
| A.H.Jones c Pycroft b Brandes | 8 | st A.Flower b Traicos | 28 |
| *M.D.Crowe c Burmester b Crocker | 140 | lbw b Traicos | 61 |
| K.R.Rutherford c A.Flower b Traicos | 74 | c Arnott b Brandes | 89 |
| D.N.Patel c Campbell b Traicos | 6 | not out | 58 |
| †A.C.Parore run out | 2 | | |
| D.J.Nash not out | 11 | | |
| M.L.Su'a c Arnott b Brandes | 1 | | |
| W.Watson b Brain | 3 | | |
| M.J.Haslam c A.Flower b Brain | 3 | | |
| Extras (LB11, NB6) | 17 | (LB2, W1) | 3 |
| **Total** | **335** | (5 wickets declared) | **262** |

## ZIMBABWE

| | | | |
|---|---:|---|---:|
| K.J.Arnott b Watson | 68 | c Watson b Nash | 10 |
| G.W.Flower lbw b Su'a | 5 | c Latham b Su'a | 1 |
| A.D.R.Campbell c Su'a b Patel | 52 | c Greatbatch b Patel | 35 |
| A.J.Pycroft b Su'a | 60 | c Latham b Watson | 5 |
| *D.L.Houghton c Parore b Su'a | 21 | c Nash b Patel | 2 |
| †A.Flower c Patel b Nash | 14 | c Parore b Patel | 9 |
| E.A.Brandes c Parore b Su'a | 0 | c and b Patel | 6 |
| G.J.Crocker b Su'a | 12 | c Greatbatch b Haslam | 33 |
| D.H.Brain c Su'a b Patel | 11 | c Su'a b Patel | 17 |
| M.G.Burmester not out | 30 | not out | 17 |
| A.J.Traicos not out | 1 | lbw b Patel | 0 |
| Extras (LB7, NB2) | 9 | (LB2) | 2 |
| **Total** (9 wickets declared) | **283** | | **137** |

| ZIMBABWE | O | M | R | W | O | M | R | W | FALL OF WICKETS | | | |
|---|---|---|---|---|---|---|---|---|---|---|---|---|
| | | | | | | | | | NZ | Z | NZ | Z |
| Brandes | 22 | 6 | 49 | 2 | 19.4 | 3 | 59 | 2 | Wkt | 1st | 1st | 2nd | 2nd |
| Brain | 18 | 5 | 49 | 3 | 16 | 2 | 52 | 1 | 1st | 44 | 7 | 21 | 3 |
| Crocker | 15 | 1 | 65 | 2 | 7 | 0 | 24 | 0 | 2nd | 73 | 114 | 27 | 15 |
| Burmester | 10 | 2 | 34 | 0 | 9 | 1 | 44 | 0 | 3rd | 131 | 136 | 77 | 28 |
| Traicos | 23 | 1 | 82 | 2 | 27 | 8 | 70 | 2 | 4th | 299 | 210 | 132 | 34 |
| G.W.Flower | 6 | 0 | 45 | 0 | 4 | 0 | 11 | 0 | 5th | 306 | 211 | 262 | 56 |
| | | | | | | | | | 6th | 313 | 211 | — | 62 |
| NEW ZEALAND | | | | | | | | | 7th | 321 | 239 | — | 71 |
| Su'a | 37 | 7 | 85 | 5 | 12 | 3 | 30 | 1 | 8th | 327 | 239 | — | 91 |
| Nash | 28 | 10 | 59 | 1 | 8 | 3 | 19 | 1 | 9th | 330 | 275 | — | 137 |
| Watson | 25 | 6 | 51 | 1 | 3 | 2 | 3 | 1 | 10th | 335 | — | — | 137 |
| Patel | 33 | 5 | 81 | 2 | 17.3 | 5 | 50 | 6 | | | | | |
| Haslam | | | | | 10 | 2 | 33 | 1 | | | | | |

**Umpires:** H.D.Bird (50), K.Kanjee (3) and I.D.Robinson (3).  Test No. 1199/2

# ZIMBABWE v NEW ZEALAND 1992-93

## ZIMBABWE – BATTING AND FIELDING

|  | M | I | NO | HS | Runs | Avge | 100 | 50 | Ct/St |
|---|---|---|---|---|---|---|---|---|---|
| K.J.Arnott | 2 | 4 | 1 | 101* | 209 | 69.66 | 1 | 1 | 2 |
| M.G.Burmester | 2 | 3 | 2 | 30* | 47 | 47.00 | – | – | 1 |
| A.D.R.Campbell | 2 | 4 | 1 | 52 | 135 | 45.00 | – | 1 | 2 |
| A.Flower | 2 | 3 | – | 81 | 104 | 34.66 | – | 1 | 5/1 |
| A.J.Pycroft | 2 | 3 | – | 60 | 67 | 22.33 | – | 1 | 1 |
| G.W.Flower | 2 | 4 | – | 45 | 80 | 20.00 | – | – | – |
| D.L.Houghton | 2 | 3 | – | 36 | 59 | 19.66 | – | – | 4 |
| G.J.Crocker | 2 | 3 | – | 33 | 46 | 15.33 | – | – | – |
| A.J.Traicos | 2 | 3 | 1 | 4 | 5 | 2.50 | – | – | – |

*Played in one Test:* D.H.Brain 11, 17; E.A.Brandes 0, 6 (1 ct); M.P.Jarvis 2* (1 ct); A.H.Shah 28.

## ZIMBABWE – BOWLING

|  | O | M | R | W | Avge | Best | 5wI | 10wM |
|---|---|---|---|---|---|---|---|---|
| D.H.Brain | 34 | 7 | 101 | 4 | 25.25 | 3-49 | – | – |
| E.A.Brandes | 41.4 | 9 | 108 | 4 | 27.00 | 2-49 | – | – |
| M.P.Jarvis | 37.1 | 4 | 125 | 3 | 41.66 | 3-38 | – | – |
| A.J.Traicos | 90.1 | 14 | 290 | 6 | 48.33 | 2-70 | – | – |
| G.J.Crocker | 41 | 2 | 176 | 2 | 88.00 | 2-65 | – | – |

*Also bowled:* M.G.Burmester 33-4-149-0; G.W.Flower 22-2-93-1; D.L.Houghton 0.5-0-0-0; A.H.Shah 21-6-82-1.

## NEW ZEALAND – BATTING AND FIELDING

|  | M | I | NO | HS | Runs | Avge | 100 | 50 | Ct/St |
|---|---|---|---|---|---|---|---|---|---|
| K.R.Rutherford | 2 | 4 | 2 | 89 | 181 | 90.50 | – | 2 | – |
| D.N.Patel | 2 | 3 | 2 | 58* | 75 | 75.00 | – | 1 | 2 |
| A.H.Jones | 2 | 4 | 2 | 67* | 142 | 71.00 | – | 1 | 1 |
| M.D.Crowe | 2 | 4 | – | 140 | 249 | 62.25 | 1 | 1 | – |
| M.J.Greatbatch | 2 | 4 | – | 88 | 243 | 60.75 | – | 3 | 2 |
| R.T.Latham | 2 | 4 | – | 119 | 192 | 48.00 | 1 | – | 4 |
| A.C.Parore | 2 | 2 | – | 12 | 14 | 7.00 | – | – | 4 |
| M.J.Haslam | 2 | 1 | – | 3 | 3 | 3.00 | – | – | 3 |
| W.Watson | 2 | 1 | – | 3 | 3 | 3.00 | – | – | 1 |
| M.L.Su'a | 2 | 1 | – | 1 | 1 | 1.00 | – | – | 3 |

*Played in one Test:* S.B.Doull 2; D.J.Nash 11* (1 ct).

## NEW ZEALAND – BOWLING

|  | O | M | R | W | Avge | Best | 5wI | 10wM |
|---|---|---|---|---|---|---|---|---|
| M.L.Su'a | 64.1 | 15 | 142 | 8 | 17.75 | 5-85 | 1 | – |
| D.N.Patel | 119.1 | 29 | 304 | 15 | 20.26 | 6-50 | 2 | – |
| D.J.Nash | 36 | 13 | 78 | 2 | 39.00 | 1-19 | – | – |
| W.Watson | 42 | 13 | 85 | 2 | 42.50 | 1-3 | – | – |

*Also bowled:* M.D.Crowe 4-0-15-0; S.B.Doull 19-7-37-1; M.J.Haslam 50-14-153-1; A.H.Jones 1-0-1-0; R.T.Latham 3-2-6-0.

# SOUTH AFRICA v INDIA (1st Test)

Played at Kingsmead, Durban, on 13, 14, 15, 16‡ 17 November 1992.
Toss: India.   Result: MATCH DRAWN.
Debuts: South Africa – S.J.Cook, O.Henry, B.M.McMillan, J.N.Rhodes,
B.N.Schultz; India – P.K.Amre, A.D.Jadeja.                    (‡ no play)

## SOUTH AFRICA

| | | | | |
|---|---|---|---|---|
| S.J.Cook c Tendulkar b Kapil Dev | 0 | c and b Kumble | 43 |
| A.C.Hudson b Kapil Dev | 14 | c More b Srinath | 55 |
| *K.C.Wessels c Azharuddin b Kumble | 118 | c More b Srinath | 32 |
| P.N.Kirsten c More b Srinath | 13 | not out | 11 |
| J.N.Rhodes c Azharuddin b Kumble | 41 | not out | 26 |
| B.M.McMillan c Prabhakar b Shastri | 3 | | |
| †D.J.Richardson lbw b Prabhakar | 15 | | |
| O.Henry c Tendulkar b Shastri | 3 | | |
| M.W.Pringle lbw b Kapil Dev | 33 | | |
| A.A.Donald lbw b Prabhakar | 1 | | |
| B.N.Schultz not out | 0 | | |
| Extras (LB6, NB7) | 13 | (B1, LB2, NB6) | 9 |
| **Total** | **254** | **(3 wickets)** | **176** |

## INDIA

| | |
|---|---|
| R.J.Shastri lbw b Pringle | 14 |
| A.D.Jadeja c McMillan b Schultz | 3 |
| S.V.Manjrekar lbw b McMillan | 0 |
| S.R.Tendulkar run out | 11 |
| *M.Azharuddin run out | 36 |
| P.K.Amre c Rhodes b McMillan | 103 |
| Kapil Dev c Richardson b McMillan | 2 |
| M.Prabhakar c McMillan b Donald | 13 |
| †K.S.More lbw b Henry | 55 |
| A.Kumble b Henry | 8 |
| J.Srinath not out | 1 |
| Extras (B1, LB7, W4, NB19) | 31 |
| **Total** | **277** |

| INDIA | O | M | R | W | O | M | R | W | FALL OF WICKETS | | | |
|---|---|---|---|---|---|---|---|---|---|---|---|---|
| Kapil Dev | 22 | 6 | 43 | 3 | 19 | 11 | 19 | 0 | | SA | I | SA |
| Prabhakar | 24.4 | 7 | 47 | 2 | 14 | 3 | 47 | 0 | Wkt | 1st | 1st | 2nd |
| Srinath | 18 | 3 | 69 | 1 | 16 | 3 | 42 | 2 | 1st | 0 | 18 | 68 |
| Kumble | 28 | 8 | 51 | 2 | 16 | 4 | 36 | 1 | 2nd | 41 | 22 | 129 |
| Shastri | 11 | 1 | 38 | 2 | 14 | 2 | 22 | 0 | 3rd | 101 | 38 | 138 |
| Tendulkar | | | | | 2 | 1 | 3 | 0 | 4th | 183 | 38 | – |
| Manjrekar | | | | | 1 | 0 | 4 | 0 | 5th | 194 | 125 | – |
| | | | | | | | | | 6th | 206 | 127 | – |
| SOUTH AFRICA | | | | | | | | | 7th | 215 | 146 | – |
| Donald | 29 | 6 | 69 | 1 | | | | | 8th | 251 | 247 | – |
| Schultz | 14.5 | 7 | 25 | 1 | | | | | 9th | 253 | 274 | – |
| McMillan | 37 | 18 | 52 | 3 | | | | | 10th | 254 | 277 | – |
| Pringle | 34 | 10 | 67 | 1 | | | | | | | | |
| Henry | 19.1 | 3 | 56 | 2 | | | | | | | | |

Umpires: S.U. Bucknor (6), K.E.Liebenberg (1) and C.J.Mitchley (1)‡.
‡Liebenberg 1st, 3rd and 5th days, Mitchley 2nd and 4th days.        Test No. 1200/1

# SOUTH AFRICA v INDIA (2nd Test)

**Played at New Wanderers, Johannesburg, on 26, 27, 28, 29, 30 November 1992.**
**Toss: South Africa.   Result: MATCH DRAWN.**
**Debuts: South Africa – C.R.Matthews.**

## SOUTH AFRICA

| | | | | |
|---|---|---|---|---|
| S.J.Cook c More b Prabhakar | 2 | | c More b Srinath | 31 |
| A.C.Hudson c Azharuddin b Prabhakar | 8 | | b Kumble | 53 |
| *K.C.Wessels c Azharuddin b Srinath | 5 | (4) | run out | 11 |
| P.N.Kirsten lbw b Prabhakar | 0 | (5) | b Kumble | 26 |
| J.N.Rhodes lbw b Kumble | 91 | (6) | b Kumble | 13 |
| W.J.Cronje c and b Kapil Dev | 8 | (7) | b Kumble | 15 |
| B.M.McMillan c Manjrekar b Srinath | 98 | (8) | c Prabhakar b Kumble | 5 |
| †D.J.Richardson lbw b Kumble | 9 | (3) | b Kumble | 50 |
| C.R.Matthews b Prabhakar | 31 | | c Tendulkar b Prabhakar | 18 |
| M.W.Pringle retired hurt | 3 | | absent hurt | |
| A.A.Donald not out | 14 | (10) | not out | 7 |
| Extras (LB10, W4, NB9) | 23 | | (B1, LB14, W1, NB7) | 23 |
| **Total** | **292** | | | **252** |

## INDIA

| | | | | |
|---|---|---|---|---|
| R.J.Shastri c Wessels b Matthews | 7 | | b Matthews | 23 |
| A.D.Jadeja lbw b McMillan | 14 | | c Wessels b Donald | 43 |
| S.V.Manjrekar b McMillan | 7 | (5) | not out | 32 |
| S.R.Tendulkar c Hudson b Cronje | 111 | | lbw b Donald | 1 |
| *M.Azharuddin c Wessels b Matthews | 9 | (3) | c Richardson b Matthews | 1 |
| P.K.Amre lbw b McMillan | 7 | | not out | 35 |
| M.Prabhakar c Richardson b Donald | 2 | | | |
| Kapil Dev c McMillan b Donald | 25 | | | |
| †K.S.More c Richardson b McMillan | 10 | | | |
| A.Kumble not out | 21 | | | |
| J.Srinath c Richardson b Donald | 5 | | | |
| Extras (LB4, W4, NB1) | 9 | | (B2, LB2, NB2) | 6 |
| **Total** | **227** | | (4 wickets) | **141** |

| INDIA | O | M | R | W | O | M | R | W | | FALL OF WICKETS | | | |
|---|---|---|---|---|---|---|---|---|---|---|---|---|---|
| Kapil Dev | 25 | 4 | 62 | 1 | 24 | 6 | 50 | 0 | | | *SA* | *I* | *SA* | *I* |
| Prabhakar | 29 | 3 | 90 | 4 | 23.2 | 3 | 74 | 1 | *Wkt* | *1st* | *1st* | *2nd* | *2nd* |
| Srinath | 26.5 | 6 | 60 | 2 | 26 | 2 | 58 | 1 | 1st | 10 | 27 | 73 | 68 |
| Kumble | 26 | 8 | 60 | 2 | 44 | 12 | 53 | 6 | 2nd | 11 | 27 | 108 | 70 |
| Shastri | 4 | 0 | 10 | 0 | | | | | 3rd | 11 | 44 | 138 | 71 |
| Tendulkar | | | | | 1 | 0 | 2 | 0 | 4th | 26 | 77 | 170 | 73 |
| | | | | | | | | | 5th | 73 | 124 | 194 | – |
| SOUTH AFRICA | | | | | | | | | 6th | 158 | 127 | 199 | – |
| Donald | 31 | 9 | 78 | 3 | 20 | 6 | 43 | 2 | 7th | 186 | 155 | 209 | – |
| McMillan | 29 | 11 | 74 | 4 | 21 | 6 | 34 | 0 | 8th | 251 | 174 | 239 | – |
| Matthews | 29 | 13 | 41 | 2 | 20 | 10 | 23 | 2 | 9th | 292 | 212 | 252 | – |
| Cronje | 17 | 10 | 22 | 1 | 18 | 7 | 32 | 0 | 10th | – | 227 | – | – |
| Kirsten | 2 | 0 | 8 | 0 | 3 | 1 | 5 | 0 | | | | | |

**Umpires: S.U.Bucknor (7), S.B.Lambson (1) and C.J.Mitchley (2).**
In South Africa's first innings, Pringle retired hurt at 261-8.      Test No. 1201/2

# SOUTH AFRICA v INDIA (3rd Test)

**Played at St George's Park, Port Elizabeth, on 26, 27, 28, 29 December 1992.**
**Toss: South Africa.   Result: SOUTH AFRICA won by 9 wickets.**
**Debuts: Nil.**

## INDIA

| | | | | |
|---|---|---|---|---|
| R.J.Shastri c Henry b McMillan | 10 | c Richardson b McMillan | 5 |
| W.V.Raman c Richardson b Donald | 21 | b Donald | 0 |
| S.V.Manjrekar c Henry b McMillan | 23 | lbw b Donald | 6 |
| S.R.Tendulkar c Richardson b Donald | 6 | c Richardson b Schultz | 0 |
| *M.Azharuddin c Richardson b Donald | 60 | c Wessels b Donald | 7 |
| P.K.Amre c McMillan b Donald | 11 | c Richardson b Schultz | 7 |
| Kapil Dev c Kirsten b McMillan | 12 | c McMillan b Donald | 129 |
| M.Prabhakar c McMillan b Matthews | 11 | c Richardson b Donald | 17 |
| †K.S.More c Richardson b Donald | 20 | b Donald | 17 |
| A.Kumble c McMillan b Schultz | 14 | c Richardson b Donald | 17 |
| S.L.V.Raju not out | 0 | not out | 2 |
| Extras (LB13, W4, NB7) | 24 | (LB4, W1, NB3) | 8 |
| **Total** | **212** | | **215** |

## SOUTH AFRICA

| | | | | |
|---|---|---|---|---|
| A.C.Hudson b Raju | 52 | c Azharuddin b Tendulkar | 33 |
| *K.C.Wessels b Prabhakar | 0 | not out | 95 |
| W.J.Cronje b Kumble | 135 | not out | 16 |
| P.N.Kirsten c More b Raju | 0 | | |
| B.M.McMillan lbw b Raju | 25 | | |
| J.N.Rhodes c Prabhakar b Kumble | 2 | | |
| †D.J.Richardson run out | 1 | | |
| O.Henry lbw b Kapil Dev | 16 | | |
| C.R.Matthews c Azharuddin b Kapil Dev | 17 | | |
| A.A.Donald b Kumble | 6 | | |
| B.N.Schultz not out | 0 | | |
| Extras (B2, LB13, NB6) | 21 | (B8, LB3) | 11 |
| **Total** | **275** | **(1 wicket)** | **155** |

| SOUTH AFRICA | O | M | R | W | O | M | R | W | FALL OF WICKETS | | | | |
|---|---|---|---|---|---|---|---|---|---|---|---|---|---|
| Donald | 27 | 11 | 55 | 5 | 28 | 4 | 84 | 7 | | *I* | *SA* | *I* | *SA* |
| Schultz | 20.5 | 4 | 39 | 1 | 16 | 5 | 37 | 2 | *Wkt* | *1st* | *1st* | *2nd* | *2nd* |
| McMillan | 20 | 9 | 41 | 3 | 12 | 2 | 30 | 1 | 1st | 43 | 0 | 1 | 98 |
| Matthews | 17 | 7 | 34 | 1 | 9 | 1 | 43 | 0 | 2nd | 49 | 117 | 10 | |
| Henry | 11 | 2 | 30 | 0 | 8 | 2 | 17 | 0 | 3rd | 59 | 117 | 11 | |
| | | | | | | | | | 4th | 98 | 171 | 20 | |
| **INDIA** | | | | | | | | | 5th | 143 | 182 | 27 | |
| Kapil Dev | 24 | 6 | 45 | 2 | 5 | 1 | 9 | 0 | 6th | 152 | 185 | 31 | |
| Prabhakar | 15 | 3 | 57 | 1 | 5 | 2 | 7 | 0 | 7th | 160 | 215 | 88 | |
| Kumble | 50.3 | 16 | 81 | 3 | 20 | 5 | 65 | 0 | 8th | 185 | 259 | 120 | |
| Raju | 46 | 15 | 73 | 3 | 18 | 5 | 50 | 0 | 9th | 208 | 274 | 197 | |
| Tendulkar | 1 | 1 | 0 | 0 | 3 | 0 | 9 | 1 | 10th | 212 | 275 | 215 | |
| Shastri | 2 | 1 | 4 | 0 | | | | | | | | | |
| Azharuddin | | | | | 0.1 | 0 | 4 | 0 | | | | | |

**Umpires:** W.Diedricks (1), R.E.Koertzen (1) and D.R.Shepherd (16).

Test No. 1202/3

# SOUTH AFRICA v INDIA (4th Test)

**Played at Newlands, Cape Town, on 2, 3, 4, 5, 6 January 1993.**
**Toss: South Africa.   Result: MATCH DRAWN.**
**Debuts: South Africa – D.J.Cullinan.**                          ‡(V.Yadav)

## SOUTH AFRICA

| | | | | |
|---|--:|---|--:|
| A.C.Hudson c and b Srinath | 19 | c More b Srinath | 11 |
| *K.C.Wessels b Prabhakar | 0 | c and b Srinath | 34 |
| W.J.Cronje c Manjrekar b Kumble | 33 | c More b Srinath | 0 |
| P.N.Kirsten c More b Kapil Dev | 13 | c Manjrekar b Kapil Dev | 13 |
| D.J.Cullinan c Prabhakar b Raju | 46 | c More b Srinath | 28 |
| J.N.Rhodes c More b Srinath | 86 | c Srinath b Kumble | 16 |
| B.M.McMillan c sub (‡) b Kumble | 52 | not out | 11 |
| †D.J.Richardson c Tendulkar b Kumble | 21 | not out | 10 |
| O.Henry run out | 34 | | |
| C.R.Matthews not out | 28 | | |
| A.A.Donald not out | 1 | | |
| Extras (B2, LB22, W2, NB1) | 27 | (LB4, NB3) | 7 |
| **Total** (9 wickets declared) | **360** | (6 wickets declared) | **130** |

## INDIA

| | | | | |
|---|--:|---|--:|
| A.D.Jadeja c Kirsten b McMillan | 19 | not out | 20 |
| M.Prabhakar c Wessels b Henry | 62 | c Richardson b Matthews | 7 |
| S.V.Manjrekar c Hudson b Donald | 46 | not out | 2 |
| P.K.Amre c McMillan b Donald | 6 | | |
| S.R.Tendulkar c Hudson b Cronje | 73 | | |
| *M.Azharuddin c Richardson b McMillan | 7 | | |
| S.L.V.Raju c Cullinan b Matthews | 18 | | |
| Kapil Dev c Hudson b Cronje | 34 | | |
| †K.S.More lbw b Matthews | 0 | | |
| A.Kumble c Hudson b Matthews | 0 | | |
| J.Srinath not out | 0 | | |
| Extras (LB7, W3, NB1) | 11 | | |
| **Total** | **276** | (1 wicket) | **29** |

| INDIA | O | M | R | W | O | M | R | W | | FALL OF WICKETS | | | |
|---|--:|--:|--:|--:|--:|--:|--:|--:|---|---|---|---|---|
| Kapil Dev | 29 | 8 | 42 | 1 | 17 | 4 | 29 | 1 | | | *SA* | *I* | *SA* | *I* |
| Prabhakar | 23 | 6 | 48 | 1 | 10 | 4 | 19 | 0 | | *Wkt* | *1st* | *1st* | *2nd* | *2nd* |
| Raju | 47 | 15 | 94 | 1 | 20 | 8 | 25 | 0 | | 1st | 0 | 44 | 20 | 21 |
| Srinath | 25 | 6 | 51 | 2 | 27 | 10 | 33 | 4 | | 2nd | 28 | 129 | 28 | – |
| Kumble | 47 | 13 | 101 | 3 | 23 | 11 | 20 | 1 | | 3rd | 57 | 138 | 61 | – |
| | | | | | | | | | | 4th | 78 | 144 | 61 | – |
| **SOUTH AFRICA** | | | | | | | | | | 5th | 177 | 153 | 95 | – |
| Donald | 36 | 13 | 58 | 2 | 4 | 0 | 7 | 0 | | 6th | 245 | 200 | 107 | – |
| McMillan | 36 | 9 | 76 | 2 | | | | | | 7th | 282 | 275 | – | – |
| Matthews | 28 | 12 | 32 | 3 | 6 | 1 | 17 | 1 | | 8th | 319 | 276 | – | – |
| Cronje | 18.4 | 8 | 17 | 2 | 3 | 0 | 0 | 0 | | 9th | 345 | 276 | – | – |
| Henry | 33 | 8 | 86 | 1 | | | | | | 10th | – | 276 | – | – |
| Rhodes | | | | | 1 | 0 | 5 | 0 | | | | | | |

**Umpires:** S.B.Lambson (2), K.E.Liebenberg (2) and D.R.Shepherd (17).

Test No. 1203/4

# SOUTH AFRICA v INDIA 1992-93

## SOUTH AFRICA – BATTING AND FIELDING

| | M | I | NO | HS | Runs | Avge | 100 | 50 | Ct/St |
|---|---|---|---|---|---|---|---|---|---|
| J.N.Rhodes | 4 | 7 | 1 | 91 | 275 | 45.83 | – | 2 | 1 |
| K.C.Wessels | 4 | 8 | 1 | 118 | 295 | 42.14 | 1 | 1 | 5 |
| W.J.Cronje | 3 | 6 | 1 | 135 | 207 | 41.40 | 1 | – | – |
| B.M.McMillan | 4 | 6 | 1 | 98 | 194 | 38.80 | – | 2 | 8 |
| C.R.Matthews | 3 | 4 | 1 | 31 | 94 | 31.33 | – | – | – |
| A.C.Hudson | 4 | 8 | – | 55 | 245 | 30.62 | – | 3 | 5 |
| D.J.Richardson | 4 | 6 | 1 | 50 | 106 | 21.20 | – | 1 | 16 |
| S.J.Cook | 2 | 4 | – | 43 | 76 | 19.00 | – | – | – |
| O.Henry | 3 | 3 | – | 34 | 53 | 17.66 | – | – | 2 |
| A.A.Donald | 4 | 5 | 3 | 14* | 29 | 14.50 | – | – | 2 |
| P.N.Kirsten | 4 | 7 | 1 | 26 | 76 | 12.66 | – | – | 2 |

*Also played* (2 Tests): M.W.Pringle 33, 3*; B.N.Schultz 0*, 0*; (1 Test) D.J.Cullinan 46, 28 (1 ct).

## SOUTH AFRICA – BOWLING

| | O | M | R | W | Avge | Best | 5wI | 10wM |
|---|---|---|---|---|---|---|---|---|
| A.A.Donald | 175 | 49 | 394 | 20 | 19.70 | 7-84 | 2 | – |
| C.R.Matthews | 109 | 44 | 190 | 9 | 21.11 | 3-32 | – | – |
| B.M.McMillan | 155 | 55 | 307 | 13 | 23.61 | 4-74 | – | – |

*Also bowled*: W.J.Cronje 56.4-28-71-3; O.Henry 71.1-15-189-3; P.N.Kirsten 5-1-13-0; M.W.Pringle 34-10-67-1; J.N.Rhodes 1-0-5-0; B.N.Schultz 51.4-16-101-4.

## INDIA – BATTING AND FIELDING

| | M | I | NO | HS | Runs | Avge | 100 | 50 | Ct/St |
|---|---|---|---|---|---|---|---|---|---|
| Kapil Dev | 4 | 5 | – | 129 | 202 | 40.40 | 1 | – | 1 |
| P.K.Amre | 4 | 6 | 1 | 103 | 169 | 33.80 | 1 | – | – |
| S.R.Tendulkar | 4 | 6 | – | 111 | 202 | 33.66 | 1 | 1 | 4 |
| A.D.Jadeja | 3 | 5 | 1 | 43 | 99 | 24.75 | – | – | – |
| S.V.Manjrekar | 4 | 7 | 2 | 46 | 116 | 23.20 | – | – | 3 |
| K.S.More | 4 | 6 | – | 55 | 102 | 20.40 | – | 1 | 11 |
| M.Azharuddin | 4 | 6 | – | 60 | 120 | 20.00 | – | 1 | 6 |
| S.L.V.Raju | 2 | 3 | 2 | 18 | 20 | 20.00 | – | – | – |
| M.Prabhakar | 4 | 6 | – | 62 | 112 | 18.66 | – | 1 | 4 |
| A.Kumble | 4 | 5 | 1 | 21* | 60 | 15.00 | – | – | 1 |
| R.J.Shastri | 3 | 5 | – | 23 | 59 | 11.80 | – | – | – |
| J.Srinath | 3 | 3 | 2 | 5 | 6 | 6.00 | – | – | 3 |

*Played in one Test*: W.V.Raman 21, 0.

## INDIA – BOWLING

| | O | M | R | W | Avge | Best | 5wI | 10wM |
|---|---|---|---|---|---|---|---|---|
| A.Kumble | 254.3 | 87 | 467 | 18 | 25.94 | 6-53 | 1 | – |
| J.Srinath | 138.5 | 30 | 313 | 12 | 26.08 | 4-33 | – | – |
| Kapil Dev | 165 | 46 | 299 | 8 | 37.37 | 3-43 | – | – |
| M.Prabhakar | 144 | 31 | 389 | 9 | 43.22 | 4-90 | – | – |

*Also bowled*: M.Azharuddin 0.1-0-4-0; S.V.Manjrekar 1-0-4-0; S.L.V.Raju 131-43-242-4; R.J.Shastri 31-4-74-2; S.R.Tendulkar 7-2-14-1.

# AUSTRALIA v WEST INDIES (1st Test)

**Played at Woolloongabba, Brisbane, on 27, 28, 29, 30 November, 1 December 1992.**
**Toss: Australia.   Result: MATCH DRAWN.**
**Debuts: Australia – D.R.Martyn.**

## AUSTRALIA

| | | | | |
|---|---|---|---|---|
| M.A.Taylor c Williams b Bishop | 7 (2) | c Williams b Walsh | 34 |
| D.C.Boon c Simmons b Hooper | 48 (1) | c Arthurton b Bishop | 111 |
| S.R.Waugh c Williams b Ambrose | 10 | c Williams b Ambrose | 20 |
| M.E.Waugh c and b Hooper | 39 | c Haynes b Ambrose | 60 |
| D.R.Martyn c Lara b Ambrose | 36 | lbw b Ambrose | 15 |
| *A.R.Border run out | 73 | c Williams b Walsh | 17 |
| G.R.J.Matthews c Arthurton b Bishop | 30 | lbw b Ambrose | 0 |
| †I.A.Healy c Lara b Hooper | 17 | c Williams b Bishop | 18 |
| M.G.Hughes c Bishop b Hooper | 10 | c Williams b Ambrose | 1 |
| C.J.McDermott c Hooper b Patterson | 3 | not out | 16 |
| B.A.Reid not out | 1 | c Richardson b Hooper | 1 |
| Extras (B3, LB4, NB12) | 19 | (B4, LB2, NB9) | 15 |
| **Total** | **293** | | **308** |

## WEST INDIES

| | | | | |
|---|---|---|---|---|
| D.L.Haynes c Taylor b Reid | 8 | c Healy b McDermott | 1 |
| P.V.Simmons b Reid | 27 | c Healy b Reid | 1 |
| *R.B.Richardson c Matthews b Hughes | 17 (5) | c Healy b Hughes | 66 |
| B.C.Lara st Healy b Matthews | 58 (3) | c Taylor b McDermott | 0 |
| K.L.T.Arthurton not out | 157 (4) | b McDermott | 0 |
| C.L.Hooper b S.R.Waugh | 47 | c Boon b Matthews | 32 |
| †D.Williams c Hughes b Reid | 15 | lbw b McDermott | 0 |
| I.R.Bishop b McDermott | 5 | not out | 16 |
| C.E.L.Ambrose lbw b Reid | 4 | c Hughes b Reid | 4 |
| B.P.Patterson c M.E.Waugh b Reid | 0 | | |
| C.A.Walsh b Hughes | 17 (10) | not out | 0 |
| Extras (LB6, NB10) | 16 | (LB7, NB6) | 13 |
| **Total** | **371** | **(8 wickets)** | **133** |

| WEST INDIES | O | M | R | W | O | M | R | W | FALL OF WICKETS | | | | |
|---|---|---|---|---|---|---|---|---|---|---|---|---|---|
| | | | | | | | | | | A | WI | A | WI |
| Ambrose | 29.1 | 12 | 53 | 2 | 32 | 8 | 66 | 5 | Wkt | 1st | 1st | 2nd | 2nd |
| Bishop | 23 | 3 | 51 | 2 | 27 | 6 | 58 | 2 | 1st | 8 | 25 | 64 | 2 |
| Patterson | 19 | 0 | 83 | 1 | 7 | 0 | 44 | 0 | 2nd | 21 | 50 | 114 | 2 |
| Walsh | 0.5 | 0 | 2 | 0 | 24 | 3 | 64 | 2 | 3rd | 88 | 58 | 224 | 3 |
| Hooper | 30.1 | 4 | 75 | 4 | 28.2 | 8 | 63 | 1 | 4th | 125 | 170 | 250 | 9 |
| Simmons | 7 | 2 | 16 | 0 | 1 | 0 | 5 | 0 | 5th | 180 | 265 | 255 | 95 |
| Arthurton | 3 | 0 | 6 | 0 | 1 | 0 | 2 | 0 | 6th | 252 | 293 | 255 | 96 |
| | | | | | | | | | 7th | 264 | 307 | 280 | 123 |
| AUSTRALIA | | | | | | | | | 8th | 285 | 321 | 287 | 128 |
| McDermott | 25 | 4 | 93 | 1 | 18 | 7 | 35 | 4 | 9th | 285 | 331 | 295 | – |
| Reid | 37 | 2 | 112 | 5 | 16 | 7 | 39 | 2 | 10th | 293 | 371 | 308 | – |
| Hughes | 18.3 | 3 | 58 | 2 | 13 | 4 | 28 | 1 | | | | | |
| Matthews | 27 | 12 | 41 | 1 | 13 | 4 | 18 | 1 | | | | | |
| Border | 1 | 0 | 7 | 0 | | | | | | | | | |
| S.R.Waugh | 14 | 2 | 46 | 1 | 5 | 1 | 6 | 0 | | | | | |
| M.E.Waugh | 2 | 0 | 8 | 0 | | | | | | | | | |

**Umpires: T.A.Prue (6) and S.G.Randell (11).**                    Test No. 1204/73

# AUSTRALIA v WEST INDIES (2nd Test)

Played at Melbourne Cricket Ground, on 26, 27, 28, 29, 30 December 1992.
Toss: Australia.   Result: AUSTRALIA won by 139 runs.
Debuts: Nil.

## AUSTRALIA

| | | | |
|---|---|---|---|
| M.A.Taylor c Lara b Walsh | 13 | (2) b Bishop | 42 |
| D.C.Boon c Williams b Walsh | 46 | (1) b Simmons | 11 |
| S.R.Waugh c Lara b Ambrose | 38 | (4) c Simmons b Bishop | 1 |
| M.E.Waugh c Williams b Ambrose | 112 | (5) c Adams b Walsh | 16 |
| D.R.Martyn c Simmons b Ambrose | 7 | (6) not out | 67 |
| *A.R.Border c Williams b Bishop | 110 | (7) b Bishop | 4 |
| †I.A.Healy c Hooper b Walsh | 24 | (8) c and b Walsh | 8 |
| S.K.Warne c Adams b Bishop | 1 | (3) c Arthurton b Ambrose | 5 |
| M.G.Hughes not out | 9 | c Williams b Ambrose | 15 |
| C.J.McDermott b Walsh | 17 | c Arthurton b Simmons | 4 |
| M.R.Whitney lbw b Bishop | 0 | run out | 13 |
| Extras (LB14, W1, NB3) | 18 | (B1, LB8, NB1) | 10 |
| **Total** | **395** | | **196** |

## WEST INDIES

| | | | |
|---|---|---|---|
| D.L.Haynes b Hughes | 7 | c Healy b Hughes | 5 |
| P.V.Simmons c Boon b Hughes | 6 | c Boon b Warne | 110 |
| *R.B.Richardson c Healy b Hughes | 15 | b Warne | 52 |
| B.C.Lara lbw b Whitney | 52 | c Boon b Whitney | 4 |
| K.L.T.Arthurton c Healy b McDermott | 71 | st Healy b Warne | 13 |
| C.L.Hooper c and b S.R.Waugh | 3 | c Whitney b Warne | 0 |
| J.C.Adams c Boon b McDermott | 47 | c Taylor b McDermott | 16 |
| †D.Williams c Healy b McDermott | 0 | c M.E.Waugh b Warne | 0 |
| I.R.Bishop b McDermott | 9 | c Taylor b Warne | 7 |
| C.E.L.Ambrose c McDermott b Warne | 7 | not out | 6 |
| C.A.Walsh not out | 0 | c Hughes b Warne | 6 |
| Extras (LB10, NB6) | 16 | (B3, LB2, NB1) | 6 |
| **Total** | **233** | | **219** |

| WEST INDIES | O | M | R | W | O | M | R | W |
|---|---|---|---|---|---|---|---|---|
| Ambrose | 35 | 10 | 70 | 3 | 30 | 9 | 57 | 2 |
| Bishop | 29 | 2 | 84 | 3 | 20 | 5 | 45 | 3 |
| Simmons | 10 | 2 | 23 | 0 | 18 | 6 | 34 | 2 |
| Walsh | 39 | 10 | 91 | 4 | 21 | 7 | 42 | 2 |
| Hooper | 36 | 3 | 95 | 0 | 2.4 | 1 | 9 | 0 |
| Adams | 4 | 0 | 18 | 0 | | | | |
| AUSTRALIA | | | | | | | | |
| McDermott | 25.1 | 8 | 66 | 4 | 17 | 6 | 66 | 1 |
| Hughes | 19 | 5 | 51 | 3 | 18 | 7 | 41 | 1 |
| Whitney | 13 | 4 | 27 | 1 | 10 | 2 | 32 | 1 |
| Warne | 24 | 7 | 65 | 1 | 23.2 | 8 | 52 | 7 |
| S.R.Waugh | 4 | 1 | 14 | 1 | | | | |
| M.E.Waugh | | | | | 3 | 0 | 23 | 0 |

### FALL OF WICKETS

| | A | WI | A | WI |
|---|---|---|---|---|
| Wkt | 1st | 1st | 2nd | 2nd |
| 1st | 38 | 11 | 22 | 9 |
| 2nd | 100 | 28 | 40 | 143 |
| 3rd | 104 | 33 | 41 | 148 |
| 4th | 115 | 139 | 73 | 165 |
| 5th | 319 | 144 | 90 | 177 |
| 6th | 362 | 192 | 102 | 198 |
| 7th | 366 | 192 | 121 | 206 |
| 8th | 369 | 206 | 154 | 206 |
| 9th | 394 | 233 | 167 | 219 |
| 10th | 395 | 233 | 196 | 219 |

**Umpires:** S.G.Randell (12) and C.D.Timmins (3).          Test No. 1205/74

# AUSTRALIA v WEST INDIES (3rd Test)

**Played at Sydney Cricket Ground, on 2, 3, 4, 5, 6 January 1993.**
**Toss: Australia.   Result: MATCH DRAWN.**
**Debuts: West Indies – J.R.Murray.**

## AUSTRALIA

| | | | | |
|---|---|---|---|---|
| M.A.Taylor c Murray b Bishop | 20 | not out | | 46 |
| D.C.Boon c Murray b Adams | 76 | not out | | 63 |
| S.R.Waugh c Simmons b Ambrose | 100 | | | |
| M.E.Waugh run out | 57 | | | |
| D.R.Martyn b Ambrose | 0 | | | |
| * A.R.Border c Murray b Hooper | 74 | | | |
| G.R.J.Matthews c Murray b Hooper | 79 | | | |
| †I.A.Healy not out | 36 | | | |
| M.G.Hughes c Haynes b Bishop | 17 | | | |
| S.K.Warne c Simmons b Hooper | 14 | | | |
| C.J.McDermott did not bat | | | | |
| Extras (B2, LB23, NB5) | 30 | (B1, LB2, NB5) | | 8 |
| **Total (9 wickets declared)** | **503** | **(0 wickets)** | | **117** |

## WEST INDIES

| | |
|---|---|
| D.L.Haynes b Matthews | 22 |
| P.V.Simmons c Taylor b McDermott | 3 |
| * R.B.Richardson c Warne b Hughes | 109 |
| B.C.Lara run out | 277 |
| K.L.T.Arthurton c Healy b Matthews | 47 |
| C.L.Hooper b Warne | 21 |
| J.C.Adams not out | 77 |
| †J.R.Murray c Healy b Hughes | 11 |
| I.R.Bishop run out | 1 |
| C.E.L.Ambrose c Martyn b M.E.Waugh | 16 |
| C.A.Walsh c Healy b Hughes | 0 |
| Extras (B4, LB9, W1, NB8) | 22 |
| **Total** | **606** |

| WEST INDIES | O | M | R | W | O | M | R | W | FALL OF WICKETS | | | |
|---|---|---|---|---|---|---|---|---|---|---|---|---|
| Ambrose | 35 | 8 | 87 | 2 | 6 | 2 | 10 | 0 | | *A* | *WI* | *A* |
| Bishop | 36 | 6 | 87 | 2 | 4 | 1 | 9 | 0 | *Wkt* | *1st* | *1st* | *2nd* |
| Walsh | 30 | 8 | 86 | 0 | 8 | 3 | 13 | 0 | 1st | 42 | 13 | – |
| Hooper | 45.4 | 6 | 137 | 3 | 10 | 2 | 22 | 0 | 2nd | 160 | 31 | – |
| Adams | 15 | 2 | 56 | 1 | 8 | 1 | 29 | 0 | 3rd | 254 | 324 | – |
| Simmons | 10 | 2 | 25 | 0 | 3 | 2 | 9 | 0 | 4th | 261 | 448 | – |
| Arthurton | | | | | 5 | 1 | 14 | 0 | 5th | 270 | 481 | – |
| Lara | | | | | 2 | 0 | 4 | 0 | 6th | 425 | 537 | – |
| Richardson | | | | | 1 | 0 | 4 | 0 | 7th | 440 | 573 | – |
| | | | | | | | | | 8th | 469 | 577 | – |
| **AUSTRALIA** | 33 | 3 | 119 | 1 | | | | | 9th | 503 | 603 | – |
| McDermott | 16.4 | 1 | 76 | 3 | | | | | 10th | – | 606 | – |
| Hughes | 59 | 12 | 169 | 2 | | | | | | | | |
| Matthews | 11 | 1 | 43 | 0 | | | | | | | | |
| S.R.Waugh | 41 | 6 | 116 | 1 | | | | | | | | |
| Warne | 14 | 1 | 41 | 0 | | | | | | | | |
| Border | 10 | 1 | 29 | 1 | | | | | | | | |
| M.E.Waugh | | | | | | | | | | | | |

**Umpires: D.B.Hair (2) and T.A.Prue (7).**                    Test No. 1206/75

# AUSTRALIA v WEST INDIES (4th Test)

**Played at Adelaide Oval, on 23, 24, 25, 26 January 1993.**
**Toss: West Indies.   Result: WEST INDIES won by 1 run.**
**Debuts: Australia – J.L.Langer.**

## WEST INDIES

| | | | |
|---|---|---|---|
| D.L.Haynes st Healy b May | 45 | c Healy b McDermott | 11 |
| P.V.Simmons c Hughes b S.R.Waugh | 46 | b McDermott | 10 |
| *R.B.Richardson lbw b Hughes | 2 | c Healy b Warne | 72 |
| B.C.Lara c Healy b McDermott | 52 | c S.R.Waugh b Hughes | 7 |
| K.L.T.Arthurton c S.R.Waugh b May | 0 | c Healy b McDermott | 0 |
| C.L.Hooper c Healy b Hughes | 2 | c Hughes b May | 25 |
| †J.R.Murray not out | 49 | c M.E.Waugh b May | 0 |
| I.R.Bishop c M.E.Waugh b Hughes | 13 | c M.E.Waugh b May | 6 |
| C.E.L.Ambrose c Healy b Hughes | 0 | st Healy b May | 1 |
| K.C.G.Benjamin b M.E.Waugh | 15 | c Warne b May | 0 |
| C.A.Walsh lbw b Hughes | 5 | not out | 0 |
| Extras (LB11, NB12) | 23 | (LB2, NB12) | 14 |
| **Total** | **252** | | **146** |

## AUSTRALIA

| | | | |
|---|---|---|---|
| M.A.Taylor c Hooper b Bishop | 1 | (2) c Murray b Benjamin | 7 |
| D.C.Boon not out | 39 | (1) lbw b Ambrose | 0 |
| J.L.Langer c Murray b Benjamin | 20 | c Murray b Bishop | 54 |
| M.E.Waugh c Simmons b Ambrose | 0 | c Hooper b Walsh | 26 |
| S.R.Waugh c Murray b Ambrose | 42 | c Arthurton b Ambrose | 4 |
| *A.R.Border c Hooper b Ambrose | 19 | c Haynes b Ambrose | 1 |
| †I.A.Healy c Murray b Ambrose | 0 | b Walsh | 0 |
| M.G.Hughes c Murray b Hooper | 43 | lbw b Ambrose | 1 |
| S.K.Warne lbw b Hooper | 0 | lbw b Bishop | 9 |
| T.B.A.May c Murray b Ambrose | 6 | not out | 42 |
| C.J.McDermott b Ambrose | 14 | c Murray b Walsh | 18 |
| Extras (B7, LB3, NB19) | 29 | (B1, LB8, NB13) | 22 |
| **Total** | **213** | | **184** |

| AUSTRALIA | O | M | R | W | O | M | R | W |
|---|---|---|---|---|---|---|---|---|
| McDermott | 16 | 1 | 85 | 1 | 11 | 0 | 66 | 3 |
| Hughes | 21.3 | 3 | 64 | 5 | 13 | 1 | 43 | 1 |
| S.R.Waugh | 13 | 4 | 37 | 1 | 5 | 1 | 8 | 0 |
| May | 14 | 1 | 41 | 2 | 6.5 | 3 | 9 | 5 |
| Warne | 2 | 0 | 11 | 0 | 6 | 2 | 18 | 1 |
| M.E.Waugh | 1 | 0 | 3 | 1 | | | | |
| WEST INDIES | | | | | | | | |
| Ambrose | 28.2 | 6 | 74 | 6 | 26 | 5 | 46 | 4 |
| Bishop | 18 | 3 | 48 | 1 | 17 | 3 | 41 | 2 |
| Benjamin | 6 | 0 | 22 | 1 | 12 | 2 | 32 | 1 |
| Walsh | 10 | 3 | 34 | 0 | 19 | 4 | 44 | 3 |
| Hooper | 13 | 4 | 25 | 2 | 5 | 1 | 12 | 0 |

### FALL OF WICKETS

| | WI | A | WI | A |
|---|---|---|---|---|
| Wkt | 1st | 1st | 2nd | 2nd |
| 1st | 84 | 1 | 14 | 5 |
| 2nd | 99 | 16 | 49 | 16 |
| 3rd | 129 | 46 | 63 | 54 |
| 4th | 130 | 108 | 65 | 64 |
| 5th | 134 | 108 | 124 | 72 |
| 6th | 189 | 112 | 137 | 73 |
| 7th | 206 | 181 | 145 | 74 |
| 8th | 206 | 181 | 146 | 102 |
| 9th | 247 | 197 | 146 | 184 |
| 10th | 252 | 213 | 146 | 184 |

**Umpires: D.B.Hair (3) and L.J.King (6).**                Test No. 1207/76
In the first innings D.C.Boon (2) retired hurt at 16 and resumed at 108-5.

# AUSTRALIA v WEST INDIES (5th Test)

Played at W.A.C.A.Ground, Perth, on 30, 31 January, 1 February 1993.
Toss: Australia.   Result: WEST INDIES won by an innings and 25 runs.
Debuts: Australia – J.Angel; West Indies – A.C.Cummins.                    ‡(A.L.Logie)

## AUSTRALIA

| | | | | |
|---|---|---:|---|---:|
| J.L.Langer c Murray b Bishop | 10 | (2) | c sub ‡ b Ambrose | 1 |
| D.C.Boon c Richardson b Ambrose | 44 | (1) | b Bishop | 52 |
| S.R.Waugh c Murray b Bishop | 13 | | c sub ‡ b Bishop | 0 |
| M.E.Waugh c Murray b Ambrose | 9 | | c Richardson b Bishop | 21 |
| D.R.Martyn c Simmons b Ambrose | 13 | (6) | c Ambrose b Cummins | 31 |
| *A.R.Border c Murray b Ambrose | 0 | (7) | b Bishop | 0 |
| †I.A.Healy c Lara b Ambrose | 0 | (8) | c Murray b Bishop | 27 |
| M.G.Hughes c Arthurton b Ambrose | 0 | (9) | c Murray b Walsh | 22 |
| S.K.Warne run out (Walsh) | 13 | (5) | c Murray b Ambrose | 0 |
| J.Angel c Murray b Ambrose | 0 | | not out | 4 |
| C.J.McDermott not out | 2 | | c Lara b Bishop | 8 |
| Extras (LB8, W1, NB6) | 15 | | (B1, LB6, NB5) | 12 |
| **Total** | **119** | | | **178** |

## WEST INDIES

| | |
|---|---:|
| D.L.Haynes c Healy b Hughes | 24 |
| P.V.Simmons c S.R.Waugh b Angel | 80 |
| *R.B.Richardson c Langer b McDermott | 47 |
| B.C.Lara c Warne b McDermott | 16 |
| K.L.T.Arthurton c S.R.Waugh b McDermott | 77 |
| J.C.Adams b Hughes | 8 |
| †J.R.Murray c Healy b M.E.Waugh | 37 |
| I.R.Bishop c Healy b M.E.Waugh | 0 |
| A.C.Cummins c M.E.Waugh b Hughes | 3 |
| C.E.L.Ambrose not out | 9 |
| C.A.Walsh b Hughes | 1 |
| Extras (B4, LB10, NB6) | 20 |
| **Total** | **322** |

| WEST INDIES | O | M | R | W | O | M | R | W | FALL OF WICKETS | | | |
|---|---|---|---|---|---|---|---|---|---|---|---|---|
| Ambrose | 18 | 9 | 25 | 7 | 21 | 8 | 54 | 2 | | A | WI | A |
| Bishop | 11 | 6 | 17 | 2 | 16 | 4 | 40 | 6 | Wkt | 1st | 1st | 2nd |
| Walsh | 11.2 | 2 | 45 | 0 | 12 | 2 | 46 | 1 | 1st | 27 | 111 | 13 |
| Cummins | 7 | 0 | 24 | 0 | 8 | 3 | 31 | 1 | 2nd | 58 | 136 | 14 |
| | | | | | | | | | 3rd | 85 | 184 | 66 |
| AUSTRALIA | | | | | | | | | 4th | 90 | 195 | 67 |
| McDermott | 22 | 4 | 85 | 3 | | | | | 5th | 90 | 205 | 95 |
| Hughes | 25.4 | 6 | 71 | 4 | | | | | 6th | 100 | 280 | 95 |
| Angel | 19 | 4 | 72 | 1 | | | | | 7th | 102 | 286 | 130 |
| Warne | 12 | 0 | 51 | 0 | | | | | 8th | 104 | 301 | 162 |
| S.R.Waugh | 6 | 3 | 8 | 0 | | | | | 9th | 104 | 319 | 170 |
| M.E.Waugh | 6 | 1 | 21 | 2 | | | | | 10th | 119 | 322 | 178 |

Umpires: S.G.Randell (13) and C.D.Timmins (4).
D.L.Haynes retired hurt when 21* at 34-0 and resumed at 195-4.   Test No. 1208/77

# AUSTRALIA v WEST INDIES 1992-93

## AUSTRALIA – BATTING AND FIELDING

| | M | I | NO | HS | Runs | Avge | 100 | 50 | Ct/St |
|---|---|---|---|---|---|---|---|---|---|
| D.C.Boon | 5 | 10 | 2 | 111 | 490 | 61.25 | 1 | 3 | 5 |
| M.E.Waugh | 5 | 9 | – | 112 | 340 | 37.77 | 1 | 2 | 6 |
| G.R.J.Matthews | 2 | 3 | – | 79 | 109 | 36.33 | – | 1 | 1 |
| A.R.Border | 5 | 9 | – | 110 | 298 | 33.11 | 1 | 2 | – |
| D.R.Martyn | 4 | 7 | 1 | 67* | 169 | 28.16 | – | 1 | 1 |
| S.R.Waugh | 5 | 9 | – | 100 | 228 | 25.33 | 1 | – | 5 |
| M.A.Taylor | 4 | 8 | 1 | 46* | 170 | 24.28 | – | – | 5 |
| J.L.Langer | 2 | 4 | – | 54 | 85 | 21.25 | – | 1 | 1 |
| I.A.Healy | 5 | 9 | 1 | 36* | 130 | 16.25 | – | – | 19/4 |
| M.G.Hughes | 5 | 9 | 1 | 43 | 118 | 14.75 | – | – | 5 |
| C.J.McDermott | 5 | 8 | 2 | 18 | 82 | 13.66 | – | – | 1 |
| S.K.Warne | 4 | 7 | – | 14 | 42 | 6.00 | – | – | 3 |

*Played in one Test:* J.Angel 0, 4*; T.B.A.May 6, 42*; B.A.Reid 1*, 1; M.R.Whitney 0, 13 (1 ct).

## AUSTRALIA – BOWLING

| | O | M | R | W | Avge | Best | 5wI | 10wM |
|---|---|---|---|---|---|---|---|---|
| T.B.A.May | 20.5 | 4 | 50 | 7 | 7.14 | 5-9 | 1 | – |
| B.A.Reid | 53 | 9 | 151 | 7 | 21.57 | 5-112 | 1 | – |
| M.G.Hughes | 145.2 | 30 | 432 | 20 | 21.60 | 5-64 | 1 | – |
| S.K.Warne | 108.2 | 23 | 313 | 10 | 31.30 | 7-52 | 1 | – |
| C.J.McDermott | 167.1 | 33 | 615 | 18 | 34.16 | 4-35 | – | – |

*Also bowled:* J.Angel 19-4-72-1; A.R.Border 15-1-48-0; G.R.J.Matthews 99-28-228-4; M.E.Waugh 22-2-84-4; S.R.Waugh 58-13-162-3; M.R.Whitney 23-6-59-2.

## WEST INDIES – BATTING AND FIELDING

| | M | I | NO | HS | Runs | Avge | 100 | 50 | Ct/St |
|---|---|---|---|---|---|---|---|---|---|
| B.C.Lara | 5 | 8 | – | 277 | 466 | 58.25 | 1 | 3 | 6 |
| K.L.T.Arthurton | 5 | 8 | 1 | 157* | 365 | 52.14 | 1 | 2 | 6 |
| J.C.Adams | 3 | 4 | 1 | 77* | 148 | 49.33 | – | 1 | 2 |
| R.B.Richardson | 5 | 8 | – | 109 | 380 | 47.50 | 1 | 3 | 3 |
| P.V.Simmons | 5 | 8 | – | 110 | 283 | 35.37 | 1 | 1 | 7 |
| J.R.Murray | 3 | 4 | 1 | 49* | 97 | 32.33 | – | – | 19 |
| C.L.Hooper | 4 | 7 | – | 47 | 130 | 18.57 | – | – | 7 |
| D.L.Haynes | 5 | 8 | – | 45 | 123 | 15.37 | – | – | 1 |
| I.R.Bishop | 5 | 8 | 1 | 16* | 57 | 8.14 | – | – | 1 |
| C.E.L.Ambrose | 5 | 8 | 2 | 16 | 47 | 7.83 | – | – | 1 |
| C.A.Walsh | 5 | 8 | 3 | 17 | 23 | 4.60 | – | – | 1 |
| D.Williams | 2 | 4 | – | 15 | 15 | 3.75 | – | – | 11 |

*Played in one Test:* K.C.G.Benjamin 15, 0; A.C.Cummins 3; B.P.Patterson 0.

## WEST INDIES – BOWLING

| | O | M | R | W | Avge | Best | 5wI | 10wM |
|---|---|---|---|---|---|---|---|---|
| C.E.L.Ambrose | 260.3 | 77 | 542 | 33 | 16.42 | 7-25 | 3 | 1 |
| I.R.Bishop | 201 | 39 | 480 | 23 | 20.86 | 6-40 | 1 | – |
| C.A.Walsh | 175.1 | 42 | 467 | 12 | 38.91 | 4-91 | – | – |
| C.L.Hooper | 170.5 | 29 | 438 | 10 | 43.80 | 4-75 | – | – |

*Also bowled:* J.C.Adams 27-3-103-1; K.L.T.Arthurton 9-1-22-0; K.C.G.Benjamin 18-2-54-2; A.C.Cummins 15-3-55-1; B.C.Lara 2-0-4-0; B.P.Patterson 26-0-127-1; R.B.Richardson 1-0-4-0; P.V.Simmons 49-14-112-2.

# SRI LANKA v NEW ZEALAND (1st Test)

**Played at Tyronne Fernando Stadium, Moratuwa, on 27, 28, 29 Nov., 1, 2 Dec. 1992.**
**Toss: Sri Lanka.   Result: MATCH DRAWN.**
**Debuts: New Zealand – C.Z.Harris, M.B.Owens, J.T.C.Vaughan.**

### NEW ZEALAND

| | | | |
|---|---|---|---|
| B.R.Hartland c De Silva b Liyanage | 3 | lbw b Ramanayake | 52 |
| J.G.Wright c Gurusinha b Ramanayake | 11 | st Wickremasinghe b Anurasiri | 42 |
| A.H.Jones c Mahanama b Liyanage | 35 | c Wickremasinghe b Ramanayake | 14 |
| *M.D.Crowe c Ranatunga b Warnaweera | 19 | c Tillekeratne b Anurasiri | 19 |
| K.R.Rutherford c Wickremasinghe b Hathurusinghe | 105 | lbw b Warnaweera | 53 |
| C.Z.Harris b Warnaweera | 56 | (7) not out | 0 |
| J.T.C.Vaughan b Liyanage | 17 | (6) not out | 0 |
| †A.C.Parore c Wickremasinghe b Anurasiri | 3 | | |
| D.J.Nash c Wickremasinghe b Liyanage | 4 | | |
| M.L.Su'a b Anurasiri | 0 | | |
| M.B.Owens not out | 0 | | |
| Extras (B5, LB12, W2, NB16) | 35 | (LB8, W1, NB14) | 23 |
| **Total** | **288** | **(5 wickets)** | **195** |

### SRI LANKA

| | |
|---|---|
| R.S.Mahanama run out | 153 |
| U.C.Hathurusinghe c Jones b Nash | 10 |
| A.P.Gurusinha c Vaughan b Su'a | 43 |
| P.A.De Silva c Nash b Su'a | 62 |
| H.P.Tillekeratne b Owens | 1 |
| *A.Ranatunga c Parore b Owens | 3 |
| †A.G.D.Wickremasinghe not out | 13 |
| C.P.H.Ramanayake not out | 10 |
| D.K.Liyanage | |
| S.D.Anurasiri } did not bat | |
| K.P.J.Warnaweera | |
| Extras (LB7, W9, NB16) | 32 |
| **Total (6 wickets declared)** | **327** |

| SRI LANKA | O | M | R | W | O | M | R | W | FALL OF WICKETS | | | |
|---|---|---|---|---|---|---|---|---|---|---|---|---|
| | | | | | | | | | | NZ | SL | NZ |
| Ramanayake | 23 | 2 | 57 | 1 | 17 | 6 | 27 | 2 | Wkt | 1st | 1st | 2nd |
| Liyanage | 26.5 | 6 | 82 | 4 | 17 | 4 | 48 | 0 | 1st | 6 | 27 | 110 |
| Hathurusinghe | 8 | 4 | 12 | 1 | 10 | 6 | 22 | 0 | 2nd | 44 | 164 | 122 |
| Anurasiri | 34 | 11 | 55 | 2 | 26 | 11 | 32 | 2 | 3rd | 297 | 136 |
| Warnaweera | 34 | 15 | 46 | 2 | 25 | 15 | 31 | 1 | 4th | 87 | 299 | 160 |
| De Silva | 4 | 2 | 8 | 0 | | | | | 5th | 138 | 300 | 194 |
| Gurusinha | 1 | 0 | 6 | 0 | | | | | 6th | 265 | 309 | – |
| Ranatunga | 3 | 2 | 5 | 0 | 7 | 2 | 26 | 0 | 7th | 273 | – | – |
| Tillekeratne | | | | | 1 | 0 | 1 | 0 | 8th | 283 | – | – |
| NEW ZEALAND | | | | | | | | | 9th | 286 | – | – |
| Su'a | 25 | 6 | 62 | 2 | | | | | 10th | 288 | – | – |
| Owens | 17 | 3 | 63 | 2 | | | | | | | | |
| Nash | 18 | 2 | 62 | 1 | | | | | | | | |
| Vaughan | 14 | 0 | 56 | 0 | | | | | | | | |
| Harris | 15 | 5 | 64 | 0 | | | | | | | | |
| Jones | 1 | 0 | 3 | 0 | | | | | | | | |
| Crowe | 1 | 0 | 2 | 0 | | | | | | | | |

**Umpires: K.T.Francis (7) and T.M.Samarasinghe (2).**          Test No. 1209/10

# SRI LANKA v NEW ZEALAND (2nd Test)

**Played at Sinhalese Sports Club, Colombo, on 6, 7, 8, 9 December 1992.**
**Toss: Sri Lanka.    Result: SRI LANKA won by 9 wickets.**
**Debuts: Nil.**                                                    ‡(S.T.Jayasuriya)

## SRI LANKA

| | | | |
|---|---:|---|---:|
| R.S.Mahanama c Bradburn b Owens | 109 | c Parore b Owens | 29 |
| U.C.Hathurusinghe c Harris b Owens | 27 | not out | 23 |
| A.P.Gurusinha st Parore b Bradburn | 22 | not out | 14 |
| P.A.DeSilva c Parore b Pringle | 3 | | |
| *A.Ranatunga c Parore b Su'a | 76 | | |
| H.P.Tillekeratne c Parore b Bradburn | 93 | | |
| †A.G.D.Wickremasinghe c Rutherford b Owens | 2 | | |
| D.K.Liyanage c Parore b Su'a | 16 | | |
| S.D.Anurasiri c Su'a b Owens | 24 | | |
| M.Muralitharan not out | 4 | | |
| K.P.J.Warnaweera c Crowe b Bradburn | 5 | | |
| Extras (B3, LB4, W3, NB3) | 13 | (LB2, NB2) | 4 |
| **Total** | **394** | (1 wicket) | **70** |

## NEW ZEALAND

| | | | |
|---|---:|---|---:|
| B.R.Hartland c Gurusinha b Warnaweera | 21 | c Muralitharan b Gurusinha | 21 |
| J.G.Wright c Wickremasinghe b Warnaweera | 30 | c Mahanama b Muralitharan | 50 |
| A.H.Jones c Tillekeratne b Warnaweera | 20 | c Tillekeratne b Warnaweera | 5 |
| *M.D.Crowe b Muralitharan | 0 | c Tillekeratne b Muralitharan | 107 |
| K.R.Rutherford c Tillekeratne b Warnaweera | 0 | c sub ‡ b Warnaweera | 38 |
| C.Z.Harris run out | 0 | lbw b Anurasiri | 19 |
| †A.C.Parore lbw b Muralitharan | 5 | c Tillekeratne b Muralitharan | 60 |
| G.E.Bradburn c Tillekeratne b Liyanage | 1 | c Wickremasinghe b Anurasiri | 7 |
| M.L.Su'a not out | 2 | b Muralitharan | 0 |
| C.Pringle b Liyanage | 0 | c Tillekeratne b Liyanage | 23 |
| M.B.Owens c Anurasiri b Muralitharan | 0 | not out | 8 |
| Extras (LB4, W1, NB9) | 14 | (B2, LB8, NB13) | 23 |
| **Total** | **102** | | **361** |

| NEW ZEALAND | O | M | R | W | O | M | R | W | FALL OF WICKETS | | | | |
|---|---|---|---|---|---|---|---|---|---|---|---|---|---|
| Su'a | 26 | 7 | 50 | 2 | 2 | 0 | 14 | 0 | | | | | |
| Owens | 30 | 7 | 101 | 4 | 6 | 1 | 36 | 1 | Wkt | 1st | 1st | 2nd | 2nd |
| Pringle | 32 | 7 | 85 | 1 | 2 | 1 | 5 | 0 | 1st | 102 | 58 | 23 | 36 |
| Bradburn | 37.4 | 4 | 134 | 3 | 3 | 1 | 8 | 0 | 2nd | 160 | 61 | 30 | – |
| Harris | 3 | 0 | 17 | 0 | | | | | 3rd | 167 | 64 | 189 | – |
| Jones | | | | | 1.4 | 0 | 5 | 0 | 4th | 182 | 65 | 196 | – |
| | | | | | | | | | 5th | 274 | 89 | 240 | – |
| SRI LANKA | | | | | | | | | 6th | 287 | 98 | 261 | – |
| Liyanage | 9 | 3 | 9 | 2 | 12 | 3 | 35 | 1 | 7th | 316 | 100 | 285 | – |
| Gurusinha | 4 | 1 | 15 | 0 | 8 | 1 | 19 | 1 | 8th | 385 | 101 | 286 | – |
| Anurasiri | 6 | 1 | 13 | 0 | 22 | 4 | 54 | 2 | 9th | 385 | 101 | 317 | – |
| Hathurusinghe | 7 | 3 | 14 | 0 | 3 | 2 | 2 | 0 | 10th | 394 | 102 | 361 | – |
| Warnaweera | 14 | 3 | 25 | 4 | 34 | 4 | 107 | 2 | | | | | |
| Muralitharan | 12.1 | 3 | 22 | 3 | 40 | 5 | 134 | 4 | | | | | |

**Umpires:** I.Anandappa (2) and T.M.Samarasinghe (3).        Test No. 1210/11

# SRI LANKA v NEW ZEALAND 1992-93

## SRI LANKA – BATTING AND FIELDING

| | M | I | NO | HS | Runs | Avge | 100 | 50 | Ct/St |
|---|---|---|---|---|---|---|---|---|---|
| R.S.Mahanama | 2 | 3 | – | 153 | 291 | 97.00 | 2 | – | 2 |
| H.P.Tillekeratne | 2 | 2 | – | 93 | 94 | 47.00 | – | 1 | 8 |
| A.P.Gurusinha | 2 | 3 | 1 | 43 | 79 | 39.50 | – | – | 2 |
| A.Ranatunga | 2 | 2 | – | 76 | 79 | 39.50 | – | 1 | 1 |
| P.A.De Silva | 2 | 2 | – | 62 | 65 | 32.50 | – | 1 | 1 |
| U.C.Hathurusinghe | 2 | 3 | 1 | 27 | 60 | 30.00 | – | – | – |
| S.D.Anurasiri | 2 | 1 | – | 24 | 24 | 24.00 | – | – | 1 |
| D.K.Liyanage | 2 | 1 | – | 16 | 16 | 16.00 | – | – | – |
| A.G.D.Wickremasinghe | 2 | 2 | 1 | 13* | 15 | 15.00 | – | – | 6/1 |
| K.P.J.Warnaweera | 2 | 1 | – | 5 | 5 | 5.00 | – | – | – |

Played in one Test: C.P.H.Ramanayake 10*; M.Muralitharan 4* (1 ct).

## SRI LANKA – BOWLING

| | O | M | R | W | Avge | Best | 5wI | 10wM |
|---|---|---|---|---|---|---|---|---|
| M.Muralitharan | 52.1 | 8 | 156 | 7 | 22.28 | 4-134 | – | – |
| K.P.J.Warnaweera | 107 | 37 | 209 | 9 | 23.22 | 4-25 | – | – |
| D.K.Liyanage | 64.5 | 16 | 174 | 7 | 24.85 | 4-82 | – | – |
| S.D.Anurasiri | 88 | 27 | 154 | 6 | 25.66 | 2-32 | – | – |
| C.P.H.Ramanayake | 40 | 8 | 84 | 3 | 28.00 | 2-27 | – | – |

Also bowled: A.P. Gurusinha 13-2-40-1; U.C.Hathurusinghe 28-15-50-1; P.A.De Silva 4-2-8-0; A.Ranatunga 10-4-31-0; H.P.Tillekeratne 1-0-1-0.

## NEW ZEALAND – BATTING AND FIELDING

| | M | I | NO | HS | Runs | Avge | 100 | 50 | Ct/St |
|---|---|---|---|---|---|---|---|---|---|
| K.R.Rutherford | 2 | 4 | – | 105 | 196 | 49.00 | 1 | 1 | 1 |
| M.D.Crowe | 2 | 4 | – | 107 | 137 | 34.25 | 1 | – | 1 |
| J.G.Wright | 2 | 4 | – | 50 | 133 | 33.25 | – | 1 | – |
| C.Z.Harris | 2 | 4 | 1 | 56 | 84 | 28.00 | – | 1 | 1 |
| B.R.Hartland | 2 | 4 | – | 52 | 97 | 24.25 | – | 1 | – |
| A.C.Parore | 2 | 3 | – | 60 | 68 | 22.66 | – | 1 | 6/1 |
| A.H.Jones | 2 | 4 | – | 35 | 74 | 18.50 | – | – | 1 |
| M.B.Owens | 2 | 3 | 2 | 8* | 8 | 8.00 | – | – | – |
| M.L.Su'a | 2 | 3 | 2 | 2* | 2 | 1.00 | – | – | 1 |

Played in one Test: G.E.Bradburn 1, 7 (1 ct); D.J.Nash 4 (1 ct); C.Pringle 0, 23; J.T.C.Vaughan 17, 0* (1 ct).

## NEW ZEALAND – BOWLING

| | O | M | R | W | Avge | Best | 5wI | 10wM |
|---|---|---|---|---|---|---|---|---|
| M.B.Owens | 53 | 11 | 200 | 7 | 28.57 | 4-101 | – | – |
| M.L.Su'a | 53 | 13 | 126 | 4 | 31.50 | 2-50 | – | – |
| G.E.Bradburn | 40.4 | 5 | 142 | 3 | 47.33 | 3-134 | – | – |

Also bowled: M.D.Crowe 2-0-10-0; C.Z.Harris 18-5-81-0; A.H.Jones 2.4-0-8-0; D.J.Nash 18-2-62-1; C.Pringle 34-8-90-1; J.T.C.Vaughan 14-0-56-0.

# NEW ZEALAND v PAKISTAN (Only Test)

**Played at Trust Bank Park, Hamilton, on 2, 3, 4, 5 January 1993.**
**Toss: New Zealand.  Result: PAKISTAN won by 33 runs.**
**Debuts: Nil.**                                                    ‡(W.V.Raman)

## PAKISTAN

| | | | |
|---|---|---|---|
| Ramiz Raja c Rutherford b Su'a | 4 | (2) c Parore b Morrison | 8 |
| Aamir Sohail c Owens b Morrison | 0 | (1) b Morrison | 0 |
| Asif Mujtaba c Owens b Su'a | 0 | lbw b Morrison | 11 |
| *Javed Miandad b Su'a | 92 | lbw b Su'a | 12 |
| Salim Malik c Parore b Morrison | 14 | c Su'a b Morrison | 0 |
| Inzamam-ul-Haq c Morrison b Su'a | 23 | lbw b Owens | 75 |
| Wasim Akram c Greatbatch b Patel | 27 | (8) b Patel | 15 |
| †Rashid Latif not out | 32 | (7) c Rutherford b Su'a | 33 |
| Waqar Younis run out | 13 | not out | 4 |
| Mushtaq Ahmed lbw b Su'a | 2 | c Rutherford b Morrison | 10 |
| Aqib Javed c Greatbatch b Morrison | 1 | c Hartland b Patel | 2 |
| Extras (W4, NB4) | 8 | (LB2, NB2) | 4 |
| **Total** | **216** | | **174** |

## NEW ZEALAND

| | | | |
|---|---|---|---|
| M.J.Greatbatch lbw b Waqar | 133 | (2) c Aamir b Wasim | 8 |
| B.R.Hartland st Rashid b Mushtaq | 43 | (1) b Wasim | 9 |
| A.H.Jones lbw b Wasim | 2 | c Asif b Waqar | 19 |
| R.T.Latham lbw b Wasim | 2 | (6) b Waqar | 0 |
| *K.R.Rutherford c Rashid b Mushtaq | 14 | (7) c Aamir b Wasim | 9 |
| C.Z.Harris lbw b Waqar | 6 | (8) b Waqar | 9 |
| D.N.Patel lbw b Waqar | 12 | (9) b Waqar | 4 |
| †A.C.Parore lbw b Wasim | 16 | (5) c Rashid b Wasim | 13 |
| M.L.Su'a c Rashid b Waqar | 0 | (10) lbw b Waqar | 0 |
| D.K.Morrison not out | 3 | (4) lbw b Wasim | 0 |
| M.B.Owens b Waqar | 0 | not out | 0 |
| Extras (B1, LB15, W1, NB16) | 33 | (B1, LB11, NB10) | 22 |
| **Total** | **264** | | **93** |

| NEW ZEALAND | O | M | R | W | O | M | R | W | FALL OF WICKETS | | | | |
|---|---|---|---|---|---|---|---|---|---|---|---|---|---|
| Morrison | 19.3 | 4 | 42 | 3 | 15 | 2 | 41 | 5 | | P | NZ | P | NZ |
| Su'a | 24 | 2 | 73 | 5 | 13 | 1 | 47 | 2 | Wkt | 1st | 1st | 2nd | 2nd |
| Owens | 12 | 3 | 48 | 0 | 7 | 0 | 19 | 1 | 1st | 4 | 108 | 0 | 19 |
| Patel | 14 | 2 | 53 | 1 | 20.1 | 5 | 65 | 2 | 2nd | 4 | 111 | 20 | 31 |
| **PAKISTAN** | | | | | | | | | 3rd | 12 | 117 | 25 | 32 |
| | | | | | | | | | 4th | 45 | 147 | 25 | 65 |
| Wasim | 31 | 9 | 66 | 3 | 22 | 4 | 45 | 5 | 5th | 87 | 164 | 39 | 67 |
| Waqar | 28 | 11 | 59 | 4 | 13.3 | 4 | 22 | 5 | 6th | 158 | 193 | 119 | 71 |
| Mushtaq | 38 | 10 | 87 | 3 | | | | | 7th | 176 | 254 | 158 | 88 |
| Aqib | 7 | 2 | 24 | 0 | 8 | 2 | 14 | 0 | 8th | 202 | 256 | 158 | 88 |
| Aamir | 5 | 2 | 12 | 0 | | | | | 9th | 208 | 257 | 171 | 88 |
| | | | | | | | | | 10th | 216 | 264 | 174 | 93 |

**Umpires: B.L.Aldridge (14) and R.S.Dunne (9).**                **Test No. 1211/33**

# INDIA v ENGLAND (1st Test)

Played at Eden Gardens, Calcutta, on 29, 30, 31 January, 1, 2 February 1993.
Toss: India.   Result: INDIA won by 8 wickets.
Debuts: India–R.K.Chauhan, V.G.Kambli.                               ‡(W.V.Raman)

## INDIA

| | | | |
|---|---|---|---|
| M.Prabhakar c Lewis b Salisbury | 46 | b Hick | 13 |
| N.S.Sidhu c Hick b Taylor | 13 | st Stewart b Hick | 37 |
| V.G.Kambli c Hick b Jarvis | 16 | not out | 18 |
| S.R.Tendulkar c Hick b Malcolm | 50 | not out | 9 |
| *M.Azharuddin c Gooch b Hick | 182 | | |
| P.K.Amre c Hick b Jarvis | 12 | | |
| Kapil Dev c Lewis b Hick | 13 | | |
| †K.S.More not out | 4 | | |
| A.Kumble b Malcolm | 0 | | |
| R.K.Chauhan b Malcolm | 2 | | |
| S.L.V.Raju c Salisbury b Hick | 1 | | |
| Extras (B6, LB6, W10, NB10) | 32 | (LB4, NB1) | 5 |
| **Total** (122.5 overs; 543 minutes) | 371 | (29.2 overs; 120 minutes) | 82-2 |

## ENGLAND

| | | | |
|---|---|---|---|
| *G.A.Gooch c Azharuddin b Raju | 17 | st More b Kumble | 18 |
| †A.J.Stewart b Prabhakar | 0 | c Tendulkar b Kumble | 49 |
| M.W.Gatting b Chauhan | 33 | b Chauhan | 81 |
| R.A.Smith c Amre b Kumble | 1 | c More b Chauhan | 8 |
| G.A.Hick b Kumble | 1 | lbw b Raju | 25 |
| N.H.Fairbrother c More b Kumble | 17 | c sub‡ b Kumble | 25 |
| I.D.K.Salisbury c More b Chauhan | 28 | (9) c More b Kapil Dev | 26 |
| C.C.Lewis b Raju | 21 | (7) c Amre b Raju | 16 |
| P.W.Jarvis c Prabhakar b Raju | 4 | (8) lbw b Raju | 6 |
| J.P.Taylor st More b Chauhan | 17 | not out | 17 |
| D.E.Malcolm not out | 4 | lbw b Kapil Dev | 0 |
| Extras (B8, LB8, W4) | 20 | (LB13, NB2) | 15 |
| **Total** (100.1 overs; 353 minutes) | 163 | (137.2 overs; 458 minutes) | 286 |

| ENGLAND | O | M | R | W | O | M | R | W |
|---|---|---|---|---|---|---|---|---|
| Malcolm | 24 | 3 | 67 | 3 | 6 | 1 | 16 | 0 |
| Jarvis | 27 | 5 | 72 | 2 | 5.2 | 1 | 23 | 0 |
| Lewis | 23 | 5 | 64 | 0 | 3 | 1 | 5 | 0 |
| Taylor | 19 | 2 | 65 | 1 | 3 | 1 | 9 | 0 |
| Salisbury | 17 | 2 | 72 | 1 | 6 | 3 | 16 | 0 |
| Hick | 12.5 | 5 | 19 | 3 | 6 | 1 | 9 | 2 |

| INDIA | O | M | R | W | O | M | R | W |
|---|---|---|---|---|---|---|---|---|
| Kapil Dev | 6 | 1 | 18 | 0 | 8.2 | 5 | 12 | 2 |
| Prabhakar | 9 | 3 | 10 | 1 | 9 | 4 | 26 | 0 |
| Kumble | 29 | 8 | 50 | 3 | 40 | 16 | 76 | 3 |
| Raju | 27 | 14 | 39 | 3 | 35 | 9 | 80 | 3 |
| Chauhan | 29.1 | 15 | 30 | 3 | 45 | 17 | 79 | 2 |

### FALL OF WICKETS

| Wkt | I 1st | E 1st | E 2nd | I 2nd |
|---|---|---|---|---|
| 1st | 49 | 8 | 48 | 51 |
| 2nd | 78 | 37 | 111 | 62 |
| 3rd | 93 | 38 | 145 | — |
| 4th | 216 | 40 | 192 | — |
| 5th | 280 | 87 | 192 | — |
| 6th | 346 | 89 | 216 | — |
| 7th | 362 | 111 | 234 | — |
| 8th | 368 | 119 | 254 | — |
| 9th | 370 | 149 | 286 | — |
| 10th | 371 | 163 | 286 | — |

Umpires: P.D.Reporter (13) and S.Venkataraghavan (1).        Test No. 1212/79

# INDIA v ENGLAND (2nd Test)

**Played at M.A.Chidambaram Stadium, Madras, on 11, 12, 13, 14, 15 February 1993.**
**Toss: India.    Result: INDIA won by an innings and 22 runs.**
**Debuts: England – R.J.Blakey.**

‡(W.V.Raman)

## INDIA

| | |
|---|---|
| M.Prabhakar c Blakey b Lewis | 27 |
| N.S.Sidhu c Hick b Jarvis | 106 |
| V.G.Kambli lbw b Hick | 59 |
| S.R.Tendulkar c and b Salisbury | 165 |
| *M.Azharuddin c Smith b Jarvis | 6 |
| P.K.Amre c Jarvis b Salisbury | 78 |
| Kapil Dev not out | 66 |
| †K.S.More not out | 26 |
| A.Kumble | |
| R.K.Chauhan  } did not bat | |
| S.L.V.Raju | |
| Extras (LB10, W2, NB15) | 27 |
| **Total** (165 overs; 689 minutes) | **560-6 dec** |

## ENGLAND

| | | | |
|---|---|---|---|
| R.A.Smith lbw b Kumble | 17 | c Amre b Kumble | 56 |
| *A.J.Stewart c sub‡ b Raju | 74 | lbw b Kapil Dev | 0 |
| G.A.Hick lbw b Chauhan | 64 | b Tendulkar b Kapil Dev | 0 |
| M.W.Gatting run out (Amre/More) | 2 | lbw b Raju | 19 |
| N.H.Fairbrother c Kapil Dev b Chauhan | 83 | c Prabhakar b Kumble | 9 |
| †R.J.Blakey b Raju | 0 | b Kumble | 6 |
| C.C.Lewis c Azharuddin b Raju | 0 | c and b Kumble | 117 |
| I.D.K.Salisbury lbw b Kumble | 4 | b Kumble | 12 |
| P.W.Jarvis c sub‡ b Raju | 8 | c Tendulkar b Kumble | 2 |
| P.C.R.Tufnell c Azharuddin b Chauhan | 2 | not out | 22 |
| D.E.Malcolm not out | 0 | c sub‡ b Raju | 0 |
| Extras (B14, LB16, NB2) | 32 | (B4, LB5) | 9 |
| **Total** (127.3 overs; 475 minutes) | **286** | (81.1 overs; 307 minutes) | **252** |

| ENGLAND | O | M | R | W | O | M | R | W |
|---|---|---|---|---|---|---|---|---|
| Malcolm | 27 | 7 | 87 | 0 | | | | |
| Jarvis | 28 | 7 | 72 | 2 | | | | |
| Lewis | 11 | 1 | 40 | 1 | | | | |
| Tufnell | 41 | 3 | 132 | 0 | | | | |
| Hick | 29 | 2 | 77 | 1 | | | | |
| Salisbury | 29 | 1 | 142 | 2 | | | | |
| | | | | | | | | |
| INDIA | | | | | | | | |
| Prabhakar | 3 | 2 | 7 | 0 | 3 | 2 | 4 | 0 |
| Kumble | 25 | 9 | 61 | 2 | 21 | 7 | 64 | 6 |
| Chauhan | 39.3 | 16 | 69 | 3 | 21 | 4 | 59 | 0 |
| Raju | 54 | 21 | 103 | 4 | 23.1 | 3 | 76 | 2 |
| Kapil Dev | 4 | 0 | 11 | 0 | 11 | 5 | 36 | 2 |
| Tendulkar | 2 | 1 | 5 | 0 | 1 | 4 | 0 | |

| FALL OF WICKETS | | | |
|---|---|---|---|
| | I | E | E |
| Wkt | 1st | 1st | 2nd |
| 1st | 41 | 46 | 10 |
| 2nd | 149 | 157 | 12 |
| 3rd | 296 | 166 | 71 |
| 4th | 324 | 175 | 82 |
| 5th | 442 | 179 | 88 |
| 6th | 499 | 179 | 99 |
| 7th | – | 220 | 172 |
| 8th | – | 277 | 186 |
| 9th | – | 279 | 241 |
| 10th | – | 286 | 252 |

**Umpires:** V.K.Ramaswamy (13) and R.S.Rathore (2).     Test No. 1213/80

# INDIA v ENGLAND (3rd Test)

Played at Wankhede Stadium, Bombay, on 19, 20, 21, 22, 23 February 1993.
Toss: England.   Result: INDIA won by an innings and 15 runs.
Debuts: Nil.

## ENGLAND

| | | | | |
|---|---|---|---|---|
| *G.A.Gooch c More b Kapil Dev | 4 | b Prabhakar | 8 |
| A.J.Stewart run out (Tendulkar/Amre) | 13 | lbw b Prabhakar | 10 |
| M.A.Atherton c Prabhakar b Kumble | 37 | c More b Prabhakar | 11 |
| R.A.Smith c More b Raju | 2 | b Kumble | 62 |
| M.W.Gatting c Kapil Dev b Raju | 23 | st More b Chauhan | 61 |
| G.A.Hick c Kapil Dev b Prabhakar | 178 | c Amre b Kumble | 47 |
| †R.J.Blakey lbw b Kumble | 1 | b Kumble | 0 |
| C.C.Lewis lbw b Kumble | 49 | c More b Raju | 3 |
| J.E.Emburey c More b Kapil Dev | 12 | c Tendulkar b Kumble | 1 |
| P.A.J.DeFreitas lbw b Kapil Dev | 11 | st More b Raju | 12 |
| P.C.R.Tufnell not out | 2 | not out | 2 |
| Extras (B4, LB5, W2, NB4) | 15 | (B4, LB6, W1, NB1) | 12 |
| Total (135 overs; 502 minutes) | 347 | (82.5 overs; 307 minutes) | 229 |

## INDIA

| | |
|---|---|
| N.S.Sidhu c Smith b Tufnell | 79 |
| M.Prabhakar c Blakey b Hick | 44 |
| V.G.Kambli c Gatting b Lewis | 224 |
| S.R.Tendulkar lbw b Tufnell | 78 |
| *M.Azharuddin lbw b Lewis | 26 |
| P.K.Amre c DeFreitas b Hick | 57 |
| Kapil Dev c DeFreitas b Emburey | 22 |
| †K.S.More c Lewis b Emburey | 0 |
| A.Kumble c Atherton b Tufnell | 16 |
| R.K.Chauhan c Atherton b Tufnell | 15 |
| S.L.V.Raju not out | 0 |
| Extras (B5, LB14, W5, NB6) | 30 |
| Total (189.3 overs; 795 minutes) | 591 |

| INDIA | O | M | R | W | O | M | R | W | FALL OF WICKETS | | | |
|---|---|---|---|---|---|---|---|---|---|---|---|---|
| | | | | | | | | | | E | I | E |
| Kapil Dev | 15 | 3 | 35 | 3 | 7 | 1 | 21 | 0 | | 1st | 1st | 2nd |
| Prabhakar | 13 | 2 | 52 | 1 | 11 | 4 | 28 | 3 | Wkt | 1st | 1st | 2nd |
| Raju | 44 | 8 | 102 | 2 | 26.5 | 7 | 68 | 2 | 1st | 11 | 109 | 17 |
| Kumble | 40 | 4 | 95 | 3 | 26 | 9 | 70 | 4 | 2nd | 25 | 174 | 26 |
| Chauhan | 23 | 7 | 54 | 0 | 12 | 5 | 32 | 1 | 3rd | 30 | 368 | 34 |
| | | | | | | | | | 4th | 58 | 418 | 155 |
| ENGLAND | | | | | | | | | 5th | 116 | 519 | 181 |
| DeFreitas | 20 | 4 | 75 | 0 | | | | | 6th | 118 | 560 | 181 |
| Lewis | 42 | 9 | 114 | 2 | | | | | 7th | 211 | 560 | 206 |
| Emburey | 59 | 14 | 144 | 2 | | | | | 8th | 262 | 563 | 214 |
| Tufnell | 39.3 | 6 | 142 | 4 | | | | | 9th | 279 | 591 | 215 |
| Hick | 29 | 3 | 97 | 2 | | | | | 10th | 347 | 591 | 229 |

Umpires: P.D.Reporter (14) and S.Venkataraghavan (2).          Test No. 1214/81

# INDIA v ENGLAND 1992-93

## INDIA – BATTING AND FIELDING

|              | M | I | NO | HS  | Runs | Avge   | 100 | 50 | Ct/St |
|--------------|---|---|----|-----|------|--------|-----|----|-------|
| V.G.Kambli   | 3 | 4 | 1  | 224 | 317  | 105.66 | 1   | 1  | –     |
| S.R.Tendulkar| 3 | 4 | 1  | 165 | 302  | 100.66 | 1   | 2  | 4     |
| M.Azharuddin | 3 | 3 | –  | 182 | 214  | 71.33  | 1   | –  | 3     |
| N.S.Sidhu    | 3 | 4 | –  | 106 | 235  | 58.75  | 1   | 1  | –     |
| Kapil Dev    | 3 | 3 | 1  | 66* | 101  | 50.50  | –   | 1  | 3     |
| P.K.Amre     | 3 | 3 | –  | 78  | 147  | 49.00  | –   | 2  | 4     |
| M.Prabhakar  | 3 | 4 | –  | 46  | 130  | 32.50  | –   | –  | 3     |
| K.S.More     | 3 | 3 | 2  | 26* | 30   | 30.00  | –   | –  | 9/4   |
| R.K.Chauhan  | 3 | 2 | –  | 15  | 17   | 8.50   | –   | –  | –     |
| A.Kumble     | 3 | 2 | –  | 16  | 16   | 8.00   | –   | –  | 1     |
| S.L.V.Raju   | 3 | 2 | 1  | 1   | 1    | 1.00   | –   | –  | –     |

## INDIA – BOWLING

|              | O     | M  | R   | W  | Avge  | Best  | 5wI | 10wM |
|--------------|-------|----|-----|----|-------|-------|-----|------|
| Kapil Dev    | 51.2  | 15 | 133 | 7  | 19.00 | 3-35  | –   | –    |
| A.Kumble     | 181   | 53 | 416 | 21 | 19.80 | 6-64  | 1   | –    |
| M.Prabhakar  | 48    | 17 | 127 | 5  | 25.40 | 3-28  | –   | –    |
| S.L.V.Raju   | 210   | 62 | 468 | 16 | 29.25 | 4-103 | –   | –    |
| R.K.Chauhan  | 169.4 | 64 | 323 | 9  | 35.88 | 3-30  | –   | –    |

*Also bowled:* S.R.Tendulkar 4-2-9-0.

## ENGLAND – BATTING AND FIELDING

|               | M | I | NO | HS  | Runs | Avge  | 100 | 50 | Ct/St |
|---------------|---|---|----|-----|------|-------|-----|----|-------|
| G.A.Hick      | 3 | 6 | –  | 178 | 315  | 52.50 | 1   | 1  | 5     |
| M.W.Gatting   | 3 | 6 | –  | 81  | 219  | 36.50 | –   | 2  | 1     |
| C.C.Lewis     | 3 | 6 | –  | 117 | 206  | 34.33 | 1   | –  | 3     |
| N.H.Fairbrother| 2| 4 | –  | 83  | 134  | 33.50 | –   | 1  | –     |
| P.C.R.Tufnell | 2 | 4 | 3  | 22* | 28   | 28.00 | –   | –  | –     |
| R.A.Smith     | 3 | 6 | –  | 62  | 146  | 24.33 | –   | 2  | 2     |
| A.J.Stewart   | 3 | 6 | –  | 74  | 146  | 24.33 | –   | 1  | –     |
| I.D.K.Salisbury| 2| 4 | –  | 28  | 70   | 17.50 | –   | –  | 1     |
| G.A.Gooch     | 2 | 4 | –  | 18  | 47   | 11.75 | –   | –  | 1     |
| P.W.Jarvis    | 2 | 4 | –  | 8   | 20   | 5.00  | –   | –  | 1     |
| D.E.Malcolm   | 2 | 4 | 2  | 4*  | 4    | 2.00  | –   | –  | –     |
| R.J.Blakey    | 2 | 4 | –  | 6   | 7    | 1.75  | –   | –  | 2     |

*Played in one Test:* M.A.Atherton 37, 11 (2 ct); P.A.J.DeFreitas 11, 12 (2 ct); J.E.Emburey 12, 1; J.P.Taylor 17, 17*.

## ENGLAND – BOWLING

|               | O    | M  | R   | W | Avge  | Best  | 5wI | 10wM |
|---------------|------|----|-----|---|-------|-------|-----|------|
| G.A.Hick      | 76.5 | 11 | 202 | 8 | 25.25 | 3-19  | –   | –    |
| P.W.Jarvis    | 60.2 | 13 | 167 | 4 | 41.75 | 2-72  | –   | –    |
| D.E.Malcolm   | 57   | 11 | 170 | 3 | 56.66 | 3-67  | –   | –    |
| P.C.R.Tufnell | 80.3 | 9  | 274 | 4 | 68.50 | 4-142 | –   | –    |
| C.C.Lewis     | 79   | 16 | 223 | 3 | 74.33 | 2-114 | –   | –    |
| I.D.K.Salisbury| 52  | 6  | 230 | 3 | 76.66 | 2-142 | –   | –    |

*Also bowled:* P.A.J.DeFreitas 20-4-75-0; J.E.Emburey 59-14-144-2; J.P.Taylor 22-3-74-1.

# THE 1992 FIRST-CLASS SEASON
## STATISTICAL HIGHLIGHTS

**HIGHEST INNINGS TOTALS**

| | | |
|---|---|---|
| 616-7d | Somerset v Nottinghamshire | Taunton |
| 603-8d | Kent v Warwickshire | Birmingham |
| 563 | Sussex v Lancashire | Manchester |
| 562 | Lancashire v Durham | Gateshead |
| 557 | Surrey v Somerset | The Oval |
| 552-9d | Hampshire v Surrey | Southampton |
| 534 | Somerset v Durham | Taunton |
| 526 | Essex v Kent | Chelmsford |
| 521-9d | Durham v Glamorgan | Cardiff |
| 510-2d | Essex v Lancashire | Ilford |
| 508 | Yorkshire v Northamptonshire | Scarborough |
| 507 | Kent v Gloucestershire | Bristol |
| 505-9d | Pakistan v England | Manchester |
| 502-4d | Kent v Leicestershire | Leicester |
| 500-9d | Derbyshire v Nottinghamshire | Derby |

**HIGHEST FOURTH INNINGS TOTAL**

| | | |
|---|---|---|
| 442-6 | Essex v Derbyshire (set 440) | Derby |

**LOWEST INNINGS TOTALS**

| | | |
|---|---|---|
| 70 | Hampshire v Kent | Canterbury |
| 74 | Derbyshire v Yorkshire | Harrogate |
| 75 | Cambridge University v Essex | Cambridge |
| 75 | Essex v Leicestershire | Leicester |
| 76 | Surrey v Kent | Guildford |
| 77 | Leicestershire v Northamptonshire | Northampton |
| 80 | Hampshire v Essex | Bournemouth |
| 83 | Essex v Yorkshire | Leeds |
| 85 | Derbyshire v Warwickshire | Birmingham |
| 93† | Pakistanis v Worcestershire | Worcester |
| 95 | Middlesex v Northamptonshire | Northampton |
| 96 | Essex v Derbyshire | Derby |

† One man absent hurt.

**MATCH AGGREGATE OF 1400 RUNS**

Runs-Wkts

| | | |
|---|---|---|
| 1409-24 | Sussex v Kent | Hove |

**VICTORY AFTER FOLLOWING-ON**

Essex (149, 310) beat Hampshire (300-8d, 80)     Bournemouth
Kent (117, 332) beat Surrey (301-8d, 76)          Guildford

**FIRST TO INDIVIDUAL TARGETS**

| | | | |
|---|---|---|---|
| **1000 RUNS** | T.C.Middleton | Hampshire | June 17 |
| **2000 RUNS** | P.D.Bowler | Derbyshire | September 3 |
| **100 WICKETS** | Not achieved. Most: 92 by C.A.Walsh for Gloucestershire | | |

**DOUBLE HUNDREDS (14)**

| | | | |
|---|---|---|---|
| Aamir Sohail | 205 | Pakistan v England | Manchester |
| P.D.Bowler | 241* | Derbyshire v Hampshire | Portsmouth |
| T.S.Curtis | 228* | Worcestershire v Derbyshire | Derby |

| G.A.Hick | 213* | Worcestershire v Nottinghamshire | Nottingham |
| Inzamam-ul-Haq | 200* | Pakistanis v Combined Universities | Cambridge |
| A.J.Lamb | 209 | Northamptonshire v Warwickshire | Northampton |
| N.J.Lenham | 222* | Sussex v Kent | Hove |
| T.C.Middleton | 221 | Hampshire v Surrey | Southampton |
| M.R.Ramprakash | 233 | Middlesex v Surrey | Lord's |
| D.M.Smith | 213 | Sussex v Essex | Southend |
| N.J.Speak | 232 | Lancashire v Leicestershire | Leicester |
| G.P.Thorpe | 216 | Surrey v Somerset | The Oval |
| R.G.Twose | 233 | Warwickshire v Leicestershire | Birmingham |
| M.E.Waugh | 219* | Essex v Lancashire | Ilford |

## HUNDRED ON FIRST-CLASS DEBUT (2)

| J.D.Glendenen | 117 | Durham v Oxford University | Oxford |
| J.R.Wileman | 109 | Nottinghamshire v Cambridge U | Nottingham |

## HUNDREDS IN THREE CONSECUTIVE INNINGS (4)

| M.W.Gatting | Middlesex v Warwickshire and Lancashire | 117, 163*, 126* |
| G.A.Gooch | Essex v Sussex and Leicestershire | 102, 108*, 135 |
| M.A.Roseberry | Middlesex v Worcs, Derbyshire and Durham | 118, 100*, 173 |
| A.P.Wells | Sussex v Kent, Surrey and Warwickshire | 144, 165*, 115 |

## SIX FIFTIES IN SUCCESSIVE INNINGS

| P.D.Bowler | Derbyshire | 91, 112, 53, 104*, 155, 90* |

## HUNDRED IN EACH INNINGS OF A MATCH (5)

| M.W.Gatting | 117 | 163* | Middlesex v Warwickshire | Coventry |
| G.A.Gooch | 102 | 108* | Essex v Sussex | Southend |
| D.M.Jones | 134* | 105 | Durham v Pakistanis | Chester-le-St |
| A.J.Lamb | 209 | 107 | Northamptonshire v Warwickshire | Northampton |
| J.P.Stephenson | 113* | 159* | Essex v Somerset | Taunton |

## FASTEST HUNDRED (WALTER LAWRENCE TROPHY)

| M.P.Speight | 62 balls | Sussex v Lancashire | Hove |

In 56 minutes, including 5 sixes and 12 fours, in contrived circumstances.

## HUNDRED BEFORE LUNCH (6)

|  |  | Day |  |  |
| C.J.Adams | 103* | 2 | Derbyshire v Middlesex | Derby |
| M.A.Atherton | 111* | 3 | Lancashire v Derbyshire | Blackpool |
| G.A.Gooch | 105* | 2 | Essex v Leicestershire | Chelmsford |
| N.J.Lenham | 122*† | 3 | Sussex v Kent | Hove |
| T.M.Moody | 100* | 2 | Worcestershire v Oxford University | Oxford |
| M.P.Speight | 119*† | 3 | Sussex v Lancashire | Hove |

† In contrived circumstances.

## HUNDRED ENTIRELY WITH THE AID OF A RUNNER (2)

| W.Larkins | 117 | Durham v Somerset | Taunton |
| N.J.Lenham | 118 | Sussex v Durham | Horsham |

## CARRYING BAT THROUGH COMPLETED INNINGS (4)

| K.J.Barnett | 156* | Derbyshire (330) v Nottinghamshire | Nottingham |
| N.E.Briers | 73* | Leicestershire (160) v Derbyshire | Ilkeston |
| J.P.Stephenson | 113* | Essex (259) v Somerset | Taunton |
| A.J.Stewart | 69* | England (175) v Pakistan | Lord's |

## FIRST-WICKET PARTNERSHIP OF 100 IN EACH INNINGS
122    156    T.S.Curtis/W.P.C.Weston    Worcestershire v Derbys    Worcester

## OTHER NOTABLE PARTNERSHIPS
### First Wicket
| | | | |
|---|---|---|---|
| 290 | T.R.Ward/M.R.Benson | Kent v Warwickshire | Birmingham |
| 285 | A.J.Moles/R.G.Twose | Warwickshire v Leics | Birmingham |
| 267 | V.P.Terry/T.C.Middleton | Hampshire v Surrey | Southampton |
| 266 | D.L.Haynes/M.A.Roseberry | Middlesex v Nottinghamshire | Nottingham |
| 250 | S.P.James/H.Morris | Glamorgan v Lancashire | Colwyn Bay |

### Second Wicket
| | | | |
|---|---|---|---|
| 259 | P.D.Bowler/J.E.Morris | Derbyshire v Somerset | Taunton |

### Third Wicket
| | | | |
|---|---|---|---|
| 347*† | M.E.Waugh/N.Hussain | Essex v Lancashire | Ilford |
| 265 | R.J.Harden/C.J.Tavaré | Somerset v Nottinghamshire | Taunton |
| 263 | N.J.Lenham/A.P.Wells | Sussex v Lancashire | Manchester |
| 259 | P.D.Bowler/T.J.G.O'Gorman | Derbyshire v Hampshire | Portsmouth |

### Fourth Wicket
| | | | |
|---|---|---|---|
| 322 | Javed Miandad/Salim Malik | Pakistan v England | Birmingham |

### Fifth Wicket
| | | | |
|---|---|---|---|
| 251 | D.M.Smith/P.Moores | Sussex v Essex | Southend |

### Sixth Wicket
| | | | |
|---|---|---|---|
| 235 | G.R.Cowdrey/S.A.Marsh | Kent v Yorkshire | Canterbury |

### Seventh Wicket
| | | | |
|---|---|---|---|
| 243 | M.A.Atherton/P.J.Martin | Lancashire v Durham | Gateshead |

### Tenth Wicket
| | | | |
|---|---|---|---|
| 109 | E.E.Hemmings/R.A.Pick | Nottinghamshire v Warwicks | Nottingham |

† County record.

## EIGHT OR MORE WICKETS IN AN INNINGS (7)
| | | | |
|---|---|---|---|
| A.M.Babington | 8-107 | Gloucestershire v Kent | Bristol |
| R.D.B.Croft | 8-66 | Glamorgan v Warwickshire | Swansea |
| P.J.Hartley | 8-111 | Yorkshire v Sussex | Hove |
| M.J.McCague | 8-26 | Kent v Hampshire | Canterbury |
| K.J.Shine | 8-47 | Hampshire v Lancashire | Manchester |
| S.D.Udal | 8-50 | Hampshire v Sussex | Southampton |
| N.F.Williams | 8-75 | Middlesex v Gloucestershire | Lord's |

## TEN OR MORE WICKETS IN A MATCH (25)
| | | | |
|---|---|---|---|
| J.A.Afford | 10-185 | Nottinghamshire v Sussex | Nottingham |
| P.J.Berry | 10-191 | Durham v Middlesex | Lord's |
| J.Boiling | 10-203 | Surrey v Gloucestershire | Bristol |
| A.R.Caddick | 10-157 | Somerset v Kent | Canterbury |
| N.G.B.Cook | 10-97 | Northamptonshire v Essex | Chelmsford |
| R.D.B.Croft | 14-169 | Glamorgan v Warwickshire | Swansea |
| C.C.Lewis | 10-155 | Nottinghamshire v Surrey | Nottingham |
| M.J.McCague | 10-86 | Kent v Gloucestershire | Canterbury |
| D.J.Millns | 10-87 | Leicestershire v Durham | Leicester |
| T.A.Munton | 12-110 | Warwickshire v Leicestershire | Birmingham |

| N.V.Radford | 11-155 | Worcestershire v Derbyshire | Derby |
| M.A.Robinson | 10-101 | Yorkshire v Durham | Durham |
| I.D.K.Salisbury (2) | 11-83 | Sussex v Lancashire | Manchester |
| | 12-138 | Sussex v Yorkshire | Hove |
| K.J.Shine | 13-105 | Hampshire v Lancashire | Manchester |
| R.D.Stemp | 11-146 | Worcestershire v Gloucestershire | Gloucester |
| F.D.Stephenson | 11-107 | Sussex v Worcestershire | Worcester |
| J.P.Taylor | 10-54 | Northamptonshire v Middlesex | Northampton |
| H.R.J.Trump | 14-104 | Somerset v Gloucestershire | Gloucester |
| C.A.Walsh (2) | 11-104 | Gloucestershire v Yorkshire | Leeds |
| | 10-85 | Gloucestershire v Somerset | Gloucester |
| Wasim Akram (2) | 10-117 | Pakistanis v Northamptonshire | Northampton |
| | 11-76 | Pakistanis v Gloucestershire | Bristol |
| M.Watkinson | 10-103 | Lancashire v Warwickshire | Birmingham |
| N.F.Williams | 12-139 | Middlesex v Gloucestershire | Lord's |

## HAT-TRICKS (3)

| K.J.Shine† | Hampshire v Lancashire | Manchester |
| H.R.J.Trump | Somerset v Gloucestershire | Gloucester |
| M.Watkinson | Lancashire v Warwickshire | Birmingham |

† Also four wickets in five balls and eight wickets in 38 balls.

## SIX OR MORE WICKET-KEEPING DISMISSALS IN AN INNINGS (2)

| R.J.Blakey | 5 ct/1 st | Yorkshire v Gloucestershire | Cheltenham |
| B.N.French | 6 ct | Nottinghamshire v Warwickshire | Birmingham |

## NINE OR MORE WICKET-KEEPING DISMISSALS IN A MATCH (2)

| B.N.French | 9 ct | Nottinghamshire v Warwickshire | Birmingham |
| P.A.Nixon | 9 ct | Leicestershire v Essex | Leicester |

## MATCH DOUBLE (100 RUNS AND 10 WICKETS)

| F.D.Stephenson | 87*, 29; 4-78, 7-29 | Sussex v Worcestershire | Worcester |

## NO BYES CONCEDED IN TOTAL OF 500 OR MORE

| N.D.Burns | | Somerset v Surrey (557) | The Oval |
| C.W.Scott | | Durham v Somerset (534) | Taunton |

## FIFTY EXTRAS IN AN INNINGS

| | B | LB | W | NB | | |
|---|---|---|---|---|---|---|
| 55 | 8 | 22 | 3 | 22 | Warwickshire v Middlesex | Lord's |
| 53 | 8 | 8 | 2 | 35 | England v Pakistan | Manchester |

# ESSEX RETAIN TITLE

At 3.35pm on 3 September, John Stephenson dabbed a leg-break from Robin Smith towards backward point, scampered the run which completed Hampshire's defeat and assured Essex of their sixth County Championship. After 102 barren years, the last 14 seasons have produced all six of their pennants, as well as five major limited-overs trophies. For the second year running, they were the only team to win half their matches.

In many respects this fifth title in ten summers, and their second in succession, was the most meritorious. It was finally achieved by the emphatic margin of 41 points, after a dismal start in which only two of the first seven matches were won and in spite of key players missing many of the 22 matches. A combined total of 45 matches was missed by Neil Foster (12), Graham Gooch (11), Derek Pringle (10), Mark Waugh (7) and Nasser Hussain (5) because of national honours or injury. No side could have withstood such losses without an immense reserve strength. Guided by Keith Fletcher for the last time before assuming the mantle of England Team Manager, Foster and Paul Prichard proved able deputy captains. After spending ten years in the wings (for three counties), Peter Such's off-spin at last earned top billing with 37 wickets in nine matches, a performance which gained him an England 'A' flight to Australia.

By 20 July, Essex had stormed to a 51-point lead to threaten the earliest date by which the Championship has been decided (12 August 1912 by Kent). Thankfully, a monotonous one-horse race was averted by the removal of Waugh (Australia's Sri Lanka mission) and Foster (injured) from the cast list for the remainder of the programme. The juggernaut faltered to such an extent that within three weeks the contest was wide open, with just 45 points separating the top half of the table.

By winning four of their last seven matches, Kent finished worthy runners-up. Their position owed much to the form of their Irish Australian, Martin McCague. A strong 23-year-old fast-medium bowler, he took 33 wickets at 15.57 during August, a tally which included the season's best innings analysis of eight for 26.

Too many three-day matches degenerated into final-day farce. This sickening formula involved the two captains conniving an acceptable runs-per-over equation and reaching the starting point for the fourth innings thrash by employing tripe bowling to donate quick runs. Whatever its shortcomings, the four-day game should rid the first-class scene of this nauseating manipulation of the playing conditions.

Mike Gatting (1980 for Middlesex) scored most Championship runs and Courtney Walsh (92 for Gloucestershire) took most wickets. Derbyshire's unheralded Peter Bowler recorded the season's highest innings (241 not out), while David Ripley (69 dismissals for Northamptonshire) and John Carr (39 catches for Middlesex) were the most successful wicket-keeper and fielder respectively.

# BRITANNIC ASSURANCE
# COUNTY CHAMPIONSHIP 1992
# FINAL TABLE

|  | P | W | L | D | Bonus Points Bat | Points Bowl | Total Points |
|---|---|---|---|---|---|---|---|
| 1 ESSEX (1) | 22 | 11 | 6 | 5 | 60 | 64 | 300 |
| 2 Kent (6) | 22 | 9 | 3 | 10 | 60 | 55 | 259 |
| 3 Northamptonshire (10) | 22 | 8 | 4 | 10 | 62 | 58 | 248 |
| 4 Nottinghamshire (4) | 22 | 7 | 7 | 8 | 54 | 58 | 224 |
| 5 Derbyshire (3) | 22 | 7 | 6 | 9 | 47 | 63 | 222 |
| 6 Warwickshire (2) | 22 | 6 | 8 | 8 | 55 | 68 | 219 |
| 7 Sussex (11) | 22 | 6 | 7 | 9 | 60 | 61 | 217 |
| 8 Leicestershire (16) | 22 | 7 | 7 | 8 | 39 | 60 | 211 |
| 9 Somerset (17) | 22 | 5 | 4 | 13 | 64 | 62 | 206 |
| 10 Gloucestershire (13) | 21 | 6 | 6 | 9 | 48 | 62 | 202 |
| 11 Middlesex (15) | 22 | 5 | 3 | 14 | 62 | 60 | 202 |
| 12 Lancashire (8) | 22 | 4 | 6 | 12 | 73 | 51 | 188 |
| 13 Surrey (5) | 22 | 5 | 7 | 10 | 56 | 50 | 186 |
| 14 Glamorgan (12) | 22 | 5 | 4 | 13 | 53 | 49 | 182 |
| 15 Hampshire (9) | 22 | 4 | 6 | 12 | 61 | 57 | 182 |
| 16 Yorkshire (14) | 22 | 4 | 6 | 12 | 56 | 52 | 172 |
| 17 Worcestershire (6) | 21 | 3 | 4 | 14 | 54 | 65 | 167 |
| 18 Durham (–) | 22 | 2 | 10 | 10 | 46 | 53 | 131 |

1991 final positions are shown in brackets.
The following match was abandoned and is not included in the above table:
29, 30 May, 1 June – Worcestershire v Gloucestershire at Worcester.

## SCORING OF POINTS 1992
(a) For a win, 16 points, plus any points scored in the first innings.
(b) In a tie, each side to score eight points, plus any points scored in the first innings.
(c) If the scores are equal in a drawn match, the side batting in the fourth innings to score eight points, plus any points scored in the first innings.
(d) First Innings Points (awarded only for performances **in the first 100 overs** of each first innings and retained whatever the result of the match).

| (i) A maximum of four batting points to be available as under:– | (ii) A maximum of four bowling points to be available as under:– |
|---|---|
| 150 to 199 runs – 1 point | 3 to 4 wickets taken – 1 point |
| 200 to 249 runs – 2 points | 5 to 6 wickets taken – 2 points |
| 250 to 299 runs – 3 points | 7 to 8 wickets taken – 3 points |
| 300 runs or over – 4 points | 9 to 10 wickets taken – 4 points |

(e) If play starts when less than eight hours playing time remains and a one innings match is played, no first innings points shall be scored. The side winning on the one innings to score 12 points.
(f) A County which is adjudged to have prepared a pitch unsuitable for First-Class Cricket shall be liable to have 25 points deducted from its aggregate of points under the procedure agreed by the TCCB in December 1988.
(g) The side which has the highest aggregate of points gained at the end of the season shall be the Champion County. Should any sides in the Championship table be equal on points, the side with most wins will have priority.

# COUNTY CHAMPIONS

The English County Championship was not officially constituted until December 1889. Prior to that date there was no generally accepted method of awarding the title; although the 'least matches lost' method existed, it was not consistently applied. Rules governing playing qualifications were not agreed until 1873, and the first unofficial points system was not introduced until 1888.

Research has produced a list of champions dating back to 1826, but at least seven different versions exist for the period from 1864 to 1889 (see *The Wisden Book of Cricket Records*). Only from 1890 can any authorised list of county champions commence.

That first official Championship was contested between eight counties: Gloucestershire, Kent, Lancashire, Middlesex, Nottinghamshire, Surrey, Sussex and Yorkshire. The remaining counties were admitted in the following seasons: 1891 – Somerset, 1895 – Derbyshire, Essex, Hampshire, Leicestershire and Warwickshire, 1899 – Worcestershire, 1905 – Northamptonshire, 1921 – Glamorgan, and 1992 – Durham.

From 1977 to 1983 the Championship was sponsored by Schweppes. BRITANNIC ASSURANCE have been its benefactors since 1984.

| | | | | | |
|---|---|---|---|---|---|
| 1890 | Surrey | 1927 | Lancashire | 1964 | Worcestershire |
| 1891 | Surrey | 1928 | Lancashire | 1965 | Worcestershire |
| 1892 | Surrey | 1929 | Nottinghamshire | 1966 | Yorkshire |
| 1893 | Yorkshire | 1930 | Lancashire | 1967 | Yorkshire |
| 1894 | Surrey | 1931 | Yorkshire | 1968 | Yorkshire |
| 1895 | Surrey | 1932 | Yorkshire | 1969 | Glamorgan |
| 1896 | Yorkshire | 1933 | Yorkshire | 1970 | Kent |
| 1897 | Lancashire | 1934 | Lancashire | 1971 | Surrey |
| 1898 | Yorkshire | 1935 | Yorkshire | 1972 | Warwickshire |
| 1899 | Surrey | 1936 | Derbyshire | 1973 | Hampshire |
| 1900 | Yorkshire | 1937 | Yorkshire | 1974 | Worcestershire |
| 1901 | Yorkshire | 1938 | Yorkshire | 1975 | Leicestershire |
| 1902 | Yorkshire | 1939 | Yorkshire | 1976 | Middlesex |
| 1903 | Middlesex | 1946 | Yorkshire | 1977 | { Kent |
| 1904 | Lancashire | 1947 | Middlesex | | { Middlesex |
| 1905 | Yorkshire | 1948 | Glamorgan | 1978 | Kent |
| 1906 | Kent | 1949 | { Middlesex | 1979 | Essex |
| 1907 | Nottinghamshire | | { Yorkshire | 1980 | Middlesex |
| 1908 | Yorkshire | 1950 | { Lancashire | 1981 | Nottinghamshire |
| 1909 | Kent | | { Surrey | 1982 | Middlesex |
| 1910 | Kent | 1951 | Warwickshire | 1983 | Essex |
| 1911 | Warwickshire | 1952 | Surrey | 1984 | Essex |
| 1912 | Yorkshire | 1953 | Surrey | 1985 | Middlesex |
| 1913 | Kent | 1954 | Surrey | 1986 | Essex |
| 1914 | Surrey | 1955 | Surrey | 1987 | Nottinghamshire |
| 1919 | Yorkshire | 1956 | Surrey | 1988 | Worcestershire |
| 1920 | Middlesex | 1957 | Surrey | 1989 | Worcestershire |
| 1921 | Middlesex | 1958 | Surrey | 1990 | Middlesex |
| 1922 | Yorkshire | 1959 | Yorkshire | 1991 | Essex |
| 1923 | Yorkshire | 1960 | Yorkshire | 1992 | Essex |
| 1924 | Yorkshire | 1961 | Hampshire | | |
| 1925 | Yorkshire | 1962 | Yorkshire | | |
| 1926 | Lancashire | 1963 | Yorkshire | | |

# LAMB SLAUGHTERS THE FOX

For once the NatWest final produced more drama behind the scenes than it did on the field. Just 30 minutes before the toss, Leicestershire's chief executive, Mike Turner, desperately trying to find eleven fit players after key all-rounder Vince Wells had been hospitalised with a viral infection and fast bowler David Millns had strained his back, had dashed to the TCCB office and re-registered Peter Willey.

Although the Millns back happily responded to liniment, the fates continued to abuse Leicestershire by condemning them to face Curtly Ambrose in the dismal knowledge that the previous six September finals had been won by the side batting second. Although the bowling proved unexceptional and conditions on a crisp, sunny morning actually favoured the bat, the Running Fox did a fair impression of a three-legged race, just seven runs accruing from the first seven overs. Boon, having refused two suicidal calls from his captain, succumbed to a third, and Briers was beginning to gain confidence and momentum, adding 20 off his final 31 balls, when he fell victim to an outstanding stop and running throw by Bailey.

It was left to a brace of Yorkshiremen, James Whitaker and the newly recruited Phil Robinson, to provide a semblance of a contest. But even their stand of 130 from 206 balls could not set a serious target for the powerful Northamptonshire batting array, especially when the last ten overs produced only 46 runs.

Reprieved by two blunders at slip, man of the match Alan Fordham (yet another astonishing omission from both England tours) and vice-captain Bailey virtually settled the issue with a stand of 144 off 212 balls.

Eventually, Fordham's miscued pull allowed Lamb a 22-ball cameo but the result was never in doubt from the first hour of the match. Set a modest goal of 3.48 runs an over, Northamptonshire cantered home by eight wickets with 10.2 overs in hand, thus allowing the presentations to be completed in reasonable light by 6.30pm.

## GILLETTE CUP WINNERS

| | | | | | |
|---|---|---|---|---|---|
| 1963 | Sussex | 1969 | Yorkshire | 1975 | Lancashire |
| 1964 | Sussex | 1970 | Lancashire | 1976 | Northamptonshire |
| 1965 | Yorkshire | 1971 | Lancashire | 1977 | Middlesex |
| 1966 | Warwickshire | 1972 | Lancashire | 1978 | Sussex |
| 1967 | Kent | 1973 | Gloucestershire | 1979 | Somerset |
| 1968 | Warwickshire | 1974 | Kent | 1980 | Middlesex |

## NATWEST TROPHY WINNERS

| | | | | | |
|---|---|---|---|---|---|
| 1981 | Derbyshire | 1985 | Essex | 1989 | Warwickshire |
| 1982 | Surrey | 1986 | Sussex | 1990 | Lancashire |
| 1983 | Somerset | 1987 | Nottinghamshire | 1991 | Hampshire |
| 1984 | Middlesex | 1988 | Middlesex | 1992 | Northamptonshire |

# 1992 NATWEST TROPHY FINAL

## LEICESTERSHIRE v NORTHAMPTONSHIRE

Played at Lord's, London, on 5 September.
Toss: Northamptonshire. Result: NORTHAMPTONSHIRE won by 8 wickets.
Match Award: A.Fordham (Adjudicator: R.Illingworth).

| LEICESTERSHIRE | Runs | Min | Balls | 6s | 4s | Fall |
|---|---|---|---|---|---|---|
| T.J.Boon run out (Curran) | 3 | 9 | 6 | – | – | 1-3 |
| *N.E.Briers run out (Bailey) | 25 | 68 | 59 | – | 3 | 2-45 |
| J.J.Whitaker c Taylor b Curran | 84 | 169 | 160 | – | 7 | 3-175 |
| P.E.Robinson c Felton b Ambrose | 62 | 133 | 106 | – | 3 | 7-200 |
| J.D.R.Benson b Ambrose | 0 | 5 | 4 | – | – | 4-178 |
| L.Potter c Capel b Curran | 12 | 11 | 15 | – | 1 | 5-197 |
| W.K.M.Benjamin b Curran | 0 | 1 | 1 | – | – | 6198 |
| †P.A.Nixon not out | 7 | 9 | 7 | – | 1 | – |
| G.J.Parsons not out | 1 | 6 | 3 | – | – | – |
| A.D.Mullally \ did not bat | | | | | | |
| D.J.Millns / | | | | | | |
| Extras (B1, LB8, W3, NB2) | 14 | | | | | |
| **Total** (60 overs; 210 minutes) | 208-7 closed | | | | | |

| NORTHAMPTONSHIRE | Runs | Min | Balls | 6s | 4s | Fall |
|---|---|---|---|---|---|---|
| A.Fordham c Potter b Mullally | 91 | 159 | 141 | – | 13 | 2-173 |
| N.A.Felton b Mullally | 6 | 30 | 21 | – | – | 1-29 |
| R.J.Bailey not out | 72 | 152 | 114 | – | 5 | – |
| *A.J.Lamb not out | 24 | 24 | 22 | – | 4 | – |
| D.J.Capel | | | | | | |
| K.M.Curran | | | | | | |
| A.L.Penberthy | | | | | | |
| †D.Ripley \ did not bat | | | | | | |
| C.E.L.Ambrose | | | | | | |
| J.P.Taylor | | | | | | |
| N.G.B.Cook / | | | | | | |
| Extras (LB9, W9) | 18 | | | | | |
| **Total** (49.4 overs; 183 minutes) | 2112 | | | | | |

| NORTHAMPTONSHIRE | O | M | R | W | LEICESTERSHIRE | O | M | R | W |
|---|---|---|---|---|---|---|---|---|---|
| Ambrose | 12 | 0 | 35 | 2 | Benjamin | 12 | 0 | 65 | 0 |
| Taylor | 7 | 1 | 19 | 0 | Mullally | 10 | 2 | 22 | 2 |
| Capel | 11 | 3 | 39 | 0 | Millns | 10 | 0 | 43 | 0 |
| Curran | 12 | 1 | 41 | 3 | Parsons | 9 | 1 | 31 | 0 |
| Cook | 12 | 0 | 43 | 0 | Potter | 4 | 0 | 18 | 0 |
| Penberthy | 6 | 0 | 22 | 0 | Benson | 4.4 | 1 | 23 | 0 |

Umpires: D.J.Constant and D.R.Shepherd.

# THE NATWEST TROPHY 1992

| FIRST ROUND 24 June | SECOND ROUND 9, 10 July | QUARTER-FINALS 29 July | SEMI-FINALS 12, 13 August | FINAL 5 September |
|---|---|---|---|---|
| LEICESTERSHIRE† | LEICESTERSHIRE | LEICESTERSHIRE† | LEICESTERSHIRE | Leicestershire (£13,500) |
| Norfolk | Derbyshire† | | | |
| DERBYSHIRE† | | | | |
| Berkshire | | | | |
| DURHAM | DURHAM | Durham (£3,375) | | |
| Ireland† | Middlesex† | | | |
| MIDDLESEX | | | | |
| Shropshire† | | | | |
| ESSEX† | ESSEX† | ESSEX | Essex (£6,750) | |
| Cumberland | Lancashire | | | |
| LANCASHIRE | | | | |
| Oxfordshire | | | | |
| GLOUCESTERSHIRE† | GLOUCESTERSHIRE | Gloucestershire† (£3,375) | | |
| Cheshire | Somerset† | | | |
| SOMERSET† | | | | |
| Scotland | | | | |
| KENT† | KENT | Kent (£3,375) | Warwickshire† (£6,750) | NORTHAMPTONSHIRE (£27,500) |
| Devon | Hampshire† | | | |
| HAMPSHIRE† | | | | |
| Dorset | | | | |
| WARWICKSHIRE† | WARWICKSHIRE† | WARWICKSHIRE† | | |
| Staffordshire | Sussex | | | |
| SUSSEX | | | | |
| Buckinghamshire† | | | | |
| NOTTINGHAMSHIRE† | Nottinghamshire† | Glamorgan† (£3,375) | NORTHAMPTONSHIRE | |
| Worcestershire | GLAMORGAN | | | |
| GLAMORGAN† | | | | |
| Surrey | | | | |
| YORKSHIRE† | Yorkshire | NORTHAMPTONSHIRE | | |
| Northumberland | NORTHAMPTONSHIRE† | | | |
| NORTHAMPTONSHIRE† | | | | |
| Cambridgeshire | | | | |

† Home team. Winning teams are in capitals. Prize-money shown in brackets.

# Congratulations Northamptonshire on winning the 1992 NatWest Trophy.

 **National Westminster Bank**
*We're here to make life easier*

# NATWEST TROPHY
# PRINCIPAL RECORDS 1963-92
### (Including The Gillette Cup)

| | | | | | |
|---|---|---|---|---|---|
| **Highest Total** | | 413-4 | Somerset v Devon | Torquay | 1990 |
| **Highest Total in a Final** | | 317-4 | Yorkshire v Surrey | Lord's | 1965 |
| **Highest Total by a Minor County** | | 305-9 | Durham v Glam | Darlington | 1991 |
| **Highest Total Batting Second** | | 326-9 | Hampshire v Leics | Leicester | 1987 |
| **Highest Total to Win Batting 2nd** | | 319-9 | Essex v Lancashire | Chelmsford | 1992 |
| **Lowest Total** | | 39 | Ireland v Sussex | Hove | 1985 |
| **Lowest Total in a Final** | | 118 | Lancashire v Kent | Lord's | 1974 |
| **Lowest Total to Win Batting First** | | 98 | Worcs v Durham | Chester-le-St | 1968 |
| **Highest Score** | | 206 | A.I.Kallicharran | Warwicks v Oxon | Birmingham | 1984 |
| **HS (Minor County)** | | 132 | G.Robinson | Lincs v Northumb | Jesmond | 1971 |
| **Hundreds** | | 216 | have been scored in GC (93) and NWT (123) matches | | |
| **Fastest Hundred** | | 36 balls – G.D.Rose | Somerset v Devon | Torquay | 1990 |
| **Most Hundreds** | | 7 C.L.Smith | Hampshire | | 1980-91 |

**Highest Partnership for each Wicket**

| | | | | | |
|---|---|---|---|---|---|
| 1st | 242* | M.D.Moxon/A.A.Metcalfe | Yorks v Warwicks | Leeds | 1990 |
| 2nd | 286 | I.S.Anderson/A.Hill | Derbys v Cornwall | Derby | 1986 |
| 3rd | 259* | H.Morris/M.P.Maynard | Glam v Durham | Darlington | 1991 |
| 4th | 234* | D.Lloyd/C.H.Lloyd | Lancashire v Glos | Manchester | 1978 |
| 5th | 166 | M.A.Lynch/G.R.J.Roope | Surrey v Durham | The Oval | 1982 |
| 6th | 105 | G.St A.Sobers/R.A.White | Notts v Worcs | Worcester | 1974 |
| 7th | 160* | C.J.Richards/I.R.Payne | Surrey v Lincs | Sleaford | 1983 |
| 8th | 83 | J.Hartley/D.A.Hale | Oxon v Glos | Oxford | 1989 |
| 9th | 87 | M.A.Nash/A.E.Cordle | Glamorgan v Lincs | Swansea | 1974 |
| 10th | 81 | S.Turner/R.E.East | Essex v Yorkshire | Leeds | 1982 |

| | | | | | |
|---|---|---|---|---|---|
| **Most Runs** | | 2261 (av 53.83) | | G.A.Gooch | Essex | 1973-92 |
| **Best Bowling** | 8-21 | M.A.Holding | Derbys v Sussex | Hove | 1988 |
| | 8-31 | D.L.Underwood | Kent v Scotland | Edinburgh | 1987 |
| **Hat-Tricks** | | J.D.F.Larter | Northants v Sussex | Northampton | 1963 |
| | | D.A.D.Sydenham | Surrey v Cheshire | Hoylake | 1964 |
| | | R.N.S.Hobbs | Essex v Middlesex | Lord's | 1968 |
| | | N.M.McVicker | Warwicks v Lincs | Birmingham | 1971 |
| | | G.S.Le Roux | Sussex v Ireland | Hove | 1985 |
| | | M.Jean-Jacques | Derbyshire v Notts | Derby | 1987 |
| | | J.F.M.O'Brien | Cheshire v Derbys | Chester | 1988 |
| **Most Wickets** | | 81 (av 14.85) | | G.G.Arnold | Surrey | 1963-80 |

**Most Wicket-Keeping Dismissals in an Innings**

| | | | | |
|---|---|---|---|---|
| 6 (5ct, 1st) | R.W.Taylor | Derbyshire v Essex | Derby | 1981 |
| 6 (4ct, 2st) | T.Davies | Glamorgan v Staffs | Stone | 1986 |

**Most Catches in an Innings**

| | | | | |
|---|---|---|---|---|
| 4 | A.S.Brown | Glos v Middlesex | Bristol | 1963 |
| 4 | G.Cook | Northants v Glam | Northampton | 1972 |
| 4 | C.G.Greenidge | Hants v Cheshire | Southampton | 1981 |
| 4 | D.C.Jackson | Durham v Northants | Darlington | 1984 |
| 4 | T.S.Smith | Herts v Somerset | St Albans | 1984 |
| 4 | H.Morris | Glam v Scotland | Edinburgh | 1988 |

| | | | | |
|---|---|---|---|---|
| **Most Appearances** | 61 | | D.P.Hughes | Lancashire | 1969-91 |
| **Most Match Awards** | 9 | | G.A.Gooch | Essex | 1973-92 |
| **Most Match Wins** | 60 – Lancashire | | **Most Cup/Trophy Wins** | 5 – Lancashire |

# NATWEST
## MAKING A REAL CONTRIBUTION TO THE WHOLE COMMUNITY.

This year as in previous years, NatWest is taking an active role in the community. And this support comes in various forms covering a wide range of environmental, social, arts and sporting projects all over the country.

Cash donations, and the secondment of around 100 of our senior staff to help with the day to day running of community projects are just two of the ways our resources are put to good use.

If our contribution helps the community in which we live and work, then we at NatWest believe it's money well spent.

National Westminster Bank PLC Registered Office 41 Lothbury, London EC2P 2BP

NatWest

# 1992 BENSON AND HEDGES CUP FINAL

## HAMPSHIRE v KENT

**Played at Lord's, London, on 11, 12 July.**
**Toss: Kent. Result: HAMPSHIRE won by 41 runs.**
Match Award: R.A.Smith (Adjudicator: M.J.Stewart).

| HAMPSHIRE | Runs | Min | Balls | 6s | 4s | Fall |
|---|---|---|---|---|---|---|
| V.P.Terry b Igglesden | 41 | 84 | 77 | – | 5 | 2-86 |
| T.C.Middleton lbw b Hooper | 27 | 65 | 51 | – | 1 | 1-68 |
| R.A.Smith run out (Taylor/Fleming) | 90 | 131 | 109 | 1 | 6 | 5-234 |
| D.I.Gower lbw b Fleming | 29 | 69 | 52 | – | – | 3-171 |
| *M.C.J.Nicholas c Ealham b Fleming | 25 | 23 | 22 | 1 | 2 | 4-205 |
| M.D.Marshall not out | 29 | 24 | 22 | – | 2 | – |
| K.D.James not out | 2 | 7 | 2 | – | – | – |
| J.R.Ayling | | | | | | |
| †R.J.Parks | | | | | | |
| S.D.Udal } did not bat | | | | | | |
| C.A.Connor | | | | | | |
| Extras (LB3, W3, NB4) | 10 | | | | | |
| Total (55 overs; 206 minutes) | 253-5 | closed | | | | |

| KENT | Runs | Min | Balls | 6s | 4s | Fall |
|---|---|---|---|---|---|---|
| T.R.Ward c Parks b Marshall | 5 | 30 | 26 | – | – | 1-17 |
| *M.R.Benson b James | 59 | 131 | 91 | – | 7 | 3-116 |
| N.R.Taylor c Parks b Ayling | 8 | 37 | 32 | – | 1 | 2-38 |
| C.L.Hooper b Udal | 28 | 65 | 56 | – | 2 | 4-116 |
| G.R.Cowdrey c Gower b Marshall | 27 | 62 | 50 | – | – | 7-186 |
| M.V.Fleming c Nicholas b Ayling | 32 | 39 | 34 | – | 2 | 5-171 |
| †S.A.Marsh b Udal | 7 | 11 | 10 | – | – | 6-182 |
| M.A.Ealham b Connor | 23 | 22 | 14 | 1 | 2 | 10-212 |
| M.J.McCague b Udal | 0 | 2 | 1 | – | – | 8-194 |
| R.P.Davis c Gower b Marshall | 1 | 6 | 3 | – | – | 9-204 |
| A.P.Igglesden not out | 1 | 4 | 2 | – | – | – |
| Extras (B1, LB11, W5, NB4) | 21 | | | | | |
| Total (52.3 overs; 213 minutes) | 212 | | | | | |

| KENT | O | M | R | W | HAMPSHIRE | O | M | R | W |
|---|---|---|---|---|---|---|---|---|---|
| Igglesden | 11 | 1 | 39 | 1 | Connor | 9.3 | 2 | 27 | 1 |
| Ealham | 9 | 0 | 46 | 0 | Marshall | 10 | 1 | 33 | 3 |
| McCague | 11 | 0 | 43 | 0 | Ayling | 11 | 0 | 38 | 2 |
| Hooper | 11 | 1 | 41 | 1 | James | 11 | 1 | 35 | 1 |
| Davis | 5 | 0 | 18 | 0 | Udal | 11 | 0 | 67 | 3 |
| Fleming | 8 | 0 | 63 | 2 | | | | | |

**Umpires:** J.H.Hampshire and M.J.Kitchen.

54

# 1992 BENSON AND HEDGES CUP

## ZONAL POINTS TABLE

| | P | W | L | NR | Pts | Run Rate |
|---|---|---|---|---|---|---|
| **GROUP A** | | | | | | |
| SURREY | 5 | 4 | 1 | – | 8 | 82.55 |
| MIDDLESEX | 5 | 4 | 1 | – | 8 | 74.48 |
| Leicestershire | 5 | 3 | 2 | – | 6 | 63.45 |
| Sussex | 5 | 2 | 3 | – | 4 | 63.83 |
| Minor Counties | 5 | 1 | 4 | – | 2 | 59.45 |
| Gloucestershire | 5 | 1 | 4 | – | 2 | 58.74 |
| **GROUP B** | | | | | | |
| HAMPSHIRE | 4 | 3 | – | 1 | 7 | 70.58 |
| LANCASHIRE | 4 | 3 | 1 | – | 6 | 64.87 |
| Essex | 4 | 2 | 2 | – | 4 | 64.31 |
| Northamptonshire | 4 | 1 | 3 | – | 2 | 73.48 |
| Scotland | 4 | – | 3 | 1 | 1 | 51.21 |
| **GROUP C** | | | | | | |
| KENT | 4 | 4 | – | – | 8 | 65.98 |
| SOMERSET | 4 | 2 | 2 | – | 4 | 62.11 |
| Nottinghamshire | 4 | 2 | 2 | – | 4 | 61.39 |
| Warwickshire | 4 | 1 | 3 | – | 2 | 61.51 |
| Yorkshire | 4 | 1 | 3 | – | 2 | 48.03 |
| **GROUP D** | | | | | | |
| WORCESTERSHIRE | 4 | 3 | 1 | – | 6 | 63.45 |
| DERBYSHIRE | 4 | 3 | 1 | – | 6 | 62.02 |
| Durham | 4 | 2 | 2 | – | 4 | 64.95 |
| Glamorgan | 4 | 2 | 2 | – | 4 | 58.96 |
| Combined Universities | 4 | – | 4 | – | 0 | 54.01 |

## FINAL ROUNDS

| QUARTER-FINALS 27 May | SEMI-FINALS 10 June | FINAL 11, 12 July |
|---|---|---|
| HAMPSHIRE†<br>Middlesex<br>(£3,375) | } HAMPSHIRE† | |
| SOMERSET<br>Worcestershire†<br>(£3,375) | } Somerset<br>(£6,750) | **HAMPSHIRE**<br>(£27,500) |
| KENT†<br>Derbyshire<br>(£3,375) | } KENT† | |
| SURREY†<br>Lancashire<br>(£3,375) | } Surrey<br>(£6,750) | Kent<br>(£13,500) |

† Home team. Winning teams are in capitals. Prize-money shown in brackets.

# BENSON AND HEDGES CUP
## PRINCIPAL RECORDS 1972-92

| | | | |
|---|---|---|---|
| **Highest Total** | 388-7 | Essex v Scotland | Chelmsford | 1992 |
| **Highest Total Batting Second** ⎫ | 303-7 | Derbys v Somerset | Taunton | 1990 |
| **Highest Losing Total** ⎭ | | | | |
| **Lowest Total** | 50 | Hampshire v Yorks | Leeds | 1991 |
| **Highest Score** 198* G.A.Gooch | | Essex v Sussex | Hove | 1982 |
| **Hundreds** | 226 have been scored in Benson and Hedges Cup matches | | | |
| **Fastest Hundred** | 62 min – M.A.Nash | Glamorgan v Hants | Swansea | 1976 |

**Highest Partnership for each Wicket**

| | | | | | |
|---|---|---|---|---|---|
| 1st | 252 | V.P.Terry/C.L.Smith | Hants v Comb Us | Southampton | 1990 |
| 2nd | 285* | C.G.Greenidge/D.R.Turner | Hants v Minor C (S) | Amersham | 1973 |
| 3rd | 269* | P.M.Roebuck/M.D.Crowe | Somerset v Hants | Southampton | 1987 |
| 4th | 184* | D.Lloyd/B.W.Reidy | Lancashire v Derbys | Chesterfield | 1980 |
| 5th | 160 | A.J.Lamb/D.J.Capel | Northants v Leics | Northampton | 1986 |
| 6th | 121 | P.A.Neale/S.J.Rhodes | Worcs v Yorkshire | Worcester | 1988 |
| 7th | 149* | J.D.Love/C.M.Old | Yorks v Scotland | Bradford | 1981 |
| 8th | 109 | R.E.East/N.Smith | Essex v Northants | Chelmsford | 1977 |
| 9th | 83 | P.G.Newman/M.A.Holding | Derbyshire v Notts | Nottingham | 1985 |
| 10th | 80* | D.L.Bairstow/M.Johnson | Yorkshire v Derbys | Derby | 1981 |

**Best Bowling**

| | | | | | |
|---|---|---|---|---|---|
| **Best Bowling** | 7-12 | W.W.Daniel | Middx v Minor C (E) | Ipswich | 1978 |
| | 7-22 | J.R.Thomson | Middx v Hampshire | Lord's | 1981 |
| | 7-32 | R.G.D.Willis | Warwicks v Yorks | Birmingham | 1981 |
| **Hat-Tricks** | | G.D.McKenzie | Leics v Worcs | Worcester | 1972 |
| | | K.Higgs | Leics v Surrey | Lord's | 1974 |
| | | A.A.Jones | Middlesex v Essex | Lord's | 1977 |
| | | M.J.Procter | Glos v Hampshire | Southampton | 1977 |
| | | W.Larkins | Northants v Comb Us | Northampton | 1980 |
| | | E.A.Moseley | Glamorgan v Kent | Cardiff | 1981 |
| | | G.C.Small | Warwickshire v Leics | Leicester | 1984 |
| | | N.A.Mallender | Somerset v Comb Us | Taunton | 1987 |
| | | W.K.M.Benjamin | Leics v Notts | Leicester | 1987 |
| | | A.R.C.Fraser | Middlesex v Sussex | Lord's | 1988 |

**Most Wicket-Keeping Dismissals in an Innings**

| | | | | |
|---|---|---|---|---|
| 8 (8ct) | D.J.S.Taylor | Somerset v Comb Us | Taunton | 1982 |

**Most Catches in an Innings**

| | | | | |
|---|---|---|---|---|
| 5 | V.J.Marks | Comb Us v Kent | Oxford | 1976 |

**Most Match Awards** 20 G.A.Gooch | | Essex | 1973-92

# BENSON AND HEDGES CUP WINNERS

| | | | | | |
|---|---|---|---|---|---|
| 1972 | Leicestershire | 1979 | Essex | 1986 | Middlesex |
| 1973 | Kent | 1980 | Northamptonshire | 1987 | Yorkshire |
| 1974 | Surrey | 1981 | Somerset | 1988 | Hampshire |
| 1975 | Leicestershire | 1982 | Somerset | 1989 | Nottinghamshire |
| 1976 | Kent | 1983 | Middlesex | 1990 | Lancashire |
| 1977 | Gloucestershire | 1984 | Lancashire | 1991 | Worcestershire |
| 1978 | Kent | 1985 | Leicestershire | 1992 | Hampshire |

# SUNDAY LEAGUE
# FINAL TABLE 1992

| | P | W | L | T | NR | Pts | Away Wins | Runs/ 100 bl |
|---|---|---|---|---|---|---|---|---|
| 1 **MIDDLESEX** (11) | 17 | 14 | 2 | – | 1 | 58 | 6 | 93.91 |
| 2 Essex (6) | 17 | 11 | 5 | – | 1 | 46 | 4 | 83.33 |
| 3 Hampshire (17) | 17 | 10 | 6 | – | 1 | 42 | 3 | 76.71 |
| 4 Surrey (8) | 17 | 10 | 7 | – | – | 40 | 7 | 90.46 |
| 5 Somerset (9) | 17 | 9 | 6 | – | 2 | 40 | 3 | 81.23 |
| 5 Kent (10) | 17 | 8 | 5 | – | 4 | 40 | 5 | 89.84 |
| 7 Worcestershire (4) | 17 | 7 | 6 | 1 | 3 | 36 | 3 | 74.48 |
| 8 Gloucestershire (12) | 17 | 8 | 8 | – | 1 | 34 | 3 | 76.04 |
| 8 Durham (–) | 17 | 7 | 7 | – | 3 | 34 | 4 | 89.11 |
| 8 Warwickshire (5) | 17 | 7 | 7 | 1 | 2 | 34 | 2 | 82.55 |
| 11 Sussex (12) | 17 | 7 | 8 | – | 2 | 32 | 3 | 82.54 |
| 11 Lancashire (2) | 17 | 6 | 7 | – | 4 | 32 | 3 | 84.05 |
| 13 Northamptonshire (3) | 17 | 7 | 9 | – | 1 | 30 | 3 | 83.21 |
| 13 Derbyshire (15) | 17 | 7 | 9 | – | 1 | 30 | 1 | 81.06 |
| 15 Yorkshire (7) | 17 | 6 | 9 | – | 2 | 28 | 3 | 79.53 |
| 16 Glamorgan (16) | 17 | 4 | 10 | – | 3 | 22 | 3 | 86.21 |
| 17 Nottinghamshire (1) | 17 | 3 | 11 | – | 3 | 18 | 1 | 81.17 |
| 18 Leicestershire (14) | 17 | 3 | 12 | – | 2 | 16 | 2 | 81.08 |

1991 final positions are shown in brackets.

Win = 4 points. Tie/No Result = 2 points. When two or more counties finish with an equal number of points, the first four places are decided by (a) most wins, (b) most away wins, (c) runs per 100 balls.

The Sunday League has been sponsored by John Player & Sons (1969-86) and by Refuge Assurance (1987-91). It endured an unsponsored interregnum in 1992. This season, under the patronage of AXA Equity & Law Insurance, it will be extended from 40 to 50 overs per innings and staged in coloured suits.

## WINNERS

| | | |
|---|---|---|
| 1969 Lancashire | 1977 Leicestershire | 1985 Essex |
| 1970 Lancashire | 1978 Hampshire | 1986 Hampshire |
| 1971 Worcestershire | 1979 Somerset | 1987 Worcestershire |
| 1972 Kent | 1980 Warwickshire | 1988 Worcestershire |
| 1973 Kent | 1981 Essex | 1989 Lancashire |
| 1974 Leicestershire | 1982 Sussex | 1990 Derbyshire |
| 1975 Hampshire | 1983 Yorkshire | 1991 Nottinghamshire |
| 1976 Kent | 1984 Essex | 1992 Middlesex |

# SUNDAY LEAGUE

## PRINCIPAL RECORDS 1969-92

| | | | | | |
|---|---|---|---|---|---|
| **Highest Total** | | 360-3 | Somerset v Glam | Neath | 1990 |
| **Highest Total Batting Second** | | 301-6 | Warwicks v Essex | Colchester | 1982 |
| **Lowest Total** | | 23 | Middlesex v Yorks | Leeds | 1974 |
| **Highest Score** | 176 | | G.A.Gooch Essex v Glamorgan | Southend | 1983 |
| **Hundreds** | | 420 have been scored in Sunday League matches | | | |
| **Fastest Hundred** | 46 balls | G.D.Rose | Somerset v Glam | Neath | 1990 |

**Highest Partnership for each Wicket**

| | | | | | |
|---|---|---|---|---|---|
| 1st | 239 | G.A.Gooch/B.R.Hardie | Essex v Notts | Nottingham | 1985 |
| 2nd | 273 | G.A.Gooch/K.S.McEwan | Essex v Notts | Nottingham | 1983 |
| 3rd | 223 | S.J.Cook/G.D.Rose | Somerset v Glam | Neath | 1990 |
| 4th | 219 | C.G.Greenidge/C.L.Smith | Hampshire v Surrey | Southampton | 1987 |
| 5th | 185* | B.M.McMillan/Asif Din | Warwicks v Essex | Chelmsford | 1986 |
| 6th | 124* | J.J.Whitaker/P.A.Nixon | Leics v Surrey | The Oval | 1992 |
| 7th | 132 | K.R.Brown/N.F.Williams | Middx v Somerset | Lord's | 1988 |
| 8th | 105 | W.K.Hegg/I.D.Austin | Lancashire v Middx | Lord's | 1991 |
| 9th | 105 | D.G.Moir/R.W.Taylor | Derbyshire v Kent | Derby | 1984 |
| 10th | 57 | D.A.Graveney/J.B.Mortimore | Glos v Lancashire | Tewkesbury | 1973 |

| **Most Wickets** | 8-26 | K.D.Boyce | Essex v Lancashire | Manchester | 1971 |
|---|---|---|---|---|---|
| | 7-15 | R.A.Hutton | Yorkshire v Worcs | Leeds | 1969 |
| | 7-39 | A.Hodgson | Northants v Somerset | Northampton | 1976 |
| | 7-41 | A.N.Jones | Sussex v Notts | Nottingham | 1986 |

**Four Wkts in Four Balls**  A.Ward   Derbyshire v Sussex   Derby   1970

**Hat-Tricks (21):** Derbyshire – A.Ward (1970), C.J.Tunnicliffe (1979); Essex – K.D.Boyce (1971); Glamorgan – M.A.Nash (1975), A.E.Cordle (1979), G.C.Holmes (1987); Gloucestershire – K.M.Curran (1989); Hampshire – J.M.Rice (1975), M.D.Marshall (1981); Kent – R.M.Ellison (1983), M.J.McCague (1992); Leicestershire – G.D.McKenzie (1972); Northamptonshire – A.Hodgson (1976); Nottinghamshire – K.Saxelby (1987); Somerset – R.Palmer (1970), I.V.A.Richards (1982); Surrey – M.P.Bicknell (1992); Sussex – A.Buss (1970); Warwickshire – R.G.D.Willis (1973), W.Blenkiron (1974); Yorkshire – P.W.Jarvis (1982).

**Most Economical Analysis**

| O | M | R | W | | | | |
|---|---|---|---|---|---|---|---|
| 8 | 8 | 0 | 0 | B.A.Langford | Somerset v Essex | Yeovil | 1969 |

**Most Expensive Analyses**

| O | M | R | W | | | | |
|---|---|---|---|---|---|---|---|
| 7.5 | 0 | 89 | 3 | G.Miller | Derbyshire v Glos | Gloucester | 1984 |
| 8 | 0 | 88 | 1 | E.E.Hemmings | Notts v Somerset | Nottingham | 1983 |

**Most Wicket-Keeping Dismissals**

7 (6 ct, 1 st)   R.W.Taylor   Derbyshire v Lancs   Manchester   1975

**Most Catches in the Field**

5   J.M.Rice   Hampshire v Warwicks   Southampton   1978

# COUNTY CAPS AWARDED IN 1992

| | |
|---|---|
| Derbyshire | C.J.Adams, K.M.Krikken, T.J.O'Gorman |
| Durham | Entire playing staff |
| Essex | – |
| Glamorgan | P.A.Cottey, R.D.B.Croft, A.Dale, S.P.James |
| Gloucestershire | G.D.Hodgson |
| Hampshire | S.D.Udal |
| Kent | M.A.Ealham, C.L.Hooper, M.J.McCague |
| Lancashire | G.D.Lloyd, N.J.Speak |
| Leicestershire | – |
| Middlesex | – |
| Northamptonshire | K.M.Curran, J.P.Taylor |
| Nottinghamshire | P.R.Pollard |
| Somerset | A.R.Caddick, M.N.Lathwell |
| Surrey | – |
| Sussex | J.W.Hall, F.D.Stephenson |
| Warwickshire | K.J.Piper, R.G.Twose |
| Worcestershire | – |
| Yorkshire | S.A.Kellett, M.A.Robinson, S.R.Tendulkar |

# MINOR COUNTIES CHAMPIONSHIP

## FINAL TABLE 1992

| | | P | W | L | D | NR | Bonus Points Bat | Bonus Points Bowl | Total Points |
|---|---|---|---|---|---|---|---|---|---|
| **EASTERN DIVISION** | | | | | | | | | |
| Staffordshire | NW | 9 | 3 | – | 4 | 2* | 27 | 21 | 101 |
| Hertfordshire | NW | 9 | 3 | – | 6 | – | 13 | 25 | 86 |
| Suffolk | NW | 9 | 2 | 1 | 5 | 1 | 14 | 19 | 70 |
| Norfolk | NW | 9 | 2 | 1 | 5 | 1 | 9 | 21 | 67 |
| Buckinghamshire | NW | 9 | 2 | 2 | 5 | – | 15 | 17 | 64 |
| Cumberland | | 9 | 1 | 2 | 6 | – | 20 | 28 | 64 |
| Lincolnshire | | 9 | 1 | 2 | 6 | – | 18 | 27 | 61 |
| Cambridgeshire | | 9 | 1 | 1 | 7 | – | 10 | 25 | 51 |
| Northumberland | | 9 | 1 | 3 | 5 | – | 13 | 18 | 47 |
| Bedfordshire | | 9 | – | 4 | 5 | – | 11 | 20 | 31 |
| **WESTERN DIVISION** | | | | | | | | | |
| Devon | NW | 9 | 3 | 1 | 3 | 2 | 24 | 15 | 97 |
| Oxfordshire | NW | 9 | 3 | – | 3 | 3 | 10 | 12 | 85 |
| Cheshire | NW | 9 | 2 | 4 | 2 | 1 | 18 | 25 | 80 |
| Wiltshire | NW | 9 | 2 | 1 | 6 | – | 20 | 25 | 77 |
| Wales | NW | 9 | 2 | 1 | 5 | 1 | 12 | 26 | 75 |
| Dorset | NW | 9 | 3 | 1 | 5 | – | 4 | 22 | 74 |
| Shropshire | NW | 9 | 2 | 2 | 4 | 1 | 12 | 25 | 74 |
| Berkshire | | 9 | 2 | 2 | 5 | – | 12 | 19 | 63 |
| Herefordshire | | 9 | 1 | 2 | 6 | – | 12 | 24 | 52 |
| Cornwall | | 9 | – | 6 | 3 | – | 9 | 15 | 24 |

NW signifies qualification for the 1993 NatWest Trophy.
* Signifies points for one No Result match included in bonus columns.

# 1992 CHAMPIONSHIP FINAL
## DEVON v STAFFORDSHIRE

**Played at Worcester, Monday 14 September 1992.**
**Toss: Devon. Result: STAFFORDSHIRE won by 79 runs.**

| STAFFORDSHIRE | | | WKT | FALL |
|---|---|---|---|---|
| S.J.Dean | c Donohue b Allin | 30 | 1 | 58 |
| D.Cartledge | c Folland b White | 36 | 2 | 74 |
| D.A.Banks | c Donohue b Allin | 11 | 3 | 91 |
| S.D.Myles | lbw b Dawson | 14 | 4 | 97 |
| A.J.Dutton | c Pritchard b Allin | 2 | 5 | 97 |
| *N.J.Archer | c White b Woodman | 34 | 6 | 178 |
| P.G.Newman | b Donohue | 41 | 7 | 200 |
| †M.I.Humphries | not out | 17 | 8 | 201 |
| R.A.Spiers | run out | 1 | 9 | – |
| N.P.Hackett | did not bat | | 10 | – |
| I.S.Worthington | did not bat | | | |
| Extras | (LB11, W3, NB1) | 15 | | |
| **Total** | (55 overs; 8 wickets) | 201 | | |

| DEVON | | | WKT | FALL |
|---|---|---|---|---|
| N.R.Gaywood | b Hackett | 1 | 1 | 1 |
| R.I.Dawson | c Dean b Newman | 0 | 2 | 6 |
| *N.A.Folland | b Newman | 73 | 3 | 48 |
| A.J.Pugh | c Humphries b Worthington | 8 | 4 | 48 |
| S.M.Willis | b Worthington | 0 | 5 | 66 |
| G.W.White | lbw b Myles | 10 | 6 | 91 |
| O.Le Fleming | c Worthington b Myles | 8 | 7 | 106 |
| A.W.Allin | b Spiers | 3 | 8 | 113 |
| M.C.Woodman | lbw b Newman | 0 | 8 | 113 |
| †C.S.Pritchard | not out | 0 | 9 | 122 |
| K.Donohue | absent hurt | 0 | 10 | – |
| Extras | (LB8, W6, NB5) | 19 | | |
| **Total** | (42.2 overs) | 122 | | |

| DEVON | O | M | R | W | STAFFS | O | M | R | W |
|---|---|---|---|---|---|---|---|---|---|
| Donohue | 10.1 | 2 | 47 | 1 | Newman | 6.2 | 1 | 12 | 3 |
| Woodman | 10.5 | 1 | 43 | 1 | Hackett | 8 | 3 | 20 | 1 |
| Le Fleming | 8 | 0 | 22 | 0 | Worthington | 8 | 3 | 21 | 2 |
| Allin | 11 | 4 | 15 | 3 | Spiers | 7 | 2 | 17 | 1 |
| White | 4 | 0 | 16 | 1 | Myles | 6 | 0 | 20 | 2 |
| Dawson | 11 | 2 | 47 | 1 | Dutton | 7 | 0 | 24 | 0 |

**Umpires: R.K.Curtis and D.J.Halfyard.**

| | Mins | Balls | 6 | 4 |
|---|---|---|---|---|
| Dean | 52 | 47 | – | 5 |
| Cartledge | 68 | 54 | 1 | 4 |
| Archer | 94 | 78 | – | 1 |
| Newman | 80 | 68 | – | 3 |
| Humphries | 16 | 9 | 2 | – |
| Folland | 148 | 122 | – | 7 |

# MINOR COUNTIES CHAMPIONS

| | | | | | |
|---|---|---|---|---|---|
| 1895 | Norfolk | 1927 | Staffordshire | 1964 | Lancashire II |
| | Durham | 1928 | Berkshire | 1965 | Somerset II |
| | Worcestershire | 1929 | Oxfordshire | 1966 | Lincolnshire |
| 1896 | Worcestershire | 1930 | Durham | 1967 | Cheshire |
| 1897 | Worcestershire | 1931 | Leicestershire II | 1968 | Yorkshire II |
| 1898 | Worcestershire | 1932 | Buckinghamshire | 1969 | Buckinghamshire |
| 1899 | Northamptonshire | 1933 | Undecided | 1970 | Bedfordshire |
| | Buckinghamshire | 1934 | Lancashire II | 1971 | Yorkshire II |
| 1900 | Glamorgan | 1935 | Middlesex II | 1972 | Bedfordshire |
| | Durham | 1936 | Hertfordshire | 1973 | Shropshire |
| | Northamptonshire | 1937 | Lancashire II | 1974 | Oxfordshire |
| 1901 | Durham | 1938 | Buckinghamshire | 1975 | Hertfordshire |
| 1902 | Wiltshire | 1939 | Surrey II | 1976 | Durham |
| 1903 | Northamptonshire | 1946 | Suffolk | 1977 | Suffolk |
| 1904 | Northamptonshire | 1947 | Yorkshire II | 1978 | Devon |
| 1905 | Norfolk | 1948 | Lancashire II | 1979 | Suffolk |
| 1906 | Staffordshire | 1949 | Lancashire II | 1980 | Durham |
| 1907 | Lancashire II | 1950 | Surrey II | 1981 | Durham |
| 1908 | Staffordshire | 1951 | Kent II | 1982 | Oxfordshire |
| 1909 | Wiltshire | 1952 | Buckinghamshire | 1983 | Hertfordshire |
| 1910 | Norfolk | 1953 | Berkshire | 1984 | Durham |
| 1911 | Staffordshire | 1954 | Surrey II | 1985 | Cheshire |
| 1912 | In abeyance | 1955 | Surrey II | 1986 | Cumberland |
| 1913 | Norfolk | 1956 | Kent II | 1987 | Buckinghamshire |
| 1920 | Staffordshire | 1957 | Yorkshire II | 1988 | Cheshire |
| 1921 | Staffordshire | 1958 | Yorkshire II | 1989 | Oxfordshire |
| 1922 | Buckinghamshire | 1959 | Warwickshire II | 1990 | Hertfordshire |
| 1923 | Buckinghamshire | 1960 | Lancashire II | 1991 | Staffordshire |
| 1924 | Berkshire | 1961 | Somerset II | 1992 | Staffordshire |
| 1925 | Buckinghamshire | 1962 | Warwickshire II | | |
| 1926 | Durham | 1963 | Cambridgeshire | | |

# MINOR COUNTIES CHAMPIONSHIP RECORDS

| | | | | | |
|---|---|---|---|---|---|
| **Highest Total** | | 621 | | Surrey II v Devon | The Oval | 1928 |
| **Lowest Total** | | 14 | | Cheshire v Staffordshire | Stoke | 1909 |
| **Highest Score** | | 282 | E.Garnett | Berkshire v Wiltshire | Reading | 1908 |
| **Most Runs – Season** | | 1212 | A.F.Brazier | Surrey II | | 1949 |
| **Record Partnership** | | | | | | |
| 2nd | 388* | T.H.Clark and A.F.Brazier | | Surrey II v Sussex II | The Oval | 1949 |
| **Best Bowling – Innings** | 10-11 | S.Turner | Cambs v Cumberland | Penrith | 1987 |
| – Match | 18-100 | N.W.Harding | Kent II v Wiltshire | Swindon | 1937 |
| **Most Wickets – Season** | 119 | S.F.Barnes | Staffordshire | | 1906 |

# 1992 MINOR COUNTIES CHAMPIONSHIP

## LEADING BATTING AVERAGES
(Qualification: 8 completed innings, average 36.00)

|  |  | I | NO | HS | Runs | Avge |
|---|---|---|---|---|---|---|
| N.A.Folland | Devon | 13 | 4 | 118 | 734 | 81.55 |
| N.R.Gaywood | Devon | 13 | 1 | 125 | 933 | 77.75 |
| J.D.Love | Lincs | 15 | 4 | 114 | 733 | 66.63 |
| S.N.V.Waterton | Oxon | 15 | 3 | 110* | 756 | 63.00 |
| M.R.Davies | Shropshire | 16 | 7 | 101* | 561 | 62.33 |
| J.Derrick | Wales | 12 | 2 | 123 | 551 | 55.10 |
| A.J.Pugh | Devon | 16 | 7 | 95 | 495 | 55.00 |
| I.Cockbain | Cheshire | 15 | 1 | 100* | 755 | 53.92 |
| G.D.Reynolds | Dorset | 12 | 3 | 156* | 477 | 53.00 |
| G.R.Morris | N'land | 16 | – | 106 | 818 | 51.12 |
| N.T.Gadsby | Cambs | 16 | 1 | 118 | 758 | 50.53 |
| D.A.J.Wise | Oxon | 15 | 2 | 153* | 636 | 48.92 |
| S.Sharp | Cumberland | 12 | 1 | 113* | 533 | 48.45 |
| D.J.M.Mercer | Berkshire | 18 | 1 | 105 | 806 | 47.41 |
| P.J.Caley | Suffolk | 16 | 2 | 100 | 663 | 47.35 |
| S.M.Shearman | Bucks | 17 | 6 | 75* | 487 | 44.27 |
| S.Wherry | Cornwall | 18 | 1 | 172* | 736 | 43.29 |
| K.N.Foyle | Wiltshire | 14 | 3 | 98* | 467 | 42.45 |
| D.P.Norman | Cambs | 15 | 5 | 85* | 420 | 42.00 |
| D.Cartledge | Staffs | 9 | 1 | 120* | 336 | 42.00 |
| M.J.Roberts | Bucks | 9 | – | 78 | 371 | 41.22 |
| T.Parton | Shropshire | 17 | 3 | 101* | 571 | 40.78 |
| D.B.Storer | Lincs | 14 | 2 | 119* | 482 | 40.16 |
| P.Robinson | Cumberland | 10 | 1 | 75 | 361 | 40.11 |
| S.G.Plumb | Norfolk | 12 | – | 78 | 468 | 39.00 |
| R.P.Skyrme | Hereford | 18 | 6 | 78 | 466 | 38.83 |
| M.James | Herts | 15 | – | 116 | 576 | 38.40 |
| G.A.Buchanan | Herts | 15 | 3 | 88 | 454 | 37.83 |
| A.J.Squire | Suffolk | 12 | 1 | 139 | 412 | 37.45 |
| R.R.Savage | Wiltshire | 14 | 3 | 120* | 403 | 36.63 |
| R.T.Walton | Cornwall | 13 | 2 | 127* | 398 | 36.18 |

## LEADING BOWLING AVERAGES
(Qualification: 20 wickets, average 30.00)

|  |  | O | M | R | W | Avge |
|---|---|---|---|---|---|---|
| G.Miller | Cheshire | 291 | 84 | 636 | 49 | 12.97 |
| N.P.Hackett | Staffs | 128.4 | 33 | 351 | 24 | 14.62 |
| S.R.Walbridge | Dorset | 251.4 | 72 | 658 | 41 | 16.04 |
| J.F.M.O'Brien | Cheshire | 242 | 47 | 700 | 42 | 16.66 |
| A.Smith | Wales | 203.4 | 76 | 459 | 26 | 17.65 |
| A.Needham | Herts | 219.3 | 83 | 448 | 25 | 17.92 |
| D.Surridge | Herts | 212.1 | 51 | 521 | 28 | 18.60 |
| D.A.Christmas | Lincs | 124.3 | 28 | 401 | 21 | 19.09 |
| P.Bent | Hereford | 112.4 | 20 | 391 | 20 | 19.55 |
| J.H.Shackleton | Dorset | 250.2 | 61 | 653 | 32 | 20.40 |
| P.C.Graham | N'land | 212.1 | 63 | 568 | 26 | 21.84 |
| R.A.Bunting | Norfolk | 213.1 | 39 | 658 | 30 | 21.93 |
| J.Derrick | Wales | 178.5 | 39 | 507 | 23 | 22.04 |
| C.Miller | Suffolk | 153.5 | 16 | 605 | 26 | 23.26 |
| T.J.A.Scriven | Bucks | 185.1 | 39 | 624 | 26 | 24.00 |

| | | O | M | R | W | Avge |
|---|---|---|---|---|---|---|
| D.J.B.Hartley | Berkshire | 186 | 25 | 799 | 32 | 24.96 |
| A.B.Byram | Shropshire | 235.4 | 47 | 778 | 31 | 25.09 |
| A. Akhtar | Cambs | 168.1 | 38 | 507 | 20 | 25.35 |
| C.K.Bullen | Beds | 236.2 | 80 | 675 | 25 | 27.00 |
| K.A.Arnold | Oxon | 198.5 | 44 | 627 | 23 | 27.26 |
| I.J.Curtis | Oxon | 208.5 | 29 | 756 | 27 | 28.00 |
| P.J.Lewington | Berkshire | 254 | 73 | 661 | 23 | 28.73 |
| A.R.K.Pierson | Cambs | 263.4 | 54 | 837 | 29 | 28.86 |
| R.Kingshott | Norfolk | 237 | 43 | 809 | 28 | 28.89 |

# SECOND XI CHAMPIONSHIP 1992
# RAPID CRICKETLINE FINAL TABLE

| | | P | W | L | D | Bonus Bat | Points Bowl | Total Points |
|---|---|---|---|---|---|---|---|---|
| 1 | SURREY (6) | 17 | 8 | 2 | 7 | 47 | 45 | 220 |
| 2 | Northamptonshire (17) | 17 | 7 | 1 | 9 | 52 | 50 | 214 |
| 3 | Gloucestershire (16) | 17 | 6 | 2 | 9 | 38 | 52 | 186 |
| 4 | Hampshire (4) | 17 | 6 | 3 | 8 | 48 | 36 | 180 |
| 5 | Yorkshire (1) | 17 | 5 | 2 | 10 | 48 | 48 | 176 |
| 6 | Middlesex (12) | 17 | 5 | 2 | 10 | 44 | 50 | 174 |
| 6 | Durham (–) | 17 | 5 | 3 | 9 | 42 | 52 | 174 |
| 8 | Kent (14) | 17 | 4 | 5 | 8 | 38 | 55 | 157 |
| 9 | Sussex (7) | 17 | 3 | 4 | 10 | 47 | 52 | 147 |
| 10 | Lancashire (11) | 17 | 3 | 1 | 13 | 47 | 48 | 143 |
| 11 | Derbyshire (8) | 17 | 3 | 5 | 9 | 43 | 51 | 142 |
| 12 | Warwickshire (2) | 17 | 3 | 4 | 10 | 33 | 47 | 128 |
| 13 | Somerset (3) | 16 | 3 | 5 | 8 | 36 | 36 | 120 |
| 14 | Nottinghamshire (5) | 17 | 1 | 5 | 11 | 47 | 39 | 110 |
| 15 | Leicestershire (10) | 17 | 1 | 4 | 12 | 37 | 46 | 99 |
| 16 | Worcestershire (9) | 17 | 1 | 4 | 12 | 39 | 37 | 92 |
| 17 | Glamorgan (13) | 17 | 1 | 4 | 12 | 21 | 44 | 81 |
| 18 | Essex (15) | 16 | – | 9 | 7 | 32 | 40 | 72 |

1991 final positions are shown in brackets.
Win = 16 points. Nottinghamshire's total includes 8 points for match drawn with scores level.

## RAPID CRICKETLINE CHAMPIONSHIP PLAYER OF THE SEASON:
### R.C.J.Williams (Gloucestershire)

### SECOND XI CHAMPIONS

| | | | | | |
|---|---|---|---|---|---|
| 1959 | Gloucestershire | 1971 | Hampshire | 1983 | Leicestershire |
| 1960 | Northamptonshire | 1972 | Nottinghamshire | 1984 | Yorkshire |
| 1961 | Kent | 1973 | Essex | 1985 | Nottinghamshire |
| 1962 | Worcestershire | 1974 | Middlesex | 1986 | Lancashire |
| 1963 | Worcestershire | 1975 | Surrey | 1987 | Kent/Yorkshire |
| 1964 | Lancashire | 1976 | Kent | 1988 | Surrey |
| 1965 | Glamorgan | 1977 | Yorkshire | 1989 | Middlesex |
| 1966 | Surrey | 1978 | Sussex | 1990 | Sussex |
| 1967 | Hampshire | 1979 | Warwickshire | 1991 | Yorkshire |
| 1968 | Surrey | 1980 | Glamorgan | 1992 | Surrey |
| 1969 | Kent | 1981 | Hampshire | | |
| 1970 | Kent | 1982 | Worcestershire | | |

# THE FIRST-CLASS COUNTIES HONOURS, REGISTER, RECORDS AND 1992 AVERAGES

Records exclude all performances during the 1992-93 overseas season.

## ABBREVIATIONS

### General

| | | | |
|---|---|---|---|
| * | not out/unbroken partnership | f-c | first-class |
| b | born | HS | Highest Score |
| BB | Best innings bowling analysis | LOI | Limited-Overs Internationals |
| Cap | Awarded 1st XI County Cap | Tests | Official Test Matches |
| Tours | Overseas tours involving first-class appearances | | |

### Awards

| | |
|---|---|
| BHC | Benson and Hedges Cup 'Gold' Award |
| NWT | NatWest Trophy/Gillette Cup 'Man of the Match' Award |
| Wisden 1992 | One of Wisden Cricketers' Almanack's Five Cricketers of 1992 |
| YC 1992 | Cricket Writers' Club Young Cricketer of 1992 |

### Competitions

| | |
|---|---|
| BHC | Benson and Hedges Cup |
| GC | Gillette Cup |
| NWT | NatWest Trophy |
| SL | Sunday League |

### Playing Categories

| | |
|---|---|
| LB | Bowls right-arm leg-breaks |
| LF | Bowls left-arm fast |
| LFM | Bowls left-arm fast-medium |
| LHB | Bats left-handed |
| LM | Bowls left-arm medium pace |
| LMF | Bowls left-arm medium-fast |
| OB | Bowls right-arm off-breaks |
| RF | Bowls right-arm fast |
| RFM | Bowls right-arm fast-medium |
| RHB | Bats right-handed |
| RM | Bowls right-arm medium pace |
| RMF | Bowls right-arm medium-fast |
| RSM | Bowls right-arm slow-medium |
| SLA | Bowls left-arm leg-breaks |
| WK | Wicket-keeper |

### Education

| | |
|---|---|
| BHS | Boys' High School |
| BS | Boys' School |
| C | College |
| CE | College of Education |
| CFE | College of Further Education |
| CHE | College of Higher Education |
| CS | Comprehensive School |
| GS | Grammar School |
| HS | High School |
| IHE | Institute of Higher Education |
| LSE | London School of Economics |
| RGS | Royal Grammar School |
| S | School |
| TC | Technical College |
| T(H)S | Technical (High) School |
| SFC | Sixth Form College |
| SM | Secondary Modern School |
| SS | Secondary School |
| U | University |

### Teams (see also p 164)

| | | | |
|---|---|---|---|
| Cav | Cavaliers | ND | Northern Districts |
| CD | Central Districts | NSW | New South Wales |
| DHR | D.H.Robins' XI | OFS | Orange Free State |
| DN | Duke of Norfolk's XI | PIA | Pakistan International Airlines |
| Eng Co | English Counties XI | RW | Rest of the World XI |
| EP | Eastern Province | SAB | South African Breweries XI |
| GW | Griqualand West | SAU | South African Universities |
| Int XI | International XI | Zim | Zimbabwe (Rhodesia) |
| IW | International Wanderers | | |

# DERBYSHIRE

**Formation of Present Club:** 4 November 1870
**Colours:** Chocolate, Amber and Pale Blue
**Badge:** Rose and Crown
**Championships:** (1) 1936
**NatWest Trophy/Gillette Cup Winners:** (1) 1981
**Benson and Hedges Cup Winners:** (0) Finalists 1978, 1988
**Sunday League Champions:** (1) 1990
**Match Awards:** NWT 30; BHC 53

**Chief Executive:** R.J.Lark, County Cricket Ground, Nottingham Road, Derby DE2 6DA (☎ 0332–383211)
**Captain:** K.J.Barnett
**Scorer:** S.W.Tacey
**1993 Beneficiary:** –

**ADAMS, Christopher** John (Repton S), b Whitwell, 6 May 1970. 6′0″. RHB, OB. Debut 1988. Cap 1992. 1000 runs (1): 1109 (1992). HS 140* v Worcs (Worcester) 1992. BB 4-29 v Lancs (Derby) 1991. **NWT:** HS 106* and BB 1-15 v Berks (Derby) 1992. **BHC:** HS 44 Minor C (Wellington) 1990. **SL:** HS 141* v Kent (Chesterfield) 1992.

**BARNETT, Kim** John (Leek HS), b Stoke-on-Trent, 17 Jul 1960. 5′11″. RHB, LB. Debut 1979. Cap 1982. Captain 1983-. Boland 1982-83/1987-88. Staffordshire 1976. Wisden 1988. Benefit 1992. **Tests:** 4 (1988 to 1989); HS 80 v A (Leeds) 1989. **LOI:** 1. Tours: SA 1989-90 (Eng XI); NZ 1979-80 (DHR); SL 1985-86 (Eng B). 1000 runs (10); most – 1734 (1984). HS 239* v Leics (Leicester) 1988. BB 6-28 v Glam (Chesterfield) 1991. Awards: NWT 2; BHC 10. **NWT:** HS 88 v Middx (Derby) 1983. BB 6-24 v Cumberland (Kendal) 1984. **BHC:** HS 115 v Glos (Derby) 1987. BB 1-10. **SL:** HS 131* v Essex (Derby) 1984. BB 3-39 v Yorks (Chesterfield) 1979.

**BASE, Simon** John (Fish Hoek HS, Cape Town), b Maidstone, Kent 2 Jan 1960. 6′2″. RHB, RMF. W Province 1981-82/1983-84. Glamorgan 1986-87. Boland 1987-88/ 1988-89. Border 1989-90 to date. Derbyshire debut 1988. Cap 1990. HS 58 v Yorks (Chesterfield) 1990. 50 wkts (1): 60 (1989). BB 7-60 v Yorks (Chesterfield) 1989. **NWT:** HS 4. BB 2-49 Gm v Sussex (Hove) 1986. **BHC:** HS 15* v Somerset (Taunton) 1990. BB 3-33 v Minor C (Wellington) 1990. **SL:** HS 19 Gm v Kent (Swansea) 1987. BB 4-14 v Northants (Derby) 1991.

**BISHOP, Ian** Raphael (Belmont SS), b Port-of-Spain, Trinidad 24 Oct 1967. Nephew of R.J. (Trinidad 1986-87). 6′5″. RHB, RF. Trinidad 1986-87/ 1990-91. Derbyshire debut 1989. Cap 1989. **Tests** (WI): 11 (1988-89 to 1990-91); HS 30* v I (P-of-S) 1988-89; BB 6-87 v I (Bridgetown) 1988-89. LOI (WI): 35. Tours (WI): E 1988; A 1988-89; P 1990-91. HS 103* v Yorks (Scarborough) 1990. 50 wkts (2); most – 64 (1992). BB 7-34 v Hants (Portsmouth) 1992. **NWT:** HS 6. BB –. **BHC:** HS 42 v Durham (Jesmond) 1992. BB 4-30 v Kent (Canterbury) 1992. **SL:** HS 36* v Notts (Derby) 1992. BB 3-18 v Glos (Derby) 1992.

**BOWLER, Peter** Duncan (Educated at Canberra, Australia), b Plymouth, Devon 30 Jul 1963. 6′1″. RHB, OB. Leicestershire 1986 – first to score hundred on f-c debut for Leics (100* and 62 v Hants). Tasmania 1986-87. Derbyshire debut 1988 scoring 155* v CU at Cambridge - first to score hundreds on debut for two counties. Cap 1990. 1000 runs (5) inc 2000 (1); most – 2044 (1992). HS 241* v Hants (Portsmouth) 1992. BB 3-41 v Leics (Leicester) 1991 and v Yorks (Chesterfield) 1991. Awards: BHC 2. **NWT:** HS 111 v Berks (Derby) 1992. **BHC:** HS 109 v Somerset (Taunton) 1990. BB 1-15. **SL:** HS 91* v Lancs (Manchester) 1992. BB 3-31 v Glos (Cheltenham) 1991.

**CORK, Dominic** Gerald (St Joseph's C, Stoke-on-Trent), b Newcastle-under-Lyme, Staffs 7 Aug 1971. 6'2". RHB, RFM. Debut 1990. Staffs 1989-90. LOI: 1. Tour: WI 1991-92 (Eng A). HS 72* v Warwks (Birmingham) 1992. 50 wkts (1): 57 (1991). BB 8-53 (before lunch on his 20th birthday) v Essex (Derby) 1991. Award: NWT 1. **NWT:** HS 11 v Leics (Derby) 1992. BB 5-18 v Berks (Derby) 1992. **BHC:** HS 8*. BB 4-26 v Durham (Jesmond) 1992. **SL:** HS 30 v Warwks (Birmingham) 1991. BB 3-26 v Glos (Derby) 1992.

**GRIFFITH, Frank** Alexander (Beaconsfield HS; Wm Morris HS; Haringey Cricket C), b Whipps Cross, Essex 15 Aug 1968. 6'0". RHB, RM. Debut 1988. HS 81 v Glam (Chesterfield) 1992. BB 4-33 v Leics (Ilkeston) 1992. **BHC:** HS 10 v Notts (Nottingham) 1989. **SL:** HS 20 v Northants (Derby) 1991. BB 3-37 v Somerset (Derby) 1991.

**KRIKKEN, Karl** Matthew (Rivington & Blackrod HS & SFC), b Bolton, Lancs 9 Apr 1969. Son of B.E. (Lancs and Worcs 1966-69). 5'9". RHB, WK. GW 1988-89. Derbyshire debut 1989. Cap 1992. HS 77* v Somerset (Taunton) 1990. **NWT:** HS 18 v Leics (Derby) 1992. **BHC:** HS 37* v Worcs (Worcester) 1992. **SL:** HS 44* v Essex (Chelmsford) 1991.

**MAHER, Bernard** Joseph Michael (Abbotsfield CS; Bishopshalt GS; Loughborough U), b Hillingdon, Middx 11 Feb 1958. 5'10". RHB, WK. Derbyshire 1981-91 (cap 1987). HS 126 v NZ (Derby) 1986. BAC HS 121* v Leics (Derby) 1988. BB 2-69 v Glam (Abergavenny) 1986. **NWT:** HS 44 v Hants (Derby) 1988. **BHC:** HS 50 v Northants (Derby) 1987. **SL:** HS 78 v Lancs (Manchester) 1987.

**MALCOLM, Devon** Eugene (Richmond C, Sheffield), b Kingston, Jamaica 22 Feb 1963. 6'2". RHB, RF. Debut 1984. Cap 1989. **Tests:** 21 (1989 to 1992). HS 15* v I (Oval) 1990. BB 6-77 v WI (P-of-S) 1989-90. LOI: 4. Tours: A 1990-91; WI 1989-90, 1991-92 (Eng A). HS 51 v Surrey (Derby) 1989. 50 wkts (2); most – 56 (1988). BB 7-74 v Australian XI (Hobart) 1990-91. De BB 6-68 v Warwks (Derby) 1988. Award: BHC 1. **NWT:** HS 10* v Leics (Derby) 1992. BB 3-54 v Lancs (Derby) 1990. **BHC:** HS 15 v Comb Us (Oxford) 1991. BB 5-27 v Middx (Derby) 1988. **SL:** HS 18 v Essex (Chelmsford) 1991. BB 4-21 v Surrey (Derby) 1989 and v Leics (Knypersley) 1990.

**MORRIS, John** Edward (Shavington CS; Dane Bank CFE), b Crewe, Cheshire 1 Apr 1964. 5'10". RHB, RM. Debut 1982. Cap 1986. GW 1988-89. **Tests:** 3 (1990); HS 32 v I (Oval) 1990. LOI: 8. Tour: A 1990-91. 1000 runs (7); most - 1739 (1986). HS 191 v Kent (Derby) 1986. BB 1-13. Awards: NWT 1; BHC 1. **NWT:** HS 94* v Salop (Chesterfield) 1990. **BHC:** HS 123 v Somerset (Taunton) 1990. **SL:** HS 134 v Somerset (Taunton) 1990.

**MORTENSEN, Ole** Henrek (Brondbyoster S; Abedore C, Copenhagen), b Vejle, Denmark 29 Jan 1958. 6'3". RHB, RFM. Debut 1983. Cap 1986. Benefit 1994. Denmark 1975-82. HS 74* v Yorks (Chesterfield) 1987. 50 wkts (2); most – 58 (1991). BB 6-27 v Yorks (Sheffield) 1983. Hat-trick 1987. Awards: NWT 2. **NWT:** HS 11 v Surrey (Derby) 1986. BB 6-14 v Ire (Derby) 1989. **BHC:** HS 5*. BB 3-17 v Leics (Chesterfield) 1986. **SL:** HS 11 v Worcs (Worcester) 1989. BB 4-10 v Leics (Chesterfield) 1985.

**O'GORMAN, Timothy** Joseph Gerard (St George's C, Weybridge; Durham U), b Woking, Surrey 15 May 1967. Grandson of J.G. (Surrey 1927). 6'2". RHB, OB. Debut 1987. Cap 1992. Comb Us (BHC) 1988-89. 1000 runs (1); most – 1116 (1991). HS 148 v Lancs (Manchester) 1991. BB 1-7. **NWT:** HS 1. **BHC:** HS 49 v Northants (Derby) 1991. **SL:** HS 69 v Northants (Northampton) 1992.

**RICHARDSON, Alastair** William (Oundle S; Durham U), b Derby 23 Oct 1972. Son of G.W (Derbys 1959-65); grandson of A.W. (Derbys 1928-36). 6'3". RHB, RFM. Debut 1992. HS 5 and BB 2-38 v Glam (Cardiff) 1992.

**SLADDIN, Richard** William (Sowerby Bridge HS), b Halifax, Yorks 8 Jan 1969. 6'0". RHB, SLA. Debut 1991. HS 39 v Glam (Cardiff) 1992. BB 6-58 v CU (Cambridge) 1992. BAC BB 5-186 v Essex (Chelmsford) 1991. **SL:** HS 3*. BB 2-35 v Sussex (Eastbourne) 1992.

**STEER, Ian Gary** Samuel (St Edmund Campion S), b Aston, Birmingham 17 Aug 1970. 5'7". RHB, RM. Warwickshire staff 1990-91. Derbyshire debut in Sunday League 1992. Awaiting f-c debut. **SL:** HS -.

**TWEATS, Timothy** Andrew (Endon HS; Stoke-on-Trent SFC), b Stoke-on-Trent, Staffs 18 Apr 1974. 6'3". RHB, RM. Debut 1992. HS 24 v Glam (Cardiff) 1992.

**WARNER, Allan** Esmond (Tabernacle S, St Kitts), b Birmingham 12 May 1957. 5'7". RHB, RFM. Worcestershire 1982-84. Derbyshire debut 1985. Cap 1987. HS 91 v Leics (Chesterfield) 1986. BB 5-27 Wo v Glam (Worcester) 1984. De BB 5-51 v Essex (Colchester) 1985. Award: NWT 1. **NWT:** HS 32 v Kent (Canterbury) 1987. BB 4-39 v Salop (Chesterfield) 1990. **BHC:** HS 35* v Comb Us (Oxford) 1991. BB 4-36 v Notts (Nottingham) 1987. **SL:** HS 68 v Hants (Heanor) 1986. BB 5-39 v Worcs (Knypersley) 1985.

**WHITAKER, Paul** Robert (Whitcliffe Mount S), b Keighley, Yorks 28 Jun 1973. 5'9". LHB, OB. No 1st XI appearances - joined staff 1992.

### NEWCOMERS

**AGRAWALLA, Amritash** (Kelvinside Academy, Glasgow; Strathclyde U), b Calcutta, India 2 Mar 1971. 5'6½". RHB, LB.

**HARRIS, Andrew** John (Glossop Dale Community S), b Ashton-under-Lyne, Lancs 26 Jun 1973. RHB, RM.

**LOVELL, David** John (Kelmscott Sr HS, Perth, WA), b Adelaide, Australia 16 Feb 1969. 5'10". RHB, SLA.

**ROLLINS, Adrian** Stewart (Little Ilford CS), b Barking, Essex 8 Feb 1972. Brother of R.J. (see ESSEX). 6'5". RHB, RM.

### DEPARTURES

**BROWN, Andrew** Mark (Aldercar CS; SE Derbyshire C), b Heanor 6 Nov 1964. 5'9". LHB, OB. Derbyshire 1985-92. HS 139* v Northants (Chesterfield) 1990. **SL:** HS 2*.

**GOLDSMITH, Steven** Clive (Simon Langton GS, Canterbury), b Ashford, Kent 19 Dec 1964. 5'10". RHB, RM. Kent 1987. Derbyshire 1988-92. 1000 runs (1): 1071 (1988). HS 127 v SL (Derby) 1991. BAC HS 100* v Worcs (Derby) 1992. BB 3-42 v Yorks (Scarborough) 1991. Award: BHC 1. **NWT:** HS 21 and BB 1-20 v Lancs (Derby) 1990. **BHC:** HS 45* and BB 3-38 v Minor C (Wellington) 1990. **SL:** HS 67* v Glos (Cheltenham) 1991. BB 3-48 v Surrey (Chesterfield) 1991.

**JEAN-JACQUES, M.** – see HAMPSHIRE.

# DERBYSHIRE 1992

## RESULTS SUMMARY

|  | Place | Won | Lost | Drew | Abandoned |
|---|---|---|---|---|---|
| **Britannic Assurance Championship** | 5th | 7 | 6 | 9 | |
| **All First-class Matches** | | 7 | 6 | 11 | |
| **Sunday League** | 13th | 7 | 9 | | 1 |
| **NatWest Trophy** | 2nd Round | | | | |
| **Benson and Hedges Cup** | Quarter-Finalist | | | | |

# BRITANNIC ASSURANCE CHAMPIONSHIP AVERAGES

### BATTING AND FIELDING

| Cap | | M | I | NO | HS | Runs | Avge | 100 | 50 | Ct/St |
|---|---|---|---|---|---|---|---|---|---|---|
| 1989 | P.D.Bowler | 22 | 35 | 7 | 241* | 1862 | 66.50 | 6 | 9 | 13 |
| 1982 | K.J.Barnett | 18 | 29 | 5 | 160 | 1270 | 52.91 | 4 | 4 | 4 |
| 1986 | J.E.Morris | 21 | 30 | – | 120 | 1236 | 41.20 | 3 | 11 | 6 |
| – | S.C.Goldsmith | 9 | 10 | 3 | 100* | 270 | 38.57 | 1 | 1 | 2 |
| 1992 | C.J.Adams | 21 | 29 | 4 | 140* | 924 | 36.96 | 4 | | 20 |
| – | F.A.Griffith | 6 | 8 | 1 | 81 | 242 | 34.57 | – | 1 | 6 |
| 1992 | T.J.G.O'Gorman | 22 | 33 | 6 | 95 | 880 | 32.59 | – | 7 | 10 |
| – | D.G.Cork | 17 | 19 | 2 | 72* | 504 | 29.64 | – | 3 | 9 |
| 1986 | O.H.Mortensen | 13 | 12 | 10 | 13* | 47 | 23.50 | – | – | 3 |
| 1990 | I.R.Bishop | 20 | 21 | 2 | 90 | 388 | 20.42 | – | 1 | 6 |
| 1989 | D.E.Malcolm | 14 | 13 | 4 | 26 | 144 | 16.00 | – | – | 4 |
| 1992 | K.M.Krikken | 21 | 24 | 3 | 57* | 323 | 15.38 | – | 1 | 49/5 |
| 1987 | A.E.Warner | 15 | 13 | 2 | 29 | 151 | 13.72 | – | – | 2 |
| – | A.M.Brown | 6 | 6 | – | 36 | 74 | 12.33 | – | – | 6 |
| – | R.W.Sladdin | 11 | 13 | 2 | 39 | 126 | 11.45 | – | – | 5 |

*Also played:* S.J.Base (2 matches – cap 1990) 3, 0* (2 ct); M.Jean-Jacques
(2 matches) 0, 6 (2 ct); A.W.Richardson (1 match) 5; T.A.Tweats (1 match) 24 (1 ct).

### BOWLING

| | O | M | R | W | Avge | Best | 5wI | 10wM |
|---|---|---|---|---|---|---|---|---|
| I.R.Bishop | 483 | 116 | 1118 | 64 | 17.46 | 7-34 | 4 | – |
| F.A.Griffith | 102 | 25 | 350 | 14 | 25.00 | 4-33 | – | – |
| D.G.Cork | 406.2 | 67 | 1237 | 44 | 28.11 | 5-36 | 2 | – |
| A.E.Warner | 335.5 | 79 | 817 | 27 | 30.25 | 4-52 | – | – |
| O.H.Mortensen | 307 | 76 | 736 | 19 | 38.73 | 2-22 | – | – |
| D.E.Malcolm | 318.2 | 48 | 1130 | 29 | 38.96 | 5-45 | 1 | – |
| R.W.Sladdin | 420.2 | 110 | 1212 | 30 | 40.40 | 4-102 | – | – |

*Also bowled:* C.J.Adams 56-3-229-2;  K.J.Barnett 77.4-11-250-4;  S.J.Base
35-8-100-7;  P.D.Bowler 17-3-69-0;  A.M.Brown 3-0-9-0;  S.C.Goldsmith
113-21-391-3;  M.Jean-Jacques 35.4-5-135-5;  T.J.G.O'Gorman 27-0-141-1;
A.W.Richardson 13-2-38-2.

The First-Class Averages (pp 164-178) give the records of Derbyshire players in
all first-class county matches (their other opponents being the Pakistanis and
Cambridge U), with the exception of:
  D.G.Cork 18-20-2-72*-551-30.61-0-3-12ct. 430.4-72-1295-46-28.15-5/36-2-0.
  D.E.Malcolm 15-14-4-26-144-14.40-0-0-5ct. 334.2-50-1192-32-37.25-5/45-1-0.

# DERBYSHIRE RECORDS

## FIRST-CLASS CRICKET

| | | | | | |
|---|---|---|---|---|---|
| **Highest Total** | For 645 | | v Hampshire | Derby | 1898 |
| | V 662 | | by Yorkshire | Chesterfield | 1898 |
| **Lowest Total** | For 16 | | v Notts | Nottingham | 1879 |
| | V 23 | | by Hampshire | Burton upon T | 1958 |
| **Highest Innings** | For 274 | G.A.Davidson | v Lancashire | Manchester | 1896 |
| | V 343* | P.A.Perrin | for Essex | Chesterfield | 1904 |

**Highest Partnership for each Wicket**

| | | | | | |
|---|---|---|---|---|---|
| 1st | 322 | H.Storer/J.Bowden | v Essex | Derby | 1929 |
| 2nd | 349 | C.S.Elliott/J.D.Eggar | v Notts | Nottingham | 1947 |
| 3rd | 291 | P.N.Kirsten/D.S.Steele | v Somerset | Taunton | 1981 |
| 4th | 328 | P.Vaulkhard/D.Smith | v Notts | Nottingham | 1946 |
| 5th | 203 | C.P.Wilkins/I.R.Buxton | v Lancashire | Manchester | 1971 |
| 6th | 212 | G.M.Lee/T.S.Worthington | v Essex | Chesterfield | 1932 |
| 7th | 241* | G.H.Pope/A.E.G.Rhodes | v Hampshire | Portsmouth | 1948 |
| 8th | 182 | A.H.M.Jackson/W.Carter | v Leics | Leicester | 1922 |
| 9th | 283 | A.Warren/J.Chapman | v Warwicks | Blackwell | 1910 |
| 10th | 132 | A.Hill/M.Jean-Jacques | v Yorkshire | Sheffield | 1986 |

| | | | | | |
|---|---|---|---|---|---|
| **Best Bowling** | For 10-40 | W.Bestwick | v Glamorgan | Cardiff | 1921 |
| **(Innings)** | V 10-47 | T.F.Smailes | for Yorkshire | Sheffield | 1939 |
| **Best Bowling** | For 17-103 | W.Mycroft | v Hampshire | Southampton | 1876 |
| **(Match)** | V 16-101 | G.Giffen | for Australians | Derby | 1886 |

| | | | | |
|---|---|---|---|---|
| **Most Runs – Season** | 2,165 | D.B.Carr | (av 48.11) | 1959 |
| **Most Runs – Career** | 20,516 | D.Smith | (av 31.41) | 1927-1952 |
| **Most 100s – Season** | 8 | P.N.Kirsten | | 1982 |
| **Most 100s – Career** | 38 | K.J.Barnett | | 1979-1992 |
| **Most Wkts – Season** | 168 | T.B.Mitchell | (av 19.55) | 1935 |
| **Most Wkts – Career** | 1,670 | H.L.Jackson | (av 17.11) | 1947-1963 |

## LIMITED-OVERS CRICKET

| | | | | | |
|---|---|---|---|---|---|
| **Highest Total** | NWT | 365-3 | v Cornwall | Derby | 1986 |
| | BHC | 366-4 | v Comb Univs | Oxford | 1991 |
| | SL | 292-9 | v Worcs | Knypersley | 1985 |
| **Lowest Total** | NWT | 79 | v Surrey | The Oval | 1967 |
| | BHC | 102 | v Yorkshire | Bradford | 1975 |
| | SL | 61 | v Hampshire | Portsmouth | 1990 |
| **Highest Innings** | NWT | 153 A.Hill | v Cornwall | Derby | 1986 |
| | BHC | 123 J.E.Morris | v Somerset | Taunton | 1990 |
| | SL | 141* C.J.Adams | v Kent | Chesterfield | 1992 |
| **Best Bowling** | NWT | 8-21 M.A.Holding | v Sussex | Hove | 1988 |
| | BHC | 6-33 E.J.Barlow | v Glos | Bristol | 1978 |
| | SL | 6-7 M.Hendrick | v Notts | Nottingham | 1972 |

# DURHAM

**Formation of Present Club:** 10 May 1882
**Colours:** Navy Blue, Yellow and Maroon
**Badge:** Coat of Arms of the County of Durham
**Championships:** (0) 18th 1992
**NatWest Trophy/Gillette Cup Winners:** (0) Quarter-Finalist 1992
**Benson and Hedges Cup Winners:** (0) Third in Group 1992
**Sunday League Champions:** (0) Eighth 1992
**Match Awards:** NWT 15; BHC 3.

**Chief Executive:** tba, County Ground, Riverside, Chester-le-Street, Co Durham
DH3 3QR. (☎ 091-387 1717)
**Captain:** D.A.Graveney
**Scorer:** B.Hunt
**1993 Beneficiary:** –

**BAINBRIDGE, Philip** (Hanley HS; Stoke-on-Trent SFC, Borough Road CE),
b Sneyd Green, Stoke-on-Trent, Staffs 16 Apr 1958. 5'10''. RHB, RM. Gloucestershire 1977-90 (cap 1981; benefit 1989). Durham debut/cap 1992. Wisden 1985.
Tours: SL 1986-87 (Gs); Z 1984-85 (EC). 1000 runs (8); most – 1644 (1985). HS
169 Gs v Yorks (Cheltenham) 1988. Du HS 92* v Northants (Stockton) 1992. BB
8-53 Gs v Somerset (Bristol) 1986. Du BB 5-100 v Lancs (Gateshead) 1992. Awards:
NWT 1; BHC 3. **NWT:** HS 89 Gs v Leics (Leicester) 1988. BB 3-49 Gs v Scot
(Bristol) 1983. **BHC:** HS 96 Gs v Hants (Southampton) 1988. BB 4-38 v Worcs
(Worcester) 1992. **SL:** HS 106* Gs v Somerset (Bristol) 1986. BB 5-22 Gs v Middx
(Lord's) 1987.

**BERRY, Philip** John (Saltscar CS; Longlands CFE, Redcar), b Saltburn, Yorks
28 Dec 1966. 6'0''. RHB, OB. Yorkshire 1986-90. Durham debut/cap 1992. HS 76
and BB 7-113 v Middx (Lord's) 1992. **NWT:** HS 9. **BHC:** HS -. **SL:** HS 6. BB 1-35.

**BLENKIRON, Darren** Andrew (Bishop Barrington CS, Bishop Auckland), b Solihull,
Warwks 4 Feb 1974. 5'10''. Cap 1992 – awaiting f-c debut. Son of W. (Warwks
1964-74, Durham 1975-76). LHB, RM. **NWT:** HS 56 v Glam (Darlington) 1991.

**BOTHAM, Ian** Terence (Buckler's Mead SS, Yeovil), b Heswall, Cheshire 24 Nov
1955. 6'1''. RHB, RM. Somerset 1974-86 (cap 1976; captain 1984-85; benefit 1984).
Worcestershire 1987-91 (cap 1987). Durham debut/cap 1992. Queensland 1987-88.
Wisden 1977. YC 1977. MCC YC. OBE 1992. **Tests:** 102 (1977 to 1992, 12 as
captain); HS 208 v I (Oval) 1982; BB 8-34 v P (Lord's) 1978. LOI: 116. Tours: A
1978-79, 1979-80, 1982-83, 1986-87; WI 1980-81 (capt), 1985-86; NZ 1977-78,
1983-84, 1991-92; I 1979-80, 1981-82; P 1977-78, 1983-84; SL 1981-82; Z 1990-91
(Wo). 1000 runs (4); most – 1530 (1985). Hit 80 sixes 1985 (f-c record). HS 228
Sm v Glos (Taunton) 1980. Du HS 105 v Leics (Durham) 1992 (on Du debut).
Shared in 2 Somerset record stands: 310 (4th) with P.W.Denning and 172 (8th)
with I.V.A.Richards. 50 wkts (8) inc 100 (1): 100 (1978). BB 8-34 (Tests). BAC
BB 7-54 Wo v Warwks (Worcester) 1991. Du BB 4-72 v Yorks (Durham) 1992. Hat-
trick 1978 (MCC). Awards: NWT 4; BHC 10. **NWT:** HS 101 Wo v Devon
(Worcester) 1987. BB 5-51 Wo v Lancs (Worcester) 1989. **BHC:** HS 138* Wo v
Glos (Bristol) 1990. BB 5-41 Wo v Yorks (Worcester) 1988. **SL:** HS 175* Sm v
Northants (Wellingborough) 1986. BB 5-27 Wo v Glos (Gloucester) 1987.

**BRIERS, Mark** Paul (Hind Leys C, Shepshed; Loughborough TC), b Loughborough,
Leics 21 Apr 1968. 6'0''. RHB, LB. Worcestershire staff 1988. Bedfordshire 1990.
Debut/cap 1992. HS 62* v Sussex (Horsham) 1992. BB 3-109 v Glos (Stockton)
1992. **NWT:** HS 54* v Ireland (Dublin) 1992. BB 1-0. **SL:** HS 69 v Surrey (Durham)
1992. BB 1-47.

70

**BROWN, Simon** John Emmerson (Boldon CS), b South Shields 29 Jun 1969. 6'3".
RHB, LFM. Northamptonshire 1987-90. Durham debut/cap 1992. HS 47* v Surrey
(Durham) 1992. 50 wkts (1): 58 (1992). BB 7-105 v Kent (Canterbury) 1992. **NWT:**
HS 7*. BB 1-43. **BHC:** HS 4*. BB 2-36 v Glam (Durham) 1992. **SL:** HS 3*. BB
3-26 Nh v Leics (Leicester) 1990.

**DALEY, James** Arthur (Hetton CS), b Sunderland 24 Sep 1973. 5'10". RHB, RM.
Debut/cap 1992. MCC YC 1991. HS 88 v Somerset (Taunton) 1992 – on debut.

**FOTHERGILL, Andrew** Robert (Eastbourne CS), b Newcastle upon Tyne,
Northumberland 10 Feb 1962. 6'0". RHB, WK. Debut for Minor C v Indians
(Trowbridge) 1990. Durham debut/cap 1992. HS 23 v Kent (Canterbury) 1992.
Soccer for Bishop Auckland 1986-91. **NWT:** HS 24 v Glam (Darlington) 1991. **BHC:**
HS 45* Minor C v Somerset (Taunton) 1990. **SL:** HS 42* v Leics (Gateshead) 1992.

**GLENDENEN, John** David (Ormesby SS), b Middlesbrough, Yorks 20 Jun 1965.
6'0". RHB, RM. Debut v OU (Oxford) 1992, scoring 117. Cap 1992. Scored 200*
v Victoria (Durham) 1991 (not f-c). HS 117 (above). BAC HS 76 v Lancs
(Gateshead) 1992. **NWT:** HS 109 v Glam (Darlington) 1991 – first 100 by Durham
batsman in NWT/GC. **BHC:** HS 60 v Comb Us (Cambridge) 1992. **SL:** HS 78 v
Warwks (Birmingham) 1992.

**GRAVENEY, David** Anthony (Millfield S), b Bristol 2 Jan 1953. Son of J.K (Glos
1947-64); nephew of T.W. (Glos, Worcs, Queensland and England 1948/1971-72).
6'4". RHB, SLA. Gloucestershire 1972-90 (cap 1976; captain 1981-88; benefit
1986). Somerset 1991. Durham debut/cap 1992. Captain 1992–. Tours: SA 1989-90
(Eng XI – manager); SL 1986-87 (Gs – capt). HS 119 Gs v OU (Oxford) 1980.
BAC HS 105* Gs v Northants (Bristol) 1981. Du HS 36 v Surrey (Durham) 1992.
50 wkts (6); most – 73 (1976). BB 8-85 Gs v Notts (Cheltenham) 1974. Du BB
3-22 v Leics (Leicester) 1992. Hat-trick 1983. Awards: NWT 2. **NWT:** HS 44 Gs v
Surrey (Bristol) 1973. BB 5-11 Gs v Ire (Dublin) 1981. **BHC:** HS 49* Gs v Somerset
(Taunton) 1982. BB 3-13 Gs v Scot (Glasgow) 1983. **SL:** HS 56* Gs v Notts (Bristol)
1985. BB 4-22 Gs v Hants (Lydney) 1974.

**HENDERSON, Paul** William (Billingham Campus S; Bede C), b Stockton-on-Tees
22 Oct 1974. 6'0". RHB, RFM. Debut/cap 1992 – when aged 17. HS 46 v Glam
(Cardiff) 1992 – on debut. BB 3-59 v Somerset (Darlington) 1992. **SL:** HS 10* and
BB 3-47 v Notts (Nottingham) 1992.

**HUGHES, Simon** Peter (Latymer Upper S, Hammersmith; Durham U), b Kingston
upon Thames, Surrey 20 Dec 1959. 5'10". RHB, RFM. Middlesex 1980-91 (cap
1981; benefit 1991). Durham debut/cap 1992. N Transvaal 1982-83. Tours: I 1980-81
(Overseas XI); Z 1980-81 (M). HS 53 M v CU (Cambridge) 1988. BAC HS 47 M
v Warwks (Uxbridge) 1986. Du HS 42 v Lancs (Gateshead) 1992. 50 wkts (2); most
– 63 (1986). BB 7-35 M v Surrey (Oval) 1986. Du BB 5-25 v Yorks (Durham) 1992.
Award: NWT 1. **NWT:** HS 11 and BB 4-20 M v Durham (Darlington) 1989. **BHC:**
HS 22 M v Somerset (Taunton) 1990. BB 4-34 M v Somerset (Lord's) 1987. **SL:**
HS 22* M v Surrey (Lord's) 1985. BB 5-23 M v Worcs (Worcester) 1989.

**HUTTON, Stewart** (De Brus S, Skelton; Cleveland TC), b Stockton-on-Tees
30 Nov 1969. 5'11". LHB, RM. Debut/cap 1992. HS 78 v Sussex (Horsham) 1992. **SL:**
HS 70 v Glam (Hartlepool) 1992.

**LARKINS, Wayne** (Bushmead SS, Eaton Socon), b Roxton, Beds 22 Nov 1953.
5'11". RHB, RM. Northamptonshire 1972-91 (cap 1976; benefit 1986). Durham
debut/cap 1992. E Province 1982-83/1983-84. **Tests:** 13 (1979-80 to 1990-91); HS
64 v A (Melbourne) 1990-91. LOI: 25. Tours: A 1979-80, 1990-91; SA 1981-82
(SAB); WI 1989-90; I 1979-80, 1980-81 (Overseas XI). 1000 runs (12); most –
1863 (1982). HS 252 Nh v Glam (Cardiff) 1983. Du HS 143 v Glam (Cardiff) 1992.
BB 5-59 Nh v Worcs (Worcester) 1984. Awards: NWT 2; BHC 6. **NWT:** HS 121*
Nh v Essex (Chelmsford) 1987. BB 2-38 Nh v Glos (Bristol) 1985. **BHC:** HS 132

LARKINS – continued:
Nh v Warwks (Birmingham) 1982. BB 4-37 Nh v Comb Us (Northampton) 1980. **SL:** HS 172* Nh v Warwks (Luton) 1983. BB 5-32 Nh v Essex (Ilford) 1978.

**McEWAN, Steven** Michael (Worcester RGS), b Worcester 5 May 1962. 6'1". RHB, RFM. Worcestershire 1985-90 (cap 1989). Durham debut/cap 1992. HS 54 Wo v Yorks (Worcester) 1990. Du HS 22 v Northants (Stockton) 1992. 50 wkts (1): 52 (1989). BB 6-34 Wo v Leics (Kidderminster) 1989. Du BB 3-52 v P (Chester-le-St) 1992. Hat-trick 1990. Award: NWT 1. **NWT:** HS 34* and 4-41 v Ireland (Dublin) 1992. **BHC:** HS 29* and BB 3-45 v Worcs (Worcester) 1992. **SL:** HS 18* Wo v Yorks (Worcester) 1990. BB 4-35 Wo v Derbys (Worcester) 1986.

**PARKER, Paul** William Giles (Collyer's GS; St Catharine's C, Cambridge), b Bulawayo, Rhodesia 15 Jan 1956. 5'10". RHB, RM. Cambridge U 1976-78 (blue 1976-77-78). Sussex 1976-91 (cap 1979; captain 1988-91; benefit 1988). Durham debut/cap 1992. YC 1979. **Tests:** 1 (1981); HS 13 v A (Oval) 1981. 1000 runs (9); most – 1692 (1984). HS 215 CU v Essex (Cambridge) 1976. BAC HS 140 Sx v Glos (Hove) 1984. Du HS 124 v Glam (Cardiff) 1992. BB 2-21 Sx v Surrey (Guildford) 1984. Awards: NWT 5; BHC 5. **NWT:** HS 109 Sx v Ire (Hove) 1985. BB 1-10. **BHC:** HS 87 Sx v Leics (Hove) 1991. BB 2-3 Sx v Minor C (Hove) 1987. **SL:** HS 121* Sx v Northants (Hastings) 1983. BB 1-2.

**SCOTT, Christopher** Wilmot (Robert Pattinson CS), b Thorpe-on-the-Hill, Lincs 23 Jan 1964. 5'8". RHB, WK. Nottinghamshire 1981-91 (cap 1988). Durham debut/cap 1992. HS 78 Nt v CU (Cambridge) 1983. BAC HS 69* Nt v Warwks (Nottingham) 1986. Du HS 57* v Somerset (Darlington) 1992. Held 10 catches for Notts in match v Derbys (Derby) 1988. **BHC:** HS 18 Nt v Northants (Northampton) 1988. **SL:** HS 26 Nt v Yorks (Nottingham) 1987.

**SMITH, Ian** (Ryton CS), b Shotley Bridge 11 Mar 1967. 6'2". RHB, RM. Glamorgan 1985-91. Durham debut/cap 1992. Tour: Z 1990-91 (Gm). HS 116 Gm v Kent (Canterbury) 1989. Du HS 110 v Somerset (Taunton) 1992. BB 3-48 Gm v Hants (Cardiff) 1989. Du BB 3-85 v Lancs (Gateshead) 1992. **NWT:** HS 33 Gm v Hants (Cardiff) 1989. BB 3-60 Gm v Durham (Darlington) 1991. **BHC:** HS 51 Gm v Hants (Southampton) 1991. BB 1-21. **SL:** HS 56* Gm v Warwks (Aberystwyth) 1989. BB 3-22 Gm v Hants (Cardiff) 1989.

**WIGHAM, Gary** (Barrington CS, Bishop Auckland), b Bishop Auckland 2 Mar 1973. 6'7". RHB, RMF. MCC YC 1991. Durham debut in Sunday League 1992. Awaiting f-c debut. **SL:** HS -. BB 1-43.

**WOOD, John** (Crofton HS; Wakefield District C; Leeds Poly), b Wakefield, Yorks 22 Jul 1970. 6'2¼". RHB, RFM. GW in Nissan Shield 1990-91. Début/cap 1992. HS 28 v Worcs (Worcester) 1992. BB 5-68 v Hants (Southampton) 1992. **NWT:** HS 1. BB 2-22 v Ireland (Dublin) 1992. **SL:** HS 4*. BB 2-58 v Sussex (Horsham) 1992.

## NEWCOMERS

**COX, David** Matthew (Greenford HS), b Southall, Middx 2 Mar 1972. 5'11". LHB, SLA. Hertfordshire. MCC YC 1990-92.

**CUMMINS, Anderson** Cleophas, b Packer's Valley, Barbados 7 May 1966. RHB, RFM. Barbados 1988-89 to date. LOI (WI): 19. Tour (WI): A 1991-92. HS 45* Barbados v Leeward Is (Bridgetown) 1991-92. BB 4-26 Barbados v Leeward Is (St John's) 1990-91.

**FOWLER, Graeme** (Accrington GS; Durham U), b Accrington, Lancs 20 Apr 1957. 5'9½". LHB, RM. Lancashire 1979-92 (cap 1981; benefit 1991). **Tests:** 21 (1982 to 1984-85); HS 201 v I (Madras) 1984-85. LOI: 26. Tours: A 1982-83; WI 1982-83 (Int); NZ 1983-84; I/SL 1984-85; P 1983-84; Z 1988-89 (La). 1000 runs (8); most – 1800 (1987). HS 226 La v Kent (Maidstone) 1984. BB 2-34 La v Warwks (Manchester) 1986. Awards: NWT 2; BHC 3. **NWT:** HS 122 La v Glos (Bristol) 1984. **BHC:** HS 136 La v Sussex (Manchester) 1991. **SL:** HS 112 La v Kent (Canterbury) 1986.

**SEARLE, Jason** Paul (John Bentley S), b Bath, Somerset 16 May 1976. 5'9". RHB, OB.

DEPARTURES – see p 155

# DURHAM 1992

## RESULTS SUMMARY

|  | Place | Won | Lost | Drew | Abandoned |
|---|---|---|---|---|---|
| Britannic Assurance Championship | 18th | 2 | 10 | 10 | |
| All First-class Matches | | 2 | 11 | 11 | |
| Sunday League | 8th | 7 | 7 | | 3 |
| NatWest Trophy | Quarter-Finalist | | | | |
| Benson and Hedges Cup | 3rd in Group D | | | | |

# BRITANNIC ASSURANCE CHAMPIONSHIP AVERAGES

## BATTING AND FIELDING

| Cap | | M | I | NO | HS | Runs | Avge | 100 | 50 | Ct/St |
|---|---|---|---|---|---|---|---|---|---|---|
| 1992 | J.A.Daley | 2 | 4 | 1 | 88 | 190 | 63.33 | – | 2 | 2 |
| 1992 | D.M.Jones | 12 | 20 | 5 | 157 | 904 | 60.26 | 2 | 5 | 12 |
| 1992 | P.Bainbridge | 16 | 29 | 8 | 92* | 899 | 42.81 | – | 8 | 8 |
| 1992 | P.W.G.Parker | 18 | 32 | 2 | 124 | 1218 | 40.60 | 2 | 8 | 12 |
| 1992 | W.Larkins | 21 | 39 | – | 143 | 1417 | 36.33 | 3 | 8 | 15 |
| 1992 | I.T.Botham | 14 | 23 | 2 | 105 | 705 | 33.57 | 1 | 4 | 7 |
| 1992 | I.Smith | 11 | 16 | 1 | 110 | 435 | 29.00 | 1 | 2 | 4 |
| 1992 | S.Hutton | 8 | 15 | – | 78 | 406 | 27.06 | – | 2 | 3 |
| 1992 | C.W.Scott | 17 | 24 | 5 | 57* | 433 | 22.78 | – | 2 | 26/2 |
| 1992 | G.K.Brown | 3 | 6 | – | 48 | 136 | 22.66 | – | – | 3 |
| 1992 | M.P.Briers | 15 | 26 | 4 | 62* | 447 | 20.31 | – | 4 | 7 |
| 1992 | S.J.E.Brown | 19 | 23 | 13 | 47* | 195 | 19.50 | – | – | 3 |
| 1992 | J.D.Glendenen | 15 | 25 | 1 | 76 | 421 | 17.54 | – | 3 | 4 |
| 1992 | P.W.Henderson | 5 | 7 | – | 46 | 119 | 17.00 | – | – | 1 |
| 1992 | P.J.Berry | 7 | 13 | 2 | 76 | 184 | 16.72 | – | 1 | – |
| 1992 | D.A.Graveney | 20 | 29 | 9 | 36 | 333 | 16.65 | – | – | 13 |
| 1992 | J.Wood | 7 | 6 | 1 | 28 | 80 | 16.00 | – | – | 1 |
| 1992 | S.P.Hughes | 19 | 24 | 4 | 42 | 227 | 11.35 | – | – | 5 |
| 1992 | A.R.Fothergill | 5 | 7 | 1 | 23 | 58 | 9.66 | – | – | 7/1 |
| 1992 | S.M.McEwan | 8 | 12 | 1 | 22 | 58 | 5.27 | – | – | 7 |

## BOWLING

| | O | M | R | W | Avge | Best | 5wI | 10wM |
|---|---|---|---|---|---|---|---|---|
| J.Wood | 120.2 | 12 | 510 | 16 | 31.87 | 5-68 | 1 | – |
| S.J.E.Brown | 476.1 | 70 | 1847 | 56 | 32.98 | 7-105 | 3 | – |
| P.J.Berry | 141.3 | 20 | 527 | 15 | 35.13 | 7-113 | 1 | 1 |
| P.W.Henderson | 96 | 14 | 405 | 10 | 40.50 | 3-59 | – | – |
| I.T.Botham | 303 | 60 | 1010 | 24 | 42.08 | 4-72 | – | – |
| P.Bainbridge | 177.1 | 36 | 555 | 13 | 42.69 | 5-100 | 1 | – |
| D.A.Graveney | 376.4 | 86 | 1196 | 28 | 42.71 | 3-22 | – | – |
| M.P.Briers | 121.3 | 22 | 485 | 11 | 44.09 | 3-109 | – | – |
| S.P.Hughes | 519.3 | 94 | 1594 | 34 | 46.88 | 5-25 | 1 | – |
| S.M.McEwan | 180 | 30 | 657 | 12 | 54.75 | 3-107 | – | – |

*Also bowled:* G.K.Brown 9-1-64-0; S.Hutton 0.1-0-4-0; D.M.Jones 16.3-1-67-0; W.Larkins 2-1-4-0; P.W.G.Parker 3.2-0-31-0; I.Smith 82-17-231-8.

The First-Class Averages (pp 164-178) give the records of Durham players in all first-class county matches (their other opponents being the Pakistanis and Oxford U), with the exception of:

I.T.Botham 15-23-2-105-705-33.57-1-4-7ct. 322-62-1083-26-41.65-4/72.

73

# DURHAM RECORDS

## FIRST-CLASS CRICKET

| | | | | | |
|---|---|---|---|---|---|
| **Highest Total** | For | 521-9d | v Glamorgan | Cardiff | 1992 |
| | V | 562 | by Lancashire | Gateshead | 1992 |
| **Lowest Total** | For | 116 | v Leics | Leicester | 1992 |
| | V | 108 | by Yorkshire | Durham | 1992 |
| **Highest Innings** | For | 157 D.M.Jones | v Northants | Stockton | 1992 |
| | V | 199 M.A.Atherton | for Lancashire | Gateshead | 1992 |

### Highest Partnership for each Wicket

| | | | | |
|---|---|---|---|---|
| 1st | 222 P.W.G.Parker/J.D.Glendenen | v Oxford U | Oxford | 1992 |
| 2nd | 206 W.Larkins/D.M.Jones | v Glamorgan | Cardiff | 1992 |
| 3rd | 137 D.M.Jones/P.W.G.Parker | v Derbyshire | Chesterfield | 1992 |
| 4th | 201 W.Larkins/J.A.Daley | v Somerset | Taunton | 1992 |
| 5th | 178 P.W.G.Parker/I.T.Botham | v Leics | Durham | 1992 |
| 6th | 98 S.Hutton/C.W.Scott | v Sussex | Horsham | 1992 |
| 7th | 106 I.Smith/D.A.Graveney | v Somerset | Taunton | 1992 |
| 8th | 89 P.J.Berry/S.P.Hughes | v Middlesex | Lord's | 1992 |
| 9th | 87 D.M.Jones/S.P.Hughes | v Northants | Stockton | 1992 |
| 10th | 70 D.A.Graveney/S.J.E.Brown | v Surrey | Durham | 1992 |

| | | | | | |
|---|---|---|---|---|---|
| **Best Bowling** | For | 7-105 S.J.E.Brown | v Kent | Canterbury | 1992 |
| **(Innings)** | V | 7-37 A.A.Donald | for Warwicks | Birmingham | 1992 |
| **Best Bowling** | For | 10-191 P.J.Berry | v Middlesex | Lord's | 1992 |
| **(Match)** | V | 10-87 D.J.Millns | for Leics | Leicester | 1992 |

| | | | |
|---|---|---|---|
| **Most Runs – Season** }<br>**Most Runs – Career** } | 1,536 W.Larkins | (av 37.46) | 1992 |
| **Most 100s – Season** }<br>**Most 100s – Career** } | 4 D.M.Jones<br>4 W.Larkins | | 1992<br>1992 |
| **Most Wkts – Season** }<br>**Most Wkts – Career** } | 58 S.J.E.Brown | (av 34.01) | 1992 |

## LIMITED-OVERS CRICKET

| | | | | | |
|---|---|---|---|---|---|
| **Highest Total** | NWT | 305-6 | v Ireland | Dublin | 1992 |
| | | 305-9 | v Glamorgan | Darlington | 1991 |
| | BHC | 271-6 | v Comb Univs | Cambridge | 1992 |
| | SL | 275-4 | v Sussex | Horsham | 1992 |
| **Lowest Total** | NWT | 82 | v Worcs | Chester-le-St | 1968 |
| | BHC | 201 | v Derbyshire | Jesmond | 1992 |
| | SL | 124 | v Northants | Stockton | 1992 |
| **Highest Innings** | NWT | 113 W.Larkins | v Ireland | Dublin | 1992 |
| | BHC | 86 I.T.Botham | v Glamorgan | Durham | 1992 |
| | SL | 114 D.M.Jones | v Lancashire | Durham | 1992 |
| **Best Bowling** | NWT | 7-32 S.P.Davis | v Lancashire | Chester-le-St | 1983 |
| | BHC | 4-38 P.Bainbridge | v Worcs | Worcester | 1992 |
| | SL | 3-26 S.P.Hughes | v Warwicks | Birmingham | 1992 |

# ESSEX

**Formation of Present Club:** 14 January 1876
**Colours:** Blue, Gold and Red
**Badge:** Three Seaxes above Scroll bearing 'Essex'
**Championships:** (6) 1979, 1983, 1984, 1986, 1991, 1992
**NatWest Trophy/Gillette Cup Winners:** (1) 1985
**Benson and Hedges Cup Winners:** (1) 1979
**Sunday League Champions:** (3) 1981, 1984, 1985
**Match Awards:** NWT 35; BHC 70

**Secretary/General Manager:** P.J.Edwards, County Ground, New Writtle Street, Chelmsford CM2 0PG (☎ 0245-252420)
**Captain:** G.A.Gooch
**Scorer:** C.F.Driver
**1993 Beneficiary:** N.A.Foster

**ANDREW, Stephen** Jon Walter (Milton Abbey S; Portchester SS), b London 27 Jan 1966. 6'3". RHB, RMF. Hampshire 1984-89. Essex debut 1990. HS 35 v Northants (Chelmsford) 1990. BB 7-92 H v Glos (Southampton) 1987. Ex BB 5-55 v Yorks (Middlesbrough) 1990. Awards: BHC 2. **NWT:** HS 0*. BB 2-34 v Scot (Chelmsford) 1990. **BHC:** HS 4*. BB 5-24 H v Essex (Chelmsford) 1987. **SL:** HS 8. BB 4-50 H v Middx (Southampton) 1988.

**BODEN, David** Jonathan Peter (Alleynes HS, Stone; Stafford CFE), b Eccleshall, Staffs 26 Nov 1970. 6'3". RHB, RMF. Middlesex 1989. Essex debut 1992. HS 5. BB 4-11 M v OU (Oxford) 1989 – on debut. Awaiting BAC debut – joined staff 1990.

**CHILDS, John** Henry (Audley Park SM, Torquay), b Plymouth, Devon 15 Aug 1951. 6'0". LHB, SLA. Gloucestershire 1975-84 (cap 1977). Essex debut 1985. Cap 1986. Devon 1973-74. Wisden 1986. **Tests:** 2 (1988); HS 2*; BB 1-13. HS 43 v Hants (Chelmsford) 1992. 50 wkts (7); most – 89 (1986). BB 9-56 Gs v Somerset (Bristol) 1981. Ex BB 8-58 v Glos (Colchester) 1986. Awards: BHC 1. **NWT:** HS 14* Gs v Hants (Bristol) 1983. BB 2-15 Gs v Ire (Dublin) 1981. **BHC:** HS 10 Gs v Somerset (Bristol) 1979. BB 3-36 Gs v Glam (Bristol) 1982. **SL:** HS 16* Gs v Warwks (Bristol) 1981. BB 4-15 Gs v Northants (Northampton) 1976.

**COUSINS, Darren** Mark (Netherhall CS; Impington Village C), b Cambridge 24 Sep 1971. 6'2". RHB, RMF. Cambridgeshire 1990. No 1st XI appearances – joined staff 1992.

**FOSTER, Neil** Alan (Philip Morant CS), b Colchester 6 May 1962. 6'3". RHB, RFM. Debut 1980. Cap 1983. Benefit 1993. YC 1983. Wisden 1987. Transvaal 1991-92. **Tests:** 28 (1983 to 1989); HS 39 v P (Lahore) 1987-88 and v A (Manchester) 1989; BB 8-107 v P (Leeds) 1987. LOI: 48. Tours: A 1986-87, 1987-88; SA 1989-90 (Eng XI); WI 1985-86; NZ 1983-84, 1987-88; I/SL 1984-85; P 1983-84, 1987-88. HS 107* v Sussex (Horsham) 1991. 50 wkts (9) inc 100 (2); most – 105 (1986). BB 8-99 v Lancs (Manchester) 1991. Awards: NWT 1; BHC 3. **NWT:** HS 26 v Worcs (Chelmsford) 1987. BB 4-9 v Northumb (Jesmond) 1987. **BHC:** HS 62 v Scot (Chelmsford) 1992. BB 5-32 v Surrey (Oval) 1988. **SL:** HS 57 v Northants (Northampton) 1991. BB 5-17 v Derbys (Derby) 1986.

**FRASER, Alastair** Gregory James (Gayton HS, John Lyon S, Harrow; Harrow Weald SFC), b Edgware, Middx 17 Oct 1967. Brother of A.R.C. (Middlesex and England). 6'1". RHB, RFM. Middlesex 1986-89. Essex debut 1991. HS 52* v Sussex (Horsham) 1991. BB 3-46 M v NZ (Lord's) 1986. BAC BB 2-12 M v Lancs (Lord's) 1986. Ex BB 2-37 v CU (Cambridge) 1992. **BHC:** HS 6. BB 1-31. **SL:** HS 12 v Middx (Lord's) 1992. BB 2-35 Mx v Northants (Lord's) 1989.

**GARNHAM, Michael** Anthony (Camberwell GS, Melbourne; Scotch C, Perth; Barnstaple GS; N Devon SFC; East Anglia U), b Johannesburg, SA 20 Aug 1960. 5'10". RHB, WK. Gloucestershire 1979. Leicestershire 1980-85 and 1988. Essex debut 1989. Cap 1990. Cambridgeshire 1986-88. HS 123 v Leics (Leicester) 1991. Shared Essex record 5th wkt stand of 316 with N.Hussain v Leics (Leicester) 1991. Awards: NWT 2; BHC 1. **NWT:** HS 110 Cambs v Warwks (Birmingham) 1988. **BHC:** HS 55 Le v Derbys (Leicester) 1982. **SL:** HS 79* Le v Lancs (Leicester) 1982.

**GOOCH, Graham** Alan (Norlington Jr HS), b Leytonstone 23 Jul 1953. 6'0". RHB, RM. Debut 1973. Cap 1975. Captain 1986-87, 1989-. Benefit 1985. W Province 1982-83/1983-84. Wisden 1979. OBE 1991. **Tests:** 99 (1975 to 1992, 28 as captain); HS 333 and record match aggregate of 456 v I (Lord's) 1990; BB 3-39 v P (Manchester) 1992. LOI: 111. Tours (C=captain): A 1978-79, 1979-80, 1990-91C; SA 1981-82 (SAB); WI 1980-81, 1985-86, 1989-90C; NZ 1991-92C; I 1979-80, 1981-82; P 1987-88; SL 1981-82. 1000 runs (16+1) inc 2000 (4); most – 2746 (1990). HS 333 (Tests). Ex HS 275 v Kent (Chelmsford) 1988. Shared Essex record 2nd wkt stand of 403 with P.J.Prichard v Leics (Chelmsford) 1990. HB 7-14 v Worcs (Ilford) 1982. Awards: NWT 9 (record); BHC 20 (record). **NWT:** HS 144 v Hants (Chelmsford) 1990. BB 3-31 v Warwks (Birmingham) 1986. **BHC:** HS 198* v Sussex (Hove) 1982. BB 3-24 v Sussex (Hove) 1982. **SL:** HS 176 v Glam (Southend) 1983. BB 4-33 v Worcs (Chelmsford) 1984.

**HUSSAIN, Nasser** (Forest S, Snaresbrook; Durham U), b Madras, India 28 Mar 1968. Brother of M. (Worcs 1985). 5'11". RHB, LB. Debut 1987. Cap 1989. Comb Us (BHC) 1987-89. YC 1989. **Tests:** 3 (1989-90); HS 35 v WI (St John's) 1989-90. LOI: 2. Tours: WI 1989-90, 1991-92 (Eng A); P 1990-91 (Eng A); SL 1990-91 (Eng A). 1000 runs (1): 1354 (1991). HS 197 v Surrey (Oval) 1990. Shared in 3 record Essex stands: 347* (3rd) with M.E.Waugh; 314 (4th) with Salim Malik and 316 (5th) with M.A.Garnham. BB 1-38. Awards: NWT 1; BHC 1. **NWT:** HS 108 v Cumberland (Chelmsford) 1992. **BHC:** HS 118 Comb Us v Somerset (Taunton) 1989. **SL:** HS 66* v Yorks (Middlesbrough) 1990.

**ILOTT, Mark** Christopher (Francis Combe S, Garston), b Watford, Herts 27 Aug 1970. 6'0¾". LHB, LMF. Debut 1988. Hertfordshire 1987-88. Tour: SL 1990-91 (Eng A). HS 42* v Kent (Chelmsford) 1990. 50 wkts (1): 64 (1992). BB 6-87 v Derbys (Derby) 1992. **NWT:** HS 10* v Leics (Leicester) 1992. BB 2-23 v Cumberland (Chelmsford) 1992. **BHC:** HS 5*. BB 4-31 v Scot (Chelmsford) 1992. **SL:** HS 7. BB 4-15 v Derbys (Derby) 1992.

**KNIGHT, Nicholas** Verity (Felsted S; Forest County C, Loughborough U), b Watford, Herts 28 Nov 1969. 6'0". LHB. Debut 1991. Comb Us (BHC) 1990-91 (captain 1991). HS 109 v Middx (Ilford) 1992. **NWT:** HS 81* v Cumberland (Chelmsford) 1992. **BHC:** HS 36 v Glos (Bristol) 1991. **SL:** HS 35 v Northants (Chelmsford) 1992.

**LEWIS, Jonathan** James Benjamin (King Edward VI S, Chelmsford; Roehampton IHE), b Isleworth, Middx 21 May 1970. 5'9½". RHB, RSM. Debut 1990 scoring 116* v Surrey (Oval). HS 133 v Sussex (Hove) 1992. **NWT:** HS 21 v Leics (Leicester) 1992. **SL:** HS 19 v Lancs (Manchester) 1991.

**PRICHARD, Paul** John (Brentwood HS), b Billericay 7 Jan 1965. 5'10". RHB. Debut 1984. Cap 1986. 1000 runs (5); most – 1485 (1992). HS 245 v Leics (Chelmsford) 1990, sharing Essex record 2nd wkt stand of 403 with G.A.Gooch. BB 1-28. Awards: BHC 2. **NWT:** HS 94 v Oxon (Chelmsford) 1985. **BHC:** HS 107 v Scot (Glasgow) 1990. **SL:** HS 103* v Lancs (Manchester) 1986.

**PRINGLE, Derek** Raymond (Felsted S; Fitzwilliam C, Cambridge), b Nairobi, Kenya 18 Sep 1958. Son of D.J. (East Africa). 6'4½". RHB, RMF. Debut 1978. Cap 1982. Benefit 1992. Cambridge U 1979-82 (blue 1979-80-81; capt 1982). **Tests:** 30 (1982 to 1992); HS 63 v I (Lord's) 1982. BB 5-95 v WI (Leeds) 1988. LOI: 42. Tours: A 1982-83; NZ 1991-92; SL 1985-86 (Eng B); Z 1989-90 (Eng A). HS 128 v Kent (Chelmsford) 1988. 50 wkts (6); most – 94 (1989). BB 7-18 v Glam (Swansea)

PRINGLE – continued:
1989. Awards: NWT 2; BHC 4. **NWT:** HS 80* v Wilts (Chelmsford) 1988. BB 5-12 v Oxon (Chelmsford) 1985. **BHC:** HS 77* v Scot (Glasgow) 1990. BB 5-35 v Lancs (Chelmsford) 1984. **SL:** HS 81* v Warwks (Birmingham) 1985. BB 5-41 v Glos (Southend) 1985.

**ROBINSON, Darren** David John (Tabor HS, Braintree; Chelmsford CFE), b Braintree 2 Mar 1973. 5'10½". RHB, RMF. No 1st XI appearances – joined staff 1992.

**ROLLINS, Robert** John (Little Ilford CS), b Plaistow 30 Jan 1974. Brother of A.S. (see DERBYSHIRE). 5'9". RHB, WK. Debut 1992. HS 13 v P (Chelmsford) 1992.

**SALIM MALIK** (Government C, Lahore), b Lahore, Pakistan 16 Apr 1963. 5'9". RHB, RSM. Lahore 1978-79/1985-86. Habib Bank 1982-83 to date. Essex 1991 (cap 1991). **Tests** (P): 71 (1981-82 to 1992); HS 165 v E (Birmingham) 1992. BB 1-3. LOI (P): 152. Tours (P): E 1982, 1987, 1992; A 1981-82, 1983-84, 1989-90, 1991-92; WI 1987-88; NZ 1984-85, 1988-89; I 1983-84, 1986-87; SL 1984-85 (P U-23), 1985-86. 1000 runs (2+1); most – 1972 (1991). HS 215 v Leics (Ilford) 1991. Shared Essex record 4th wkt stand of 314 with N.Hussain v Surrey (Oval) 1991. BB 5-19 Habib Bank v Karachi (Karachi) 1985-86. Ex BB 3-26 v Northants (Colchester) 1991. Award: BHC 1. **NWT:** HS 26 v Surrey (Oval) 1991. **BHC:** HS 90* v Surrey (Oval) 1991. BB 1-7. **SL:** HS 89 v Worcs (Ilford) 1991. BB 1-25.

**SHAHID, Nadeem** (Ipswich S), b Karachi, Pakistan 23 Apr 1969. 6'0". RHB, LB. Debut 1989. Suffolk 1988. 1000 runs (1): 1003 (1990). HS 132 v Kent (Chelmsford) 1992. BB 3-91 v Surrey (Oval) 1990. **NWT:** HS 18 and BB 1-0 v Cumberland (Chelmsford) 1992. **BHC:** HS 42 v Hants (Chelmsford) 1991. **SL:** HS 36 v Glos (Cheltenham) 1991.

**STEPHENSON, John** Patrick (Felsted S; Durham U), b Stebbing 14 Mar 1965. 6'1". RHB, RM. Debut 1985. Cap 1989. Comb Us (BHC) 1987. Boland 1988-89. **Tests:** 1 (1989); HS 25 v A (Oval) 1989. Tours: WI 1991-92 (Eng A); Z 1989-90 (Eng A). 1000 runs (4); most – 1887 (1990). HS 202* v Somerset (Bath) 1990. BB 6-54 v Notts (Colchester) 1992. Awards: BHC 2. **NWT:** HS 75 and BB 3-78 v Lancs (Chelmsford) 1992. **BHC:** HS 142 v Warwks (Birmingham) 1991. BB 3-22 v Northants (Northampton) 1990. **SL:** HS 109 v Lancs (Colchester) 1990. BB 5-58 v Glos (Chelmsford) 1992.

**SUCH, Peter** Mark (Harry Carlton CS, Ex Leake, Notts), b Helensburgh, Dumbartonshire 12 Jun 1964. 5'11". RHB, OB. Nottinghamshire 1982-86. Leicestershire 1987-89. Essex debut 1990. Cap 1991. HS 35* v Hants (Chelmsford) 1992. BB 6-17 v Sussex (Southend) 1992. **NWT:** HS 0*. BB 2-29 v Devon (Exmouth) 1991. **BHC:** HS 4. BB 4-43 v Northants (Northampton) 1992. **SL:** HS 9*. BB 4-30 v Derbys (Chelmsford) 1991.

**TENNANT, Lloyd** (Shelfield CS), b Walsall, Staffs 9 Apr 1968. 5'11". RHB, RMF. Leicestershire 1986-91. HS 23* Le v Sussex (Hove) 1991. BB 4-54 Le v CU (Cambridge) 1991. BAC BB 3-65 Le v Notts (Nottingham) 1991. No Essex 1st XI appearances – joined staff 1992. **SL:** HS 17* Le v Somerset (Leicester) 1988. BB 3-25 Le v Somerset (Leicester) 1986.

**TOPLEY, Thomas Donald** (Royal Hospital S, Holbrook, Suffolk), b Canterbury, Kent 25 Feb 1964. Brother of P.A. (Kent 1972-75). 6'3". RHB, RMF. Surrey (v CU) and Essex debuts 1985. Cap 1988. GW 1987-88. Norfolk 1984-85. MCC YC. HS 66 v Yorks (Leeds) 1987. 50 wkts (3); most – 77 (1989). BB 7-75 v Derbys (Chesterfield) 1988. Awards: NWT 1; BHC 2. **NWT:** HS 19* v Leics (Leicester) 1992. BB 4-21 v Northumb (Jesmond) 1987. **BHC:** HS 10* v Notts (Chelmsford) 1990. BB 4-22 v Surrey (Chelmsford) 1988. **SL:** HS 38* v Lancs (Manchester) 1991. BB 6-33 v Notts (Colchester) 1988.

## NEWCOMERS

**DIWAN, Muneeb** (Sr George Monoux S, Walthamstow), b St Stephens, Canada 20 Mar 1972. 5'9". RHB, RM.

**KHAN, Gul** Abbass (Valentine S, Ilford; Ipswich S; Swansea U), b Gujrat, Pakistan 31 Dec 1973. 5'8". RHB, LB.                    DEPARTURES – see p 155

# ESSEX 1992

## RESULTS SUMMARY

| | Place | Won | Lost | Drew | Abandoned |
|---|---|---|---|---|---|
| Britannic Assurance Championship | 1st | 11 | 6 | 5 | |
| All First-class Matches | | 11 | 7 | 7 | |
| Sunday League | 2nd | 11 | 5 | | 1 |
| NatWest Trophy | Semi-Finalist | | | | |
| Benson and Hedges Cup | 3rd in Group B | | | | |

# BRITANNIC ASSURANCE CHAMPIONSHIP AVERAGES

## BATTING AND FIELDING

| Cap | | M | I | NO | HS | Runs | Avge | 100 | 50 | Ct/St |
|---|---|---|---|---|---|---|---|---|---|---|
| 1975 | G.A.Gooch | 11 | 18 | 3 | 160 | 1246 | 83.06 | 6 | 4 | 17 |
| 1989 | M.E.Waugh | 15 | 23 | 7 | 219* | 1253 | 78.31 | 4 | 5 | 25 |
| 1989 | J.P.Stephenson | 19 | 33 | 5 | 159* | 1309 | 46.75 | 3 | 8 | 9 |
| 1989 | N.Hussain | 17 | 21 | 3 | 172* | 833 | 46.27 | 1 | 5 | 19 |
| – | J.J.B.Lewis | 11 | 16 | 4 | 133 | 555 | 46.25 | 1 | 4 | 3 |
| 1982 | D.R.Pringle | 12 | 12 | 3 | 112* | 405 | 45.00 | 1 | 2 | 4 |
| 1986 | P.J.Prichard | 21 | 36 | 4 | 136 | 1399 | 43.71 | 4 | 8 | 18 |
| – | N.V.Knight | 18 | 27 | 5 | 109 | 603 | 27.40 | 1 | 2 | 17 |
| – | N.Shahid | 13 | 18 | – | 132 | 467 | 25.94 | 1 | 2 | 8 |
| 1983 | N.A.Foster | 10 | 13 | – | 54 | 290 | 22.30 | – | 2 | 12 |
| 1990 | M.A.Garnham | 21 | 24 | 3 | 66 | 445 | 21.19 | – | 3 | 35/3 |
| 1991 | P.M.Such | 13 | 11 | 3 | 35* | 100 | 12.50 | – | – | 6 |
| 1986 | J.H.Childs | 19 | 15 | 6 | 43 | 105 | 11.66 | – | – | 5 |
| 1988 | T.D.Topley | 10 | 11 | 2 | 29 | 99 | 11.00 | – | – | 8 |
| – | M.C.Ilott | 21 | 19 | 3 | 28 | 143 | 8.93 | – | – | 7 |
| – | S.J.W.Andrew | 9 | 10 | 4 | 14* | 29 | 4.83 | – | – | – |

*Also played* (1 match each): A.D.Brown did not bat (4 ct, 1 st); A.G.J.Fraser 2.

## BOWLING

| | O | M | R | W | Avge | Best | 5wI | 10wM |
|---|---|---|---|---|---|---|---|---|
| D.R.Pringle | 324.5 | 83 | 870 | 39 | 22.30 | 5-63 | 1 | – |
| P.M.Such | 391.1 | 125 | 895 | 39 | 22.94 | 6-17 | 3 | – |
| J.H.Childs | 624.5 | 197 | 1598 | 64 | 24.96 | 6-82 | 3 | – |
| N.A.Foster | 226 | 56 | 634 | 23 | 27.56 | 4-47 | – | – |
| M.E.Waugh | 173.4 | 31 | 614 | 21 | 29.23 | 3-38 | – | – |
| M.C.Ilott | 625.3 | 137 | 2077 | 62 | 33.50 | 6-87 | 3 | – |
| S.J.W.Andrew | 247 | 43 | 779 | 21 | 37.09 | 4-54 | – | – |
| T.D.Topley | 223.4 | 47 | 753 | 18 | 41.83 | 4-67 | – | – |
| J.P.Stephenson | 226.4 | 45 | 773 | 18 | 42.94 | 6-54 | 1 | – |

*Also bowled*: A.G.J.Fraser 11-3-58-1; G.A.Gooch 69-21-149-3; N.Hussain 4-0-38-1; P.J.Prichard 8-0-100-0; N.Shahid 34-4-143-7.

The First-Class Averages (pp 164-178) give the records of Essex players in all first-class county matches (their other opponents being England A, the Pakistanis and Cambridge U), with the exception of:
G.A.Gooch 13-21-3-160-1466-81.44-7-5-17ct. 83-23-211-4-52.75-1/4.
D.R.Pringle 13-13-4-112*-507-56.33-2-2-4ct. 353.5-89-950-42-22.61-5/63-1-0.

# ESSEX RECORDS

## FIRST-CLASS CRICKET

| | | | | | |
|---|---|---|---|---|---|
| **Highest Total** | For 761-6d | | v Leics | Chelmsford | 1990 |
| | V 803-4d | | by Kent | Brentwood | 1934 |
| **Lowest Total** | For 30 | | v Yorkshire | Leyton | 1901 |
| | V 14 | | by Surrey | Chelmsford | 1983 |
| **Highest Innings** | For 343* | P.A.Perrin | v Derbyshire | Chesterfield | 1904 |
| | 332 | W.H.Ashdown | for Kent | Brentwood | 1934 |

### Highest Partnership for each Wicket

| | | | | | |
|---|---|---|---|---|---|
| 1st | 270 | A.V.Avery/T.C.Dodds | v Surrey | The Oval | 1946 |
| 2nd | 403 | G.A.Gooch/P.J.Prichard | v Leics | Chelmsford | 1990 |
| 3rd | 347* | M.E.Waugh/N.Hussain | v Lancashire | Ilford | 1992 |
| 4th | 314 | Salim Malik/N.Hussain | v Surrey | The Oval | 1991 |
| 5th | 316 | N.Hussain/M.A.Garnham | v Leics | Leicester | 1991 |
| 6th | 206 | J.W.H.T.Douglas/J.O'Connor | v Glos | Cheltenham | 1923 |
| | 206 | B.R.Knight/R.A.G.Luckin | v Middlesex | Brentwood | 1962 |
| 7th | 261 | J.W.H.T.Douglas/J.Freeman | v Lancashire | Leyton | 1914 |
| 8th | 263 | D.R.Wilcox/R.M.Taylor | v Warwicks | Southend | 1946 |
| 9th | 251 | J.W.H.T.Douglas/S.N.Hare | v Derbyshire | Leyton | 1921 |
| 10th | 218 | F.H.Vigar/T.P.B.Smith | v Derbyshire | Chesterfield | 1947 |

| | | | | | |
|---|---|---|---|---|---|
| **Best Bowling** | For 10-32 | H.Pickett | v Leics | Leyton | 1895 |
| **(Innings)** | V 10-40 | E.G.Dennett | for Glos | Bristol | 1906 |
| **Best Bowling** | For 17-119 | W.Mead | v Hampshire | Southampton | 1895 |
| **(Match)** | V 17-56 | C.W.L.Parker | for Glos | Gloucester | 1925 |

| | | | | |
|---|---|---|---|---|
| **Most Runs – Season** | 2,559 | G.A.Gooch | (av 67.34) | 1984 |
| **Most Runs – Career** | 29,434† | K.W.R.Fletcher | (av 36.88) | 1962-1988 |
| **Most 100s – Season** | 9 | J.O'Connor | | 1934 |
| | 9 | D.J.Insole | | 1955 |
| **Most 100s – Career** | 71† | J.O'Connor | | 1921-1939 |
| **Most Wkts – Season** | 172 | T.P.B.Smith | (av 27.13) | 1947 |
| **Most Wkts – Career** | 1,610 | T.P.B.Smith | (av 26.68) | 1929-1951 |

†G.A.Gooch has scored 23,984 runs, including 70 hundreds, 1973-1992.

## LIMITED-OVERS CRICKET

| | | | | | |
|---|---|---|---|---|---|
| **Highest Total** | NWT | 386-5 | v Wiltshire | Chelmsford | 1988 |
| | BHC | 388-7 | v Scotland | Chelmsford | 1992 |
| | SL | 310-5 | v Glamorgan | Southend | 1983 |
| **Lowest Total** | NWT | 100 | v Derbyshire | Brentwood | 1965 |
| | BHC | 61 | v Lancashire | Chelmsford | 1992 |
| | SL | 69 | v Derbyshire | Chesterfield | 1974 |
| **Highest Innings** | NWT | 144 G.A.Gooch | v Hampshire | Chelmsford | 1990 |
| | BHC | 198* G.A.Gooch | v Sussex | Hove | 1982 |
| | SL | 176 G.A.Gooch | v Glamorgan | Southend | 1983 |
| **Best Bowling** | NWT | 5-8 J.K.Lever | v Middlesex | Westcliff | 1972 |
| | BHC | 5-13 J.K.Lever | v Middlesex | Lord's | 1985 |
| | SL | 8-26 K.D.Boyce | v Lancashire | Manchester | 1971 |

# GLAMORGAN

**Formation of Present Club:** 6 July 1888
**Colours:** Blue and Gold
**Badge:** Gold Daffodil
**Championships:** (2) 1948, 1969
**NatWest Trophy/Gillette Cup Winners:** (0) Finalists 1977
**Benson and Hedges Cup Winners:** (0) Semi-Finalists 1988
**Sunday League Champions:** (0) Fifth 1988
**Match Awards:** NWT 28; BHC 41

**Cricket Secretary:** M.Fatkin, Sophia Gardens, Cardiff, CF1 9XR (☎ 0222–343478)
**Captain:** H.Morris
**Scorer:** B.T.Denning
**1993 Beneficiary:** –

**BARWICK, Stephen** Royston (Cwrt Sart CS; Dwr-y-Felin CS), b Neath 6 Sep 1960. 6'2". RHB, RMF. Debut 1981. Cap 1987. HS 30 v Hants (Bournemouth) 1988. 50 wkts (2); most – 64 (1989). BB 8-42 v Worcs (Worcester) 1983. Award: BHC 1. **NWT:** HS 6. BB 5-26 v Surrey (Swansea) 1992. **BHC:** HS 18 v Kent (Canterbury) 1984. BB 4-11 v Minor C (Swansea) 1985. **SL:** HS 48* v Worcs (Worcester) 1989. BB 4-23 v Yorks (Cardiff) 1987.

**BASTIEN, Steven** (St Bonaventure S, Forest Gate; Haringey Cricket C), b Stepney, London 13 Mar 1963 (of Dominican parents). 6'1". RHB, RMF. Debut 1988. Tour: Z 1990-91 (Gm). HS 36* v Warwks (Birmingham) 1988 (his first innings). BB 6-75 v Worcs (Worcester) 1990. **NWT:** HS 7*. BB 1-42. **BHC:** HS 7. BB 1-29. **SL:** HS 1. BB 2-42 v Kent (Maidstone) 1991.

**BISHOP, Jamie** (Pontardulais CS; Gorseinon Tertiary C; Cardiff IHE), b Swansea 14 Jan 1971. LHB. Debut v OU (Oxford) 1992, scoring 51*. Wales (Minor Counties) 1991. HS 51* (above).

**COTTEY, Phillip Anthony** (Bishopston CS), b Swansea 2 Jun 1966. 5'4". RHB, OB. Debut 1986. Cap 1992. E Transvaal 1991-92. Tour: Z 1990-91 (Gm). 1000 runs (2); most – 1076 (1992). HS 156 v OU (Oxford) 1990. BAC HS 141 v Kent (Canterbury) 1992. BB 2-42 E Transvaal v W Transvaal (Potchefstroom) 1991-92. **NWT:** HS 27 v Sussex (Cardiff) 1990. **BHC:** HS 68 v Hants (Southampton) 1989. **SL:** 92* v Hants (Ebbw Vale) 1992. BB 2-30 v Sussex (Hove) 1992.

**CROFT, Robert** Damien Bale (St John Lloyd Catholic CS; W Glam IHE), b Morriston 25 May 1970. 5'10½". RHB, OB. Debut 1989. Cap 1992. Tours: WI 1991-92 (Eng A); Z 1990-91 (Gm). HS 91* v Worcs (Abergavenny) 1990. 50 wkts (1): 68 (1992). BB 8-66 (14-169 match) v Warwks (Swansea) 1992. **NWT:** HS 26 v Middx (Lord's) 1990. BB 2-28 v Worcs (Worcester) 1991. **BHC:** HS 30* v Durham (Durham) 1992. BB 3-28 v Comb Us (Cardiff) 1992. **SL:** HS 31* v Yorks (Ebbw Vale) 1992. BB 2-30 v Glos (Swansea) 1991.

**DALE, Adrian** (Chepstow CS; Swansea U), b Germiston, SA 24 Oct 1968 (to UK at 6 mths). 5'11½". RHB, RM. Debut 1989. Cap 1992. Comb Us (Dev) 1989-90. Tour: Z 1990-91 (Gm). 1000 runs (1): 1159 (1992). HS 150* v Notts (Nottingham) 1992. BB 3-21 v I (Swansea) 1992. BAC BB 3-30 v Leics (Swansea) 1992. Award: NWT 1. **NWT:** HS 86 v Worcs (Worcester) 1991. BB 2-32 v Staffs (Cardiff) 1989. **BHC:** HS 53 v Comb Us (Cardiff) 1992. BB 3-24 Comb Us v Surrey (Cambridge) 1989. **SL:** HS 67* v Derbys (Heanor) 1989. BB 4-27 v Leics (Swansea) 1992.

**FROST, Mark** (Alexander HS, Tipton; St Peter's S, Wolverhampton; Durham U), b Barking, Essex 21 Oct 1962. 6'2". RHB, RMF. Surrey 1988-89. Glamorgan debut 1990. Cap 1991. Staffordshire 1987. Tour: Z 1990-91 (Gm). HS 12 v Warwks (Birmingham) 1990. 50 wkts (2); most – 65 (1991). BB 7-99 (11-143 match) v Glos (Cheltenham) 1991. Award: BHC 1. **NWT:** HS 3. BB 3-50 v Dorset (Swansea) 1990. **BHC:** HS 4. BB 4-25 v Worcs (Worcester) 1990. **SL:** HS 6*. BB 4-30 v Northants (Northampton) 1990.

**HEMP, David** Lloyd (Olchfa CS; Millfield S; W Glamorgan C), b Bermuda 8 Nov 1970. UK resident since 1976. 6'0". LHB, RM. Debut 1991. Scored 4 successive hundreds for Wales U-19 1990. Scored 68 and 258* for Wales v MCC (High Wycombe) 1991. HS 84* v Hants (Portsmouth) 1992. **SL:** HS 10 v Notts (Nottingham) 1992.

**JAMES, Stephen** Peter (Monmouth S; Swansea U; Hughes Hall, Cambridge), b Lydney, Glos 7 Sep 1967. 6'0". RHB. Debut 1985. Cap 1992. Cambridge U 1989-90; blue 1989-90. Comb Us (BHC) 1989-90. Tour: Z 1990-91 (Gm). 1000 runs (2); most – 1376 (1992). HS 152* v Lancs (Colwyn Bay) 1992. Shared Glam record 2nd wkt stand of 249 with H.Morris v OU (Oxford) 1987. Award: BHC 1. **NWT:** HS 26 v Cheshire (Cardiff) 1987. **BHC:** HS 135 v Comb Us (Cardiff) 1992. **SL:** HS 74 v Leics (Swansea) 1992.

**MAYNARD, Matthew** Peter (David Hughes S, Anglesey), b Oldham, Lancs 21 Mar 1966. 5'10½". RHB, RM. Debut 1985 scoring 102 out of 117 in 87 min v Yorks (Swansea), reaching 100 with 3 sixes off successive balls. Cap 1987. N Districts 1990-91/1991-92. YC 1988. **Tests:** 1 (1988); HS 10 v WI (Oval) 1988. Tour: SA 1989-90 (Eng XI). 1000 runs (7); most – 1803 (1991). HS 243 v Hants (Southampton) 1991. BB 3-21 v OU (Oxford) 1987. BAC BB 1-3. Awards: NWT 2; BHC 4. **NWT:** HS 151* v Durham (Darlington) 1991. **BHC:** HS 115 v Comb Us (Cardiff) 1988. **SL:** HS 122* v Leics (Swansea) 1992.

**METSON, Colin** Peter (Enfield GS; Stanborough S, Welwyn Garden City; Durham U), b Goffs Oak, Herts 2 Jul 1963. 5'5½". RHB, WK. Middlesex 1981-86. Glamorgan debut/cap 1987. HS 96 M v Glos (Uxbridge) 1984. Gm HS 84 v Kent (Maidstone) 1991. **NWT:** HS 21 v Notts (Nottingham) 1992. **BHC:** HS 23 v Kent (Swansea) 1990. **SL:** HS 30* v Hants (Bournemouth) 1990.

**MORRIS, Hugh** (Blundell's S), b Cardiff 5 Oct 1963. 5'8". LHB, RM. Debut 1981. Cap 1986. Captain 1986-89 and 1993. **Tests:** 3 (1991); HS 44 v WI (Oval) 1991. Tours: WI 1991-92 (Eng A); SL 1990-91 (Eng A). 1000 runs (6) inc 2000 (1): 2276 – inc 10 hundreds – both Gm records (1990). HS 160* v Derbys (Cardiff) 1990. Shared Glam record 2nd wkt stand of 249 with S.P.James v OU (Oxford) 1987. BB 1-6. BAC BB 1-45. Awards: NWT 1; BHC 3. **NWT:** HS 154* v Staffs (Cardiff) 1989. **BHC:** HS 143* v Hants (Southampton) 1989. BB 1-14. **SL:** HS 104* v Derbys (Pontypridd) 1992.

**RICHARDS, Isaac Vivian** Alexander (Antigua GS), b St John's, Antigua 7 Mar 1952. 5'11". RHB, OB. Leeward Is 1971-72/1990-91 (captain 1981-82/1990-91). Somerset 1974-86 (cap 1974; benefit 1982). Glamorgan debut/cap 1990. Queensland 1976-77. Wisden 1976. **Tests** (WI): 121 (1974-75 to 1991, 50 as captain); HS 291 v E (Oval) 1976; BB 2-17 v P (P-of-S) 1987-88. LOI (WI): 187. Tours: WI (C=captain): E 1976, 1980, 1984, 1988C, 1991C; A 1975-76, 1979-80, 1981-82, 1984-85, 1986-87C, 1988-89C; NZ 1986-87C; I 1974-75, 1983-84, 1987-88C; P 1974-75, 1980-81, 1986-87C; SL 1974-75. 1000 runs (13+3) inc 2000 (1): 2161 (1977). Only West Indian to score 100 f-c hundreds (111). HS 322 (Sm record) v Warwks (Taunton) 1985. Gm HS 164* v Hants (Southampton) 1990. Shared record Somerset 8th wkt stand of 172 with I.T.Botham v Leics (Leicester) 1983. BB 5-88 WI v Queensland (Brisbane) 1981-82. BAC BB 4-36 Sm v Derbys (Chesterfield) 1986. Gm BB 2-27 v Sussex (Hove) 1990. Awards: NWT 6; BHC 6. **NWT:** HS 139* Sm v Warwks (Taunton) 1978. BB 3-15 Sm v Beds (Bedford) 1982. **BHC:** HS 132* Sm v Surrey (Lord's) 1981. BB 3-24 v Warwks (Birmingham) 1990. **SL:** HS 126* Sm v Glos (Bristol Imp) 1975. BB 6-24 Sm v Lancs (Manchester) 1983.

**SHAW, Adrian** David (Neath Tertiary C), b Neath 17 Feb 1972. 5'11". RHB, WK. Wales 1990-91. Awaiting f-c debut. **SL:** HS –.

**THOMAS, Stuart Darren** (Graig CS, Llanelli; Neath Tertiary C), b Morriston 25 Jan 1975. 6'0". LHB, RFM. Debut v Derbys (Chesterfield) 1992, taking 5-80 when aged 17yr 217d. HS 10 v Derbys (Cardiff) 1992. BB 5-79 v Kent (Canterbury) 1992. **SL:** HS -. BB 1-34.

**WATKIN, Steven** Llewellyn (Cymer Afan CS; S Glamorgan CHE), b Maesteg 15 Sep 1964. 6'3". RHB, RMF. Debut 1986. Cap 1989. **Tests:** 2 (1991); HS 6; BB 3-38 v WI (Leeds) 1991 – on debut. Tours: WI 1991-92 (Eng A); P 1990-91 (Eng A); Z 1989-90 (Eng A), 1990-91 (Gm). HS 41 v Worcs (Worcester) 1992. 50 wkts (4); most – 94 (1989). BB 8-59 v Warwks (Birmingham) 1988. Award: NWT 1. **NWT:** HS 9. BB 3-18 v Sussex (Cardiff) 1990. **BHC:** HS 15 v Hants (Southampton) 1991. BB 3-28 v Minor C (Trowbridge) 1991. **SL:** 31* v Derbys (Checkley) 1991. BB 5-23 v Warwks (Birmingham) 1990.

## NEWCOMERS

**BUTCHER, Gary** Paul (Trinity S; Riddlesdown S; Heath Clark C), b Clapham, London 11 Mar 1975. Son of A.R. (see below); brother of M.A. (see SURREY). 5'9". RHB, RM.

**DALTON, Alistair** John (Millfield S), b Bridgend 27 Apr 1973. 5'7". RHB, RM. Wales 1992.

**JONES, Robin** Owen (Millfield S; Durham U), b Crewe, Cheshire 4 Oct 1973. Brother of G.W. (see CAMBRIDGE U). 5'10". RHB, OB.

**LEFEBVRE, Roland** Philippe (Montessori Lyceum, Rotterdam; Hague Accademie of Physiotherapy), b Rotterdam, Holland 7 Feb 1963. 6'1". RHB, RMF. Somerset 1990-92 (cap 1991). Holland 1983-90; ICC Trophy 1986 and 1989. Canterbury 1990-91. HS 100 Sm v Worcs (W-s-M) 1991. BB 6-53 Canterbury v Auckland (Auckland) 1990-91. Sm BB 5-30 v Glos (Taunton) 1990. **NWT:** HS 21* Sm v Warwks (Birmingham) 1991. BB 7-15 Sm v Devon (Torquay) 1990. **BHC:** HS 37 Sm v Middx (Lord's) 1990. BB 3-44 Sm v Surrey (Taunton) 1991. **SL:** HS 28 Sm v Yorks (Scarborough) 1990. BB 4-35 Sm v Northants (Taunton) 1990.

**PURDIE, Scott** (St Kentigern C, NZ), b Baillieston, Glasgow 18 Apr 1974. 6'3". RHB, RMF.

## DEPARTURES

**BUTCHER, Alan** Raymond (Heath Clark GS), b Croydon, Surrey 7 Jan 1954. Brother of I.P. (Leics 1980-87 and Glos 1988-90) and M.S. (Surrey 1982), father of M.A. (see Surrey) and G.P. (see above). 5'8½". LHB, SLA/LM. Surrey 1972-86 (cap 1975; benefit 1985). Glamorgan 1987-92 (cap 1987; captain 1989-92). Wisden 1990. **Tests:** 1 (1979); HS 20 v I (Oval) 1979. LOI: 1. Tours: WI 1982-83 (Int); I 1980-81 (Overseas XI); Z 1990-91 (Gm – captain). 1000 runs (12) inc 2000 (1): 2116 (1990). HS 216* Sy v CU (Cambridge) 1980. BAC HS 188 Sy v Sussex (Hove) 1978. Gm HS 171* v Warwks (Birmingham) 1989. BB 6-48 Sy v Hants (Guildford) 1972. Gm BB 3-35 v Middx (Cardiff) 1987. Awards: NWT 3; BHC 6. **NWT:** HS 104* v Middx (Lord's) 1990. BB 1-27. **BHC:** HS 127 v Yorks (Cardiff) 1991. BB 4-36 Sy v Middx (Lord's) 1985. **SL:** HS 113* Sy v Warwks (Birmingham) 1978. BB 5-19 Sy v Glos (Bristol) 1975. Appointed captain/coach Essex 2nd XI 1993.

continued on p 155

# GLAMORGAN 1992

## RESULTS SUMMARY

| | Place | Won | Lost | Drew | Abandoned |
|---|---|---|---|---|---|
| Britannic Assurance Championship | 14th | 5 | 4 | 13 | |
| All First-class Matches | | 5 | 5 | 14 | |
| Sunday League | 16th | 4 | 10 | | 3 |
| NatWest Trophy | Quarter-Finalist | | | | |
| Benson and Hedges Cup | 4th in Group D | | | | |

# BRITANNIC ASSURANCE CHAMPIONSHIP AVERAGES

## BATTING AND FIELDING

| Cap | | M | I | NO | HS | Runs | Avge | 100 | 50 | Ct/St |
|---|---|---|---|---|---|---|---|---|---|---|
| 1992 | P.A.Cottey | 18 | 25 | 5 | 141 | 1008 | 50.40 | 2 | 5 | 9 |
| 1986 | H.Morris | 22 | 36 | 3 | 146 | 1546 | 46.84 | 6 | 5 | 15 |
| 1992 | A.Dale | 20 | 30 | 4 | 150* | 1056 | 40.61 | 2 | 6 | 7 |
| 1987 | M.P.Maynard | 22 | 35 | 4 | 176 | 1191 | 38.41 | 2 | 7 | 19 |
| 1992 | S.P.James | 22 | 37 | 4 | 152* | 1238 | 37.51 | 2 | 6 | 20 |
| 1990 | I.V.A.Richards | 14 | 23 | – | 127 | 722 | 31.39 | 1 | 4 | 18 |
| 1992 | R.D.B.Croft | 22 | 32 | 9 | 60* | 592 | 25.73 | – | 2 | 10 |
| – | D.L.Hemp | 10 | 15 | 2 | 84* | 276 | 21.23 | – | 2 | 6 |
| 1987 | C.P.Metson | 22 | 27 | 6 | 46* | 417 | 19.85 | – | – | 48/5 |
| – | D.J.Foster | 7 | 4 | 1 | 17* | 40 | 13.33 | – | – | – |
| 1989 | S.L.Watkin | 21 | 23 | 4 | 41 | 147 | 7.73 | – | – | 5 |
| – | S.D.Thomas | 6 | 7 | 2 | 10 | 25 | 5.00 | – | – | 1 |
| 1987 | S.R.Barwick | 17 | 14 | 4 | 9* | 31 | 3.10 | – | – | 6 |
| – | S.Bastien | 10 | 10 | 3 | 9* | 21 | 3.00 | – | – | 3 |
| 1991 | M.Frost | 6 | 4 | 1 | 4 | 4 | 1.33 | – | – | 2 |

*Also played:* A.R.Butcher (2 matches – cap 1987) 23, 8, 59* (1 ct); C.S.Cowdrey (1 match) did not bat (1 ct).

## BOWLING

| | O | M | R | W | Avge | Best | 5wI | 10wM |
|---|---|---|---|---|---|---|---|---|
| S.D.Thomas | 113.2 | 18 | 404 | 18 | 22.44 | 5-79 | 2 | – |
| R.D.B.Croft | 610.4 | 114 | 2010 | 65 | 30.92 | 8-66 | 5 | 1 |
| S.L.Watkin | 665.3 | 146 | 2046 | 66 | 31.00 | 6-97 | 1 | – |
| A.Dale | 211 | 53 | 594 | 15 | 39.60 | 3-30 | – | – |
| S.R.Barwick | 578 | 152 | 1545 | 36 | 42.91 | 4-67 | – | – |
| D.J.Foster | 171.3 | 25 | 737 | 17 | 43.35 | 5-87 | 1 | – |
| S.Bastien | 305.3 | 73 | 954 | 19 | 50.21 | 5-95 | 1 | – |

*Also bowled:* P.A.Cottey 6-2-25-0; M.Frost 155.1-24-664-9; M.P.Maynard 7-0-72-1; C.P.Metson 1-1-0-0; H.Morris 4.5-0-57-0; I.V.A.Richards 12-2-34-0.

The First-Class Averages (pp 164-178) give the records of Glamorgan players in all first-class county matches (their other opponents being the Pakistanis and Oxford U), with the exception of H.Morris whose full county figures are as above.

# GLAMORGAN RECORDS

## FIRST-CLASS CRICKET

| | | | | | |
|---|---|---|---|---|---|
| **Highest Total** | For | 587-8d | | v Derbyshire | Cardiff | 1951 |
| | V | 653-6d | | by Glos | Bristol | 1928 |
| **Lowest Total** | For | 22 | | v Lancashire | Liverpool | 1924 |
| | V | 33 | | by Leics | Ebbw Vale | 1965 |
| **Highest Innings** | For | 287* | D.E.Davies | v Glos | Newport | 1939 |
| | V | 313* | S.J.Cook | for Somerset | Cardiff | 1990 |

### Highest Partnership for each Wicket

| | | | | | |
|---|---|---|---|---|---|
| 1st | 330 | A.Jones/R.C.Fredericks | v Northants | Swansea | 1972 |
| 2nd | 249 | S.P.James/H.Morris | v Oxford U | Oxford | 1987 |
| 3rd | 313 | D.E.Davies/W.E.Jones | v Essex | Brentwood | 1948 |
| 4th | 306* | Javed Miandad/Younis Ahmed | v Australians | Neath | 1985 |
| 5th | 264 | M.Robinson/S.W.Montgomery | v Hampshire | Bournemouth | 1949 |
| 6th | 230 | W.E.Jones/B.L.Muncer | v Worcs | Worcester | 1953 |
| 7th | 195* | W.Wooller/W.E.Jones | v Lancashire | Liverpool | 1947 |
| 8th | 202 | D.Davies/J.J.Hills | v Sussex | Eastbourne | 1928 |
| 9th | 203* | J.J.Hills/J.C.Clay | v Worcs | Swansea | 1929 |
| 10th | 143 | T.Davies/S.A.B.Daniels | v Glos | Swansea | 1982 |

| | | | | | |
|---|---|---|---|---|---|
| **Best Bowling** | For | 10-51 | J.Mercer | v Worcs | Worcester | 1936 |
| **(Innings)** | V | 10-18 | G.Geary | for Leics | Pontypridd | 1929 |
| **Best Bowling** | For | 17-212 | J.C.Clay | v Worcs | Swansea | 1937 |
| **(Match)** | V | 16-96 | G.Geary | for Leics | Pontypridd | 1929 |

| | | | | |
|---|---|---|---|---|
| **Most Runs – Season** | 2,276 | H.Morris | (av 55.51) | 1990 |
| **Most Runs – Career** | 34,056 | A.Jones | (av 33.03) | 1957-1983 |
| **Most 100s – Season** | 10 | H.Morris | | 1990 |
| **Most 100s – Career** | 52 | A.Jones | | 1957-1983 |
| **Most Wkts – Season** | 176 | J.C.Clay | (av 17.34) | 1937 |
| **Most Wkts – Career** | 2,174 | D.J.Shepherd | (av 20.95) | 1950-1972 |

## LIMITED-OVERS CRICKET

| | | | | | |
|---|---|---|---|---|---|
| **Highest Total** | NWT | 345-2 | | v Durham | Darlington | 1991 |
| | BHC | 302-6 | | v Comb Univs | Cardiff | 1988 |
| | SL | 277-6 | | v Derbyshire | Ebbw Vale | 1984 |
| **Lowest Total** | NWT | 76 | | v Northants | Northampton | 1968 |
| | BHC | 68 | | v Lancashire | Manchester | 1973 |
| | SL | 42 | | v Derbyshire | Swansea | 1979 |
| **Highest Innings** | NWT | 154* | H.Morris | v Staffs | Cardiff | 1989 |
| | BHC | 143* | H.Morris | v Hampshire | Southampton | 1989 |
| | SL | 130* | J.A.Hopkins | v Somerset | Bath | 1983 |
| **Best Bowling** | NWT | 5-13 | R.J.Shastri | v Scotland | Edinburgh | 1988 |
| | BHC | 5-17 | A.H.Wilkins | v Worcs | Worcester | 1978 |
| | SL | 6-29 | M.A.Nash | v Worcs | Worcester | 1975 |

# GLOUCESTERSHIRE

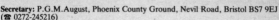

**Formation of Present Club:** 1871
**Colours:** Blue, Gold, Brown, Silver, Green and Red
**Badge:** Coat of Arms of the City and County of Bristol
**Championships (since 1890):** (0) Second 1930, 1931, 1947, 1959, 1969, 1986
**NatWest Trophy/Gillette Cup Winners:** (1) 1973
**Benson and Hedges Cup Winners:** (1) 1977
**Sunday League Champions:** (0) Second 1988
**Match Awards:** NWT 36; BHC 43

**Secretary:** P.G.M.August, Phoenix County Ground, Nevil Road, Bristol BS7 9EJ (☎ 0272-245216)
**Captain:** A.J.Wright
**Scorer:** B.H.Jenkins
**1993 Beneficiary:** D.V.Lawrence

**ALLEYNE, Mark** Wayne (Harrison C, Barbados; Cardinal Pole S, London E9; Haringey Cricket C), b Tottenham, London 23 May 1968. 5'10". RHB, RM. Debut 1986. Cap 1990. Tour: SL 1986-87 (Gs). 1000 runs (2); most – 1121 (1991). HS 256 v Northants (Northampton) 1990. BB 4-48 v Glam (Bristol) 1988. **NWT:** HS 45 v Notts (Bristol) 1991. BB 5-30 v Lincs (Gloucester) 1990. **BHC:** HS 36 v Derbys (Derby) 1987. BB 5-27 v Comb Us (Bristol) 1988. **SL:** HS 134* v Leics (Bristol) 1992. BB 4-35 v Lancs (Manchester) 1992.

**BABINGTON, Andrew** Mark (Reigate GS; Borough Road PE College), b Middlesex Hospital, London 22 Jul 1963. 6'2". LHB, RFM. Sussex 1986-90. Gloucestershire debut 1991. HS 58 v Sussex (Cheltenham) 1991. BB 8-107 v Kent (Bristol) 1992. Hat-trick 1986. **NWT:** HS 4*. BB 3-8 v Cheshire (Bristol) 1992. **BHC:** HS 27 v Leics (Cheltenham) 1992. BB 4-29 Sx v Surrey (Hove) 1988. **SL:** HS 11 v Essex (Cheltenham) 1991. BB 4-21 v Northants (Moreton) 1992.

**BALL, Martyn** Charles John (King Edmund SS; Bath CFE), b Bristol 26 Apr 1970. 5'8". RHB, OB. Debut 1988. HS 54 v Somerset (Taunton) 1992. BB 5-101 v Sussex (Cheltenham) 1992. **NWT:** 16* v Essex (Cheltenham) 1992. BB 3-42 v Lancs (Gloucester) 1989. **BHC:** HS 13 v Middx (Lord's) 1992. BB 1-39. **SL:** HS 19 v Surrey (Bristol) 1992. BB 2-33 v Worcs (Worcester) 1992.

**BROAD, Brian Christopher** (Colston's S, Bristol; St. Paul's C, Cheltenham), b Knowle, Bristol 29 Sep 1957. 6'4". LHB, RM. Gloucestershire 1979-83 (cap 1981). Nottinghamshire 1984-92 (cap 1984). OFS 1985-86 (captain). **Tests:** 25 (1984 to 1989); HS 162 v A (Perth) 1986-87. LOI: 34. Tours: A 1986-87, 1987-88; SA 1989-90 (Eng XI); NZ 1987-88; P 1987-88; Z 1984-85 (EC). 1000 runs (10) inc 2000 (1): 2226 (1990). HS 227* Nt v Kent (Tunbridge W) 1990. Gs HS 145 v Notts (Bristol) 1983. BB 2-14 v WI (Bristol) 1980. Awards: NWT 4; BHC 2. **NWT:** HS 115 Nt v Bucks (Marlow) 1990. **BHC:** HS 122 Nt v Derbys (Derby) 1984. BB 2-73 Nt v Lancs (Nottingham) 1984. **SL:** HS 108 Nt v Glam (Cardiff) 1991. BB 3-46 v Worcs (Bristol) 1982.

**DAVIES, Mark** (Cwrt Sart CS; Neath Tertiary C), b Neath, Glam 18 Apr 1969. 5'6". RHB, SLA. Glamorgan 1990. Gloucestershire debut 1992. MCC YC. HS 32* v Yorks (Cheltenham) 1992. 50 wkts (1): 56 (1992). BB 4-73 v Durham (Stockton) 1992. **SL:** HS -.

**DAWSON, Robert** Ian (Millfield S; Newcastle Poly), b Exmouth, Devon 29 Mar 1970. 5'11". RHB, RM. Debut 1992. Devon 1988-91. HS 29 v Middx (Lord's) 1992. **NWT:** HS -. **SL:** HS 35 v Sussex (Cheltenham) 1992.

**De La PENA, Jason** Michael (Stowe S; Bournside S), b London 16 Sep 1972. 6'4". RHB, RFM. Debut 1991. HS 1*. BB 2-69 v Leics (Hinckley) 1991.

**GERRARD, Martin** James (Grittleton House S; St Brendan's SFC; Wales Poly), b Southmead, Bristol 19 May 1967. 6'3". RHB, LMF. Debut 1991. W Transvaal 1991-92. HS 42 v Somerset (Bristol) 1991. BB 6-40 (10-60 match) v SL (Bristol) 1991. BAC BB 2-25 v Sussex (Cheltenham) 1991. **BHC:** HS 1*. **SL:** HS 7. BB 2-35 v Surrey (Bristol) 1992.

**HANCOCK, Timothy** Harold Coulter (St Edward's S, Oxford; Henley C), b Reading, Berkshire 20 Apr 1972. 5'10". RHB, RM. Debut 1991. Oxfordshire 1990. HS 102 v Somerset (Taunton) 1992. BB 2-43 v Northants (Bristol) 1992. **BHC:** HS 12 (twice) 1992. **SL:** HS 20 v Warwks (Birmingham) 1991.

**HINKS, Simon** Graham (St George's S, Gravesend), b Northfleet, Kent 12 Oct 1960. 6'2". LHB, RM. Kent 1982-91 (cap 1985). Gloucestershire debut 1992. 1000 runs (3); most – 1588 (1990). HS 234 K v Middx (Canterbury) 1990 sharing in Kent record 2nd wkt stand of 366 with N.R.Taylor. Gs HS 88* v Lancs (Manchester) 1992. BB 2-18 K v Notts (Nottingham) 1989. Awards: NWT 1; BHC 1. **NWT:** HS 95 K v Surrey (Canterbury) 1985. **BHC:** HS 85 K v Sussex (Canterbury) 1987. BB 1-15. **SL:** HS 99 K v Glam (Maidstone) 1986. BB 1-3.

**HODGSON, Geoffrey** Dean (Nelson Thomlinson CS, Wigton; Loughborough U), b Carlisle, Cumberland 22 Oct 1966. 6'1". RHB. Debut 1989. Cap 1992. Cumberland 1984-88 (cap 1987 when aged 20 – county record). Warwickshire (SL only) 1987. 1000 runs (3); most – 1320 (1990). HS 147 v Essex (Southend) 1992. Awards: BHC 2. **NWT:** HS 52 v Lancs (Manchester) 1990. **BHC:** HS 103* v Minor C (Cheltenham) 1992. **SL:** HS 84* v Notts (Nottingham) 1992.

**HORRELL, Ryan** (Pilton Community C), b Barnstaple, Devon 7 Apr 1973. 5'10". LHB, SLA. Devon 1991. Awaiting f-c debut. No 1st XI appearances – joined staff 1992.

**LAWRENCE, David** Valentine (Linden S), b Gloucester 28 Jan 1964. 6'2". RHB, RF. Debut 1981. Cap 1985. Benefit 1993. YC 1985. **Tests:** 5 (1988 to 1991-92); HS 34 v WI (Nottingham) 1991; BB 5-106 v WI (Oval) 1991. LOI: 1. Tours: NZ 1991-92; SL 1985-86 (Eng B); 1986-87 (Gs). HS 66 v Glam (Abergavenny) 1991. 50 wkts (5); most – 85 (1985). BB 7-47 v Surrey (Cheltenham) 1988. Hat-trick 1990. Awards: NWT 2; BHC 2. **NWT:** HS 5*. BB 5-17 v Norfolk (Bristol) 1991. **BHC:** HS 23 and BB 6-20 v Comb Us (Bristol) 1991. **SL:** HS 38* v Yorks (Scarborough) 1991. BB 5-18 v Somerset (Bristol) 1990. Missed 1992 season (fractured kneecap).

**RUSSELL, Robert** Charles (**Jack**) (Archway CS), b Stroud 15 Aug 1963. 5'8½". LHB, WK, occ OB. Debut 1981. Cap 1985. Wisden 1989. **Tests:** 31 (1988 to 1992); HS 128* v A (Manchester) 1989. LOI: 26. Tours: A 1990-91; WI 1989-90; NZ 1991-92; P 1987-88; SL 1986-87 (Gs). HS 128* (Tests). Gs HS 120 v Somerset (Bristol) 1990. BB 1-4. Award: BHC 1. **NWT:** HS 42* v Lancs (Gloucester) 1989. **BHC:** HS 51 v Worcs (Worcester) 1991. **SL:** HS 108 v Worcs (Hereford) 1986.

**SCOTT, Richard** John (Queen Elizabeth S, Bournemouth), b Bournemouth, Hants 2 Nov 1963. 5'11". LHB, RM. Hampshire 1988-90. Gloucestershire debut 1991. Dorset 1981-85. HS 127 v Worcs (Worcester) 1991 – on Gs debut. BB 3-43 v Sussex (Hove) 1991. **NWT:** HS 25 v Cheshire (Bristol) 1992. BB 4-22 v Norfolk (Bristol) 1991. **BHC:** HS 69 H v Sussex (Hove) 1989. BB 1-42. **SL:** HS 116* H v Yorks (Southampton) 1989. BB 3-23 v Northants (Moreton) 1992.

**SMITH, Andrew Michael** (Queen Elizabeth GS, Wakefield; Exeter U), b Dewsbury, Yorks 1 Oct 1967. 5'9". RHB, LM. Debut 1991. Comb Us (BHC) 1988-90. HS 51* v Warwks (Bristol) 1992. BB 4-41 v Leics (Hinckley) 1991. **NWT:** HS 6 and BB 3-45 v Somerset (Taunton) 1992. **BHC:** HS 15* Comb Us v Surrey (Oxford) 1990. BB 4-49 Comb Us v Somerset (Oxford) 1988. **SL:** HS 15* v Essex (Cheltenham) 1991. BB 4-38 v Leics (Bristol) 1992.

**WALSH, Courtney** Andrew (Excelsior HS), b Kingston, Jamaica 30 Oct 1962. 6'5½". RHB, RF. Jamaica 1981-82 to date (captain 1990-91 to date). Gloucestershire debut 1984. Cap 1985. Benefit 1992. Wisden 1986. **Tests** (WI): 51 (1984-85 to 1991-92); HS 30* v A (Melbourne) 1988-89; BB 6-62 v I (Kingston) 1988-89. LOI (WI): 97. Tours (WI): E 1984, 1988, 1991; A 1984-85, 1986-87, 1988-89; NZ 1986-87; I 1987-88; P 1986-87, 1990-91; Z 1983-84 (Young WI). HS 63* v Yorks (Cheltenham) 1990. 50 wkts (6) inc 100 (1): 118 (1986). BB 9-72 v Somerset (Bristol) 1986. Awards: NWT 2. **NWT:** HS 25* v Berks (Reading) 1986. BB 6-21 v Kent (Bristol) 1990 and v Cheshire (Bristol) 1992. **BHC:** HS 28 v Comb Us (Bristol) 1989. BB 2-19 v Scot (Bristol) 1985. **SL:** HS 35 v Glam (Cardiff) 1986. BB 4-19 v Kent (Cheltenham) 1987.

**WILLIAMS, Ricardo** Cecil (Ellerslie SS, Barbados; Haringey Cricket C), b Camberwell, London 3 Feb 1968. 5'9". RHB, RMF. HS 44 v Notts (Worksop) 1992. BB 3-44 v P (Bristol) 1992. BAC BB 1-46. **SL:** HS -.

**WILLIAMS, Richard** Charles James (Millfield S), b Southmead, Bristol 8 Aug 1969. 5'8". LHB, WK. Debut 1990. HS 55* v Derbys (Gloucester) 1991. **SL:** HS 17 v Warwks (Bristol) 1992.

**WINDOWS, Matthew** Guy Newman (Clifton C), b Bristol 5 Apr 1973. Son of A.R. (Glos and CU 1960-68). 5'7". RHB. Debut 1992. HS 71 v Essex (Bristol) 1992 – on debut.

**WRIGHT, Anthony** John (Alleyn's GS) b Stevenage, Herts 27 Jun 1962. 6'0". RHB, RM. Gloucestershire debut 1982. Cap 1987. Captain 1990-. Tour: SL 1986-87 (Gs). 1000 runs (4): most – 1596 (1991). HS 161 v Glam (Bristol) 1987. BB 1-16. Awards: NWT 1; BHC 1. **NWT:** HS 107* v Cheshire (Bristol) 1992. **BHC:** HS 97 v Worcs (Bristol) 1990. **SL:** HS 93 v Durham (Stockton) 1992.

### NEWCOMERS

**CUNLIFFE, Robert** John (Banbury S; Banbury TC), b Oxford 8 Nov 1973. 5'10". RHB, RM. Oxfordshire 1991-92.

**WIGHT, Robert Marcus** (KCS, Wimbledon; Exeter U; Trinity Hall, Cambridge), b London 12 Sep 1969. Nephew of P.B. (British Guiana, Somerset & Canterbury 1950/51-1965). 6'2". RHB, OB. Debut/blue Cambridge U 1992. HS 62* CU v OU (Lord's) 1992. BB 3-65 CU v Kent (Cambridge) 1992. Hockey for Devon 1989-91; CU blue 1991-92 (captain 1992).

### DEPARTURES

**ATHEY, C.W.J.** – see SUSSEX.

**VAUGHAN, Justin** Thomas Caldwell (Westlake BHS, Auckland; Auckland U), b Hereford 30 Aug 1967. 6'1". LHB, RM. Auckland 1989-90 to date. Gloucestershire 1992. HS 106* Auckland v Wellington 1989-90 – on debut. Gs HS 99 v Northants (Bristol) 1992. BB 5-72 Auckland v Otago (Auckland) 1991-92. Gs BB 3-46 v Middx (Lord's) 1992. **NWT:** HS 54* v Essex (Cheltenham) 1992. **BHC:** HS 12 v Leics (Cheltenham) 1992. BB 3-61 v Sussex (Hove) 1992. **SL:** HS 20 v Hants (Southampton) 1992. BB 3-31 v Sussex (Cheltenham) 1992.

# GLOUCESTERSHIRE 1992

## RESULTS SUMMARY

| | Place | Won | Lost | Drew | Abandoned |
|---|---|---|---|---|---|
| Britannic Assurance Championship | 10th | 6 | 6 | 9 | 1 |
| All First-class Matches | | 6 | 7 | 9 | 1 |
| Sunday League | 8th | 8 | 8 | | 1 |
| NatWest Trophy | Quarter-Finalist | | | | |
| Benson and Hedges Cup | 6th in Group A | | | | |

# BRITANNIC ASSURANCE CHAMPIONSHIP AVERAGES

## BATTING AND FIELDING

| Cap | | M | I | NO | HS | Runs | Avge | 100 | 50 | Ct/St |
|---|---|---|---|---|---|---|---|---|---|---|
| 1985 | R.C.Russell | 16 | 28 | 9 | 75 | 904 | 47.57 | – | 5 | 30/2 |
| – | J.T.C.Vaughan | 10 | 16 | 4 | 99 | 450 | 37.50 | – | 4 | 9 |
| 1992 | G.D.Hodgson | 20 | 34 | 1 | 147 | 1214 | 36.78 | 2 | 8 | 10 |
| 1990 | M.W.Alleyne | 21 | 34 | 3 | 93 | 1030 | 33.22 | – | 7 | 21 |
| 1985 | C.W.J.Athey | 20 | 32 | 4 | 181 | 1022 | 31.93 | 2 | 4 | 19 |
| – | S.G.Hinks | 10 | 16 | 3 | 88* | 402 | 30.92 | – | 3 | 3 |
| – | T.H.C.Hancock | 9 | 15 | 1 | 102 | 396 | 28.28 | 1 | 2 | 8 |
| 1987 | A.J.Wright | 18 | 31 | 3 | 128 | 754 | 26.92 | 1 | 3 | 10 |
| – | R.J.Scott | 19 | 31 | 3 | 73 | 751 | 26.82 | – | 4 | 7 |
| – | A.M.Smith | 11 | 12 | 5 | 51* | 165 | 23.57 | – | 1 | 2 |
| – | R.C.J.Williams | 5 | 5 | 2 | 18* | 51 | 17.00 | – | – | 9/4 |
| – | M.C.J.Ball | 12 | 21 | 6 | 54 | 201 | 13.40 | – | 2 | 6 |
| – | R.C.Williams | 6 | 9 | 1 | 44 | 100 | 12.50 | – | – | – |
| 1985 | C.A.Walsh | 18 | 27 | 3 | 51 | 280 | 11.66 | – | 1 | 7 |
| – | A.M.Babington | 8 | 9 | 3 | 24 | 63 | 10.50 | – | – | 3 |
| – | M.Davies | 18 | 21 | 9 | 32* | 123 | 10.25 | – | – | 9 |
| – | R.I.Dawson | 5 | 6 | – | 29 | 58 | 9.66 | – | – | 2 |
| – | M.J.Gerrard | 4 | 4 | 1 | 4 | 6 | 2.00 | – | – | 1 |

*Also played:* M.G.N.Windows (1 match) 71 (1 ct).

## BOWLING

| | O | M | R | W | Avge | Best | 5wI | 10wM |
|---|---|---|---|---|---|---|---|---|
| C.A.Walsh | 587.2 | 138 | 1469 | 92 | 15.96 | 7-27 | 8 | 2 |
| M.Davies | 529.5 | 138 | 1537 | 55 | 27.94 | 4-73 | – | – |
| A.M.Smith | 232.2 | 35 | 764 | 23 | 33.21 | 3-53 | – | – |
| J.T.C.Vaughan | 178.4 | 40 | 499 | 15 | 33.26 | 3-46 | – | – |
| M.W.Alleyne | 133.1 | 29 | 489 | 14 | 34.92 | 3-25 | – | – |
| M.C.J.Ball | 322 | 61 | 1072 | 28 | 38.28 | 5-101 | 1 | – |
| A.M.Babington | 162 | 17 | 642 | 14 | 45.85 | 8-107 | 1 | – |
| R.J.Scott | 267.4 | 40 | 959 | 20 | 47.95 | 2-9 | – | – |

*Also bowled:* C.W.J.Athey 58-7-184-2; M.J.Gerrard 93-20-297-7; T.H.C.Hancock 26.4-2-102-3; S.G.Hinks 2.5-1-14-0; G.D.Hodgson 4-0-65-0; R.C.Williams 48-5-209-2; A.J.Wright 2-0-27-0.

The First-Class Averages (pp 164-178) give the records of Gloucestershire players in all first-class county matches (their other opponents being the Pakistanis), with the exception of:

R.C.Russell 17-30-9-75-929-44.23-0-5-34ct/2st. Did not bowl.

# GLOUCESTERSHIRE RECORDS

## FIRST-CLASS CRICKET

| | | | | | |
|---|---|---|---|---|---|
| **Highest Total** | For 653-6d | | v Glamorgan | Bristol | 1928 |
| | V 774-7d | | by Australians | Bristol | 1948 |
| **Lowest Total** | For 17 | | v Australians | Cheltenham | 1896 |
| | V 12 | | by Northants | Gloucester | 1907 |
| **Highest Innings** | For 318* | W.G.Grace | v Yorkshire | Cheltenham | 1876 |
| | V 296 | A.O.Jones | for Notts | Nottingham | 1903 |

**Highest Partnership for each Wicket**

| | | | | | |
|---|---|---|---|---|---|
| 1st | 395 | D.M.Young/R.B.Nicholls | v Oxford U | Oxford | 1962 |
| 2nd | 256 | C.T.M.Pugh/T.W.Graveney | v Derbyshire | Chesterfield | 1960 |
| 3rd | 336 | W.R.Hammond/B.H.Lyon | v Leics | Leicester | 1933 |
| 4th | 321 | W.R.Hammond/W.L.Neale | v Leics | Gloucester | 1937 |
| 5th | 261 | W.G.Grace/W.O.Moberley | v Yorkshire | Cheltenham | 1876 |
| 6th | 320 | G.L.Jessop/J.H.Board | v Sussex | Hove | 1903 |
| 7th | 248 | W.G.Grace/E.L.Thomas | v Sussex | Hove | 1896 |
| 8th | 239 | W.R.Hammond/A.E.Wilson | v Lancashire | Bristol | 1938 |
| 9th | 193 | W.G.Grace/S.A.P.Kitcat | v Sussex | Bristol | 1896 |
| 10th | 131 | W.R.Gouldsworthy/J.G.Bessant | v Somerset | Bristol | 1923 |

| | | | | | |
|---|---|---|---|---|---|
| **Best Bowling** | For | 10-40 E.G.Dennett | v Essex | Bristol | 1906 |
| (Innings) | V | 10-66 A.A.Mailey | for Australians | Cheltenham | 1921 |
| | | 10-66 K.Smales | for Notts | Stroud | 1956 |
| **Best Bowling** | For | 17-56 C.W.L.Parker | v Essex | Gloucester | 1925 |
| (Match) | V | 15-87 A.J.Conway | for Worcs | Moreton-in-M | 1914 |

| | | | | |
|---|---|---|---|---|
| **Most Runs – Season** | 2,860 | W.R.Hammond (av 69.75) | | 1933 |
| **Most Runs – Career** | 33,664 | W.R.Hammond (av 57.05) | | 1920-1951 |
| **Most 100s – Season** | 13 | W.R.Hammond | | 1938 |
| **Most 100s – Career** | 113 | W.R.Hammond | | 1920-1951 |
| **Most Wkts – Season** | 222 | T.W.J.Goddard (av 16.80) | | 1937 |
| | 222 | T.W.J.Goddard (av 16.37) | | 1947 |
| **Most Wkts – Career** | 3,170 | C.W.L.Parker (av 19.43) | | 1903-1935 |

## LIMITED-OVERS CRICKET

| | | | | | |
|---|---|---|---|---|---|
| **Highest Total** | NWT | 327-7 | v Berkshire | Reading | 1966 |
| | BHC | 300-4 | v Comb Univs | Oxford | 1982 |
| | SL | 281-2 | v Hampshire | Swindon | 1991 |
| **Lowest Total** | NWT | 82 | v Notts | Bristol | 1987 |
| | BHC | 62 | v Hampshire | Bristol | 1975 |
| | SL | 49 | v Middlesex | Bristol | 1978 |
| **Highest Innings** | NWT | 158 Zaheer Abbas | v Leics | Leicester | 1983 |
| | BHC | 154* M.J.Procter | v Somerset | Taunton | 1972 |
| | SL | 134* M.W.Alleyne | v Leics | Bristol | 1992 |
| **Best Bowling** | NWT | 6-21 C.A.Walsh | v Kent | Bristol | 1990 |
| | | 6-21 C.A.Walsh | v Cheshire | Bristol | 1992 |
| | BHC | 6-13 M.J.Procter | v Hampshire | Southampton | 1977 |
| | SL | 6-52 J.N.Shepherd | v Kent | Bristol | 1983 |

# HAMPSHIRE

**Formation of Present Club:** 12 August 1863
**Colours:** Blue, Gold and White
**Badge:** Tudor Rose and Crown
**Championships:** (2) 1961, 1973
**NatWest Trophy/Gillette Cup Winners:** (1) 1991
**Benson and Hedges Cup Winners:** (2) 1988, 1992
**Sunday League Champions:** (3) 1975, 1978, 1986
**Match Awards:** NWT 48; BHC 54

**Chief Executive:** A.F.Baker, County Cricket Ground, Northlands Road, Southampton SO9 2TY (☎ 0703-333788/9)
**Captain:** M.C.J.Nicholas
**Scorer:** V.H Isaacs
**1993 Beneficiary:** T.M.Tremlett (Coach)

**AYLING, Jonathan** Richard (Portsmouth GS), b Portsmouth 13 Jun 1967. 6′4″. RHB, RM. Debut 1988. Cap 1991. Took wicket of D.A.Polkinghorne (OU) with first ball in f-c cricket. HS 121 v OU (Oxford) 1992. BAC HS 90 v Durham (Darlington) 1992. BB 5-12 v Middx (Bournemouth) 1992. **NWT:** HS 29 v Leics (Leicester) 1990. BB 3-30 v Yorks (Southampton) 1990. **BHC:** HS 18* v Lancs (Manchester) 1992. BB 2-22 v Lancs (Manchester) 1990. **SL:** HS 56 v Surrey (Oval) 1991. BB 4-37 v Notts (Southampton) 1990.

**AYMES, Adrian** Nigel (Bellemoor SM, Southampton), b Southampton 4 Jun 1964. 6′0″. RHB, WK. Debut 1987. Cap 1991. HS 75* v Glam (Pontypridd) 1990. BB 1-75. **NWT:** HS 2. **BHC:** HS 11 v Essex (Southampton) 1992. **SL:** HS 33* v Northants (Northampton) 1991.

**CONNOR, Cardigan** Adolphus (The Valley SS, Anguilla; Langley C, Berkshire), b The Valley, Anguilla 24 Mar 1961. 5′9″. RHB, RFM. Debut 1984. Cap 1988. Buckinghamshire 1979-83. HS 51 v Yorks (Leeds) 1992. 50 wkts (2); most – 62 (1984). BB 7-31 v Glos (Portsmouth) 1989. **NWT:** HS 13 v Yorks (Southampton) 1990. BB 4-29 v Warwks (Birmingham) 1991. **BHC:** HS 5*. BB 4-19 v Sussex (Hove) 1989. **SL:** HS 19 v Glos (Trowbridge) 1989. BB 4-11 v Derbys (Portsmouth) 1990.

**COX, Rupert** Michael FIENNES- (Bradfield C), b Guildford, Surrey 20 Aug 1967. 5′9″. LHB, OB. Debut 1990. HS 104* v Worcs (Worcester) 1990 – in second match. **SL:** 13 v Surrey (Oval) 1991.

**FLINT, Darren** Peter John (Queen Mary's SFC), b Basingstoke 14 Jun 1970. 6′0″. RHB, SLA. No 1st XI appearances – joined staff 1990.

**GOWER, David** Ivon (King's S, Canterbury; London U), b Tunbridge Wells, Kent 1 Apr 1957. 6′0″. LHB, OB. Leicestershire 1975-89 (cap 1977; captain 1984-86, 1988-89; benefit 1987). Hampshire debut/cap 1990. Wisden 1978. YC 1978. OBE 1992. **Tests:** 117 (1978 to 1992, 32 as captain); England record aggregate (8231 runs), HS 215 v A (Birmingham) 1985; BB 1-1. **LOI:** 114. Tours (C=captain): A 1978-79, 1979-80, 1982-83, 1986-87, 1990-91; WI 1980-81, 1985-86C, 1989-90 (part); NZ 1983-84; I 1979-80, 1981-82, 1984-85C; P 1983-84; SL 1977-78 (DHR), 1981-82, 1984-85C. 1000 runs (12); most – 1530 (1982). HS 228 Le v Glam (Leicester) 1989. H HS 155 v Yorks (Basingstoke) 1992. Shared record Leics 2nd wkt stand of 289* with J.C.Balderstone v Essex (Leicester) 1981. BB 3-47 Le v Essex (Leicester) 1977. Awards: NWT 5; BHC 3 **NWT:** HS 156 Le v Derbys (Leicester) 1984. **BHC:** HS 118* v Northants (Southampton) 1992. **SL:** HS 135* Le v Warwks (Leicester) 1977.

**JAMES, Kevan** David (Edmonton County HS), b Lambeth, London 18 Mar 1961. 6′0″. LHB, LMF. Middlesex 1980-84. Wellington 1982-83. Hampshire debut 1985. Cap 1989. 1000 runs (1); most – 1274 (1991). Shared record Hants 8th wkt stand of 227 with T.M.Tremlett v Somerset (Taunton) 1985. HS 162 v Glam (Cardiff)

90

JAMES – continued:
1989. BB 6-22 v A (Southampton) 1985. BAC BB 5-25 v Glos (Southampton) 1988. **NWT:** HS 42 v Glam (Cardiff) 1989. BB 3-22 v Dorset (Southampton) 1987. **BHC:** HS 45 v Essex (Chelmsford) 1989. BB 3-31 v Middx 1987 and v Glam 1988. **SL:** HS 66 v Glos (Trowbridge) 1989. BB 4-23 v Lancs (Southampton) 1986.

**MARSHALL, Malcolm** Denzil (Parkinson CS, Barbados), b St Michael, Barbados 18 Apr 1958. 5'11". RHB, RF. Barbados 1977-78/1990-91 (capt 1987-88). Hampshire debut 1979. Cap 1981. Benefit 1987. Wisden 1982. **Tests** (WI): 81 (1978-79 to 1991); HS 92 v I (Kanpur) 1983-84; BB 7-22 v E (Manchester) 1988. LOI (WI): 136. Tours (WI): E 1980, 1984, 1988, 1991; A 1979-80, 1981-82, 1984-85, 1988-89; NZ 1979-80, 1986-87; I 1978-79, 1983-84; P 1980-81, 1986-87, 1990-91; SL 1978-79; Z 1981-82 (Young WI). HS 117 v Yorks (Leeds) 1990. 50 wkts (8+4) inc 100 (2); most – 134 (1982). 2 hat-tricks: 1978-79 (Barbados), 1983 (4 wkts in 5 balls). BB 8-71 v Worcs (Southampton) 1982. Awards: NWT 1; BHC 1. **NWT:** HS 77 v Northants (Southampton) 1990. BB 4-15 v Kent (Canterbury) 1983. **BHC:** HS 34 v Essex (Chelmsford) 1987. BB 4-26 v Kent (Canterbury) 1983. **SL:** HS 46 v Leics 1982 and v Middx 1990. BB 5-13 v Glam (Portsmouth) 1979.

**MARU, Rajesh** Jamandass (Rook's Heath HS, Harrow; Pinner SFC), b Nairobi, Kenya 28 Oct 1962. 5'6". RHB. SLA. Middlesex 1980-82. Hampshire debut 1984. Cap 1986. Tour: Z 1980-81 (M). HS 74 v Glos (Gloucester) 1988. 50 wkts (4); most – 73 (1985). BB 8-41 v Kent (Southampton) 1989. **NWT:** HS 22 v Yorks (Southampton) 1990. BB 3-46 v Leics (Leicester) 1990. **BHC:** HS 9. BB 3-46 v Comb Us (Southampton) 1990. **SL:** HS 33* v Glam (Ebbw Vale) 1991. BB 3-30 v Leics (Leicester) 1988.

**MIDDLETON, Tony** Charles (Montgomery of Alamein S, and Peter Symonds SFC, Winchester), b Winchester 1 Feb 1964. 5'10½". RHB, SLA. Debut 1984. Cap 1990. 1000 runs (2); most – 1780 (1992). HS 221 v Surrey (Southampton) 1992. BB 2-41 v Kent (Canterbury) 1991. **NWT:** HS 78 v Surrey (Lord's) 1991 (on debut). **BHC:** HS 65 v Middx (Southampton) 1992. **SL:** HS 98 v Northants (Bournemouth) 1992.

**MORRIS, Robert Sean** Millner (Stowe S; Durham U), b Great Horwood, Bucks 10 Sep 1968. RHB, OB. 6'0". Debut 1992. HS 74 v Worcs (Southampton) 1992. **SL:** HS 4*.

**NICHOLAS, Mark** Charles Jefford (Bradfield C), b London 29 Sep 1957. Grandson of F.W.H. (Essex 1912-29). 5'11". RHB, RM. Debut 1978. Cap 1982. Captain 1985-. Benefit 1991. Tours (C=captain): SL 1985-86C (Eng B); Z 1984-85C (EC), 1989-90 (Eng A). 1000 runs (8); most – 1559 (1984). HS 206* v OU (Oxford) 1982. BAC HS 158 v Lancs (Portsmouth) 1984. BB 6-37 v Somerset (Southampton) 1989. Award: BHC 1. **NWT:** HS 71 v Surrey (Oval) 1989. BB 2-39 v Berks (Southampton) 1985. **BHC:** HS 74 v Glam (Southampton) 1985. BB 4-34 v Minor C (Reading) 1985. **SL:** HS 108 v Glos (Bristol) 1984. BB 4-30 v Glos (Trowbridge) 1989.

**SHINE, Kevin** James (Maiden Erlegh CS), b Bracknell, Berkshire 22 Feb 1969. 6'2½". RHB, RFM. Debut 1989. Berkshire 1986. HS 26* v Middx (Lord's) 1989. BB 8-47 (8 wkts in 38 balls inc hat-trick and 4 in 5; 13-105 match) v Lancs (Manchester) 1992. **BHC:** HS 0. BB 4-68 v Surrey (Oval) 1990. **SL:** HS 2*. BB 2-35 v Lancs (Southampton) 1991.

**SMITH, Robin** Arnold (Northlands HS), b Durban, SA 13 Sep 1963. Brother of C.L. (Natal, Glam, Hants and England 1977/78-92) and grandson of Dr V.L.Shearer (Natal). 5'11". RHB, LB. Natal 1980-81/1984-85. Hampshire debut 1982. Cap 1985. Wisden 1989. **Tests:** 36 (1988 to 1992); HS 148* v WI (Lord's) 1991. LOI: 47. Tours: A 1990-91; WI 1989-90; NZ 1991-92. 1000 (6); most – 1577 (1989). HS 209* v Essex (Southend) 1987. BB 2-11 v Surrey (Southampton) 1985. Awards: NWT 5; BHC 3. **NWT:** HS 125* v Surrey (Oval) 1989. BB 2-13 v Berks (Southampton) 1988. **BHC:** HS 155* v Glam (Southampton) 1989. **SL:** HS 131 v Notts (Nottingham) 1989. BB 1-0.

**TERRY, Vivian Paul** (Millfield S), b Osnabruck, W Germany 14 Jan 1959. 6'0". RHB, RM. Debut 1978. Cap 1983. **Tests**: 2 (1984); HS 8. Tour: Z 1984-85 (EC). 1000 runs (8); most – 1382 (1987). HS 190 v SL (Southampton) 1988. BAC HS 180 v Derbys (Derby) 1990. Shared record Hants 1st wkt stand of 347 with C.L.Smith v Warwks (Birmingham) 1987. Awards: NWT 4; BHC 4. **NWT**: HS 165* v Berks (Southampton) 1985. **BHC**: HS 134 v Comb Us (Southampton) 1990. **SL**: HS 142 v Leics (Southampton) 1986.

**THURSFIELD, Martin John** (Boldon CS), b South Shields, Co Durham 14 Dec 1971. 6'3". RHB, RM. Middlesex 1990. Hampshire debut 1992. MCC YC. HS -. BB 1-11.

**TURNER, Ian John** (Cowplain SS; Southdown C), b Denmead 18 Jul 1968. 6'1". RHB, SLA. Debut 1989. HS 39* v Glam (Swansea) 1991. BB 5-81 v Essex (Chelmsford) 1992. **SL**: HS -. BB 2-31 v Northants (Bournemouth) 1992.

**UDAL, Shaun David** (Cove CS), b Farnborough 18 Mar 1969. Grandson of G.F. (Middx 1932 and Leics 1946). 6'2". RHB, OB. Debut 1989. Cap 1992. HS 44 v Essex (Chelmsford) 1992. 50 wkts (1): 58 (1992). BB 8-50 v Sussex (Southampton) 1992. Awards: NWT 1; BHC 1. **NWT**: HS 2. BB 3-39 v Kent (Southampton) 1992. **BHC**: HS 9. BB 4-40 v Middx (Southampton) 1992. **SL**: HS 23 v Glam (Ebbw Vale) 1991. BB 4-51 v Northants (Bournemouth) 1992.

**WOOD, Julian Ross** (Leighton Park S, Reading), b Winchester 21 Nov 1968. 5'8". LHB, RM. Debut 1989. MCC YC. HS 96 v Northants (Northampton) 1989. BB 1-5. Award: BHC 1. **NWT**: HS 3*. **BHC**: HS 70* v Minor C (Trowbridge) 1991. **SL**: HS 66 v Notts (Nottingham) 1989.

## NEWCOMERS

**BOVILL, James Noel Bruce** (Charterhouse S; Durham U), b High Wycombe, Bucks 2 Jun 1971. Son of M.E. (Dorset 1957-60). 6'1". RHB, RFM. Buckinghamshire 1990-92. Comb US (BHC) 1992. **BHC**: HS 14* and BB 1-39 Comb Us v Glam (Cardiff) 1992.

**BYRNE, James Robert** (St Paul's RCS; Salford TC), b Wythenshawe, Manchester 1 Apr 1973. 5'10". RHB, RFM.

**GARAWAY, Mark** (Sandown HS, I.o.W.), b Swindon, Wilts 20 Jul 1973. 5'8". RHB, WK. MCC YC.

**JEAN-JACQUES, Martin** (Aylestone SS, London), b Soufriere, Dominica 2 Jul 1960. 6'0". RHB, RMF. Derbyshire 1986-92. Buckinghamshire 1983-85. HS 73 De v Yorks (Sheffield) 1986 (on debut, sharing Derbys record 10th wkt stand of 132 with A.Hill). BB 8-77 De v Kent (Derby) 1986. **NWT**: HS 16 De v Surrey (Derby) 1986. BB 3-23 De v Cambs (Wisbech) 1987. **BHC**: HS 2*. BB 3-22 De v Notts (Nottingham) 1987. **SL**: HS 23 De v Lancs (Derby) 1991. BB 3-36 De v Worcs (Worcester) 1986.

## DEPARTURES

**BAKKER, Paul-Jan** (Hugo De Groot C, The Hague), b Vlaardingen, Holland 19 Aug 1957. 5'11". RHB, RMF. Hampshire 1986-92 (cap 1989). HS 22 v Yorks (Southampton) 1989 and v Glam (Portsmouth) 1992. 50 wkts (1): 77 (1989). BB 7-31 v Kent (Bournemouth) 1987. **NWT**: HS 3*. BB 3-34 v Worcs (Worcester) 1988. **BHC**: HS 7. BB 2-19 v Comb Us (Oxford) 1986. **SL**: HS 14 v Glam (Portsmouth) 1992. BB 5-17 v Derbys (Derby) 1989.

**PARKS, Robert James** (Eastbourne GS; Southampton Inst of Technology), b Cuckfield, Sussex 15 Jun 1959. Son of J.M. (Sussex, Somerset and England 1949-76) and grandson of J.H. (Sussex and England 1924-52). 5'8". RHB, WK. Hampshire 1980-92. (cap 1982; benefit 1992). Tour: Z 1984-85 (EC). Held 10 catches in match v Derbys (Portsmouth) 1981. Holds career record Hampshire aggregate of dismissals (700 – 630ct, 70st). HS 89 v CU (Cambridge) 1984. BAC HS 80 v Derbys (Portsmouth) 1986. Award: BHC 1. **NWT**: HS 27* v Yorks (Southampton) 1990. **BHC**: HS 23* v Somerset (Taunton) 1988. **SL**: HS 38* v Essex (Portsmouth) 1987.

# HAMPSHIRE 1992

## RESULTS SUMMARY

| | Place | Won | Lost | Drew | Abandoned |
|---|---|---|---|---|---|
| Britannic Assurance Championship | 15th | 4 | 6 | 12 | |
| All First-class Matches | | 5 | 7 | 12 | |
| Sunday League | 3rd | 10 | 6 | | 1 |
| NatWest Trophy | 2nd Round | | | | |
| Benson and Hedges Cup | Winners | | | | |

# BRITANNIC ASSURANCE CHAMPIONSHIP AVERAGES

## BATTING AND FIELDING

| Cap | | M | I | NO | HS | Runs | Avge | 100 | 50 | Ct/St |
|---|---|---|---|---|---|---|---|---|---|---|
| 1983 | V.P.Terry | 11 | 17 | 2 | 141 | 766 | 51.06 | 3 | 3 | 7 |
| 1990 | T.C.Middleton | 22 | 37 | 4 | 221 | 1628 | 49.33 | 5 | 7 | 15 |
| 1990 | D.I.Gower | 16 | 26 | 5 | 155 | 1005 | 47.85 | 1 | 6 | 13 |
| 1982 | M.C.J.Nicholas | 20 | 30 | 5 | 95* | 972 | 38.88 | – | 6 | 9 |
| 1985 | R.A.Smith | 11 | 18 | 2 | 107* | 599 | 37.43 | 1 | 4 | 5 |
| 1989 | K.D.James | 21 | 33 | 2 | 116 | 1006 | 32.45 | 1 | 7 | 10 |
| – | J.R.Wood | 8 | 9 | 1 | 57 | 244 | 30.50 | – | 1 | 4 |
| 1981 | M.D.Marshall | 19 | 25 | 5 | 70 | 513 | 25.65 | – | 2 | 11 |
| 1982 | R.J.Parks | 5 | 7 | 2 | 33 | 125 | 25.00 | – | – | 15/1 |
| – | R.S.M.Morris | 4 | 8 | – | 74 | 198 | 24.75 | – | 2 | 6 |
| 1991 | A.N.Aymes | 17 | 21 | 4 | 65 | 336 | 19.76 | – | 2 | 46/4 |
| 1991 | J.R.Ayling | 17 | 25 | 1 | 90 | 472 | 19.66 | – | 2 | 4 |
| 1992 | S.D.Udal | 21 | 26 | 8 | 44 | 346 | 19.22 | – | – | 4 |
| 1988 | C.A.Connor | 16 | 13 | 5 | 51 | 127 | 15.87 | – | 1 | 5 |
| 1989 | P-J.Bakker | 5 | 5 | 1 | 22 | 63 | 15.75 | – | – | – |
| – | K.J.Shine | 14 | 10 | 6 | 22* | 59 | 14.75 | – | – | 7 |
| 1986 | R.J.Maru | 6 | 8 | 3 | 23* | 71 | 14.20 | – | – | 7 |
| – | I.J.Turner | 6 | 7 | 1 | 16 | 31 | 5.16 | – | – | 4 |

*Also played:* R.M.F.Cox (3 matches) 1, 13, 12 (1 ct).

## BOWLING

| | O | M | R | W | Avge | Best | 5wI | 10wM |
|---|---|---|---|---|---|---|---|---|
| J.R.Ayling | 326.2 | 69 | 939 | 43 | 21.83 | 5-12 | 1 | – |
| R.J.Maru | 157.2 | 54 | 331 | 15 | 22.06 | 4-8 | – | – |
| I.J.Turner | 182.4 | 51 | 519 | 19 | 27.31 | 5-81 | 1 | – |
| M.D.Marshall | 529 | 134 | 1348 | 49 | 27.51 | 6-58 | 1 | – |
| K.J.Shine | 289.5 | 40 | 1161 | 38 | 30.55 | 8-47 | 3 | 1 |
| P-J.Bakker | 137 | 43 | 363 | 11 | 33.00 | 4-38 | – | – |
| S.D.Udal | 637.2 | 156 | 1867 | 50 | 37.34 | 8-50 | 1 | – |
| C.A.Connor | 417.2 | 69 | 1386 | 32 | 43.31 | 5-58 | 1 | – |
| K.D.James | 230.3 | 52 | 705 | 12 | 58.75 | 2-23 | – | – |

*Also bowled:* A.N.Aymes 7-0-75-1; T.C.Middleton 10-0-57-0; M.C.J.Nicholas 22.3-2-71-2; R.A.Smith 8.1-0-41-0.

The First-Class Averages (pp 164-178) give the records of Hampshire players in all first-class county matches (their other opponents being the Pakistanis and Oxford U), with the exception of:
D.I.Gower 17-28-5-155-1075-46.73-1-7-13ct. Did not bowl.
R.A.Smith 12-20-2-107*-636-35.33-1-4-5ct. 8.1-0-41-0.

# HAMPSHIRE RECORDS

## FIRST-CLASS CRICKET

| | | | | | | |
|---|---|---|---|---|---|---|
| **Highest Total** | For | 672-7d | | v Somerset | Taunton | 1899 |
| | V | 742 | | by Surrey | The Oval | 1909 |
| **Lowest Total** | For | 15 | | v Warwicks | Birmingham | 1922 |
| | V | 23 | | by Yorkshire | Middlesbrough | 1965 |
| **Highest Innings** | For | 316 | R.H.Moore | v Warwicks | Bournemouth | 1937 |
| | V | 302* | P.Holmes | for Yorkshire | Portsmouth | 1920 |

### Highest Partnership for each Wicket

| | | | | | |
|---|---|---|---|---|---|
| 1st | 347 | V.P.Terry/C.L.Smith | v Warwicks | Birmingham | 1987 |
| 2nd | 321 | G.Brown/E.I.M.Barrett | v Glos | Southampton | 1920 |
| 3rd | 344 | C.P.Mead/G.Brown | v Yorkshire | Portsmouth | 1927 |
| 4th | 263 | R.E.Marshall/D.A.Livingstone | v Middlesex | Lord's | 1970 |
| 5th | 235 | G.Hill/D.F.Walker | v Sussex | Portsmouth | 1937 |
| 6th | 411 | R.M.Poore/E.G.Wynyard | v Somerset | Taunton | 1899 |
| 7th | 325 | G.Brown/C.H.Abercrombie | v Essex | Leyton | 1913 |
| 8th | 227 | K.D.James/T.M.Tremlett | v Somerset | Taunton | 1985 |
| 9th | 230 | D.A.Livingstone/A.T.Castell | v Surrey | Southampton | 1962 |
| 10th | 192 | H.A.W.Bowell/W.H.Livsey | v Worcs | Bournemouth | 1921 |

| | | | | | | |
|---|---|---|---|---|---|---|
| **Best Bowling** | For | 9-25 | R.M.H.Cottam | v Lancashire | Manchester | 1965 |
| **(Innings)** | V | 10-46 | W.Hickton | for Lancashire | Manchester | 1870 |
| **Best Bowling** | For | 16-88 | J.A.Newman | v Somerset | Weston-s-Mare | 1927 |
| **(Match)** | V | 17-119 | W.Mead | for Essex | Southampton | 1895 |

| | | | | |
|---|---|---|---|---|
| **Most Runs – Season** | 2,854 | C.P.Mead | (av 79.27) | 1928 |
| **Most Runs – Career** | 48,892 | C.P.Mead | (av 48.84) | 1905-1936 |
| **Most 100s – Season** | 12 | C.P.Mead | | 1928 |
| **Most 100s – Career** | 138 | C.P.Mead | | 1905-1936 |
| **Most Wkts – Season** | 190 | A.S.Kennedy | (av 15.61) | 1922 |
| **Most Wkts – Career** | 2,669 | D.Shackleton | (av 18.23) | 1948-1969 |

## LIMITED-OVERS CRICKET

| | | | | | |
|---|---|---|---|---|---|
| **Highest Total** | NWT | 371-4 | | v Glamorgan | Southampton | 1975 |
| | BHC | 321-1 | | v Minor C (S) | Amersham | 1973 |
| | SL | 292-1 | | v Surrey | Portsmouth | 1983 |
| **Lowest Total** | NWT | 98 | | v Lancashire | Manchester | 1975 |
| | BHC | 50 | | v Yorkshire | Leeds | 1991 |
| | SL | 43 | | v Essex | Basingstoke | 1972 |
| **Highest Innings** | NWT | 177 | C.G.Greenidge | v Glamorgan | Southampton | 1975 |
| | BHC | 173* | C.G.Greenidge | v Minor C (S) | Amersham | 1973 |
| | SL | 172 | C.G.Greenidge | v Surrey | Southampton | 1987 |
| **Best Bowling** | NWT | 7-30 | P.J.Sainsbury | v Norfolk | Southampton | 1965 |
| | BHC | 5-13 | S.T.Jefferies | v Derbyshire | Lord's | 1988 |
| | SL | 6-20 | T.E.Jesty | v Glamorgan | Cardiff | 1975 |

# KENT

**Formation of Present Club:** 1 March 1859
**Substantial Reorganisation:** 6 December 1870
**Colours:** Maroon and White
**Badge:** White Horse on a Red Ground
**Championships:** (6) 1906, 1909, 1910, 1913, 1970, 1978
**Joint Championship:** (1) 1977
**NatWest Trophy/Gillette Cup Winners:** (2) 1967, 1974
**Benson and Hedges Cup Winners:** (3) 1973, 1976, 1978
**Sunday League Champions:** (3) 1972, 1973, 1976
**Match Awards:** NWT 43; BHC 70

**Secretary:** S.T.W.Anderson OBE, MC, St Lawrence Ground, Canterbury, CT1 3NZ (☎ 0227-456886)
**Captain:** M.R.Benson
**Scorer:** J.Foley
**1993 Beneficiary:** R.M.Ellison

**BENSON, Mark** Richard (Sutton Valence S), b Shoreham, Sussex 6 Jul 1958. 5'10". LHB, OB. Debut 1980. Cap 1981. Captain 1991-. Benefit 1991. **Tests:** 1 (1986); HS 30 v I (Birmingham) 1986. LOI: 1. 1000 runs (11); most – 1725 (1987). HS 257 v Hants (Southampton) 1991. Shared Kent record 1st wkt stand of 300 with N.R.Taylor v Derbys (Canterbury) 1991. BB 2-55 v Surrey (Dartford) 1986. Awards: NWT 2; BHC 4. **NWT:** HS 113* v Warwks (Birmingham) 1984. **BHC:** HS 118 v Glam (Swansea) 1990. **SL:** HS 97 v Surrey (Oval) 1982.

**COWDREY, Graham** Robert (Tonbridge S; Durham U), b Farnborough 27 Jun 1964. Brother of C.S. (see GLAMORGAN), son of M.C. (Kent and England 1950-76), grandson of E.A (Europeans). 5'11". RHB, RM. Debut 1984. Cap 1988. 1000 runs (3); most – 1576 (1990). HS 147 v Glos (Bristol) 1992. BB 1-5. Award: BHC 1. **NWT:** HS 37 v Glos (Bristol) 1990. BB 2-4 v Devon (Canterbury) 1992. **BHC:** HS 70* v Leics (Canterbury) 1991. BB 1-6. **SL:** HS 102* v Leics (Folkestone) 1989. BB 4-15 v Essex (Ilford) 1987.

**DAVIS, Richard** Peter (King Ethelbert's S, Birchington; Thanet TC), b Westbrook, Margate 18 Mar 1966. 6'3". RHB, SLA. Debut 1986. Cap 1990. HS 67 v Hants (Southampton) 1989. 50 wkts (2); most – 74 (1992). BB 7-64 v Durham (Gateshead) 1992. Award: BHC 1. **NWT:** HS 22 v Warwks (Birmingham) 1992. BB 3-19 v Bucks (Canterbury) 1988. **BHC:** HS 12* v Surrey (Canterbury) 1992. BB 2-33 v Sussex (Hove) 1988. **SL:** HS 40* v Northants (Canterbury) 1991. BB 5-52 v Somerset (Bath) 1989.

**EALHAM, Mark** Alan (Stour Valley SS, Chartham), b Willesborough, Ashford 27 Aug 1969. Son of A.G.E. (Kent 1966-82). 5'9". RHB, RMF. Debut 1989. Cap 1992. HS 67* v Glos (Bristol) 1992. BB 5-39 v Sussex (Hove) 1991. Award: NWT 1. **NWT:** HS 33* v Hants (Southampton) 1992. BB 2-33 v Warwks (Birmingham) 1992. **BHC:** HS 26 v Yorks (Leeds) 1992. BB 4-29 v Somerset (Canterbury) 1992. **SL:** HS 43* v Derbys (Chesterfield) 1992. BB 3-24 v Hants (Canterbury) 1992.

**ELLISON, Richard** Mark (Tonbridge S; Exeter U), b Willesborough, Ashford 21 Sep 1959. Brother of C.C. (Cambridge U 1982-83). 6'2". LHB, RMF. Debut 1981. Cap 1983. Benefit 1993. Tasmania 1986-87. Wisden 1985. **Tests:** 11 (1984 to 1986); HS 41 v SL (Lord's) 1984; BB 6-77 v A (Birmingham) 1985. LOI: 14. Tours: SA 1989-90 (Eng XI); WI 1985-86; I/SL 1984-85. HS 108 v OU (Oxford) 1984. BAC HS 98 v Notts (Nottingham) 1985. 50 wkts (4); most – 71 (1988). BB 7-33 v Warwks (Tunbridge W) 1991. Awards: NWT 1; BHC 5. **NWT:** HS 49* v Warwks

95

ELLISON – continued:
(Birmingham) 1984. BB 4-19 v Cheshire (Canterbury) 1983. **BHC:** HS 72 v Middx (Lord's) 1984. BB 4-28 v Glam (Canterbury) 1984. **SL:** HS 84 v Glos (Canterbury) 1984. BB 4-25 v Hants (Canterbury) 1983.

**FLEMING, Matthew** Valentine (St Aubyns S, Rottingdean; Eton C), b Macclesfield, Cheshire 12 Dec 1964. 5'11½". RHB, RM. Debut 1989. Cap 1990. HS 116 v WI (Canterbury) 1991. BAC HS 113 v Surrey (Canterbury) 1991. BB 4-63 v Glam (Canterbury) 1992. Awards: NWT 1; BHC 3. **NWT:** HS 53 v Devon (Canterbury) 1992. BB 3-34 v Hants (Southampton) 1992. **BHC:** HS 69 v Somerset (Canterbury) 1992. BB 2-32 v Surrey (Canterbury) 1992. **SL:** HS 77 v Sussex (Hove) 1991. BB 4-45 v Somerset (Taunton) 1991.

**FULTON, David** Paul (The Judd S; Kent U), b Lewisham 15 Nov 1971. 6'2". RHB. Debut 1992. HS 42 v CU (Cambridge) 1992 – on debut. Awaiting BAC debut.

**HOOPER, Carl** Llewellyn (Christchurch SS, Georgetown), b Georgetown, Guyana 15 Dec 1966. 6'1". RHB, OB. Debut (Demerara) 1983-84. Guyana 1984-85 to date. Kent debut/cap 1992. **Tests** (WI): 32 (1987-88 to 1991); HS 134 v P (Lahore) 1990-91; BB 2-28 v A (Bridgetown) 1990-91. LOI (WI): 80. Tours (WI): E 1988, 1991; A 1988-89, 1991-92; NZ 1986-87; I 1987-88; P 1990-91; Z 1986-87 (WI B). 1000 runs (2); most – 1501 (1991). HS 196 WI v Hants (Southampton) 1991. K HS 131 v Surrey (Guildford) 1992. BB 5-33 WI v Queensland (Brisbane) 1988-89. K BB 4-57 v Warwks (Birmingham) 1992. Award: BHC 1. **NWT:** HS 40 v Hants (Southampton) 1992. BB 1-19. **BHC:** HS 50 v Surrey (Canterbury) 1992. BB 3-28 v Yorks (Leeds) 1992. **SL:** HS 90 v Surrey (Oval) 1992. BB 2-23 v Northants (Northampton) 1992.

**IGGLESDEN, Alan** Paul (Churchill S, Westerham), b Farnborough 8 Oct 1964. 6'6". RHB, RFM. Debut 1986. Cap 1989. W Province 1987-88. **Tests:** 1 (1989); HS 2* and BB 2-91 v A (Oval). Tour: Z 1989-90 (Eng A). HS 41 and BB 6-34 v Surrey (Canterbury) 1988. 50 wkts (3); most – 56 (1989). **NWT:** HS 12* v Oxon (Oxford) 1990. BB 4-29 v Cambs (Canterbury) 1991. **BHC:** HS 5* v Worcs (Worcester) 1991. BB 3-24 v Scot 1991 and v Notts 1992. **SL:** HS 13* (twice). BB 5-13 v Sussex (Hove) 1989.

**LLONG, Nigel** James (Ashford North S), b Ashford 11 Feb 1969. 6'0". LHB, OB. Debut 1990. HS 92 v Durham (Gateshead) 1992. BB 3-50 v CU (Cambridge) 1992. BAC BB 3-70 v Worcs (Tunbridge Wells) 1992. **NWT:** HS 13* and BB 1-11 v Devon (Canterbury) 1992. **SL:** HS 44* v Essex (Chelmsford) 1992. BB 1-20.

**LONGLEY, Jonathan** Ian (Tonbridge S; Durham U), b New Brunswick, New Jersey, USA 12 Apr 1969. 5'7". RHB. Debut 1989. Comb Us (BHC) 1989-91. HS 110 v CU (Cambridge) 1992. BAC HS 35 v Somerset (Canterbury) 1992. **BHC:** HS 57 v Somerset (Canterbury) 1992. **SL:** HS 71 v Northants (Northampton) 1992.

**McCAGUE, Martin** John (Hedland Sr HS; Carine Tafe C), b Larne, N Ireland 24 May 1969. 6'5". RHB, RFM. W Australia 1990-91/1991-92. Kent debut 1991. Cap 1992. HS 34 WA v Victoria (Perth) 1991-92. K HS 29 v Leics (Leicester) 1991. 50 wkts (1): 53 (1992). BB 8-26 v Hants (Canterbury) 1992. **NWT:** HS 14 v Warwks (Birmingham) 1992. BB 2-16 v Devon (Canterbury) 1992. **BHC:** HS 30 v Derbys (Canterbury) 1992. BB 5-43 v Somerset (Canterbury) 1992. **SL:** HS 22* v Glam (Swansea) 1992. BB 4-35 v Leics (Leicester) 1992.

**MARSH, Steven** Andrew (Walderslade SS; Mid-Kent CFE), b Westminster, London 27 Jan 1961. 5'10". RHB, WK. Debut 1982. Cap 1986. HS 125 v Yorks (Canterbury) 1990. BB 2-20 v Warwks (Birmingham) 1990. Set world f-c record by holding eight catches in an innings AND scoring a hundred (v Middx at Lord's) 1991. **NWT:** HS 24* v Middx (Lord's) 1988. **BHC:** HS 71 v Lancs (Manchester) 1991. **SL:** HS 59 v Leics (Canterbury) 1991.

**PATEL, Minal** Mahesh (Dartford GS; Erith TC), b Bombay, India 7 Jul 1970. 5'9".
RHB, SLA. Debut 1989. HS 43 v Leics (Leicester) 1991. BB 6-57 v Leics (Dartford)
1990. **NWT:** HS -. BB 2-29 v Oxon (Oxford) 1990.

**PENN, Christopher** (Dover GS), b Dover 19 Jun 1963. 6'1". LHB, RFM. Debut
1982. Cap 1987. HS 115 v Lancs (Manchester) 1984. 50 wkts (2); most – 81 (1988).
BB 7-70 v Middx (Lord's) 1988. **NWT:** HS 20* v Surrey (Oval) 1991. BB 3-30 v
Warwks (Canterbury) 1988. **BHC:** HS 24* v Northants (Northampton) 1989. BB
4-34 v Surrey (Canterbury) 1982. **SL:** HS 40 v Sussex (Maidstone) 1982. BB 4-15
v Glos (Maidstone) 1989.

**PRESTON, Nicholas** William (Meopham SS; Gravesend GS), b Dartford 22 Jan
1972. 6'1". RHB, RFM. No 1st XI appearances – joined staff 1991.

**TAYLOR, Neil** Royston (Cray Valley THS), b Orpington 21 Jul 1959. 6'1". RHB,
OB. Debut 1979, scoring 110 and 11 v SL at Canterbury. Cap 1982. Benefit 1992.
1000 runs (9); most – 1979 (1990). HS 204 v Surrey (Canterbury) 1990. Shared in
2 Kent record stands: 300 (1st) with M.R.Benson and 366 (2nd) with S.G.Hinks.
BB 2-20 v Somerset (Canterbury) 1985. Awards: BHC 8. **NWT:** HS 85 v Derbys
(Canterbury) 1987. BB 3-29 v Dorset (Canterbury) 1989. **BHC:** HS 137 v Surrey
(Oval) 1988. **SL:** HS 95 v Hants (Canterbury) 1990.

**WARD, Trevor** Robert (Hextable CS, nr Swanley), b Farningham 18 Jan 1968.
5'11". RHB, OB. Debut 1986. Cap 1989. 1000 runs (3); most – 1648 (1992). HS
235* v Middx (Canterbury) 1991. BB 2-48 v Worcs (Canterbury) 1990. Awards:
NWT 1; BHC 1. **NWT:** HS 92 v Hants (Southampton) 1992. BB 1-58. **BHC:** HS
94 v Worcs (Worcester) 1990. **SL:** HS 80 v Derbys (Chesterfield) 1990. BB 3-20
v Glam (Canterbury) 1989.

## NEWCOMERS

**HEADLEY, Dean** Warren (Worcester RGS), b Norton, Stourbridge, Worcs 27 Jan
1970. Son of R.G.A. (Worcs, Jamaica and WI 1958-74); grandson of G.A (Jamaica
and WI 1927-28/1953-54). 6'4". RHB, RFM. Middlesex 1991-92. HS 91 M v Leics
(Leicester) 1992. BB 5-46 M v Yorks (Lord's) 1991 – on BAC debut. Award: BHC
1. **NWT:** HS 11* M v Somerset (Taunton) 1991. BB 5-20 M v Salop (Telford) 1992.
**BHC:** HS 26 M v Surrey (Lord's) 1991. BB 4-19 M v Sussex (Hove) 1992. **SL:** HS
6*. BB 4-23 M v Essex (Lord's) 1992.

**SPENCER, Duncan** John, b Burnley, Lancs 5 Apr 1972. RHB, RF.

## DEPARTURES

**KERSEY, Graham** James (Bexley & Erith Technical HS), b Plumstead, London
19 May 1971. 5'7". RHB, WK. Kent 1991-92. HS 27* v Surrey (Oval) 1991 – on
debut. **SL:** HS 0*.

**TUTT, Andrew** (St Columba RC S; Erith Tech C), b Bermondsey, London 21 Feb
1968. 6'0". RHB, RM. Kent 1992. HS -.

**WREN, Timothy** Neil, b Folkestone 26 Mar 1970. 6'3". RHB, LM. Kent 1990-92.
HS 16 v Essex (Chelmsford) 1990. BB 3-14 v OU (Oxford) 1991. BAC BB 2-78
v Worcs (Canterbury) 1990. **SL:** HS 0*. BB 1-31.

# KENT 1992

## RESULTS SUMMARY

| | Place | Won | Lost | Drew | Abandoned |
|---|---|---|---|---|---|
| Britannic Assurance Championship | 2nd | 9 | 3 | 10 | |
| All First-class Matches | | 9 | 4 | 10 | |
| Sunday League | 5th | 8 | 5 | | 4 |
| NatWest Trophy | Quarter-Finalist | | | | |
| Benson and Hedges Cup | Finalist | | | | |

# BRITANNIC ASSURANCE CHAMPIONSHIP AVERAGES

## BATTING AND FIELDING

| Cap | | M | I | NO | HS | Runs | Avge | 100 | 50 | Ct/St |
|---|---|---|---|---|---|---|---|---|---|---|
| 1982 | N.R.Taylor | 21 | 35 | 7 | 144 | 1508 | 53.85 | 1 | 11 | 10 |
| 1988 | G.R.Cowdrey | 21 | 31 | 6 | 147 | 1291 | 51.64 | 3 | 7 | 6 |
| 1989 | T.R.Ward | 21 | 37 | 3 | 153 | 1648 | 48.47 | 5 | 9 | 25 |
| 1992 | C.L.Hooper | 21 | 32 | 4 | 131 | 1329 | 47.46 | 5 | 7 | 25 |
| 1981 | M.R.Benson | 21 | 35 | 2 | 139 | 1482 | 44.90 | 4 | 6 | 15 |
| 1986 | S.A.Marsh | 21 | 28 | 3 | 125 | 816 | 32.64 | 1 | 6 | 43/8 |
| 1990 | M.V.Fleming | 21 | 32 | 2 | 100* | 797 | 26.56 | 1 | 4 | 13 |
| 1990 | R.P.Davis | 17 | 23 | 11 | 54* | 297 | 24.75 | – | 1 | 11 |
| 1992 | M.A.Ealham | 16 | 25 | 5 | 67* | 426 | 21.30 | – | 4 | 2 |
| 1983 | R.M.Ellison | 18 | 20 | 7 | 41 | 258 | 19.84 | – | – | 12 |
| 1992 | M.J.McCague | 16 | 18 | 5 | 25* | 120 | 9.23 | – | – | 12 |
| 1989 | A.P.Igglesden | 16 | 13 | 5 | 16 | 67 | 8.37 | – | – | 5 |
| 1987 | C.Penn | 6 | 4 | 1 | 9 | 12 | 4.00 | – | 1 | 3 |

*Also played*: G.J.Kersey (1 match) did not bat (5 ct, 1 st); N.J.Llong (3 matches) 0, 2, 92 (3 ct); J.I.Longley (2 matches) 5, 35, 19 (3 ct).

## BOWLING

| | O | M | R | W | Avge | Best | 5wI | 10wM |
|---|---|---|---|---|---|---|---|---|
| R.P.Davis | 536 | 141 | 1469 | 67 | 21.92 | 7-64 | 5 | – |
| M.J.McCague | 457.2 | 86 | 1430 | 53 | 26.98 | 8-26 | 5 | 1 |
| M.V.Fleming | 245 | 46 | 696 | 24 | 29.00 | 4-63 | – | – |
| A.P.Igglesden | 480.4 | 95 | 1413 | 46 | 30.71 | 5-41 | 3 | – |
| M.A.Ealham | 392.3 | 69 | 1193 | 36 | 33.13 | 4-67 | – | – |
| C.L.Hooper | 500.5 | 114 | 1307 | 35 | 37.34 | 4-57 | – | – |
| R.M.Ellison | 401.5 | 80 | 1204 | 29 | 41.51 | 6-95 | 2 | – |

*Also bowled*: M.R.Benson 3-0-25-1; G.R.Cowdrey 48-9-213-2; N.J.Llong 28-4-109-3; S.A.Marsh 8-0-126-0; C.Penn 141-22-460-5; T.R.Ward 39.5-4-109-0.

The First-Class Averages (pp 164-178) give the records of Kent players in all first-class county matches (their other opponents being Cambridge U).

# KENT RECORDS

## FIRST-CLASS CRICKET

| Highest Total | For | 803-4d | | v | Essex | Brentwood | 1934 |
|---|---|---|---|---|---|---|---|
| | V | 676 | | by | Australians | Canterbury | 1921 |
| Lowest Total | For | 18 | | v | Sussex | Gravesend | 1867 |
| | V | 16 | | by | Warwicks | Tonbridge | 1913 |
| Highest Innings | For | 332 | W.H.Ashdown | v | Essex | Brentwood | 1934 |
| | V | 344 | W.G.Grace | for | MCC | Canterbury | 1876 |

### Highest Partnership for each Wicket

| 1st | 300 | N.R.Taylor/M.R.Benson | v | Derbyshire | Canterbury | 1991 |
|---|---|---|---|---|---|---|
| 2nd | 366 | S.G.Hinks/N.R.Taylor | v | Middlesex | Canterbury | 1990 |
| 3rd | 321* | A.Hearne/J.R.Mason | v | Notts | Nottingham | 1899 |
| 4th | 297 | H.T.W.Harding/A.P.F.Chapman | v | Hampshire | Southampton | 1926 |
| 5th | 277 | F.E.Woolley/L.E.G.Ames | v | New Zealand | Canterbury | 1931 |
| 6th | 284 | A.P.F.Chapman/G.B.Legge | v | Lancashire | Maidstone | 1927 |
| 7th | 248 | A.P.Day/E.Humphreys | v | Somerset | Taunton | 1908 |
| 8th | 157 | A.L.Hilder/A.C.Wright | v | Essex | Gravesend | 1924 |
| 9th | 161 | B.R.Edrich/F.Ridgway | v | Sussex | Tunbridge W | 1949 |
| 10th | 235 | F.E.Woolley/A.Fielder | v | Worcs | Stourbridge | 1909 |

| Best Bowling | For | 10-30 | C.Blythe | v | Northants | Northampton | 1907 |
|---|---|---|---|---|---|---|---|
| (Innings) | V | 10-48 | C.H.G.Bland | for | Sussex | Tonbridge | 1899 |
| Best Bowling | For | 17-48 | C.Blythe | v | Northants | Northampton | 1907 |
| (Match) | V | 17-106 | T.W.J.Goddard | for | Glos | Bristol | 1939 |

| Most Runs – Season | 2,894 | F.E.Woolley | (av 59.06) | | 1928 |
|---|---|---|---|---|---|
| Most Runs – Career | 47,868 | F.E.Woolley | (av 41.77) | | 1906-1938 |
| Most 100s – Season | 10 | F.E.Woolley | | | 1928 |
| | 10 | F.E.Woolley | | | 1934 |
| Most 100s – Career | 122 | F.E.Woolley | | | 1906-1938 |
| Most Wkts – Season | 262 | A.P.Freeman | (av 14.74) | | 1933 |
| Most Wkts – Career | 3,340 | A.P.Freeman | (av 17.64) | | 1914-1936 |

## LIMITED-OVERS CRICKET

| Highest Total | NWT | 359-4 | | v | Dorset | Canterbury | 1989 |
|---|---|---|---|---|---|---|---|
| | BHC | 319-8 | | v | Scotland | Glasgow | 1991 |
| | SL | 290-4 | | v | Lancashire | Manchester | 1987 |
| Lowest Total | NWT | 60 | | v | Somerset | Taunton | 1979 |
| | BHC | 73 | | v | Middlesex | Canterbury | 1979 |
| | SL | 83 | | v | Middlesex | Lord's | 1984 |
| Highest Innings | NWT | 129* | B.W.Luckhurst | v | Durham | Canterbury | 1974 |
| | BHC | 143 | C.J.Tavaré | v | Somerset | Taunton | 1985 |
| | SL | 142 | B.W.Luckhurst | v | Somerset | Weston-s-Mare | 1970 |
| Best Bowling | NWT | 8-31 | D.L.Underwood | v | Scotland | Edinburgh | 1987 |
| | BHC | 5-21 | B.D.Julien | v | Surrey | The Oval | 1973 |
| | SL | 6-9 | R.A.Woolmer | v | Derbyshire | Chesterfield | 1979 |

# LANCASHIRE

**Formation of Present Club:** 12 January 1864
**Colours:** Red, Green and Blue
**Badge:** Red Rose
**Championships (since 1890):** (7) 1897, 1904, 1926, 1927, 1928, 1930, 1934
**Joint Championship:** (1) 1950
**NatWest Trophy/Gillette Cup Winners:** (5) 1970, 1971, 1972, 1975, 1990
**Benson and Hedges Cup Winners:** (2) 1984, 1990
**Sunday League Champions:** (3) 1969, 1970, 1989
**Match Awards:** NWT 55; BHC 55

**Cricket Secretary:** Miss R. Fitzgibbon, Old Trafford, Manchester M16 0PX
(☎ 061-848 7021)
**Captain:** N.H.Fairbrother
**Scorer:** W.Davies
**1993 Beneficiary:** G.D.Mendis

**ATHERTON, Michael** Andrew (Manchester GS; Downing C, Cambridge), b Manchester 23 Mar 1968. 5'11". RHB, LB. Cambridge U 1987-89 (blue 1987-88-89; captain 1988-89). Lancashire debut 1987. Cap 1989. YC 1990. Wisden 1990. Comb Us (BHC) 1987-89 (captain 1988-89). **Tests:** 21 (1989 to 1992); HS 151 v NZ (Nottingham) 1990; BB 1-60. LOI: 10. Tours: A 1990-91; Z 1989-90 (Eng A). 1000 runs (1): most – 1924 (1990). Scored 1193 in season of f-c debut. HS 199 v Durham (Gateshead) 1992. Shared in Lancs record 3rd wkt stand of 364 with N.H.Fairbrother v Surrey (Oval) 1990. BB 6-78 v Notts (Nottingham) 1990. Award: NWT 1. **NWT:** HS 109* v Oxon (Oxford) 1992. BB 2-15 v Glos (Manchester) 1990. **BHC:** HS 91 v Sussex (Manchester) 1991. BB 4-42 Comb Us v Somerset (Taunton) 1989. **SL:** HS 111 v Essex (Colchester) 1990. BB 3-33 v Notts (Nottingham) 1992.

**AUSTIN, Ian** David (Haslingden HS), b Haslingden 30 May 1966. 5'10". LHB, RM. Debut 1987. Cap 1990. Tour: Z 1988-89 (La). HS 115* v Derbys (Blackpool) 1992. BB 5-79 v Surrey (Oval) 1988. **NWT:** HS 33* v Essex (Chelmsford) 1992. BB 3-36 v Durham (Manchester) 1990. **BHC:** HS 80 v Worcs (Worcester) 1991. BB 4-25 v Surrey (Manchester) 1990. **SL:** HS 48 v Middx (Lord's) 1991. BB 5-56 v Derbys (Derby) 1991.

**BARNETT, Alexander** Anthony (William Ellis S), b Malaga, Spain, 11 Sep 1970. Great nephew of C.J. (Glos and England 1927-54). 5'11". RHB, SLA. Middlesex 1988-91. Lancashire debut 1992. HS 17 v Kent (Manchester) 1992. BB 5-78 v Leics (Leicester) 1992. **BHC:** HS -. **SL:** HS -.

**CHAPPLE, Glen** (West Craven HS; Nelson & Colne C), b Skipton, Yorks 23 Jan 1974. 6'1". RHB, RMF. Debut 1992. HS 18 v Sussex (Hove) 1992. BB 3-40 v Warwks (Birmingham) 1992.

**CORDINGLEY, Gareth** John (Queen Elizabeth GS, Blackburn; Trinity C, Leeds), b Blackburn 23 Jan 1973. 5'10". RHB, RM. No 1st XI appearances – joined staff 1992.

**CRAWLEY, John** Paul (Manchester GS; Trinity C, Cambridge), b Maldon, Essex 21 Sep 1971. Brother of M.A. (see NOTTS) and P.M. (CU 1992). 6'1". RHB, RM. Debut 1990. Cambridge U 1991-92 (captain 1992-93; blue 1991-92). Comb Us (BHC) 1991-92 (captain 1992). 1000 runs (1): 1175 (1992). HS 172 v Surrey (Lytham) 1992. BB 1-90. **BHC:** HS 42 Comb Us v Durham (Cambridge) 1992. **SL:** HS 8.

**DeFREITAS, Phillip** Anthony Jason (Willesden HS, London), b Scotts Head, Dominica 18 Feb 1966. 6'0". RHB, RFM. UK resident since 1976. Leicestershire 1985-88 (cap 1986). Lancashire debut 1989. Cap 1989. Wisden 1991. MCC YC. **Tests:** 31 (1986-87 to 1992); HS 55* v WI (Nottingham) 1991; BB 7-70 v SL (Lord's) 1991. LOI: 78. Tours: A 1986-87, 1990-91; WI 1989-90; NZ 1987-88, 1991-92; P 1987-88; Z 1988-89 (La). HS 113 Le v Notts (Worksop) 1988. La HS 102 v OU

100

DeFREITAS – continued:
(Oxford) 1990. 50 wkts (5); most – 94 (1986). BB 7-21 v Middx (Lord's) 1989.
Awards: NWT 3; BHC 4. **NWT:** HS 69 Le v Lancs (Leicester) 1986. BB 5-13 v
Cumberland (Kendal) 1989. **BHC:** HS 75* v Hants (Manchester) 1990. BB 5-16 v
Essex (Chelmsford) 1992. **SL:** HS 49* v Hants (Manchester) 1992. BB 4-20 Le v
Middx and v Worcs 1986.

**DERBYSHIRE, Nicholas** Alexander (Ampleforth C; London U); b Ramsbottom
11 Sep 1970. 5'11½". RHB, RFM. No 1st XI appearances – joined staff 1990.

**FAIRBROTHER, Neil** Harvey (Lymm GS) b Warrington 9 Sep 1963. 5'8".  RHB, LHB,
LM. Debut 1982. Cap 1985. Captain 1992-. **Tests:** 7 (1987 to 1990); HS 33* v NZ
(Lord's) 1990. **LOI:** 29. Tours: NZ 1987-88, 1991-92; P 1987-88, 1990-91 (Eng
A); SL 1990-91 (Eng A). 1000 runs (8); most – 1740 (1990). HS 366 v Surrey
(Oval) 1990, ground record including 311 in a day and 100 or more in each session,
and sharing in Lancs record 3rd wkt stand of 364 with M.A.Atherton. BB 2-91 v
Notts (Manchester) 1987. Awards: NWT 5; BHC 5. **NWT:** HS 93* v Leics
(Leicester) 1986. **BHC:** HS 116* v Scot (Manchester) 1988. **SL:** HS 116* v Notts
(Nottingham) 1988.

**FIELDING, Jonathan** Mark (Woodhey HS; Bury C), b Bury 13 Mar 1973. 6'1".
RHB, SLA. No 1st XI appearances – joined staff 1992.

**FITTON, John Dexter** (Redbrook HS; Oulder Hill S), b Littleborough 24 Aug
1965. 5'10". LHB, OB. Debut 1987. HS 60 v Northants (Lytham) 1991. BB 6-59
v Yorks (Manchester) 1988. **NWT:** HS 17* and 1-49 v Essex (Chelmsford) 1992.
**BHC:** HS 14 and BB 2-56 v Surrey (Oval) 1992. **SL:** HS 36 v Sussex (Hove) 1992.
BB 4-26 v Middx (Manchester) 1992.

**FLETCHER, Stuart** David (Reins Wood SS), b Keighley, Yorks 8 Jun 1964. 5'10".
RHB, RMF. Yorkshire 1983-91 (cap 1988). Lancashire debut 1992. HS 28* Y v Kent
(Tunbridge Wells) 1984. 50 wkts (1): 59 (1988). BB 8-58 Y v Essex (Sheffield)
1988. La HS 23 and BB 2-53 v Notts (Nottingham) 1992. Award: NWT 1. **NWT:**
HS 16* Y v Surrey (Oval) 1989. BB 3-20 Y v Berks (Finchampstead) 1988. **BHC:**
HS 15* Y v Lancs (Leeds) 1990. BB 4-34 Y v Scot (Glasgow) 1987. **SL:** HS 11*
Y v Essex (Chelmsford) 1991. BB 4-11 Y v Kent (Canterbury) 1988.

**GALLIAN, Jason** Edward Riche (Pittwater House S, Sydney; Keble C, Oxford),
b Manly, Sydney, Australia 25 Jun 1971. 6'0". RHB, RM. Debut 1990 taking wicket
of D.A.Hagan (OU) with his first ball. Qualifies for Lancs in 1994. Captained
Australia YC v England YC 1989-90 scoring 158* in 1st 'Test'. OU debut 1992;
blue 1992; captain 1993. Comb Us (BHC) 1992. HS 112 OU v Worcs (Oxford)
1992. BB 4-29 OU v Lancs (Oxford) 1992. La HS 17* and BB 1-50 v OU (Oxford)
1990. **BHC:** HS 50 Comb Us v Derbys and Durham 1992. BB 1-26.

**HARVEY, Mark** Edward (Habergham HS), b Burnley 26 Jun 1974. 5'9". RHB,
RM/LB. No 1st XI appearances – joined staff 1992.

**HEGG, Warren** Kevin (Unsworth HS, Bury; Stand C, Whitefield), b Whitefield
23 Feb 1968. 5'8". RHB, WK. Debut 1986. Cap 1989. Tours: WI 1986-87 (La);
SL 1990-91 (Eng A); Z 1988-89 (La). HS 130 v Northants (Northampton) 1987.
Held 11 catches (equalling world f-c match record) v Derbys (Chesterfield) 1989.
**NWT:** HS 29 v Glos (Gloucester) 1989. **BHC:** HS 31* v Worcs (Lord's) 1990. **SL:**
HS 47* v Middx (Lord's) 1991.

**IRANI, Ronald** Charles (Smithills CS, Bolton), b Leigh 26 Oct 1971. 6'3". RHB,
RM. Debut 1990. HS 31* v OU (Oxford) 1991. BAC HS 22 v Sussex (Hove) 1992.
BB 2-21 v Notts (Nottingham) 1992. **SL:** HS 3. BB 1-21.

101

**LLOYD, Graham** David (Hollins County HS), b Accrington 1 Jul 1969. Son of D. (Lancs and England 1965-83). 5'9". RHB, RM. Debut 1988. Cap 1992. 1000 runs (1): 1389 (1992). HS 132 v Kent (Manchester) 1992. BB 1-57. **NWT:** HS 39 v Hants (Southampton) 1991. **BHC:** HS 26 v Surrey (Oval) 1992. **SL:** HS 100* v Kent (Maidstone) 1990.

**MARTIN, Peter** James (Danum S, Doncaster), b Accrington 15 Nov 1968. 6'4". RHB, RFM. Debut 1989. HS 133 v Durham (Gateshead) 1992. BB 4-30 v Worcs (Blackpool) 1991. **NWT:** BB 2-19 v Dorset (Bournemouth) 1991. **SL:** HS 18* v Sussex (Hove) 1992. BB 2-17 v Derbys (Manchester) 1992.

**MENDIS, Gehan** Dixon (St Thomas C, Colombo; Brighton, Hove & Sussex GS; Durham U), b Colombo, Ceylon 24 Apr 1955. 5'9". RHB, RM. Sussex 1974-85 (cap 1980). Lancashire debut/cap 1986. Benefit 1993. Tours: WI 1982-83 (Int), 1986-87(La); P 1981-82 (Int); Z 1988-89 (La). 1000 runs (12): most – 1756 (1985). HS 209* Sx v Somerset (Hove) 1984. La HS 203* v Middx (Manchester) 1987. BB 1-65. Awards: NWT 4; BHC 5. **NWT:** HS 141* Sx v Warwks (Hove) 1980. **BHC:** HS 125* v Northants (Manchester) 1991. **SL:** HS 125* Sx v Glos (Hove) 1981.

**SHARP, Marcus** Anthony (Clitheroe RGS; Edgehill CHE, Ormskirk), b Oxford 1 Jun 1970. 6'6½". LHB, RM. Debut 1991. HS –. BB 1-21.

**SPEAK, Nicholas** Jason (Parrs Wood HS, Manchester), b Manchester 21 Nov 1966. 6'0". RHB, RM/OB. Debut v Jamaica (Kingston) 1986-87. Cap 1992. Tour: WI 1986-87 (La). 1000 runs (1): 1892 (1992). HS 232 v Leics (Leicester) 1992. BB 1-0. **NWT:** HS 60 v Essex (Chelmsford) 1992. **BHC:** HS 82 v Hants (Manchester) 1992. **SL:** HS 102* v Yorks (Leeds) 1992.

**STANWORTH, John** (Chadderton GS), b Oldham 30 Sep 1960. 5'10". RHB, WK. Debut 1983. Cap 1989. HS 50* v Glos (Bristol) 1985. **NWT:** HS 0. **BHC:** HS 8*. **SL:** HS 4*.

**TITCHARD, Stephen** Paul (Lymm County HS; Priestley C), b Warrington 17 Dec 1967. 6'3". RHB, RM. Debut 1990. HS 135 v Notts (Manchester) 1991. **NWT:** HS 20 v Oxon (Oxford) 1992. **BHC:** HS 82 v Surrey (Oval) 1992. **SL:** HS 20 v Somerset (Manchester) 1992.

**WASIM AKRAM** (Islamia C), b Lahore, Pakistan 3 Jun 1966. 6'3". LHB, LF. PACO 1984-85/1985-86. Lahore Whites 1985-86. Lancashire debut 1988. Cap 1989. Wisden 1992. **Tests** (P): 44 (1984-85 to 1992). HS 123 v A (Adelaide) 1989-90; BB 6-62 v A (Melbourne) 1989-90. LOI (P): 126. Tours (P): E 1987, 1992; A 1988-89, 1989-90, 1991-92; WI 1987-88; NZ 1984-85; I 1986-87; SL 1984-85 (P U-23), 1985-86. HS 123 (Tests). La HS 122 v Hants (Basingstoke) 1991. 50 wkts (3); most – 82 (1992). BB 7-42 World XI v MCC (Scarborough) 1989. La BB 7-53 v Northants (Northampton) 1988. Hat-trick 1988. **NWT:** HS 29 v Hants (Southampton) 1991. BB 4-27 v Lincs (Manchester) 1988. **BHC:** HS 52 v Northants (Northampton) 1989. BB 5-27 v Scot (Perth) 1989. **SL:** HS 50 v Glam (Colwyn Bay) 1990. BB 4-19 v Yorks (Scarborough) 1990.

**WATKINSON, Michael** (Rivington and Blackrod HS, Horwich), b Westhoughton 1 Aug 1961. 6'1". RHB, RMF. Debut 1982. Cap 1987. Cheshire 1982. HS 138 v Yorks (Manchester) 1990. 50 wkts (4); most – 66 (1992). Hat-trick 1992. BB 7-25 v Sussex (Lytham) 1987. Awards: NWT 2; BHC 2. **NWT:** HS 90 and BB 3-14 v Glos (Manchester) 1990. **BHC:** HS 76 v Northants (Northampton) 1992. BB 5-49 v Yorks (Manchester) 1991. **SL:** HS 83 v Sussex (Manchester) 1991. BB 5-46 v Warwks (Manchester) 1990.

**YATES, Gary** (Manchester GS), b Ashton-under-Lyne 20 Sep 1967. 6'0". RHB, OB. Debut 1990. HS 106 v Notts (Nottingham) 1990 – on BAC debut. BB 4-94 v SL (Manchester) 1990. BAC BB 3-47 v Warwks (Birmingham) 1991. **BHC:** BB 2-50 v Sussex (Manchester) 1991. **SL:** BB 2-45 v Worcs (Worcester) 1991.

NEWCOMERS/DEPARTURES – see p 156

# LANCASHIRE 1992

## RESULTS SUMMARY

| | Place | Won | Lost | Drew | Abandoned |
|---|---|---|---|---|---|
| Britannic Assurance Championship | 12th | 4 | 6 | 12 | |
| All First-class Matches | | 4 | 6 | 13 | |
| Sunday League | 11th | 6 | 7 | | 4 |
| NatWest Trophy | 2nd Round | | | | |
| Benson and Hedges Cup | Quarter-Finalist | | | | |

## BRITANNIC ASSURANCE CHAMPIONSHIP AVERAGES

### BATTING AND FIELDING

| Cap | | M | I | NO | HS | Runs | Avge | 100 | 50 | Ct/St |
|---|---|---|---|---|---|---|---|---|---|---|
| 1985 | N.H.Fairbrother | 11 | 16 | 5 | 166* | 644 | 58.54 | 1 | 5 | 7 |
| 1992 | N.J.Speak | 22 | 36 | 3 | 232 | 1892 | 57.33 | 4 | 12 | 18 |
| – | J.P.Crawley | 7 | 10 | – | 172 | 558 | 55.80 | 1 | 3 | 5 |
| 1989 | M.A.Atherton | 17 | 30 | 5 | 199 | 1351 | 54.04 | 5 | 4 | 16 |
| 1992 | G.D.Lloyd | 22 | 35 | 9 | 132 | 1310 | 50.38 | 4 | 9 | 21 |
| 1989 | W.K.Hegg | 18 | 24 | 7 | 80 | 618 | 36.35 | – | 4 | 33/6 |
| – | S.P.Titchard | 13 | 22 | 3 | 74 | 647 | 34.05 | – | 6 | 8 |
| 1981 | G.Fowler | 10 | 18 | 2 | 66 | 502 | 31.37 | – | 4 | 6 |
| 1989 | P.A.J.DeFreitas | 11 | 12 | 1 | 72 | 322 | 29.27 | – | 3 | 1 |
| 1990 | I.D.Austin | 8 | 10 | 2 | 115* | 230 | 28.75 | 1 | 1 | – |
| – | P.J.Martin | 21 | 24 | 6 | 133 | 492 | 27.33 | 1 | 2 | 4 |
| – | J.D.Fitton | 7 | 8 | 2 | 48* | 135 | 22.50 | – | – | 1 |
| 1986 | G.D.Mendis | 5 | 8 | 1 | 45 | 145 | 20.71 | – | – | – |
| – | S.D.Fletcher | 5 | 4 | 1 | 23 | 62 | 20.66 | – | – | 2 |
| 1987 | M.Watkinson | 19 | 24 | 1 | 96 | 466 | 20.26 | – | 1 | 10 |
| – | R.C.Irani | 5 | 6 | – | 22 | 68 | 11.33 | – | – | 4 |
| – | D.K.Morrison | 14 | 12 | 1 | 30 | 113 | 10.27 | – | – | 4 |
| – | A.A.Barnett | 21 | 16 | 10 | 17 | 61 | 10.16 | – | – | 7 |

*Also played*: G.Chapple (2 matches) 1*, 18; J.Stanworth (4 matches – cap 1989) 21 (7 ct, 1 st).

### BOWLING

| | O | M | R | W | Avge | Best | 5wI | 10wM |
|---|---|---|---|---|---|---|---|---|
| D.K.Morrison | 335.4 | 52 | 1209 | 36 | 33.58 | 6-48 | 1 | – |
| P.A.J.DeFreitas | 290.5 | 52 | 912 | 27 | 33.77 | 6-94 | 1 | – |
| J.D.Fitton | 166.1 | 37 | 453 | 13 | 34.84 | 4-81 | – | – |
| M.Watkinson | 629.2 | 128 | 2118 | 59 | 35.89 | 6-62 | 3 | 1 |
| P.J.Martin | 512.3 | 128 | 1476 | 36 | 41.00 | 4-45 | – | – |
| I.D.Austin | 164.5 | 41 | 522 | 12 | 43.50 | 3-44 | – | – |
| A.A.Barnett | 571.5 | 79 | 2092 | 43 | 48.65 | 5-78 | 2 | – |

*Also bowled*: M.A.Atherton 66.1-4-337-3; G.Chapple 48-17-128-5; J.P.Crawley 10-0-90-1; S.D.Fletcher 83-16-363-4; G.Fowler 5-0-60-1; R.C.Irani 33.5-5-137-3; G.D.Lloyd 7-0-45-0; N.J.Speak 6-0-66-0.

The First-Class Averages (pp 164-178) give the records of Lancashire players in all first-class county matches (their other opponents being Oxford U), with the exception of J.P.Crawley and P.A.J.DeFreitas whose full county figures are as above, and:

  M.A.Atherton 18-32-6-199-1453-55.88-5-5-19ct. 74.1-9-343-4-85.75-2/109.

103

# LANCASHIRE RECORDS

## FIRST-CLASS CRICKET

| | | | | | |
|---|---|---|---|---|---|
| **Highest Total** | For | 863 | | v Surrey | The Oval | 1990 |
| | V | 707-9d | | by Surrey | The Oval | 1990 |
| **Lowest Total** | For | 25 | | v Derbyshire | Manchester | 1871 |
| | V | 22 | | by Glamorgan | Liverpool | 1924 |
| **Highest Innings** | For | 424 | A.C.MacLaren | v Somerset | Taunton | 1895 |
| | V | 315* | T.W.Hayward | for Surrey | The Oval | 1898 |

### Highest Partnership for each Wicket

| | | | | | |
|---|---|---|---|---|---|
| 1st | 368 | A.C.MacLaren/R.H.Spooner | v Glos | Liverpool | 1903 |
| 2nd | 371 | F.B.Watson/G.E.Tyldesley | v Surrey | Manchester | 1928 |
| 3rd | 364 | M.A.Atherton/N.H.Fairbrother | v Surrey | The Oval | 1990 |
| 4th | 324 | A.C.MacLaren/J.T.Tyldesley | v Notts | Nottingham | 1904 |
| 5th | 249 | B.Wood/A.Kennedy | v Warwicks | Birmingham | 1975 |
| 6th | 278 | J.Iddon/H.R.W.Butterworth | v Sussex | Manchester | 1932 |
| 7th | 245 | A.H.Hornby/J.Sharp | v Leics | Manchester | 1912 |
| 8th | 158 | J.Lyon/R.M.Ratcliffe | v Warwicks | Manchester | 1979 |
| 9th | 142 | L.O.S.Poidevin/A.Kermode | v Sussex | Eastbourne | 1907 |
| 10th | 173 | J.Briggs/R.Pilling | v Surrey | Liverpool | 1885 |

| | | | | | |
|---|---|---|---|---|---|
| **Best Bowling** | For | 10-46 | W.Hickton | v Hampshire | Manchester | 1870 |
| **(Innings)** | V | 10-40 | G.O.B.Allen | for Middlesex | Lord's | 1929 |
| **Best Bowling** | For | 17-91 | H.Dean | v Yorkshire | Liverpool | 1913 |
| **(Match)** | V | 16-65 | G.Giffen | for Australians | Manchester | 1886 |

| | | | | |
|---|---|---|---|---|
| **Most Runs – Season** | 2,633 | J.T.Tyldesley | (av 56.02) | 1901 |
| **Most Runs – Career** | 34,222 | G.E.Tyldesley | (av 45.20) | 1909-1936 |
| **Most 100s – Season** | 11 | C.Hallows | | 1928 |
| **Most 100s – Career** | 90 | G.E.Tyldesley | | 1909-1936 |
| **Most Wkts – Season** | 198 | E.A.McDonald | (av 18.55) | 1925 |
| **Most Wkts – Career** | 1,816 | J.B.Statham | (av 15.12) | 1950-1968 |

## LIMITED-OVERS CRICKET

| | | | | | | |
|---|---|---|---|---|---|---|
| **Highest Total** | NWT | 372-5 | | v Glos | Manchester | 1990 |
| | BHC | 330-4 | | v Sussex | Manchester | 1991 |
| | SL | 276-6 | | v Derbys | Derby | 1991 |
| **Lowest Total** | NWT | 59 | | v Worcs | Worcester | 1963 |
| | BHC | 82 | | v Yorkshire | Bradford | 1972 |
| | SL | 71 | | v Essex | Chelmsford | 1987 |
| **Highest Innings** | NWT | 131 | A.Kennedy | v Middlesex | Manchester | 1978 |
| | BHC | 136 | G.Fowler | v Sussex | Manchester | 1991 |
| | SL | 134* | C.H.Lloyd | v Somerset | Manchester | 1970 |
| **Best Bowling** | NWT | 5-13 | P.A.DeFreitas | v Cumberland | Kendal | 1989 |
| | BHC | 6-10 | C.E.H.Croft | v Scotland | Manchester | 1982 |
| | SL | 6-29 | D.P.Hughes | v Somerset | Manchester | 1977 |

# LEICESTERSHIRE

**Formation of Present Club:** 25 March 1879
**Colours:** Dark Green and Scarlet
**Badge:** Gold Running Fox on Green Ground
**Championships:** (1) 1975
**NatWest Trophy/Gillette Cup Winners:** (0) Finalists 1992
**Benson and Hedges Cup Winners:** (3) 1972, 1975, 1985
**Sunday League Champions:** (2) 1974, 1977
**Match Awards:** NWT 33; BHC 56

**Chief Executive:** F.M.Turner. **Administrative Secretary:** K.P.Hill, County Ground, Grace Road, Leicester LE2 8AD (☎ 0533-831880)
**Captain:** N.E.Briers
**Scorer:** G.R.Blackburn
**1993 Beneficiary:** J.J.Whitaker

**BENJAMIN, Winston** Keithroy Matthew (All Saints S, Antigua), b St John's, Antigua 31 Dec 1964. 6'3". RHB, RFM. Debut (Rest of World XI) 1985. Leicestershire 1986-90 (cap 1989) and 1992. Leeward Is 1985-86 to date. Cheshire 1985. **Tests** (WI): 8 (1987-88 to 1988-89); HS 40* v P (Bridgetown) 1987-88; BB 4-52 v Eng (Oval) 1988. LOI (WI): 60. Tours (WI): E 1988; A 1986-87, 1988-89; I 1987-88; P 1986-87. HS 101* v Derbys (Leicester) 1990. 50 wkts (1): 69 (1989). BB 7-54 (inc hat-trick) v A (Leicester) 1989. BAC BB 6-26 v Derbys (Chesterfield) 1989. Award: BHC 1. **NWT:** HS 24* v Durham (Leicester) 1992. BB 5-32 v Derbys (Derby) 1992. **BHC:** HS 45 v Middx (Leicester) 1992. BB 5-17 v Minor C (Leicester) 1986. **SL:** HS 41* v Essex (Chelmsford) 1989. BB 4-19 v Lancs (Leicester) 1986.

**BENSON, Justin** David Ramsay (The Leys S, Cambridge), b Dublin, Ireland 1 Mar 1967. 6'2". RHB, RM. Debut 1988. Cambridgeshire 1984-87. HS 133* v Hants (Bournemouth) 1991, sharing Leics record 7th wkt stand of 219* with P.Whitticase. BB 2-24 v Yorks (Sheffield) 1992. Awards: NWT 2. **NWT:** HS 85 Cambs v Yorks (Leeds) 1986. BB 2-18 v Norfolk (Leicester) 1992. **BHC:** HS 43 v Notts (Nottingham) 1990. BB 2-27 v Glos (Cheltenham) 1992. **SL:** HS 67 v Surrey (Oval) 1990. BB 3-37 v Warwks (Leicester) 1991.

**BOON, Timothy** James (Edlington CS, Doncaster), b Doncaster, Yorks 1 Nov 1961. 6'0". RHB, RM. Debut 1980. Cap 1986. Tour: Z 1980-81 (Le). 1000 runs (7); most – 1539 (1990). HS 144 v Glos (Leicester) 1984. Shared Leics record 4th wkt stand of 290* with P.Willey v Warwks (Leicester) 1984. BB 3-40 v Yorks (Leicester) 1986. Awards: NWT 1; BHC 1. **NWT:** HS 76* v Salop (Leicester) 1991. **BHC:** HS 103 v Scot (Leicester) 1991. **SL:** HS 97 v Kent (Leicester) 1990. BB 1-23.

**BRIERS, Nigel** Edwin (Lutterworth GS; Borough Road CE), b Leicester 15 Jan 1955. 6'0". RHB, RM. Debut 1971 (aged 16yr 103d – youngest Leicestershire player). Cap 1981. Captain 1990-. Benefit 1990. Wisden 1992. Tour: Z 1980-81 (Le). 1000 runs (9); most – 1996 (1990). HS 201* v Warwks (Birmingham) 1983. Shared record Leics 5th wkt stand of 233 with R.W.Tolchard v Somerset (Leicester) 1979. BB 4-29 v Derbys (Leicester) 1985. Awards: NWT 1; BHC 5. **NWT:** HS 88 v Essex (Leicester) 1992. BB 2-6 v Worcs (Leicester) 1979. **BHC:** HS 102 v Minor C (Stone) 1992. BB 1-26. **SL:** HS 119* v Hants (Bournemouth) 1981. BB 3-29 v Middx (Leicester) 1984.

**BRIMSON, Matthew** Thomas (Chislehurst & Sidcup GS; Durham U), b Plumstead, London 1 Dec 1970. 6'0". RHB, SLA. Kent staff 1991. No 1st XI appearances – joined staff 1992.

**COBB, Russell** Alan (Trent C), b Leicester 18 May 1961. 5'11". RHB, SLA. Leicestershire 1980-89 (cap 1986). Natal B 1988-89. Tours: NZ 1979-80 (DHR); Z 1980-81 (Le). 1000 runs (1): 1092 (1986). HS 91 v Northants (Leicester) 1986.

COBB – continued:
Award: NWT 1. **NWT:** HS 66* v Oxon (Leicester) 1987. **BHC:** HS 22 v Warwks (Leicester) 1986. **SL:** HS 24 v Worcs (Leicester) 1981.

**HAYE, Andrew** Fitzpatrick (Copland HS; Elm Park C), b St Ann's, Jamaica 10 Nov 1972. 6'1″. RHB, RMF. MCC YC. No 1st XI appearances – joined staff 1992.

**HEPWORTH, Peter** Nash, b Ackworth, Yorks 4 May 1967. 6'1″. RHB, OB. Debut 1988. 1000 runs (1): 1119 (1991). HS 115 v CU (Cambridge) 1991 and v Essex (Leicester) 1991. BB 3-51 v Kent (Canterbury) 1991. **BHC:** HS 33 v Sussex (Hove) 1991. BB 4-39 v Scot (Leicester) 1991. **SL:** HS 38 v Sussex (Leicester) 1988. BB 2-33 v Notts (Leicester) 1991.

**MADDY, Darren** Lee (Wreake Valley C), b Leicester 23 May 1974. 5'9″. RHB, RM. No 1st XI appearances – joined staff 1992.

**MILLNS, David** James (Garibaldi CS), b Clipstone, Notts 27 Feb 1965. 6'3″. LHB, RMF. Nottinghamshire 1988-89. Leicestershire debut 1990. Cap 1991. HS 44 v Middx (Uxbridge) 1991. 50 wkts (2); most – 74 (1992). BB 9-37 (12-91 match) v Derbys (Derby) 1991. Award: NWT 1. **NWT:** HS 29* v Derbys (Derby) 1992. BB 3-22 v Norfolk (Leicester) 1992. **BHC:** HS 11* v Sussex (Hove) 1991. BB 4-51 v Minor C (Stone) 1992. **SL:** HS 20* v Notts (Leicester) 1991. BB 2-20 v Warwks (Leicester) 1991.

**MULLALLY, Alan** David (Educated in Perth, Aus), b Southend-on-Sea, Essex 12 Jul 1969. 6'3¼″. RHB, LFM. W Australia 1987-88/1989-90. Victoria 1990-91. Hampshire (1 match) 1988. Leicestershire debut 1990. HS 34 WA v Tasmania (Perth) 1989-90. Le HS 29 v Hants (Leicester) 1990. BB 5-119 v Warwks (Birmingham) 1992. **NWT:** HS 1*. BB 2-22 v Derbys and v Northants 1992. **BHC:** HS 11 v Surrey (Leicester) 1992. BB 1-8. **SL:** HS 10* (twice). BB 2-19 v Somerset (W-s-M) 1991.

**NIXON, Paul** Andrew (Ullswater HS, Penrith), b Carlisle, Cumberland 21 Oct 1970. 6'0″. LHB, WK. Debut 1989. Cumberland 1987. MCC YC. HS 107* v Hants (Leicester) 1992. **NWT:** HS 32 v Derbys (Derby) 1992. **BHC:** HS 5. **SL:** HS 60 v Notts (Nottingham) 1992.

**PARSONS, Gordon** James (Woodside County SS, Slough), b Slough, Bucks 17 Oct 1959. 6'1″. LHB, RMF. Leicestershire 1978-85 and 1989 (cap 1984). Warwickshire 1986-88 (cap 1987). Boland 1983-84/1984-85. GW 1985-86/1986-87. OFS 1988-89/ 1990-91. Buckinghamshire 1977. Tours: NZ 1979-80 (DHR); Z 1980-81 (Le). HS 76 Boland v W Province B (Cape Town) 1984-85. Le HS 69 v Glos (Leicester) 1989. 50 wkts (2); most – 67 (1984). BB 9-72 Boland v Transvaal B (Johannesburg) 1984-85. Le BB 6-11 v OU (Oxford) 1985. BAC BB 6-70 v Surrey (Oval) 1992. Awards: BHC 2. **NWT:** HS 23 v Northants (Northampton) 1984. BB 2-11 v Wilts (Swindon) 1984. **BHC:** HS 63* and BB 4-12 v Scot (Leicester) 1989. **SL:** HS 31* v Sussex (Leicester) 1992. BB 4-19 v Essex (Harlow) 1982.

**POTTER, Laurie** (Kelmscott HS, Perth, Aus), b Bexleyheath, Kent 7 Nov 1962. 6'1″. RHB, SLA. Kent 1981-85. Leicestershire debut 1986. Cap 1988. GW 1984-85/ 1985-86 (captain 1985-86). OFS 1987-88. 1000 runs (3); most – 1093 (1989). HS 165* GW v Border (East London) 1984-85. Le HS 121* v Notts (Leicester) 1989. BB 4-52 GW v Boland (Stellenbosch) 1985-86. Le BB 4-73 v Surrey (Oval) 1992. Award: BHC 1. **NWT:** HS 57 v Northants (Northampton) 1991. BB 1-28. **BHC:** HS 112 and BB 2-70 v Minor C (Leicester) 1986. **SL:** HS 105 v Derbys (Leicester) 1986. BB 4-9 K v Derbys (Folkestone) 1985.

**ROBINSON, Phillip** Edward (Greenhead GS, Keighley), b Keighley, Yorks 3 Aug 1963. 5'9″. RHB, LM. Yorkshire 1984-91 (cap 1988). Leicestershire debut 1992. Cumberland 1992. 1000 runs (3); most – 1402 (1990). HS 189 Y v Lancs (Scarborough) 1991. Le HS 19 v Kent (Leicester) 1992. BB 1-10. Awards: NWT 1; BHC 1. **NWT:** HS 73 v Norfolk (Leicester) 1992. **BHC:** HS 73* Y v Hants (Southampton) 1990. **SL:** HS 104 v Lancs (Manchester) 1992.

**SMITH, Benjamin** Francis (Kibworth HS), b Corby, Northants 3 Apr 1972. 5'9".
RHB, RM. Debut 1990. HS 100* v Durham (Durham) 1992. BB 1-5. **NWT:** HS
49 v Norfolk (Leicester) 1992. **BHC:** HS 2. **SL:** HS 37 v Yorks (Sheffield) 1992.

**WELLS, Vincent** John (Sir William Nottidge S, Whitstable), b Dartford, Kent
6 Aug 1965. 6'0". RHB, RMF, occ WK. Kent 1988-9i. Leicestershire debut 1992.
HS 58 K v Hants (Bournemouth) 1990 and K v OU (Oxford) 1991. Le HS 56 v
Surrey (Oval) 1992. BB 5-43 K v Leics (Leicester) 1990. Le BB 4-26 v Northants
(Northampton) 1992. Awards: NWT 1; BHC 1. **NWT:** 100* K v Oxon (Oxford)
1990. BB 3-38 v Durham (Leicester) 1992. **BHC:** HS 25 K v Sussex (Canterbury)
1991. BB 3-13 v Glos (Cheltenham) 1992. **SL:** HS 29* v Essex (Leicester) 1992.
BB 3-17 K v Somerset (Canterbury) 1988.

**WHITAKER, John James** (Uppingham S), b Skipton, Yorks 5 May 1962. 5'10".
RHB, OB. Debut 1983. Cap 1986. Benefit 1993. Wisden 1986. YC 1986. **Tests:** 1
(1986-87); HS 11 v A (Adelaide) 1986-87. LOI: 2. Tours: A 1986-87; Z 1989-90
(Eng A). 1000 runs (8); most – 1767 (1990). HS 200* v Notts (Leicester) 1986. BB
1-29. Awards: NWT 1; BHC 1. **NWT:** HS 155 v Wilts (Swindon) 1984. **BHC:** HS
100 v Kent (Canterbury) 1991. **SL:** HS 132 v Glam (Swansea) 1984.

**WHITTICASE, Philip** (Crestwood CS, Kingswinford), b Marston Green, Solihull
15 Mar 1965. 5'8". RHB, WK. Debut 1984. Cap 1987. HS 114* v Hants
(Bournemouth) 1991, sharing Leics record 7th wkt stand of 219* with J.D.R.Benson.
**NWT:** HS 32 v Lancs (Leicester) 1986. **BHC:** HS 45 v Notts (Nottingham) 1990.
**SL:** HS 38 v Northants (Leicester) 1990.

## NEWCOMERS

**DAKIN, J.** and **DE SILVA, N.** (no details furnished).

**PIERSON, Adrian** Roger Kirshaw (Kent C, Canterbury; Hatfield Polytechnic), b
Enfield, Middx 21 Jul 1963. 6'4". RHB, OB. Warwickshire 1985-91. Cambridgeshire
1992. MCC YC. HS 42* Wa v Northants (Northampton) 1986. BB 6-82 Wa v
Derbys (Nuneaton) 1989. Award: BHC 1. **NWT:** HS 1*. BB 3-20 Wa v Wilts
(Birmingham) 1989. **BHC:** HS 11 Wa v Minor C (Walsall) 1986. BB 3-34 Wa v
Lancs (Birmingham) 1988. **SL:** HS 21* Wa v Hants (Birmingham) 1987. BB 3-21
Wa v Leics (Birmingham) 1988.

## DEPARTURES

**GIDLEY, Martyn** Ian (Loughborough GS), b Leicester 30 Sep 1968. 6'1". LHB,
OB. Leicestershire 1989-92. OFS B 1990-91. HS 80 and Le BB 2-58 v Derbys
(Leicester) 1991. BB 3-51 OFS B v W Province B (Bloemfontein) 1990-91. **BHC:**
HS 20* v Notts (Nottingham) 1990. **SL:** HS 55* v Northants (Leicester) 1992. BB
3-45 v Surrey (Oval) 1990.

**GOFTON, Robert** Paul (Wolfreton S, Hull), b Scarborough, Yorks 10 Sep 1968. 5'10".
RHB, RM. MCC YC 1988-89. Leicestershire 1992. Worcestershire staff 1991. HS 75
v Surrey (Oval) 1992. BB 4-81 v Derbys (Ilkeston) 1992. **SL:** HS 2*. BB 1-33.

**HAWKES, Christopher** James (Loughborough GS; Durham U), b Loughborough
14 Jul 1972. 6'3". LHB, SLA. Leicestershire 1990-92. HS 18 v Somerset (Leicester)
1992. BB 4-18 v Lancs (Southport) 1992.

**ROSEBERRY, Andrew** (Durham S), b Sunderland, Co Durham 2 Apr 1971. 6'0".
Younger brother of M.A. (see MIDDLESEX). RHB, RM. Leicestershire 1992.
HS 14 v P (Leicester) 1992. No BAC appearances.

# LEICESTERSHIRE 1992

## RESULTS SUMMARY

| | Place | Won | Lost | Drew | Abandoned |
|---|---|---|---|---|---|
| **Britannic Assurance Championship** | 8th | 7 | 7 | 8 | |
| **All First-class Matches** | | 8 | 8 | 8 | |
| **Sunday League** | 18th | 3 | 12 | | 2 |
| **NatWest Trophy** | Finalist | | | | |
| **Benson and Hedges Cup** | 3rd in Group A | | | | |

# BRITANNIC ASSURANCE CHAMPIONSHIP AVERAGES

## BATTING AND FIELDING

| Cap | | M | I | NO | HS | Runs | Avge | 100 | 50 | Ct/St |
|---|---|---|---|---|---|---|---|---|---|---|
| 1986 | T.J.Boon | 22 | 38 | 3 | 139 | 1383 | 39.51 | 2 | 9 | 12 |
| 1981 | N.E.Briers | 22 | 39 | 6 | 122* | 1092 | 33.09 | 1 | 9 | 11 |
| – | V.J.Wells | 16 | 23 | 3 | 56 | 526 | 30.94 | – | 3 | 2 |
| 1988 | L.Potter | 21 | 33 | 3 | 96 | 797 | 26.56 | – | 4 | 9 |
| – | P.A.Nixon | 15 | 23 | 6 | 107* | 451 | 26.52 | 1 | 1 | 40/5 |
| – | B.F.Smith | 14 | 20 | 3 | 100* | 441 | 25.94 | 1 | 3 | 9 |
| 1986 | J.J.Whitaker | 20 | 31 | 2 | 74 | 701 | 24.17 | – | 1 | 10 |
| – | J.D.R.Benson | 17 | 26 | 1 | 122 | 571 | 22.84 | 1 | 1 | 28 |
| 1989 | W.K.M.Benjamin | 20 | 25 | 3 | 72 | 453 | 20.59 | – | 4 | 15 |
| – | C.J.Hawkes | 3 | 4 | 1 | 18 | 60 | 20.00 | – | – | 1 |
| – | M.I.Gidley | 5 | 10 | 2 | 39 | 143 | 17.87 | – | – | 2 |
| 1991 | D.J.Millns | 17 | 17 | 9 | 33* | 143 | 17.87 | – | – | 11 |
| – | R.P.Gofton | 4 | 6 | – | 75 | 100 | 16.66 | – | 1 | 1 |
| 1984 | G.J.Parsons | 13 | 14 | 2 | 35 | 142 | 11.83 | – | – | 6 |
| – | P.N.Hepworth | 8 | 13 | 1 | 29 | 131 | 10.91 | – | – | 5 |
| 1987 | P.Whitticase | 7 | 10 | 3 | 18* | 62 | 8.85 | – | – | 18 |
| – | A.D.Mullally | 17 | 21 | 6 | 21 | 112 | 7.46 | – | – | 4 |

*Also played*: P.E.Robinson (1 match) 0, 19.

## BOWLING

| | O | M | R | W | Avge | Best | 5wI | 10wM |
|---|---|---|---|---|---|---|---|---|
| D.J.Millns | 436.3 | 103 | 1401 | 68 | 20.60 | 6-87 | 6 | 1 |
| V.J.Wells | 293 | 90 | 738 | 33 | 22.36 | 4-26 | – | – |
| G.J.Parsons | 335.2 | 88 | 943 | 36 | 26.19 | 6-70 | 2 | – |
| W.K.M.Benjamin | 489 | 102 | 1498 | 47 | 31.87 | 4-34 | – | – |
| A.D.Mullally | 476 | 115 | 1365 | 38 | 35.92 | 5-119 | 1 | – |
| L.Potter | 344.1 | 78 | 1021 | 25 | 40.84 | 4-73 | – | – |

*Also bowled*: J.D.R.Benson 35-4-109-3; T.J.Boon 29-4-175-4; M.I.Gidley 80-20-248-2; R.P.Gofton 46-10-203-5; C.J.Hawkes 42-11-122-5; P.N.Hepworth 68.4-9-301-3; J.J.Whitaker 8-0-86-1.

The First-Class Averages (pp 164-178) give the records of Leicestershire players in all first-class county matches (their other opponents being the Pakistanis and Cambridge U)

# LEICESTERSHIRE RECORDS

## FIRST-CLASS CRICKET

| | | | | | |
|---|---|---|---|---|---|
| **Highest Total** | For | 701-4d | v Worcs | Worcester | 1906 |
| | V | 761-6d | by Essex | Chelmsford | 1990 |
| **Lowest Total** | For | 25 | v Kent | Leicester | 1912 |
| | V | 24 | by Glamorgan | Leicester | 1971 |
| | | 24 | by Oxford U | Oxford | 1985 |
| **Highest Innings** | For 252* | S.Coe | v Northants | Leicester | 1914 |
| | V 341 | G.H.Hirst | for Yorkshire | Leicester | 1905 |

### Highest Partnership for each Wicket

| | | | | | |
|---|---|---|---|---|---|
| 1st | 390 | B.Dudleston/J.F.Steele | v Derbyshire | Leicester | 1979 |
| 2nd | 289* | J.C.Balderstone/D.I.Gower | v Essex | Leicester | 1981 |
| 3rd | 316* | W.Watson/A.Wharton | v Somerset | Taunton | 1961 |
| 4th | 290* | P.Willey/T.J.Boon | v Warwicks | Leicester | 1984 |
| 5th | 233 | N.E.Briers/R.W.Tolchard | v Somerset | Leicester | 1979 |
| 6th | 262 | A.T.Sharpe/G.H.S.Fowke | v Derbyshire | Chesterfield | 1911 |
| 7th | 219* | J.D.R.Benson/P.Whitticase | v Hampshire | Bournemouth | 1991 |
| 8th | 164 | M.R.Hallam/C.T.Spencer | v Essex | Leicester | 1964 |
| 9th | 160 | W.W.Odell/R.T.Crawford | v Worcs | Leicester | 1902 |
| 10th | 228 | R.Illingworth/K.Higgs | v Northants | Leicester | 1977 |

| | | | | | |
|---|---|---|---|---|---|
| **Best Bowling** | For 10-18 | G.Geary | v Glamorgan | Pontypridd | 1929 |
| **(Innings)** | V 10-32 | H.Pickett | for Essex | Leyton | 1905 |
| **Best Bowling** | For 16-96 | G.Geary | v Glamorgan | Pontypridd | 1929 |
| **(Match)** | V 16-102 | C.Blythe | for Kent | Leicester | 1909 |

| | | | | | |
|---|---|---|---|---|---|
| **Most Runs – Season** | 2,446 | L.G.Berry | (av 52.04) | | 1937 |
| **Most Runs – Career** | 30,143 | L.G.Berry | (av 30.32) | | 1924-1951 |
| **Most 100s – Season** | 7 | L.G.Berry | | | 1937 |
| | 7 | W.Watson | | | 1959 |
| | 7 | B.F.Davison | | | 1982 |
| **Most 100s – Career** | 45 | L.G.Berry | | | 1924-1951 |
| **Most Wkts – Season** | 170 | J.E.Walsh | (av 18.96) | | 1948 |
| **Most Wkts – Career** | 2,130 | W.E.Astill | (av 23.19) | | 1906-1939 |

## LIMITED-OVERS CRICKET

| | | | | | | |
|---|---|---|---|---|---|---|
| **Highest Total** | NWT | 354-7 | | v Wiltshire | Swindon | 1984 |
| | BHC | 327-4 | | v Warwicks | Coventry | 1972 |
| | SL | 291-5 | | v Glamorgan | Swansea | 1984 |
| **Lowest Total** | NWT | 56 | | v Northants | Leicester | 1964 |
| | BHC | 56 | | v Minor C | Wellington | 1982 |
| | SL | 36 | | v Sussex | Leicester | 1973 |
| **Highest Innings** | NWT | 156 | D.I.Gower | v Derbyshire | Leicester | 1984 |
| | BHC | 158* | B.F.Davison | v Warwicks | Coventry | 1972 |
| | SL | 152 | B.Dudleston | v Lancashire | Manchester | 1975 |
| **Best Bowling** | NWT | 6-20 | K.Higgs | v Staffs | Longton | 1975 |
| | BHC | 6-35 | L.B.Taylor | v Worcs | Worcester | 1982 |
| | SL | 6-17 | K.Higgs | v Glamorgan | Leicester | 1973 |

# MIDDLESEX

**Formation of Present Club:** 2 February 1864
**Colours:** Blue
**Badge:** Three Seaxes
**Championships (since 1890):** (9) 1903, 1920, 1921, 1947, 1976, 1980, 1982, 1985, 1990
**Joint Championships:** (2) 1949, 1977
**NatWest Trophy/Gillette Cup Winners:** (4) 1977, 1980, 1984, 1988
**Benson and Hedges Cup Winners:** (2) 1983, 1986
**Sunday League Champions:** (1) 1992
**Match Awards:** NWT 47; BHC 52

**Secretary:** J.Hardstaff MBE, Lord's Cricket Ground, London NW8 8QN
(**☎** 071-289 1300 and 071-286 1310)
**Captain:** M.W.Gatting
**Scorer:** H.P.H.Sharp
**1993 Beneficiary:** N.G.Cowans

**BROWN, Keith** Robert (Chace S, Enfield), b Edmonton 18 Mar 1963. Brother of G.K. (Middx 1986 and Durham 1992). 5'11''. RHB, WK, RSM. Debut 1984. Cap 1990. MCC YC. 1000 runs (2); most – 1505 (1990). HS 200* v Notts (Lord's) 1990. BB 2-7 v Glos (Bristol) 1987. **Award:** NWT 1. **NWT:** HS 103* v Surrey (Uxbridge) 1990. **BHC:** HS 56 v Minor C (Lord's) 1990. **SL:** HS 102 v Somerset (Lord's) 1988.
**CARR, John** Donald (Repton S; Worcester C, Oxford), b St John's Wood 15 Jun 1963. Son of D.B. (Derbys, OU and England 1945-63). 5'11''. RHB, RM. Oxford U 1983-85 (blue 1983-84-85). Middlesex 1983-89 (cap 1987) and 1992. Hertfordshire 1982-84 and 1991. 1000 runs (3); most – 1541 (1987). HS 156 v Essex (Lord's) 1987. BB 6-61 v Glos (Lord's) 1985. **NWT:** HS 83 v Hants (Southampton) 1989. BB 2-19 v Surrey (Oval) 1988. **BHC:** HS 70 v Leics (Leicester) 1992. BB 3-22 Comb Us v Glos (Bristol) 1984. **SL:** HS 104* v Warwks (Lord's) 1992. BB 4-21 v Surrey (Lord's) 1989.
**COWANS, Norman** George (Park High SS, Stanmore), b Enfield St Mary, Jamaica 17 Apr 1961. 6'3''. RHB, RF. Debut 1980. Cap 1984. Benefit 1993. YC 1982. MCC YC. **Tests:** 19 (1982-83 to 1985); HS 36 v A (Perth) 1982-83; BB 6-77 v A (Melbourne) 1982-83. LOI: 23. Tours: A 1982-83; NZ 1983-84; I 1984-85; P 1983-84; SL 1984-85, 1985-86 (Eng B); Z 1980-81 (M). HS 66 v Surrey (Lord's) 1984. 50 wkts (6); most – 73 (1984, 1985). BB 6-31 v Leics (Leicester) 1985. **Awards:** NWT 1; BHC 1. **NWT:** HS 12* v Lancs (Lord's) 1984. BB 4-24 v Yorks (Leeds) 1986. **BHC:** HS 12 v Derbys (Derby) 1990. BB 4-33 v Lancs (Lord's) 1983. **SL:** HS 27 v Notts (Lord's) 1990. BB 6-9 v Lancs (Lord's) 1991.
**EMBUREY, John** Ernest (Peckham Manor SS), b Peckham, London 20 Aug 1952. 6'2''. RHB, OB. Debut 1973. Cap 1977. Wisden 1983. W Province 1982-83/1983-84. Benefit 1986. **Tests:** 60 (1978 to 1989, 2 as captain); HS 75 v NZ (Nottingham) 1986; BB 7-78 v A (Sydney) 1986-87. LOI: 58. Tours: A 1978-79, 1979-80, 1986-87, 1987-88; SA 1981-82 (SAB), 1989-90 (Eng XI); WI 1980-81, 1985-86; NZ 1987-88; I 1979-80, 1981-82; P 1987-88; SL 1977-78 (DHR), 1981-82; Z 1980-81 (M). HS 133 v Essex (Chelmsford) 1983. 50 wkts (14) inc 100 (1): 103 (1983). BB 7-27 (12-66 match) v Glos (Cheltenham) 1983. **Awards:** NWT 1; BHC 6. **NWT:** HS 36* v Lancs (Manchester) 1978. BB 3-11 v Sussex (Lord's) 1989. **BHC:** HS 50 v Kent (Lord's) 1984. BB 5-37 v Somerset (Taunton) 1991. **SL:** HS 50 v Lancs (Blackpool) 1988. BB 5-23 v Somerset (Taunton) 1991.
**FARBRACE, Paul** (Geoffrey Chaucer S, Canterbury), b Ash, Kent 7 Jul 1967. 5'10''. RHB, WK. Kent 1987-89. Middlesex debut 1990. HS 79 v CU (Cambridge) 1990. BAC HS 75* K v Yorks (Canterbury) 1987. BB 1-64. **NWT:** HS 17 v Berks (Lord's) 1990. **SL:** HS 26* v Lancs (Lord's) 1991.

110

**FRASER, Angus** Robert Charles (Gayton HS, Harrow), b Billinge, Lancs 8 Aug 1965. Brother of A.G.J. (see ESSEX). 6'5". RHB, RFM. Debut 1984. Cap 1988. **Tests:** 11 (1989 to 1990-91); HS 29 v A (Nottingham) 1989; BB 6-82 v A (Melbourne) 1990-91. LOI: 24. Tours: A 1990-91; WI 1989-90. HS 92 v Surrey (Oval) 1990. 50 wkts (3); most – 92 (1989). BB 7-77 v Kent (Canterbury) 1989. **NWT:** HS 19 v Durham (Darlington) 1989. BB 4-34 v Yorks (Leeds) 1988. **BHC:** HS 13* v Essex (Lord's) 1988. BB 3-30 v Glos (Lord's) 1992. **SL:** HS 30* v Kent (Canterbury) 1988. BB 4-28 v Glam (Lord's) 1990.

**GATTING, Michael** William (John Kelly HS), b Kingsbury 6 Jun 1957. 5'10". RHB, RM. Debut 1975. Cap 1977. Captain 1983-. Benefit 1988. YC 1981. Wisden 1983. OBE 1987. **Tests:** 68 (1977-78 to 1989, 23 as captain); HS 207 v I (Madras) 1984-85; BB 1-14. LOI: 85. Tours (C=captain): A 1986-87C, 1987-88C; SA 1989-90C (Eng XI); WI 1980-81, 1985-86; NZ 1977-78, 1983-84, 1987-88C; I/SL 1981-82, 1984-85; P 1977-78, 1983-84, 1987-88C; Z 1980-81 (M). 1000 runs (14+1) inc 2000 (3); most – 2257 (1984). HS 258 v Somerset (Bath) 1984. BB 5-34 v Glam (Swansea) 1982. Awards: NWT 6; BHC 11. **NWT:** HS 132* v Sussex (Lord's) 1989. BB 2-14 (twice). **BHC:** HS 143* v Sussex (Hove) 1985. BB 4-49 v Sussex (Lord's) 1984. **SL:** HS 124* v Leics (Leicester) 1990. BB 4-30 v Glos (Bristol) 1989.

**HABIB, Aftab** (Millfield S; Taunton S), b Reading, Berkshire 7 Feb 1972. 5'11". Cousin of Zahid Sadiq (Surrey and Derbys 1988-90). RHB, RMF. Debut 1992. HS 12 v Surrey (Oval) 1992.

**HARRISON, Jason** Christian (Great Marlow SM; Bucks CHE), b Amersham, Bucks 15 Jan 1972. 6'3". RHB, OB. No 1st XI appearances – joined staff 1992. Buckinghamshire 1991-92.

**HAYNES, Desmond** Leo (Barbados Academy; Federal HS), b Holder's Hill, Barbados 15 Feb 1956. 5'11". RHB, RM/LB. Barbados 1976-77 to date (captain 1990-91). Middlesex debut/cap 1989. Scotland (BHC) 1983. Wisden 1990. **Tests** (WI): 103 (1977-78 to 1991-92, 4 as captain); HS 184 v E (Lord's) 1980; BB 1-2. LOI (WI): 203. Tours (WI): E 1980, 1984, 1988, 1991; A 1979-80, 1981-82, 1984-85, 1986-87, 1988-89, 1991-92; NZ 1979-80, 1986-87; I 1983-84, 1987-88; P 1980-81, 1986-87, 1990-91 (captain); Z 1981-82 (WI B). 1000 runs (3+4) inc 2000 (1): 2346 (1990). HS 255* v Sussex (Lord's) 1990. BB 1-2 (Tests). M BB 1-4. Awards: NWT 1; BHC 3. **NWT:** HS 149* v Lancs (Manchester) 1990. **BHC:** HS 131 v Sussex (Hove) 1990. BB 1-21. **SL:** HS 107* v Lancs (Manchester) 1990.

**JOHNSON, Richard** Leonard (Sunbury Manor S; S Pelthorne C), b Chertsey, Surrey 29 Dec 1974. 6'2". RHB, RMF. Debut 1992. HS 1. BB 1-25.

**KEECH, Matthew** (Northumberland Park S), b Hampstead 21 Oct 1970. 6'0". RHB, RM. Debut 1991. MCC YC. HS 58* v Notts (Lord's) 1991. **BHC:** HS 47 v Warwks (Lord's) 1991. **SL:** HS 49* v Somerset (Taunton) 1991.

**POOLEY, Jason** Calvin (Acton HS), b Hammersmith 8 Aug 1969. 6'0". LHB. Debut 1989. HS 88 v Derbys (Lord's) 1991. **BHC:** HS 8. **SL:** HS 109 v Derbys (Lord's) 1991.

**RADFORD, Toby** Alexander (St Bartholomew's S, Newbury; Loughborough U), b Caerphilly, Glam 3 Dec 1971. 5'10". RHB, OB. No 1st XI appearances – joined staff 1992.

**RAMPRAKASH, Mark** Ravin (Gayton HS; Harrow Weald SFC), b Bushey, Herts 5 Sep 1969. 5'9". RHB, RM. Debut 1987. Cap 1990. YC 1991. **Tests:** 9 (1991 to 1992); HS 29 v WI (Birmingham) 1991. LOI: 2. Tours: WI 1991-92 (Eng A); NZ 1991-92; P 1990-91 (Eng A); SL 1990-91 (Eng A). 1000 runs (4); most – 1541 (1990). HS 233 v Surrey (Lord's) 1992. BB 1-0. Awards: NWT 1; BHC 1. **NWT:**

**RAMPRAKASH** – continued:
HS 104 v Surrey (Uxbridge) 1990. BB 2-15 v Ire (Dublin) 1991. **BHC:** HS 108* v Leics (Leicester) 1992. **SL:** HS 147* v Worcs (Lord's) 1990. BB 2-32 v Sussex (Hove) 1991.

**ROSEBERRY, Michael** Anthony (Durham S), b Houghton-le-Spring, Co Durham 28 Nov 1966. Elder brother of A. (see LEICS). 6'1". RHB, RM. Debut 1986. Cap 1990. 1000 runs (3) inc 2000 (1): 2044 (1992). HS 173 v Durham (Lord's) 1992. BB 1-1. Award: BHC 1. **NWT:** HS 112 and BB 1-22 v Salop (Telford) 1992. **BHC:** HS 84 v Minor C (Lord's) 1992. **SL:** HS 106* v Yorks (Lord's) 1991.

**SIMS, Robin** Jason (Vyners SS), b Hillingdon 22 Nov 1970. 5'8". LHB, WK. Debut 1992. MCC YC (held long-leg catch as substitute to dismiss A.R.Border in Lord's Test 1989). HS 3. Awaiting BAC debut. **NWT:** HS 13* v Salop (Telford) 1992. **BHC:** HS –. **SL:** HS 27* v Derbys (Derby) 1992.

**TAYLOR, Charles** William (Spendlove S, Charlbury), b Banbury, Oxon 12 Aug 1966. 6'5½". LHB, LMF. Debut 1990. Oxfordshire 1986 and 1990. HS 21 v Kent (Lord's) 1991. BB 5-33 v Yorks (Leeds) 1990. **SL:** HS –. BB 1-54. **SL:** 3*. BB 1-14.

**TUFNELL, Philip** Clive Roderick (Highgate S), b Barnet, Herts 29 Apr 1966. 6'0". RHB, SLA. Debut 1986. Cap 1990. MCC YC. **Tests:** 10 (1990-91 to 1992); HS 8; BB 7-47 (11-147 match) v NZ (Christchurch) 1991-92. LOI: 15. Tours: A 1990-91; NZ 1991-92. HS 37 v Leics (Leicester) and v Yorks (Leeds) 1990. 50 wkts (3); most – 88 (1991). BB 7-47 (Tests). M BB 7-116 (11-228 match) v Hants (Lord's) 1991. Award: NWT 1. **NWT:** HS 8. BB 3-29 v Herts (Lord's) 1988. **BHC:** HS 18 v Warwks (Lord's) 1991. BB 3-50 v Surrey (Lord's) 1991. **SL:** HS 13* v Glam (Merthyr Tydfil) 1989. BB 3-28 v Surrey (Lord's) 1991.

**WALKER, David** Anthony (John Kelly S; Willesden C), b Hackney 18 Jun 1975. 5'11". RHB, RMF. No 1st XI appearances – joined staff 1991.

**WEEKES, Paul** Nicholas (Homerton House SS, Hackney), b Hackney, London 8 Jul 1969. 5'10". LHB, OB. Debut 1990. MCC YC. HS 95 v OU (Oxford) 1992. BAC HS 89* v Surrey (Lord's) 1992. BB 3-57 v Worcs (Worcester) 1991. Award: BHC 1. **NWT:** HS 7. BB 1-30. **BHC:** HS 44* v Glos (Lord's) 1992. BB 2-29 v Hants (Southampton) 1992. **SL:** HS 32* v Yorks (Lord's) 1991. BB 4-37 v Somerset (Lord's) 1992.

**WILLIAMS, Neil** FitzGerald (Acland Burghley CS), b Hope Well, St Vincent 2 Jul 1962. 5'11". RHB, RFM. Debut 1982. Cap 1984. Windward Is 1982-83 and 1989-90 to date. Tasmania 1983-84. MCC YC. **Tests:** 1 (1990); HS 38 and BB 2-148 v I (Oval) 1990. Tour: Z 1984-85 (EC). HS 77 v Warwks (Birmingham) 1991. 50 wkts (3); most – 63 (1983). BB 8-75 (12-139 match) v Glos (Lord's) 1992. Award: BHC 1. **NWT:** HS 10 v Northumb (Jesmond) 1984. BB 4-36 v Derbys (Derby) 1983. **BHC:** HS 29* v Surrey (Lord's) 1985. BB 3-16 v Comb Us (Cambridge) 1982. **SL:** HS 43 v Somerset (Lord's) 1988. BB 4-39 v Surrey (Oval) 1988.

### NEWCOMERS

**BALLINGER, Richard** John (Millfield S; Durham U), b Wimbledon, Surrey 18 Sep 1973. 6'2". RHB, RFM.

**DUTCH, Keith** Philip (Nower Hill HS; Weald C), b Harrow 21 Mar 1973. 5'10". RHB, OB. MCC YC 1992.

**FELTHAM, Mark** Andrew (Tiffin S), b St John's Wood 26 June 1963. 6'2¼". RHB, RMF. Surrey 1983-92 (cap 1990). MCC YC. HS 101 Sy v Middx (Oval) 1990. 50 wkts (1): 56 (1988). BB 6-53 Sy v Leics (Oval) 1990. Awards: BHC 2. **NWT:** HS 19* Sy v Hants (Oval) 1991. BB 2-27 Sy v Cheshire (Birkenhead) 1986. **BHC:** HS 35 Sy v Kent (Canterbury) 1992. BB 5-28 Sy v Comb Us (Cambridge) 1989. **SL:** HS 61 Sy v Warwks (Oval) 1990. BB 4-35 Sy v Sussex (Guildford) 1986.

DEPARTURES – see p 156

# MIDDLESEX 1992

## RESULTS SUMMARY

|  | Place | Won | Lost | Drew | Abandoned |
|---|---|---|---|---|---|
| Britannic Assurance Championship | 11th | 5 | 3 | 14 | |
| All First-class Matches | | 5 | 4 | 16 | |
| Sunday League | 1st | 14 | 2 | | 1 |
| NatWest Trophy | 2nd Round | | | | |
| Benson and Hedges Cup | Quarter-Finalist | | | | |

# BRITANNIC ASSURANCE CHAMPIONSHIP AVERAGES

## BATTING AND FIELDING

| Cap | | M | I | NO | HS | Runs | Avge | 100 | 50 | Ct/St |
|---|---|---|---|---|---|---|---|---|---|---|
| 1977 | M.W.Gatting | 22 | 35 | 6 | 170 | 1980 | 68.27 | 6 | 10 | 15 |
| – | J.C.Pooley | 2 | 4 | 1 | 69 | 149 | 49.66 | – | 2 | – |
| 1990 | M.A.Roseberry | 22 | 38 | 3 | 173 | 1724 | 49.25 | 6 | 8 | 13 |
| 1990 | M.R.Ramprakash | 14 | 24 | 2 | 233 | 1042 | 47.36 | 3 | 5 | 6 |
| 1989 | D.L.Haynes | 20 | 35 | 2 | 177 | 1513 | 45.84 | 3 | 10 | 8 |
| 1987 | J.D.Carr | 22 | 34 | 6 | 114 | 1068 | 38.14 | 2 | 7 | 39 |
| – | P.N.Weekes | 14 | 17 | 5 | 89* | 431 | 35.91 | – | 2 | 14 |
| – | D.W.Headley | 14 | 12 | 3 | 91 | 268 | 29.77 | – | 1 | 5 |
| 1977 | J.E.Emburey | 22 | 27 | 6 | 102 | 554 | 26.38 | 1 | 3 | 21 |
| 1990 | K.R.Brown | 22 | 33 | 5 | 106 | 651 | 23.25 | 1 | 2 | 36/11 |
| 1988 | A.R.C.Fraser | 16 | 18 | 7 | 33 | 188 | 17.09 | – | – | 3 |
| 1984 | N.F.Williams | 17 | 17 | 3 | 46* | 186 | 13.28 | – | – | 9 |
| 1990 | P.C.R.Tufnell | 14 | 13 | 7 | 12 | 55 | 9.16 | – | – | 2 |
| – | C.W.Taylor | 16 | 13 | 6 | 14 | 64 | 9.14 | – | – | 3 |

*Also played*: P.H.Edmonds (1 match – cap 1974) did not bat; A.Habib (1 match) 12, 7*; R.L.Johnson (1 match) 1 (1 ct); S.A.Sylvester (2 matches) 0* (1 ct).

## BOWLING

| | O | M | R | W | Avge | Best | 5wI | 10wM |
|---|---|---|---|---|---|---|---|---|
| J.E.Emburey | 848.5 | 245 | 2064 | 80 | 25.80 | 5-23 | 3 | – |
| N.F.Williams | 437 | 86 | 1283 | 48 | 26.72 | 8-75 | 2 | 1 |
| P.C.R.Tufnell | 517.2 | 122 | 1366 | 41 | 33.31 | 5-83 | 2 | – |
| D.W.Headley | 304.3 | 62 | 968 | 26 | 37.23 | 3-31 | – | – |
| C.W.Taylor | 379.2 | 74 | 1337 | 32 | 41.78 | 4-50 | – | – |
| P.N.Weekes | 155 | 36 | 428 | 10 | 42.80 | 3-61 | – | – |
| A.R.C.Fraser | 366.2 | 69 | 1158 | 18 | 64.33 | 3-59 | – | – |

*Also bowled*: J.D.Carr 41-14-100-3; P.H.Edmonds 28-10-48-4; M.W.Gatting 6-0-38-0; D.L.Haynes 2.4-0-5-1; R.L.Johnson 14-2-71-1; M.R.Ramprakash 10-1-41-0; M.A.Roseberry 10-2-71-0; S.A.Sylvester 42-9-123-2.

The First-Class Averages (pp 164-178) give the records of Middlesex players in all first-class county matches (their other opponents being the Pakistanis, Cambridge U and Oxford U), with the exception of:
    M.R.Ramprakash 16-27-2-233-1156-46.24-3-5-7ct. 10-1-41-0.
    P.C.R.Tufnell 15-13-7-12-55-9.16-0-0-2ct. 562.2-135-1472-42-35.04-5/83-2-0.

# MIDDLESEX RECORDS

## FIRST-CLASS CRICKET

| | | | | |
|---|---|---|---|---|
| **Highest Total** | For 642-3d | v Hampshire | Southampton | 1923 |
| | V 665 | by W Indians | Lord's | 1939 |
| **Lowest Total** | For 20 | v MCC | Lord's | 1864 |
| | V 31 | by Glos | Bristol | 1924 |
| **Highest Innings** | For 331* J.D.B.Robertson | v Worcs | Worcester | 1949 |
| | V 316* J.B.Hobbs | for Surrey | Lord's | 1926 |

**Highest Partnership for each Wicket**

| | | | | |
|---|---|---|---|---|
| 1st | 367* G.D.Barlow/W.N.Slack | v Kent | Lord's | 1981 |
| 2nd | 380 F.A.Tarrant/J.W.Hearne | v Lancashire | Lord's | 1914 |
| 3rd | 424* W.J.Edrich/D.C.S.Compton | v Somerset | Lord's | 1948 |
| 4th | 325 J.W.Hearne/E.H.Hendren | v Hampshire | Lord's | 1919 |
| 5th | 338 R.S.Lucas/T.C.O'Brien | v Sussex | Hove | 1895 |
| 6th | 227 C.T.Radley/F.J.Titmus | v S Africans | Lord's | 1965 |
| 7th | 271* E.H.Hendren/F.T.Mann | v Notts | Nottingham | 1925 |
| 8th | 182* M.H.C.Doll/H.R.Murrell | v Notts | Lord's | 1913 |
| 9th | 160* E.H.Hendren/T.J.Durston | v Essex | Leyton | 1927 |
| 10th | 230 R.W.Nicholls/W.Roche | v Kent | Lord's | 1899 |

| | | | | |
|---|---|---|---|---|
| **Best Bowling** | For 10-40 G.O.B.Allen | v Lancashire | Lord's | 1929 |
| **(Innings)** | V 9-38 R.C.Glasgow† | for Somerset | Lord's | 1924 |
| **Best Bowling** | For 16-114 G.Burton | v Yorkshire | Sheffield | 1888 |
| **(Match)** | 16-114 J.T.Hearne | v Lancashire | Manchester | 1898 |
| | V 16-109 C.W.L.Parker | for Glos | Cheltenham | 1930 |

| | | | |
|---|---|---|---|
| **Most Runs – Season** | 2,669 | E.H.Hendren (av 83.41) | 1923 |
| **Most Runs – Career** | 40,302 | E.H.Hendren (av 48.81) | 1907-1937 |
| **Most 100s – Season** | 13 | D.C.S.Compton | 1947 |
| **Most 100s – Career** | 119 | E.H.Hendren | 1907-1937 |
| **Most Wkts – Season** | 158 | F.J.Titmus (av 14.63) | 1955 |
| **Most Wkts – Career** | 2,361 | F.J.Titmus (av 21.27) | 1949-1982 |

## LIMITED-OVERS CRICKET

| | | | | | |
|---|---|---|---|---|---|
| **Highest Total** | NWT | 296-4 | v Lancashire | Manchester | 1990 |
| | BHC | 325-5 | v Leics | Leicester | 1992 |
| | SL | 290-6 | v Worcs | Lord's | 1990 |
| **Lowest Total** | NWT | 41 | v Essex | Westcliff | 1972 |
| | BHC | 73 | v Essex | Lord's | 1985 |
| | SL | 23 | v Yorkshire | Leeds | 1974 |
| **Highest Innings** | NWT | 158 G.D.Barlow | v Lancashire | Lord's | 1984 |
| | BHC | 143* M.W.Gatting | v Sussex | Hove | 1985 |
| | SL | 147* M.Ramprakash | v Worcs | Lord's | 1990 |
| **Best Bowling** | NWT | 6-15 W.W.Daniel | v Sussex | Hove | 1980 |
| | BHC | 7-12 W.W.Daniel | v Minor C (E) | Ipswich | 1978 |
| | SL | 6-6 R.W.Hooker | v Surrey | Lord's | 1969 |

† R.C.Robertson-Glasgow

# NORTHAMPTONSHIRE

**Formation of Present Club:** 31 July 1878
**Colours:** Maroon
**Badge:** Tudor Rose
**Championships:** (0) Second 1912, 1957, 1965, 1976
**NatWest Trophy/Gillette Cup Winners:** (2) 1976, 1992
**Benson and Hedges Cup Winners:** (1) 1980
**Sunday League Champions:** (0) Third 1991
**Match Awards:** NWT 42; BHC 41
**Chief Executive:** S.P.Coverdale, County Ground, Wantage Road, Northampton, NN1 4TJ (☎ 0604-32917)
**Captain:** A.J.Lamb
**Scorer:** A.C.Kingston
**1993 Beneficiary:** R.J.Bailey

**AMBROSE,** Curtly Elconn Lynwall (All Saints Village SS), b Swetes Village, Antigua 21 Sep 1963. Cousin of R.M.Otto (Leeward Is 1979-80/1990-91). 6'7". LHB, RF. Leeward Is 1985-86 to date. Northamptonshire debut 1989. Cap 1990. Wisden 1991. **Tests** (WI): 34 (1987-88 to 1991-92); HS 53 v A (P-of-S) 1990-91; BB 8-45 v E (Bridgetown) 1989-90. LOI (WI): 71. Tours (WI): E 1988, 1991; A 1988-89; P 1990-91. HS 59 WI v Sussex (Hove) 1988. Nh HS 55* v Leics (Leicester) 1990. 50 wkts (3); most – 61 (1990). BB 8-45 (Tests). Nh BB 7-89 v Leics (Leicester) 1990. Award: NWT 1. **NWT:** HS 48 v Lancs (Lord's) 1990. BB 4-7 v Yorks (Northampton) 1992. **BHC:** HS 17* v Kent (Northampton) 1989. BB 4-31 v Essex (Northampton) 1992. **SL:** HS 14* v Glos (Moreton) 1992. BB 3-15 v Notts (Finedon) 1989.

**BAILEY,** Robert John (Biddulph HS), b Biddulph, Staffs 28 Oct 1963. 6'3". RHB, OB. Debut 1982. Cap 1985. Benefit 1993. Staffordshire 1980. YC 1984. **Tests:** 4 (1988 to 1989-90); HS 43 v WI (Oval) 1988. LOI: 4. Tours: SA 1991-92 (Nh); WI 1989-90. 1000 runs (9); most – 1987 (1990). HS 224* v Glam (Swansea) 1986. BB 3-27 v Glam (Wellingborough) 1988. Awards: NWT 3; BHC 5. **NWT:** HS 145 v Staffs (Stone) 1991. BB 3-47 v Notts (Northampton) 1990. **BHC:** HS 134 v Glos (Northampton) 1987. BB 1-22. **SL:** HS 125* v Derbys (Derby) 1987. BB 3-23 v Leics (Leicester) 1987.

**BOWEN,** Mark Nicholas (Sacred Heart, Redcar; St Mary's C; Teesside Poly), b Redcar, Yorks 6 Dec 1967. 6'2". RHB, RM. Debut v Natal (Durban) 1991-92. Tour: SA 1991-92 (Nh). HS 13* and BB 1-23 on debut. BAC HS 5. BAC BB 1-35. **SL:** HS 9. BB 1-33.

**CAPEL,** David John (Roade CS), b Northampton 6 Feb 1963. 5'11". RHB, RMF. Debut 1981. Cap 1986. E Province 1985-86/1986-87. **Tests:** 15 (1987 to 1990); HS 98 v P (Karachi) 1987-88; BB 3-88 v WI (Bridgetown) 1989-90. LOI: 23. Tours: A 1987-88; WI 1989-90; NZ 1987-88; P 1987-88. 1000 runs (3); most – 1311 (1989). HS 134 EP v W Province (Port Elizabeth) 1986-87. Nh HS 126 v Sussex (Hove) 1989. 50 wkts (3); most – 63 (1986). BB 7-46 v Yorks (Northampton) 1987. Awards: NWT 3. **NWT:** HS 101 v Notts (Northampton) 1990. BB 3-21 v Glam (Swansea) 1992. **BHC:** HS 97 v Yorks (Lord's) 1987. BB 4-29 v Warwks (Birmingham) 1986. **SL:** HS 121 v Glam (Northampton) 1990. BB 4-30 v Yorks (Middlesbrough) 1982.

**COOK,** Nicholas Grant Billson (Lutterworth GS), b Leicester 17 Jun 1956. 6'0". RHB, SLA. Leicestershire 1978-85 (cap 1982). Northamptonshire debut 1986. Cap 1987. **Tests:** 15 (1983 to 1989); HS 31 v A (Oval) 1989; BB 6-65 (11-83 match) v P (Karachi) 1983-84. LOI: 3. Tours: NZ 1979-80 (DHR), 1983-84; P 1983-84, 1987-88; SL 1985-86 (Eng B); Z 1980-81 (Le), 1984-85 (EC). HS 75 Le v Somerset (Taunton) 1988. Nh HS 64 v Lancs (Manchester) 1987. 50 wkts (8); most – 90 (1982). BB 7-34 (10-97 match) v Essex (Chelmsford) 1992. **NWT:** HS 13 v Middx (Northampton) 1986. BB 4-24 v Ire (Northampton) 1987. **BHC:** HS 23 Le v Warwks (Leicester) 1984. BB 3-35 v Kent (Northampton) 1989. **SL:** HS 17* v Surrey (Tring) 1991. BB 3-20 v Kent (Canterbury) 1989.

115

**CURRAN, Kevin** Malcolm (Marandellas HS), b Rusape, S Rhodesia 7 Sep 1959. Son of K.P. (Rhodesia 1947-48/1953-54). 6'1". RHB, RMF. Zimbabwe 1980-81/ 1987-88. Natal 1988-89. Gloucestershire 1985-90 (cap 1985). Northamptonshire debut 1991; cap 1992. Qualifies for England in 1994. LOI (Z): 11. Tours (Z): E 1982; SL 1983-84. 1000 runs (5); most – 1353 (1986). HS 144* Gs v Sussex (Bristol) 1990. Nh HS 89* v Lancs (Lytham) 1991. 50 wkts (4); most – 65 (1988). BB 7-47 Natal v Transvaal (Johannesburg) 1988-89. BAC BB 7-54 Gs v Leics (Gloucester) 1988. Nh BB 6-45 v Hants (Bournemouth) 1992. Awards: NWT 2; BHC 2. **NWT:** HS 78* v Cambs (Northampton) 1992. BB 4-34 Gs v Northants (Bristol) 1985. **BHC:** HS 57 Gs v Derbys (Derby) 1987. BB 4-41 Gs v Notts (Bristol) 1989. **SL:** HS 92 Gs v Northants (Northampton) 1990. BB 5-15 Gs v Leics (Gloucester) 1988.

**FELTON, Nigel** Alfred (Millfield S; Loughborough U), b Guildford, Surrey 24 Oct 1960. 5'8". LHB, OB. Somerset 1982-88 (cap 1986). Northamptonshire debut 1989. Cap 1990. Tour: SA 1991-92 (Nh). 1000 runs (4); most – 1538 (1990). HS 173* Sm v Kent (Taunton) 1983. Nh HS 122 v Glam (Northampton) 1990. BB 1-48. Awards: NWT 2. **NWT:** HS 87 Sm v Kent (Taunton) 1984. **BHC:** HS 82 v Lancs (Northampton) 1992. **SL:** HS 96 Sm v Essex (Chelmsford) 1986.

**FORDHAM, Alan** (Bedford Modern S; Durham U), b Bedford 9 Nov 1964. 6'1". RHB, RM. Debut 1986. Cap 1990. Bedfordshire 1982-85. Comb Us (BHC) 1987. Tour: SA 1991-92 (Nh). 1000 runs (3); most – 1840 (1991). HS 206* v Yorks (Leeds) 1990, sharing in Northants record 3rd wkt stand of 393 with A.J.Lamb. BB 1-25. Nh 2nd XI record score: 236 (158 balls) v Worcs (Kidderminster) 1989. Awards: NWT 4; BHC 3. **NWT:** HS 132* v Leics (Northampton) 1991. BB 1-3. **BHC:** HS 103 v Scot (Forfar) 1992. **SL:** HS 89 v Notts (Nottingham) 1992.

**HUGHES, John** Gareth (Sir Christopher Hatton SS, Wellingborough; Sheffield City Poly), b Wellingborough 3 May 1971. 6'1". RHB, RM. Debut 1990. Tour: SA 1991-92 (Nh). HS 6 and BB 3-56 v Natal (Durban) 1991-92. BAC HS 2. BAC BB 2-57 v Derbys (Chesterfield) 1990. SL 1*.

**INNES, Kevin** John (Weston Favell Upper S), b Wellingborough 24 Sep 1975. 5'10". RHB, RM. 2nd XI debut 1990 (aged 14yr 8mth – Northamptonshire record). No 1st XI appearances – joined staff 1992.

**LAMB, Allan** Joseph (Wynberg HS; Abbotts C) b Langebaanweg, Cape Province, SA 20 Jun 1954. 5'8". RHB, RM. W Province 1972-73/1981-82. OFS 1987-88. Northamptonshire debut/cap 1978. Benefit 1988. Captain 1989-. Wisden 1980. **Tests:** 79 (1982 to 1992, 3 as captain); HS 142 v NZ (Wellington) 1991-92; BB 1-6. LOI: 122. Tours: A 1982-83, 1986-87, 1990-91; WI 1985-86, 1989-90; NZ 1983-84, 1991-92; I/SL 1984-85; P 1983-84. 1000 runs (11) inc 2000 (1); 2049 (1981). HS 294 OFS v E Province (Bloemfontein) 1987-88 – sharing record SA 5th wkt stand of 355 with J.J.Strydom. Nh HS 235 v Yorks (Leeds) 1990 sharing in Northants record 3rd wkt stand of 393 with A.Fordham. BB 2-29 v Lancs (Lytham) 1991. Awards: NWT 2; BHC 9. **NWT:** HS 103 v Suffolk (Bury St E) 1989. BB 1-4. **BHC:** HS 126* v Kent (Canterbury) 1987. BB 1-11. **SL:** HS 132* v Surrey (Guildford) 1985.

**LOYE, Malachy** Bernhard (Moulton S), b Northampton 27 Sep 1972. 6'2". RHB, OB. Debut 1991. HS 46 v Durham (Stockton) 1992. **SL:** HS 27* v Essex (Chelmsford) 1992.

**MONTGOMERIE, Richard** Robert (Rugby S; Worcester C, Oxford), b Rugby, Warwks 3 Jul 1971. 5'10½". RHB, OB. Oxford U 1991-92 (blue 1991-92). Northants debut 1991. Comb Us (BHC) 1992. Rackets blue 1990. HS 103* OU v Middx (Oxford) 1992. Nh HS 7. **BHC:** HS 75 Comb Us v Worcs (Oxford) 1992.

**NOON, Wayne** Michael (Caistor S), b Grimsby, Lincs 5 Feb 1971. 5'9". RHB, WK. Debut 1989. Worcs 2nd XI debut when aged 15yr 199d. Tour: SA 1991-92 (Nh). HS 37 v A (Northampton) 1989. BAC HS 36 v Glos (Bristol) 1991. **BHC:** HS –. **SL:** HS 21 v Surrey (Oval) 1990.

116

**PEARSON, Richard** Michael (Batley GS; St John's, Cambridge), b Batley, Yorks 27 Jan 1972. 6'3". RHB, OB. Cambridge U 1991-92 (blue 1991-92) Northamptonshire debut 1992. Comb Us (BHC) 1991-92. HS 33* CU v Surrey (Cambridge) 1992. Nh HS –. BB 5-108 CU v Warwks (Cambridge) 1992. Nh BB 2-90 v Warwks (Northampton) 1992. **BHC:** HS 8. BB 2-31 Comb Us v Durham (Cambridge) 1992. **SL:** HS –.

**PENBERTHY, Anthony** Leonard (Camborne CS), b Troon, Cornwall 1 Sep 1969. 6'1". LHB, RM. Debut 1989. Cornwall 1987-89. Tour: SA 1991-92 (Nh). HS 101* v CU (Cambridge) 1990. BAC HS 83 v Essex (Chelmsford) 1990. Nh BB 4-91 v Warwks (Northampton) 1990. Dismissed M.A.Taylor with his first ball in f-c cricket. **NWT:** HS 36 v Yorks (Northampton) 1992. BB 2-29 v Glam (Swansea) 1992. **BHC:** HS 10 v Notts (Nottingham) 1990. BB 2-22 v Comb Us (Northampton) 1991. **SL:** HS 43 v Warwks (Northampton) 1992. BB 3-26 v Essex (Northampton) 1989.

**RIPLEY, David** (Royds SS, Leeds), b Leeds, Yorks 13 Sep 1966. 5'9". RHB, WK. Debut 1984. Cap 1987. Tour: SA 1991-92 (Nh). HS 134* v Yorks (Scarborough) 1986. BB 2-89 v Essex (Ilford) 1987. Award: BHC 1. **NWT:** HS 27* v Durham (Darlington) 1984. **BHC:** HS 36* v Glos (Bristol) 1991. **SL:** HS 36* v Hants (Southampton) 1986.

**ROBERTS, Andrew** Richard, b Kettering 16 Apr 1971. 5'5". RHB, LB. Debut 1989. Tour: SA 1991-92 (Nh). HS 62 v Notts (Nottingham) 1992. BB 6-72 v Lancs (Lytham) 1991. **NWT:** HS –. BB 1-23. **SL:** HS 14 v Worcs (Northampton) 1991. BB 3-26 v Hants (Northampton) 1991.

**SNAPE, Jeremy** Nicholas (Denstone C; Durham U), b Stoke-on-Trent, Staffs 27 Apr 1973. 5'8½". RHB, OB. Debut 1992. Comb Us (BHC) 1992. HS –. BB 1-20. Award: BHC 1. **NWT:** HS 5*. **BHC:** HS 26 Comb Us v Durham (Cambridge) 1992. BB 3-35 Comb Us v Worcs (Oxford) 1992. **SL:** HS 6. BB 3-33 v Warwks (Northampton) 1992.

**STANLEY, Neil** Alan (Bedford Modern S), b Bedford 16 May 1968. 6'2". RHB, RM. Debut 1988. Bedfordshire 1987. Tour: SA 1991-92 (Nh). HS 132 v Lancs (Lytham) 1991. **BHC:** HS 8. BB 1-3. **SL:** HS 18 v Warwks (Birmingham) 1988.

**TAYLOR, Jonathan Paul** (Pingle S, Swadlincote), b Ashby-de-la-Zouch 8 Aug 1964. 6'2". LHB, LFM. Derbyshire 1984-86. Northamptonshire debut 1991; cap 1992. Staffordshire 1989-90 (cap 1989). HS 74* v Notts (Northampton) 1992. 50 wkts (1): 68 (1992). BB 7-23 v Hants (Bournemouth) 1992. **NWT:** HS 9. BB 3-41 v Glam (Swansea) 1992. **BHC:** HS 3. BB 3-38 v Lancs (Northampton) 1992. **SL:** HS 16 v Surrey (Tring) 1991. BB 3-14 D v Glos (Gloucester) 1986.

**WALKER, Alan** (Shelley HS), b Emley, Yorks 7 Jul 1962. 5'11". LHB, RFM. Debut 1983. Cap 1987. Tour: SA 1991-92 (Nh). HS 41* v Warwks (Birmingham) 1987. 50 wkts (1): 54 (1988). BB 6-50 v Lancs (Northampton) 1986. Award: NWT 1. **NWT:** HS 11 v Surrey (Oval) 1991. BB 4-7 v Ire (Northampton) 1987. **BHC:** HS 15* v Notts (Nottingham) 1987. BB 4-46 v Glos (Northampton) 1985. **SL:** HS 13 v Yorks (Tring) 1983. BB 4-21 v Worcs (Worcester) 1985.

**WALTON, Timothy** Charles (Leeds GS), b Low Head, Yorks 8 Nov 1972. 6'0½". RHB, RM. Awaiting f-c debut. **SL:** HS –. BB 2-27 v Leics (Leicester) 1992.

**WARREN, Russell** John (Kingsthorpe Upper S), b Northampton 10 Sep 1971. 6'1". RHB, OB. Debut 1992. HS 19 v Glos (Bristol) 1992.

## NEWCOMERS

**RIKA, Craig** Justin (Woodhouse Grove S, Bradford), b Staincliffe, Yorks 18 Jan 1974. 6'2½". RHB, RM.

**TOMLINSON, Jamie** (St Ninian's HS, I.o.M.; Ballakermeen HS, I.o.M.), b Warrington, Cheshire 14 Aug 1971. 6'3". RHB, RFM.

DEPARTURE – see p 157

# NORTHAMPTONSHIRE 1992

## RESULTS SUMMARY

|  | Place | Won | Lost | Drew | Abandoned |
|---|---|---|---|---|---|
| **Britannic Assurance Championship** | 3rd | 8 | 4 | 10 | |
| **All First-class Matches** | | 8 | 5 | 10 | |
| **Sunday League** | 13th | 7 | 9 | | |
| **NatWest Trophy** | Winners | | | | |
| **Benson and Hedges Cup** | 4th in Group B | | | | |

# BRITANNIC ASSURANCE CHAMPIONSHIP AVERAGES

### BATTING AND FIELDING

| Cap | | M | I | NO | HS | Runs | Avge | 100 | 50 | Ct/St |
|---|---|---|---|---|---|---|---|---|---|---|
| 1978 | A.J.Lamb | 15 | 23 | 4 | 209 | 1350 | 71.05 | 6 | 5 | 11 |
| 1985 | R.J.Bailey | 22 | 37 | 7 | 167* | 1514 | 50.46 | 2 | 7 | 20 |
| 1990 | A.Fordham | 22 | 39 | 2 | 192 | 1693 | 45.75 | 4 | 7 | 12 |
| 1987 | D.Ripley | 21 | 29 | 9 | 107* | 782 | 39.10 | 2 | 3 | 64/5 |
| 1990 | N.A.Felton | 21 | 35 | 3 | 103 | 1075 | 33.59 | 1 | 9 | 18 |
| 1986 | D.J.Capel | 22 | 32 | 4 | 103 | 888 | 31.71 | 1 | 5 | 15 |
| 1987 | N.G.B.Cook | 16 | 9 | 5 | 37 | 108 | 27.00 | – | – | 3 |
| 1992 | K.M.Curran | 20 | 28 | 1 | 82 | 685 | 25.37 | – | 5 | 9 |
| 1990 | C.E.L.Ambrose | 18 | 20 | 10 | 49* | 200 | 20.00 | – | – | 5 |
| 1992 | J.P.Taylor | 22 | 17 | 8 | 74* | 180 | 20.00 | – | 1 | 9 |
| – | A.R.Roberts | 13 | 17 | 3 | 62 | 259 | 18.50 | – | 1 | 5 |
| – | M.B.Loye | 10 | 14 | 1 | 46 | 195 | 15.00 | – | – | 7 |
| – | A.L.Penberthy | 9 | 12 | 1 | 33 | 147 | 13.36 | – | – | 5 |

*Also played*: M.N.Bowen (2 matches) 5; W.M.Noon (1 match) did not bat (2 ct); R.M.Pearson (1 match) did not bat (1 ct); J.N.Snape (1 match) did not bat (1 ct); N.A.Stanley (1 match) 16, 7*; A.Walker (1 match – cap 1987) 39; R.J.Warren (2 matches) 19, 5, 3*; R.G.Williams (2 matches – cap 1979) 12, 3, 14.

### BOWLING

| | O | M | R | W | Avge | Best | 5wI | 10wM |
|---|---|---|---|---|---|---|---|---|
| N.G.B.Cook | 285.1 | 79 | 831 | 34 | 24.44 | 7-34 | 1 | 1 |
| D.J.Capel | 440 | 91 | 1181 | 48 | 24.60 | 5-61 | 1 | – |
| C.E.L.Ambrose | 543.4 | 151 | 1307 | 50 | 26.14 | 4-53 | – | – |
| K.M.Curran | 436.4 | 95 | 1318 | 48 | 27.45 | 6-45 | 1 | – |
| J.P.Taylor | 630.2 | 117 | 1977 | 68 | 29.07 | 7-23 | 3 | 1 |
| A.R.Roberts | 298.2 | 55 | 982 | 20 | 49.10 | 4-101 | – | – |

*Also bowled*: R.J.Bailey 120.1-31-291-9; M.N.Bowen 43-6-159-1; N.A.Felton 14-2-93-0; A.Fordham 12.2-0-72-0; R.M.Pearson 35.4-2-130-2; A.L.Penberthy 94-18-279-5; D.Ripley 1-0-14-0; J.N.Snape 26-8-62-1; A.Walker 45-14-90-2; R.G.Williams 31-5-83-4.

The First-Class Averages (pp 164-178) give the records of Northamptonshire players in all first-class county matches (their other opponents being the Pakistanis), with the exception of R.M.Pearson, whose full county figures are as above, and:
A.J.Lamb 16-25-4-209-1406-66.95-6-5-12ct. Did not bowl.

# NORTHAMPTONSHIRE RECORDS

## FIRST-CLASS CRICKET

| | | | | | |
|---|---|---|---|---|---|
| **Highest Total** | For 636-6d | | v Essex | Chelmsford | 1990 |
| | V 670-9d | | by Sussex | Hove | 1921 |
| **Lowest Total** | For 12 | | v Glos | Gloucester | 1907 |
| | V 33 | | by Lancashire | Northampton | 1977 |
| **Highest Innings** | For 300 | R.Subba Row | v Surrey | The Oval | 1958 |
| | V 333 | K.S.Duleepsinhji | for Sussex | Hove | 1930 |

**Highest Partnership for each Wicket**

| | | | | | | |
|---|---|---|---|---|---|---|
| 1st | 361 | N.Oldfield/V.Broderick | v | Scotland | Peterborough | 1953 |
| 2nd | 344 | G.Cook/R.J.Boyd-Moss | v | Lancashire | Northampton | 1986 |
| 3rd | 393 | A.Fordham/A.J.Lamb | v | Yorkshire | Leeds | 1990 |
| 4th | 370 | R.T.Virgin/P.Willey | v | Somerset | Northampton | 1976 |
| 5th | 347 | D.Brookes/D.W.Barrick | v | Essex | Northampton | 1952 |
| 6th | 376 | R.Subba Row/A.Lightfoot | v | Surrey | The Oval | 1958 |
| 7th | 229 | W.W.Timms/F.A.Walden | v | Warwicks | Northampton | 1926 |
| 8th | 164 | D.Ripley/N.G.B.Cook | v | Lancashire | Manchester | 1987 |
| 9th | 156 | R.Subba Row/S.Starkie | v | Lancashire | Northampton | 1955 |
| 10th | 148 | B.W.Bellamy/J.V.Murdin | v | Glamorgan | Northampton | 1925 |

| | | | | | |
|---|---|---|---|---|---|
| **Best Bowling** | For 10-127 | V.W.C.Jupp | v Kent | Tunbridge W | 1932 |
| **(Innings)** | V 10-30 | C.Blythe | for Kent | Northampton | 1907 |
| **Best Bowling** | For 15-31 | G.E.Tribe | v Yorkshire | Northampton | 1958 |
| **(Match)** | V 17-48 | C.Blythe | for Kent | Northampton | 1907 |

| | | | | | |
|---|---|---|---|---|---|
| **Most Runs – Season** | 2,198 | D.Brookes | (av 51.11) | | 1952 |
| **Most Runs – Career** | 28,980 | D.Brookes | (av 36.13) | | 1934-1959 |
| **Most 100s – Season** | 8 | R.A.Haywood | | | 1921 |
| **Most 100s – Career** | 67 | D.Brookes | | | 1934-1959 |
| **Most Wkts – Season** | 175 | G.E.Tribe | (av 18.70) | | 1955 |
| **Most Wkts – Career** | 1,097 | E.W.Clark | (av 21.31) | | 1922-1947 |

## LIMITED-OVERS CRICKET

| | | | | | | |
|---|---|---|---|---|---|---|
| **Highest Total** | NWT | 360-2 | | v Staffs | Northampton | 1990 |
| | BHC | 300-9 | | v Derbyshire | Derby | 1987 |
| | SL | 306-2 | | v Surrey | Guildford | 1985 |
| **Lowest Total** | NWT | 62 | | v Leics | Leicester | 1974 |
| | BHC | 85 | | v Sussex | Northampton | 1978 |
| | SL | 41 | | v Middlesex | Northampton | 1972 |
| **Highest Innings** | NWT | 145 | R.J.Bailey | v Staffs | Stone | 1991 |
| | BHC | 134 | R.J.Bailey | v Glos | Northampton | 1987 |
| | SL | 172* | W.Larkins | v Warwicks | Luton | 1983 |
| **Best Bowling** | NWT | 7-37 | N.A.Mallender | v Worcs | Northampton | 1984 |
| | BHC | 5-21 | Sarfraz Nawaz | v Middlesex | Lord's | 1980 |
| | SL | 7-39 | A.Hodgson | v Somerset | Northampton | 1976 |

# NOTTINGHAMSHIRE

**Formation of Present Club:** March/April 1841
**Substantial Reorganisation:** 11 December 1866
**Colours:** Green and Gold
**Badge:** County Badge of Nottinghamshire
**Championships (since 1890):** (4) 1907, 1929, 1981, 1987
**NatWest Trophy/Gillette Cup Winners:** (1) 1987
**Benson and Hedges Cup Winners:** (1) 1989
**Sunday League Champions:** (1) 1991
**Match Awards:** NWT 33; BHC 57

**Secretary/General Manager:** B.Robson, Trent Bridge, Nottingham NG2 6AG
(☎ 0602-821525)
**Captain:** R.T.Robinson
**Scorer:** L.Beaumont
**1993 Beneficiary:** D.W.Randall (testimonial)

**AFFORD, John Andrew** (Spalding GS; Stamford CFE), b Crowland, Lincs 12 May 1964. 6'1½". RHB, SLA. Debut 1984. Cap 1990. Tour: Z 1989-90 (Eng A). HS 22* v Leics (Nottingham) 1989. 50 wkts (3); most – 57 (1991). BB 6-68 (10-185 match) v Sussex (Nottingham) 1992. Award: BHC 1. **NWT:** HS 2*. BB 3-32 v Herts (Hitchin) 1989. **BHC:** HS 1*. BB 4-38 v Kent (Nottingham) 1989. **SL:** HS 0*. BB 2-39 v Glam (Nottingham) 1990.

**ARCHER, Graeme** Francis (Heron Brook Middle S; King Edward VI HS, Stafford), b Carlisle, Cumberland 26 Sep 1970. 6'1". RHB, OB. Debut 1992. Staffordshire 1990. HS 117 v Derbys (Nottingham) 1992. **SL:** HS 9.

**BATES, Richard** Terry (Bourne GS; Stamford CFE), b Stamford, Lincs 17 Jun 1972. 6'1". RHB, OB. No 1st XI appearances – joined staff 1991.

**BRAMHALL, Stephen** (Stockton Heath CHS; Newcastle U), b Warrington, Cheshire 26 Nov 1967. 6'1". RHB, WK. Lancashire 1990. Nottinghamshire debut 1992. Cheshire 1988-91. HS 37* v Surrey (Nottingham) 1992. **SL:** HS 1.

**CAIRNS, Christopher** Lance (Christchurch BHS), b Picton, NZ 13 Jun 1970. Son of B.L. (CD, Otago, ND and NZ 1971-86). 6'2". RHB, RFM. Nottinghamshire 1988-89 and 1992. N Districts 1988-89. Canterbury 1990-91 to date. **Tests** (NZ): 5 (1989-90 to 1991-92); HS 61 v E (Christchurch) 1991-92; BB 6-52 v E (Auckland) 1991-92. LOI (NZ): 10. Tour (NZ): A 1989-90. HS 110 ND v Auckland (Hamilton) 1988-89. Nt HS 107* v Glos (Worksop) 1992. 50 wkts (1): 56 (1992). BB 7-34 (11-100 match) Canterbury v CD (New Plymouth) 1991-92. Nt BB 6-70 v Lancs (Nottingham) 1992. **NWT:** HS 77 and BB 2-38 v Glam (Nottingham) 1992. **BHC:** HS 16 v Kent (Nottingham) 1992. BB 1-34. **SL:** HS 55* v Glos (Nottingham) 1992. BB 4-26 v Glam (Nottingham) 1992.

**CHAPMAN, Robert** James (Farnborough CS; S Notts CFE), b Nottingham 28 Jul 1972. Son of footballer R.O. ('Sammy') Chapman (Nottingham Forest, Notts County and Shrewsbury Town). 6'1". RHB, RFM. Debut 1992. HS –. BB 1-38.

**CRAWLEY, Mark** Andrew (Manchester GS; Oriel C, Oxford), b Newton-le-Willows, Lancs 16 Dec 1967. Brother of J.P. (see LANCS & CU) and P.M. (CU 1992). 6'3". RHB, RM. Oxford U 1987-90 (captain 1988-89-90; captain 1989). Lancashire 1990. Nottinghamshire debut 1991. Comb Us (BHC) 1987-89 (captain 1990). 1000 runs (1): 1297 (1992). HS 160* v Derbys (Derby) 1992. BB 6-92 OU v Glam (Oxford) 1990. Nt BB 3-18 v OU (Oxford) 1992. BAC BB 3-21 v Derbys (Derby) 1991. Awards: NWT 1; BHC 1. **NWT:** HS 74* and 4-26 v Lincs (Nottingham) 1991 (on debut). **BHC:** HS 58 v Glam (Cardiff) 1991. BB 2-72 Comb Us v Worcs (Worcester) 1989. **SL:** HS 94* and BB 3-41 v Leics (Nottingham) 1992.

**DESSAUR, Wayne** Anthony (Loughborough GS), b Nottingham 4 Feb 1971. 6'0". RHB, RM. Debut 1992. HS 148 v CU (Nottingham) 1992. BAC HS 15 v Northants (Nottingham) 1992. **SL:** HS 13* v Somerset (Bath) 1992.

**EVANS, Kevin** Paul (Colonel Frank Seely S) b Calverton 10 Sep 1963. Elder brother of R.J. (Notts 1987-90). 6'2". RHB, RMF. Debut 1984. Cap 1990. HS 104 v Surrey (Nottingham) 1988. BB 5-27 v Northants (Northampton) 1992. **NWT:** HS 20 v Hants (Southampton) 1991. BB 4-30 v Kent (Nottingham) 1986. **BHC:** HS 31* v Northants (Northampton) 1988. BB 4-43 v Glam (Cardiff) 1991. **SL:** HS 30 v Kent 1990 and v Hants 1992. BB 4-28 v Derbys (Nottingham) 1989.

**FIELD-BUSS, Michael** Gwyn (Wanstead HS), b Mtarfa, Malta 23 Sep 1964. 5'10". RHB, OB. Essex 1987. Nottinghamshire debut 1989. HS 34* Ex v Middx (Lord's) 1987. Nt HS 25 v Middx (Lord's) 1991. BB 4-33 v Somerset (Nottingham) 1989. **NWT:** HS 1. BB 4-62 v Worcs (Nottingham) 1992. **SL:** HS 10* v Hants (Southampton) 1992. BB 2-22 v Yorks (Scarborough) 1991.

**FRENCH, Bruce** Nicholas (The Meden CS), b Warsop 13 Aug 1959. 5'6". RHB, WK. Debut 1976 (aged 16yr 287d). Cap 1980. Benefit 1991. **Tests:** 16 (1986 to 1987-88); HS 59 v P (Manchester) 1987. LOI: 13. Tours: A 1986-87, 1987-88; SA 1989-90 (Eng XI); WI 1985-86; NZ 1987-88; I/SL 1984-85; P 1987-88. HS 105* v Derbys (Derby) 1990. BB 1-37. Awards: BHC 1. **NWT:** HS 49 v Staffs (Nottingham) 1985. **BHC:** HS 48* v Worcs (Nottingham) 1984. **SL:** HS 37 v Glos (Bristol) 1985.

**HINDSON, James** Edward (Toot Hill CS, Bingham), b Huddersfield, Yorks 13 Sep 1973. RHB, SLA. Debut 1992. HS -. BB 5-42 v CU (Nottingham) 1992. Awaiting BAC debut.

**JOHNSON, Paul** (Grove CS, Balderton), b Newark 24 Apr 1965. 5'7". RHB, RM. Debut 1982. Cap 1986. Tour: WI 1991-92 (Eng A). 1000 runs (6); most – 1518 (1990). HS 165* v Northants (Nottingham) 1990. BB 1-9. BAC HS 1-14. Awards: NWT 1; BHC 3. **NWT:** HS 101* v Staffs (Nottingham) 1985. **BHC:** HS 104* v Essex (Chelmsford) 1990. **SL:** HS 114 v Warwks (Birmingham) 1990.

**LEWIS, Clairmonte Christopher** (Willesden HS, London), b Georgetown, Guyana 14 Feb 1968. 6'2½". RHB, RFM. Leicestershire 1987-91 (cap 1990). Nottinghamshire debut 1992. **Tests:** 14 (1990 to 1992); HS 70 v NZ (Christchurch) 1991-92; BB 6-111 v WI (Birmingham) 1991. LOI: 30. Tours: A 1990-91 (part); WI 1989-90 (part); NZ 1991-92. HS 189* Le v Essex (Chelmsford) 1990. Nt HS 134* v Northants (Northampton) 1992. 50 wkts (2); most – 56 (1990). BB 6-22 Le v OU (Oxford) 1988. BAC BB 6-55 Le v Glam (Cardiff) 1990. Nt BB 6-90 v Surrey (Nottingham) 1992. Award: NWT 1. **NWT:** HS 53 Le v Glos (Leicester) 1988. BB 3-28 Le v Salop (Leicester) 1991. **BHC:** HS 26 v Somerset (Nottingham) 1992. BB 5-46 v Kent (Nottingham) 1992. **SL:** HS 93* Le v Essex (Leicester) 1990. BB 4-13 Le v Essex (Leicester) 1988.

**MIKE, Gregory** Wentworth, b Nottingham 14 Jul 1966. 6'0". RHB, RMF. Debut 1989. HS 61* and BB 3-48 v Warwks (Birmingham) 1992. **BHC:** HS 29 v Kent (Nottingham) 1989. **SL:** HS 26* v Durham (Nottingham) 1992. BB 3-30 v Glos (Nottingham) 1990.

**NEWELL, Michael** (West Bridgford CS), b Blackburn, Lancs 25 Feb 1965. 5'8". RHB, LB. Debut 1984. Cap 1987. 1000 runs (1): 1054 (1987). HS 203* v Derbys (Derby) 1987. BB 2-38 v SL (Nottingham) 1988. BB BB 1-0. **NWT:** HS 60 v Derbys (Derby) 1987. **BHC:** HS 39 v Somerset (Taunton) 1989. **SL:** HS 109* v Essex (Southend) 1990.

**PENNETT, David** Barrington (Benton Park GS, Rawdon), b Leeds, Yorks 26 Oct 1969. 6'0". RHB, RMF. Debut 1992. Yorks Cricket Academy. **NWT:** HS 29 v Derbys (Nottingham) 1992. BB 4-58 v Warwks (Birmingham) 1992. **SL:** HS 12* and BB 2-28 v Durham (Nottingham) 1992.

**PICK, Robert Andrew** (Alderman Derbyshire CS; High Pavement SFC), b Nottingham 19 Nov 1963. 5'10". LHB, RMF. Debut 1983. Cap 1987. Wellington 1989-90. Tours: WI 1991-92 (Eng A); SL 1990-91 (Eng A). HS 63 v Warwks (Nuneaton) 1985. 50 wkts (3); most – 67 (1991). BB 7-128 v Leics (Leicester) 1990. Awards: NWT 1; BHC 1. **NWT:** HS 34* v Sussex (Hove) 1983. BB 5-22 v Glos (Bristol) 1987. **BHC:** HS 25* v Hants (Southampton) 1991. BB 4-42 v Northants (Nottingham) 1987. **SL:** HS 24 v Yorks 1986 and v Hants 1992. BB 4-32 v Glos (Moreton) 1987.

**POLLARD, Paul** Raymond (Gedling CS), b Carlton, Nottingham, 24 Sep 1968. 5'11". LHB, RM. Debut 1987. Cap 1992. 1000 runs (2); most – 1255 (1991). HS 153 v CU (Cambridge) 1989. BAC HS 145 v Lancs (Nottingham) 1991. BB 1-46. **NWT:** HS 28 v Worcs (Nottingham) 1992. **BHC:** HS 77 v Kent (Nottingham) 1989. **SL:** HS 123* v Surrey (Oval) 1989.

**RANDALL, Derek** William (Sir Frederick Milner SS), b Retford 24 Feb 1951. 5'9". RHB, RM. Debut 1972. Cap 1973. Benefit 1983. Testimonial 1993. Wisden 1979. Tests: 47 (1976-77 to 1984); HS 174 v A (Melbourne) 1976-77. LOI: 49. Tours: A 1976-77, 1978-79, 1979-80, 1982-83; SA 1975-76 (DHR); NZ 1977-78, 1983-84; I/SL 1976-77; P 1977-78, 1983-84; Z 1985-86 (Eng B). 1000 runs (13) inc 2000 (1); 2151 (1985). HS 237 v Derbys (Nottingham) 1988. BB 3-15 v MCC (Lord's) 1982. BAC BB 3-43 v Sussex (Hove) 1984. Awards: NWT 3; BHC 6. **NWT:** HS 149* v Devon (Torquay) 1988. **BHC:** HS 103* v Minor C (N) (Nottingham) 1979. **SL:** HS 123 v Yorks (Nottingham) 1987.

**ROBINSON, Robert Timothy** (Dunstable GS; High Pavement SFC; Sheffield U), b Sutton in Ashfield 21 Nov 1958. 6'0". RHB, RM. Debut 1978. Cap 1983. Captain 1988-. Benefit 1992. Wisden 1985. Tests: 29 (1984-85 to 1989); HS 175 v A (Leeds) 1985. LOI: 26. Tours: A 1987-88; SA 1989-90 (Eng XI); NZ 1987-88; WI 1985-86; I/SL 1984-85; P 1987-88. 1000 runs (10) inc 2000 (1): 2032 (1984). HS 220* v Yorks (Nottingham) 1990. BB 1-22. Awards: NWT 4; BHC 6. **NWT:** HS 139 v Worcs (Worcester) 1985. **BHC:** HS 120 v Scot (Glasgow) 1985. **SL:** HS 116 v Derbys (Derby) 1990.

**SAXELBY, Mark** (Nottingham HS), b Worksop 4 Jan 1969. 6'3". LHB, RM. Younger brother of K. (Notts 1978-90). Debut 1989. HS 73 v CU (Cambridge) 1990 and v OU (Oxford) 1992. BAC HS 66 v Warwks (Birmingham) 1992. BB 3-41 v Derbys (Derby) 1991. **NWT:** HS 41 v Bucks (Marlow) 1990. BB 2-42 v Lincs (Nottingham) 1991. **BHC:** HS 32 v Hants (Southampton) 1991. BB 1-36. **SL:** HS 55 v Yorks (Scarborough) 1991. BB 4-29 v Leics (Leicester) 1991.

### NEWCOMER

**DOWMAN, Mathew** Peter (Grantham C), b Grantham, Lincs 10 May 1974. LHB, RMF.

### DEPARTURES

**BROAD, B.C.** – see GLOUCESTERSHIRE.

**COOPER, Kevin** Edwin (Hucknall National SS), b Hucknall 27 Dec 1957. 6'1". LHB, RFM. Nottinghamshire 1976-92 (cap 1980; benefit 1990). HS 46 v Middx (Nottingham) 1985. 50 wkts (8) inc 100 (1): 101 (1988). BB 8-44 v Middx (Lord's) 1984. Awards: NWT 1; BHC 2. **NWT:** HS 11 v Glos (Nottingham) 1982. BB 4-49 v Warwks (Nottingham) 1985. **BHC:** HS 25* v Lancs (Manchester) 1983. BB 4-9 v Yorks (Nottingham) 1989. **SL:** HS 31 v Glos (Nottingham) 1984. BB 4-25 v Hants (Nottingham) 1976.

**HEMMINGS, E.E.** – see SUSSEX.

**WILEMAN, Jonathan** Ritchie (Stancliffe Hall S, Darley Dale; Malvern C; Salford U), b Sheffield, Yorks 18 Aug 1970. 6'1". RHB, RSM. Nottinghamshire 1992. Scored 109 v CU (Nottingham) in his only f-c innings. HS 109 (above). No BAC appearances.

# NOTTINGHAMSHIRE 1992

## RESULTS SUMMARY

| | Place | Won | Lost | Drew | Abandoned |
|---|---|---|---|---|---|
| Britannic Assurance Championship | 4th | 7 | 7 | 8 | |
| All First-class Matches | | 8 | 8 | 9 | |
| Sunday League | 17th | 3 | 11 | | 3 |
| NatWest Trophy | 2nd Round | | | | |
| Benson and Hedges Cup | 3rd in Group C | | | | |

# BRITANNIC ASSURANCE CHAMPIONSHIP AVERAGES

## BATTING AND FIELDING

| Cap | | M | I | NO | HS | Runs | Avge | 100 | 50 | Ct/St |
|---|---|---|---|---|---|---|---|---|---|---|
| 1983 | R.T.Robinson | 18 | 31 | 5 | 189 | 1510 | 58.07 | 4 | 8 | 13 |
| – | C.C.Lewis | 10 | 15 | 3 | 134* | 591 | 49.25 | 2 | 3 | 7 |
| – | G.F.Archer | 6 | 11 | 2 | 117 | 424 | 47.11 | 1 | 3 | 5 |
| 1986 | P.Johnson | 15 | 24 | 3 | 107* | 963 | 45.85 | 2 | 7 | 6 |
| 1984 | B.C.Broad | 13 | 25 | 3 | 159* | 1000 | 45.45 | 5 | – | 5 |
| – | C.L.Cairns | 20 | 29 | 6 | 107* | 983 | 42.73 | 2 | 6 | 6 |
| 1973 | D.W.Randall | 18 | 27 | 3 | 133* | 865 | 36.04 | 1 | 5 | 11 |
| – | M.Saxelby | 7 | 12 | 1 | 66 | 389 | 35.36 | – | 4 | 1 |
| – | M.A.Crawley | 22 | 39 | 7 | 160* | 1115 | 34.84 | 3 | 4 | 18 |
| 1992 | P.R.Pollard | 18 | 32 | 3 | 75 | 828 | 28.55 | – | 4 | 19 |
| – | G.W.Mike | 4 | 5 | 1 | 61* | 102 | 25.50 | – | 1 | 2 |
| 1990 | K.P.Evans | 18 | 22 | 4 | 104 | 419 | 23.27 | 1 | 2 | 12 |
| 1980 | E.E.Hemmings | 7 | 11 | 5 | 52* | 132 | 22.00 | – | 1 | 1 |
| 1987 | R.A.Pick | 9 | 10 | 4 | 52 | 117 | 19.50 | – | 1 | 1 |
| – | S.Bramhall | 6 | 9 | 3 | 37* | 113 | 18.83 | – | – | 13/5 |
| 1980 | B.N.French | 16 | 18 | 3 | 55 | 246 | 16.40 | – | 1 | 36/4 |
| – | D.B.Pennett | 11 | 11 | 1 | 29 | 69 | 6.90 | – | – | 3 |
| – | M.G.Field-Buss | 7 | 7 | 2 | 13 | 27 | 5.40 | – | – | 5 |
| 1990 | J.A.Afford | 15 | 15 | 5 | 12 | 33 | 3.30 | – | – | 4 |

*Also played* (1 match each): R.J.Chapman did not bat; W.A.Dessaur 1, 15 (1 ct).

## BOWLING

| | O | M | R | W | Avge | Best | 5wI | 10wM |
|---|---|---|---|---|---|---|---|---|
| C.C.Lewis | 370.3 | 67 | 991 | 40 | 24.77 | 6-90 | 2 | 1 |
| J.A.Afford | 445.1 | 111 | 1434 | 43 | 33.34 | 6-68 | 1 | 1 |
| E.E.Hemmings | 259.5 | 95 | 602 | 18 | 33.44 | 4-30 | – | – |
| C.L.Cairns | 576.3 | 104 | 1945 | 54 | 36.01 | 6-70 | 2 | – |
| D.B.Pennett | 272.2 | 49 | 924 | 25 | 36.96 | 4-58 | – | – |
| M.A.Crawley | 206 | 52 | 601 | 16 | 37.56 | 3-38 | – | – |
| K.P.Evans | 558.5 | 124 | 1633 | 43 | 37.97 | 5-27 | 1 | – |
| R.A.Pick | 234.1 | 46 | 784 | 15 | 52.26 | 3-33 | – | – |
| M.G.Field-Buss | 159 | 24 | 571 | 10 | 57.10 | 4-71 | – | – |

*Also bowled:* R.J.Chapman 13-1-77-2; P.Johnson 5-0-30-0; G.W.Mike 68.2-9-276-8; P.R.Pollard 4-0-33-0; D.W.Randall 1-0-8-0; R.T.Robinson 1-0-4-0.

The First-Class Averages (pp 164-178) give the records of Nottinghamshire players in all first-class county matches (their other opponents being the Pakistanis, Cambridge U and Oxford U), with the exception of:
P.Johnson 18-28-4-107*-1094-45.58-2-9.9ct. 5-0-30-0.
C.C.Lewis 12-19-4-134*-722-48.13-2-4-9ct. 406.3-79-1089-41-26.56-6/90-2-1.

# NOTTINGHAMSHIRE RECORDS

## FIRST-CLASS CRICKET

| | | | | | |
|---|---|---|---|---|---|
| **Highest Total** | For 739-7d | | v Leics | Nottingham | 1903 |
| | V 706-4d | | by Surrey | Nottingham | 1947 |
| **Lowest Total** | For 13 | | v Yorkshire | Nottingham | 1901 |
| | V 16 | | by Derbyshire | Nottingham | 1879 |
| | 16 | | by Surrey | The Oval | 1880 |
| **Highest Innings** | For 312* | W.W.Keeton | v Middlesex | The Oval | 1939 |
| | V 345 | C.G.Macartney | for Australians | Nottingham | 1921 |

### Highest Partnership for each Wicket

| | | | | | |
|---|---|---|---|---|---|
| 1st | 391 | A.O.Jones/A.Shrewsbury | v Glos | Bristol | 1899 |
| 2nd | 398 | A.Shrewsbury/W.Gunn | v Sussex | Nottingham | 1890 |
| 3rd | 369 | W.Gunn/J.R.Gunn | v Leics | Nottingham | 1903 |
| 4th | 361 | A.O.Jones/J.R.Gunn | v Essex | Leyton | 1905 |
| 5th | 266 | A.Shrewsbury/W.Gunn | v Sussex | Hove | 1884 |
| 6th | 303* | F.H.Winrow/P.F.Harvey | v Derbyshire | Nottingham | 1947 |
| 7th | 204 | M.J.Smedley/R.A.White | v Surrey | The Oval | 1967 |
| 8th | 220 | G.F.H.Heane/R.Winrow | v Somerset | Nottingham | 1935 |
| 9th | 165 | W.McIntyre/G.Wootton | v Kent | Nottingham | 1869 |
| 10th | 152 | E.B.Alletson/W.Riley | v Sussex | Hove | 1911 |

| | | | | | |
|---|---|---|---|---|---|
| **Best Bowling** | For 10-66 | K.Smales | v Glos | Stroud | 1956 |
| (Innings) | V 10-10 | H.Verity | for Yorkshire | Leeds | 1932 |
| **Best Bowling** | For 17-89 | F.C.Matthews | v Northants | Nottingham | 1923 |
| (Match) | V 17-89 | W.G.Grace | for Glos | Cheltenham | 1877 |

| | | | | |
|---|---|---|---|---|
| **Most Runs – Season** | 2,620 | W.W.Whysall | (av 53.46) | 1929 |
| **Most Runs – Career** | 31,592 | G.Gunn | (av 35.69) | 1902-1932 |
| **Most 100s – Season** | 9 | W.W.Whysall | | 1928 |
| | 9 | M.J.Harris | | 1971 |
| | 9 | B.C.Broad | | 1990 |
| **Most 100s – Career** | 65 | J.Hardstaff, jr | | 1930-1955 |
| **Most Wkts – Season** | 181 | B.Dooland | (av 14.96) | 1954 |
| **Most Wkts – Career** | 1,653 | T.G.Wass | (av 20.34) | 1896-1920 |

## LIMITED-OVERS CRICKET

| | | | | | |
|---|---|---|---|---|---|
| **Highest Total** | NWT 312-9 | | v Bucks | Marlow | 1990 |
| | BHC 296-6 | | v Kent | Nottingham | 1989 |
| | SL 283-6 | | v Yorkshire | Nottingham | 1987 |
| **Lowest Total** | NWT 123 | | v Yorkshire | Scarborough | 1969 |
| | BHC 74 | | v Leics | Leicester | 1987 |
| | SL 66 | | v Yorkshire | Bradford | 1969 |
| **Highest Innings** | NWT 149* | D.W.Randall | v Devon | Torquay | 1988 |
| | BHC 130* | C.E.B.Rice | v Scotland | Glasgow | 1982 |
| | SL 123* | P.R.Pollard | v Surrey | The Oval | 1989 |
| **Best Bowling** | NWT 6-18 | C.E.B.Rice | v Sussex | Hove | 1982 |
| | BHC 6-22 | M.K.Bore | v Leics | Leicester | 1980 |
| | 6-22 | C.E.B.Rice | v Northants | Northampton | 1981 |
| | SL 6-12 | R.J.Hadlee | v Lancashire | Nottingham | 1980 |

# SOMERSET

**Formation of Present Club:** 18 August 1875
**Colours:** Black, White and Maroon
**Badge:** Somerset Dragon
**Championships:** (0) Third 1892, 1958, 1963, 1966, 1981
**NatWest Trophy/Gillette Cup Winners:** (2) 1979, 1983
**Benson and Hedges Cup Winners:** (2) 1981, 1982
**Sunday League Champions:** (1) 1979
**Match Awards:** NWT 42; BHC 54

**Chief Executive:** P.W.Anderson, The County Ground, Taunton TA1 1JT
(☎ 0823-272946)
**Captain:** C.J.Tavaré
**Scorer:** D.A.Oldam
**1993 Beneficiary:** –

**BURNS, Neil** David (Moulsham HS, Chelmsford), b Chelmsford, Essex 19 Sep 1965. 5'10". LHB, WK, occ SLA. W Province B 1985-86. Essex 1986. Somerset debut/cap 1987. HS 166 v Glos (Taunton) 1990. **NWT:** HS 25* v Glos (Taunton) 1990. **BHC:** HS 51 v Middx (Lord's) 1987. **SL:** HS 58 v Sussex (Hove) 1990.

**CADDICK, Andrew** Richard, b Christchurch, NZ 21 Nov 1968. Son of English emigrants – qualified for England 1992. 6'5". RHB, RFM. Debut 1991. Cap 1992. Represented NZ in 1987-88 Youth World Cup. Took 96 wkts (av 12.84) in 1991 2nd XI Championship. HS 54* v Worcs (W-s-M) 1992. 50 wkts (1): 71 (1992). BB 6-52 (10-157 match) v Kent (Canterbury) 1992. Award: NWT 1. HS 0. BB 6-30 v Glos (Taunton) 1992. **BHC:** HS 6*. BB 2-20 v Yorks (Taunton) 1992. **SL:** HS 4*. BB 4-18 v Lancs (Manchester) 1992.

**COTTAM, Andrew** Colin (Axminster SS), b Northampton 14 Jul 1973. Son of R.M.H. (Hants, Northants and England 1963-76). 6'1". RHB, SLA. Debut 1992. HS 31 v Glos (Gloucester) 1992. BB 1-1. **BHC:** HS -.

**FLETCHER, Ian** (Millfield S; Loughborough U), b Sawbridgeworth, Herts 31 Aug 1971. 5'11". RHB, RM. Debut 1991. Hertfordshire 1990. Comb Us (BHC) 1991. HS 56 v Hants (Southampton) 1991 – on debut. **NWT:** (Herts) HS 1. **BHC:** HS 9.

**FOLLAND, Nicholas** Arthur (Exmouth S; Loughborough U), b Bristol 17 Sep 1963. 6'0½". LHB, RM. Debut for Minor Counties v Indians (Trowbridge) 1990 scoring 26 and 82. Somerset debut 1992. Devon 1981-92. England Amateurs 1992. Master at Blundell's S. HS 82* v Worcs (W-s-M) 1992. Awards: NWT 1; BHC 1. **NWT:** HS 55 Devon v Essex (Exmouth) 1991. **BHC:** HS 100* Minor C v Notts (Nottingham) 1991. **SL:** HS 3.

**HALLETT, Jeremy** Charles (Millfield S; Durham U), b Yeovil 18 Oct 1970. 6'2". RHB, RMF. Debut 1990. Comb Us (BHC) 1991-92. HS 15 v Glos (Bristol) 1991. BB 3-154 v Worcs (Worcester) 1991. **BHC:** HS 5*. BB 3-36 Comb Us v Worcs (Cambridge) 1991. **SL:** HS 4*. BB 3-41 v Glam (Neath) 1992.

**HARDEN, Richard** John (King's C, Taunton), b Bridgwater 16 Aug 1965. 5'11". RHB, SLA. Debut 1985. Cap 1989. C Districts 1987-88. 1000 runs (4); most – 1460 (1990). HS 187 v Notts (Taunton) 1992. BB 2-7 CD v Canterbury (Blenheim) 1987-88. Sm BB 2-24 v Hants (Taunton) 1986. Award: NWT 1. **NWT:** HS 108* v Scot (Taunton) 1992. **BHC:** HS 76 v Kent (Canterbury) 1992. **SL:** HS 90* v Surrey (Bath) 1992.

**HAYHURST, Andrew** Neil (Worsley Wardley HS; Eccles SFC; Leeds Poly), b Davyhulme, Manchester 23 Nov 1962. 5'11". RHB, RM. Lancashire 1985-89. Somerset debut/cap 1990. Tours: WI 1986-87 (La); Z 1988-89 (La). 1000 runs (2); most – 1559 (1990). HS 172* v Glos (Bath) 1991. BB 4-27 La v Middx (Manchester) 1987. Sm BB 3-27 v Yorks (Middlesbrough) 1992. **NWT:** HS 91* and BB 5-60 v Warwks (Birmingham) 1991. **BHC:** HS 95 v Notts (Nottingham) 1992. BB 4-50 La v Worcs (Worcester) 1987. **SL:** HS 84 La v Leics (Manchester) 1988. BB 4-37 La v Glam 1988 and Sm v Sussex 1990.

**KERR, Jason** Ian Douglas (Withins HS; Bolton C), b Bolton, Lancs 7 Apr 1974. 6'2". RHB, RM. No 1st XI appearances – joined staff 1992.

**LATHWELL, Mark** Nicholas (Braunton S, Devon), b Bletchley, Bucks 26 Dec 1971. 5'8". RHB, RM. Debut 1991. Cap 1992. MCC YC. 1000 runs (1): 1176 (1992). HS 114 v Surrey (Bath) 1992. BB 1-9. **NWT:** HS 85 v Glos (Taunton) 1992. **BHC:** HS 93 v Worcs (Worcester) 1992. **SL:** HS 96 v Leics (Leicester) 1992.

**MALLENDER, Neil** Alan (Beverley GS), b Kirk Sandall, Yorks 13 Aug 1961. 6'0". RHB, RFM. Northamptonshire 1980-86 (cap 1984). Somerset debut/cap 1987. Otago 1983-84 to date (captain 1990-91 to 1991-92). **Tests:** 2 (1992); HS 4; BB 5-50 v P (Leeds) 1992 – on debut. HS 100* Otago v CD (Palmerston N) 1991-92. Sm HS 87* v Sussex (Hove) 1990 sharing in Somerset record 9th wkt stand of 183 with C.J.Tavaré. 50 wkts (6); most – 56 (1983). BB 7-27 Otago v Auckland (Auckland) 1984-85. BAC BB 7-41 Nh v Derbys (Northampton) 1982. Sm BB 7-61 v Derbys (Taunton) 1987. Award: NWT 1. **NWT:** HS 11* Nh v Yorks (Leeds) 1983. BB 7-37 Nh v Worcs (Northampton) 1984. **BHC:** HS 16* v Hants (Taunton) 1988. BB 5-53 Nh v Leics (Northampton) 1986. **SL:** HS 24 v Glos (Bristol) 1990. BB 5-34 Nh v Middx (Tring) 1981.

**PARSONS, Keith** Alan (The Castle S, Taunton; Richard Huish SFC), b Taunton 2 May 1973. Identical twin brother of Kevin (Somerset staff). 6'1". RHB, RM. Debut 1992. HS 1. Awaiting BAC debut.

**PARSONS, Kevin** John (The Castle S, Taunton; Richard Huish's SFC), b Taunton 2 May 1973. Identical twin brother of Keith. 6'1". RHB, OB. Awaiting f-c debut. **SL:** HS –.

**PAYNE, Andrew** (Accrington & Rossendale C), b Rawtenstall, Lancs 20 Oct 1973. 5'10". RHB, RMF. Debut 1992. HS 51* and BB 1-71 v Glos (Taunton) 1992. **SL:** HS 6*.

**ROSE, Graham** David (Northumberland Park S, Tottenham), b Tottenham, London 12 Apr 1964. 6'4". RHB, RM. Middlesex 1985-86. Somerset debut 1987. Cap 1988. 1000 runs (1): 1000 (1990). HS 132 v Surrey (Oval) 1992. 50 wkts (2); most – 57 (1988). BB 6-41 M v Worcs (Worcester) 1985 – on debut. Sm BB 6-47 v Warwks (Bath) 1988. Award: BHC 2. **NWT:** HS 110 v Devon (Torquay) 1990. BB 2-30 v Bucks (High Wycombe) 1987. **BHC:** HS 65 v Hants (Southampton) 1992. BB 4-37 v Sussex (Hove) 1990. **SL:** HS 148 v Glam (Neath) 1990. BB 4-28 v Derbys (Derby) 1987.

**TAVARÉ, Christopher** James (Sevenoaks S; St John's, Oxford), b Orpington, Kent 27 Oct 1954. 6'1½". RHB, RM. Kent 1974-88 (cap 1978; captain 1983-84; benefit 1988). Oxford U 1975-77 (blue 1975-76-77). Somerset debut/cap 1989. Captain 1990-. **Tests:** 31 (1980 to 1989); HS 149 v I (Delhi) 1981-82. LOI: 29. Tours: A 1982-83; NZ 1983-84; I/SL 1981-82; P 1983-84. 1000 runs (16); most – 1770 (1981). HS 219 v Sussex (Hove) 1990 sharing in Somerset record 9th wkt stand of 183 with N.A.Mallender. BB 1-3. Awards: NWT 4; BHC 9. **NWT:** HS 162* v Devon (Torquay) 1990. **BHC:** HS 143 K v Somerset (Taunton) 1985. **SL:** HS 136* K v Glos (Canterbury) 1978.

**TRUMP, Harvey** Russell John (Millfield S), b Taunton 11 Oct 1968. 6'0". RHB, OB. Debut 1988. HS 48 v Notts (Taunton) 1988 – on debut. 50 wkts (1): 51 (1991). BB 7-52 (inc hat-trick; 14-104 match) v Glos (Gloucester) 1992. **NWT:** HS 1*. BB 2-44 v Essex (Taunton) 1989. **BHC:** HS 1. BB 2-23 v Yorks (Taunton) 1992. **SL:** HS 19 v Kent (Taunton) 1991. BB 2-8 v Lancs (Manchester) 1992.

**TURNER, Robert** Julian (Millfield S; Magdalene C, Cambridge), b Malvern, Worcs 25 Nov 1967. 6'1¾". RHB, WK. Brother of S.J. (Somerset 1984-85). Cambridge U 1988-91 (blue 1988-89-90-91; captain 1991). Somerset debut 1991. Comb Us (BHC) 1990. HS 101* v Notts (Taunton) 1992. **BHC:** HS 25* Comb Us v Surrey (Oxford) 1990.

**VAN TROOST, Adrianus** Pelrus, b Schiedam, Holland 2 Oct 1972. RHB, RFM. Holland 1990 (opened bowling in ICC Trophy final v Zimbabwe). Debut 1991. HS 12 v P (Taunton) 1992; also 12 and BB 6-48 v Essex (Taunton) 1992.

**WHITE, Giles** William (Millfield S), b Barnstaple, Devon 23 Mar 1972. 6'0". RHB, LB. Debut 1991. Devon 1988-92. HS 42 and BB 1-30 v SL (Taunton) 1991 – on debut. Awaiting BAC debut. **NWT:** HS 11 and BB 1-45 Devon v Kent (Canterbury) 1992.

NEWCOMERS

**CLIFFORD, Paul** Robert (Sheldon CS, Chippenham), b Swindon, Wilts 19 Sep 1976. 6'4". RHB, RFM.

**MUSHTAQ AHMED**, b Sahiwal, Pakistan 28 Jun 1970. 5'5". RHB, LB. Multan, United Bank 1986-87 to date. **Tests** (P): 8 (1989-90 to 1992); HS 11 v E (Leeds) 1992; BB 3-32 v E (Lord's) 1992. LOI (P): 48. Tours (P): E 1992; A 1989-90, 1991-92. HS 75 Multan v Hyderabad (Sahiwal) 1986-87. 50 wkts (1+1); most – 66 (1992). BB 9-93 Multan v Peshawar (Sahiwal) 1990-91.

DEPARTURES

**BARTLETT, Richard** James (Taunton S), b Ash Priors 8 Oct 1966. 5'9". RHB, OB. Somerset 1986-92 scoring 117* v OU (Oxford) on debut. HS 117* (above). BAC HS 102* v Kent (Canterbury) 1988. BB: 1-9 (twice). **NWT:** HS 85 v Hants (Southampton) 1988. **BHC:** HS 36 v Comb Us (Taunton) 1989. **SL:** HS 55 v Lancs (Manchester) 1988 and 1990.

**LEFEBVRE, R.P.** – see GLAMORGAN.

**MacLEAY, Kenneth** Hervey (Scotch C, Perth; W Australia U), b Bradford-on-Avon, Wilts 2 Apr 1959. 6'4". RHB, RM. W Australia 1981-82/1990-91. Somerset 1991-92. LOI (A) 16 – inc 1983 World Cup in England. Tours: I 1989-90 (WA); Z 1982-83 (Young A). HS 114* WA v NSW (Perth) 1986-87. Sm HS 63 v Warwks (Taunton) 1991. BB 6-93 WA v NSW (Perth) 1985-86. Sm BB 3-40 v Derbys (Derby) 1991. **NWT:** HS 25* v Middx (Taunton) 1991. BB 2-35 v Bucks (Bath) 1991. **BHC:** HS 43 v Notts (Nottingham) 1992. **SL:** HS 40* v Surrey (Bath) 1992. BB 5-20 v Worcs (Taunton) 1992.

**SNELL, Richard** Peter (Durban HS; Witwatersrand U), b Durban, SA 12 Sep 1968. 6'1". RHB, RFM. Debut for Natal B 1987-88. Transvaal 1988-89 to date. Somerset 1992. **Tests** (SA): 1 (1991-92); HS 6 and BB 4-74 v WI (Bridgetown) 1991-92. LOI (SA): 15. Tour (SA): WI 1991-92. HS 81 v Leics (Leicester) 1992. BB 6-58 Transvaal v Natal (Jo'burg) 1990-91. Sm BB 3-29 v Middx (Lord's) 1992. **NWT:** HS 19 v Glos (Taunton) 1992. **BHC:** HS 31 and BB 3-47 v Worcs (Worcester) 1992. **SL:** HS 62 v Warwks (Taunton) 1992. BB 2-24 v Northants (Taunton) 1992.

**TOWNSEND, Gareth** Terence John (Tiverton S; Birmingham U), b Tiverton, Devon 28 Jun 1968. 6'0". RHB. Somerset 1990-92. HS 53 v SL (Taunton) 1991. BAC HS 49 v Leics (Leicester) 1992. **BHC:** HS 1. **SL:** HS 33 v Northants (Taunton) 1992.

# SOMERSET 1992

## RESULTS SUMMARY

|  | Place | Won | Lost | Drew | Abandoned |
|---|---|---|---|---|---|
| Britannic Assurance Championship | 9th | 5 | 4 | 13 | |
| All First-class Matches | | 5 | 5 | 13 | |
| Sunday League | 5th | 9 | 6 | | 2 |
| NatWest Trophy | 2nd Round | | | | |
| Benson and Hedges Cup | Semi-Finalist | | | | |

# BRITANNIC ASSURANCE CHAMPIONSHIP AVERAGES

## BATTING AND FIELDING

| Cap | | M | I | NO | HS | Runs | Avge | 100 | 50 | Ct/St |
|---|---|---|---|---|---|---|---|---|---|---|
| – | R.J.Turner | 7 | 10 | 5 | 101* | 286 | 57.20 | – | 1 | 6 |
| 1989 | R.J.Harden | 19 | 31 | 5 | 187 | 1321 | 50.80 | 3 | 6 | 11 |
| 1989 | C.J.Tavaré | 21 | 32 | 2 | 125 | 1157 | 38.56 | 3 | 6 | 15 |
| 1992 | M.N.Lathwell | 19 | 33 | 1 | 114 | 1176 | 36.75 | 1 | 11 | 14 |
| 1987 | N.D.Burns | 21 | 31 | 11 | 73* | 709 | 35.45 | – | 4 | 38/3 |
| 1990 | A.N.Hayhurst | 22 | 36 | 2 | 102 | 1167 | 34.32 | 1 | 9 | 4 |
| 1988 | G.D.Rose | 21 | 32 | 4 | 132 | 925 | 33.03 | 1 | 6 | 11 |
| – | R.J.Bartlett | 7 | 11 | – | 72 | 327 | 29.72 | – | 2 | 5 |
| – | K.H.MacLeay | 11 | 17 | 3 | 74 | 386 | 27.57 | – | 3 | 6 |
| – | R.P.Snell | 16 | 20 | 4 | 81 | 436 | 27.25 | – | 3 | 6 |
| – | G.T.J.Townsend | 6 | 11 | 1 | 49 | 252 | 25.20 | – | – | 4 |
| 1992 | A.R.Caddick | 19 | 17 | 5 | 54* | 246 | 20.50 | – | 1 | 6 |
| 1991 | R.P.Lefebvre | 3 | 4 | – | 36 | 70 | 17.50 | – | – | 3 |
| – | H.R.J.Trump | 17 | 16 | 7 | 28 | 142 | 15.77 | – | – | 13 |
| – | A.P.van Troost | 10 | 7 | 5 | 12 | 30 | 15.00 | – | – | 2 |
| 1987 | N.A.Mallender | 15 | 18 | 5 | 29* | 182 | 14.00 | – | – | 3 |
| – | A.C.Cottam | 6 | 8 | 1 | 31 | 43 | 6.14 | – | – | 1 |

*Also played* (1 match each): N.A.Folland 22, 82* (1 ct); A.Payne 51*.

## BOWLING

| | O | M | R | W | Avge | Best | 5wI | 10wM |
|---|---|---|---|---|---|---|---|---|
| N.A.Mallender | 361.4 | 74 | 1067 | 45 | 23.71 | 5-29 | 3 | – |
| A.R.Caddick | 558.2 | 94 | 1797 | 64 | 28.07 | 6-52 | 2 | 1 |
| H.R.J.Trump | 553 | 133 | 1558 | 49 | 31.79 | 7-52 | 2 | 1 |
| A.P.Van Troost | 155.4 | 17 | 695 | 18 | 38.61 | 6-48 | 2 | – |
| R.P.Snell | 339.1 | 60 | 1194 | 27 | 44.22 | 3-29 | – | – |
| G.D.Rose | 373 | 77 | 1179 | 24 | 49.12 | 4-59 | – | – |

*Also bowled*: A.C.Cottam 116.1-24-280-6; R.J.Harden 3-0-31-0; A.N.Hayhurst 137-28-403-8; M.N.Lathwell 64-14-224-4; R.P.Lefebvre 41-11-96-5; K.H.MacLeay 107-27-286-9; A.Payne 27-8-71-1; C.J.Tavaré 3.2-0-33-0; R.J.Turner 2.1-0-26-0.

The First-Class Averages (pp 164-178) give the records of Somerset players in all first-class county matches (their other opponents being the Pakistanis), with the exception of N.A.Mallender, whose full county figures are as above.

# SOMERSET RECORDS

## FIRST-CLASS CRICKET

| | | | | | |
|---|---|---|---|---|---|
| **Highest Total** | For | 675-9d | v Hampshire | Bath | 1924 |
| | V | 811 | by Surrey | The Oval | 1899 |
| **Lowest Total** | For | 25 | v Glos | Bristol | 1947 |
| | V | 22 | by Glos | Bristol | 1920 |
| **Highest Innings** | For | 322 I.V.A.Richards | v Warwicks | Taunton | 1985 |
| | V | 424 A.C.MacLaren | for Lancashire | Taunton | 1895 |

### Highest Partnership for each Wicket

| | | | | | |
|---|---|---|---|---|---|
| 1st | 346 | H.T.Hewett/L.C.H.Palairet | v Yorkshire | Taunton | 1892 |
| 2nd | 290 | J.C.W.MacBryan/M.D.Lyon | v Derbyshire | Buxton | 1924 |
| 3rd | 319 | P.M.Roebuck/M.D.Crowe | v Leics | Taunton | 1984 |
| 4th | 310 | P.W.Denning/I.T.Botham | v Glos | Taunton | 1980 |
| 5th | 235 | J.C.White/C.C.C.Case | v Glos | Taunton | 1927 |
| 6th | 265 | W.E.Alley/K.E.Palmer | v Northants | Northampton | 1961 |
| 7th | 240 | S.M.J.Woods/V.T.Hill | v Kent | Taunton | 1898 |
| 8th | 172 | I.V.A.Richards/I.T.Botham | v Leics | Leicester | 1983 |
| 9th | 183 | C.H.M.Greetham/H.W.Stephenson | v Leics | Weston-s-Mare | 1963 |
| | 183 | C.J.Tavaré/N.A.Mallender | v Sussex | Hove | 1990 |
| 10th | 143 | J.J.Bridges/A.H.D.Gibbs | v Essex | Weston-s-Mare | 1919 |

| | | | | | |
|---|---|---|---|---|---|
| **Best Bowling** | For | 10-49 E.J.Tyler | v Surrey | Taunton | 1895 |
| **(Innings)** | V | 10-35 A.Drake | for Yorkshire | Weston-s-Mare | 1914 |
| **Best Bowling** | For | 16-83 J.C.White | v Worcs | Bath | 1919 |
| **(Match)** | V | 17-137 W.Brearley | for Lancashire | Manchester | 1905 |

| | | | | |
|---|---|---|---|---|
| **Most Runs – Season** | 2,761 | W.E.Alley | (av 58.74) | 1961 |
| **Most Runs – Career** | 21,142 | H.Gimblett | (av 36.96) | 1935-1954 |
| **Most 100s – Season** | 11 | S.J.Cook | | 1991 |
| **Most 100s – Career** | 49 | H.Gimblett | | 1935-1954 |
| **Most Wkts – Season** | 169 | A.W.Wellard | (av 19.24) | 1938 |
| **Most Wkts – Career** | 2,166 | J.C.White | (av 18.02) | 1909-1937 |

## LIMITED-OVERS CRICKET

| | | | | | |
|---|---|---|---|---|---|
| **Highest Total** | NWT | 413-4 | v Devon | Torquay | 1990 |
| | BHC | 321-5 | v Sussex | Hove | 1990 |
| | SL | 360-3 | v Glamorgan | Neath | 1990 |
| **Lowest Total** | NWT | 59 | v Middlesex | Lord's | 1977 |
| | BHC | 98 | v Middlesex | Lord's | 1982 |
| | SL | 58 | v Essex | Chelmsford | 1977 |
| **Highest Innings** | NWT | 162* C.J.Tavaré | v Devon | Torquay | 1990 |
| | BHC | 177 S.J.Cook | v Sussex | Hove | 1990 |
| | SL | 175* I.T.Botham | v Northants | Wellingborough | 1986 |
| **Best Bowling** | NWT | 7-15 R.P.Lefebvre | v Devon | Torquay | 1990 |
| | BHC | 5-14 J.Garner | v Surrey | Lord's | 1981 |
| | SL | 6-24 I.V.A.Richards | v Lancashire | Manchester | 1983 |

# SURREY

**Formation of Present Club:** 22 August 1845
**Colours:** Chocolate
**Badge:** Prince of Wales' Feathers
**Championships (since 1890):** (15) 1890, 1891, 1892, 1894, 1895, 1899, 1914, 1952, 1953, 1954, 1955, 1956, 1957, 1958, 1971. **Joint:** (1) 1950
**NatWest Trophy/Gillette Cup Winners:** (1) 1982
**Benson and Hedges Cup Winners:** (1) 1974
**Sunday League Champions:** (0) Fourth 1992
**Match Awards:** NWT 35; BHC 51

**Chief Executive:** G.A.Woodman, Kennington Oval, London, SE11 5SS
(☎ 071-582 6660)
**Captain:** A.J.Stewart
**Scorer:** M.R.L.W.Ayers
**1993 Beneficiary:** H.T.Brind (Head Groundsman)

**ALIKHAN, Rehan** Iqbal ('Ray') (KCS, Wimbledon), b Westminster Hospital, London 28 Dec 1962. 6'1½". RHB, OB. Sussex 1986-88. PIA 1986-87. Surrey debut 1989. 1000 runs (1): 1055 (1991). HS 138 v Essex (Oval) 1990. Sy BB 2-43 v Northants (Northampton) 1991. **NWT:** HS 41 Sx v Worcs (Worcester) 1986. **BHC:** HS 71 Sx v Glam (Swansea) 1987. **SL:** HS 23 Sx v Essex (Chelmsford) 1987.

**ATKINS, Paul** David (Aylesbury GS), b Aylesbury, Bucks 11 Jun 1966. 6'1". RHB, OB. Debut 1988 v CU (Cambridge) scoring 114* and 8. Buckinghamshire 1985-90 (cap 1986). HS 114* (above). BAC HS 99 v Lancs (Southport) 1988 and v Notts (Oval) 1992. Award: NWT 1. **NWT:** HS 82 v Glam (Oval) 1988. **BHC:** HS 9. **SL:** HS 2.

**BAINBRIDGE, Mark** Robert (Teddington S; Richmond upon Thames C), b Isleworth, Middx 11 May 1973. 5'9¾". RHB, SLA. No 1st XI appearances – joined staff 1992.

**BENJAMIN, Joseph** Emmanuel (Cayon HS, St Kitts; Mount Pleasant S, Highgate, Birmingham), b Christ Church, St Kitts 2 Feb 1961. 6'2". RHB, RMF. Warwickshire 1988-91. Surrey debut 1992. Staffordshire 1986-88. HS 42 v Kent (Guildford) 1992. BB 6-30 v Durham (Durham) 1992. **NWT:** HS 19 and BB 2-37 Staffs v Glam (Stone) 1986. **BHC:** HS 20 Wa v Worcs (Birmingham) 1990. BB 2-32 Wa v Glos (Bristol) 1990. **SL:** HS 24 Wa v Lancs (Manchester) 1990. BB 4-44 v Middx (Oval) 1992.

**BICKNELL, Darren** John (Robert Haining SS; Guildford TC), b Guildford 24 Jun 1967. Elder brother of M.P. 6'4". LHB, LM. Debut 1987. Cap 1990. Tours: WI 1991-92 (Eng A); P 1990-91 (Eng A); SL 1990-91 (Eng A); Z 1989-90 (Eng A). 1000 runs (4); most – 1888 (1991). HS 186 v Kent (Canterbury) 1990 sharing in Surrey record 3rd wkt stand of 413 with D.M.Ward. BB 2-62 v Northants (Northampton) 1991. Awards: NWT 1; BHC 2. **NWT:** HS 135* v Yorks (Oval) 1989. **BHC:** HS 119 v Hants (Oval) 1990. **SL:** HS 125 v Durham (Durham) 1992.

**BICKNELL, Martin** Paul (Robert Haining SS), b Guildford 14 Jan 1969. Younger brother of D.J. 6'3". RHB, RFM. Debut 1986. Cap 1989. LOI: 7. Tours: A 1990-91; Z 1989-90 (Eng A). HS 88 v Hants (Southampton) 1992. Shared in Surrey record 8th wkt stand of 205 with I.A.Greig v Lancs (Oval) 1990. 50 wkts (4); most – 71 (1992). BB 9-45 v CU (Oval) 1988. BAC BB 7-52 v Sussex (Oval) 1991. Award: BHC 1. **NWT:** HS 66* v Northants (Oval) 1991. BB 4-49 v Yorks (Oval) 1989. **BHC:** HS 27* v Lancs (Manchester) 1990. BB 3-28 v Middx (Lord's) 1991. **SL:** HS 20* v Northants (Tring) 1991. BB 4-14 v Middx (Oval) 1990.

**BOILING, James** (Rutlish S, Merton; Durham U), b New Delhi, India 8 Apr 1968. 6'4". RHB, OB. Debut 1988. Comb Us (BHC) 1988-90. HS 29 v Glam (Neath) 1992. BB 6-84 (10-203 match) v Glos (Bristol) 1992. Award: BHC 1. **NWT:** HS 22 and BB 2-22 v Northants (Oval) 1991. **BHC:** HS 9*. BB 3-9 Comb Us v Surrey (Cambridge) 1989. **SL:** HS 12* v Hants (Oval) 1991. BB 5-24 v Hants (Basingstoke) 1992.

**BROWN, Alistair** Duncan (Caterham S), b Beckenham, Kent 11 Feb 1970. 5'10". RHB, LB, occ WK. Debut 1992. HS 175 v Durham (Durham) 1992. **BHC:** HS 41 v Lancs (Oval) 1992. **SL:** HS 113 v Glam (Llanelli) 1992.

**BUTCHER, Mark** Alan (Trinity Sch; Archbishop Tenison's S, Croydon), b Croydon 23 Aug 1972. Son of A.R. (Surrey, Glamorgan and England 1972-92); brother of G.P. (see GLAMORGAN). 5'11". LHB, RM. Debut 1992. HS 47 and BB 1-95 v Middx (Oval) 1992. **NWT:** HS 4*. **SL:** HS 48* v Glam (Oval) 1991 (on 1st XI debut and against team captained by his father). BB 3-32 v Sussex (Oval) 1992.

**HOLLIOAKE, Adam** John (St George's S, Weybridge), b Melbourne, Australia 5 Sep 1971. 5'11". RHB, RMF. Qualified for England 1992. Awaiting f-c debut. **SL:** HS 22 and BB 1-37 v Durham (Durham) 1992.

**KENDRICK, Neil** Michael (Wilson's GS), b Bromley, Kent 11 Nov 1967. 5'11". RHB, SLA. Debut 1988. HS 55 v Middx (Lord's) 1992. 50 wkts (1): 51 (1992). BB 6-61 v Leics (Oval) 1992. **NWT:** HS -. BB 1-51. **BHC:** HS 24 and BB 2-47 v Kent (Canterbury) 1992. **SL:** HS 2*. BB 1-45.

**LYNCH, Monte** Alan (Ryden's S, Walton-on-Thames), b Georgetown, British Guiana 21 May 1958. 5'8". RHB, OB. Debut 1977. Cap 1982. Benefit 1991. Guyana 1982-83. LOI: 3. Tours: SA 1983-84 (WI XI); P 1981-82 (Int). 1000 (8); most – 1714 (1985). HS 172* v Kent (Oval) 1989. BB 3-6 v Glam (Swansea) 1981. Awards: NWT 1; BHC 4. **NWT:** HS 129 v Durham (Oval) 1982. BB 2-28 v Glam (Swansea) 1992. **BHC:** HS 112* v Kent (Oval) 1987. **SL:** HS 136 v Yorks (Bradford) 1985. BB 2-2 v Northants 1987 and v Sussex 1990.

**MURPHY, Anthony** John (Xaverian C; Swansea U), b Manchester 6 Aug 1962. 6'0". RHB, RMF. Lancashire 1985-88. Surrey debut 1989. Cheshire 1984-85. Tour: WI 1986-87 (La). HS 38 v Glos (Oval) 1989. 50 wkts (1): 65 (1989). BB 6-97 v Derbys (Derby) 1989. **NWT:** HS 1*. BB 2-34 v Hants (Oval) 1989. **BHC:** HS 5*. BB 2-23 v Middx (Lord's) 1991. **SL:** HS 9*. BB 4-22 v Glos (Oval) 1989.

**SARGEANT, Neil** Fredrick (Whitmore HS), b Hammersmith 8 Nov 1965. 5'8". RHB, WK. Debut 1989. HS 49 v Lancs (Manchester) 1991. BB 1-88. **SL:** HS 22 v Glos (Cheltenham) 1990.

**SMITH, Andrew** William (Sutton Manor HS), b Sutton 30 May 1969. Son of W.A. (Surrey 1961-70). 5'8". RHB, OB. No 1st XI appearances apart from Seeboard Trophy 1992 – joined staff 1990.

**STEWART, Alec** James (Tiffin S), b Merton 8 Apr 1963. Son of M.J. (Surrey and England 1954-72). 5'11". RHB, WK. Debut 1981. Cap 1985. Captain 1992. Wisden 1992. **Tests:** 22 (1989-90 to 1992); HS 190 v P (Birmingham) 1992. LOI: 41. Tours: A 1990-91; WI 1989-90; NZ 1991-92. 1000 runs (7); most – 1665 (1986). HS 206* v Essex (Oval) 1989. BB 1-7. Held 11 catches (equalling world f-c match record) v Leics (Leicester) 1989. Awards: NWT 1; BHC 3. **NWT:** HS 107* v Middx (Oval) 1988. **BHC:** HS 110* v Somerset (Taunton) 1991. **SL:** HS 125 v Lancs (Oval) 1990.

131

**THORPE, Graham** Paul (Weydon CS; Farnham C), b Farnham 1 Aug 1969. 5'11". LHB, RM. Debut 1988. Cap 1991. Tours (Eng A): WI 1991-92; P 1990-91; SL 1990-91; Z 1989-90. 1000 runs (3); most – 1895 (1992). HS 216 v Somerset (Oval) 1992. BB 2-31 v Essex (Oval) 1989. **NWT:** HS 93 v Hants (Lord's) 1991. **BHC:** HS 82 v Kent (Canterbury) 1992. BB 3-35 v Middx (Lord's) 1989. **SL:** HS 115* v Lancs (Manchester) 1991. BB 3-21 v Somerset (Oval) 1991.

**WAQAR YOUNIS** (Government C, Vehari), b Vehari, Pakistan 16 Nov 1971. 6'0". RHB, RF. Multan 1987-88/1990-91. United Bank 1988-89/1990-91. Surrey debut/ cap 1990. Wisden 1991. **Tests** (P): 19 (1989-90 to 1992); HS 20* v E (Lord's) 1992; BB 7-76 v NZ (Faisalabad) 1990-91. LOI (P): 47. Tours (P): E 1992; A 1989-90. HS 51 United Bank v PIA (Lahore) 1989-90 Qaid-e-Azam Final. Sy HS 31 v Yorks (Guildford) 1991. 50 wkts (2) inc 100 (1): 113 (1991). BB 7-64 United Bank v ADBP (Lahore) 1990-91. Sy BB 7-73 v Warwks (Oval) 1990. Awards: NWT 2. **NWT:** HS 26 v Essex (Oval) 1991. BB 5-40 v Northants (Oval) 1991. **BHC:** HS 5*. BB 3-29 v Somerset (Taunton) 1991. **SL:** HS 8. BB 5-26 v Kent (Oval) 1990.

**WARD, David** Mark (Haling Manor HS), b Croydon 10 Feb 1961. 6'1". RHB, OB. Debut 1985. Cap 1990. 1000 runs (2) inc 2000 (1): 2072 (1990). HS 263 v Kent (Canterbury) 1990 sharing in Surrey record 3rd wkt stand of 413 with D.J.Bicknell. BB 2-66 v Glos (Guildford) 1991. Award: NWT 1. **NWT:** HS 101* v Glam (Swansea) 1992. **BHC:** HS 46* v Yorks (Oval) 1990. **SL:** HS 102* v Hants (Southampton) 1990.

**WARD, Ian** James (Millfield S), b Plymouth, Devon 30 Sep 1972. 5'8½". LHB, RM. Debut 1992. HS 0.

## NEWCOMER

**KELLEHER, Daniel** John Michael (St Mary's GS, Sidcup; Erith TC), b Southwark 5 May 1966. Nephew of H.R.A. (Surrey 1955, Northants 1956-58). 6'1". RHB, RMF. Kent 1987-91. HS 53* K v Derbys (Dartford) 1989. BB 6-109 K v Somerset (Bath) 1987. **NWT:** HS.21 and BB 3-16 K v Oxon (Oxford) 1990. **BHC:** HS 11* K v Notts (Nottingham) 1989. BB 1-23. **SL:** HS 19 K v Notts (Nottingham) 1987. BB 2-25 (twice in 1987).

## DEPARTURES

**BRYSON, Rudi** Edwin (Springs BHS), b Springs, Transvaal, SA 25 Jul 1968. 6'1". RHB, RFM. N Transvaal 1987-88/1988-89. E Province 1988-89 to date. Surrey 1992. HS 100 EP v Boland (Worcester) 1991-92. Sy HS 76 v Notts (Nottingham) 1992. BB 7-68 (12-133 match) EP B v GW (Kimberley) 1988-89. Sy BB 5-48 v CU (Cambridge) 1992. BAC BB 5-117 v Middx (Oval) 1992. **BHC:** HS 18* v Glos (Oval) 1992. BB 4-31 v Leics (Leicester) 1992. **SL:** HS 20 and BB 2-30 v Northants (Oval) 1992.

**FELTHAM, M.A.** – see MIDDLESEX.

**LIGERTWOOD, David** George Coutts (St Peter's C, Adelaide; Adelaide U), b Oxford 16 May 1969. 5'8". RHB, WK. Surrey 1992. Hertfordshire 1990-91. HS 28 v Sussex (Oval) 1992 – on debut. **SL:** HS -.

**ROBINSON, Jonathan** David (Lancing C; West Sussex IHE), b Epsom 3 Aug 1966. Son of P.M.H. (L.C.Stevens' XI 1961). 5'10". LHB, RM. Surrey 1988-92. HS 79 v Lancs (Manchester) 1991. BB 3-22 v Somerset (Bath) 1992. Award: NWT 1. **NWT:** HS 47 v Essex (Oval) 1991. BB 3-46 v Kent (Oval) 1991. **BHC:** HS 38 v Warwks (Oval) 1991. BB 2-31 v Middx (Lord's) 1991. **SL:** HS 55* v Somerset (Oval) 1991. BB 2-32 v Glam (Oval) 1991.

# SURREY 1992

## RESULTS SUMMARY

| | Place | Won | Lost | Drew |
|---|---|---|---|---|
| Britannic Assurance Championship | 13th | 5 | 7 | 10 |
| All First-class Matches | | 6 | 7 | 10 |
| Sunday League | 4th | 10 | 7 | |
| NatWest Trophy | 1st Round | | | |
| Benson and Hedges Cup | Semi-Finalist | | | |

# BRITANNIC ASSURANCE CHAMPIONSHIP AVERAGES

## BATTING AND FIELDING

| Cap | | M | I | NO | HS | Runs | Avge | 100 | 50 | Ct/St |
|---|---|---|---|---|---|---|---|---|---|---|
| – | A.D.Brown | 11 | 16 | 1 | 175 | 740 | 49.33 | 3 | 3 | 6 |
| 1991 | G.P.Thorpe | 22 | 39 | 3 | 216 | 1749 | 48.58 | 2 | 13 | 17 |
| 1982 | M.A.Lynch | 22 | 39 | 6 | 107 | 1404 | 42.54 | 3 | 7 | 23 |
| 1985 | A.J.Stewart | 13 | 24 | 3 | 140 | 766 | 36.47 | 1 | 5 | 13 |
| 1990 | D.J.Bicknell | 22 | 40 | 5 | 120* | 1176 | 33.60 | 1 | 7 | 5 |
| 1990 | D.M.Ward | 17 | 28 | 5 | 138 | 756 | 32.86 | 2 | 1 | 3 |
| 1990 | M.A.Feltham | 12 | 17 | 5 | 50 | 392 | 32.66 | – | 1 | 3 |
| – | P.D.Atkins | 7 | 14 | – | 99 | 382 | 27.28 | – | 2 | 2 |
| – | J.D.Robinson | 9 | 17 | 5 | 65* | 307 | 25.58 | – | 2 | 8 |
| 1989 | M.P.Bicknell | 18 | 25 | 8 | 88 | 426 | 25.05 | – | 2 | 7 |
| – | R.E.Bryson | 10 | 13 | 2 | 76 | 257 | 23.36 | – | 1 | – |
| – | J.Boiling | 18 | 21 | 11 | 29 | 190 | 19.00 | – | – | 18 |
| – | N.M.Kendrick | 16 | 20 | 4 | 55 | 300 | 18.75 | – | 2 | 14 |
| – | A.J.Murphy | 5 | 5 | 2 | 32 | 45 | 15.00 | – | – | – |
| – | N.F.Sargeant | 14 | 19 | 4 | 30 | 176 | 11.73 | – | – | 35/6 |
| – | J.E.Benjamin | 18 | 18 | 8 | 42 | 116 | 11.60 | – | – | 5 |
| – | D.G.C.Ligertwood | 4 | 7 | – | 28 | 63 | 9.00 | – | – | 7/1 |

*Also played*: R.I.Alikhan (1 match) 1, 10; M.A.Butcher (2 matches) 5*, 47; I.J.Ward (1 match) 0 (1 ct).

## BOWLING

| | O | M | R | W | Avge | Best | 5wI | 10wM |
|---|---|---|---|---|---|---|---|---|
| M.P.Bicknell | 597.5 | 107 | 1734 | 67 | 25.88 | 6-107 | 4 | – |
| J.D.Robinson | 93.4 | 14 | 341 | 13 | 26.23 | 3-22 | – | – |
| N.M.Kendrick | 557.1 | 161 | 1464 | 48 | 30.50 | 6-61 | 3 | – |
| J.Boiling | 557.2 | 143 | 1506 | 41 | 36.73 | 6-84 | 1 | 1 |
| J.E.Benjamin | 582.2 | 94 | 1780 | 45 | 39.55 | 6-30 | 2 | – |
| M.A.Feltham | 310.1 | 57 | 1071 | 23 | 46.56 | 4-75 | – | – |
| A.J.Murphy | 178.4 | 34 | 531 | 11 | 48.27 | 3-97 | – | – |
| R.E.Bryson | 305.4 | 36 | 1165 | 17 | 68.52 | 5-117 | 1 | – |

*Also bowled*: D.J.Bicknell 9.2-0-90-0; A.D.Brown 16-1-78-0; M.A.Butcher 44-10-115-1; M.A.Lynch 21-4-85-1; A.J.Stewart 7-1-14-0; G.P.Thorpe 17.4-5-79-0; D.M.Ward 4-0-16-0; I.J.Ward 8-0-35-0.

The First-Class Averages (pp 164-178) give the records of Surrey players in all first-class county matches (their other opponents being Cambridge U), with the exception of:
D.J.Bicknell 23-41-5-120*-1225-34.02-1-7-5ct. 9.2-0-90-0.
A.J.Stewart 14-25-3-140-837-38.04-1-6-17ct. 7-1-14-0.
G.P.Thorpe 23-40-4-216-1863-51.75-3-13-18ct. 17.4-5-79-0.

# SURREY RECORDS

## FIRST-CLASS CRICKET

| | | | | | | |
|---|---|---|---|---|---|---|
| **Highest Total** | For | 811 | v | Somerset | The Oval | 1899 |
| | V | 863 | by | Lancashire | The Oval | 1990 |
| **Lowest Total** | For | 14 | v | Essex | Chelmsford | 1983 |
| | V | 16 | by | MCC | Lord's | 1872 |
| **Highest Innings** | For | 357* R.Abel | v | Somerset | The Oval | 1899 |
| | V | 366 N.H.Fairbrother | for | Lancashire | The Oval | 1990 |

### Highest Partnership for each Wicket

| | | | | | | |
|---|---|---|---|---|---|---|
| 1st | 428 | J.B.Hobbs/A.Sandham | v | Oxford U | The Oval | 1926 |
| 2nd | 371 | J.B.Hobbs/E.G.Hayes | v | Hampshire | The Oval | 1909 |
| 3rd | 413 | D.J.Bicknell/D.M.Ward | v | Kent | Canterbury | 1990 |
| 4th | 448 | R.Abel/T.W.Hayward | v | Yorkshire | The Oval | 1899 |
| 5th | 308 | J.N.Crawford/F.C.Holland | v | Somerset | The Oval | 1908 |
| 6th | 298 | A.Sandham/H.S.Harrison | v | Sussex | The Oval | 1913 |
| 7th | 262 | C.J.Richards/K.T.Medlycott | v | Kent | The Oval | 1987 |
| 8th | 205 | I.A.Greig/M.P.Bicknell | v | Lancashire | The Oval | 1990 |
| 9th | 168 | E.R.T.Holmes/E.W.J.Brooks | v | Hampshire | The Oval | 1936 |
| 10th | 173 | A.Ducat/A.Sandham | v | Essex | Leyton | 1921 |

| | | | | | | |
|---|---|---|---|---|---|---|
| **Best Bowling** | For | 10-43 T.Rushby | v | Somerset | Taunton | 1921 |
| **(Innings)** | V | 10-28 W.P.Howell | for | Australians | The Oval | 1899 |
| **Best Bowling** | For | 16-83 G.A.R.Lock | v | Kent | Blackheath | 1956 |
| **(Match)** | V | 15-57 W.P.Howell | for | Australians | The Oval | 1899 |

| | | | | |
|---|---|---|---|---|
| **Most Runs – Season** | 3,246 | T.W.Hayward | (av 72.13) | 1906 |
| **Most Runs – Career** | 43,554 | J.B.Hobbs | (av 49.72) | 1905-1934 |
| **Most 100s – Season** | 13 | T.W.Hayward | | 1906 |
| | 13 | J.B.Hobbs | | 1925 |
| **Most 100s – Career** | 144 | J.B.Hobbs | | 1905-1934 |
| **Most Wkts – Season** | 252 | T.Richardson | (av 13.94) | 1895 |
| **Most Wkts – Career** | 1,775 | T.Richardson | (av 17.87) | 1892-1904 |

## LIMITED-OVERS CRICKET

| | | | | | | |
|---|---|---|---|---|---|---|
| **Highest Total** | NWT | 313-5 | v | Northumb | Jesmond | 1989 |
| | BHC | 331-5 | v | Hampshire | The Oval | 1990 |
| | SL | 330-6 | v | Durham | Durham | 1992 |
| **Lowest Total** | NWT | 74 | v | Kent | The Oval | 1967 |
| | BHC | 89 | v | Notts | Nottingham | 1984 |
| | SL | 64 | v | Worcs | Worcester | 1978 |
| **Highest Innings** | NWT | 146 G.S.Clinton | v | Kent | Canterbury | 1985 |
| | BHC | 121* G.S.Clinton | v | Kent | The Oval | 1988 |
| | SL | 136 M.A.Lynch | v | Yorkshire | Bradford | 1985 |
| **Best Bowling** | NWT | 7-33 R.D.Jackman | v | Yorkshire | Harrogate | 1970 |
| | BHC | 5-21 P.H.L.Wilson | v | Comb Univs | The Oval | 1979 |
| | SL | 6-25 Intikhab Alam | v | Derbyshire | The Oval | 1974 |

# SUSSEX

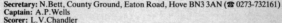

**Formation of Present Club:** 1 March 1839
**Substantial Reorganisation:** August 1857
**Colours:** Dark Blue, Light Blue and Gold
**Badge:** County Arms of Six Martlets
**Championships:** (0) Second 1902, 1903, 1932, 1933, 1934, 1953, 1981
**NatWest Trophy/Gillette Cup Winners:** (4) 1963, 1964, 1978, 1986
**Benson and Hedges Cup Winners:** (0) Semi-Finalists 1982
**Sunday League Champions:** (1) 1982
**Match Awards:** NWT 45; BHC 47

**Secretary:** N.Bett, County Ground, Eaton Road, Hove BN3 3AN (☎ 0273-732161)
**Captain:** A.P.Wells
**Scorer:** L.V.Chandler
**1993 Beneficiary:** C.M.Wells

**DEAN, Jacob** Winston (Chailey S; Haywards Heath SFC), b Cuckfield 23 Aug 1970. 5'10½". RHB, SLA. No 1st XI appearances – joined staff 1991.

**DONELAN, Bradleigh** Thomas Peter (Finchley Catholic HS), b Park Royal Hospital, Middx 3 Jan 1968. 6'1". RHB, OB. Debut 1989. MCC YC. HS 68* v Hants (Southampton) 1992. BB 6-62 (10-136 match) v Glos (Hove) 1991. **BHC:** HS 9*. BB 1-41. **SL:** HS 19 v Glos (Hove) 1991. BB 2-39 v Surrey (Oval) 1992.

**GIDDINS, Edward** Simon Hunter (Eastbourne C), b Eastbourne 20 Jul 1971. 6'4½". RHB, RMF. Debut 1991. MCC YC. HS 14* v Middx (Lord's) 1991. BB 5-32 v Derbys (Eastbourne) 1992. **BHC:** HS 0. BB 1-46. **SL:** HS 2. BB 3-37 v Glos (Cheltenham) 1992.

**GREENFIELD, Keith** (Falmer HS), b Brighton 6 Dec 1968. 6'0". RHB, RM. Debut 1987. HS 127* v CU (Hove) 1991. BAC HS 64 v Glos (Hove) 1991. **NWT:** HS 19 and BB 1-33 v Bucks (Beaconsfield) 1992. **BHC:** HS 62 v Leics (Leicester) 1992. BB 1-35. **SL:** HS 79 and BB 2-36 v Glam (Hove) 1992.

**HALL, James** William (Chichester HS), b Chichester 30 Mar 1968. 6'3". RHB, OB. Debut 1990. Cap 1992. 1000 runs (2); most – 1140 (1990 – debut season). HS 140* v Lancs (Hove) 1992. Award: BHC 1. **NWT:** HS 47 v Bucks (Beaconsfield) 1992. **BHC:** HS 81 v Surrey (Hove) 1992. **SL:** HS 77 v Notts (Nottingham) 1992.

**JONES, Adrian** Nicholas (Seaford C), b Woking, Surrey 22 Jul 1961. 6'2". LHB, RFM. Sussex 1981-86 (cap 1986). Somerset 1987-90 (cap 1987). Border 1981-82. HS 43* Sm v Leics (Taunton) 1989. Sx HS 35 v Middx (Hove) 1984. 50 wkts (5); most – 71 (1989). BB 7-30 Sm v Hants (Southampton) 1988. Sx BB 5-29 v Glos (Hove) 1984. Awards: BHC 3. **NWT:** HS 7. BB 4-26 v Yorks (Leeds) 1986. **BHC:** HS 25 Sm v Essex (Taunton) 1989. BB 5-53 Sm v Notts (Taunton) 1989. **SL:** HS 37 Sm v Surrey (Oval) 1989. BB 7-41 v Notts (Nottingham) 1986.

**LENHAM, Neil** John (Brighton C), b Worthing 17 Dec 1965. Son of L.J. (Sussex 1956-70). 5'11". RHB, RMF. Debut 1984. Cap 1990. 1000 runs (3); most – 1663 (1990). HS 222* v Kent (Hove) 1992. BB 4-85 v Leics (Leicester) 1986. Awards: NWT 1; BHC 1. **NWT:** HS 66 v Scot (Edinburgh) 1991. BB 2-12 v Ire (Downpatrick) 1990. **BHC:** HS 82 v Somerset (Hove) 1986. BB 1-3. **SL:** HS 86 v Kent (Hove) 1991. BB 2-19 v Glos (Hove) 1989.

**MOORES, Peter** (King Edward VI S, Macclesfield), b Macclesfield, Cheshire 18 Dec 1962. 6'0". RHB, WK. Worcestershire 1983-84. Sussex debut 1985. Cap 1989. OFS 1988-89. HS 116 v Somerset (Hove) 1989. **NWT:** HS 26 v Scot (Edinburgh) 1991. **BHC:** HS 76 v Middx (Hove) 1990. **SL:** HS 57 v Hants (Hove) 1992.

**NORTH, John** Andrew (Chichester HS), b Slindon 19 Nov 1970. 5'9". RHB, RM. Debut 1990. HS 63* v Hants (Hove) 1991. BB 4-47 v SL (Hove) 1991. BAC BB 3-51 v Worcs and v Hants 1992. **BHC:** HS 22 v Scot (Hove) 1991. BB 3-24 v Leics (Leicester) 1992. **SL:** HS 56 v Durham (Horsham) 1992. BB 3-29 v Kent (Hove) 1991.

**PIGOTT, Anthony** Charles Shackleton (Harrow S), b Fulham, London 4 Jun 1958. 6'1". RHB, RFM. Debut 1978. Cap 1982. Benefit 1991. Wellington 1982-83/1983-84. **Tests:** 1 (1983-84); HS 8* and BB 2-75 v NZ (Christchurch) 1983-84. Tours: NZ 1979-80 (DHR), 1983-84 (part). HS 104* v Warwks (Birmingham) 1986. 50 wkts (5); most – 74 (1988). BB 7-74 v Northants (Eastbourne) 1982. Hat-trick 1978 (his first f-c wkts). **NWT:** HS 53 v Derbys (Hove) 1988. BB 3-4 v Ire (Hove) 1985. **BHC:** HS 49* v Essex (Hove) 1989. BB 3-29 v Leics (Hove) 1991. **SL:** HS 51* v Northants (Hove) 1989. BB 5-24 v Lancs (Manchester) 1986.

**REMY, Carlos** Charles (St Aloyous C; Haringey Cricket C), b Castries, St Lucia 24 Jul 1968. 5'9". RHB, RM. Debut 1989. HS 47 v Derbys (Eastbourne) 1992. BB 4-63 v CU (Hove) 1990. BAC BB 3-27 v Lancs (Hove) 1992. **NWT:** HS 1. **SL:** HS 15 v Kent (Canterbury) 1992. BB 4-31 v Lancs (Hove) 1992.

**ROBSON, Andrew** George (Whitburn CS), b East Boldon, Co Durham 27 Apr 1971. 6'0". RHB, RFM. Surrey 1991. Sussex debut 1992. HS 3. Sx HS 0*. BB 4-37 v Somerset (Hove) 1992. **NWT:** HS -. BB 1-29. **BHC:** HS 0. BB 1-32. **SL:** HS 3. BB 3-42 Sy v Hants (Oval) 1991.

**SALISBURY, Ian** David Kenneth (Moulton CS), b Northampton 21 Jan 1970. 5'11". RHB, LB. Debut 1989. Cap 1991. MCC YC. YC 1992. Wisden 1992. **Tests:** 2 (1992); HS 50 v P (Manchester) 1992; BB 3-49 v P (Lord's) 1992. Tours (Eng A): WI 1991-92; P 1990-91; SL 1990-91. HS 68 v Derbys (Hove) 1990. 50 wkts (1): 87 (1992). BB 7-54 (12-138 match) v Yorks (Hove) 1992. **NWT:** HS 14* v Essex (Hove) 1991. BB 3-28 v Bucks (Beaconsfield) 1992. **BHC:** HS 17* and BB 3-40 v Kent (Canterbury) 1991. **SL:** HS 27* v Glos (Cheltenham) 1992. BB 5-30 v Leics (Leicester) 1992.

**SMITH, David** Mark (Battersea GS), b Balham, London 9 Jan 1956. 6'4". LHB, RM. Surrey 1973-83 and 1987-88 (cap 1980). Worcestershire 1984-86 (cap 1984). Sussex debut/cap 1989. **Tests:** 2 (1985-86); HS 47 v WI (P-of-S) 1985-86. LOI: 2. Tour: WI 1985-86. 1000 runs (7); most – 1305 (1989). HS 213 v Essex (Southend) 1992. BB 3-40 Sy v Sussex (Oval) 1976. Sx BB -. Awards: NWT 3; BHC 4. **NWT:** HS 109 Wo v Lancs (Manchester) 1985. BB 3-39 Sy v Derbys (Ilkeston) 1976. **BHC:** HS 126 Wo v Warwks (Worcester) 1985. BB 4-29 Sy v Kent (Oval) 1980. **SL:** HS 87* Sy v Hants (Oval) 1980. BB 2-21 Sy v Worcs (Byfleet) 1973.

**SPEIGHT, Martin** Peter (Hurstpierpoint C; Durham U), b Walsall, Staffs 24 Oct 1967. 5'9". RHB, WK. Debut 1986. Cap 1991. Comb Us (BHC) 1987-89. Wellington 1989-90. 1000 runs (2); most – 1375 (1990). HS 179 v Glam (Eastbourne) 1992. BB 1-2. Award: BHC 1. **NWT:** HS 48 v Leics 1989 and v Essex 1991. **BHC:** HS 83 Comb Us v Glos (Bristol) 1988. **SL:** HS 106* v Worcs (Hove) 1991.

**STEPHENSON, Franklyn** Dacosta (Samuel Jackson Prescod Polytechnic), b St James, Barbados 8 Apr 1959. 6'3¼". RHB, RFM. Barbados 1981-82 and 1989-90. Tasmania 1981-82. Gloucestershire 1982-83. Nottinghamshire 1988-91 (cap 1988). OFS 1991-92. Sussex debut/cap 1992. Staffordshire 1980. Wisden 1988. Tour (WI XI): SA 1982-83, 1983-84. 1000 runs (1): 1018 (1988). HS 165 Barbados v Leeward Is (Basseterre) 1981-82. Sx HS 133 v Somerset (Hove) 1992. 50 wkts (4) inc 100 (1): 125 (1988). BB 8-47 (15-106 match) Nt v Essex (Nottingham) 1989. Sx BB 7-29 (11-107 match) v Worcs (Worcester) 1992. Scored 111 and 117 and took 11-122 Nt v Yorks (Nottingham) 1988. Double 1988. Awards: BHC 3. **NWT:** HS 40 v Warwks (Birmingham) 1992. BB 3-8 v Bucks (Beaconsfield) 1992. **BHC:** HS 98*

STEPHENSON – continued:
Nt v Worcs (Nottingham) 1990. BB 5–30 Nt v Yorks (Nottingham) 1991. **SL:** HS 69 Nt v Hants (Nottingham) 1989. BB 5-31 Nt v Northants (Wellingborough) 1991.
**WELLS, Alan** Peter (Tideway CS, Newhaven), b Newhaven 2 Oct 1961. Younger brother of C.M. 6'0". RHB, RM. Debut 1981. Cap 1986. Captain 1992-. Border 1981-82. Tour: SA 1989-90 (Eng XI). 1000 runs (7); most – 1784 (1991). HS 253* v Yorks (Middlesbrough) 1991. BB 3-67 v Worcs (Worcester) 1987. Award: NWT 1. **NWT:** HS 119 v Bucks (Beaconsfield) 1992. **BHC:** HS 74 v Middx (Hove) 1990. BB 1-17. **SL:** HS 110* v Essex (Southend) 1992. BB 1-0.
**WELLS, Colin** Mark (Tideway CS, Newhaven), b Newhaven 3 Mar 1960. Elder brother of A.P. 5'11". RHB, RM. Debut 1979. Cap 1982. Benefit 1993. Border 1980-81. W Province 1984-85. LOI: 2. 1000 runs (6); most – 1456 (1987). HS 203 v Hants (Hove) 1984. 50 wkts (2); most – 59 (1984). BB 7-42 v Derbys (Derby) 1991. Awards: BHC 3. **NWT:** HS 76 v Ire (Hove) 1985. BB 3-16 v Scot (Edinburgh) 1991. **BHC:** HS 117 v Glam (Swansea) 1989. BB 4-21 v Middx (Lord's) 1980. **SL:** HS 104* v Warwks (Hove) 1983. BB 4-15 v Worcs (Worcester) 1983.

## NEWCOMERS

**ATHEY, Charles William** Jeffrey (Stainsby SS; Acklam Hall HS), b Middlesbrough, Yorks 27 Sep 1957. 5'9½". RHB, RM. Yorkshire 1976-83 (cap 1980). Gloucestershire 1984-92 (cap 1985; captain 1989; benefit 1990). **Tests:** 23 (1980 to 1988); HS 123 v P (Lord's) 1987. LOI: 31. Tours: A 1986-87, 1987-88; SA 1989-90 (Eng A); WI 1980-81; NZ 1979-80 (DHR), 1987-88; P 1987-88; SL 1985-86 (Eng B). 1000 runs (10); most – 1812 (1984). HS 184 Eng B v Sri Lanka (Galle) 1985-86. BAC HS 181 Gs v Sussex (Cheltenham) 1992. BB 3-3 Gs v Hants (Bristol) 1985. Awards: NWT 4; BHC 5. **NWT:** HS 115 Y v Kent (Leeds) 1980. BB 1-18. **BHC:** HS 95 Gs v Northants (Northampton) 1987. BB 4-48 Gs v Comb Us (Bristol) 1984. **SL:** HS 121* Gs v Worcs (Moreton) 1985. BB 5-35 Y v Derbys (Chesterfield) 1981.
**HEMMINGS, Edward** Ernest (Campion S), b Leamington Spa, Warwks 20 Feb 1949. 5'10". RHB, OB. Warwickshire 1966-78 (cap 1974). Nottinghamshire 1979-92 (cap 1980; benefit 1987). **Tests:** 16 (1982 to 1990-91); HS 95 v A (Sydney) 1982-83; BB 6-58 v NZ (Birmingham) 1990. LOI: 33. Tours: A 1982-83, 1987-88, 1990-91; SA 1974-75 (DHR); WI 1982-83 (Int), 1989-90; NZ 1987-88; P 1981-82 (Int), 1987-88. HS 127* Nt v Yorks (Worksop) 1982. 50 wkts (14); most – 94 (1984). BB 10-175 Int XI v WI XI (Kingston) 1982-83. BAC BB 7-23 Nt v Lancs (Nottingham) 1983. 2 hat-tricks: 1977 (Wa), 1984 (Nt). Awards: NWT 1; BHC 1. **NWT:** HS 31* Nt v Staffs (Nottingham) 1985. BB 3-27 Nt v Warwks (Nottingham) 1985. **BHC:** HS 61* Wa v Leics (Birmingham) 1974. BB 4-47 Nt v Glos (Bristol) 1989. **SL:** HS 44* Wa v Kent (Birmingham) 1971. BB 5-22 Wa v Notts (Birmingham) 1974.
**HUMPHRIES, Shaun** (The Weald, Billingshurst, Kingston C, London), b Horsham 11 Jan 1973. 5'9". RHB.
**LAW, Danny** Richard (Steyning GS), b St Thomas's Hospital, London 15 Jul 1975. 6'5". RHB, RFM.
**NEWELL, Keith** (Ifield Community C), b Crawley 25 Mar 1972. 6'0". RHB, RM.
**PEIRCE, Michael** Toby Edward (Ardingly C; Durham U), b Maidenhead, Berkshire 14 Jun 1973. 5'10". LHB, SLA.

## DEPARTURES

**HANLEY, Robin** (Willingdon S; Eastbourne SFC), b Tonbridge, Kent 5 Jan 1968. 6'2". RHB. Sussex 1990-92. HS 28 v Warwks (Eastbourne) 1990. **SL:** HS 11 v Warwks (Eastbourne) 1990.
**HANSFORD, Alan** Roderick (Oakmeeds Community S; Haywards Heath SFC; Surrey U), b Burgess Hill 1 Oct 1968. 6'0". RHB, RM. Sussex 1989-92. Comb Us (BHC) 1989-91. HS 29 v Hants (Southampton) 1990. BB 5-79 v Hants (Hove) 1989. **NWT:** HS 5* and BB 2-48 v Middx (Lord's) 1989. **BHC:** HS 13* Comb Us v Worcs (Cambridge) 1991. BB 2-11 Comb Us v Surrey (Cambridge) 1989. **SL:** HS 5*. BB 5-32 v Glos (Hove) 1989.

# SUSSEX 1992

## RESULTS SUMMARY

|  | Place | Won | Lost | Drew | Abandoned |
|---|---|---|---|---|---|
| **Britannic Assurance Championship** | 7th | 6 | 7 | 9 | |
| **All First-class Matches** | | 6 | 7 | 9 | |
| **Sunday League** | 11th | 7 | 8 | | 2 |
| **NatWest Trophy** | 2nd Round | | | | |
| **Benson and Hedges Cup** | 4th in Group A | | | | |

# BRITANNIC ASSURANCE CHAMPIONSHIP AVERAGES

## BATTING AND FIELDING

| Cap | | M | I | NO | HS | Runs | Avge | 100 | 50 | Ct/St |
|---|---|---|---|---|---|---|---|---|---|---|
| 1986 | A.P.Wells | 22 | 35 | 5 | 165* | 1465 | 48.83 | 5 | 4 | 24 |
| 1992 | J.W.Hall | 20 | 34 | 5 | 140* | 1125 | 38.79 | 1 | 8 | 7 |
| 1991 | M.P.Speight | 20 | 33 | 2 | 179 | 1180 | 38.06 | 5 | – | 16 |
| 1990 | N.J.Lenham | 20 | 34 | 2 | 222* | 1173 | 36.65 | 4 | 3 | 9 |
| 1989 | D.M.Smith | 19 | 33 | 4 | 213 | 1076 | 34.70 | 2 | 5 | 12 |
| 1989 | P.Moores | 21 | 30 | 5 | 109 | 851 | 34.04 | 1 | 3 | 32/7 |
| 1992 | F.D.Stephenson | 18 | 25 | 4 | 133 | 680 | 32.38 | 1 | 2 | 10 |
| – | K.Greenfield | 6 | 10 | 2 | 48 | 205 | 25.62 | – | – | 5 |
| 1982 | C.M.Wells | 6 | 7 | 1 | 39 | 133 | 22.16 | – | – | 1 |
| – | B.T.P.Donelan | 16 | 25 | 6 | 68* | 421 | 22.15 | – | 2 | 2 |
| – | C.C.Remy | 7 | 9 | – | 47 | 192 | 21.33 | – | – | 1 |
| 1982 | A.C.S.Pigott | 17 | 19 | 7 | 27* | 191 | 15.91 | – | – | 5 |
| – | J.A.North | 5 | 7 | 1 | 53* | 81 | 13.50 | – | 1 | – |
| 1986 | A.N.Jones | 10 | 9 | 4 | 17 | 56 | 11.20 | – | – | 1 |
| 1991 | I.D.K.Salisbury | 17 | 18 | 2 | 42 | 177 | 11.06 | – | – | 15 |
| – | E.S.H.Giddins | 11 | 8 | 6 | 10* | 15 | 7.50 | – | – | 4 |
| – | A.G.Robson | 5 | 4 | 3 | 0* | 0 | 0.00 | – | – | 1 |

*Also played:* (1 match each): R.Hanley 1; A.R.Hansford 1.

## BOWLING

| | O | M | R | W | Avge | Best | 5wI | 10wM |
|---|---|---|---|---|---|---|---|---|
| I.D.K.Salisbury | 678.3 | 169 | 2135 | 79 | 27.02 | 7-54 | 6 | 2 |
| E.S.H.Giddins | 247.5 | 52 | 857 | 31 | 27.64 | 5-32 | 2 | – |
| J.A.North | 96.3 | 14 | 331 | 11 | 30.09 | 3-51 | – | – |
| C.M.Wells | 119 | 26 | 323 | 10 | 32.30 | 3-26 | – | – |
| F.D.Stephenson | 467.2 | 93 | 1375 | 40 | 34.37 | 7-29 | 1 | 1 |
| A.C.S.Pigott | 363 | 74 | 1063 | 27 | 39.37 | 3-34 | – | – |
| B.T.P.Donelan | 404 | 85 | 1323 | 28 | 47.25 | 6-77 | 1 | – |
| A.N.Jones | 161.5 | 17 | 745 | 11 | 67.72 | 3-76 | – | – |

*Also bowled:* K.Greenfield 17-0-84-0; J.W.Hall 2-1-14-0; A.R.Hansford 29-5-81-3; N.J.Lenham 120.1-28-362-6; C.C.Remy 96.2-12-336-6; A.G.Robson 19-24-405-8; D.M.Smith 4-1-18-0; M.P.Speight 3-0-30-1; A.P.Wells 29-7-94-0.

Sussex played no first-class fixtures outside the Britannic Assurance Championship in 1992.

# SUSSEX RECORDS

## FIRST-CLASS CRICKET

| | | | | | |
|---|---|---|---|---|---|
| **Highest Total** | For 705-8d | v | Surrey | Hastings | 1902 |
| | V 726 | by | Notts | Nottingham | 1895 |
| **Lowest Total** | For 19 | v | Surrey | Godalming | 1830 |
| | 19 | v | Notts | Hove | 1873 |
| | V 18 | by | Kent | Gravesend | 1867 |
| **Highest Innings** | For 333 K.S.Duleepsinhji | v | Northants | Hove | 1930 |
| | V 322 E.Paynter | for | Lancashire | Hove | 1937 |

### Highest Partnership for each Wicket

| | | | | | | |
|---|---|---|---|---|---|---|
| 1st | 490 | E.H.Bowley/J.G.Langridge | v | Middlesex | Hove | 1933 |
| 2nd | 385 | E.H.Bowley/M.W.Tate | v | Northants | Hove | 1921 |
| 3rd | 298 | K.S.Ranjitsinhji/E.H.Killick | v | Lancashire | Hove | 1901 |
| 4th | 326* | J.Langridge/G.Cox | v | Yorkshire | Leeds | 1949 |
| 5th | 297 | J.H.Parks/H.W.Parks | v | Hampshire | Portsmouth | 1937 |
| 6th | 255 | K.S.Duleepsinhji/M.W.Tate | v | Northants | Hove | 1930 |
| 7th | 344 | K.S.Ranjitsinhji/W.Newham | v | Essex | Leyton | 1902 |
| 8th | 229* | C.L.A.Smith/G.Brann | v | Kent | Hove | 1902 |
| 9th | 178 | H.W.Parks/A.F.Wensley | v | Derbyshire | Horsham | 1930 |
| 10th | 156 | G.R.Cox/H.R.Butt | v | Cambridge U | Cambridge | 1908 |

| | | | | | |
|---|---|---|---|---|---|
| **Best Bowling** | For 10-48 C.H.G.Bland | v | Kent | Tonbridge | 1899 |
| **(Innings)** | V 9-11 A.P.Freeman | for | Kent | Hove | 1922 |
| **Best Bowling** | For 17-106 G.R.Cox | v | Warwicks | Horsham | 1926 |
| **(Match)** | V 17-67 A.P.Freeman | for | Kent | Hove | 1922 |

| | | | | |
|---|---|---|---|---|
| **Most Runs – Season** | 2,850 | J.G.Langridge | (av 64.77) | 1949 |
| **Most Runs – Career** | 34,152 | J.G.Langridge | (av 37.69) | 1928-1955 |
| **Most 100s – Season** | 12 | J.G.Langridge | | 1949 |
| **Most 100s – Career** | 76 | J.G.Langridge | | 1928-1955 |
| **Most Wkts – Season** | 198 | M.W.Tate | (av 13.47) | 1925 |
| **Most Wkts – Career** | 2,211 | M.W.Tate | (av 17.41) | 1912-1937 |

## LIMITED-OVERS CRICKET

| | | | | | |
|---|---|---|---|---|---|
| **Highest Total** | NWT 327-6 | v | Bucks | Beaconsfield | 1992 |
| | BHC 305-6 | v | Kent | Hove | 1982 |
| | SL 293-4 | v | Worcs | Horsham | 1980 |
| **Lowest Total** | NWT 49 | v | Derbyshire | Chesterfield | 1969 |
| | BHC 61 | v | Middlesex | Hove | 1978 |
| | SL 61 | v | Derbyshire | Derby | 1978 |
| **Highest Innings** | NWT 141* G.D.Mendis | v | Warwicks | Hove | 1980 |
| | BHC 117 R.D.V.Knight | v | Surrey | The Oval | 1977 |
| | 117 C.M.Wells | v | Glamorgan | Swansea | 1989 |
| | SL 129 A.W.Greig | v | Yorkshire | Scarborough | 1976 |
| **Best Bowling** | NWT 6-9 A.I.Dodemaide | v | Ireland | Downpatrick | 1990 |
| | BHC 5-8 Imran Khan | v | Northants | Northampton | 1978 |
| | SL 7-41 A.N.Jones | v | Notts | Nottingham | 1986 |

# WARWICKSHIRE

**Formation of Present Club:** 8 April 1882
**Substantial Reorganisation:** 19 January 1884
**Colours:** Dark Blue, Gold and Silver
**Badge:** Bear and Ragged Staff
**Championships:** (3) 1911, 1951, 1972
**NatWest Trophy/Gillette Cup Winners:** (3) 1966, 1968, 1989
**Benson and Hedges Cup Winners:** (0) Finalists 1984
**Sunday League Champions:** (1) 1980
**Match Awards:** NWT 44; BHC 44

**General Secretary:** D.M.W.Heath, County Ground, Edgbaston, Birmingham, B5 7QU (☎ 021-446 4422)
**Captain:** D.A.Reeve
**Scorers:** A.E.Davis (home) and S.P.Austin (away)
**1993 Beneficiary:** –

**ASIF DIN,** Mohamed (Ladywood CS, Birmingham), b Kampala, Uganda 21 Sep 1960. 5'9¾". RHB, LB. Debut 1981. Cap 1987. MCC YC. Tour: SA 1991-92 (Wa). 1000 runs (2); most – 1425 (1988). HS 158* v CU (Cambridge) 1988. BAC HS 140 v Leics (Leicester) 1991. BB 5-100 v Glam (Birmingham) 1982. Awards: NWT 2; BHC 1. **NWT:** HS 94* v Worcs (Birmingham) 1989. BB 5-40 v Herts (St Albans) 1990. **BHC:** HS 137 v Somerset (Birmingham) 1991. BB 1-26. **SL:** HS 113 v Somerset (W-s-M) 1990. BB 1-11.

**BELL, Michael** Anthony Vincent (Bishop Milner CS; Dudley Tech C), b Birmingham 19 Dec 1966. 6'2". RHB, LMF. Debut 1992. MCC YC. HS 5 and BB 3-78 v Notts (Birmingham) 1992.

**BOOTH, Paul** Antony (Honley HS), b Huddersfield, Yorks 5 Sep 1965. 5'10". LHB, SLA. Yorkshire 1982-89. Warwickshire debut 1990. Tour: SA 1991-92 (Wa). HS 62 v Somerset (Taunton) 1991. BB 5-98 Y v Lancs (Manchester) 1988. Wa BB 4-29 v Somerset (Taunton) 1992. **NWT:** HS 6*. **BHC:** HS 13* v Glam (Birmingham) 1990. BB 2-28 Y v Worcs (Bradford) 1985. **SL:** HS -. BB 1-33.

**BROWN, Douglas** Robert (Alloa Academy; W London IHE), b Stirling, Scotland 29 Oct 1969. 6'2". RHB, RFM. Debut for Scotland 1989. Warwickshire debut. v Boland (Brackenfell) 1992. Tour: SA 1991-92 (Wa). HS 44* Scot v Ire (Dublin) 1989. Wa HS 5*. BB 3-27 v CU (Cambridge) 1992. Awaiting BAC debut. **BHC:** HS 24 Scot v Notts (Glasgow) 1990. BB 3-50 Scot v Northants (Northampton) 1990. **SL:** HS 14 v Middx (Lord's) 1992. BB 3-21 v Hants (Birmingham) 1992.

**BURNS, Michael** (Walney CS), b Barrow-in-Furness, Lancs 6 Jun 1969. 6'0". RHB, WK, occ RM. Cumberland 1988-90. Debut 1992. HS 78 v CU (Cambridge) 1992. BAC HS 4. **BHC:** HS 3. **SL:** HS 1.

**DONALD, Allan** Anthony (Grey College HS), b Bloemfontein, SA 20 Oct 1966. 6'2". RHB, RF. OFS 1985-86 to date. Warwickshire debut 1987. Cap 1989. Wisden 1991. **Tests (SA):** 1 (1991-92); HS 0 and BB 4-77 v WI (Bridgetown) 1991-92. LOI (SA): 14. Tour (SA): WI 1991-92. HS 46* OFS v W Province (Cape Town) 1990-91. Wa HS 41 v Notts (Birmingham) 1992. 50 wkts (3); most – 86 (1989). BB 8-37 OFS v Transvaal (Johannesburg) 1986-87. Wa BB 7-37 v Durham (Birmingham) 1992. Awards: NWT 3. **NWT:** HS 14* v Northants (Birmingham) 1992. BB 5-12 v Wilts (Birmingham) 1989. **BHC:** HS 23* v Leics (Leicester) 1989. BB 4-28 v Scot (Perth) 1987. **SL:** HS 18* v Middx (Lord's) 1988. BB 4-23 v Surrey (Oval) 1992.

**GILES, Ashley** Fraser (George Abbot S, Guildford), b Chertsey, Surrey 19 Mar 1973. 6'3". RHB, SLA. No 1st XI appearances – joined staff 1992.

**HOLLOWAY, Piran** Christopher Laity (Millfield S; Taunton S; Loughborough U), b Helston, Cornwall 1 Oct 1970. 5'8". LHB, WK. Debut 1988. Comb Us (BHC) 1991. HS 102* v Worcs (Birmingham) 1992. **NWT:** HS 2. **BHC:** HS 27 Comb Us v Derbys (Oxford) 1991. **SL:** HS 51 v Northants (Northampton) 1992.

**KHAN, Wasim** Gulzar (Small Heath CS; Josiah Mason SFC, Erdington), b Birmingham 26 Feb 1971. 6'0". LHB, LB. Awaiting f-c debut. **SL:** HS 7.

**MOLES, Andrew** James (Finham Park CS; Butts CHE), b Solihull 12 Feb 1961. 5'10". RHB, RM. Debut 1986. Cap 1987. GW 1986-87/1988-89. Tour: SA 1991-92 (Wa). 1000 runs (5); most – 1854 (1990). HS 230* GW v N Transvaal B (Verwoerdburg) 1988-89. Wa HS 224* v Glam (Swansea) 1990. BB 3-21 v OU (Oxford) 1987. BAC BB 3-50 v Essex (Chelmsford) 1987. Awards: NWT 1; BHC 1. **NWT:** HS 127 v Bucks (Birmingham) 1987. **BHC:** HS 72 v Scot (Perth) 1987. BB 1-11. **SL:** HS 96* v Glam (Birmingham) 1992. BB 2-24 v Worcs (Worcester) 1987.

**MUNTON, Timothy** Alan (Sarson HS; King Edward VII Upper S), b Melton Mowbray, Leics 30 Jul 1965. 6'5". RHB, RMF. Debut 1985. Cap 1989. **Tests:** 2 (1992); HS 25* v P (Manchester) 1992; BB 2-22 v P (Leeds) 1992. Tours (Eng A): WI 1991-92; P 1990-91; SL 1990-91. HS 47 v Kent (Birmingham) 1992. 50 wkts (4); most – 78 (1990). BB 8-89 (11-128 match) v Middx (Birmingham) 1991. **NWT:** HS 5. BB 3-36 v Kent (Canterbury) 1989. **BHC:** HS 13 v Leics (Leicester) 1989. BB 4-35 v Surrey (Oval) 1991. **SL:** HS 10* v Northants (Northampton) 1991. BB 5-23 v Glos (Moreton) 1990.

**OSTLER, Dominic** Piers (Princethorpe C; Solihull TC), b Solihull 15 Jul 1970. 6'3". RHB, RM. Debut 1990. Cap 1991. 1000 runs (2); most – 1284 (1991). HS 192 v Surrey (Guildford) 1992. **NWT:** HS 34* v Yorks (Birmingham) 1991. **BHC:** HS 65* v Somerset (Taunton) 1992. **SL:** HS 62* v Derbys (Birmingham) 1991.

**PENNEY, Trevor** Lionel (Prince Edward S, Salisbury), b Salisbury, Rhodesia 12 Jun 1968. 6'0". RHB, RM. Gained England qualification 1992. Debut for Boland 1991-92. Warwickshire debut v Boland (Brackenfell) 1991-92. UK debut v Cambridge U (Cambridge) scoring 102*. Tour: SA 1991-92 (Wa). HS 151 v Middx (Lord's) 1992. **NWT:** HS 7. **BHC:** HS 17 v Yorks (Birmingham) 1992. **SL:** HS 53* v Yorks (Scarborough) 1992.

**PIPER, Keith** John (Haringey Cricket C), b Leicester 18 Dec 1969. 5'6". RHB, WK. Debut 1989. Cap 1992. Tour: SA 1991-92 (Wa). HS 111 v Somerset (Birmingham) 1990. BB 1-57. **NWT:** HS 12 v Northants (Birmingham) 1992. **BHC:** HS 11* v Surrey (Oval) 1991. **SL:** HS 30 v Lancs (Manchester) 1990.

**RATCLIFFE, Jason** David (Sharman's Cross SS; Solihull SFC), b Solihull 19 Jun 1969. Son of D.P. (Warwks 1957-68). 6'4". RHB, RM. Debut 1988. Tour: SA 1991-92 (Wa). HS 127* v CU (Cambridge) 1989. BAC HS 94 v Middx (Birmingham) 1991. BB 1-15. Award: NWT 1. **NWT:** HS 68* v Herts (Birmingham) 1991. **BHC:** HS 29 v Surrey (Oval) 1991. **SL:** HS 37 v Somerset (Birmingham) 1989. BB 1-8.

**REEVE, Dermot** Alexander (King George V S, Kowloon), b Kowloon, Hong Kong 2 Apr 1963. 6'0". RHB, RMF. Sussex 1983-87 (cap 1986). Warwickshire debut 1988. Cap 1989. Captain 1993. Hong Kong 1982 (ICC Trophy). MCC YC. **Tests:** 3 (1991-92); HS 59 v NZ (Christchurch) 1991-92 (on debut); BB 1-4. **LOI:** 15. Tour: NZ 1991-92. 1000 runs (2); most – 1412 (1990). HS 202* v Northants (Northampton) 1990. 50 wkts (2); most – 55 (1984). BB 7-37 Sx v Lancs (Lytham) 1987. Wa BB

REEVE – continued:
6-73 v Kent (Tunbridge W) 1991. Awards: NWT 3; BHC 1. **NWT:** HS 57* v Hants (Birmingham) 1991. BB 4-20 Sx v Lancs (Lord's) 1986. **BHC:** HS 80 v Essex (Birmingham) 1991. BB 4-42 Sx v Kent (Canterbury) 1987. **SL:** HS 100 v Lancs (Birmingham) 1991. BB 5-23 v Essex (Birmingham) 1988.

**SMALL, Gladstone** Cleophas (Moseley S; Hall Green TC), b St George, Barbados 18 Oct 1961. 5'11". RHB, RFM. Debut 1979-80 (DHR XI in NZ). Warwickshire debut 1980. Cap 1982. Benefit 1992. S Australia 1985-86. **Tests:** 17 (1986 to 1990); HS 59 v A (Oval) 1989; BB 5-48 v A (Melbourne) 1986-87. LOI: 53. Tours: A 1986-87, 1990-91; WI 1989-90; NZ 1979-80 (DHR); P 1981-82 (Int). HS 70 v Lancs (Manchester) 1988. 50 wkts (6); most – 80 (1988). BB 7-15 v Notts (Birmingham) 1988. Award: NWT 1. **NWT:** HS 33 v Surrey (Lord's) 1982. BB 3-22 v Glam (Cardiff) 1982. **BHC:** HS 22 v Kent (Canterbury) 1990. BB 4-22 v Glam (Birmingham) 1990. **SL:** HS 40* v Essex (Ilford) 1984. BB 5-29 v Surrey (Birmingham) 1980.

**SMITH, Neil** Michael Knight (Warwick S), b Birmingham 27 Jul 1967. Son of M.J.K. (Leics, Warwks and England 1951-75). 6'0". RHB, OB. Debut 1987. MCC YC. Tour: SA 1991-92 (Wa). HS 161 v Yorks (Leeds) 1989. BB 5-61 v Middx (Lord's) 1992. Award: BHC 1. **NWT:** HS 52 v Yorks (Leeds) 1990. BB 1-6. **BHC:** HS 32 and BB 3-45 v Somerset (Taunton) 1992. **SL:** HS 44 v Durham (Birmingham) 1992. BB 4-25 v Essex (Birmingham) 1992.

**SMITH, Paul** Andrew (Heaton GS), b Jesmond, Northumb 15 Apr 1964. Son of K.D. sr (Leics 1950-51) and brother of K.D. jr (Warwks 1973-85). 6'2". RHB, RFM. Debut 1982. Cap 1986. MCC YC. Tour: SA 1991-92 (Wa). 1000 runs (2); most – 1508 (1986). HS 140 v Worcs (Worcester) 1989. BB 6-91 v Derbys (Birmingham) 1992. 2 hat-tricks: 1989, 1990. Awards: BHC 2. **NWT:** HS 79 v Durham (Birmingham) 1986. BB 3-10 v Salop (Birmingham) 1984. **BHC:** HS 74 v Northants (Birmingham) 1989. BB 3-28 v Middx (Lord's) 1991. **SL:** HS 93* v Middx (Birmingham) 1989. BB 4-21 v Somerset (Birmingham) 1991.

**TWOSE, Roger** Graham (King's C, Taunton), b Torquay, Devon 17 Apr 1968. Nephew of R.W.Tolchard (Leics and England 1965-83). 6'0". LHB, RM. Debut 1989. Cap 1992. N Districts 1989-90. C Districts 1991-92. Devon 1988-89. MCC YC. Tour: SA 1991-92 (Wa). 1000 runs (1): 1412 (1992). HS 233 v Leics (Birmingham) 1992. BB 6-63 v Middx (Coventry) 1992. Award: NWT 1. **NWT:** HS 107* v Staffs (Birmingham) 1992. BB 3-39 v Sussex (Birmingham) 1992. **BHC:** HS 62 v Yorks (Birmingham) 1992. **SL:** HS 100 v Leics (Birmingham) 1992. BB 2-11 v Derbys (Derby) 1990.

**WELCH, Graeme** (Hetton CS), b Durham 21 Mar 1972. 5'11½". RHB, RM. Awaiting f-c debut. **SL:** HS 23 v Durham (Birmingham) 1992. BB 1-24.

## NEWCOMERS

**MULRAINE, Charles** E., b Leamington Spa 24 Dec 1973. LHB.

**ROBINSON, Matthew** Fitz David (King's C, Taunton), b Cardiff, Glam 2 Apr 1973. RHB, RM. Somerset staff 1992.

## DEPARTURE

**LLOYD, Timothy Andrew** (Oswestry HS; Dorset CHE), b Oswestry, Salop 5 Nov 1956. 5'10". LHB, RM/OB. Warwickshire 1977-92 (cap 1980; captain 1988-92; benefit 1990). OFS 1978-79/1979-80. Salop 1975. **Tests:** 1 (1984); HS 10* (rtd hurt) v WI (Birmingham) 1984. LOI: 3. Tours: SA 1991-92 (Wa); Z 1984-85 (EC). 1000 runs (9); most – 1673 (1983). HS 208* v Glos (Birmingham) 1983. BB 3-7 v Middx (Lord's) 1992. Awards: NWT 3. **NWT:** HS 121 v Cambs (Birmingham) 1988. BB 1-4. **BHC:** HS 137* v Lancs (Birmingham) 1985. **SL:** HS 90 v Kent (Birmingham) 1980. BB 2-37 v Yorks (Scarborough) 1992.

# WARWICKSHIRE 1992

## RESULTS SUMMARY

| | Place | Won | Lost | Tied | Drew | Abandoned |
|---|---|---|---|---|---|---|
| Britannic Assurance Championship | 6th | 6 | 8 | | 8 | |
| All First-class Matches | | 6 | 8 | | 9 | |
| Sunday League | 8th | 7 | 7 | 1 | | 2 |
| NatWest Trophy | Semi-Finalist | | | | | |
| Benson and Hedges Cup | 4th in Group C | | | | | |

# BRITANNIC ASSURANCE CHAMPIONSHIP AVERAGES

## BATTING AND FIELDING

| Cap | | M | I | NO | HS | Runs | Avge | 100 | 50 | Ct/St |
|---|---|---|---|---|---|---|---|---|---|---|
| – | T.L.Penney | 15 | 23 | 6 | 151 | 802 | 47.17 | 2 | 4 | 4 |
| 1992 | R.G.Twose | 22 | 37 | 3 | 233 | 1368 | 40.23 | 1 | 10 | 16 |
| 1987 | A.J.Moles | 22 | 39 | 3 | 122 | 1292 | 35.88 | 1 | 11 | 18 |
| 1989 | D.A.Reeve | 17 | 28 | 4 | 79 | 833 | 34.70 | – | 7 | 15 |
| 1991 | D.P.Ostler | 21 | 35 | 1 | 192 | 1172 | 34.47 | 3 | 4 | 20 |
| 1980 | T.A.Lloyd | 22 | 38 | 2 | 84* | 914 | 25.38 | – | 5 | 5 |
| – | N.M.K.Smith | 12 | 20 | 2 | 67 | 454 | 25.22 | – | 1 | 5 |
| 1992 | K.J.Piper | 19 | 25 | 8 | 72 | 345 | 20.29 | – | 2 | 41/2 |
| 1989 | A.A.Donald | 21 | 22 | 10 | 41 | 234 | 19.50 | – | – | 14 |
| 1986 | P.A.Smith | 18 | 25 | 4 | 45 | 394 | 18.76 | – | – | 6 |
| – | J.D.Ratcliffe | 6 | 12 | – | 50 | 219 | 18.25 | – | 1 | 3 |
| 1982 | G.C.Small | 17 | 17 | 6 | 31* | 181 | 16.45 | – | – | 6 |
| 1989 | T.A.Munton | 15 | 17 | 6 | 47 | 123 | 11.18 | – | – | 6 |
| – | P.A.Booth | 7 | 10 | 4 | 22* | 64 | 10.66 | – | – | – |
| – | M.A.V.Bell | 3 | 5 | 2 | 5 | 10 | 3.33 | – | – | – |

*Also played*: Asif Din (2 matches – cap 1987) 40, 35, 28; M.Burns (1 match) 3, 4 (5 ct); P.C.L.Holloway (2 matches) 16, 102*, 15 (8 ct).

## BOWLING

| | O | M | R | W | Avge | Best | 5wI | 10wM |
|---|---|---|---|---|---|---|---|---|
| A.A.Donald | 576.2 | 139 | 1647 | 74 | 22.25 | 7-37 | 6 | – |
| P.A.Smith | 364 | 55 | 1334 | 42 | 31.76 | 6-91 | 4 | – |
| R.G.Twose | 221.3 | 37 | 735 | 23 | 31.95 | 6-63 | 1 | – |
| T.A.Munton | 520.2 | 145 | 1389 | 42 | 33.07 | 7-64 | 3 | 1 |
| G.C.Small | 367.2 | 83 | 1003 | 30 | 33.43 | 3-43 | – | – |
| P.A.Booth | 231.4 | 60 | 723 | 16 | 45.18 | 4-29 | – | – |
| D.A.Reeve | 267 | 80 | 632 | 13 | 48.61 | 2-4 | – | – |
| N.M.K.Smith | 332.3 | 63 | 1178 | 24 | 49.08 | 5-61 | 1 | – |

*Also bowled*: M.A.V.Bell 79.2-17-247-8; T.A.Lloyd 68.5-8-295-6; A.J.Moles 42-8-167-2; D.P.Ostler 9-0-54-0; T.L.Penney 5-0-35-0; K.J.Piper 4.4-0-57-1.

The First-Class Averages (pp 164-178) give the records of Warwickshire players in all first-class county matches (their other opponents being Cambridge U), with the exception of:
    T.A.Munton 16-17-6-47-123-11.18-0-0-7ct. 550.1-154-1441-44-32.75-7/64-3-1.

# WARWICKSHIRE RECORDS

## FIRST-CLASS CRICKET

| | | | | | |
|---|---|---|---|---|---|
| **Highest Total** | For | 657-6d | v Hampshire | Birmingham | 1899 |
| | V | 887 | by Yorkshire | Birmingham | 1896 |
| **Lowest Total** | For | 16 | v Kent | Tonbridge | 1913 |
| | V | 15 | by Hampshire | Birmingham | 1922 |
| **Highest Innings** | For | 305* F.R.Foster | v Worcs | Dudley | 1914 |
| | V | 322 I.V.A.Richards | for Somerset | Taunton | 1985 |

### Highest Partnership for each Wicket

| | | | | | |
|---|---|---|---|---|---|
| 1st | 377* | N.F.Horner/K.Ibadulla | v Surrey | The Oval | 1960 |
| 2nd | 465* | J.A.Jameson/R.B.Kanhai | v Glos | Birmingham | 1974 |
| 3rd | 327 | S.P.Kinneir/W.G.Quaife | v Lancashire | Birmingham | 1901 |
| 4th | 470 | A.I.Kallicharran/G.W.Humpage | v Lancashire | Southport | 1982 |
| 5th | 268 | W.Quaife/W.G.Quaife | v Essex | Leyton | 1900 |
| 6th | 220 | H.E.Dollery/J.Buckingham | v Derbyshire | Derby | 1938 |
| 7th | 250 | H.E.Dollery/J.S.Ord | v Kent | Maidstone | 1953 |
| 8th | 228 | A.J.W.Croom/R.E.S.Wyatt | v Worcs | Dudley | 1925 |
| 9th | 154 | G.W.Stephens/A.J.W.Croom | v Derbyshire | Birmingham | 1925 |
| 10th | 128 | F.R.Santall/W.Sanders | v Yorkshire | Birmingham | 1930 |

| | | | | | |
|---|---|---|---|---|---|
| **Best Bowling** | For | 10-41 J.D.Bannister | v Comb Servs | Birmingham | 1959 |
| (Innings) | V | 10-36 H.Verity | for Yorkshire | Leeds | 1931 |
| **Best Bowling** | For | 15-76 S.Hargreave | v Surrey | The Oval | 1903 |
| (Match) | V | 17-92 A.P.Freeman | for Kent | Folkestone | 1932 |

| | | | | |
|---|---|---|---|---|
| **Most Runs – Season** | 2,417 | M.J.K.Smith | (av 60.42) | 1959 |
| **Most Runs – Career** | 35,146 | D.L.Amiss | (av 41.64) | 1960-1987 |
| **Most 100s – Season** | 9 | A.I.Kallicharran | | 1984 |
| **Most 100s – Career** | 78 | D.L.Amiss | | 1960-1987 |
| **Most Wkts – Season** | 180 | W.E.Hollies | (av 15.13) | 1946 |
| **Most Wkts – Career** | 2,201 | W.E.Hollies | (av 20.45) | 1932-1957 |

## LIMITED-OVERS CRICKET

| | | | | | |
|---|---|---|---|---|---|
| **Highest Total** | NWT | 392-5 | v Oxfordshire | Birmingham | 1984 |
| | BHC | 308-4 | v Scotland | Birmingham | 1988 |
| | SL | 301-6 | v Essex | Colchester | 1982 |
| **Lowest Total** | NWT | 109 | v Kent | Canterbury | 1971 |
| | BHC | 96 | v Leics | Leicester | 1972 |
| | SL | 65 | v Kent | Maidstone | 1979 |
| **Highest Innings** | NWT | 206 A.I.Kallicharran | v Oxfordshire | Birmingham | 1984 |
| | BHC | 137* T.A.Lloyd | v Lancashire | Birmingham | 1985 |
| | SL | 123* J.A.Jameson | v Notts | Nottingham | 1973 |
| **Best Bowling** | NWT | 6-32 K.Ibadulla | v Hampshire | Birmingham | 1965 |
| | | 6-32 A.I.Kallicharran | v Oxfordshire | Birmingham | 1984 |
| | BHC | 7-32 R.G.D.Willis | v Yorkshire | Birmingham | 1981 |
| | SL | 6-20 N.Gifford | v Northants | Birmingham | 1985 |

# WORCESTERSHIRE

**Formation of Present Club:** 11 March 1865
**Colours:** Dark Green and Black
**Badge:** Shield Argent a Fess between three Pears Sable
**Championships:** (5) 1964, 1965, 1974, 1988, 1989
**NatWest Trophy/Gillette Cup Winners:** (0) Finalists 1963, 1966, 1988
**Benson and Hedges Cup Winners:** (1) 1991
**Sunday League Champions:** (3) 1971, 1987, 1988
**Match Awards:** NWT 35; BHC 54

**Secretary:** Revd M.D.Vockins, County Ground, New Road, Worcester, WR2 4QQ
(☎ 0905-422694)
**Captain:** T.S.Curtis
**Scorer:** J.W.Sewter
**1993 Beneficiaries:** D.B.D'Oliveira and M.J.Weston

**CURTIS, Timothy** Stephen (Worcester RGS; Durham U; Magdalene C, Cambridge), b Chislehurst, Kent 15 Jan 1960. 5'11". RHB, LB. Debut 1979. Cap 1984. Captain 1992-. Cambridge U 1983 (blue). **Tests:** 5 (1988 to 1989); HS 41 v A (Birmingham) 1989. **Tour:** Z 1990-91 (Wo). 1000 runs (9); most – 1829 (1992). HS 248 v Somerset (Worcester) 1991. Shared record Worcs 2nd wkt stand of 287* with G.A.Hick v Glam (Neath) 1986. **BB** 2-17 v OU (Oxford) 1991. **BAC BB** 2-72 v Warwks 1987 and v Derbys 1992. **Awards:** NWT 5; BHC 2. **NWT:** HS 120 v Notts (Nottingham) 1988. **BB** 1-6. **BHC:** HS 97 v Warwks (Birmingham) 1990. **SL:** HS 124 v Somerset (Taunton) 1990.

**D'OLIVEIRA, Damian** Basil (Blessed Edward Oldcorne SS), b Cape Town, SA 19 Oct 1960. Son of B.L. (Worcs and England 1964-80). 5'9". RHB, OB. Debut 1982. Cap 1985. Benefit 1993. MCC YC. **Tours:** Z 1984-85 (EC), 1990-91 (Wo). 1000 runs (4); most – 1263 (1990). HS 237 v OU (Oxford) 1991. **BAC** HS 155 v Lancs (Manchester) 1990. **BB** 2-17 v Glos (Bristol) 1986. **Awards:** NWT 2; BHC 2. **NWT:** HS 99 v Oxon (Worcester) 1986. **BB** 2-17 v Suffolk (Bury St E) 1990. **BHC:** HS 66 v Yorks (Leeds) 1986. **BB** 3-12 v Scot (Glasgow) 1986. **SL:** HS 103 v Surrey (Worcester) 1985. **BB** 3-23 v Derbys (Derby) 1983.

**HAYNES, Gavin** Richard (High Park S; King Edward VI S, Stourbridge), b Stourbridge 29 Sep 1969. 5'10". RHB, RM. Debut 1991. HS 66 v Glam (Worcester) 1992. **NWT:** HS 5. **BHC:** HS 19* v Somerset (Worcester) 1992. **BB** 2-22 v Glam (Cardiff) 1992. **SL:** HS 26 v Surrey (Oval) 1992. **BB** 1-18.

**HICK, Graeme** Ashley (Prince Edward HS, Salisbury), b Salisbury, Rhodesia 23 May 1966. 6'3". RHB, OB. Zimbabwe 1983-84/1985-86. Worcestershire debut 1984. Cap 1986. N Districts 1987-88/1988-89. Queensland 1990-91. Wisden 1986. **Tests:** 11 (1991 to 1992); HS 51 v P (Birmingham) 1992; BB 4-126 v NZ (Wellington) 1991-92. **LOI:** 21. **Tours:** E 1985 (Z); NZ 1991-92; SL 1983-84 (Z); Z 1990-91 (Wo). 1000 runs (8+1) inc 2000 runs (3); most – 2713 (1988); youngest to score 2000 (1986). 1019 runs before June 1988. HS 405* (Worcs record and 2nd highest in UK f-c matches) v Somerset (Taunton) 1988. Shared in 4 record Worcs wkt stands: 287* (2nd) with T.S.Curtis; 265 (6th) with S.J.Rhodes; 205 (7th) with P.J.Newport; and 177* (8th) with R.K.Illingworth. **BB** 5-37 v Glos (Worcester) 1990. **Awards:** NWT 2; BHC 7. **NWT:** HS 172* v Devon (Worcester) 1987. **BB** 4-54 v Hants (Worcester) 1988. **BHC:** HS 109 v Comb U (Worcester) 1989. **BB** 3-36 v Warwks (Birmingham) 1990. **SL:** HS 114* v Notts (Worcester) 1990. **BB** 4-42 v Sussex (Worcester) 1988.

**ILLINGWORTH, Richard** Keith (Salts GS), b Bradford, Yorks 23 Aug 1963. 5'11". RHB, SLA. Debut 1982. Cap 1986. Natal 1988-89. **Tests:** 2 (1991); HS 13 (twice) and BB 3-110 (including wicket of P.V.Simmons with first ball) v WI (Nottingham) 1991 – on debut. LOI: 16. Tours: NZ 1991-92; P 1990-91 (Eng A); SL 1990-91 (Eng A); Z 1989-90 (Eng A), 1990-91 (Wo). HS 120* v Warwks (Worcester) 1987. Shared record Worcs 8th wkt stand of 177* with G.A.Hick v Somerset (Taunton) 1988. 50 wkts (3); most – 75 (1990). BB 7-50 v OU (Oxford) 1985. BAC BB 5-23 v Hants (Bournemouth) 1989. **NWT:** HS 22 v Northants (Northampton) 1984. BB 4-20 v Devon (Worcester) 1987. **BHC:** HS 36* v Kent (Worcester) 1990. BB 4-36 v Yorks (Bradford) 1985. **SL:** HS 25* v Essex (Ilford) 1991. BB 5-24 v Somerset (Worcester) 1983.

**LAMPITT, Stuart** Richard (Kingswinford S; Dudley TC), b Wolverhampton, Staffs 29 Jul 1966. 5'11". RHB, RM. Debut 1985. Cap 1989. Tour: Z 1990-91 (Wo). HS 93 v Derbys (Kidderminster) 1991, sharing record Worcs 8th wkt stand of 184 with S.J.Rhodes. 50 wkts (2); most – 58 (1990). BB 5-32 v Kent (Worcester) 1989. Awards: NWT 1; BHC 2. **NWT:** HS 14 v Notts (Nottingham) 1992. BB 5-22 v Suffolk (Bury St E) 1990. **BHC:** HS 41 v Glam (Worcester) 1990. BB 4-46 v Glos (Worcester) 1991. **SL:** HS 25* and BB 5-67 v Middx (Lord's) 1990.

**LEATHERDALE, David** Anthony (Pudsey Grangefield S), b Bradford, Yorks 26 Nov 1967. 5'10½". RHB, RM. Debut 1988. HS 157 v Somerset (Worcester) 1991. BB 1-12. **NWT:** HS 43 v Hants (Worcester) 1988. **BHC:** HS 14 (thrice in 1992). **SL:** HS 62* v Kent (Folkestone) 1988.

**NEWPORT, Philip** John (High Wycombe RGS; Portsmouth Polytechnic), b High Wycombe, Bucks 11 Oct 1962. 6'3". RHB, RFM. Debut 1982. Cap 1986. Boland 1987-88. Buckinghamshire 1981-82. **Tests:** 3 (1988 to 1990-91); HS 40* v A (Perth) 1990-91; BB 4-87 v SL (Lord's) 1988 (on debut). Tours: A 1990-91 (part); P 1990-91 (Eng A); SL 1990-91 (Eng A). HS 98 v NZ (Worcester) 1990. BAC HS 96 v Essex (Worcester) 1990. Shared record Worcs 7th wkt stand of 205 with G.A.Hick v Yorks (Worcester) 1988. 50 wkts (5); most – 93 (1988). BB 8-52 v Middx (Lord's) 1988. **NWT:** HS 25 v Northants (Northampton) 1984. BB 4-46 v Northants (Northampton) 1990. **BHC:** HS 28 v Kent (Worcester) 1990. BB 5-22 v Warwks (Birmingham) 1987. **SL:** HS 26* v Leics (Leicester) 1987. BB 4-18 v Glam (Worcester) 1989.

**RADFORD, Neal** Victor (Athlone BHS, Johannesburg), b Luanshya, N Rhodesia 7 Jun 1957. Brother of W.R. (OFS). 5'11". RHB, RFM. Transvaal 1978-79/1988-89. Lancashire 1980-84. Worcestershire debut/cap 1985. Wisden 1985. **Tests:** 3 (1986 to 1987-88); HS 12* v NZ (Lord's); BB 2-131 v I (Birmingham). LOI: 6. Tours: NZ 1987-88; Z 1990-91 (Wo). HS 76* La v Derbys (Blackpool) 1981. Wo HS 73* v Notts (Nottingham) 1992. 50 wkts (6) inc 100 (2); most – 109 (1987). BB 9-70 v Somerset (Worcester) 1986. Award: NWT 1. **NWT:** HS 37 v Essex (Chelmsford) 1987. BB 7-19 v Beds (Bedford) 1991. **BHC:** HS 40 v Glam (Worcester) 1990. BB 4-25 v Northants (Northampton) 1988. **SL:** HS 55 v Kent (Canterbury) 1992. BB 5-32 v Warwks (Worcester) 1987.

**RHODES, Steven** John (Lapage Middle S; Carlton-Bolling S, Bradford), b Bradford, Yorks 17 Jun 1964. Son of W.E. (Notts 1961-64). 5'7". RHB, WK. Yorkshire 1981-84. Worcestershire debut 1985. Cap 1986. LOI 3. Tours: WI 1991-92 (Eng A); SL 1985-86 (Eng B), 1990-91 (Eng A), 1990-91 (Wo); Z 1989-90 (Eng A), 1990-91 (Wo). HS 116* v Warwks (Worcester) 1992. Shared in 2 record Worcs stands: 265 (6th) with G.A.Hick and 184 (8th) with S.R.Lampitt. Award: BHC 1. **NWT:** HS 61 v Derbys (Worcester) 1989. **BHC:** HS 51* v Warwks (Birmingham) 1987. **SL:** HS 48* v Kent (Worcester) 1989.

**SEYMOUR, Adam** Charles Hylton (Millfield S), b Royston, Cambs 7 Dec 1967. 6'2". LHB, RM. Essex 1988-91. Worcestershire debut 1992. HS 157 Ex v Glam (Cardiff) 1991. Wo HS 133 v OU (Oxford) 1992 – on Wo debut. **NWT:** HS 0. **BHC:** HS 23 v Comb Us (Oxford) 1992. **SL:** HS 25 Ex v Lancs (Manchester) 1991.

**TOLLEY, Christopher** Mark (King Edward VI C, Stourbridge; Loughborough U), b Kidderminster 30 Dec 1967. 5'9". RHB, LMF. Debut 1989. Comb Us (BHC) 1989-90. Tour: Z 1990-91 (Wo). HS 37 v Kent (Worcester) 1989. BB 4-69 v SL (Worcester) 1991. BAC BB 3-38 v Hants (Southampton) 1992. Award: BHC 1. **BHC:** HS 77 Comb Us v Lancs (Cambridge) 1990. BB 1-12. **SL:** HS 1*. BB 3-28 v Leics (Leicester) 1992.

**WESTON, Martin** John (Samuel Southall SS), b Worcester 8 Apr 1959. 6'1". RHB, RM. Debut 1979. Cap 1986. Benefit 1993. 1000 runs (1): 1061 (1984). HS 145* v Northants (Worcester) 1984. BB 4-24 v Warwks (Birmingham) 1988. Awards: NWT 1; BHC 1. **NWT:** HS 98 v Somerset (Taunton) 1990. BB 4-30 v Suffolk (Worcester) 1984. **BHC:** HS 99* v Notts (Nottingham) 1990. B 2-27 v Yorks (Bradford) 1985. **SL:** HS 109 v Somerset (Taunton) 1982. BB 4-11 v Hants (Worcester) 1988.

**WESTON, William Philip** Christopher (Durham S), b Durham 16 Jun 1973. Son of M.P. (Durham; England RFU). 6'3". LHB, LM. Debut 1991. HS 66* v Somerset (W-s-M) 1992. BB 2-39 v P (Worcester) 1992. BAC BB -.

**WYLIE, Alex** (Bromsgrove S; Warwick C of Ag), b Tamworth, Staffs 20 Feb 1973. 6'2½". LHB, RFM. No 1st XI appearances – joined staff 1991.

## NEWCOMERS

**AYRES, Christopher** John (Worcester RGS), b Aylesbury, Bucks 28 Mar 1972. RHB, RM.

**BENJAMIN, Kenneth** Charlie Griffith, b Antigua 8 Apr 1967. RHB, RF. Leeward Is 1988-89 to date. **Tests** (WI): 1 (1991-92); HS 7 and BB 2-87 v SA (Bridgetown) 1991-92. Tour (WI): E 1992 (RW). HS 52* Leeward Is v Trinidad (Basseterre) 1991-92. BB 7-51 Leeward Is v Jamaica (Basseterre) 1990-91.

**BRINKLEY, James** Edward, b Scotland 13 Mar 1974.

**EDWARDS, Timothy,** b 24 Jun 1974. RHB, WK. Somerset staff 1991-92 (YTS trainee). No 1st XI appearances.

**SOLANKI, Vikram** Singh, (Regis S, Wolverhampton), b India 1 Apr 1976. RHB, OB.

**SPIRING, Ruben,** b Southport, Lancs 13 Nov 1974.

## DEPARTURES

**DILLEY, Graham** Roy (Dartford West SS), b Dartford, Kent 18 May 1959. 6'3". LHB, RF. Kent 1977-86 (cap 1980). Worcestershire 1987-92 (cap 1987). Natal 1985-86. YC 1980. **Tests:** 41 (1979-80 to 1989); HS 56 v A (Leeds) 1981; BB 6-38 v NZ (Christchurch) 1987-88. LOI: 36. Tours: A 1979-80, 1986-87, 1987-88; SA 1989-90 (Eng XI); WI 1980-81; NZ 1983-84, 1987-88; I 1979-80, 1981-82; P 1983-84, 1987-88; SL 1981-82. HS 81 K v Northants (Northampton) 1979. Wo HS 45* v Glam (Worcester) 1990. 50 wkts (3); most – 64 (1982). BB 7-63 Natal v Transvaal (Johannesburg) 1985-86. Wo/BAC BB 6-43 v Leics (Worcester) 1987. 2 hat-tricks (Kent): 1985, 1986. Awards: NWT 1; BHC 1. **NWT:** HS 25 v Essex (Chelmsford) 1987. BB 5-29 K v Scot 1986 and Wo v Middx 1988. **BHC:** HS 37* K v Hants (Canterbury) 1983. BB 4-14 K v Comb Us (Canterbury) 1981. **SL:** HS 33 K v Northants (Northampton) 1980. BB 4-20 K v Glos (Canterbury) 1980.

continued on p 157

# WORCESTERSHIRE 1992

## RESULTS SUMMARY

| | Place | Won | Lost | Tied | Drew | Abandoned |
|---|---|---|---|---|---|---|
| Britannic Assurance Championship | 17th | 3 | 4 | | 14 | 1 |
| All First-class Matches | | 4 | 4 | | 15 | 1 |
| Sunday League | 7th | 7 | 6 | 1 | | 3 |
| NatWest Trophy | 1st Round | | | | | |
| Benson and Hedges Cup | Quarter-Finalist | | | | | |

# BRITANNIC ASSURANCE CHAMPIONSHIP AVERAGES

## BATTING AND FIELDING

| Cap | | M | I | NO | HS | Runs | Avge | 100 | 50 | Ct/St |
|---|---|---|---|---|---|---|---|---|---|---|
| 1986 | G.A.Hick | 11 | 19 | 2 | 213* | 1179 | 69.35 | 4 | 4 | 20 |
| 1984 | T.S.Curtis | 21 | 37 | 4 | 228* | 1622 | 49.15 | 4 | 5 | 14 |
| 1991 | T.M.Moody | 10 | 18 | 1 | 178 | 624 | 36.70 | 3 | 1 | 11 |
| – | R.D.Stemp | 11 | 6 | 4 | 16* | 70 | 35.00 | – | – | 4 |
| – | W.P.C.Weston | 13 | 21 | 3 | 66* | 579 | 32.16 | – | 4 | 2 |
| 1986 | S.J.Rhodes | 21 | 29 | 7 | 116* | 703 | 31.95 | 2 | 2 | 41/5 |
| 1985 | D.B.D'Oliveira | 12 | 17 | 1 | 100 | 502 | 31.37 | 1 | 2 | 11 |
| – | D.A.Leatherdale | 21 | 36 | 3 | 112 | 882 | 26.72 | 1 | 4 | 15 |
| – | G.R.Haynes | 9 | 13 | 2 | 66 | 288 | 26.18 | – | 2 | 3 |
| 1986 | P.J.Newport | 20 | 24 | 6 | 75* | 463 | 25.72 | – | 3 | 4 |
| 1989 | S.R.Lampitt | 18 | 28 | 5 | 71* | 562 | 24.43 | – | 4 | 5 |
| – | A.C.H.Seymour | 9 | 17 | – | 62 | 373 | 21.94 | – | 1 | 8 |
| 1986 | R.K.Illingworth | 18 | 19 | 6 | 43 | 282 | 21.69 | – | – | 7 |
| 1985 | N.V.Radford | 20 | 18 | 7 | 73* | 195 | 17.72 | – | 1 | 3 |
| – | C.M.Tolley | 12 | 10 | 4 | 27 | 89 | 14.83 | – | – | 7 |

*Also played*: G.R.Dilley (1 match – cap 1987) 18, 4*; P.A.Neale (2 matches – cap 1978) 24, 17, 38; M.J.Weston (2 matches – cap 1986) 17*, 8*, 1* (1 ct).

## BOWLING

| | O | M | R | W | Avge | Best | 5wI | 10wM |
|---|---|---|---|---|---|---|---|---|
| P.J.Newport | 576.1 | 121 | 1655 | 61 | 27.13 | 5-45 | 3 | – |
| N.V.Radford | 497.2 | 91 | 1553 | 57 | 27.24 | 6-88 | 4 | 1 |
| S.R.Lampitt | 356 | 39 | 1239 | 33 | 37.54 | 4-57 | – | – |
| R.D.Stemp | 331.5 | 80 | 1054 | 28 | 37.64 | 6-67 | 3 | 1 |
| C.M.Tolley | 217 | 52 | 650 | 17 | 38.23 | 3-38 | – | – |
| R.K.Illingworth | 570.3 | 170 | 1420 | 36 | 39.44 | 4-43 | – | – |
| D.B.D'Oliveira | 153.4 | 29 | 536 | 10 | 53.60 | 2-44 | – | – |

*Also bowled*: T.S.Curtis 24-2-116-2; G.R.Dilley 11-3-34-0; G.R.Haynes 45.2-13-128-0; G.A.Hick 104.3-33-304-7; D.A.Leatherdale 10-2-33-0; T.M.Moody 67-12-235-8; M.J.Weston 19-3-58-1; W.P.C.Weston 46-6-125-0.

The First-Class Averages (pp 164-178) give the records of Worcestershire players in all first-class county matches (their other opponents being the Pakistanis and Oxford U), with the exception of:
G.A.Hick 13-22-2-213*-1239-61.95-4-4-22ct. 124.3-37-352-8-44.00-3/32.
S.J.Rhodes 23-33-10-116*-776-33.73-2-2-45ct/5st. Did not bowl.

# WORCESTERSHIRE RECORDS

## FIRST-CLASS CRICKET

| | | | | | | |
|---|---|---|---|---|---|---|
| **Highest Total** | For | 633 | | v Warwicks | Worcester | 1906 |
| | V | 701-4d | | by Leics | Worcester | 1906 |
| **Lowest Total** | For | 24 | | v Yorkshire | Huddersfield | 1903 |
| | V | 30 | | by Hampshire | Worcester | 1903 |
| **Highest Innings** | For | 405* | G.A.Hick | v Somerset | Taunton | 1988 |
| | V | 331* | J.D.B.Robertson | for Middlesex | Worcester | 1949 |

### Highest Partnership for each Wicket

| | | | | | | |
|---|---|---|---|---|---|---|
| 1st | 309 | F.L.Bowley/H.K.Foster | v Derbyshire | Derby | 1901 |
| 2nd | 287* | T.S.Curtis/G.A.Hick | v Glamorgan | Neath | 1986 |
| 3rd | 314 | M.J.Horton/T.W.Graveney | v Somerset | Worcester | 1962 |
| 4th | 281 | J.A.Ormrod/Younis Ahmed | v Notts | Nottingham | 1979 |
| 5th | 393 | E.G.Arnold/W.B.Burns | v Warwicks | Birmingham | 1909 |
| 6th | 265 | G.A.Hick/S.J.Rhodes | v Somerset | Taunton | 1988 |
| 7th | 205 | G.A.Hick/P.J.Newport | v Yorkshire | Worcester | 1988 |
| 8th | 184 | S.J.Rhodes/S.R.Lampitt | v Derbyshire | Kidderminster | 1991 |
| 9th | 181 | J.A.Cuffe/R.D.Burrows | v Glos | Worcester | 1907 |
| 10th | 119 | W.B.Burns/G.A.Wilson | v Somerset | Worcester | 1906 |

| | | | | | | |
|---|---|---|---|---|---|---|
| **Best Bowling** | For | 9-23 | C.F.Root | v Lancashire | Worcester | 1931 |
| (Innings) | V | 10-51 | J.Mercer | for Glamorgan | Worcester | 1936 |
| **Best Bowling** | For | 15-87 | A.J.Conway | v Glos | Moreton-in-M | 1914 |
| (Match) | V | 17-212 | J.C.Clay | for Glamorgan | Swansea | 1937 |

| | | | | | |
|---|---|---|---|---|---|
| **Most Runs – Season** | 2,654 | H.H.I.Gibbons | (av 52.03) | | 1934 |
| **Most Runs – Career** | 33,490 | D.Kenyon | (av 33.19) | | 1946-1967 |
| **Most 100s – Season** | 10 | G.M.Turner | | | 1970 |
| | 10 | G.A.Hick | | | 1988 |
| **Most 100s – Career** | 72 | G.M.Turner | | | 1967-1982 |
| **Most Wkts – Season** | 207 | C.F.Root | (av 17.52) | | 1925 |
| **Most Wkts – Career** | 2,143 | R.T.D.Perks | (av 23.73) | | 1930-1955 |

## LIMITED-OVERS CRICKET

| | | | | | | |
|---|---|---|---|---|---|---|
| **Highest Total** | NWT | 404-3 | | v Devon | Worcester | 1987 |
| | BHC | 314-5 | | v Lancashire | Manchester | 1980 |
| | SL | 307-4 | | v Derbyshire | Worcester | 1975 |
| **Lowest Total** | NWT | 98 | | v Durham | Chester-le-St | 1968 |
| | BHC | 81 | | v Leics | Worcester | 1983 |
| | SL | 86 | | v Yorkshire | Leeds | 1969 |
| **Highest Innings** | NWT | 172* | G.A.Hick | v Devon | Worcester | 1987 |
| | BHC | 143* | G.M.Turner | v Warwicks | Birmingham | 1976 |
| | SL | 160 | T.M.Moody | v Kent | Worcester | 1991 |
| **Best Bowling** | NWT | 7-19 | N.V.Radford | v Beds | Bedford | 1991 |
| | BHC | 6-8 | N.Gifford | v Minor C (S) | High Wycombe | 1979 |
| | SL | 6-26 | A.P.Pridgeon | v Surrey | Worcester | 1978 |

# YORKSHIRE

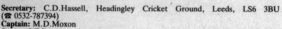

**Formation of Present Club:** 8 January 1863
**Substantial Reorganisation:** 10 December 1891
**Colours:** Dark Blue, Light Blue and Gold
**Badge:** White Rose
**Championships (since 1890):** (29) 1893, 1896, 1898, 1900,
1901, 1902, 1905, 1908, 1912, 1919, 1922, 1923, 1924,
1925, 1931, 1932, 1933, 1935, 1937, 1938, 1939, 1946,
1959, 1960, 1962, 1963, 1966, 1967, 1968. **Joint:** (1) 1949
**NatWest Trophy/Gillette Cup Winners:** (2) 1965, 1969
**Benson and Hedges Cup Winners:** (1) 1987
**Sunday League Champions:** (1) 1983
**Match Awards:** NWT 25; BHC 55

**Secretary:** C.D.Hassell, Headingley Cricket Ground, Leeds, LS6 3BU
(☎ 0532-787394)
**Captain:** M.D.Moxon
**Scorer:** J.T.Potter
**1993 Beneficiary:** M.D.Moxon

**BATTY, Jeremy** David (Bingley GS; Horsforth C), b Bradford 15 May 1971. 6'1".
RHB, OB. Debut 1989. Tour: SA 1991-92 (Y). HS 51 v SL (Leeds) 1991. BAC
HS 49 v Essex (Leeds) 1992. BB 6-48 v Notts (Worksop) 1991. **NWT:** HS 4. BB
1-17. **BHC:** HS 2*. BB 1-34. **SL:** HS 13* and BB 4-33 v Kent (Scarborough) 1991.

**BLAKEY, Richard** John (Rastrick GS), b Huddersfield 15 Jan 1967. 5'9". RHB,
WK. Debut 1985. Cap 1987. YC 1987. LOI: 1. Tours: SA 1991-92 (Y); WI 1986-87
(Y); P 1990-91 (Eng A); SL 1990-91 (Eng A); Z 1989-90 (Eng A). 1000 runs
(4); most – 1361 (1987). HS 221 Eng A v Z (Bulawayo) 1989-90. Y HS 204* v
Glos (Leeds) 1987. BB 1-68. Awards: BHC 2. **NWT:** HS 64 v Northants
(Northampton) 1992. **BHC:** HS 79 v Surrey (Oval) 1990. **SL:** HS 130* v Kent
(Scarborough) 1991.

**BROADHURST, Mark** (Kingstone S, Barnsley), b Worsborough Common, Barnsley
20 Jun 1974. 6'0". RHB, RFM. Debut 1991. Awaiting BAC debut. HS 1. BB
3-61 v OU (Oxford) 1991. **SL:** HS -.

**BYAS, David** (Scarborough C), b Kilham 26 Aug 1963. 6'4". LHB, RM. Debut
1986. Cap 1991. Tour: SA 1991-92 (Y). 1000 runs (1): 1557 (1991). HS 153 v Notts
(Worksop) 1991. BB 3-55 v Derbys (Chesterfield) 1990. **NWT:** HS 54 v Scot (Leeds)
1989. BB 1-23. **BHC:** HS 92 v Hants (Leeds) 1991. BB 2-38 v Somerset (Leeds)
1989. **SL:** HS 80 v Somerset (Middlesbrough) 1992. BB 3-19 v Notts (Leeds) 1989.

**CARRICK, Phillip** (Bramley SS; Intake SS; Park Lane CPE), b Armley 16 Jul
1952. 5'11½". RHB, SLA. Debut 1970. Cap 1976. Captain 1987-89. Benefit 1985.
E Province 1976-77. N Transvaal 1982-83. Tours: SA 1975-76 (DIIR), 1991-92
(Y); WI 1986-87 (Y – captain); SL 1977-78 (DHR). HS 131* v Northants
(Northampton) 1980. 50 wkts (11); most – 79 (1975). BB 8-33 v CU (Cambridge)
1973. BAC BB 8-72 v Derbys (Scarborough) 1975. Awards: NWT 1; BHC 1. **NWT:**
HS 54 v Sussex (Leeds) 1986. BB 3-8 v Norfolk (Leeds) 1990. **BHC:** HS 53 v
Warwks (Leeds) 1985. BB 3-22 v Warwks (Leeds) 1991. **SL:** HS 48* v Worcs
(Scarborough) 1989. BB 5-22 v Glam (Leeds) 1991.

**CHAPMAN, Colin** Anthony (Beckfoot GS, Bingley; Bradford & Ilkley Art C),
b Bradford 8 Jun 1971. 5'8½". RHB, WK. Debut 1990. HS 20 v Middx (Uxbridge)
1990. **SL:** HS 36* v Middx (Scarborough) 1990.

**GOUGH, Darren** (Priory CS, Lundwood), b Barnsley 18 Sep 1970. 5'11". RHB, RMF. Debut 1989. Tour: SA 1991-92 (Y). HS 72 v Northants (Northampton) 1991. BB 5-41 v Lancs (Scarborough) 1991. **NWT:** HS 4. BB 2-18 v Northumb (Leeds) 1992. **BHC:** HS 7*. BB 2-29 v Somerset and v Kent 1992. **SL:** HS 72* v Leics (Leicester) 1991. BB 3-30 v Derbys (Leeds) 1992.

**GRAYSON, Adrian Paul** (Bedale CS), b Ripon 31 Mar 1971. 6'1". RHB, SLA. Debut 1990. Tour: SA 1991-92 (Y). HS 57 v Surrey (Oval) 1992. BB 1-3. **BHC:** HS 22 v Warwks (Birmingham) 1992. **SL:** HS 8. BB 1-32.

**HARTLEY, Peter** John (Greenhead GS; Bradford C), b Keighley 18 Apr 1960. 6'0". RHB, RMF. Warwickshire 1982. Yorkshire debut 1985. Cap 1987. Tours (Y): SA 1991-92; WI 1986-87. HS 127* v Lancs (Manchester) 1988. 50 wkts (3); most – 56 (1992). BB 8-111 v Sussex (Hove) 1992. Awards: NWT 1; BHC 1. **NWT:** HS 52 and BB 5-46 v Hants (Southampton) 1990. **BHC:** HS 29* v Notts (Nottingham) 1986. BB 5-43 v Scot (Leeds) 1986. **SL:** HS 51 v Northants (Tring) 1990. BB 5-38 v Worcs (Worcester) 1990.

**JARVIS, Paul** William (Bydales CS, Marske), b Redcar 29 Jun 1965. 5'10". RHB, RFM. Debut 1981 aged 16yr 75d (youngest Yorkshire player). Cap 1986. **Tests:** 6 (1987-88 to 1989); HS 29* and BB 4-107 v WI (Lord's) 1988. LOI: 5. Tours: SA 1989-90 (Eng XI); WI 1986-87 (Y); Ind 1987-88; P 1987-88. HS 80 v Northants (Scarborough) 1992. 50 wkts (3); most – 81 (1987). BB 7-55 v Surrey (Leeds) 1986. Hat-trick 1985. **NWT:** HS 16 v Somerset (Leeds) 1985. BB 4-41 v Leics (Leeds) 1987. **BHC:** HS 42 v Lancs (Leeds) 1990. BB 4-34 v Warwks (Birmingham) 1992. **SL:** HS 29* v Somerset (Taunton) 1987. BB 6-27 v Somerset (Taunton) 1989.

**KELLETT, Simon** Andrew (Whitcliffe Mount S), b Mirfield 16 Oct 1967. 6'2". RHB. Debut 1989. Cap 1992. Wellington 1991-92. Tour: SA 1991-92 (Y). 1000 runs (2); most – 1326 (1992). HS 125* v Derbys (Chesterfield) 1991. **NWT:** HS 38 v Northumb (Leeds) 1992. **BHC:** HS 45 v Surrey (Oval) 1990. **SL:** HS 118* v Derbys (Leeds) 1992.

**METCALFE, Ashley** Anthony (Bradford GS; University C, London), b Horsforth 25 Dec 1963. 5'8". RHB, OB. Debut 1983 scoring 122 v Notts (Bradford). Cap 1986. YC 1986. OFS 1988-89. Tours (Y): SA 1991-92; WI 1986-87. 1000 runs (6) inc 2000 (1): 2047 (1990). HS 216* v Middx (Leeds) 1988. BB 2-18 v Warwks (Scarborough) 1987. Awards: NWT 1; BHC 5. **NWT:** HS 127* v Warwks (Leeds) 1990. BB 2-44 v Wilts (Trowbridge) 1987. **BHC:** HS 114 v Lancs (Manchester) 1991. **SL:** HS 116 v Middx (Lord's) 1991.

**MILBURN, Stuart** Mark (Upper Nidderdale HS), b Harrogate 29 Sep 1972. 6'1". RHB, RMF. Debut 1992. HS 5. BB 1-54.

**MOXON, Martyn** Douglas (Holgate GS, Barnsley), b Barnsley 4 May 1960. 6'0". RHB, RM. Debut 1981 scoring 5 and 116 v Essex (Leeds). Cap 1984. Captain 1990–. Benefit 1993. GW 1982-83/1983-84. Wisden 1992. **Tests:** 10 (1986 to 1989); HS 99 v NZ (Auckland) 1987-88. LOI: 8. Tours: A 1987-88; WI 1986-87 (Y); NZ 1987-88; I 1984-85; SL 1984-85, 1985-86 (Eng B). 1000 runs (8); most – 1669 (1991). HS 218* v Sussex (Eastbourne) 1990. BB 3-24 v Hants (Southampton) 1989. Awards: NWT 4; BHC 7. **NWT:** HS 107* v Warwks (Leeds) 1990. BB 2-19 v Norfolk (Leeds) 1990. **BHC:** HS 141* v Glam (Cardiff) 1991. BB 5-31 v Warwks (Leeds) 1991. **SL:** HS 129* v Surrey (Oval) 1991. BB 3-29 v Sussex (Hove) 1990.

**PARKER, Bradley** (Bingley GS), b Mirfield 23 Jun 1970. 5'11". RHB, RM. Debut 1992. Yorkshire CA. HS 30 v Kent (Canterbury) 1992.

**ROBINSON, Mark** Andrew (Hull GS), b Hull 23 Nov 1966. 6'3". RHB, RFM. Northamptonshire 1987-90 (cap 1990). Canterbury 1988-89. Yorkshire debut 1991. Cap 1992. Tour: SA 1991-92 (Y). Failed to score in 12 successive f-c innings 1990 – world record. HS 19* Nh v Essex (Chelmsford) 1988. Y HS 12 v Hants (Leeds) 1992. 50 wkts (1): 50 (1992). BB 6-57 (10-101 match) v Durham (Durham) 1992. Award: BHC 1. **NWT:** HS 3*. BB 4-32 Nh v Somerset (Taunton) 1989. **BHC:** HS 1*. BB 3-20 Nh v Scot (Glasgow) 1989. **SL:** HS 3. BB 4-33 v Surrey (Oval) 1991.

**WHITE, Craig** (Flora Hill HS, Bendigo, Australia; Bendigo HS), b Morley Hall 16 Dec 1969. 6'0". RHB, OB. Debut 1990. Victoria 1990-91. Tour: SA 1991-92 (Y). HS 79* v Worcs (Worcester) 1992. BB 5-74 v Surrey (Harrogate) 1990. **NWT:** HS 41 v Northants (Northampton) 1992. **BHC:** HS 26 v Notts (Leeds) 1992. BB 1-31. **SL:** HS 63 v Surrey (Scarborough) 1992. BB 2-49 v Kent (Canterbury) 1990.

## NEWCOMERS

**BARTLE, Stephen** (Blackfoot GS), b Shipley 5 Sep 1971. 6'4". LHB, RMF. Yorkshire CA.

**FOSTER, Michael** James (New C, Pontefract), b Leeds 17 Sep 1972. 6'1". RHB, RMF. Yorkshire CA.

**KETTLEBOROUGH, Richard** Allan (Worksop C), b Sheffield 15 Mar 1973. 6'0". LHB, RM. Yorkshire CA.

**RICHARDSON, Richard** Benjamin ('Richie'), b Five Islands, Antigua 12 Jan 1962. RHB, RM. Leeward Is 1981-82 to date. **Tests** (WI): 63 (1983-84 to 1991-92, 1 as captain); HS 194 v I (Georgetown) 1988-89. LOI (WI): 163. Tours (WI): E 1984, 1988, 1990 (RW), 1991; A 1984-85, 1986-87, 1988-89; NZ 1986-87; I 1983-84, 1987-88; P 1986-87, 1990-91. 1000 runs (1+2); most – 1403 (1991). HS 194 (Tests). BB 5-40 Leeward Is v E (St John's) 1985-86 (his first f-c wkts).

**STEMP, Richard** David (Brittania HS, Rowley Regis), b Erdington, Birmingham 11 Dec 1967. 6'0". RHB, SLA. Worcestershire 1990-92. HS 16* Wo v Leics (Leicester) and Wo v Middx (Uxbridge) 1992. BB 6-67 (11-146 match) Wo v Glos (Gloucester) 1992. **BHC:** HS -. **SL:** HS 3*. BB 3-18 Wo v Derbys (Worcester) 1991.

**VAUGHAN, Michael** Paul, b Manchester, Lancs 29 Oct 1974. 6'2". RHB, OB. Yorkshire CA.

## DEPARTURES

**PICKLES, Christopher** Stephen (Whitcliffe Mount S), b Mirfield 30 Jan 1966. 6'1". RHB, RM. Yorkshire 1985-92. HS 66 v Somerset (Taunton) 1989. BB 4-40 v Northants (Northampton) 1992. **NWT:** HS 12 v Warwks (Birmingham) 1991. BB 2-40 v Northumb (Leeds) 1992. **BHC:** HS 37* v Warwks (Birmingham) 1992. BB 2-49 v Minor C (Leeds) 1991. **SL:** HS 30* v Worcs (Sheffield) 1991. BB 4-36 v Somerset (Scarborough) 1990.

**PRIESTLEY, Iain** Martin (Priesthorpe SS, Farsley), b Horsforth 25 Sep 1967. 6'3". RHB, RMF. Yorkshire 1989. HS 23 v Northants (Northampton) 1989. BB 4-27 v Notts (Leeds) 1989 (on debut).

continued on p 157

152

# YORKSHIRE 1992

## RESULTS SUMMARY

|  | Place | Won | Lost | Drew | Abandoned |
|---|---|---|---|---|---|
| Britannic Assurance Championship | 16th | 4 | 6 | 12 | |
| All First-class Matches | | 4 | 6 | 12 | 1 |
| Sunday League | 15th | 6 | 9 | | 2 |
| NatWest Trophy | 2nd Round | | | | |
| Benson and Hedges Cup | 5th in Group C | | | | |

# BRITANNIC ASSURANCE CHAMPIONSHIP AVERAGES

## BATTING AND FIELDING

| Cap | | M | I | NO | HS | Runs | Avge | 100 | 50 | Ct/St |
|---|---|---|---|---|---|---|---|---|---|---|
| 1984 | M.D.Moxon | 18 | 27 | 2 | 183 | 1314 | 52.56 | 5 | 4 | 8 |
| – | C.White | 19 | 26 | 8 | 79* | 859 | 47.72 | – | 7 | 14 |
| 1992 | S.R.Tendulkar | 16 | 25 | 2 | 100 | 1070 | 46.52 | 1 | 7 | 10 |
| 1987 | R.J.Blakey | 21 | 32 | 9 | 125* | 1065 | 46.30 | 2 | 5 | 44/5 |
| 1992 | S.A.Kellett | 22 | 36 | 1 | 96 | 1326 | 37.88 | – | 9 | 23 |
| 1986 | P.W.Jarvis | 15 | 14 | 4 | 80 | 374 | 37.40 | – | 3 | 2 |
| 1991 | D.Byas | 20 | 30 | 4 | 100 | 784 | 30.15 | 1 | 6 | 30 |
| 1986 | A.A.Metcalfe | 11 | 17 | 1 | 73 | 422 | 26.37 | – | 1 | 4 |
| – | A.P.Grayson | 6 | 6 | – | 57 | 116 | 19.33 | – | 1 | 3 |
| 1987 | P.J.Hartley | 20 | 23 | 3 | 69 | 353 | 17.65 | – | 2 | 6 |
| – | C.S.Pickles | 6 | 9 | 1 | 49 | 131 | 16.37 | – | – | 2 |
| – | J.D.Batty | 18 | 24 | 4 | 49 | 155 | 14.09 | – | – | 3 |
| 1976 | P.Carrick | 19 | 25 | 5 | 46 | 261 | 13.05 | – | – | 7 |
| – | D.Gough | 11 | 12 | 4 | 22* | 72 | 9.00 | – | – | 3 |
| 1992 | M.A.Robinson | 17 | 12 | 5 | 12 | 31 | 4.42 | – | – | 4 |

*Also played* (1 match each): C.A.Chapman 8* (1 ct); S.M.Milburn 2*, 5; B.Parker 7, 30 (1 ct).

## BOWLING

| | O | M | R | W | Avge | Best | 5wI | 10wM |
|---|---|---|---|---|---|---|---|---|
| M.A.Robinson | 413.5 | 79 | 1134 | 50 | 22.68 | 6-57 | 3 | 1 |
| C.S.Pickles | 120.1 | 27 | 387 | 14 | 27.64 | 4-40 | – | – |
| P.W.Jarvis | 393.4 | 89 | 1164 | 40 | 29.10 | 4-27 | – | – |
| P.Carrick | 630.1 | 202 | 1375 | 47 | 29.25 | 6-58 | 1 | – |
| P.J.Hartley | 549.5 | 101 | 1690 | 56 | 30.17 | 8-111 | 3 | – |
| D.Gough | 255.1 | 53 | 910 | 25 | 36.40 | 4-43 | – | – |
| J.D.Batty | 426 | 87 | 1408 | 33 | 42.66 | 4-34 | – | – |

*Also bowled:* A.P.Grayson 50-5-186-1; S.M.Milburn 28-2-115-1; M.D.Moxon 3-0-7-0-; S.R.Tendulkar 62.3-10-195-4; C.White 3-0-22-0.

Yorkshire played no first-class fixtures outside the Britannic Assurance Championship in 1992, their match against Oxford U being abandoned without a ball bowled.

# YORKSHIRE RECORDS

## FIRST-CLASS CRICKET

| | | | | | |
|---|---|---|---|---|---|
| **Highest Total** | For 887 | | v Warwicks | Birmingham | 1896 |
| | V 630 | | by Somerset | Leeds | 1901 |
| **Lowest Total** | For 23 | | v Hampshire | Middlesbrough | 1965 |
| | V 13 | | by Notts | Nottingham | 1901 |
| **Highest Innings** | For 341 | G.H.Hirst | v Leics | Leicester | 1905 |
| | V 318* | W.G.Grace | for Glos | Cheltenham | 1876 |

**Highest Partnership for each Wicket**

| | | | | | |
|---|---|---|---|---|---|
| 1st | 555 | P.Holmes/H.Sutcliffe | v Essex | Leyton | 1932 |
| 2nd | 346 | W.Barber/M.Leyland | v Middlesex | Sheffield | 1932 |
| 3rd | 323* | H.Sutcliffe/M.Leyland | v Glamorgan | Huddersfield | 1928 |
| 4th | 312 | D.Denton/G.H.Hirst | v Hampshire | Southampton | 1914 |
| 5th | 340 | E.Wainwright/G.H.Hirst | v Surrey | The Oval | 1899 |
| 6th | 276 | M.Leyland/E.Robinson | v Glamorgan | Swansea | 1926 |
| 7th | 254 | W.Rhodes/D.C.F.Burton | v Hampshire | Dewsbury | 1919 |
| 8th | 292 | R.Peel/Lord Hawke | v Warwicks | Birmingham | 1896 |
| 9th | 192 | G.H.Hirst/S.Haigh | v Surrey | Bradford | 1898 |
| 10th | 149 | G.Boycott/G.B.Stevenson | v Warwicks | Birmingham | 1982 |

| | | | | | |
|---|---|---|---|---|---|
| **Best Bowling** | For 10-10 | H.Verity | v Notts | Leeds | 1932 |
| **(Innings)** | V 10-37 | C.V.Grimmett | for Australians | Sheffield | 1930 |
| **Best Bowling** | For 17-91 | H.Verity | v Essex | Leyton | 1933 |
| **(Match)** | V 17-91 | H.Dean | for Lancashire | Liverpool | 1913 |

| | | | | | |
|---|---|---|---|---|---|
| **Most Runs – Season** | 2,883 | H.Sutcliffe | (av 80.08) | | 1932 |
| **Most Runs – Career** | 38,561 | H.Sutcliffe | (av 50.20) | | 1919-1945 |
| **Most 100s – Season** | 12 | H.Sutcliffe | | | 1932 |
| **Most 100s – Career** | 112 | H.Sutcliffe | | | 1919-1945 |
| **Most Wkts – Season** | 240 | W.Rhodes | (av 12.72) | | 1900 |
| **Most Wkts – Career** | 3,608 | W.Rhodes | (av 16.00) | | 1898-1930 |

## LIMITED-OVERS CRICKET

| | | | | | |
|---|---|---|---|---|---|
| **Highest Total** | NWT | 317-4 | v Surrey | Lord's | 1965 |
| | BHC | 317-5 | v Scotland | Leeds | 1986 |
| | SL | 274-8 | v Sussex | Middlesbrough | 1991 |
| **Lowest Total** | NWT | 76 | v Surrey | Harrogate | 1970 |
| | BHC | 111 | v Notts | Nottingham | 1989 |
| | SL | 74 | v Warwicks | Birmingham | 1972 |
| **Highest Innings** | NWT | 146 G.Boycott | v Surrey | Lord's | 1965 |
| | BHC | 142 G.Boycott | v Worcs | Worcester | 1980 |
| | SL | 130* R.J.Blakey | v Kent | Scarborough | 1991 |
| **Best Bowling** | NWT | 6-15 F.S.Trueman | v Somerset | Taunton | 1965 |
| | BHC | 6-27 A.G.Nicholson | v Minor C (N) | Middlesbrough | 1972 |
| | SL | 7-15 R.A.Hutton | v Worcs | Leeds | 1969 |

## DURHAM – DEPARTURES (continued from p 72)

**BROWN, Gary** Kevin (Chace S, Enfield), b Welling, Kent 16 Jun 1965. Brother of K.R. (Middlesex). 5'11". RHB, RM. Middlesex 1986 (1 match). Durham debut/cap 1992. HS 103 and BB 1-39 Minor C v Indians (Trowbridge) 1990. Du HS 48 v Kent (Gateshead) 1992. NWT: HS 42 v Lancs (Manchester) 1990. BHC: HS 82 Minor C v Hants (Trowbridge) 1991.

**JONES, Dean** Mervyn, b Coburg, Victoria, Australia 24 Mar 1961. RHB, OB. Victoria 1981-82 to date. Durham 1992 (cap 1992). Tests (A): 49 (1983-84 to 1991-92); HS 216 v WI (Adelaide) 1988-89; BB 1-5. LOI (A): 132. Tours (A): E 1987 (RW), 1989, 1991 (Vic); WI 1983-84, 1990-91; NZ 1989-90; I 1986-87; P 1988-89; Z 1985-86 (Young A). 1000 runs (2+3); most – 1510 (1989). HS 248 A v Warwks (Birmingham) 1989. Du HS 157 v Northants (Stockton) 1992. BB 1-0. Du BB 1-4. NWT: HS 46 v Ireland (Dublin) 1992. BHC: HS 13 v Worcs (Worcester) 1992. BB 2-34 v Comb Us (Cambridge) 1992. SL: HS 114 v Lancs (Durham) 1992. BB 1-37.

## ESSEX – DEPARTURES (continued from p 77)

**BROWN, Adrian** Desmond (Clacton County HS; Magdalene C, CU), b Clacton on Sea 18 May 1962. 5'10½". RHB, WK. CU debut/blue 1986. Essex 1988 and 1992. Suffolk 1984 to date. HS 30 CU v Surrey (Cambridge) 1986. Ex HS 6*. NWT: HS 9. BHC: HS 10* Comb Us v Surrey (Oval) 1986. SL: HS 1*.

**BUTLER, Keith** Andrew (Dagenham Priory CS), b Camden Town, London 20 Jan 1971. 5'8". RHB, RM. Essex 1989. HS 10* v CU (Cambridge) 1989. SL: HS 5*.

**WAUGH, Mark** Edward (E Hills HS), b Canterbury, Sydney, Australia 2 Jun 1965. Younger twin of S.R. (NSW, Somerset and Australia). 6'1". RHB, RM. NSW 1985-86 to date. Essex 1988-90 (cap 1989) and 1992. Wisden 1990. Tests (A): 11 (1990-91 to 1991-92); HS 139* v WI (St John's) 1990-91; BB 4-80 v WI (Bridgetown) 1990-91. LOI (A): 33. Tours (A): WI 1990-91; Z 1985-86 (Young A), 1987-88 (Young A). 1000 runs (3+2) inc 2000 (1): 2072 (1990). HS 229* NSW v WA (Perth) 1990-91, sharing Australian record 5th wkt stand of 464* with S.R.Waugh. Ex HS 219* v Lancs (Ilford) 1992, sharing Essex record 3rd wkt stand of 347* with N.Hussain. BB 5-37 v Northants (Chelmsford) 1990. Awards: BHC 2. NWT: HS 47 v Hants (Chelmsford) 1990. BB 1-51. BHC: HS 100 v Northants (Northampton) 1992. BB 3-31 v Scot (Chelmsford) 1992. SL: HS 112* v Glam (Neath) 1989. BB 3-26 v Worcs (Worcester) 1992.

## GLAMORGAN – DEPARTURES (continued from p 82)

**COWDREY, Christopher** Stuart (Tonbridge S), b Farnborough, Kent 20 Oct 1957. Brother of G.R. (see KENT), son of M.C. (Kent and England 1950-76), grandson of E.A (Europeans). 6'1". RHB, RM. Kent 2nd XI debut when aged 15. Kent 1977-91 (captain; captain 1985-90; benefit 1989). Glamorgan 1992. Tests: 6 (1984-85 to 1988, 1 as captain); HS 38 v I (Delhi) 1984-85; BB 2-65 v I (Madras) 1984-85. LOI: 3. Tours: SA 1989-90 (Eng XI); NZ 1979-80. (DHR); I/SL 1984-85; SL 1977-78 (DHR). 1000 runs (4); most – 1364 (1983). HS 159 K v Surrey (Canterbury) 1985. Gm HS 50 v OU (Oxford) 1992 (only inns). BB 5-46 K v Hants (Canterbury) 1988. Awards: NWT 3; BHC 7. NWT: HS 122* K v Essex (Chelmsford) 1983. BB 4-36 K v Hants (Canterbury) 1983. BHC: HS 114 K v Sussex (Canterbury) 1977. BB 4-14 K v Sussex (Canterbury) 1987. SL: HS 95 K v Worcs (Canterbury) 1983. BB 5-28 K v Leics (Canterbury) 1984.

**DOBSON, Mark** Christopher (Simon Langton GS), b Canterbury, Kent 24 Oct 1967. 5'10". RHB, SLA. Kent 1989-91. Glamorgan 1992. HS 52 and BB 2-20 K v Glam (Canterbury) 1989. Gm HS 5* and BB 1-42 v OU (Oxford) 1992 – only match. SL: HS 21 K v Glos (Maidstone) 1989.

GLAMORGAN – DEPARTURES – continued:

**FOSTER, Daren** Joseph (Somerset S; Southgate TC; Haringey Cricket C), b Tottenham, London 14 Mar 1966. 5'9". RHB, RFM. Somerset 1986-89. Glamorgan 1991-92. HS 20 Sm v Hants (Southampton) 1988. Gm HS 17* v Notts (Nottingham) 1992. BB 6-84 v Somerset (Taunton) 1991. **NWT:** HS 2. BB 1-15. **BHC:** HS 0. BB 2-26 Sm v Yorks (Leeds) 1989. **SL:** HS 10* v Kent (Swansea) 1992. BB 4-26 Sm v Glos (Bath) 1989.

**KIRNON, Samuel** (Montserrat SS, West Indies), b Fulwood, Preston, Lancs 25 Dec 1962. 5'10". RHB, RMF. Glamorgan 1992 (1 match). Made Sunday League debut 1991 while a British Army PT Instructor serving in Germany. HS - and BB 1-14 v OU (Oxford) 1992. **SL:** HS 1. BB 2-48 v Surrey (Oval) 1991.

### LANCASHIRE – NEWCOMERS (continued from p 102)

**HENDERSON, Jonathan** Andrew Lloyd (Hulme GS, Oldham), b Cardiff, Glam 16 Jan 1975. Son of A.A. (Sussex 1972). 6'4". RHB, RM.

**WOOD, Nathan** Theo (Wm Hulme's GS), b Thornhill Edge, Yorks 4 Oct 1974. Son of B. (Yorks, Lancs, Derbys and England 1964-83). 5'8". LHB, OB.

### DEPARTURES

**FOWLER, G.** – see DURHAM.

**MORRISON, Daniel** Kyle (Takapuna GS), b Auckland, NZ 3 Feb 1966. 5'10". RHB, RFM. Auckland 1985-86 to date. Lancashire debut 1992. **Tests** (NZ): 25 (1987-88 to 1991-92); HS 27* v I (Bombay) 1988-89; BB 5-69 v E (Christchurch) 1987-88. Tours (NZ): E 1990, 1991 (RW); A 1987-88, 1989-90; I 1988-89; P 1990-91; Z 1988-89 (Young NZ). LOI (NZ): 46. HS 36 Auckland v Wellington (Auckland) 1986-87. La HS 30 v Notts (Nottingham) 1992. BB 7-82 Auckland v Canterbury (Rangiora) 1986-87. La BB 6-48 v Kent (Maidstone) 1992. **NWT:** HS –. BB 3-17 v Oxon (Oxford) 1992. **BHC:** HS 0*. BB 2-17 v Essex (Chelmsford) 1992. **SL:** HS 0*. BB 1-41.

### MIDDLESEX – DEPARTURES (continued from p 112)

**EDMONDS, Philippe** Henri (Gilbert Rennie HS, Lusaka; Skinners S, Tunbridge Wells; Cranbrook S; Fitzwilliam C, Cambridge), b Lusaka, N Rhodesia 8 Mar 1951. 6'1½". RHB, SLA. CU 1971-73; blue 1971-72-73 (capt 1973). Middlesex 1971-87 and 1992 (cap 1974; benefit 1983). YC 1974. E Province 1975-76. **Tests:** 51 (1975 to 1987); HS 64 v I (Lord's) 1982; BB 7-66 v P (Karachi) 1977-78. LOI: 29. Tours: A 1978-79, 1986-87; SA 1975-76 (IW); WI 1985-86; NZ 1977-78; I/SL 1984-85; P 1977-78. HS 142 v Glam (Swansea) 1984. BB 8-53 v Hants (Bournemouth) 1984. Awards: NWT 1; BHC 3. **NWT:** HS 63* v Somerset (Lord's) 1979. BB 5-12 v Cheshire (Enfield) 1982. **BHC:** HS 44* v Notts (Newark) 1976. BB 5-43 v Comb Us (Cambridge) 1985. **SL:** HS 52 v Somerset (Taunton) 1980. BB 3-19 v Leics (Lord's) 1973.

**HEADLEY, D.W.** – see KENT.

**SYLVESTER, Steven** Antony (Wellesbourne SM; Buckinghamshire C; Goldsmiths' C, London U), b Chalfont St Giles, Bucks, 26 Sep 1968. 5'11". RHB, LFM. Middlesex 1991-92. Buckinghamshire 1991. HS 0*. BB 2-34 v CU (Cambridge) 1992. BAC BB 2-35 v Lancs (Lord's) 1992. **BHC:** HS 0. BB 1-31.

**WHITTINGTON, Jonathan** Mark Smith (Eton C; Manchester U), b Middlesex Hospital, London 17 Aug 1973. 6'2". LHB, SLA. Middlesex 1992. HS –. No BAC appearances.

## NORTHAMPTONSHIRE – DEPARTURE (continued from p 117)

**WILLIAMS, Richard** Grenville (Ellesmere Port GS), b Bangor, Caernarvonshire 10 Aug 1957. 5'6½". RHB, OB. Debut 1974. Cap 1979. Benefit 1989. Tours: NZ 1979-80 (DHR); Z 1984-85 (EC). 1000 runs (6); most – 1262 (1980). HS 175* v Leics (Leicester) 1980. BB 7-73 v CU (Cambridge) 1980. BAC BB 6-65 v Glos (Northampton) 1990. Hat-trick 1980. Awards: NWT 1; BHC 4. **NWT:** HS 94 v Worcs (Northampton) 1984. BB 4-10 v Leics (Leicester) 1987. **BHC:** HS 83 v Yorks (Bradford) 1980. BB 4-41 v Glos (Northampton) 1987. **SL:** HS 82 v Glos (Bristol) 1982. BB 5-30 v Warwks (Luton) 1983.

## WORCESTERSHIRE – DEPARTURES (continued from p 147)

**MOODY, Thomas** Masson (Guildford GS, WA), b Adelaide, Australia 2 Oct 1965. 6'6½". RHB, RM. W Australia 1985-86 to date. Warwickshire 1990 (cap 1990). Worcestershire debut/cap 1991. Tests (A): 5 (1989-90 to 1991-92); HS 106 v SL (Brisbane) 1989-90; BB 1-23. LOI (A): 13. Tours (A): E 1989; I 1989-90 (WA). 1000 runs (2+1); most – 1887 (1991). HS 210 v Warwks (Worcester) 1991. BB 7-43 (10-109 match) WA v Victoria (Perth) 1990-91. BAC BB 4-50 v Warwks (Birmingham) 1992. Awards: BHC 5. **NWT:** HS 58 Wa v Herts (St Albans) 1990. BB 1-7. **BHC:** HS 110* v Derbys (Worcester) 1991. BB 4-59 v Somerset (Worcester) 1992. **SL:** HS 160 v Kent (Worcester) 1991 (on Wo debut in all competitions). BB 2-33 v Yorks (Worcester) 1992.

**NEALE, Phillip** Anthony (Frederick Gough CS; John Leggott SFC; Leeds U), b Scunthorpe, Lincs 5 Jun 1954. 5'11". RHB, RM. Worcestershire 1975-92 (cap 1978; captain 1982-91; benefit 1988). Lincolnshire 1972. Wisden 1988. Tour: Z 1990-91 (Wo – captain). 1000 runs (8); most – 1706 (1984). HS 167 v Sussex (Kidderminster) 1988. BB 1-15. Awards: NWT 1; BHC 2. **NWT:** HS 98 v Cumberland (Worcester) 1988. **BHC:** HS 128 v Lancs (Manchester) 1980. **SL:** HS 102 v Northants (Luton) 1982. BB 2-46 v Warwks (Worcester) 1976.

**STEMP, R.D.** – see YORKSHIRE.

## YORKSHIRE – DEPARTURES (continued from p 152)

**TENDULKAR, Sachin** Ramesh (Kirti C), b Bombay, India 24 Apr 1973. 5'5". RHB, RM. Bombay 1988-89 (scoring 100* v Gujarat when record 15yr 232d) to date. Yorkshire debut/cap 1992. Tests (I): 16 (1989-90 to 1991-92); HS 148* v A (Sydney) 1991-92; BB 2-10 v A (Adelaide) 1991-92. LOI (I): 39. Tours (I): E 1990, 1991 (RW); A 1991-92; NZ 1989-90; P 1989-90. 1000 runs (1): 1070 (1992). HS 159 W Zone v C Zone (Gauhati) 1990-91. Y HS 100 v Durham (Durham) 1992. W Zone v S Zone (Rourkela) 1990-91. Y BB 2-35 v Glos (Leeds) 1992. **NWT:** HS 32* v Northumb (Leeds) 1992. **BHC:** HS 16 v Notts (Leeds) 1992. BB 2-21 v Kent (Leeds) 1992. **SL:** HS 107 v Lancs (Leeds) 1992. BB 2-28 v Derbys (Leeds) 1992.

# UNIVERSITY MATCH RESULTS

Played: 147. Wins: Cambridge 55; Oxford 46. Drawn: 46. Abandoned: 1.
This, the oldest surviving first-class fixture, dates from 1827 and, wartime interruptions apart, it has been played annually since 1838. With the exception of five matches played in the area of Oxford (1829, 1843, 1846, 1848 and 1850), all the fixtures have been played at Lord's.

| Year | Result | Year | Result | Year | Result |
|------|--------|------|--------|------|--------|
| 1827 | Drawn | 1885 | Cambridge | 1939 | Oxford |
| 1829 | Oxford | 1886 | Oxford | 1946 | Oxford |
| 1836 | Oxford | 1887 | Oxford | 1947 | Drawn |
| 1838 | Oxford | 1888 | Drawn | 1948 | Oxford |
| 1839 | Cambridge | 1889 | Cambridge | 1949 | Cambridge |
| 1840 | Cambridge | 1890 | Cambridge | 1950 | Drawn |
| 1841 | Cambridge | 1891 | Cambridge | 1951 | Oxford |
| 1842 | Cambridge | 1892 | Oxford | 1952 | Drawn |
| 1843 | Cambridge | 1893 | Cambridge | 1953 | Cambridge |
| 1844 | Drawn | 1894 | Oxford | 1954 | Drawn |
| 1845 | Cambridge | 1895 | Cambridge | 1955 | Drawn |
| 1846 | Oxford | 1896 | Oxford | 1956 | Drawn |
| 1847 | Cambridge | 1897 | Cambridge | 1957 | Cambridge |
| 1848 | Oxford | 1898 | Oxford | 1958 | Cambridge |
| 1849 | Cambridge | 1899 | Drawn | 1959 | Oxford |
| 1850 | Oxford | 1900 | Drawn | 1960 | Drawn |
| 1851 | Cambridge | 1901 | Drawn | 1961 | Drawn |
| 1852 | Oxford | 1902 | Cambridge | 1962 | Drawn |
| 1853 | Oxford | 1903 | Oxford | 1963 | Drawn |
| 1854 | Oxford | 1904 | Drawn | 1964 | Drawn |
| 1855 | Oxford | 1905 | Cambridge | 1965 | Drawn |
| 1856 | Cambridge | 1906 | Cambridge | 1966 | Oxford |
| 1857 | Oxford | 1907 | Cambridge | 1967 | Drawn |
| 1858 | Oxford | 1908 | Oxford | 1968 | Drawn |
| 1859 | Cambridge | 1909 | Drawn | 1969 | Drawn |
| 1860 | Cambridge | 1910 | Oxford | 1970 | Drawn |
| 1861 | Cambridge | 1911 | Oxford | 1971 | Drawn |
| 1862 | Cambridge | 1912 | Cambridge | 1972 | Cambridge |
| 1863 | Oxford | 1913 | Cambridge | 1973 | Drawn |
| 1864 | Oxford | 1914 | Oxford | 1974 | Drawn |
| 1865 | Oxford | 1919 | Oxford | 1975 | Drawn |
| 1866 | Oxford | 1920 | Drawn | 1976 | Oxford |
| 1867 | Cambridge | 1921 | Cambridge | 1977 | Drawn |
| 1868 | Cambridge | 1922 | Cambridge | 1978 | Drawn |
| 1869 | Cambridge | 1923 | Oxford | 1979 | Cambridge |
| 1870 | Cambridge | 1924 | Cambridge | 1980 | Drawn |
| 1871 | Oxford | 1925 | Drawn | 1981 | Drawn |
| 1872 | Cambridge | 1926 | Cambridge | 1982 | Cambridge |
| 1873 | Oxford | 1927 | Cambridge | 1983 | Drawn |
| 1874 | Oxford | 1928 | Drawn | 1984 | Oxford |
| 1875 | Oxford | 1929 | Drawn | 1985 | Drawn |
| 1876 | Cambridge | 1930 | Cambridge | 1986 | Cambridge |
| 1877 | Oxford | 1931 | Oxford | 1987 | Drawn |
| 1878 | Cambridge | 1932 | Drawn | 1988 | Abandoned |
| 1879 | Cambridge | 1933 | Drawn | 1989 | Drawn |
| 1880 | Cambridge | 1934 | Drawn | 1990 | Drawn |
| 1881 | Oxford | 1935 | Cambridge | 1991 | Drawn |
| 1882 | Cambridge | 1936 | Cambridge | 1992 | Cambridge |
| 1883 | Cambridge | 1937 | Oxford | | |
| 1884 | Oxford | 1938 | Drawn | | |

# CAMBRIDGE v OXFORD
## (147th UNIVERSITY MATCH)

Played at Lord's, London, on 30 June, 1, 2 July.
Toss: Oxford.  Result: CAMBRIDGE won by 7 wickets.

### OXFORD UNIVERSITY

| | | | | |
|---|---|---|---|---|
| R.R.Montgomerie c Pearson b Johnson | 16 | not out | | 45 |
| J.E.R.Gallian c Jones b Johnson | 1 | st Arscott b Wight | | 66 |
| A.C.Storie c Johnson b Hooper | 5 | | | |
| *G.B.T.Lovell c Crawley b Pitcher | 32 | | | |
| C.L.Keey lbw b Pearson | 33 | | | |
| H.R.Davies lbw b Abington | 39 | | | |
| M.P.W.Jeh c Pearson b Johnson | 8 | | | |
| R.H.MacDonald not out | 8 | | | |
| D.J.Anderson not out | 8 | | | |
| †C.J.Townsend } did not bat | | | | |
| B.S.Wood | | | | |
| Extras (B15, LB11, W6) | 32 | (LB3, W1) | | 4 |
| **Total (7 wickets declared)** | **182** | **(1 wicket declared)** | | **115** |

### CAMBRIDGE UNIVERSITY

| | | | | |
|---|---|---|---|---|
| A.M.Hooper c Montgomerie b Gallian | 1 | b Jeh | | 17 |
| G.W.Jones c Townsend b Gallian | 12 | lbw b MacDonald | | 18 |
| *J.P.Crawley c Gallian b Jeh | 1 | (4) not out | | 106 |
| R.M.Wight c Storie b Jeh | 5 | (5) not out | | 62 |
| J.P.Carroll c Townsend b Wood | 7 | | | |
| †J.P.Arscott c Gallian b MacDonald | 5 | | | |
| M.E.D.Jarrett not out | 7 | (3) c Anderson b Gallian | | 22 |
| S.W.Johnson c Anderson b MacDonald | 14 | | | |
| C.M.Pitcher | | | | |
| R.M.Pearson } did not bat | | | | |
| M.B.Abington | | | | |
| Extras (LB3, NB5) | 8 | (B3, LB4, W4, NB2) | | 13 |
| **Total (7 wickets declared)** | **60** | **(3 wickets)** | | **238** |

| CAMBRIDGE | O | M | R | W | O | M | R | W |
|---|---|---|---|---|---|---|---|---|
| Johnson | 18 | 4 | 62 | 3 | 6 | 0 | 22 | 0 |
| Pitcher | 17 | 5 | 36 | 1 | 11 | 0 | 39 | 0 |
| Pearson | 14 | 4 | 37 | 1 | 0 | | 31 | 0 |
| Hooper | 5 | 2 | 5 | 1 | | | | |
| Wight | 11 | 5 | 14 | 0 | 5 | 0 | 13 | 1 |
| Abington | 2 | 1 | 2 | 1 | 2 | 0 | 7 | 0 |

| OXFORD | O | M | R | W | O | M | R | W |
|---|---|---|---|---|---|---|---|---|
| Jeh | 8 | 1 | 15 | 2 | 6 | 0 | 27 | 1 |
| Gallian | 8 | 4 | 10 | 2 | 16 | 1 | 89 | 1 |
| Wood | 6 | 0 | 19 | 1 | 12.5 | 0 | 56 | 0 |
| MacDonald | 5.4 | 3 | 13 | 2 | 12 | 3 | 30 | 1 |
| Anderson | | | | | 4 | 0 | 29 | 0 |

**FALL OF WICKETS**

| | OU | CU | OU | CU |
|---|---|---|---|---|
| Wkt | 1st | 1st | 2nd | 2nd |
| 1st | 14 | 5 | 115 | 25 |
| 2nd | 21 | 11 | – | 56 |
| 3rd | 35 | 24 | – | 72 |
| 4th | 66 | 25 | – | – |
| 5th | 130 | 35 | – | – |
| 6th | 149 | 37 | – | – |
| 7th | 166 | 60 | – | – |
| 8th | – | – | – | – |
| 9th | | | | |
| 10th | | | | |

Umpires: J.D.Bond and V.A.Holder.

# CAMBRIDGE UNIVERSITY

**ABINGTON, Michael** Barringer (Bedford S; Brighton Poly; Homerton C), b Lusaka, Zambia 8 Mar 1965. 6'3". RHB, SLA. Sussex U-25. British Polytechnics. Debut 1992; blue 1992. HS 6. BB 3-33 v Derbys (Cambridge) 1992.

**ARSCOTT, Jonathan** Paul (Tonbridge S; Magdalene C), b Tooting, London 4 Jul 1970. 5'10". RHB, RM, WK. Debut 1990; blue 1991-92. HS 79 v Surrey (Cambridge) 1992. BB 1-17.

**CARROLL, John** Paul (Rendcomb C, Cirencester; Homerton C), b Bebington, Cheshire 14 Jul 1972. 6'2". RHB, RM. Debut 1992; blue 1992. HS 92 v Kent (Cambridge) 1992.

**CRAWLEY, John** Paul (Manchester GS; Trinity C), b Maldon, Essex 21 Sep 1971. Brother of M.A. (see NOTTS) and P.M. (CU 1992). 6'1". RHB, RM. Lancashire 1990-91. CU debut 1991; blue 1991-92; captain 1992-93. 1000 runs (1): 1175 (1992). HS 172 La v Surrey (Lytham) 1992. CU HS 106* v OU (Lord's) 1992. BB 1-90.

**CRAWLEY, Peter** Matthew (Manchester GS; St Andrews U; Trinity Hall), b Newton-le-Willows, Lancs 4 Jan 1969. Brother of M.A. (see NOTTS) and J.P. (see above). 6'5". RHB, RM. Golf blue 1991. Debut 1992. HS 45 v Surrey (Cambridge) 1992. BB 2-36 v Middx (Cambridge) 1992.

**DAS, Shonu** Sanjeev Kumar (QEGS Wakefield; QMW London; Hughes Hall), b Newcastle upon Tyne, Northumb 15 Nov 1967. 5'10". RHB, RM. Debut 1992. HS 24* v Middx (Cambridge) 1992.

**HOOPER, Anthony** Mark (Latymer Upper S; St John's C), b Perivale, Middx 5 Sep 1967. 5'7". RHB, RM. Debut 1987; blue 1987-91-92. HS 125 v Surrey (Cambridge) 1991. BB 1-5.

**JARRETT, Michael** Eugene Dominic (Harrow S; Girton C), b St Thomas' Hospital, London 18 Sep 1972. 5'9". RHB, RM. Debut 1992; blue 1992. HS 27 v Warwks (Cambridge) 1992.

**JENKINS, Rory** Harry John (Oundle S; Downing C), b Leicester 29 Jun 1970. 6'2". RHB, RM. Debut 1990; blue 1990-91. Athletics and Rugby blue. HS 20 v Northants (Cambridge) 1991. BB 5-100 v Middx (Cambridge) 1990.

**JOHNSON, Simon** Wolseley (Newcastle RGS; Magdalene C), b Newcastle upon Tyne, Northumb 29 Jan 1970. 6'2". RHB, RMF. Debut 1990; blue 1990-91-92. HS 50 v Leics (Cambridge) 1992. BB 3-62 v OU (Lord's) 1992.

**JONES, Garri** Wyn (King's S, Chester; Gonville & Caius C), b Birmingham 1 May 1970. Brother of R.O. (see GLAMORGAN). 5'7". LHB, OB. Debut 1991; blue 1992. HS 44 v Derbys (Cambridge) 1992.

**KEMP, Trevor** Rodney (Colchester RGS; Christ's C), b Colchester, Essex 22 Sep 1971. 6'2". RHB, OB. Essex II 1991. Debut 1992. HS 0. BB 1-35.

**PEARSON, Richard** Michael (Batley GS; St John's C), b Batley, Yorks 27 Jan 1972. 6'3". RHB, OB. Debut 1991; blue 1991-92. Northamptonshire debut 1992. HS 33* v Surrey (Cambridge) 1992. BB 5-108 v Warwks (Cambridge) 1992.

**PITCHER, Christopher** Michael (St Edward's S, Oxford; Selwyn C), b Croydon, Surrey 26 Aug 1973. 6'2". RHB, RM. Debut 1992; blue 1992. HS 32* v Leics (Cambridge) 1992 – on debut. BB 1-35.

**THWAITES, Guy** Edward (Eastbourne C; Girton C), b Brighton, Sussex 19 Jan 1971. Son of I.G. (CU 1963-64). 5'9". RHB. Debut 1991. HS 32 v Derbys (Cambridge) 1991.

**WIGHT, Robert Marcus** (KCS, Wimbledon; Exeter U; Trinity Hall), b London 12 Sep 1969. Nephew of P.B. (British Guiana, Somerset & Canterbury 1950/51-1965). 6'2". RHB, OB. Debut 1992; blue 1992. Worcs II 1990. Derbys II 1991. Joins Glos 1993 (2 year contract). Hockey for Devon 1989-91; CU blue 1991-92 (captain 1992). HS 62* v OU (Lord's) 1992. BB 3-65 v Kent (Cambridge) 1992.

# CAMBRIDGE UNIVERSITY 1992

### RESULTS SUMMARY

|  | Played | Won | Lost | Drew |
|---|---|---|---|---|
| All first-class matches | 9 | 2 | 3 | 4 |

## FIRST-CLASS AVERAGES
### BATTING AND FIELDING

|  | M | I | NO | HS | Runs | Avge | 100 | 50 | Ct/St |
|---|---|---|---|---|---|---|---|---|---|
| †J.P.Crawley | 9 | 17 | 3 | 106* | 541 | 38.64 | 1 | 3 | 5 |
| †J.P.Arscott | 9 | 12 | 2 | 79 | 318 | 31.80 | – | 3 | 10/6 |
| P.M.Crawley | 4 | 6 | 2 | 45 | 118 | 29.50 | – | – | – |
| †R.M.Wight | 9 | 15 | 2 | 62* | 366 | 28.15 | – | 2 | 3 |
| †G.W.Jones | 6 | 12 | – | 44 | 249 | 20.75 | – | – | 1 |
| †J.P.Carroll | 5 | 9 | – | 92 | 175 | 19.44 | – | 1 | 1 |
| †S.W.Johnson | 9 | 13 | 2 | 50 | 201 | 18.27 | – | 1 | 4 |
| †A.M.Hooper | 9 | 17 | 1 | 48 | 243 | 15.18 | – | – | 1 |
| †R.M.Pearson | 9 | 11 | 5 | 33* | 88 | 14.66 | – | – | 3 |
| †C.M.Pitcher | 6 | 8 | 3 | 32* | 62 | 12.40 | – | – | – |
| †M.E.D.Jarrett | 9 | 13 | 2 | 27 | 106 | 9.63 | – | – | 2 |
| S.S.K.Das | 3 | 5 | 1 | 24* | 38 | 9.50 | – | – | 1 |
| †M.B.Abington | 7 | 7 | – | 6 | 20 | 2.85 | – | – | 4 |

*Also played:* R.H.J.Jenkins (2 matches) 1 (1ct): T.R.Kemp (2 matches) 0 (1 ct); G.E.Thwaites (1 match) 0.

### BOWLING

|  | O | M | R | W | Avge | Best | 5wI | 10wM |
|---|---|---|---|---|---|---|---|---|
| R.M.Wight | 213.3 | 36 | 677 | 18 | 37.61 | 3-65 | – | – |
| M.B.Abington | 146.4 | 23 | 530 | 10 | 53.00 | 3-33 | – | – |
| S.W.Johnson | 164 | 27 | 541 | 10 | 54.10 | 3-62 | – | – |
| R.M.Pearson | 337.5 | 57 | 1021 | 18 | 56.72 | 5-108 | 1 | – |

*Also bowled:* P.M.Crawley 66-13-236-3; A.M.Hooper 20.2-7-63-3; R.H.J.Jenkins 32-5-137-2; T.R.Kemp 29-2-128-1; C.M.Pitcher 131-20-453-3.
† Blue 1992.

The following appeared in other first-class matches in 1992:
J.P.Arscott, J.P.Crawley, A.M.Hooper, R.M.Pearson and R.M.Wight for Combined Universities v Pakistanis; J.P.Crawley also appeared in seven matches for Lancashire and R.M.Pearson in one match for Northamptonshire. Their records in all first-class matches appear on pp 164-178.

# OXFORD UNIVERSITY

**ANDERSON, Desmond** John (Repton S; Reading U; St Edmund Hall), b Johannesburg, SA 17 Oct 1968. 5'11". RHB, RM. Debut 1992; blue 1992. British Us football (OU blue 1992). HS 9. BB 2-68 v Worcs (Oxford) 1992.

**DAVIES, Henry** Richard (St Dunstan's C; Christ Church), b Camberwell, London 2 Sep 1970. 5'10". LHB, OB. Debut 1990; blue 1992. HS 39 v CU (Lord's) 1992. BB 3-93 v Hants (Oxford) 1990 – on debut.

**GALLIAN, Jason** Edward Riche (Pittwater House S, Sydney; Keble C), b Manly, Sydney, Australia 25 Jun 1971. 6'0". RHB, RM. Debut 1990 for Lancashire, taking wicket of D.A.Hagan (OU) with his first ball. Qualifies for Lancs in 1994. Captained Australia YC v England YC 1989-90 scoring 158* in 1st 'Test'. OU debut 1992; blue 1992; captain 1993. HS 112 v Worcs (Oxford) 1992. BB 4-29 v Lancs (Oxford) 1992.

**GUPTE, Chinmay** Madhukar (John Lyon S, Harrow; Pembroke C), b Poona, India 5 Jul 1972. Son of M.S. (Maharashtra). 5'7". RHB, SLA. Debut 1991; blue 1991. HS 55* v Glos (Oxford) 1991. BB 2-41 v Notts (Oxford) 1991.

**JEH, Michael** Pradeep Williams (Brisbane State HS; Griffith U, Brisbane; Keble C), b Colombo, Ceylon 21 Apr 1968. 6'1". RHB, RFM. Debut 1992; blue 1992. HS 23 Comb Us v P (Cambridge) 1992. OU HS 16 v Hants (Oxford) 1992. BB 3-44 v Worcs (Oxford) 1992.

**KEEY, Christopher** Leyton (Harrow S; Durham U; Keble C), b Johannesburg, SA 27 Dec 1969. 5'10". RHB, OB. Debut 1992; blue 1992. HS 64 v Middx (Oxford) 1992.

**LOVELL, Geoffrey** Bruce Tasman (Sydney C of E GS; Sydney U; Exeter C), b Sydney, Australia 11 Jul 1966. 5'10½". RHB, RM. Debut 1991; blue 1991-92; captain 1992. Inaugural Bradman Scholarship. HS 110* v Glam (Oxford) 1992. BB 1-13.

**MACDONALD, Robert** Hepburn (Rondebosch BHS; Cape Town U; Durham U; Keble C), b Cape Town, SA 18 Jul 1965. 6'2". RHB, RMF. Debut 1991; blue 1991-92. Squash blue 1990. HS 20 v Hants (Oxford) 1991. BB 3-66 v Glos (Oxford) 1991.

**MALIK, Hasnain** Siddiq (KCS, Wimbledon; Keble C), b Harrow, Middx 1 Dec 1971. 5'11". LHB, OB. Debut 1992. HS 4.

**MONTGOMERIE, Richard** Robert (Rugby S; Worcester C), b Rugby, Warwks 3 Jul 1971. 5'10½". RHB, OB. Debut 1991; blue 1991-92. Northamptonshire 1991. Rackets blue 1990. HS 103* v Middx (Oxford) 1992.

**OLIPHANT-CALLUM, Ralph** David (Brighton C; Brasenose C), b Twickenham, Middx 26 Sep 1971. 5'8". RHB, WK. Debut 1992. HS 19 v Worcs (Oxford) 1992.

**SANDIFORD, David** Charles (Bolton S; St Edmund Hall), b Bolton, Lancs 24 Dec 1970. 5'9". RHB, WK. Debut 1991; blue 1991. HS 83 v Yorks (Oxford) 1991.

**STORIE, Alastair** Caleb (St Stithians C, Johannesburg; Keble C), b Bishopbriggs, Glasgow 25 Jul 1965. 5'9". RHB, RM. Northamptonshire 1985-86. Warwickshire 1987-88. OFS 1987-88. OU debut 1992; blue 1992. HS 106 Nh v Hants (Northampton) 1985 – on debut. OU HS 29 v Hants (Oxford) 1992. BB 1-17.

**TOWNSEND, Christopher** James (Dean Close S; Brasenose C), b Wokingham, Berks 1 Dec 1972. 6'0". RHB, WK. Grandson of W.D.Wickson (Surrey President 1992). Debut 1992; blue 1992. HS 8.

**WARLEY, Simon** Nicholas (Kent C, Canterbury; Oriel C), b Sittingbourne, Kent 6 Jan 1972. 6'4". RHB, RMF. Debut 1991. HS 35 v Notts (Oxford) 1992.

**WOOD, Benjamin** Shaw (Batley GS; Worcester C), b Dewsbury, Yorks 25 Jan 1971. 6'0". RHB, RMF. Debut 1991; blue 1991-92. HS 13 v Hants (Oxford) and v CU (Lord's) 1992. BB 2-24 v CU (Lord's) 1991.

# OXFORD UNIVERSITY 1992

## RESULTS SUMMARY

| | Played | Won | Lost | Drew | Abandoned |
|---|---|---|---|---|---|
| All first-class matches | 8 | 1 | 2 | 5 | 1 |

## FIRST-CLASS AVERAGES
### BATTING AND FIELDING

| | M | I | NO | HS | Runs | Avge | 100 | 50 | Ct/St |
|---|---|---|---|---|---|---|---|---|---|
| †R.R.Montgomerie | 8 | 13 | 3 | 103* | 447 | 44.70 | 1 | 1 | 3 |
| †G.B.T.Lovell | 8 | 11 | 1 | 110* | 324 | 32.40 | 1 | 1 | 7 |
| †J.E.R.Gallian | 8 | 13 | – | 112 | 374 | 28.76 | 1 | 2 | 5 |
| †C.L.Keey | 7 | 11 | 1 | 64 | 271 | 27.10 | – | 3 | 1 |
| †B.S.Wood | 3 | 2 | 1 | 13 | 16 | 16.00 | – | – | – |
| S.N.Warley | 7 | 10 | 2 | 35 | 117 | 14.62 | – | – | 2 |
| R.D.Oliphant-Callum | 3 | 2 | – | 19 | 28 | 14.00 | – | – | 1 |
| †A.C.Storie | 7 | 10 | 1 | 29 | 113 | 12.55 | – | – | 4 |
| †H.R.Davies | 6 | 7 | 1 | 39 | 62 | 10.33 | – | – | – |
| †M.P.W.Jeh | 8 | 9 | 2 | 16 | 51 | 7.28 | – | – | 3 |
| C.M.Gupte | 5 | 6 | 1 | 11 | 36 | 7.20 | – | – | 1 |
| †R.H.MacDonald | 3 | 3 | 1 | 8* | 13 | 6.50 | – | – | – |
| †D.J.Anderson | 8 | 8 | 4 | 9 | 18 | 4.50 | – | – | 3 |
| †C.J.Townsend | 5 | 4 | 1 | 8 | 8 | 2.66 | – | – | 8 |

*Played in one match*: H.S.Malik 4; D.C.Sandiford 20, 1.

### BOWLING

| | O | M | R | W | Avge | Best | 5wI | 10wM |
|---|---|---|---|---|---|---|---|---|
| J.E.R.Gallian | 193 | 39 | 570 | 17 | 33.52 | 4-29 | – | – |
| R.H.MacDonald | 79.4 | 22 | 188 | 5 | 37.60 | 2-13 | – | – |
| M.P.W.Jeh | 212.5 | 37 | 736 | 15 | 49.06 | 3-44 | – | – |
| D.J.Anderson | 164.5 | 38 | 511 | 9 | 56.77 | 2-68 | – | – |
| H.R.Davies | 146.3 | 18 | 640 | 6 | 106.66 | 3-118 | – | – |

*Also bowled*: C.M.Gupte 28-2-133-1; H.S.Malik 25-4-88-0; R.R.Montgomerie 10-2-31-0; A.C.Storie 40-5-128-2; B.S.Wood 73.2-7-254-4.
† Blue 1992.

The following appeared in other first-class matches in 1992:
J.E.R.Gallian, M.P.W.Jeh, C.L.Keey, G.B.T.Lovell, R.R.Montgomerie and B.S.Wood for Combined Universities v Pakistanis. Their records in all first-class matches appear on pp 164-178.

# 1992 FIRST-CLASS AVERAGES

These averages include performances in all first-class matches played in the British Isles in 1992.

'Cap' denotes the season in which the player was awarded a 1st XI cap by the county he represented in 1992. Durham do not award caps on merit; each player receives his cap on joining the staff.

Team abbreviations: CU – Cambridge University: De – Derbyshire; Du – Durham; E – England; EA – England A; Ex – Essex; Gm – Glamorgan; Gs – Gloucestershire; H – Hampshire; Ire – Ireland; K – Kent; La – Lancashire; Le – Leicestershire; M – Middlesex; MCC – Marylebone Cricket Club; Nh – Northamptonshire; Nt – Nottinghamshire; OU – Oxford University; P – Pakistan(is); Sc – Scotland; Sm – Somerset; Sy – Surrey; Sx – Sussex; Us – Combined (Oxbridge) Universities; W – World XI; Wa – Warwickshire; Wo – Worcestershire; Y – Yorkshire.

† Left-handed batsman.

## BATTING AND FIELDING

| | Cap | M | I | NO | HS | Runs | Avge | 100 | 50 | Ct/St |
|---|---|---|---|---|---|---|---|---|---|---|
| †Aamir Sohail (P) | — | 17 | 28 | 2 | 205 | 1110 | 42.69 | 2 | 4 | 14 |
| Abington, M.B.(CU) | — | 7 | 7 | – | 6 | 20 | 2.85 | – | – | 4 |
| Adams, C.J.(De) | 1992 | 23 | 33 | 6 | 140* | 1109 | 41.07 | 4 | 4 | 20 |
| Afford, J.A.(Nt) | 1990 | 18 | 17 | 6 | 12 | 42 | 3.81 | – | – | 4 |
| Alikhan, R.I.(Sy) | — | 2 | 3 | – | 54 | 65 | 21.66 | – | 1 | 2 |
| Alleyne, M.W.(Gs) | 1990 | 22 | 36 | 3 | 93 | 1065 | 32.27 | – | 7 | 23 |
| †Ambrose, C.E.L.(Nh) | 1990 | 18 | 20 | 10 | 49* | 200 | 20.00 | – | – | 5 |
| Anderson, D.J.(OU) | — | 8 | 8 | 4 | 9 | 18 | 4.50 | – | – | 3 |
| Andrew, S.J.W.(Ex) | — | 10 | 12 | 4 | 14* | 38 | 4.75 | – | – | – |
| Aqib Javed (P) | — | 14 | 8 | 3 | 5* | 10 | 2.00 | – | – | 1 |
| Archer, G.F.(Nt) | — | 7 | 13 | 3 | 117 | 475 | 47.50 | 1 | 4 | 6 |
| Arscott, J.P.(CU/Us) | — | 10 | 14 | 3 | 79 | 341 | 31.00 | – | 3 | 11/6 |
| Asif Din (Wa) | 1987 | 2 | 3 | – | 40 | 103 | 34.33 | – | – | – |
| †Asif Mujtaba (P) | — | 16 | 25 | 6 | 154* | 1074 | 56.52 | 2 | 6 | 6 |
| Ata-ur-Rehman (P) | — | 9 | 2 | 1 | 1* | 1 | 1.00 | – | – | 3 |
| Atherton, M.A.(La/E) | 1989 | 21 | 37 | 6 | 199 | 1598 | 51.54 | 5 | 7 | 24 |
| Athey, C.W.J.(Gs) | 1985 | 20 | 32 | – | 181 | 1022 | 31.93 | 2 | 4 | 19 |
| Atkins, P.D.(Sy) | — | 7 | 14 | – | 99 | 382 | 27.28 | – | 2 | 2 |
| †Austin, I.D.(La) | 1990 | 8 | 10 | 2 | 115* | 230 | 28.75 | 1 | 1 | – |
| Ayling, J.R.(H) | 1991 | 18 | 26 | 1 | 121 | 593 | 23.72 | 1 | 2 | 4 |
| Aymes, A.N.(H) | 1991 | 18 | 23 | 5 | 65 | 359 | 19.94 | – | 2 | 47/4 |
| †Babington, A.M.(Gs) | — | 9 | 11 | 4 | 24 | 75 | 10.71 | – | – | 3 |
| Bailey, R.J.(Nh) | 1985 | 23 | 39 | 7 | 167* | 1572 | 49.12 | 2 | 8 | 22 |
| Bainbridge, P.(Du) | 1992 | 17 | 30 | 9 | 92* | 923 | 43.95 | – | 8 | 8 |
| Bakker, P-J.(H) | 1989 | 6 | 7 | 1 | 22 | 69 | 11.50 | – | – | – |
| Ball, M.C.J.(Gs) | — | 12 | 21 | 6 | 54 | 201 | 13.40 | – | 2 | 6 |
| Barnett, A.A.(La) | — | 22 | 17 | 10 | 17 | 70 | 10.00 | – | – | 7 |
| Barnett, K.J.(De) | 1982 | 19 | 29 | 5 | 160 | 1270 | 52.91 | 4 | 4 | 5 |
| Bartlett, R.J.(Sm) | — | 8 | 13 | – | 72 | 352 | 27.07 | – | 2 | 5 |
| Barwick, S.R.(Gm) | 1987 | 18 | 15 | 4 | 9* | 31 | 2.81 | – | – | 6 |
| Base, S.J.(De) | 1990 | 2 | 2 | 1 | 3 | 3 | 3.00 | – | – | 1 |
| Bastien, S.(Gm) | — | 10 | 10 | 3 | 9* | 21 | 3.00 | – | – | – |
| Batty, J.D.(Y) | — | 18 | 15 | 4 | 49 | 155 | 14.09 | – | 1 | 3 |
| Bee, A.(Sc) | — | 1 | 1 | 1 | 1* | 1 | | – | – | – |
| Bell, M.A.V.(Wa) | — | 3 | 5 | 2 | 5 | 10 | 3.33 | – | – | – |
| Benjamin, J.E.(Sy) | — | 18 | 18 | 8 | 42 | 116 | 11.60 | – | – | 5 |

164

| | Cap | M | I | NO | HS | Runs | Avge | 100 | 50 | Ct/St |
|---|---|---|---|---|---|---|---|---|---|---|
| Benjamin, K.C.G.(W) | — | 1 | 1 | 1 | 0* | 0 | — | — | — | — |
| Benjamin, W.K.M.(Le) | 1989 | 20 | 25 | 3 | 72 | 453 | 20.59 | — | 4 | 15 |
| Benson, J.D.R.(Le) | — | 18 | 28 | 1 | 122 | 623 | 23.07 | 1 | 1 | 30 |
| †Benson, M.R.(K) | 1981 | 21 | 35 | 2 | 139 | 1482 | 44.90 | 4 | 6 | 15 |
| Berry, P.J.(Du) | 1992 | 9 | 15 | 3 | 76 | 205 | 17.08 | — | 1 | 6 |
| †Bicknell, D.J.(Sy/EA) | 1990 | 24 | 42 | 5 | 120* | 1340 | 36.21 | 2 | 7 | 6 |
| Bicknell, M.P.(Sy) | 1989 | 19 | 26 | 8 | 88 | 447 | 24.83 | — | 2 | 7 |
| Bishop, I.R.(De) | 1990 | 20 | 21 | 2 | 90 | 388 | 20.42 | — | 1 | 6 |
| †Bishop, J.(Gm) | — | 1 | 1 | 1 | 51* | 51 | — | — | 1 | 4 |
| Blakey, R.J.(Y) | 1987 | 21 | 32 | 9 | 125* | 1065 | 46.30 | 2 | 5 | 44/5 |
| Boden, D.J.P.(Ex) | — | 1 | 1 | — | 5 | 5 | 5.00 | — | — | 1 |
| Boiling, J.(Sy) | — | 19 | 21 | 11 | 29 | 190 | 19.00 | — | — | 19 |
| Boon, T.J.(Le) | 1986 | 24 | 41 | 3 | 139 | 1448 | 38.10 | 2 | 10 | 15 |
| †Booth, P.A.(Wa) | — | 8 | 11 | 4 | 22* | 78 | 11.14 | — | — | — |
| Botham, I.T.(Du/E) | 1992 | 17 | 25 | 2 | 105 | 713 | 31.00 | 1 | 4 | 9 |
| Bowen, M.N.(Nh) | — | 2 | 1 | — | 5 | 5 | 5.00 | — | — | — |
| Bowler, P.D.(De) | 1989 | 24 | 38 | 7 | 241* | 2044 | 65.93 | 6 | 11 | 13 |
| Bramhall, S.(Nt) | — | 8 | 10 | 3 | 37* | 114 | 16.28 | — | — | 16/5 |
| Briers, M.P.(Du) | 1992 | 16 | 28 | 4 | 62* | 460 | 19.16 | — | 4 | 7 |
| Briers, N.E.(Le) | 1981 | 24 | 42 | 6 | 123 | 1372 | 38.11 | 3 | 9 | 12 |
| †Broad, B.C.(Nt) | 1984 | 14 | 27 | 3 | 159* | 1040 | 43.33 | 5 | — | 7 |
| Brown, A.D.(Ex) | — | 1 | — | — | — | — | — | — | — | 4/1 |
| Brown, A.D.(Sy) | — | 11 | 16 | 1 | 175 | 740 | 49.33 | 3 | 3 | 6 |
| Brown, A.M.(De) | — | 7 | 8 | — | 43 | 144 | 18.00 | — | — | 7 |
| Brown, D.R.(Wa) | — | 1 | 1 | — | 5* | 5 | — | — | — | — |
| Brown, G.K.(Du) | 1992 | 4 | 6 | — | 48 | 136 | 22.66 | — | — | 3 |
| Brown, K.R.(M) | 1990 | 25 | 37 | 7 | 106 | 776 | 25.86 | 1 | 3 | 39/11 |
| Brown, S.J.E.(Du) | 1992 | 20 | 24 | 13 | 47* | 197 | 17.90 | — | — | 4 |
| Bryson, R.E.(Sy) | 1992 | 11 | 13 | 2 | 76 | 257 | 23.36 | — | 1 | — |
| Burns, M.(Wa) | — | 2 | 3 | — | 78 | 85 | 28.33 | — | 1 | 7/1 |
| †Burns, N.D.(Sm) | 1987 | 22 | 33 | 12 | 73* | 772 | 36.76 | — | 4 | 42/3 |
| †Butcher, A.R.(Gm) | 1987 | 3 | 3 | 1 | 59* | 90 | 45.00 | — | 1 | 2 |
| †Butcher, M.A.(Sy) | — | 2 | 2 | 1 | 47 | 52 | 52.00 | — | — | — |
| †Byas, D.(Y) | 1991 | 20 | 30 | 4 | 100 | 784 | 30.15 | 1 | 6 | 30 |
| Caddick, A.R.(Sm) | 1992 | 20 | 19 | 6 | 54* | 261 | 20.07 | — | 1 | 6 |
| Cairns, C.L.(Nt) | — | 21 | 30 | 6 | 107* | 984 | 41.00 | 2 | 6 | 8 |
| Capel, D.J.(Nh) | 1986 | 23 | 34 | 4 | 103 | 892 | 29.73 | 1 | 5 | 16 |
| Carr, J.D.(M) | 1987 | 25 | 39 | 7 | 114 | 1228 | 38.37 | 2 | 8 | 41 |
| Carrick, P.(Y) | 1976 | 19 | 25 | 5 | 46 | 261 | 13.05 | — | — | 7 |
| Carroll, J.P.(CU) | — | 5 | 9 | — | 92 | 175 | 19.44 | — | 1 | 1 |
| Chapman, C.A.(Y) | — | 1 | 1 | 1 | 8* | 8 | — | — | — | 1 |
| Chapman, R.J.(Nt) | — | 1 | — | — | — | — | — | — | — | — |
| Chapple, G.(La) | — | 2 | 2 | 1 | 18 | 19 | 19.00 | — | — | — |
| †Childs, J.H.(Ex) | 1986 | 22 | 17 | 8 | 43 | 110 | 12.22 | — | — | 5 |
| Connor, C.A.(H) | 1988 | 16 | 13 | 5 | 51 | 127 | 15.87 | — | — | 5 |
| Cook, N.G.B.(Nh) | 1987 | 17 | 11 | 6 | 37 | 118 | 23.60 | — | — | 3 |
| †Cooper, K.E.(Nt) | 1980 | 2 | 2 | — | 2 | 2 | 1.00 | — | — | — |
| Cork, D.G.(De/EA) | — | 19 | 21 | 2 | 72* | 578 | 30.42 | — | 3 | 12 |
| Cottam, A.C.(Sm) | — | 6 | 8 | 1 | 31 | 43 | 6.14 | — | — | 1 |
| Cottey, P.A.(Gm) | 1992 | 20 | 28 | 5 | 141 | 1076 | 46.78 | 2 | 6 | 9 |
| Cowans, N.G.(M) | 1984 | 1 | — | — | — | — | — | — | — | — |
| Cowdrey, C.S.(Gm) | — | 2 | 1 | — | 50 | 50 | 50.00 | — | 1 | 5 |
| Cowdrey, G.R.(K) | 1988 | 21 | 31 | 6 | 147 | 1291 | 51.64 | 3 | 7 | 6 |
| †Cox, R.M.F.(H) | — | 3 | 3 | — | 13 | 26 | 8.66 | — | — | 1 |
| Crawley, J.P.(CU/Us/La) | — | 17 | 29 | 3 | 172 | 1175 | 45.19 | 2 | 7 | 11 |

| | Cap | M | I | NO | HS | Runs | Avge | 100 | 50 | Ct/St |
|---|---|---|---|---|---|---|---|---|---|---|
| Crawley, M.A.(Nt) | — | 25 | 44 | 9 | 160* | 1297 | 37.05 | 4 | 5 | 21 |
| Crawley, P.M.(CU) | — | 4 | 6 | 2 | 45 | 118 | 29.50 | – | – | – |
| Croft, R.D.B.(Gm) | 1992 | 24 | 34 | 10 | 60* | 650 | 27.08 | – | 3 | 10 |
| Curran, K.M.(Nh) | 1992 | 21 | 30 | 1 | 82 | 730 | 25.17 | – | 5 | 10 |
| Curtis, T.S.(Wo) | 1984 | 23 | 41 | 5 | 228* | 1829 | 50.80 | 4 | 7 | 15 |
| Dale, A.(Gm) | 1992 | 22 | 33 | 5 | 150* | 1159 | 41.39 | 2 | 7 | 8 |
| Daley, J.A.(Du) | 1992 | 2 | 4 | 1 | 88 | 190 | 63.33 | – | 2 | 2 |
| Das, S.S.K.(CU) | — | 3 | 5 | 1 | 24* | 38 | 9.50 | – | – | 1 |
| †Davies, H.R.(OU) | — | 6 | 7 | 1 | 39 | 62 | 10.33 | – | – | – |
| Davies, M.(Gs) | — | 19 | 23 | 10 | 32* | 148 | 11.38 | – | – | 10 |
| Davis, R.P.(K) | 1990 | 18 | 24 | 11 | 54* | 312 | 24.00 | – | 1 | 11 |
| Dawson, R.I.(Gs) | — | 6 | 8 | – | 29 | 88 | 11.00 | – | – | 2 |
| DeFreitas, P.A.J.(La/E) | 1989 | 13 | 14 | 1 | 72 | 325 | 25.00 | – | 3 | 1 |
| Dessaur, W.A.(Nt) | — | 2 | 3 | – | 148 | 164 | 54.66 | 1 | – | 1 |
| †Dilley, G.R.(Wo) | 1987 | 2 | 3 | 1 | 39 | 61 | 30.50 | – | – | – |
| Dobson, M.C.(K) | — | 1 | 1 | 1 | 5* | 5 | – | – | – | 1 |
| D'Oliveira, D.B.(Wo) | 1985 | 13 | 19 | 1 | 100 | 535 | 29.72 | 1 | 2 | 13 |
| Donald, A.A.(Wa) | 1989 | 21 | 22 | 10 | 41 | 234 | 19.50 | – | – | 14 |
| Donelan, B.T.P.(Sx) | — | 16 | 25 | 6 | 68* | 421 | 22.15 | – | 2 | 2 |
| Dunlop, A.R.(Ire) | — | 1 | 2 | – | 37 | 52 | 26.00 | – | – | – |
| Ealham, M.A.(K) | 1992 | 17 | 27 | 5 | 67* | 452 | 20.54 | – | 4 | 4 |
| Edmonds, P.H.(M) | 1974 | 1 | | | | | | – | – | – |
| †Ellison, R.M.(K) | 1983 | 19 | 22 | 8 | 64 | 323 | 23.07 | – | 1 | 13 |
| Emburey, J.E.(M) | 1977 | 23 | 27 | 6 | 102 | 554 | 26.38 | 1 | 3 | 21 |
| Evans, K.P.(Nt) | 1990 | 19 | 24 | 4 | 104 | 438 | 21.90 | 1 | 2 | 12 |
| †Everett, J.(Sc) | — | 1 | 2 | – | 33 | 53 | 26.50 | – | – | 3 |
| †Fairbrother, N.H.(La) | 1985 | 12 | 18 | 7 | 166* | 689 | 62.63 | 1 | 5 | 8 |
| Farbrace, P.(M) | — | 2 | 1 | 1 | 51* | 51 | – | – | 1 | 5 |
| Feltham, M.A.(Sy) | 1990 | 13 | 19 | 6 | 50 | 437 | 33.61 | – | 1 | 3 |
| Felton, N.A.(Nh) | 1990 | 22 | 37 | 3 | 103 | 1076 | 31.64 | 1 | 9 | 18 |
| Field-Buss, M.G.(Nt) | — | 8 | 7 | 2 | 13 | 27 | 5.40 | – | – | 5 |
| †Fitton, J.D.(La) | — | 8 | 9 | 2 | 48* | 136 | 19.42 | – | – | 1 |
| Fleming, M.V.(K) | 1990 | 21 | 32 | 2 | 100* | 797 | 26.56 | 1 | 4 | 13 |
| Fletcher, S.D.(Y) | 1988 | 6 | 5 | 1 | 23 | 62 | 15.50 | – | – | 2 |
| †Folland, N.A.(Sm) | — | 1 | 2 | 1 | 82* | 104 | 104.00 | – | 1 | 1 |
| Fordham, A.(Nh) | 1990 | 23 | 41 | 2 | 192 | 1710 | 43.84 | 4 | 7 | 14 |
| Foster, D.J.(Gm) | — | 8 | 4 | 1 | 17* | 40 | 13.33 | – | – | 1 |
| Foster, N.A.(Ex) | 1983 | 11 | 14 | – | 54 | 326 | 23.28 | – | 2 | 12 |
| Fothergill, A.R.(Du) | 1992 | 6 | 8 | 1 | 23 | 71 | 10.14 | – | – | 10/1 |
| †Fowler, G.(La) | 1981 | 11 | 20 | 2 | 106 | 623 | 34.61 | 1 | 4 | 7 |
| Fraser, A.G.J.(Ex) | — | 2 | 3 | 1 | 5 | 11 | 5.50 | – | – | 1 |
| Fraser, A.R.C.(M) | 1988 | 18 | 20 | 7 | 33 | 218 | 16.76 | – | – | 3 |
| French, B.N.(Nt) | 1980 | 17 | 20 | 4 | 55 | 260 | 16.25 | – | 1 | 41/4 |
| Frost, M.(Gm) | 1991 | 8 | 5 | 2 | 4 | 4 | 1.33 | – | – | 2 |
| Fulton, D.P.(K) | — | 1 | 2 | – | 42 | 58 | 29.00 | – | – | 2 |
| Gallian, J.E.R.(OU/Us) | — | 9 | 15 | – | 112 | 468 | 31.20 | 1 | 3 | 6 |
| Garnham, M.A.(Ex) | 1990 | 24 | 28 | 4 | 82* | 569 | 23.70 | – | 4 | 41/3 |
| Gatting, M.W.(M) | 1977 | 24 | 36 | 6 | 170 | 2000 | 66.66 | 6 | 10 | 16 |
| Gerrard, M.J.(Gs) | — | 4 | 4 | 1 | 4 | 6 | 2.00 | – | – | 1 |
| Giddins, E.S.H.(Sx) | — | 11 | 8 | 6 | 10* | 15 | 7.50 | – | – | 4 |
| †Gidley, M.I.(Le) | — | 5 | 10 | 2 | 39 | 143 | 17.87 | – | – | 2 |
| Glendenen, J.D.(Du) | 1992 | 17 | 28 | 1 | 117 | 607 | 22.48 | 1 | 3 | 5 |
| Gofton, R.P.(Le) | — | 5 | 8 | 1 | 75 | 142 | 20.28 | – | 1 | 2 |
| Goldsmith, S.C.(De) | — | 10 | 11 | 3 | 100* | 273 | 34.12 | 1 | 1 | 3 |
| Gooch, G.A.(Ex/E) | 1975 | 18 | 29 | 3 | 160 | 1850 | 71.15 | 8 | 7 | 19 |
| Gough, D.(Y) | — | 11 | 12 | 4 | 22* | 72 | 9.00 | – | – | 3 |

166

| | Cap | M | I | NO | HS | Runs | Avge | 100 | 50 | Ct/St |
|---|---|---|---|---|---|---|---|---|---|---|
| Govan, J.W.(Sc) | — | 1 | 1 | — | 6 | 6 | 6.00 | — | — | 1 |
| †Gower, D.I.(H/E) | 1990 | 20 | 33 | 7 | 155 | 1225 | 47.11 | 1 | 8 | 14 |
| Graham, S.(Ire) | — | 1 | 2 | — | 35 | 62 | 31.00 | — | — | 1 |
| Graveney, D.A.(Du) | 1992 | 21 | 29 | 9 | 36 | 333 | 16.65 | — | — | 13 |
| Grayson, A.P.(Y) | — | 6 | 6 | — | 57 | 116 | 19.33 | — | 1 | 3 |
| †Greatbatch, M.J.(W) | — | 1 | 1 | — | 45 | 45 | 45.00 | — | — | 1 |
| Greenfield, K.(Sx) | — | 6 | 10 | 2 | 48 | 205 | 25.62 | — | — | 5 |
| Greenidge, C.G.(W) | — | 1 | 1 | — | 24 | 24 | 24.00 | — | — | — |
| Griffith, F.A.(De) | — | 7 | 10 | 3 | 81 | 248 | 35.42 | — | 1 | 6 |
| Gupte, C.M.(OU) | — | 5 | 6 | 1 | 11 | 36 | 7.20 | — | — | 1 |
| Habib, A.(M) | — | 1 | 2 | 1 | 12 | 19 | 19.00 | — | — | — |
| Hall, J.W.(Sx) | 1992 | 20 | 34 | 5 | 140* | 1125 | 38.79 | 1 | 8 | 7 |
| Hancock, T.H.C.(Gs) | — | 10 | 17 | 1 | 102 | 436 | 27.25 | 1 | 2 | 8 |
| Hanley, R.(Sx) | — | 1 | 1 | — | 1 | 1 | 1.00 | — | — | — |
| Hansford, A.R.(Sx) | — | 1 | 1 | — | 1 | 1 | 1.00 | — | — | 1 |
| Harden, R.J.(Sm) | 1989 | 20 | 33 | 5 | 187 | 1387 | 49.53 | 3 | 6 | 13 |
| Harper, R.A.(W) | — | 1 | 1 | — | 11 | 11 | 11.00 | — | — | 1 |
| Hartley, P.J.(Y) | 1987 | 20 | 23 | 3 | 69 | 353 | 17.65 | — | 2 | 6 |
| †Hawkes, C.J.(Le) | — | 3 | 4 | 1 | 18 | 60 | 20.00 | — | — | 1 |
| Hayhurst, A.N.(Sm) | 1990 | 23 | 38 | 2 | 102 | 1197 | 33.25 | 1 | 9 | 6 |
| Haynes, D.L.(M) | 1989 | 20 | 35 | 2 | 177 | 1513 | 45.84 | 3 | 10 | 8 |
| Haynes, G.R.(Wo) | — | 9 | 13 | 2 | 66 | 288 | 26.18 | — | 2 | 3 |
| Headley, D.W.(M) | — | 17 | 14 | 3 | 91 | 270 | 24.54 | — | 1 | 5 |
| Hegg, W.K.(La) | 1989 | 18 | 24 | 7 | 80 | 618 | 36.35 | — | 4 | 33/6 |
| Hemmings, E.E.(Nt) | 1980 | 7 | 11 | 5 | 52* | 132 | 22.00 | — | 1 | 2 |
| †Hemp, D.L.(Gm) | — | 12 | 17 | 2 | 84* | 326 | 21.73 | — | 2 | 8 |
| Henderson, P.W.(Du) | 1992 | 5 | 7 | — | 46 | 119 | 17.00 | — | — | 1 |
| Hepworth, P.N.(Le) | — | 10 | 15 | 1 | 38 | 173 | 12.35 | — | — | 5 |
| Hick, G.A.(Wo/E) | 1986 | 17 | 27 | 1 | 213* | 1337 | 53.48 | 4 | 5 | 32 |
| Hindson, J.E.(Nt) | — | 1 | — | — | — | — | — | — | — | — |
| †Hinks, S.G.(Gs) | — | 10 | 16 | 3 | 88* | 402 | 30.92 | — | 3 | 3 |
| Hodgson, G.D.(Gs) | 1992 | 21 | 36 | 1 | 147 | 1224 | 34.97 | 2 | 8 | 10 |
| Hoey, C.J.(Ire) | — | 1 | 2 | — | 8 | 15 | 7.50 | — | — | — |
| †Holloway, P.C.L.(Wa) | — | 2 | 3 | 1 | 102* | 133 | 66.50 | 1 | — | 8 |
| Hooper, A.M.(CU/Us) | — | 10 | 19 | 1 | 48 | 268 | 14.88 | — | — | 1 |
| Hooper, C.L.(K) | 1992 | 21 | 32 | 4 | 131 | 1329 | 47.46 | 5 | 7 | 25 |
| Hughes, S.P.(Du) | 1992 | 20 | 25 | 5 | 42 | 229 | 11.45 | — | — | 6 |
| Hussain, N.(Ex) | 1989 | 20 | 26 | 3 | 172* | 866 | 37.65 | 1 | 5 | 24 |
| †Hutton, S.(Du) | 1992 | 8 | 15 | — | 78 | 406 | 27.06 | — | 2 | 3 |
| Igglesden, A.P.(K) | 1989 | 16 | 13 | 5 | 16 | 67 | 8.37 | — | — | 5 |
| Ijaz Ahmed (P) | — | 1 | 2 | — | 36 | 67 | 33.50 | — | — | 1 |
| Illingworth, R.K.(Wo) | 1986 | 20 | 20 | 6 | 43 | 294 | 21.00 | — | — | 8 |
| †Ilott, M.C.(Ex) | — | 23 | 22 | 4 | 28 | 164 | 9.11 | — | — | 7 |
| Inzamam-ul-Haq (P) | — | 15 | 21 | 7 | 200* | 736 | 52.57 | 1 | 5 | 21 |
| Irani, R.C.(La) | — | 5 | 6 | — | 22 | 68 | 11.33 | — | — | 4 |
| †James, K.D.(H) | 1989 | 23 | 37 | 2 | 116 | 1149 | 32.82 | 1 | 8 | 10 |
| James, S.P.(Gm) | 1992 | 24 | 39 | 4 | 152* | 1376 | 39.31 | 3 | 6 | 20 |
| Jarrett, M.E.D.(CU) | — | 9 | 13 | 2 | 27 | 106 | 9.63 | — | — | 2 |
| Jarvis, P.W.(Y) | 1986 | 15 | 14 | 4 | 80 | 374 | 37.40 | — | 3 | 2 |
| Javed Miandad (P) | — | 12 | 17 | 3 | 153* | 809 | 57.78 | 2 | 4 | 8 |
| Jean-Jacques, M.(De) | — | 2 | 2 | — | 6 | 6 | 3.00 | — | — | 2 |
| Jeh, M.P.W.(OU/Us) | — | 9 | 11 | 2 | 23 | 81 | 9.00 | — | — | 3 |
| Jenkins, R.H.J.(CU) | — | 2 | 1 | — | 1 | 1 | 1.00 | — | — | 1 |
| Johnson, P.(Nt/EA) | 1986 | 19 | 29 | 4 | 107* | 1147 | 45.88 | 2 | 10 | 10 |
| Johnson, R.L.(M) | — | 1 | 1 | — | 1 | 1 | 1.00 | — | — | 1 |
| Johnson, S.W.(CU) | — | 9 | 13 | 2 | 50 | 201 | 18.27 | — | 1 | 4 |

| | Cap | M | I | NO | HS | Runs | Avge | 100 | 50 | Ct/St |
|---|---|---|---|---|---|---|---|---|---|---|
| †Jones, A.N.(Sx) | 1986 | 10 | 9 | 4 | 17 | 56 | 11.20 | – | – | 1 |
| Jones, D.M.(Du) | 1992 | 14 | 23 | 7 | 157 | 1179 | 73.68 | 4 | 5 | 12 |
| †Jones, G.W.(CU) | – | 6 | 12 | – | 44 | 249 | 20.75 | – | – | 1 |
| Keey, C.L.(OU/Us) | – | 8 | 13 | 1 | 64 | 308 | 25.66 | – | 3 | 1 |
| Kellett, S.A.(Y) | 1992 | 22 | 36 | 1 | 96 | 1326 | 37.88 | – | 9 | 23 |
| Kemp, T.R.(CU) | – | 2 | 1 | – | 0 | 0 | 0.00 | – | – | 1 |
| Kendrick, N.M.(Sy) | – | 17 | 21 | 5 | 55 | 306 | 19.12 | – | 2 | 16 |
| Kersey, G.J.(K) | – | 2 | 2 | 1 | 22 | 42 | 42.00 | – | – | 7/1 |
| Kirnon, S.(Gm) | – | 1 | – | – | – | – | – | – | – | – |
| †Knight, N.V.(Ex) | – | 20 | 30 | 6 | 109 | 774 | 32.25 | 2 | 3 | 17 |
| Krikken, K.M.(De) | 1992 | 23 | 27 | 3 | 57* | 383 | 15.95 | – | 2 | 52/5 |
| Lamb, A.J.(Nh/E) | 1978 | 18 | 28 | 4 | 209 | 1460 | 60.83 | 6 | 5 | 12 |
| Lampitt, S.R.(Wo) | 1989 | 19 | 29 | 5 | 71* | 565 | 23.54 | – | 4 | 6 |
| Larkins, W.(Du) | 1992 | 22 | 41 | – | 143 | 1536 | 37.46 | 4 | 8 | 16 |
| Lathwell, M.N.(Sm) | 1992 | 19 | 33 | 1 | 114 | 1176 | 36.75 | 1 | 11 | 14 |
| Leatherdale, D.A.(Wo) | – | 23 | 40 | 4 | 112 | 983 | 27.30 | 1 | 5 | 16 |
| Lefebvre, R.P.(Sm) | 1991 | 3 | 4 | – | 36 | 70 | 17.50 | – | – | 3 |
| Lenham, N.J.(Sx) | 1990 | 20 | 34 | 2 | 222* | 1173 | 36.65 | 4 | 3 | 9 |
| Lewis, C.C.(Nt/E) | – | 17 | 26 | 4 | 134* | 836 | 38.00 | 2 | 5 | 13 |
| Lewis, D.A.(Ire) | – | 1 | 2 | 1 | 122* | 126 | 126.00 | 1 | – | – |
| Lewis, J.J.B.(Ex) | – | 13 | 20 | 4 | 133 | 746 | 46.62 | 1 | 7 | 3 |
| Ligertwood, D.G.C.(Sy) | – | 4 | 7 | – | 28 | 63 | 9.00 | – | – | 7/1 |
| †Llong, N.J.(K) | – | 4 | 5 | – | 92 | 137 | 27.40 | – | 1 | 4 |
| Lloyd, G.D.(La) | 1992 | 23 | 37 | 10 | 132 | 1389 | 51.44 | 4 | 10 | 21 |
| †Lloyd, T.A.(Wa) | 1980 | 23 | 39 | 2 | 84* | 919 | 24.83 | – | 5 | 5 |
| Longley, J.I.(K) | – | 3 | 4 | – | 110 | 169 | 42.25 | 1 | – | 4 |
| Lovell, G.B.T.(OU/Us) | – | 9 | 13 | 1 | 110* | 422 | 35.16 | 1 | 2 | 8 |
| Loye, M.B.(Nh) | – | 10 | 14 | 1 | 46 | 195 | 15.00 | – | – | 7 |
| Lynch, M.A.(Sy) | 1982 | 23 | 40 | 6 | 107 | 1465 | 43.08 | 3 | 8 | 24 |
| McBrine, A.(Ire) | – | 1 | 2 | – | 9 | 9 | 4.50 | – | – | – |
| McCague, M.J.(K) | 1992 | 16 | 18 | 5 | 25* | 120 | 9.23 | – | – | 12 |
| McCrum, C.(Ire) | – | 1 | 2 | – | 70 | 109 | 54.50 | – | 1 | – |
| McCrum, P.(Ire) | – | 1 | 2 | 1 | 0* | 0 | 0.00 | – | – | – |
| MacDonald, R.H.(OU) | – | 3 | 3 | 1 | 8* | 13 | 6.50 | – | – | – |
| McEwan, S.M.(Du) | 1992 | 10 | 13 | 1 | 22 | 59 | 4.91 | – | – | 7 |
| MacLeay, K.H.(Sm) | – | 12 | 19 | 3 | 74 | 427 | 26.68 | – | 3 | 7 |
| Malcolm, D.E.(De/EA/E) | 1989 | 19 | 19 | 4 | 26 | 150 | 10.00 | – | – | 6 |
| †Malik, H.S.(OU) | – | 1 | 1 | – | 4 | 4 | 4.00 | – | – | – |
| Mallender, N.A.(Sm/E) | 1987 | 17 | 21 | 5 | 29* | 190 | 11.87 | – | – | 3 |
| Marsh, S.A.(K) | 1986 | 22 | 30 | 4 | 125 | 896 | 34.46 | 1 | 6 | 44/8 |
| Marshall, M.D.(H) | 1981 | 19 | 25 | 5 | 70 | 513 | 25.65 | – | 2 | 11 |
| Martin, P.J.(La) | – | 22 | 24 | 6 | 133 | 492 | 27.33 | 1 | 2 | 4 |
| †Maru, R.J.(H) | 1986 | 8 | 11 | 3 | 27 | 119 | 14.87 | – | – | 9 |
| Maynard, M.P.(Gm) | 1987 | 23 | 36 | 4 | 176 | 1219 | 38.09 | 2 | 7 | 19 |
| Mendis, G.D.(La) | 1986 | 8 | 8 | 1 | 45 | 145 | 20.71 | – | – | – |
| Metcalfe, A.A.(Y) | 1986 | 11 | 17 | 1 | 73 | 422 | 26.37 | – | 1 | 4 |
| Metson, C.P.(Gm) | 1987 | 23 | 28 | 6 | 46* | 437 | 19.86 | – | – | 49/5 |
| Middleton, T.C.(H) | 1990 | 24 | 40 | 4 | 221 | 1780 | 49.44 | 6 | 7 | 16 |
| Mike, G.W.(Nt) | – | 5 | 6 | 2 | 61* | 130 | 32.50 | – | 1 | 2 |
| Milburn, S.M.(Y) | – | 1 | 2 | 1 | 5 | 7 | 7.00 | – | – | – |
| †Millns, D.J.(Le) | 1991 | 19 | 19 | 9 | 33* | 144 | 14.40 | – | – | 12 |
| Moin Khan (P) | – | 13 | 14 | 4 | 53 | 237 | 23.70 | – | 1 | 28/1 |
| Moles, A.J.(Wa) | 1987 | 23 | 41 | 3 | 122 | 1359 | 35.76 | 1 | 12 | 18 |
| Montgomerie, R.R.(OU/Us) | – | 9 | 15 | 3 | 103* | 477 | 39.75 | 1 | 1 | 3 |
| Moody, T.M.(Wo) | 1991 | 11 | 19 | 2 | 178 | 724 | 42.58 | 4 | 1 | 13 |
| Moore, P.D.(Ire) | – | 1 | 1 | 1 | 0* | 0 | – | – | – | 2 |

168

| Name | Cap | M | I | NO | HS | Runs | Avge | 100 | 50 | Ct/St |
|---|---|---|---|---|---|---|---|---|---|---|
| Moores, P.(Sx) | 1989 | 21 | 30 | 5 | 109 | 851 | 34.04 | 1 | 3 | 32/7 |
| †Morris, H.(Gm/EA) | 1986 | 23 | 37 | 3 | 146 | 1597 | 46.97 | 6 | 6 | 16 |
| Morris, J.E.(De) | 1986 | 23 | 33 | – | 120 | 1358 | 41.15 | 3 | 12 | 6 |
| Morris, R.S.M.(H) | – | 5 | 9 | 1 | 74 | 209 | 26.12 | – | 2 | 5 |
| Morrison, D.K.(La) | – | 14 | 12 | 1 | 30 | 113 | 10.27 | – | – | 4 |
| Mortensen, O.H.(De) | 1986 | 15 | 13 | 10 | 13* | 47 | 15.66 | – | – | 3 |
| Moxon, M.D.(Y/EA) | 1984 | 19 | 28 | 2 | 183 | 1385 | 53.26 | 5 | 5 | 9 |
| Mudassar Nazar (W) | – | 1 | – | – | – | – | – | – | – | 1 |
| Mullally, A.D.(Le) | – | 19 | 23 | 6 | 21 | 118 | 6.94 | – | – | 4 |
| Munton, T.A.(Wa/EA/E) | 1989 | 19 | 19 | 7 | 47 | 148 | 12.33 | – | – | 7 |
| Murphy, A.J.(Sy) | – | 5 | 5 | 2 | 32 | 45 | 15.00 | – | – | 4 |
| Mushtaq Ahmed (P) | – | 17 | 12 | 3 | 12 | 73 | 8.11 | – | – | 6 |
| Naved Anjum (P) | – | 5 | 6 | 2 | 56 | 77 | 19.25 | – | 1 | 1 |
| Neale, P.A.(Wo) | 1978 | 2 | 3 | – | 38 | 79 | 26.33 | – | – | – |
| Newell, M.(Nt) | 1987 | 2 | 3 | 2 | 48* | 75 | 75.00 | – | – | 3 |
| Newport, P.J.(Wo) | 1986 | 22 | 25 | 6 | 75* | 467 | 24.57 | – | 3 | 5 |
| Nicholas, M.C.J.(H) | 1982 | 21 | 32 | 5 | 95* | 1003 | 37.14 | – | 6 | 9 |
| †Nixon, P.A.(Le) | – | 16 | 25 | 7 | 107* | 529 | 29.38 | 1 | 1 | 40/5 |
| Noon, W.M.(Nh) | – | 1 | – | – | – | – | – | – | – | 2 |
| North, J.A.(Sx) | – | 5 | 7 | 1 | 53* | 81 | 13.50 | – | 1 | – |
| O'Gorman, T.J.G.(De) | 1992 | 24 | 37 | 8 | 95 | 1031 | 35.55 | – | 8 | 11 |
| Oliphant-Callum, R.D.(OU) | – | 3 | 2 | – | 19 | 28 | 14.00 | – | – | 1 |
| Orr, D.A.(Sc) | – | 1 | 1 | 1 | 23* | 23 | – | – | – | 1/1 |
| Ostler, D.P.(Wa) | 1991 | 22 | 37 | 2 | 192 | 1225 | 35.00 | 3 | 4 | 20 |
| Parker, B.(Y) | – | 1 | 2 | – | 30 | 37 | 18.50 | – | – | 1 |
| Parker, P.W.G.(Du) | 1992 | 20 | 35 | 2 | 124 | 1331 | 40.33 | 3 | 8 | 16 |
| Parks, R.J.(H) | 1982 | 7 | 10 | 3 | 33 | 169 | 24.14 | – | – | 21/2 |
| Parore, A.C.(W) | – | 1 | 1 | 1 | 2* | 2 | – | – | – | –/1 |
| †Parsons, G.J.(Le) | 1984 | 14 | 14 | 2 | 35 | 142 | 11.83 | – | – | 6 |
| Parsons, K.A.(Sm) | – | 1 | 2 | – | 1 | 1 | 0.50 | – | – | – |
| Patel, D.N.(W) | – | 1 | 1 | – | 72 | 72 | 72.00 | – | 1 | – |
| Patterson, B.M.W.(Sc) | – | 1 | 2 | – | 55 | 89 | 44.50 | – | 1 | – |
| †Patterson, T.J.T.(Ire) | – | 1 | 2 | – | 28 | 28 | 14.00 | – | – | 1 |
| Payne, A.(Sm) | – | 1 | 1 | 1 | 51* | 51 | – | – | 1 | – |
| Pearson, R.M.(CU/Us/Nh) | – | 11 | 13 | 5 | 33* | 96 | 12.00 | – | – | 4 |
| †Penberthy, A.L.(Nh) | – | 10 | 14 | 1 | 33 | 164 | 12.61 | – | – | 6 |
| †Penn, C.(K) | 1987 | 5 | 7 | 2 | 14* | 26 | 8.66 | – | – | 3 |
| Pennett, D.B.(Nt) | – | 12 | 11 | 1 | 29 | 69 | 6.90 | – | – | 3 |
| Penney, T.L.(Wa) | – | 16 | 24 | 7 | 151 | 904 | 53.17 | 3 | 4 | 5 |
| Philip, I.L.(Sc) | – | 1 | 2 | – | 79 | 107 | 53.50 | – | 1 | 2 |
| †Pick, R.A.(Nt) | 1987 | 10 | 12 | 4 | 52 | 145 | 18.12 | – | 1 | 1 |
| Pickles, C.S.(Y) | – | 6 | 9 | 1 | 49 | 131 | 16.37 | – | – | 2 |
| Pigott, A.C.S.(Sx) | 1982 | 17 | 19 | 7 | 27* | 191 | 15.91 | – | – | 5 |
| Piper, K.J.(Wa) | 1992 | 19 | 25 | 8 | 72 | 345 | 20.29 | – | 2 | 41/2 |
| Pitcher, C.M.(CU) | – | 6 | 8 | 3 | 32* | 62 | 12.40 | – | – | – |
| †Pollard, P.R.(Nt) | 1992 | 19 | 33 | 3 | 75 | 900 | 30.00 | – | 5 | 20 |
| †Pooley, J.C.(M) | – | 3 | 6 | 2 | 69 | 186 | 46.50 | – | 2 | – |
| Potter, L.(Le) | 1988 | 23 | 36 | 4 | 96 | 834 | 26.06 | – | 4 | 10 |
| Prichard, P.J.(Ex) | 1986 | 23 | 38 | 4 | 136 | 1485 | 43.67 | 4 | 9 | 18 |
| Pringle, C.(W) | – | 1 | 1 | – | 0 | 0 | 0.00 | – | – | – |
| Pringle, D.R.(Ex/E) | 1982 | 16 | 17 | 5 | 112* | 509 | 42.41 | 2 | 2 | 4 |
| Radford, N.V.(Wo) | 1985 | 22 | 19 | 7 | 73* | 261 | 21.75 | – | 2 | 4 |
| Ramiz Raja (P) | – | 16 | 26 | 2 | 172 | 1036 | 43.16 | 2 | 6 | 3 |
| Ramprakash, M.R.(M/EA/E) | 1990 | 20 | 33 | 3 | 233 | 1199 | 39.96 | 3 | 5 | 8 |
| Randall, D.W.(Nt) | 1973 | 19 | 29 | 3 | 133* | 882 | 33.92 | 1 | 5 | 11 |
| Rashid Latif (P) | – | 8 | 8 | 2 | 50 | 136 | 22.66 | – | 1 | 27/2 |

169

| | Cap | M | I | NO | HS | Runs | Avge | 100 | 50 | Ct/St |
|---|---|---|---|---|---|---|---|---|---|---|
| Ratcliffe, J.D.(Wa) | — | 7 | 14 | – | 50 | 272 | 19.42 | – | 1 | 3 |
| Rea, M.P.(Ire) | — | 1 | 2 | – | 89 | 115 | 57.50 | – | 1 | 1 |
| Reeve, D.A.(Wa) | 1989 | 17 | 28 | 4 | 79 | 833 | 34.70 | – | 7 | 15 |
| Remy, C.C.(Sx) | — | 7 | 9 | – | 47 | 192 | 21.33 | – | – | 1 |
| Rhodes, S.J.(Wo/EA) | 1986 | 24 | 34 | 11 | 116* | 815 | 35.43 | 2 | 2 | 47/1 |
| Richards, I.V.A.(Gm) | 1990 | 14 | 23 | – | 127 | 722 | 31.39 | 1 | 4 | 18 |
| Richardson, A.W.(De) | — | 1 | 1 | – | 5 | 5 | 5.00 | – | – | – |
| Richardson, M.S.(Sc) | — | 1 | – | – | – | – | – | – | – | 1 |
| Richardson, R.B.(W) | — | 1 | 1 | – | 5 | 5 | 5.00 | – | – | – |
| Ripley, D.(Nh) | 1987 | 22 | 31 | 10 | 107* | 891 | 42.42 | 2 | 4 | 66/5 |
| Roberts, A.R.(Nh) | — | 14 | 19 | 3 | 62 | 304 | 19.00 | – | 1 | 5 |
| †Robinson, J.D.(Sy) | — | 9 | 17 | 5 | 65* | 307 | 25.58 | – | 2 | 8 |
| Robinson, M.A.(Y) | 1992 | 17 | 12 | 5 | 12 | 31 | 4.42 | – | – | 4 |
| Robinson, P.E.(Le) | — | 1 | 2 | – | 19 | 19 | 9.50 | – | – | – |
| Robinson, R.T.(Nt) | 1983 | 19 | 33 | 5 | 189 | 1547 | 55.25 | 4 | 8 | 13 |
| Robson, A.G.(Sx) | — | 5 | 4 | 3 | 0* | 0 | 0.00 | – | – | 1 |
| Rollins, R.J.(Ex) | — | 1 | 2 | – | 13 | 19 | 9.50 | – | – | 2 |
| Rose, G.D.(Sm) | 1988 | 22 | 34 | 4 | 132 | 930 | 31.00 | 1 | 6 | 11 |
| Roseberry, A.(Le) | — | 1 | 2 | – | 14 | 14 | 7.00 | – | – | 1 |
| Roseberry, M.A.(M) | 1990 | 25 | 41 | 3 | 173 | 2044 | 56.77 | 9 | 8 | 14 |
| Russell, A.B.(Sc) | — | 1 | 2 | 1 | 33 | 62 | 62.00 | – | – | 5 |
| †Russell, R.C.(Gs/E) | 1985 | 20 | 34 | 11 | 75 | 985 | 42.82 | – | 5 | 40/3 |
| Salim Jaffer (P) | — | 4 | 1 | 1 | 1* | 1 | – | – | – | 1 |
| Salim Malik (P) | — | 15 | 21 | 6 | 165 | 1184 | 78.93 | 2 | 8 | 4 |
| Salisbury, I.D.K.(Sx/EA/E) | 1991 | 20 | 22 | 3 | 50 | 279 | 14.68 | – | 1 | 15 |
| †Salmond, G.(Sc) | — | 1 | 2 | – | 118 | 213 | 106.50 | 1 | 1 | 1 |
| Sandiford, D.C.(OU) | — | 1 | 2 | – | 20 | 21 | 10.50 | – | – | – |
| Sargeant, N.F.(Sy) | — | 14 | 19 | 4 | 30 | 176 | 11.73 | – | – | 35/6 |
| †Saxelby, M.(Nt) | — | 8 | 13 | 1 | 73 | 462 | 38.50 | – | 5 | 1 |
| Scott, C.W.(Du) | 1992 | 18 | 24 | 5 | 57* | 433 | 22.78 | – | 2 | 27/2 |
| †Scott, R.J.(Gs) | — | 19 | 31 | 3 | 73 | 751 | 26.82 | – | 4 | 7 |
| †Seymour, A.C.H.(Wo) | — | 11 | 21 | – | 133 | 556 | 26.47 | 1 | 1 | 9 |
| Shahid, N.(Ex) | — | 15 | 21 | 1 | 132 | 561 | 28.05 | 1 | 3 | 8 |
| Sheridan, K.L.P.(Sc) | — | 1 | – | – | – | – | – | – | – | – |
| Shine, K.J.(H) | — | 16 | 12 | 6 | 22* | 59 | 9.83 | – | – | – |
| Shoaib Mohammad (P) | — | 12 | 21 | 4 | 105* | 761 | 44.76 | 1 | 7 | 2 |
| Simmons, P.V.(W) | — | 1 | 1 | – | 23 | 23 | 23.00 | – | – | 1 |
| †Sims, R.J.(M) | — | 1 | 1 | – | 3 | 3 | 3.00 | – | – | – |
| Sladdin, R.W.(De) | — | 13 | 16 | 2 | 39 | 131 | 9.35 | – | – | 6 |
| Sleep, P.R.(W) | — | 1 | – | 182 | 182 | 182.00 | 1 | – | – | |
| Small, G.C.(Wa) | 1982 | 17 | 17 | 6 | 31* | 181 | 16.45 | – | – | 6 |
| Smith, A.M.(Gs) | — | 12 | 14 | 5 | 51* | 169 | 18.77 | – | 1 | 3 |
| Smith, B.F.(Le) | — | 15 | 20 | 3 | 100* | 441 | 25.94 | 1 | 3 | 9 |
| †Smith, D.M.(Sx) | 1989 | 19 | 33 | 2 | 213 | 1076 | 34.70 | 2 | 5 | 12 |
| Smith, I.(Du) | 1992 | 12 | 16 | 1 | 110 | 435 | 29.00 | 1 | 3 | 6 |
| Smith, N.M.K.(Wa) | — | 12 | 20 | 2 | 67 | 454 | 25.22 | – | 1 | 5 |
| Smith, P.A.(Wa) | 1986 | 19 | 27 | 5 | 45 | 416 | 18.90 | – | – | 6 |
| Smith, R.A.(H/E) | 1985 | 17 | 28 | 3 | 127 | 950 | 38.00 | 2 | 5 | 12 |
| Snape, J.N.(Nh) | — | 1 | – | – | – | – | – | – | – | 1 |
| Snell, R.P.(Sm) | — | 16 | 20 | 4 | 81 | 436 | 27.25 | – | 3 | 6 |
| Speak, N.J.(La) | 1992 | 22 | 36 | 3 | 232 | 1892 | 57.33 | 4 | 12 | 18 |
| Speight, M.P.(Sx) | 1991 | 20 | 33 | 2 | 179 | 1180 | 38.06 | 5 | – | 16 |
| Stanley, N.A.(Nh) | — | 1 | 2 | 1 | 16 | 23 | 23.00 | – | – | – |
| Stanworth, J.(La) | 1989 | 5 | 2 | – | 21 | 30 | 15.00 | – | – | 7/1 |
| Stemp, R.D.(Wo) | — | 11 | 6 | 4 | 16* | 70 | 35.00 | – | – | 4 |
| Stephenson, F.D.(Sx) | 1992 | 18 | 25 | 4 | 133 | 680 | 32.38 | 1 | 2 | 10 |

| | Cap | M | I | NO | HS | Runs | Avge | 100 | 50 | Ct/St |
|---|---|---|---|---|---|---|---|---|---|---|
| Stephenson, J.P.(Ex) | 1989 | 21 | 37 | 5 | 159* | 1401 | 43.78 | 3 | 8 | 10 |
| Stewart, A.J.(Sy/E) | 1985 | 19 | 33 | 4 | 190 | 1234 | 42.55 | 2 | 8 | 22 |
| Storie, A.C.(OU) | — | 7 | 10 | 1 | 29 | 113 | 12.55 | – | – | 4 |
| Such, P.M.(Ex) | 1991 | 15 | 13 | 3 | 35* | 113 | 11.30 | – | – | 6 |
| Sylvester, S.A.(M) | — | 4 | 1 | 1 | 0* | 0 | – | – | – | 1 |
| Tanvir Mehdi (P) | — | 5 | 3 | 1 | 13* | 21 | 10.50 | – | – | 2 |
| Tavaré, C.J.(Sm) | 1989 | 21 | 32 | 2 | 125 | 1157 | 38.56 | 3 | 6 | 15 |
| †Taylor, C.W.(M) | — | 18 | 14 | 7 | 14 | 75 | 10.71 | – | – | 3 |
| †Taylor, J.P.(Nh) | 1992 | 23 | 19 | 8 | 74* | 188 | 17.09 | – | 1 | 9 |
| Taylor, N.R.(K) | 1982 | 21 | 35 | 7 | 144 | 1508 | 53.85 | 1 | 11 | 10 |
| Tendulkar, S.R.(Y) | 1992 | 16 | 25 | 2 | 100 | 1070 | 46.52 | 1 | 7 | 10 |
| Terry, V.P.(H) | 1983 | 11 | 17 | 2 | 141 | 766 | 51.06 | 3 | 3 | 7 |
| †Thomas, S.D.(Gm) | — | 6 | 7 | 2 | 10 | 25 | 5.00 | – | – | 1 |
| Thomson, K.(Sc) | — | 1 | – | – | – | – | – | – | – | – |
| †Thorpe, G.P.(Sy/EA) | 1991 | 24 | 41 | 4 | 216 | 1895 | 51.21 | 3 | 13 | 19 |
| Thursfield, M.J.(H) | — | 1 | – | – | – | – | – | – | – | – |
| Thwaites, G.E.(CU) | — | 1 | 1 | – | 0 | 0 | 0.00 | – | – | – |
| Titchard, S.P.(La) | — | 14 | 24 | 3 | 74 | 668 | 31.80 | – | 6 | 8 |
| Tolley, C.M.(Wo) | — | 13 | 10 | 4 | 27 | 89 | 14.83 | – | – | 7 |
| Topley, T.D.(Ex) | 1988 | 11 | 12 | 2 | 29 | 100 | 10.00 | – | – | 8 |
| Townsend, C.J.(OU) | — | 5 | 4 | 1 | 8 | 8 | 2.66 | – | – | 4 |
| Townsend, G.T.J.(Sm) | — | 7 | 13 | 1 | 49 | 272 | 22.66 | – | – | 4 |
| Trump, H.R.J.(Sm) | — | 18 | 18 | 7 | 28 | 154 | 14.00 | – | – | 14 |
| Tufnell, P.C.R.(M/E) | 1990 | 16 | 15 | 8 | 12 | 55 | 7.85 | – | – | 8 |
| Turner, I.J.(H) | — | 6 | 7 | 1 | 16 | 31 | 5.16 | – | – | 4 |
| Turner, R.J.(Sm) | — | 7 | 10 | 5 | 101* | 286 | 57.20 | 1 | 1 | 6 |
| Tutt, A.(K) | — | 1 | – | – | – | – | – | – | – | – |
| Tweats, T.A.(De) | — | 1 | 1 | – | 24 | 24 | 24.00 | – | – | 1 |
| †Twose, R.G.(Wa) | 1992 | 23 | 38 | 3 | 233 | 1412 | 40.34 | 1 | 10 | 17 |
| Udal, S.D.(H) | 1992 | 23 | 29 | 10 | 44 | 400 | 21.05 | – | – | 4 |
| Van Troost, A.P.(Sm) | — | 11 | 9 | 5 | 12 | 42 | 10.50 | – | – | 3 |
| †Vaughan, J.T.C.(Gs) | — | 11 | 18 | 4 | 99 | 473 | 33.78 | – | 4 | 11 |
| †Walker, A.(Nh) | 1987 | 1 | 1 | – | 39 | 39 | 39.00 | – | – | – |
| Walsh, C.A.(Gs) | 1985 | 18 | 27 | 3 | 51 | 280 | 11.66 | – | 1 | 7 |
| Waqar Younis (P) | — | 10 | 9 | 4 | 23* | 95 | 19.00 | – | – | 1 |
| Ward, D.M.(Sy) | 1990 | 18 | 30 | 6 | 138 | 879 | 36.62 | 3 | 1 | 3 |
| †Ward, I.J.(Sy) | — | 1 | 1 | – | 0 | 0 | 0.00 | – | – | 1 |
| Ward, T.R.(K) | 1989 | 21 | 37 | 3 | 153 | 1648 | 48.47 | 5 | 9 | 25 |
| Warke, S.J.S.(Ire) | — | 1 | 2 | – | 13 | 17 | 8.50 | – | – | 2 |
| Warley, S.N.(OU) | — | 7 | 10 | 2 | 35 | 117 | 14.62 | – | – | 2 |
| Warner, A.E.(De) | 1987 | 17 | 15 | 2 | 55 | 210 | 16.15 | – | 1 | 3 |
| Warren, R.J.(Nh) | — | 2 | 3 | 1 | 19 | 27 | 13.50 | – | – | – |
| †Wasim Akram (P) | — | 14 | 18 | 3 | 45* | 299 | 19.93 | – | – | 5 |
| Watkin, S.L.(Gm) | 1989 | 22 | 24 | 4 | 41 | 153 | 7.65 | – | – | 5 |
| Watkinson, M.(La) | 1987 | 20 | 25 | 1 | 96 | 482 | 20.08 | – | 1 | 10 |
| Waugh, M.E.(Ex) | 1989 | 16 | 24 | 7 | 219* | 1314 | 77.29 | 4 | 6 | 27 |
| Weekes, P.N.(M) | — | 17 | 21 | 7 | 95 | 539 | 38.50 | – | 3 | 15 |
| Wells, A.P.(Sx) | 1986 | 22 | 35 | 5 | 165* | 1465 | 48.83 | 5 | 4 | 24 |
| Wells, C.M.(Sx) | 1982 | 6 | 7 | 1 | 39 | 133 | 22.16 | – | – | 1 |
| Wells, V.J.(Le) | — | 17 | 23 | 6 | 56 | 526 | 30.94 | – | 3 | 2 |
| Weston, M.J.(Wo) | 1986 | 2 | 3 | 3 | 17* | 26 | – | – | – | 1 |
| †Weston, W.P.C.(Wo) | — | 14 | 23 | 5 | 66* | 675 | 37.50 | – | 5 | 2 |
| Whitaker, J.J.(Le) | 1986 | 22 | 34 | 3 | 74 | 830 | 26.77 | – | 2 | 13 |
| White, C.(Y) | — | 19 | 26 | 8 | 79* | 859 | 47.72 | – | 7 | 14 |
| Whitticase, P.(Le) | 1987 | 8 | 10 | 3 | 18* | 62 | 8.85 | – | – | 18/1 |
| †Whittington, J.M.S.(M) | — | 1 | – | – | – | – | – | – | – | – |

| | Cap | M | I | NO | HS | Runs | Avge | 100 | 50 | Ct/St |
|---|---|---|---|---|---|---|---|---|---|---|
| Wight, R.M.(CU/Us) | — | 10 | 17 | 3 | 62* | 388 | 27.71 | – | 2 | 3 |
| Wileman, J.R.(Nt) | — | 1 | 1 | – | 109 | 109 | 109.00 | 1 | – | 2 |
| Williams, N.F.(M) | 1984 | 17 | 17 | 3 | 46* | 186 | 13.28 | – | – | 9 |
| Williams, R.C.(Gs) | — | 7 | 11 | 1 | 44 | 117 | 11.70 | – | – | – |
| †Williams, R.C.J.(Gs) | — | 5 | 5 | 2 | 18* | 51 | 17.00 | – | – | 9/4 |
| Williams, R.G.(Nh) | 1979 | 2 | 3 | – | 14 | 29 | 9.66 | – | – | – |
| Windows, M.G.N.(Gs) | — | 1 | 1 | – | 71 | 71 | 71.00 | – | 1 | 1 |
| Wood, B.S.(OU/Us) | — | 4 | 4 | 1 | 13 | 29 | 9.66 | – | – | – |
| Wood, J.(Du) | 1992 | 8 | 6 | 1 | 28 | 80 | 16.00 | – | – | 1 |
| †Wood, J.R.(H) | — | 10 | 13 | 1 | 57 | 294 | 24.50 | – | 1 | 6 |
| Wren, T.N.(K) | — | 1 | – | – | – | – | – | – | – | 2 |
| Wright, A.J.(Gs) | 1987 | 19 | 33 | 3 | 128 | 772 | 25.73 | 1 | 3 | 11 |
| Zahid Fazal (P) | — | 6 | 8 | 3 | 51 | 115 | 23.00 | – | 1 | 7 |

## BOWLING

See BATTING and FIELDING section for details of caps and teams.

| | Cat | O | M | R | W | Avge | Best | 5 wI | 10 wM |
|---|---|---|---|---|---|---|---|---|---|
| Aamir Sohail | SLA | 103 | 29 | 251 | 9 | 27.88 | 3-31 | – | – |
| Abington, M.B. | SLA | 146.4 | 23 | 530 | 10 | 53.00 | 3-33 | – | – |
| Adams, C.J. | OB | 66 | 5 | 260 | 2 | 130.00 | 1-47 | – | – |
| Afford, J.A. | SLA | 509.1 | 128 | 1599 | 51 | 31.35 | 6-68 | 2 | 1 |
| Alleyne, M.W. | RM | 138.1 | 31 | 502 | 14 | 35.85 | 3-25 | – | – |
| Ambrose, C.E.L. | RF | 543.4 | 151 | 1307 | 50 | 26.14 | 4-53 | – | – |
| Anderson, D.J. | RM | 164.5 | 38 | 511 | 9 | 56.77 | 2-68 | – | – |
| Andrew, S.J.W. | RMF | 265 | 45 | 849 | 24 | 35.37 | 4-54 | – | – |
| Aqib Javed | RFM | 292 | 58 | 966 | 36 | 26.83 | 5-34 | 1 | – |
| Asif Mujtaba | SLA | 129.5 | 35 | 325 | 9 | 36.11 | 4-73 | – | – |
| Ata-ur-Rehman | RFM | 159.1 | 29 | 621 | 18 | 34.50 | 3-69 | – | – |
| Atherton, M.A. | LB | 74.1 | 9 | 343 | 4 | 85.75 | 2-109 | – | – |
| Athey, C.W.J. | RM | 58 | 7 | 184 | 2 | 92.00 | 1-16 | – | – |
| Austin, I.D. | RM | 164.5 | 41 | 522 | 12 | 43.50 | 3-44 | – | – |
| Ayling, J.R. | RM | 356.2 | 78 | 989 | 48 | 20.60 | 5-12 | 1 | – |
| Aymes, A.N. | (WK) | 7 | 0 | 75 | 1 | 75.00 | 1-75 | – | – |
| Babington, A.M. | RFM | 188 | 21 | 753 | 17 | 44.29 | 8-107 | 1 | – |
| Bailey, R.J. | OB | 120.1 | 31 | 291 | 9 | 32.33 | 1-0 | – | – |
| Bainbridge, P. | RM | 188.1 | 39 | 569 | 14 | 40.64 | 5-100 | 1 | – |
| Bakker, P-J. | RMF | 162 | 48 | 441 | 11 | 40.09 | 4-38 | – | – |
| Ball, M.C.J. | OB | 322 | 61 | 1072 | 28 | 38.28 | 5-101 | 1 | – |
| Barnett, A.A. | SLA | 595 | 84 | 2165 | 46 | 47.06 | 5-78 | 2 | – |
| Barnett, K.J. | LB | 77.4 | 11 | 250 | 4 | 62.50 | 3-24 | – | – |
| Barwick, S.R. | RMF | 602 | 155 | 1627 | 36 | 45.19 | 4-67 | – | – |
| Base, S.J. | RMF | 35 | 8 | 100 | 7 | 14.28 | 5-35 | 1 | – |
| Bastien, S. | RMF | 305.3 | 73 | 954 | 19 | 50.21 | 5-95 | 1 | – |
| Batty, J.D. | OB | 426 | 87 | 1408 | 33 | 42.66 | 4-34 | – | – |
| Bee, A. | RMF | 26 | 4 | 91 | 1 | 91.00 | 1-39 | – | – |
| Bell, M.A.V. | LMF | 79.2 | 17 | 247 | 8 | 30.87 | 3-78 | – | – |
| Benjamin, J.E. | RMF | 582.2 | 94 | 1780 | 45 | 39.55 | 6-30 | 2 | – |
| Benjamin, K.C.G. | RF | 12 | 0 | 55 | 3 | 18.33 | 3-55 | – | – |
| Benjamin, W.K.M. | RFM | 489 | 102 | 1498 | 47 | 31.87 | 4-34 | – | – |
| Benson, J.D.R. | RM | 43.4 | 6 | 142 | 5 | 28.40 | 2-24 | – | – |
| Benson, M.R. | OB | 3 | 0 | 25 | 1 | 25.00 | 1-18 | – | – |
| Berry, P.J. | OB | 178.3 | 27 | 649 | 17 | 38.17 | 7-113 | 1 | 1 |
| Bicknell, D.J. | LM | 9.2 | 0 | 90 | 0 | – | – | – | – |
| Bicknell, M.P. | RFM | 628.5 | 116 | 1823 | 71 | 25.67 | 6-107 | 4 | – |

| | Cat | O | M | R | W | Avge | Best | 5 wI | 10 wM |
|---|---|---|---|---|---|---|---|---|---|
| Bishop, I.R. | RF | 483 | 116 | 1118 | 64 | 17.46 | 7-34 | 4 | – |
| Boden, D.J.P. | RMF | 16 | 6 | 42 | 0 | – | – | – | – |
| Boiling, J. | OB | 591.1 | 156 | 1579 | 45 | 35.08 | 6-84 | 1 | 1 |
| Boon, T.J. | RM | 29 | 4 | 175 | 4 | 43.75 | 2-0 | – | – |
| Booth, P.A. | SLA | 279.4 | 74 | 814 | 19 | 42.84 | 4-29 | – | – |
| Botham, I.T. | RMF | 346 | 70 | 1144 | 26 | 44.00 | 4-72 | – | – |
| Bowen, M.N. | RM | 43 | 6 | 159 | 1 | 159.00 | 1-35 | – | – |
| Bowler, P.D. | OB | 23 | 3 | 92 | 0 | – | – | – | – |
| Briers, M.P. | LB | 144.3 | 22 | 621 | 12 | 51.75 | 3-109 | – | – |
| Brown, A.D.(Sy) | LB | 16 | 1 | 78 | 0 | – | – | – | – |
| Brown, A.M. | OB | 3 | 0 | 9 | 0 | – | – | – | – |
| Brown, D.R. | RFM | 34 | 14 | 70 | 5 | 14.00 | 3-27 | – | – |
| Brown, G.K. | OB | 9 | 1 | 64 | 0 | – | – | – | – |
| Brown, S.J.E. | LFM | 509.1 | 75 | 1973 | 58 | 34.01 | 7-105 | 3 | – |
| Bryson, R.E. | RF | 333.4 | 41 | 1256 | 23 | 54.60 | 5-48 | 2 | – |
| Butcher, M.A. | RM | 44 | 10 | 115 | 1 | 115.00 | 1-95 | – | – |
| Caddick, A.R. | RFM | 587.4 | 98 | 1918 | 71 | 27.01 | 6-52 | 3 | 1 |
| Cairns, C.L. | RFM | 592.3 | 110 | 1974 | 56 | 35.25 | 6-70 | 2 | – |
| Capel, D.J. | RMF | 446 | 92 | 1214 | 48 | 25.29 | 5-61 | 1 | – |
| Carr, J.D. | RM | 53 | 18 | 124 | 5 | 24.80 | 1-9 | – | – |
| Carrick, P. | SLA | 630.1 | 202 | 1375 | 47 | 29.25 | 6-58 | 1 | – |
| Chapman, R.J. | RFM | 13 | 1 | 77 | 2 | 38.50 | 1-38 | – | – |
| Chapple, G. | RMF | 48 | 17 | 128 | 5 | 25.60 | 3-40 | – | – |
| Childs, J.H. | SLA | 678.2 | 205 | 1822 | 67 | 27.19 | 6-82 | 3 | – |
| Connor, C.A. | RFM | 417.2 | 69 | 1386 | 32 | 43.31 | 5-58 | 1 | – |
| Cook, N.G.B. | SLA | 325.1 | 90 | 939 | 38 | 24.71 | 7-34 | 1 | 1 |
| Cooper, K.E. | RFM | 38 | 15 | 63 | 6 | 10.50 | 4-41 | – | – |
| Cork, D.G. | RFM | 450.4 | 74 | 1366 | 48 | 28.45 | 5-36 | 2 | – |
| Cottam, A.C. | SLA | 116.1 | 24 | 280 | 6 | 46.66 | 1-1 | – | – |
| Cottey, P.A. | OB | 7 | 2 | 26 | 0 | – | – | – | – |
| Cowans, N.G. | RF | 7 | 3 | 9 | 0 | – | – | – | – |
| Cowdrey, G.R. | RM | 48 | 9 | 213 | 2 | 106.50 | 1-15 | – | – |
| Crawley, J.P. | RM | 10 | 0 | 90 | 1 | 90.00 | 1-90 | – | – |
| Crawley, M.A. | RM | 221.4 | 56 | 647 | 19 | 34.05 | 3-18 | – | – |
| Crawley, P.M. | RM | 66 | 13 | 236 | 3 | 78.66 | 2-36 | – | – |
| Croft, R.D.B. | OB | 657.1 | 124 | 2152 | 68 | 31.64 | 8-66 | 5 | 1 |
| Curran, K.M. | RMF | 452.4 | 96 | 1376 | 50 | 27.52 | 6-45 | 1 | – |
| Curtis, T.S. | LB | 24 | 2 | 116 | 2 | 58.00 | 2-72 | – | – |
| Dale, A. | RM | 234 | 62 | 644 | 20 | 32.20 | 3-30 | – | – |
| Davies, H.R. | OB | 146.3 | 18 | 640 | 6 | 106.66 | 3-118 | – | – |
| Davies, M. | SLA | 560.5 | 143 | 1661 | 56 | 29.66 | 4-73 | – | – |
| Davis, R.P. | SLA | 582 | 150 | 1609 | 74 | 21.74 | 7-64 | 5 | – |
| DeFreitas, P.A.J. | RFM | 349.5 | 66 | 1091 | 34 | 32.08 | 6-94 | 1 | – |
| Dilley, G.R. | RF | 25 | 7 | 57 | 0 | – | – | – | – |
| Dobson, M.C. | SLA | 18 | 7 | 45 | 1 | 45.00 | 1-42 | – | – |
| D'Oliveira, D.B. | OB | 153.4 | 29 | 536 | 10 | 53.60 | 2-44 | – | – |
| Donald, A.A. | RF | 576.2 | 139 | 1647 | 74 | 22.25 | 7-37 | 6 | – |
| Donelan, B.T.P. | OB | 404 | 85 | 1323 | 28 | 47.25 | 6-77 | 1 | – |
| Dunlop, A.R. | OB | 30 | 8 | 106 | 2 | 53.00 | 1-8 | – | – |
| Ealham, M.A. | RMF | 406.1 | 70 | 1243 | 37 | 33.59 | 4-67 | – | – |
| Edmonds, P.H. | SLA | 28 | 10 | 48 | 4 | 12.00 | 4-48 | – | – |
| Ellison, R.M. | RMF | 401.5 | 80 | 1204 | 29 | 41.51 | 6-95 | 2 | – |
| Emburey, J.E. | OB | 854.5 | 249 | 2069 | 81 | 25.54 | 5-23 | 3 | – |
| Evans, K.P. | RMF | 595.4 | 133 | 1723 | 48 | 35.89 | 5-27 | 1 | – |
| Feltham, M.A. | RMF | 326.1 | 61 | 1125 | 25 | 45.00 | 4-75 | – | – |

173

| | Cat | O | M | R | W | Avge | Best | 5 wI | 10 wM |
|---|---|---|---|---|---|---|---|---|---|
| Felton, N.A. | OB | 14 | 2 | 93 | 0 | – | – | – | – |
| Field-Buss, M.G. | OB | 169 | 29 | 590 | 11 | 53.63 | 4-71 | – | – |
| Fitton, J.D. | OB | 171.1 | 38 | 465 | 13 | 35.76 | 4-81 | – | – |
| Fleming, M.V. | RM | 245 | 46 | 696 | 24 | 29.00 | 4-63 | – | – |
| Fletcher, S.D. | RMF | 101 | 23 | 409 | 6 | 68.16 | 2-53 | – | – |
| Fordham, A. | RM | 12.2 | 0 | 72 | 0 | – | – | – | – |
| Foster, D.J. | RFM | 191.3 | 27 | 820 | 22 | 37.27 | 5-87 | 1 | – |
| Foster, N.A. | RFM | 256 | 63 | 724 | 24 | 30.16 | 4-47 | – | – |
| Fowler, G. | RM | 5 | 0 | 60 | 1 | 60.00 | 1-60 | – | – |
| Fraser, A.G.J. | RFM | 20.3 | 5 | 95 | 3 | 31.66 | 2-37 | – | – |
| Fraser, A.R.C. | RFM | 426.4 | 90 | 1273 | 23 | 55.34 | 3-16 | – | – |
| Frost, M. | RMF | 198.1 | 29 | 833 | 13 | 64.07 | 3-100 | – | – |
| Gallian, J.E.R. | RM | 208 | 41 | 628 | 18 | 34.88 | 4-29 | – | – |
| Gatting, M.W. | RM | 9 | 3 | 38 | 0 | – | – | – | – |
| Gerrard, M.J. | LMF | 93 | 20 | 297 | 7 | 42.42 | 2-51 | – | – |
| Giddins, E.S.H. | RMF | 247.5 | 52 | 857 | 31 | 27.64 | 5-32 | 2 | – |
| Gidley, M.I. | OB | 80 | 20 | 248 | 2 | 124.00 | 1-51 | – | – |
| Gofton, R.P. | RM | 81.4 | 15 | 348 | 6 | 58.00 | 4-81 | – | – |
| Goldsmith, S.C. | RM | 119 | 22 | 419 | 3 | 139.66 | 1-9 | – | – |
| Gooch, G.A. | RM | 134 | 38 | 305 | 9 | 33.88 | 3-39 | – | – |
| Gough, D. | RMF | 255.1 | 53 | 910 | 25 | 36.40 | 4-43 | – | – |
| Govan, J.W. | OB | 50.3 | 13 | 156 | 9 | 17.33 | 6-70 | 1 | – |
| Graveney, D.A. | SLA | 380.4 | 87 | 1201 | 28 | 42.89 | 3-22 | – | – |
| Grayson, A.P. | SLA | 50 | 5 | 186 | 1 | 186.00 | 1-79 | – | – |
| Greenfield, K. | RM | 17 | 0 | 84 | 0 | – | – | – | – |
| Griffith, F.A. | RM | 113 | 31 | 373 | 15 | 24.86 | 4-33 | – | – |
| Gupte, C.M. | SLA | 28 | 2 | 133 | 1 | 133.00 | 1-55 | – | – |
| Hall, J.W. | OB | 2 | 1 | 14 | 0 | – | – | – | – |
| Hancock, T.H.C. | RM | 33.4 | 4 | 136 | 4 | 34.00 | 2-43 | – | – |
| Hansford, A.R. | RM | 29 | 5 | 81 | 3 | 27.00 | 3-81 | – | – |
| Harden, R.J. | SLA | 3 | 0 | 31 | 0 | – | – | – | – |
| Harper, R.A. | OB | 15 | 0 | 32 | 0 | – | – | – | – |
| Hartley, P.J. | RMF | 549.5 | 101 | 1690 | 56 | 30.17 | 8-111 | 3 | – |
| Hawkes, C.J. | SLA | 42 | 11 | 122 | 5 | 24.40 | 4-18 | – | – |
| Hayhurst, A.N. | RM | 142 | 30 | 407 | 9 | 45.22 | 3-27 | – | – |
| Haynes, D.L. | RM/LB | 2.4 | 0 | 5 | 1 | 5.00 | 1-4 | – | – |
| Haynes, G.R. | RM | 45.2 | 13 | 128 | 0 | – | – | – | – |
| Headley, D.W. | RMF | 385 | 74 | 1258 | 31 | 40.58 | 3-31 | – | – |
| Hemmings, E.E. | OB | 259.5 | 95 | 602 | 18 | 33.44 | 4-30 | – | – |
| Henderson, P.W. | RFM | 96 | 14 | 405 | 10 | 40.50 | 3-59 | – | – |
| Hepworth, P.N. | OB | 102.4 | 16 | 439 | 5 | 87.80 | 2-29 | – | – |
| Hick, G.A. | OB | 142.3 | 40 | 415 | 8 | 51.87 | 3-32 | – | – |
| Hindson, J.E. | SLA | 33.4 | 11 | 74 | 8 | 9.25 | 5-42 | 1 | – |
| Hinks, S.G. | RM | 2.5 | 1 | 14 | 0 | – | – | – | – |
| Hodgson, G.D. | RSM | 4 | 0 | 65 | 0 | – | – | – | – |
| Hoey, C.J. | LB | 19 | 6 | 59 | 2 | 29.50 | 1-15 | – | – |
| Hooper, A.M. | RM | 24 | 7 | 88 | 4 | 22.00 | 1-5 | – | – |
| Hooper, C.L. | OB | 500.5 | 114 | 1307 | 35 | 37.34 | 4-57 | – | – |
| Hughes, S.P. | RFM | 548.3 | 98 | 1672 | 34 | 49.17 | 5-25 | 1 | – |
| Hussain, N. | LB | 4 | 0 | 38 | 1 | 38.00 | 1-38 | – | – |
| Hutton, S. | RSM | 0.1 | 0 | 4 | 0 | – | – | – | – |
| Igglesden, A.P. | RF | 480.4 | 95 | 1413 | 46 | 30.71 | 5-41 | 3 | – |
| Illingworth, R.K. | SLA | 635.3 | 185 | 1580 | 42 | 37.61 | 4-43 | – | – |
| Ilott, M.C. | LMF | 675.3 | 145 | 2264 | 64 | 35.37 | 6-87 | 3 | – |
| Inzamam-ul-Haq | SLA | 2 | 0 | 13 | 1 | 13.00 | 1-5 | – | – |

174

| | Cat | O | M | R | W | Avge | Best | 5 wI | 10 wM |
|---|---|---|---|---|---|---|---|---|---|
| Irani, R.C. | RM | 33 | 5 | 137 | 3 | 45.66 | 2-21 | – | – |
| James, K.D. | LMF | 264.3 | 65 | 781 | 14 | 55.78 | 2-23 | – | – |
| Jarvis, P.W. | RFM | 393.4 | 89 | 1164 | 40 | 29.10 | 4-27 | – | – |
| Jean-Jacques, M. | RMF | 35.4 | 5 | 135 | 5 | 27.00 | 4-46 | – | – |
| Jeh, M.P.W. | RFM | 233.5 | 38 | 846 | 17 | 49.76 | 3-44 | – | – |
| Jenkins, R.H.J. | RM | 32 | 5 | 137 | 2 | 68.50 | 1-24 | – | – |
| Johnson, P. | RM | 5 | 0 | 30 | 0 | – | – | – | – |
| Johnson, R.L. | RMF | 14 | 2 | 71 | 1 | 71.00 | 1-25 | – | – |
| Johnson, S.W. | RMF | 164 | 27 | 541 | 10 | 54.10 | 3-62 | – | – |
| Jones, A.N. | RFM | 161.5 | 17 | 745 | 11 | 67.72 | 3-76 | – | – |
| Jones, D.M. | OB | 18.1 | 1 | 71 | 1 | 71.00 | 1-4 | – | – |
| Kemp, T.R. | OB | 29 | 2 | 128 | 1 | 128.00 | 1-35 | – | – |
| Kendrick, N.M. | SLA | 595.1 | 171 | 1567 | 51 | 30.72 | 6-61 | 3 | – |
| Kirnon, S. | RMF | 14 | 5 | 21 | 1 | 21.00 | 1-14 | – | – |
| Lampitt, S.R. | RMF | 369.3 | 44 | 1257 | 35 | 35.91 | 4-57 | – | – |
| Larkins, W. | RM | 2 | 1 | 4 | 0 | – | – | – | – |
| Lathwell, M.N. | RM | 64 | 14 | 224 | 4 | 56.00 | 1-9 | – | – |
| Leatherdale, D.A. | RM | 10 | 2 | 33 | 0 | – | – | – | – |
| Lefebvre, R.P. | RMF | 41 | 11 | 96 | 5 | 19.20 | 2-33 | – | – |
| Lenham, N.J. | RMF | 120.1 | 28 | 362 | 6 | 60.33 | 2-61 | – | – |
| Lewis, C.C. | RFM | 594.3 | 119 | 1633 | 53 | 30.81 | 6-90 | 2 | 1 |
| Lewis, D.A. | RM | 19 | 3 | 81 | 2 | 40.50 | 2-39 | – | – |
| Llong, N.J. | OB | 55 | 7 | 212 | 7 | 30.28 | 3-50 | – | – |
| Lloyd, G.D. | RM | 7 | 0 | 45 | 0 | – | – | – | – |
| Lloyd, T.A. | RM/OB | 68.5 | 8 | 295 | 6 | 49.16 | 3-7 | – | – |
| Lynch, M.A. | OB | 21 | 4 | 85 | 1 | 85.00 | 1-16 | – | – |
| McBrine, A. | SLA | 34 | 10 | 82 | 0 | – | – | – | – |
| McCague, M.J. | RFM | 457.2 | 86 | 1430 | 53 | 26.98 | 8-26 | 5 | 1 |
| McCrum, C. | RM | 28 | 1 | 97 | 3 | 32.33 | 3-57 | – | – |
| McCrum, P. | RFM | 35 | 5 | 145 | 1 | 145.00 | 1-80 | – | – |
| MacDonald, R.H. | RFM | 79.4 | 22 | 188 | 5 | 37.60 | 2-13 | – | – |
| McEwan, S.M. | RFM | 229 | 44 | 800 | 17 | 47.05 | 3-52 | – | – |
| MacLeay, K.H. | RM | 115 | 28 | 311 | 9 | 34.55 | 2-33 | – | – |
| Malcolm, D.E. | RF | 451.1 | 64 | 1648 | 45 | 36.62 | 5-45 | 2 | – |
| Malik, H.S. | OB | 25 | 4 | 88 | 0 | – | – | – | – |
| Mallender, N.A. | RFM | 436.3 | 94 | 1282 | 55 | 23.30 | 5-29 | 4 | – |
| Marsh, S.A. | (WK) | 8 | 0 | 126 | 0 | – | – | – | – |
| Marshall, M.D. | RF | 529 | 134 | 1348 | 49 | 27.51 | 6-58 | 1 | – |
| Martin, P.J. | RFM | 520.2 | 129 | 1490 | 37 | 40.27 | 4-45 | – | – |
| Maru, R.J. | SLA | 204.2 | 75 | 444 | 17 | 26.11 | 4-8 | – | – |
| Maynard, M.P. | RM | 7 | 0 | 72 | 1 | 72.00 | 1-3 | – | – |
| Metson, C.P. | (WK) | 1 | 1 | 0 | 0 | – | – | – | – |
| Middleton, T.C. | SLA | 10 | 0 | 57 | 0 | – | – | – | – |
| Mike, G.W. | RMF | 90.2 | 17 | 314 | 10 | 31.40 | 3-48 | – | – |
| Milburn, S.M. | RMF | 28 | 2 | 115 | 1 | 115.00 | 1-54 | – | – |
| Millns, D.J. | RF | 470.5 | 107 | 1526 | 74 | 20.62 | 6-87 | 6 | 1 |
| Moin Khan | (WK) | 1 | 0 | 3 | 0 | – | – | – | – |
| Moles, A.J. | RM | 43 | 8 | 169 | 2 | 84.50 | 1-16 | – | – |
| Montgomerie, R.R. | OB | 10 | 2 | 31 | 0 | – | – | – | – |
| Moody, T.M. | RM | 72 | 13 | 249 | 8 | 31.12 | 4-50 | – | – |
| Morris, H. | RM | 4.5 | 0 | 57 | 0 | – | – | – | – |
| Morris, J.E. | RM | 8 | 3 | 13 | 1 | 13.00 | 1-13 | – | – |
| Morrison, D.K. | RFM | 335.4 | 52 | 1209 | 36 | 33.58 | 6-48 | 1 | – |
| Mortensen, O.H. | RFM | 338.4 | 87 | 795 | 23 | 34.56 | 2-22 | – | – |
| Moxon, M.D. | RM | 3 | 0 | 7 | 0 | – | – | – | – |

| | Cat | O | M | R | W | Avge | Best | 5 wI | 10 wM |
|---|---|---|---|---|---|---|---|---|---|
| Mullally, A.D. | LFM | 518.2 | 125 | 1485 | 42 | 35.35 | 5-119 | 1 | – |
| Munton, T.A. | RMF | 640.4 | 176 | 1725 | 51 | 33.82 | 7-64 | 3 | 1 |
| Murphy, A.J. | RMF | 178.4 | 34 | 531 | 11 | 48.27 | 3-97 | – | – |
| Mushtaq Ahmed | LB | 614.4 | 158 | 1620 | 66 | 24.54 | 5-46 | 4 | – |
| Naved Anjum | RMF | 107.1 | 24 | 379 | 10 | 37.90 | 3-73 | – | – |
| Newport, P.J. | RFM | 618.2 | 130 | 1770 | 68 | 26.02 | 5-22 | 4 | – |
| Nicholas, M.C.J. | RM | 25.3 | 2 | 101 | 2 | 50.50 | 1-16 | – | – |
| North, J.A. | RM | 96.3 | 14 | 331 | 11 | 30.09 | 3-51 | – | – |
| O'Gorman, T.J.G. | OB | 28.2 | 0 | 148 | 2 | 74.00 | 1-7 | – | – |
| Ostler, D.P. | RM | 13 | 0 | 83 | 0 | – | – | – | – |
| Parker, P.W.G. | RM | 3.2 | 0 | 31 | 0 | – | – | – | – |
| Parsons, G.J. | RMF | 343.2 | 92 | 955 | 39 | 24.48 | 6-70 | 2 | – |
| Patel, D.N. | OB | 20 | 3 | 72 | 2 | 36.00 | 2-72 | – | – |
| Payne, A. | RMF | 27 | 8 | 71 | 1 | 71.00 | 1-71 | – | – |
| Pearson, R.M. | OB | 402.3 | 64 | 1271 | 20 | 63.55 | 5-108 | 1 | – |
| Penberthy, A.L. | RM | 108 | 24 | 313 | 8 | 39.12 | 3-34 | – | – |
| Penn, C. | RFM | 151 | 26 | 477 | 5 | 95.40 | 2-69 | – | – |
| Pennett, D.B. | RMF | 296.2 | 52 | 981 | 26 | 37.73 | 4-58 | – | – |
| Penney, T.L. | RM | 5 | 0 | 35 | 0 | – | – | – | – |
| Pick, R.A. | RMF | 254.1 | 50 | 862 | 18 | 47.88 | 3-33 | – | – |
| Pickles, C.S. | RM | 120.1 | 27 | 387 | 14 | 27.64 | 4-40 | – | – |
| Pigott, A.C.S. | RFM | 363 | 74 | 1063 | 27 | 39.37 | 3-34 | – | – |
| Piper, K.J. | (WK) | 4.4 | 0 | 57 | 1 | 57.00 | 1-57 | – | – |
| Pitcher, C.M. | RM | 131 | 20 | 453 | 3 | 151.00 | 1-35 | – | – |
| Pollard, P.R. | RM | 4 | 0 | 33 | 0 | – | – | – | – |
| Potter, L. | SLA | 360.1 | 80 | 1075 | 27 | 39.81 | 4-73 | – | – |
| Prichard, P.J. | RSM | 8 | 0 | 100 | 0 | – | – | – | – |
| Pringle, C. | RMF | 18 | 5 | 56 | 0 | – | – | – | – |
| Pringle, D.R. | RMF | 423.5 | 99 | 1177 | 47 | 25.04 | 5-63 | 1 | – |
| Radford, N.V. | RFM | 532.2 | 99 | 1670 | 60 | 27.83 | 6-88 | 4 | 1 |
| Ramprakash, M.R. | RM | 11.1 | 1 | 49 | 0 | – | – | – | – |
| Randall, D.W. | RM | 1.2 | 0 | 8 | 0 | – | – | – | – |
| Rashid Latif | (WK) | 8 | 2 | 17 | 2 | 8.50 | 2-17 | – | – |
| Reeve, D.A. | RMF | 267 | 80 | 632 | 13 | 48.61 | 2-4 | – | – |
| Remy, C.C. | RM | 96.2 | 12 | 336 | 6 | 56.00 | 3-27 | – | – |
| Richards, I.V.A. | OB | 12 | 2 | 34 | 0 | – | – | – | – |
| Richardson, A.W. | RFM | 13 | 2 | 38 | 2 | 19.00 | 2-38 | – | – |
| Richardson, M.S. | RMF | 24 | 7 | 64 | 2 | 32.00 | 2-49 | – | – |
| Ripley, D. | (WK) | 1 | 0 | 14 | 0 | – | – | – | – |
| Roberts, A.R. | LB | 323.2 | 60 | 1056 | 22 | 48.00 | 4-101 | – | – |
| Robinson, J.D. | RM | 93.4 | 14 | 341 | 13 | 26.23 | 3-22 | – | – |
| Robinson, M.A. | RFM | 413.5 | 79 | 1134 | 50 | 22.68 | 6-57 | 3 | 1 |
| Robinson, R.T. | RM | 1 | 0 | 4 | 0 | – | – | – | – |
| Robson, A.G. | RFM | 119 | 24 | 405 | 8 | 50.62 | 4-37 | – | – |
| Rose, G.D. | RM | 392.1 | 84 | 1250 | 28 | 44.64 | 4-59 | – | – |
| Roseberry, M.A. | RM | 13 | 5 | 71 | 0 | – | – | – | – |
| Russell, A.B. | RM | 15 | 5 | 42 | 2 | 21.00 | 2-27 | – | – |
| Salim Jaffer | LMF | 65 | 9 | 247 | 5 | 49.40 | 2-53 | – | – |
| Salim Malik | RSM | 18.1 | 0 | 71 | 3 | 23.66 | 2-15 | – | – |
| Salisbury, I.D.K. | LB | 772.4 | 176 | 2520 | 87 | 28.96 | 7-54 | 6 | 2 |
| Saxelby, M. | RM | 6 | 2 | 22 | 0 | – | – | – | – |
| Scott, R.J. | RM | 267.4 | 40 | 959 | 20 | 47.95 | 2-9 | – | – |
| Shahid, N. | LB | 40 | 4 | 167 | 9 | 18.55 | 2-22 | – | – |
| Sheridan, K.L.P. | SLA | 35 | 10 | 104 | 1 | 104.00 | 1-62 | – | – |
| Shine, K.J. | RFM | 333.5 | 49 | 1290 | 40 | 32.25 | 8-47 | 3 | 1 |

| | Cat | O | M | R | W | Avge | Best | 5 wI | 10 wM |
|---|---|---|---|---|---|---|---|---|---|
| Shoaib Mohammad | OB | 27 | 5 | 82 | 0 | – | – | – | – |
| Sladdin, R.W. | SLA | 499.3 | 138 | 1396 | 39 | 35.79 | 6-58 | 1 | – |
| Sleep, P.R. | LB | 10 | 3 | 34 | 1 | 34.00 | 1-34 | – | – |
| Small, G.C. | RFM | 367.2 | 83 | 1003 | 30 | 33.43 | 3-43 | – | – |
| Smith, A.M. | LM | 249.2 | 35 | 835 | 24 | 34.79 | 3-53 | – | – |
| Smith, D.M. | RM | 4 | 1 | 18 | 0 | – | – | – | – |
| Smith, I. | RM | 90 | 20 | 242 | 8 | 30.25 | 3-85 | – | – |
| Smith, N.M.K. | OB | 332.3 | 63 | 1178 | 24 | 49.08 | 5-61 | 1 | – |
| Smith, P.A. | RFM | 373 | 57 | 1362 | 42 | 32.42 | 6-91 | 4 | – |
| Smith, R.A. | LB | 8.1 | 0 | 41 | 0 | – | – | – | – |
| Snape, J.N. | OB | 26 | 8 | 62 | 1 | 62.00 | 1-20 | – | – |
| Snell, R.P. | RFM | 339.1 | 60 | 1194 | 27 | 44.22 | 3-29 | – | – |
| Speak, N.J. | RM/OB | 6 | 0 | 66 | 0 | – | – | – | – |
| Speight, M.P. | (WK) | 3 | 0 | 30 | 1 | 30.00 | 1-30 | – | – |
| Stemp, R.D. | SLA | 331.5 | 80 | 1054 | 28 | 37.64 | 6-67 | 3 | 1 |
| Stephenson, F.D. | RFM | 467.2 | 93 | 1375 | 40 | 34.37 | 7-29 | 1 | 1 |
| Stephenson, J.P. | RM | 251.5 | 51 | 854 | 22 | 38.81 | 6-54 | 1 | – |
| Stewart, A.J. | RSM | 7 | 1 | 14 | 0 | – | – | – | – |
| Storie, A.C. | RM | 40 | 5 | 128 | 2 | 64.00 | 1-17 | – | – |
| Such, P.M. | OB | 409.5 | 126 | 1015 | 40 | 25.37 | 6-17 | 3 | – |
| Sylvester, S.A. | LFM | 84 | 22 | 222 | 4 | 55.50 | 2-34 | – | – |
| Tanvir Mehdi | RMF | 94 | 21 | 307 | 12 | 25.58 | 3-24 | – | – |
| Tavaré, C.J. | RM | 3.2 | 0 | 33 | 0 | – | – | – | – |
| Taylor, C.W. | LMF | 409.2 | 82 | 1425 | 35 | 40.71 | 4-50 | – | – |
| Taylor, J.P. | LFM | 648.2 | 119 | 2072 | 68 | 30.47 | 7-23 | 3 | 1 |
| Tendulkar, S.R. | RSM | 62.3 | 10 | 195 | 4 | 48.75 | 2-35 | – | – |
| Thomas, S.D. | RFM | 113.2 | 18 | 404 | 18 | 22.44 | 5-79 | 2 | – |
| Thomson, K. | RMF | 26 | 5 | 82 | 2 | 41.00 | 1-27 | – | – |
| Thorpe, G.P. | RM | 17.4 | 5 | 79 | 0 | – | – | – | – |
| Thursfield, M.J. | RM | 16 | 3 | 35 | 2 | 17.50 | 1-11 | – | – |
| Tolley, C.M. | LMF | 239 | 56 | 726 | 18 | 40.33 | 3-38 | – | – |
| Topley, T.D. | RMF | 240.4 | 54 | 779 | 24 | 32.45 | 5-15 | 1 | – |
| Trump, H.R.J. | OB | 558 | 134 | 1584 | 49 | 32.32 | 7-52 | 2 | 1 |
| Tufnell, P.C.R. | SLA | 596.2 | 144 | 1559 | 43 | 36.25 | 5-83 | 2 | – |
| Turner, I.J. | SLA | 182.4 | 51 | 519 | 19 | 27.31 | 5-81 | 1 | – |
| Turner, R.J. | (WK) | 2.1 | 0 | 26 | 0 | – | – | – | – |
| Tutt, A. | RM | 19 | 5 | 53 | 0 | – | – | – | – |
| Twose, R.G. | RM | 249.3 | 48 | 794 | 28 | 28.35 | 6-63 | 1 | – |
| Udal, S.D. | OB | 692.2 | 177 | 2012 | 58 | 34.68 | 8-50 | 2 | – |
| Van Troost, A.P. | RMF | 175.4 | 20 | 766 | 21 | 36.47 | 6-48 | 2 | – |
| Vaughan, J.T.C. | RM | 202.4 | 44 | 588 | 18 | 32.66 | 3-46 | – | – |
| Walker, A. | RFM | 45 | 14 | 90 | 2 | 45.00 | 1-24 | – | – |
| Walsh, C.A. | RF | 587.2 | 138 | 1469 | 92 | 15.96 | 7-27 | 8 | 2 |
| Waqar Younis | RF | 287.1 | 50 | 913 | 37 | 24.67 | 5-22 | 4 | – |
| Ward, D.M. | OB | 4 | 0 | 16 | 0 | – | – | – | – |
| Ward, I.J. | RM | 8 | 0 | 35 | 0 | – | – | – | – |
| Ward, T.R. | OB | 39.5 | 4 | 109 | 0 | – | – | – | – |
| Warner, A.E. | RFM | 367.5 | 87 | 888 | 29 | 30.62 | 4-52 | – | – |
| Wasim Akram | LF | 499.5 | 127 | 1330 | 82 | 16.21 | 6-32 | 7 | 2 |
| Watkin, S.L. | RMF | 689.3 | 148 | 2126 | 68 | 31.26 | 6-97 | 1 | – |
| Watkinson, M. | RMF | 660 | 140 | 2178 | 66 | 33.00 | 6-62 | 4 | 1 |
| Waugh, M.E. | RM | 184.4 | 31 | 671 | 22 | 30.50 | 3-38 | – | – |
| Weekes, P.N. | OB | 222 | 51 | 595 | 12 | 49.58 | 3-61 | – | – |
| Wells, A.P. | RM | 29 | 7 | 94 | 0 | – | – | – | – |
| Wells, C.M. | RM | 119 | 26 | 323 | 10 | 32.30 | 3-26 | – | – |

177

| | Cat | O | M | R | W | Avge | Best | 5 wI | 10 wM |
|---|---|---|---|---|---|---|---|---|---|
| Wells, V.J. | RMF | 301 | 93 | 751 | 33 | 22.75 | 4-26 | – | – |
| Weston, M.J. | RM | 19 | 3 | 58 | 1 | 58.00 | 1-34 | – | – |
| Weston, W.P.C. | LM | 74 | 9 | 237 | 2 | 118.50 | 2-39 | – | – |
| Whitaker, J.J. | OB | 8 | 0 | 86 | 1 | 86.00 | 1-29 | – | – |
| White, C. | OB | 3 | 0 | 22 | 0 | | | – | – |
| Whittington, J.M.S. | SLA | 19 | 2 | 44 | 0 | | | – | – |
| Wight, R.M. | OB | 231.3 | 39 | 748 | 19 | 39.36 | 3-65 | – | – |
| Williams, N.F. | RFM | 437 | 86 | 1283 | 48 | 26.72 | 8-75 | 2 | 1 |
| Williams, R.C. | RM | 77.3 | 10 | 300 | 5 | 60.00 | 3-44 | – | – |
| Williams, R.G. | OB | 31 | 5 | 83 | 4 | 20.75 | 3-42 | – | – |
| Wood, B.S. | RMF | 87.2 | 7 | 352 | 4 | 88.00 | 2-29 | – | – |
| Wood, J. | RFM | 134.2 | 17 | 534 | 17 | 31.41 | 5-68 | 1 | – |
| Wren, T.N. | LM | 24 | 4 | 92 | 5 | 18.40 | 3-54 | – | – |
| Wright, A.J. | RM | 2 | 0 | 27 | 0 | | | – | – |
| Zahid Fazal | RM | 13 | 2 | 73 | 0 | | | – | – |

# FIRST-CLASS CAREER RECORDS

Compiled by Paul Cartwright in association with Philip Bailey

The following career records are for all players who appeared in first-class cricket during the 1992 season, and are complete to the end of that season. Some players who did not appear in 1992 but may do so in 1993, are also included.

## BATTING AND FIELDING

'1000' denotes instances of scoring 1000 runs in a season. Where these have been achieved outside the UK, they are shown after a plus sign.

| | M | I | NO | HS | Runs | Avge | 100 | 1000 | Ct/St |
|---|---|---|---|---|---|---|---|---|---|
| Aamir Sohail | 106 | 177 | 14 | 205 | 6527 | 40.04 | 14 | 1 | 79 |
| Abington, M.B. | 7 | 7 | – | 6 | 20 | 2.85 | – | – | 4 |
| Adams, C.J. | 69 | 103 | 13 | 140* | 3014 | 33.48 | 8 | 1 | 71 |
| Afford, J.A. | 115 | 99 | 41 | 22* | 208 | 3.58 | – | – | 36 |
| Alikhan, R.I. | 101 | 173 | 14 | 138 | 4547 | 28.59 | 2 | 1 | 56 |
| Alleyne, M.W. | 124 | 194 | 25 | 256 | 5082 | 30.07 | 5 | 2 | 103/2 |
| Ambrose, C.E.L. | 110 | 140 | 37 | 59 | 1603 | 15.56 | – | – | 26 |
| Anderson, D.J. | 8 | 8 | 4 | 9 | 18 | 4.50 | – | – | 3 |
| Andrew, S.J.W. | 100 | 69 | 31 | 35 | 292 | 7.68 | – | – | 21 |
| Aqib Javed | 52 | 39 | 18 | 32* | 124 | 5.90 | – | – | 4 |
| Archer, G.F. | 7 | 13 | 3 | 117 | 475 | 47.50 | 1 | – | 6 |
| Arscott, J.P. | 21 | 30 | 5 | 79 | 573 | 22.92 | – | – | 18/8 |
| Asif Din | 199 | 326 | 44 | 158* | 8423 | 29.86 | 8 | 2 | 108 |
| Asif Mujtaba | 128 | 201 | 40 | 193* | 7765 | 48.22 | 20 | 1+1 | 114 |
| Ata-ur-Rehman | 19 | 11 | 3 | 17 | 57 | 7.12 | – | – | 4 |
| Atherton, M.A. | 123 | 211 | 26 | 199 | 8424 | 45.53 | 26 | 4 | 108 |
| Athey, C.W.J. | 387 | 639 | 62 | 184 | 20129 | 34.88 | 42 | 10 | 369/2 |
| Atkins, P.D. | 17 | 32 | 3 | 114* | 853 | 29.41 | 1 | – | 5 |
| Austin, I.D. | 51 | 66 | 17 | 115* | 1249 | 25.48 | 2 | – | 7 |
| Ayling, J.R. | 56 | 84 | 11 | 121 | 1993 | 27.30 | 1 | – | 14 |
| Aymes, A.N. | 50 | 63 | 17 | 75* | 1402 | 30.47 | – | – | 121/9 |
| Babington, A.M. | 87 | 92 | 37 | 58 | 475 | 8.63 | – | – | 31 |
| Bailey, R.J. | 233 | 390 | 60 | 224* | 13725 | 41.59 | 29 | 9 | 166 |
| Bainbridge, P. | 274 | 454 | 69 | 169 | 13276 | 34.48 | 22 | 8 | 118 |

178

| | M | I | NO | HS | Runs | Avge | 100 | 1000 | Ct/St |
|---|---|---|---|---|---|---|---|---|---|
| Bakker, P-J. | 69 | 54 | 19 | 22 | 333 | 9.51 | – | – | 9 |
| Ball, M.C.J. | 32 | 44 | 9 | 54 | 379 | 10.82 | – | – | 23 |
| Barnett, A.A. | 25 | 20 | 12 | 17 | 92 | 11.50 | – | – | 7 |
| Barnett, K.J. | 333 | 533 | 47 | 239* | 18495 | 38.05 | 38 | 10 | 216 |
| Bartlett, R.J. | 51 | 82 | 6 | 117* | 1856 | 24.42 | 2 | – | 35 |
| Barwick, S.R. | 173 | 162 | 62 | 30 | 724 | 7.24 | – | – | 37 |
| Base, S.J. | 103 | 130 | 33 | 58 | 1135 | 11.70 | – | – | 45 |
| Bastien, S. | 44 | 33 | 13 | 36* | 152 | 7.60 | – | – | 5 |
| Batty, J.D. | 45 | 41 | 13 | 51 | 403 | 14.39 | – | – | 15 |
| Bee, A. | 3 | 3 | 3 | 29* | 41 | – | – | – | 1 |
| Bell, M.A.V. | 3 | 5 | 2 | 5 | 10 | 3.33 | – | – | – |
| Benjamin, J.E. | 43 | 40 | 16 | 42 | 341 | 14.20 | – | – | 12 |
| Benjamin, K.C.G. | 25 | 33 | 10 | 52* | 321 | 13.95 | – | – | 2 |
| Benjamin, W.K.M. | 124 | 148 | 34 | 101* | 2630 | 23.07 | 1 | – | 60 |
| Benson, J.D.R. | 50 | 76 | 8 | 133* | 1854 | 27.26 | 3 | – | 52 |
| Benson, M.R. | 248 | 419 | 31 | 257 | 16035 | 41.32 | 42 | 11 | 120 |
| Berry, P.J. | 16 | 22 | 9 | 76 | 281 | 21.61 | – | – | 6 |
| Bicknell, D.J. | 122 | 213 | 22 | 186 | 7364 | 38.55 | 17 | 4 | 45 |
| Bicknell, M.P. | 119 | 133 | 40 | 88 | 1563 | 16.80 | – | – | 38 |
| Bishop, I.R. | 88 | 115 | 32 | 103* | 1342 | 16.16 | 1 | – | 19 |
| Bishop, J. | 1 | 1 | 1 | 51* | 51 | – | – | – | 4 |
| Blakey, R.J. | 157 | 254 | 35 | 221 | 7242 | 33.06 | 9 | 4 | 252/25 |
| Boden, D.J.P. | 2 | 1 | – | 5 | 5 | 5.00 | – | – | 2 |
| Boiling, J. | 28 | 34 | 15 | 29 | 250 | 13.15 | – | – | 27 |
| Boon, T.J. | 208 | 350 | 39 | 144 | 10117 | 32.53 | 12 | 7 | 106 |
| Booth, P.A. | 52 | 69 | 15 | 62 | 686 | 12.70 | – | – | 15 |
| Botham, I.T. | 392 | 600 | 45 | 228 | 18983 | 34.20 | 37 | 4 | 346 |
| Bowen, M.N. | 3 | 3 | 2 | 13* | 26 | 26.00 | – | – | – |
| Bowler, P.D. | 128 | 223 | 22 | 241* | 8256 | 41.07 | 18 | 5 | 82/1 |
| Bramhall, S. | 10 | 13 | 5 | 37* | 115 | 14.37 | – | – | 18/6 |
| Briers, M.P. | 16 | 28 | 4 | 62* | 460 | 19.16 | – | – | 7 |
| Briers, N.E. | 335 | 547 | 55 | 201* | 15977 | 32.47 | 26 | 9 | 144 |
| Broad, B.C. | 311 | 557 | 38 | 227* | 20147 | 38.81 | 47 | 10 | 174 |
| Broadhurst, M. | 2 | 1 | – | 1 | 1 | 1.00 | – | – | – |
| Brown, A.D. (Sy) | 11 | 16 | 1 | 175 | 740 | 49.33 | 3 | – | 6 |
| Brown, A.D. (Ex) | 14 | 16 | 4 | 30 | 99 | 8.25 | – | – | 28/5 |
| Brown, A.M. | 22 | 31 | 3 | 139* | 815 | 29.10 | 1 | – | 19 |
| Brown, D.R. | 3 | 3 | 2 | 44* | 54 | 54.00 | – | – | 2 |
| Brown, G.K. | 6 | 10 | 1 | 103 | 345 | 38.33 | 1 | – | 5 |
| Brown, K.R. | 136 | 212 | 36 | 200* | 6059 | 34.42 | 10 | 2 | 180/11 |
| Brown, S.J.E. | 35 | 38 | 19 | 47* | 267 | 14.05 | – | – | 9 |
| Bryson, R.E. | 39 | 43 | 11 | 100 | 750 | 23.43 | 1 | – | 9 |
| Burns, M. | 2 | 3 | – | 78 | 85 | 28.33 | – | – | 7/1 |
| Burns, N.D. | 143 | 211 | 50 | 166 | 4870 | 30.24 | 4 | – | 279/28 |
| Butcher, A.R. | 401 | 682 | 60 | 216* | 22633 | 36.38 | 46 | 12 | 185 |
| Butcher, M.A. | 2 | 2 | 1 | 47 | 52 | 52.00 | – | – | – |
| Byas, D. | 99 | 161 | 17 | 153 | 4488 | 31.16 | 8 | 1 | 99 |
| Caddick, A.R. | 22 | 20 | 6 | 54* | 261 | 18.64 | – | – | 7 |
| Cairns, C.L. | 59 | 77 | 14 | 110 | 1945 | 30.87 | 3 | – | 24 |
| Capel, D.J. | 261 | 394 | 58 | 134 | 10068 | 29.96 | 12 | 3 | 126 |
| Carr, J.D. | 138 | 223 | 28 | 156 | 6623 | 33.96 | 12 | 3 | 123 |
| Carrick, P. | 441 | 568 | 102 | 131* | 10255 | 22.00 | 3 | – | 197 |
| Carroll, J.P. | 5 | 9 | – | 92 | 175 | 19.44 | – | – | 1 |
| Chapman, C.A. | 3 | 5 | 1 | 20 | 55 | 13.75 | – | – | 3 |
| Chapman, R.J. | 1 | – | – | – | – | – | – | – | – |

179

| | M | I | NO | HS | Runs | Avge | 100 | 1000 | Ct/St |
|---|---|---|---|---|---|---|---|---|---|
| Chapple, G. | 2 | 2 | 1 | 18 | 19 | 19.00 | – | – | – |
| Childs, J.H. | 326 | 290 | 136 | 43 | 1391 | 9.03 | – | – | 103 |
| Connor, C.A. | 160 | 129 | 38 | 51 | 889 | 9.76 | – | – | 47 |
| Cook, N.G.B. | 337 | 344 | 94 | 75 | 2989 | 11.95 | – | – | 191 |
| Cooper, K.E. | 273 | 281 | 67 | 46 | 2141 | 10.00 | – | – | 85 |
| Cork, D.G. | 42 | 56 | 12 | 72* | 1022 | 23.22 | – | – | 23 |
| Cottam, A.C. | 6 | 8 | 1 | 31 | 43 | 6.14 | – | – | 1 |
| Cottey, P.A. | 88 | 136 | 22 | 156 | 3582 | 31.42 | 5 | 2 | 45 |
| Cowans, N.G. | 221 | 228 | 61 | 66 | 1531 | 9.16 | – | – | 59 |
| Cowdrey, C.S. | 299 | 452 | 68 | 159 | 12252 | 31.90 | 21 | 4 | 295 |
| Cowdrey, G.R. | 124 | 193 | 27 | 147 | 6009 | 36.19 | 11 | 3 | 66 |
| Cox, R.M.F. | 9 | 12 | 2 | 104* | 287 | 28.70 | 1 | – | 5 |
| Crawley, J.P. | 32 | 52 | 6 | 172 | 2127 | 46.23 | 3 | 1 | 25 |
| Crawley, M.A. | 62 | 94 | 19 | 160* | 2900 | 38.66 | 8 | 1 | 52 |
| Crawley, P.M. | 4 | 6 | 2 | 45 | 118 | 29.50 | – | – | – |
| Croft, R.D.B. | 73 | 100 | 27 | 91* | 1902 | 26.05 | – | – | 28 |
| Cummins, A.C. | 11 | 15 | 3 | 45* | 208 | 17.33 | – | – | 3 |
| Curran, K.M. | 210 | 320 | 53 | 144* | 9441 | 35.35 | 18 | 5 | 118 |
| Curtis, T.S. | 249 | 423 | 54 | 248 | 15311 | 41.49 | 27 | 9 | 139 |
| Dale, A. | 53 | 83 | 12 | 150* | 2509 | 35.33 | 4 | 1 | 23 |
| Daley, J.A. | 2 | 4 | 1 | 88 | 190 | 63.33 | – | – | 2 |
| Das, S.S.K. | 3 | 5 | 1 | 24* | 38 | 9.50 | – | – | 1 |
| Davies, H.R. | 17 | 20 | 6 | 39 | 178 | 12.71 | – | – | – |
| Davies, M. | 20 | 24 | 11 | 32* | 153 | 11.76 | – | – | 11 |
| Davis, R.P. | 110 | 136 | 37 | 67 | 1620 | 16.36 | – | – | 94 |
| Dawson, R.I. | 6 | 8 | – | 29 | 88 | 11.00 | – | – | 2 |
| DeFreitas, P.A.J. | 167 | 224 | 24 | 113 | 4295 | 21.47 | 4 | – | 43 |
| De la Pena, J.M. | 2 | 2 | 1 | 1* | 1 | 1.00 | – | – | – |
| Dessaur, W.A. | 2 | 3 | – | 148 | 164 | 54.66 | 1 | – | 1 |
| Dilley, G.R. | 234 | 252 | 93 | 81 | 2339 | 14.71 | – | – | 75 |
| Dobson, M.C. | 10 | 15 | 3 | 52 | 211 | 17.58 | – | – | 2 |
| Doidge, M.J. | 1 | – | – | – | – | – | – | – | – |
| D'Oliveira, D.B. | 212 | 331 | 22 | 237 | 8667 | 28.04 | 10 | 4 | 187 |
| Donald, A.A. | 151 | 178 | 69 | 46* | 1282 | 11.76 | – | – | 53 |
| Donelan, B.T.P. | 49 | 62 | 20 | 68* | 1026 | 24.42 | – | – | 13 |
| Dunlop, A.R. | 2 | 3 | – | 56 | 108 | 36.00 | – | – | 1 |
| Ealham, M.A. | 25 | 39 | 8 | 67* | 656 | 21.16 | – | – | 7 |
| Edmonds, P.H. | 391 | 495 | 91 | 142 | 7651 | 18.93 | 3 | – | 345 |
| Ellison, R.M. | 204 | 280 | 71 | 108 | 4954 | 23.70 | 1 | – | 85 |
| Emburey, J.E. | 446 | 562 | 112 | 133 | 10316 | 22.92 | 5 | – | 403 |
| Evans, K.P. | 89 | 123 | 30 | 104 | 2374 | 25.52 | 2 | – | 69 |
| Everett, J. | 1 | 2 | – | 33 | 53 | 26.50 | – | – | 3 |
| Fairbrother, N.H. | 221 | 345 | 55 | 366 | 12177 | 41.98 | 26 | 8 | 140 |
| Farbrace, P. | 38 | 48 | 11 | 79 | 694 | 18.75 | – | – | 86/12 |
| Feltham, M.A. | 114 | 142 | 38 | 101 | 2526 | 24.28 | 1 | – | 48 |
| Felton, N.A. | 183 | 312 | 18 | 173* | 8771 | 29.83 | 13 | 4 | 101 |
| Field-Buss, M.G. | 18 | 18 | 4 | 34* | 136 | 9.71 | – | – | 7 |
| Fitton, J.D. | 52 | 61 | 15 | 60 | 872 | 18.95 | – | – | 11 |
| Fleming, M.V. | 68 | 108 | 14 | 116 | 2898 | 30.82 | 4 | – | 34 |
| Fletcher, I. | 1 | 2 | 1 | 56 | 58 | 58.00 | – | – | – |
| Fletcher, S.D. | 113 | 96 | 32 | 28* | 476 | 7.43 | – | – | 27 |
| Folland, N.A. | 2 | 4 | 1 | 82* | 212 | 70.66 | – | – | 1 |
| Fordham, A. | 103 | 182 | 16 | 206* | 6759 | 40.71 | 14 | 3 | 65 |
| Foster, D.J. | 45 | 39 | 15 | 20 | 201 | 8.37 | – | – | 8 |
| Foster, N.A. | 222 | 257 | 56 | 107* | 4108 | 20.43 | 2 | – | 115 |

| | M | I | NO | HS | Runs | Avge | 100 | 1000 | Ct/St |
|---|---|---|---|---|---|---|---|---|---|
| Fothergill, A.R. | 7 | 9 | 1 | 23 | 74 | 9.25 | – | – | 10/1 |
| Fowler, G. | 274 | 464 | 27 | 226 | 15803 | 36.16 | 35 | 8 | 143/5 |
| Fraser, A.G.J. | 10 | 10 | 5 | 52* | 137 | 27.40 | – | – | 1 |
| Fraser, A.R.C. | 119 | 134 | 34 | 92 | 1240 | 12.40 | – | – | 19 |
| French, B.N. | 340 | 444 | 88 | 105* | 6721 | 18.87 | 1 | – | 772/95 |
| Frost, M. | 62 | 48 | 16 | 12 | 87 | 2.71 | – | – | 7 |
| Fulton, D.P. | 1 | 2 | – | 42 | 58 | 29.00 | – | – | 2 |
| Gallian, J.E.R. | 10 | 16 | 1 | 112 | 485 | 32.33 | 1 | – | 6 |
| Garnham, M.A. | 171 | 221 | 46 | 123 | 4956 | 28.32 | 4 | – | 361/31 |
| Gatting, M.W. | 432 | 676 | 107 | 258 | 28512 | 50.10 | 72 | 14+1 | 376 |
| Gerrard, M.J. | 16 | 19 | 7 | 42 | 81 | 6.75 | – | – | 4 |
| Giddins, E.S.H. | 13 | 9 | 7 | 14* | 29 | 14.50 | – | – | 4 |
| Gidley, M.I. | 21 | 32 | 7 | 80 | 559 | 22.36 | – | – | 11 |
| Glendenen, J.D. | 17 | 28 | 1 | 117 | 607 | 22.48 | 1 | – | 5 |
| Gofton, R.P. | 5 | 8 | 1 | 75 | 142 | 20.28 | – | – | 2 |
| Goldsmith, S.C. | 75 | 118 | 12 | 127 | 2646 | 24.96 | 2 | 1 | 37 |
| Gooch, G.A. | 484 | 816 | 66 | 333 | 36126 | 48.16 | 99 | 16+1 | 478 |
| Gough, D. | 41 | 47 | 14 | 72 | 532 | 16.12 | – | – | 7 |
| Govan, J.W. | 10 | 13 | 1 | 17 | 87 | 7.25 | – | – | 6 |
| Gower, D.I. | 432 | 699 | 69 | 228 | 25203 | 40.00 | 49 | 12 | 269/1 |
| Graham, S. | 1 | 2 | – | 35 | 62 | 31.00 | – | – | – |
| Graveney, D.A. | 425 | 530 | 158 | 119 | 6501 | 17.47 | 2 | – | 224 |
| Grayson, A.P. | 14 | 18 | 5 | 57 | 291 | 22.38 | – | – | 7 |
| Greatbatch, M.J. | 104 | 179 | 22 | 202* | 5774 | 36.77 | 12 | – | 92 |
| Greenfield, K. | 25 | 42 | 5 | 127* | 995 | 26.89 | 3 | – | 27 |
| Greenidge, C.G. | 523 | 889 | 75 | 273* | 37354 | 45.88 | 92 | 15+2 | 516 |
| Griffith, F.A. | 20 | 31 | 4 | 81 | 467 | 17.29 | – | – | 12 |
| Gupte, C.M. | 13 | 15 | 2 | 55* | 236 | 18.15 | – | – | 3 |
| Habib, A. | 1 | 2 | 1 | 12 | 19 | 19.00 | – | – | – |
| Hall, J.W. | 55 | 97 | 9 | 140* | 2951 | 33.53 | 4 | 2 | 21 |
| Hallett, J.C. | 11 | 6 | 1 | 15 | 35 | 7.00 | – | – | 4 |
| Hancock, T.H.C. | 15 | 26 | 3 | 102 | 529 | 23.00 | 1 | – | 15 |
| Hanley, R. | 5 | 7 | – | 28 | 52 | 7.42 | – | – | – |
| Hansford, A.R. | 10 | 11 | 3 | 29 | 109 | 13.62 | – | – | 3 |
| Harden, R.J. | 155 | 245 | 41 | 187 | 7902 | 38.73 | 15 | 4 | 99 |
| Harper, R.A. | 174 | 226 | 39 | 234 | 6113 | 32.68 | 8 | – | 219 |
| Hartley, P.J. | 125 | 140 | 36 | 127* | 2279 | 21.91 | 1 | – | 43 |
| Hawkes, C.J. | 4 | 6 | 2 | 18 | 65 | 16.25 | – | – | 2 |
| Hayhurst, A.N. | 106 | 168 | 21 | 172* | 4851 | 33.00 | 9 | 2 | 31 |
| Haynes, D.L. | 298 | 510 | 58 | 255* | 21176 | 46.84 | 50 | 3+4 | 162/1 |
| Haynes, G.R. | 13 | 17 | 3 | 66 | 339 | 24.21 | – | – | 5 |
| Headley, D.W. | 29 | 29 | 4 | 91 | 472 | 18.88 | – | – | 10 |
| Hegg, W.K. | 127 | 179 | 34 | 130 | 3698 | 25.50 | 2 | – | 284/35 |
| Hemmings, E.E. | 482 | 627 | 146 | 127* | 9297 | 19.32 | 1 | – | 196 |
| Hemp, D.L. | 13 | 19 | 3 | 84* | 338 | 21.12 | – | – | 8 |
| Henderson, P.W. | 5 | 7 | – | 46 | 119 | 17.00 | – | – | 1 |
| Hepworth, P.N. | 46 | 75 | 7 | 115 | 1672 | 24.58 | 2 | 1 | 28 |
| Hick, G.A. | 226 | 364 | 41 | 405* | 19083 | 59.08 | 67 | 8+1 | 271 |
| Hindson, J.E. | 1 | – | – | – | – | – | – | – | – |
| Hinks, S.G. | 164 | 283 | 18 | 234 | 7971 | 30.07 | 11 | 3 | 99 |
| Hodgson, G.D. | 71 | 119 | 7 | 147 | 3705 | 33.08 | 5 | 3 | 30 |
| Hoey, C.J. | 2 | 3 | 1 | 8 | 16 | 8.00 | – | – | – |
| Holloway, P.C.L. | 11 | 17 | 6 | 102* | 436 | 39.63 | 1 | – | 25/1 |
| Hooper, A.M. | 24 | 41 | 2 | 125 | 848 | 21.74 | 1 | – | 2 |
| Hooper, C.L. | 118 | 178 | 21 | 196 | 6528 | 41.57 | 15 | 2 | 120 |

| | M | I | NO | HS | Runs | Avge | 100 | 1000 | Ct/St |
|---|---|---|---|---|---|---|---|---|---|
| Hughes, J.G. | 6 | 9 | – | 6 | 11 | 1.22 | – | – | 1 |
| Hughes, S.P. | 199 | 218 | 68 | 53 | 1738 | 11.58 | – | – | 49 |
| Hussain, N. | 99 | 142 | 22 | 197 | 5163 | 43.02 | 10 | 1 | 121 |
| Hutton, S. | 8 | 15 | – | 78 | 406 | 27.06 | – | – | 3 |
| Igglesden, A.P. | 103 | 106 | 37 | 41 | 670 | 9.71 | – | – | 29 |
| Ijaz Ahmed | 87 | 144 | 7 | 201* | 5351 | 39.05 | 11 | – | 70 |
| Illingworth, R.K. | 243 | 264 | 70 | 120* | 4094 | 21.10 | 3 | – | 105 |
| Ilott, M.C. | 42 | 39 | 11 | 42* | 331 | 11.82 | – | – | 10 |
| Inzamam-ul-Haq | 76 | 120 | 27 | 201* | 4701 | 50.54 | 14 | 0+2 | 61 |
| Irani, R.C. | 7 | 7 | 1 | 31* | 99 | 16.50 | – | – | 4 |
| James, K.D. | 140 | 197 | 36 | 162 | 5379 | 33.40 | 8 | 2 | 47 |
| James, S.P. | 77 | 131 | 11 | 152* | 4067 | 33.89 | 10 | 2 | 53 |
| Jarrett, M.E.D. | 9 | 13 | 2 | 27 | 106 | 9.63 | – | – | 2 |
| Jarvis, P.W. | 143 | 162 | 51 | 80 | 1896 | 17.08 | – | – | 36 |
| Javed Miandad | 394 | 618 | 94 | 311 | 28248 | 53.90 | 80 | 5+9 | 337/3 |
| Jean-Jacques, M. | 53 | 66 | 14 | 73 | 587 | 11.28 | – | – | 13 |
| Jeh, M.P.W. | 9 | 11 | 2 | 23 | 81 | 9.00 | – | – | 3 |
| Jenkins, R.H.J. | 17 | 21 | 6 | 20 | 123 | 8.20 | – | – | 4 |
| Johnson, P. | 215 | 353 | 37 | 165* | 11467 | 36.28 | 22 | 6 | 144/1 |
| Johnson, R.L. | 1 | 1 | – | 1 | 1 | 1.00 | – | – | 1 |
| Johnson, S.W. | 22 | 27 | 9 | 50 | 321 | 17.83 | – | – | 9 |
| Jones, A.N. | 170 | 147 | 61 | 43* | 998 | 11.60 | – | – | 42 |
| Jones, D.M. | 157 | 255 | 28 | 248 | 11790 | 51.93 | 34 | 2+3 | 119 |
| Jones, G.W. | 9 | 17 | 1 | 44 | 268. | 16.75 | – | – | 1 |
| Keech, M. | 15 | 24 | 3 | 58* | 420 | 20.00 | – | – | 4 |
| Keey, C.L. | 8 | 13 | 1 | 64 | 308 | 25.66 | – | – | 1 |
| Kellett, S.A. | 66 | 111 | 9 | 125* | 3422 | 33.54 | 2 | 2 | 57 |
| Kemp, T.R. | 2 | 1 | – | 0 | 0 | 0.00 | – | – | 1 |
| Kendrick, N.M. | 36 | 41 | 12 | 55 | 513 | 17.68 | – | – | 35 |
| Kersey, G.J. | 4 | 3 | 2 | 27* | 69 | 69.00 | – | – | 14/1 |
| Kirnon, S. | 1 | – | – | – | – | – | – | – | – |
| Knight, N.V. | 27 | 40 | 7 | 109 | 1215 | 36.81 | 3 | – | 22 |
| Krikken, K.M. | 74 | 104 | 16 | 77* | 1676 | 19.04 | – | – | 175/12 |
| Lamb, A.J. | 412 | 684 | 101 | 294 | 28495 | 48.87 | 79 | 11 | 320 |
| Lampitt, S.R. | 89 | 99 | 22 | 93 | 1665 | 21.62 | – | – | 35 |
| Larkins, W. | 436 | 762 | 48 | 252 | 24384 | 34.15 | 53 | 12 | 260 |
| Lathwell, M.N. | 21 | 36 | 1 | 114 | 1239 | 35.40 | 1 | 1 | 14 |
| Lawrence, D.V. | 181 | 205 | 35 | 66 | 1819 | 10.70 | – | – | 44 |
| Leatherdale, D.A. | 49 | 75 | 6 | 157 | 1864 | 27.01 | 2 | – | 38 |
| Lefebvre, R.P. | 43 | 44 | 10 | 100 | 715 | 21.02 | 1 | – | 20 |
| Lenham, N.J. | 128 | 218 | 21 | 222* | 6467 | 32.82 | 13 | 3 | 53 |
| Lewis, C.C. | 91 | 132 | 17 | 189* | 3282 | 28.53 | 3 | – | 65 |
| Lewis, D.A. | 5 | 9 | 1 | 122* | 260 | 32.50 | 1 | – | 1 |
| Lewis, J.J.B. | 16 | 23 | 5 | 133 | 935 | 51.94 | 2 | – | 5 |
| Ligertwood, D.G.C. | 4 | 7 | – | 28 | 63 | 9.00 | – | – | 7/1 |
| Llong, N.J. | 9 | 12 | 2 | 92 | 200 | 20.00 | – | – | 9 |
| Lloyd, G.D. | 63 | 101 | 13 | 132 | 3478 | 39.52 | 7 | 1 | 44 |
| Lloyd, T.A. | 312 | 547 | 45 | 208* | 17211 | 34.28 | 29 | 9 | 147 |
| Longley, J.I. | 7 | 12 | – | 110 | 211 | 17.58 | 1 | – | 4 |
| Lovell, G.B.T. | 18 | 26 | 4 | 110* | 672 | 30.54 | 1 | – | 13 |
| Loye, M.B. | 11 | 15 | 2 | 46 | 198 | 15.23 | – | – | 8 |
| Lynch, M.A. | 300 | 483 | 58 | 172* | 15377 | 36.18 | 34 | 8 | 289 |
| McBrine, A. | 4 | 6 | – | 102 | 155 | 25.83 | 1 | – | 1 |
| McCague, M.J. | 35 | 41 | 10 | 34 | 386 | 12.45 | – | – | 20 |
| McCrum, C. | 1 | 2 | – | 70 | 109 | 54.50 | – | – | – |

| | M | I | NO | HS | Runs | Avge | 100 | 1000 | Ct/St |
|---|---|---|---|---|---|---|---|---|---|
| McCrum, P. | 2 | 3 | 1 | 0* | 0 | 0.00 | – | – | |
| MacDonald, R.H. | 10 | 9 | 4 | 20 | 54 | 10.80 | – | – | |
| McEwan, S.M. | 65 | 48 | 17 | 54 | 407 | 13.12 | – | – | 24 |
| MacLeay, K.H. | 129 | 173 | 34 | 114* | 3750 | 26.97 | 3 | – | 79 |
| Malcolm, D.E. | 130 | 143 | 39 | 51 | 826 | 7.94 | – | – | 25 |
| Malik, H.S. | 1 | 1 | – | 4 | 4 | 4.00 | – | – | |
| Mallender, N.A. | 307 | 343 | 107 | 100* | 3868 | 16.38 | 1 | – | 103 |
| Marsh, S.A. | 172 | 240 | 45 | 125 | 5492 | 28.16 | 6 | – | 368/31 |
| Marshall, M.D. | 366 | 464 | 62 | 117 | 9863 | 24.53 | 6 | – | 131 |
| Martin, P.J. | 50 | 46 | 17 | 133 | 641 | 22.10 | 1 | – | 15 |
| Maru, R.J. | 200 | 190 | 46 | 74 | 2353 | 16.34 | – | – | 210 |
| Maynard, M.P. | 188 | 306 | 36 | 243 | 11362 | 42.08 | 25 | 7 | 161/2 |
| Mendis, G.D. | 348 | 609 | 61 | 209* | 20337 | 37.11 | 40 | 12 | 140/1 |
| Metcalfe, A.A. | 177 | 307 | 18 | 216* | 10163 | 35.16 | 23 | 6 | 66 |
| Metson, C.P. | 166 | 212 | 46 | 96 | 3001 | 18.07 | – | – | 387/30 |
| Middleton, T.C. | 78 | 130 | 13 | 221 | 4522 | 38.64 | 12 | 2 | 56 |
| Mike, G.W. | 10 | 13 | 4 | 61* | 246 | 27.33 | – | – | 6 |
| Milburn, S.M. | 1 | 1 | 1 | 5 | 7 | 7.00 | – | – | |
| Millns, D.J. | 63 | 68 | 28 | 44 | 509 | 12.72 | – | – | 30 |
| Moin Khan | 43 | 54 | 9 | 129 | 1110 | 24.66 | 1 | – | 108/7 |
| Moles, A.J. | 164 | 296 | 31 | 230* | 10814 | 40.80 | 22 | 5 | 117 |
| Montgomerie, R.R. | 18 | 28 | 5 | 103* | 786 | 34.17 | 1 | – | 12 |
| Moody, T.M. | 130 | 213 | 18 | 210 | 9424 | 48.32 | 31 | 2+1 | 103 |
| Moore, P.D. | 1 | 1 | 1 | 0* | 0 | – | – | – | 2 |
| Moores, P. | 136 | 188 | 25 | 116 | 3933 | 24.12 | 4 | – | 270/34 |
| Morris, H. | 216 | 367 | 38 | 160* | 12579 | 38.23 | 31 | 6 | 126 |
| Morris, J.E. | 218 | 359 | 26 | 191 | 12806 | 38.45 | 29 | 7 | 92 |
| Morris, R.S.M. | 5 | 9 | 1 | 74 | 209 | 26.12 | – | – | 7 |
| Morrison, D.K. | 93 | 90 | 28 | 36 | 495 | 7.98 | – | – | 33 |
| Mortensen, O.H. | 145 | 159 | 89 | 74* | 639 | 9.12 | – | – | 43 |
| Moxon, M.D. | 236 | 401 | 28 | 218* | 15234 | 40.84 | 33 | 8 | 185 |
| Mudassar Nazar | 219 | 354 | 33 | 241 | 14078 | 43.85 | 42 | 0+4 | 141 |
| Mullally, A.D. | 57 | 55 | 17 | 34 | 314 | 8.26 | – | – | 13 |
| Munton, T.A. | 147 | 150 | 58 | 47 | 892 | 9.69 | – | – | 52 |
| Murphy, A.J. | 72 | 71 | 28 | 38 | 225 | 5.23 | – | – | 12 |
| Mushtaq Ahmed | 53 | 58 | 9 | 75 | 537 | 10.95 | – | – | 30 |
| Naved Anjum | 116 | 184 | 18 | 159 | 4737 | 28.53 | 6 | – | 55 |
| Neale, P.A. | 354 | 571 | 93 | 167 | 17445 | 36.49 | 28 | 8 | 134 |
| Newell, M. | 102 | 178 | 26 | 203* | 4636 | 30.50 | 6 | 1 | 93/1 |
| Newport, P.J. | 194 | 212 | 66 | 98 | 3720 | 25.47 | – | – | 55 |
| Nicholas, M.C.J. | 321 | 526 | 76 | 206* | 14952 | 33.22 | 29 | 8 | 195 |
| Nixon, P.A. | 45 | 59 | 19 | 107* | 1081 | 27.02 | 1 | – | 109/9 |
| Noon, W.M. | 12 | 16 | 2 | 37 | 150 | 10.71 | – | – | 23/3 |
| North, J.A. | 16 | 20 | 3 | 63* | 285 | 16.76 | – | – | 2 |
| O'Gorman, T.J.G. | 71 | 120 | 16 | 148 | 3228 | 31.03 | 5 | 2 | 45 |
| Oliphant-Callum, R.D. | 3 | 2 | – | 19 | 28 | 14.00 | – | – | 1 |
| Orr, D.A. | 1 | 1 | 1 | 23* | 23 | – | – | – | 1/1 |
| Ostler, D.P. | 55 | 96 | 9 | 192 | 3019 | 34.70 | 4 | 2 | 49 |
| Parker, B | 1 | 2 | – | 30 | 37 | 18.50 | – | – | 1 |
| Parker, P.W.G. | 352 | 601 | 78 | 215 | 18495 | 35.36 | 44 | 9 | 244 |
| Parks, R.J. | 255 | 284 | 82 | 89 | 3944 | 19.52 | – | – | 638/72 |
| Parore, A.C. | 31 | 37 | 8 | 155* | 1062 | 36.62 | 1 | – | 63/9 |
| Parsons, G.J. | 260 | 341 | 77 | 76 | 4929 | 18.67 | – | – | 78 |
| Parsons, K.A. | 1 | 2 | – | 1 | 1 | 0.50 | – | – | |
| Patel, D.N. | 314 | 489 | 44 | 204 | 13951 | 31.35 | 26 | 6 | 165 |

183

| | M | I | NO | HS | Runs | Avge | 100 | 1000 | Ct/St |
|---|---|---|---|---|---|---|---|---|---|
| Patel, M.M. | 15 | 20 | 7 | 43 | 183 | 14.07 | – | – | 5 |
| Patterson, B.M.W. | 5 | 8 | – | 108 | 462 | 57.75 | 2 | – | 8 |
| Patterson, T.J.T. | 4 | 6 | 1 | 84 | 211 | 42.20 | – | – | 3 |
| Payne, A. | 1 | 1 | – | 51* | 51 | – | – | – | – |
| Pearson, R.M. | 21 | 25 | 6 | 33* | 166 | 8.73 | – | – | 6 |
| Penberthy, A.L. | 39 | 56 | 7 | 101* | 905 | 18.46 | 1 | – | 25 |
| Penn, C. | 123 | 141 | 36 | 115 | 1985 | 18.90 | 1 | – | 54 |
| Pennett, D.B. | 12 | 11 | 1 | 29 | 69 | 6.90 | – | – | 3 |
| Penney, T.L. | 22 | 33 | 10 | 151 | 1146 | 49.82 | 3 | – | 6 |
| Philip, I.L. | 7 | 11 | 1 | 145 | 574 | 57.40 | 3 | – | 7 |
| Pick, R.A. | 138 | 135 | 39 | 63 | 1430 | 14.89 | – | – | 32 |
| Pickles, C.S. | 58 | 76 | 21 | 66 | 1336 | 24.29 | – | – | 24 |
| Pierson, A.R.K. | 57 | 64 | 29 | 42* | 427 | 12.20 | – | – | 17 |
| Pigott, A.C.S. | 234 | 282 | 63 | 104* | 4452 | 20.32 | 1 | – | 115 |
| Piper, K.J. | 64 | 85 | 14 | 111 | 1388 | 19.54 | 1 | – | 158/9 |
| Pitcher, C.M. | 6 | 8 | 3 | 32* | 62 | 12.40 | – | – | – |
| Pollard, P.R. | 81 | 143 | 7 | 153 | 4056 | 29.82 | 6 | 2 | 75 |
| Pooley, J.C. | 17 | 30 | 2 | 88 | 628 | 22.42 | – | – | 9 |
| Potter, L. | 211 | 337 | 40 | 165* | 8623 | 29.03 | 7 | 3 | 178 |
| Prichard, P.J. | 194 | 306 | 38 | 245 | 9610 | 35.85 | 16 | 5 | 125 |
| Pringle, C. | 30 | 34 | 8 | 33 | 321 | 12.34 | – | – | 10 |
| Pringle, D.R. | 281 | 383 | 74 | 128 | 8633 | 27.93 | 10 | – | 142 |
| Radford, N.V. | 257 | 253 | 62 | 76* | 3140 | 16.43 | – | – | 121 |
| Ramiz Raja | 141 | 234 | 19 | 172 | 8001 | 37.21 | 15 | 1+1 | 75 |
| Ramprakash, M.R. | 117 | 193 | 32 | 233 | 6327 | 39.29 | 12 | 4 | 48 |
| Randall, D.W. | 483 | 817 | 81 | 237 | 28176 | 38.28 | 52 | 13 | 355 |
| Rashid Latif | 37 | 50 | 13 | 54* | 929 | 25.10 | – | – | 99/18 |
| Ratcliffe, J.D. | 54 | 102 | 8 | 127* | 2715 | 28.88 | 2 | – | 33 |
| Rea, M.P. | 6 | 12 | 1 | 89 | 307 | 27.90 | – | – | 1 |
| Reeve, D.A. | 189 | 248 | 63 | 202* | 6492 | 35.09 | 5 | 2 | 129 |
| Remy, C.C. | 10 | 11 | 1 | 47 | 196 | 19.60 | – | – | 2 |
| Rhodes, S.J. | 213 | 277 | 87 | 116* | 5939 | 31.25 | 3 | – | 504/62 |
| Richards, I.V.A. | 490 | 764 | 56 | 322 | 34977 | 49.40 | 112 | 13+3 | 447/1 |
| Richardson, A.W. | 1 | 1 | – | 5 | 5 | 5.00 | – | – | – |
| Richardson, M.S. | 1 | – | – | – | – | – | – | – | 1 |
| Richardson, R.B. | 151 | 250 | 22 | 194 | 9863 | 43.25 | 29 | 1+2 | 144 |
| Ripley, D. | 178 | 229 | 57 | 134* | 4268 | 24.81 | 6 | – | 372/55 |
| Roberts, A.R. | 33 | 42 | 13 | 62 | 577 | 19.89 | – | – | 15 |
| Robinson, J.D. | 31 | 49 | 10 | 79 | 898 | 23.02 | – | – | 12 |
| Robinson, M.A. | 100 | 95 | 42 | 19* | 126 | 2.37 | – | – | 22 |
| Robinson, P.E. | 133 | 219 | 31 | 189 | 6687 | 35.56 | 7 | 3 | 96 |
| Robinson, R.T. | 312 | 544 | 71 | 220* | 20209 | 42.72 | 46 | 10 | 199 |
| Robson, A.G. | 7 | 3 | 7 | 3 | 3 | 0.75 | – | – | 1 |
| Rollins, R.J. | 1 | 2 | – | 13 | 19 | 9.50 | – | – | 2 |
| Rose, G.D. | 122 | 159 | 36 | 132 | 3726 | 30.29 | 3 | 1 | 57 |
| Roseberry, A. | 1 | 2 | – | 14 | 14 | 7.00 | – | – | – |
| Roseberry, M.A. | 120 | 201 | 25 | 173 | 6782 | 38.53 | 15 | 3 | 83 |
| Russell, A.B. | 6 | 8 | 1 | 51 | 200 | 28.57 | – | – | 10 |
| Russell, R.C. | 251 | 351 | 80 | 128* | 7334 | 27.06 | 4 | – | 567/84 |
| Salim Jaffer | 69 | 61 | 27 | 33* | 332 | 9.76 | – | – | 18 |
| Salim Malik | 190 | 289 | 46 | 215 | 11875 | 48.86 | 31 | 2+1 | 124 |
| Salisbury, I.D.K. | 80 | 87 | 29 | 68 | 939 | 16.18 | – | – | 52 |
| Salmond, G. | 2 | 3 | – | 118 | 279 | 93.00 | 1 | – | 2 |
| Sandiford, D.C. | 10 | 11 | 1 | 83 | 210 | 21.00 | – | – | 11/1 |
| Sargeant, N.F. | 41 | 52 | 9 | 49 | 612 | 14.23 | – | – | 91/16 |

184

| | M | I | NO | HS | Runs | Avge | 100 | 1000 | Ct/St |
|---|---|---|---|---|---|---|---|---|---|
| Saxelby, M. | 24 | 40 | 7 | 73 | 982 | 29.75 | – | – | 4 |
| Scott, C.W. | 81 | 96 | 23 | 78 | 1696 | 23.23 | – | – | 162/11 |
| Scott, R.J. | 66 | 111 | 8 | 127 | 2516 | 24.42 | 3 | – | 33 |
| Seymour, A.C.H. | 25 | 45 | 4 | 157 | 1253 | 30.56 | 2 | – | 17 |
| Shahid, N. | 49 | 68 | 11 | 132 | 1966 | 34.49 | 2 | 1 | 42 |
| Sharp, M.A. | 1 | – | – | – | – | – | – | – | – |
| Sheridan, K.L.P. | 1 | – | – | – | – | – | – | – | – |
| Shine, K.J. | 41 | 33 | 16 | 26* | 204 | 12.00 | – | – | 3 |
| Shoaib Mohammad | 144 | 242 | 33 | 208* | 8801 | 42.11 | 27 | 0+1 | 65 |
| Simmons, P.V. | 85 | 151 | 6 | 202 | 4943 | 34.08 | 9 | 1 | 83 |
| Sims, R.J. | 1 | 1 | – | 3 | 3 | 3.00 | – | – | – |
| Sladdin, R.W. | 21 | 25 | 6 | 39 | 199 | 10.47 | – | – | 12 |
| Sleep, P.R. | 162 | 264 | 46 | 182 | 7600 | 34.86 | 14 | – | 95/1 |
| Small, G.C. | 272 | 351 | 82 | 70 | 4033 | 14.99 | – | – | 83 |
| Smith, A.M. | 26 | 27 | 7 | 51* | 229 | 11.45 | – | – | 3 |
| Smith, B.F. | 32 | 45 | 9 | 100* | 1134 | 31.50 | 1 | – | 13 |
| Smith, D.M. | 297 | 476 | 87 | 213 | 14137 | 36.34 | 27 | 7 | 183 |
| Smith, I. | 75 | 99 | 14 | 116 | 2158 | 25.38 | 4 | – | 29 |
| Smith, N.M.K. | 40 | 61 | 10 | 161 | 1399 | 27.43 | 1 | – | 14 |
| Smith, P.A. | 193 | 311 | 38 | 140 | 7377 | 27.02 | 4 | 2 | 53 |
| Smith, R.A. | 230 | 390 | 68 | 209* | 14227 | 44.18 | 33 | 6 | 153 |
| Snape, J.N. | 1 | – | – | – | – | – | – | – | 1 |
| Snell, R.P. | 41 | 53 | 10 | 81 | 724 | 16.83 | – | – | 12 |
| Speak, N.J. | 53 | 92 | 7 | 232 | 3380 | 39.76 | 6 | 1 | 35 |
| Speight, M.P. | 80 | 130 | 12 | 179 | 4164 | 35.28 | 8 | 2 | 58 |
| Stanley, N.A. | 21 | 35 | 4 | 132 | 1019 | 32.87 | 1 | – | 9 |
| Stanworth, J. | 44 | 40 | 11 | 50* | 266 | 9.17 | – | – | 63/10 |
| Stemp, R.D. | 22 | 16 | 11 | 16* | 103 | 20.60 | – | – | 5 |
| Stephenson, F.D. | 142 | 215 | 28 | 165 | 5108 | 27.31 | 6 | 1 | 60 |
| Stephenson, J.P. | 155 | 265 | 29 | 202* | 8684 | 36.79 | 15 | 4 | 84 |
| Stewart, A.J. | 222 | 366 | 45 | 206* | 12608 | 39.27 | 23 | 7 | 273/6 |
| Storie, A.C. | 53 | 86 | 13 | 106 | 1495 | 20.47 | 1 | – | 34 |
| Such, P.M. | 132 | 105 | 40 | 35* | 315 | 4.84 | – | – | 50 |
| Sylvester, S.A. | 5 | 2 | 1 | 0* | 0 | – | – | – | 2 |
| Tanvir Mehdi | 28 | 25 | 10 | 21* | 166 | 11.06 | – | – | 9 |
| Tavaré, C.J. | 418 | 692 | 74 | 219 | 24278 | 39.28 | 47 | 16 | 396 |
| Taylor, C.W. | 27 | 21 | 8 | 21 | 147 | 11.30 | – | – | 5 |
| Taylor, J.P. | 43 | 37 | 14 | 74* | 239 | 10.39 | – | – | 16 |
| Taylor, N.R.(H) | 2 | 2 | – | 0 | 0 | 0.00 | – | – | 1 |
| Taylor, N.R.(K) | 264 | 450 | 61 | 204 | 15622 | 40.15 | 38 | 9 | 143 |
| Tendulkar, S.R. | 60 | 97 | 11 | 159 | 4708 | 54.74 | 10 | 1 | 28 |
| Tennant, L. | 10 | 13 | 5 | 23* | 110 | 13.75 | – | – | 1 |
| Terry, V.P. | 227 | 379 | 38 | 190 | 12281 | 36.01 | 27 | 8 | 250 |
| Thomas, S.D. | 6 | 7 | 2 | 10 | 25 | 5.00 | – | – | 1 |
| Thomson, K. | 1 | – | – | – | – | – | – | – | – |
| Thorpe, G.P. | 96 | 157 | 26 | 216 | 5650 | 43.12 | 10 | 3 | 60 |
| Thursfield, M.J. | 3 | – | – | – | – | – | – | – | – |
| Thwaites, G.E. | 4 | 6 | – | 32 | 68 | 11.33 | – | – | 2 |
| Titchard, S.P. | 25 | 44 | 4 | 135 | 1343 | 33.57 | 1 | – | 16 |
| Tolley, C.M. | 33 | 32 | 11 | 37 | 432 | 20.57 | – | – | 14 |
| Topley, T.D. | 111 | 125 | 28 | 66 | 1536 | 15.83 | – | – | 67 |
| Townsend, C.J. | 5 | 4 | 1 | 8 | 8 | 2.66 | – | – | 8 |
| Townsend, G.T.J. | 12 | 22 | 2 | 53 | 414 | 20.70 | – | – | 10 |
| Trump, H.R.J. | 66 | 66 | 18 | 48 | 429 | 8.93 | – | – | 42 |
| Tufnell, P.C.R. | 114 | 113 | 45 | 37 | 722 | 10.61 | – | – | 49 |

185

|  | M | I | NO | HS | Runs | Avge | 100 | 1000 | Ct/St |
|---|---|---|---|---|---|---|---|---|---|
| Turner, I.J. | 20 | 22 | 7 | 39* | 142 | 9.46 | – | – | 9 |
| Turner, R.J. | 41 | 64 | 14 | 101* | 1245 | 24.90 | 1 | – | 42/12 |
| Tutt, A. | 1 | – | – | – | – | – | – | – | – |
| Tweats, T.A. | 1 | 1 | – | 24 | 24 | 24.00 | – | – | 1 |
| Twose, R.G. | 56 | 96 | 12 | 233 | 2900 | 34.52 | 3 | 1 | 36 |
| Udal, S.D. | 32 | 36 | 12 | 44 | 479 | 19.95 | – | – | 6 |
| Van Troost, A.P. | 15 | 10 | 6 | 12 | 42 | 10.50 | – | – | 4 |
| Vaughan, J.T.C. | 33 | 53 | 12 | 106* | 1462 | 35.65 | 1 | – | 32 |
| Walker, A. | 96 | 91 | 45 | 41* | 664 | 14.43 | – | – | 37 |
| Walsh, C.A. | 252 | 306 | 72 | 63* | 2969 | 12.68 | – | – | 68 |
| Waqar Younis | 80 | 78 | 31 | 51 | 634 | 13.48 | – | – | 18 |
| Ward, D.M. | 121 | 192 | 31 | 263 | 6430 | 39.93 | 14 | 2 | 100/3 |
| Ward, I.J. | 1 | 1 | – | 0 | 0 | 0.00 | – | – | 1 |
| Ward, T.R. | 93 | 160 | 12 | 235* | 5683 | 38.39 | 13 | 3 | 71 |
| Warke, S.J.S. | 11 | 20 | 2 | 144* | 832 | 46.22 | 2 | – | 7 |
| Warley, S.N. | 9 | 13 | 2 | 35 | 132 | 12.00 | – | – | 3 |
| Warner, A.E. | 163 | 221 | 40 | 91 | 3164 | 17.48 | – | – | 39 |
| Warren, R.J. | 2 | 3 | 1 | 19 | 27 | 13.50 | – | – | – |
| Wasim Akram | 122 | 158 | 24 | 123 | 2981 | 22.24 | 3 | – | 39 |
| Watkin, S.L. | 117 | 122 | 33 | 41 | 738 | 8.29 | – | – | 24 |
| Watkinson, M. | 200 | 292 | 36 | 138 | 6192 | 24.18 | 3 | – | 99 |
| Waugh, M.E. | 139 | 217 | 33 | 229* | 10448 | 56.78 | 35 | 3+2 | 175 |
| Weekes, P.N. | 26 | 35 | 8 | 95 | 863 | 31.96 | – | – | 23 |
| Wells, A.P. | 234 | 386 | 64 | 253* | 12481 | 38.76 | 26 | 7 | 131 |
| Wells, C.M. | 276 | 436 | 69 | 203 | 12203 | 33.25 | 20 | 6 | 86 |
| Wells, V.J. | 31 | 48 | 7 | 58 | 1008 | 24.58 | – | – | 13 |
| Weston, M.J. | 154 | 245 | 23 | 145* | 5320 | 23.96 | 3 | 1 | 73 |
| Weston, W.P.C. | 16 | 26 | 5 | 66* | 703 | 33.47 | – | – | 2 |
| Whitaker, J.J. | 225 | 357 | 43 | 200* | 12003 | 38.22 | 24 | 8 | 142 |
| White, C. | 32 | 41 | 10 | 79* | 1045 | 33.70 | – | – | 20 |
| White, G.W. | 1 | 1 | – | 42 | 42 | 42.00 | – | – | – |
| Whitticase, P. | 129 | 169 | 39 | 114* | 2963 | 22.79 | 1 | – | 302/13 |
| Whittington, J.M.S. | 1 | – | – | – | – | – | – | – | – |
| Wight, R.M. | 10 | 17 | 3 | 62* | 388 | 27.71 | – | – | 3 |
| Wileman, J.R. | 1 | 1 | – | 109 | 109 | 109.00 | 1 | – | 2 |
| Williams, N.F. | 198 | 232 | 46 | 77 | 3629 | 19.51 | – | – | 54 |
| Williams, R.C. | 8 | 13 | 1 | 44 | 130 | 10.83 | – | – | – |
| Williams, R.C.J. | 23 | 25 | 8 | 55* | 278 | 16.35 | – | – | 54/11 |
| Williams, R.G. | 284 | 447 | 65 | 175* | 11817 | 30.93 | 18 | 6 | 99 |
| Windows, M.G.N. | 1 | 1 | – | 71 | 71 | 71.00 | – | – | 1 |
| Wood, B.S. | 13 | 10 | 2 | 13 | 37 | 4.62 | – | – | – |
| Wood, J. | 8 | 6 | 1 | 28 | 80 | 16.00 | – | – | 1 |
| Wood, J.R. | 26 | 35 | 3 | 96 | 935 | 29.21 | – | – | 13 |
| Wren, T.N. | 7 | 5 | 2 | 16 | 23 | 7.66 | – | – | 4 |
| Wright, A.J. | 205 | 352 | 26 | 161 | 9337 | 28.64 | 12 | 4 | 140 |
| Yates, G. | 25 | 30 | 15 | 106 | 480 | 32.00 | 2 | – | 10 |
| Zahid Fazal | 29 | 42 | 7 | 115 | 1197 | 34.20 | 3 | – | 19 |

## BOWLING

'100wS' denotes instances of taking 100 or more wickets in a season.

|  | Runs | Wkts | Avge | Best | 5wI | 10wM | 100wS |
|---|---|---|---|---|---|---|---|
| Aamir Sohail | 3256 | 90 | 36.17 | 7-53 | 1 | 1 | – |
| Abington, M.B. | 530 | 10 | 53.00 | 3-33 | – | – | – |
| Adams, C.J. | 375 | 10 | 37.50 | 4-29 | – | – | – |

| | Runs | Wkts | Avge | Best | 5wI | 10wM | 100wS |
|---|---|---|---|---|---|---|---|
| Afford, J.A. | 9900 | 296 | 33.44 | 6-68 | 9 | 2 | – |
| Alikhan, R.I. | 274 | 7 | 39.14 | 2-19 | – | – | – |
| Alleyne, M.W. | 2505 | 62 | 40.40 | 4-48 | – | – | – |
| Ambrose, C.E.L. | 9293 | 420 | 22.12 | 8-45 | 19 | 3 | – |
| Anderson, D.J. | 511 | 9 | 56.77 | 2-68 | – | – | – |
| Andrew, S.J.W. | 8349 | 260 | 32.11 | 7-92 | 5 | – | – |
| Aqib Javed | 4105 | 122 | 33.64 | 6-91 | 4 | – | – |
| Arscott, J.P. | 252 | 7 | 36.00 | 1-17 | – | – | – |
| Asif Din | 4256 | 73 | 58.30 | 5-100 | 1 | – | – |
| Asif Mujtaba | 3960 | 178 | 22.24 | 6-19 | 10 | 2 | – |
| Ata-ur-Rehman | 1335 | 40 | 33.37 | 8-87 | 1 | – | – |
| Atherton, M.A. | 4666 | 106 | 44.01 | 6-78 | 3 | – | – |
| Athey, C.W.J. | 2339 | 45 | 51.97 | 3-3 | – | – | – |
| Austin, I.D. | 2919 | 78 | 37.42 | 5-79 | 1 | – | – |
| Ayling, J.R. | 3254 | 131 | 24.83 | 5-12 | 1 | – | – |
| Aymes, A.N. | 75 | 1 | 75.00 | 1-75 | – | – | – |
| Babington, A.M. | 6911 | 194 | 35.62 | 8-107 | 3 | – | – |
| Bailey, R.J. | 2361 | 55 | 42.92 | 3-27 | – | – | – |
| Bainbridge, P. | 10554 | 287 | 36.77 | 8-53 | 8 | – | – |
| Bakker, P-J. | 5406 | 193 | 28.01 | 7-31 | 7 | – | – |
| Ball, M.C.J. | 2499 | 70 | 34.98 | 5-101 | 2 | – | – |
| Barnett, A.A. | 2559 | 56 | 45.69 | 5-78 | 2 | – | – |
| Barnett, K.J. | 5324 | 137 | 38.86 | 6-28 | 2 | – | – |
| Bartlett, R.J. | 145 | 4 | 36.25 | 1-9 | – | – | – |
| Barwick, S.R. | 12931 | 378 | 34.20 | 8-42 | 9 | 1 | – |
| Base, S.J. | 8915 | 323 | 27.60 | 7-60 | 12 | 1 | – |
| Bastien, S. | 3715 | 96 | 38.69 | 6-75 | 5 | – | – |
| Batty, J.D. | 3864 | 99 | 39.03 | 6-48 | 2 | – | – |
| Bee, A. | 219 | 3 | 73.00 | 2-20 | – | – | – |
| Bell, M.A.V. | 247 | 8 | 30.87 | 3-78 | – | – | – |
| Benjamin, J.E. | 3800 | 109 | 34.86 | 6-30 | 6 | – | – |
| Benjamin, K.C.G. | 1943 | 81 | 23.98 | 7-51 | 2 | – | – |
| Benjamin, W.K.M. | 8946 | 343 | 26.08 | 7-54 | 17 | 2 | – |
| Benson, J.D.R. | 488 | 8 | 61.00 | 2-24 | – | – | – |
| Benson, M.R. | 493 | 5 | 98.60 | 2-55 | – | – | – |
| Berry, P.J. | 1050 | 24 | 43.75 | 7-113 | 1 | 1 | – |
| Bicknell, D.J. | 265 | 3 | 88.33 | 2-62 | – | – | – |
| Bicknell, M.P. | 10298 | 383 | 26.88 | 9-45 | 13 | – | – |
| Bishop, I.R. | 6660 | 325 | 20.49 | 7-34 | 18 | 1 | – |
| Blakey, R.J. | 68 | 1 | 68.00 | 1-68 | – | – | – |
| Boden, D.J.P. | 68 | 4 | 17.00 | 4-11 | – | – | – |
| Boiling, J. | 2286 | 62 | 36.87 | 6-84 | 1 | 1 | – |
| Boon, T.J. | 525 | 11 | 47.72 | 3-40 | – | – | – |
| Booth, P.A. | 3804 | 91 | 41.80 | 5-98 | 1 | – | – |
| Botham, I.T. | 31386 | 1159 | 27.08 | 8-34 | 59 | 8 | 1 |
| Bowen, M.N. | 247 | 2 | 123.50 | 1-23 | – | – | – |
| Bowler, P.D. | 1449 | 20 | 72.45 | 3-41 | – | – | – |
| Briers, M.P. | 621 | 12 | 51.75 | 3-109 | – | – | – |
| Briers, N.E. | 988 | 32 | 30.87 | 4-29 | – | – | – |
| Broad, B.C. | 1036 | 16 | 64.75 | 2-14 | – | – | – |
| Broadhurst, M. | 130 | 6 | 21.66 | 3-61 | – | – | – |
| Brown, A.D. (Sy) | 78 | 0 | – | – | – | – | – |
| Brown, A.M. | 9 | 0 | – | – | – | – | – |
| Brown, D.R. | 204 | 8 | 25.50 | 3-27 | – | – | – |
| Brown, G.K. | 103 | 1 | 103.00 | 1-39 | – | – | – |

| | Runs | Wkts | Avge | Best | 5wI | 10wM | 100wS |
|---|---|---|---|---|---|---|---|
| Brown, K.R. | 162 | 5 | 32.40 | 2-7 | – | – | – |
| Brown, S.J.E. | 2787 | 83 | 33.57 | 7-105 | 3 | – | – |
| Bryson, R.E. | 3735 | 136 | 27.46 | 7-68 | 10 | 2 | – |
| Burns, N.D. | 8 | 0 | – | – | – | – | – |
| Butcher, A.R. | 5433 | 141 | 38.53 | 6-48 | 1 | – | – |
| Butcher, M.A. | 115 | 1 | 115.00 | 1-95 | – | – | – |
| Byas, D. | 612 | 10 | 61.20 | 3-55 | – | – | – |
| Caddick, A.R. | 2169 | 76 | 28.53 | 6-52 | 3 | 1 | – |
| Cairns, C.L. | 5619 | 187 | 30.04 | 7-34 | 6 | 2 | – |
| Capel, D.J. | 14350 | 439 | 32.68 | 7-46 | 12 | – | – |
| Carr, J.D. | 2866 | 64 | 44.78 | 6-61 | 3 | – | – |
| Carrick, P. | 32115 | 1078 | 29.79 | 8-33 | 47 | 5 | – |
| Chapman, R.J. | 77 | 2 | 38.50 | 1-38 | – | – | – |
| Chapple, G. | 128 | 5 | 25.60 | 3-40 | – | – | – |
| Childs, J.H. | 25095 | 840 | 29.87 | 9-56 | 45 | 8 | – |
| Connor, C.A. | 13326 | 405 | 32.90 | 7-31 | 10 | 1 | – |
| Cook, N.G.B. | 24380 | 854 | 28.54 | 7-34 | 31 | 4 | – |
| Cooper, K.E. | 19332 | 711 | 27.18 | 8-44 | 25 | 1 | 1 |
| Cork, D.G. | 3135 | 115 | 27.26 | 8-53 | 3 | 1 | – |
| Cottam, A.C. | 280 | 6 | 46.66 | 1-1 | – | – | – |
| Cottey, P.A. | 303 | 6 | 50.50 | 2-42 | – | – | – |
| Cowans, N.G. | 15241 | 620 | 24.58 | 6-31 | 23 | 1 | – |
| Cowdrey, C.S. | 7962 | 200 | 39.81 | 5-46 | 2 | – | – |
| Cowdrey, G.R. | 749 | 11 | 68.09 | 1-5 | – | – | – |
| Cox, R.M.F. | 1 | 0 | – | – | – | – | – |
| Crawley, J.P. | 104 | 1 | 104.00 | 1-90 | – | – | – |
| Crawley, M.A. | 2682 | 57 | 47.05 | 6-92 | 1 | – | – |
| Crawley, P.M. | 236 | 3 | 78.66 | 2-36 | – | – | – |
| Croft, R.D.B. | 6076 | 143 | 42.48 | 8-66 | 6 | 1 | – |
| Cummins, A.C. | 964 | 38 | 25.36 | 4-26 | – | – | – |
| Curran, K.M. | 10589 | 409 | 25.88 | 7-47 | 12 | 4 | – |
| Curtis, T.S. | 657 | 11 | 59.72 | 2-17 | – | – | – |
| Dale, A. | 1547 | 38 | 40.71 | 3-21 | – | – | – |
| Davies, H.R. | 1377 | 13 | 105.92 | 3-93 | – | – | – |
| Davies, M. | 1677 | 56 | 29.94 | 4-73 | – | – | – |
| Davis, R.P. | 10010 | 280 | 35.75 | 7-64 | 11 | 1 | – |
| DeFreitas, P.A.J. | 14847 | 542 | 27.39 | 7-21 | 27 | 2 | – |
| De la Pena, J.M. | 138 | 3 | 46.00 | 2-69 | – | – | – |
| Dilley, G.R. | 17395 | 648 | 26.84 | 7-63 | 34 | 3 | – |
| Dobson, M.C. | 486 | 9 | 54.00 | 2-20 | – | – | – |
| Doidge, M.J. | 106 | 0 | – | – | – | – | – |
| D'Oliveira, D.B. | 1712 | 37 | 46.27 | 2-17 | – | – | – |
| Donald, A.A. | 12586 | 546 | 23.05 | 8-37 | 30 | 3 | – |
| Donelan, B.T.P. | 4118 | 96 | 42.89 | 6-62 | 3 | 1 | – |
| Dunlop, A.R. | 143 | 2 | 71.50 | 1-8 | – | – | – |
| Ealham, M.A. | 1835 | 58 | 31.63 | 5-39 | 2 | – | – |
| Edmonds, P.H. | 31981 | 1246 | 25.66 | 8-53 | 47 | 9 | – |
| Ellison, R.M. | 13604 | 471 | 28.88 | 7-33 | 18 | 2 | – |
| Emburey, J.E. | 35599 | 1366 | 26.06 | 7-27 | 63 | 9 | 1 |
| Evans, K.P. | 6405 | 182 | 35.19 | 5-27 | 3 | – | – |
| Fairbrother, N.H. | 423 | 5 | 84.60 | 2-91 | – | – | – |
| Farbrace, P. | 64 | 1 | 64.00 | 1-64 | – | – | – |
| Feltham, M.A. | 9266 | 292 | 31.73 | 6-53 | 6 | – | – |
| Felton, N.A. | 345 | 2 | 172.50 | 1-48 | – | – | – |
| Field-Buss, M.G. | 1004 | 22 | 45.63 | 4-33 | – | – | – |

188

|  | Runs | Wkts | Avge | Best | 5wI | 10wM | 100wS |
|---|---|---|---|---|---|---|---|
| Fitton, J.D. | 4359 | 82 | 53.15 | 6-59 | 3 | – | – |
| Fleming, M.V. | 2786 | 68 | 40.97 | 4-63 | – | – | – |
| Fletcher, S.D. | 8375 | 240 | 34.89 | 8-58 | 5 | – | – |
| Fordham, A. | 238 | 3 | 79.33 | 1-25 | – | – | – |
| Foster, D.J. | 3844 | 96 | 40.04 | 6-84 | 2 | – | – |
| Foster, N.A. | 21473 | 896 | 23.96 | 8-99 | 49 | 8 | 2 |
| Fowler, G. | 366 | 10 | 36.60 | 2-34 | – | – | – |
| Fraser, A.G.J. | 386 | 12 | 32.16 | 3-46 | – | – | – |
| Fraser, A.R.C. | 9376 | 355 | 26.41 | 7-77 | 16 | 2 | – |
| French, B.N. | 70 | 1 | 70.00 | 1-37 | – | – | – |
| Frost, M. | 5825 | 162 | 35.95 | 7-99 | 4 | 2 | – |
| Gallian, J.E.R. | 693 | 19 | 36.47 | 4-29 | – | – | – |
| Garnham, M.A. | 39 | 0 | – | – | – | – | – |
| Gatting, M.W. | 4466 | 154 | 29.00 | 5-34 | 2 | – | – |
| Gerrard, M.J. | 1016 | 26 | 39.07 | 6-40 | 1 | 1 | – |
| Giddins, E.S.H. | 1043 | 33 | 31.60 | 5-32 | 2 | – | – |
| Gidley, M.I. | 1116 | 16 | 69.75 | 3-51 | – | – | – |
| Gofton, R.P. | 348 | 6 | 58.00 | 4-81 | – | – | – |
| Goldsmith, S.C. | 1571 | 29 | 54.17 | 3-42 | – | – | – |
| Gooch, G.A. | 8034 | 231 | 34.77 | 7-14 | 3 | – | – |
| Gough, D. | 3105 | 79 | 39.30 | 5-41 | 1 | – | – |
| Govan, J.W. | 846 | 35 | 24.17 | 6-70 | 2 | – | – |
| Gower, D.I. | 227 | 4 | 56.75 | 3-47 | – | – | – |
| Graveney, D.A. | 27314 | 912 | 29.94 | 8-85 | 38 | 7 | – |
| Grayson, A.P. | 523 | 3 | 174.33 | 1-3 | – | – | – |
| Greatbatch, M.J. | 65 | 0 | – | – | – | – | – |
| Greenfield, K. | 133 | 0 | – | – | – | – | – |
| Greenidge, C.G. | 479 | 18 | 26.61 | 5-49 | 1 | – | – |
| Griffith, F.A. | 1017 | 33 | 30.81 | 4-33 | – | – | – |
| Gupte, C.M. | 253 | 4 | 63.25 | 2-41 | – | – | – |
| Hall, J.W. | 14 | 0 | – | – | – | – | – |
| Hallett, J.C. | 875 | 18 | 48.61 | 3-154 | – | – | – |
| Hancock, T.H.C. | 136 | 4 | 34.00 | 2-43 | – | – | – |
| Hansford, A.R. | 991 | 30 | 33.03 | 5-79 | 1 | – | – |
| Harden, R.J. | 952 | 19 | 50.10 | 2-7 | – | – | – |
| Harper, R.A. | 13085 | 475 | 27.54 | 6-57 | 20 | 2 | – |
| Hartley, P.J. | 10863 | 318 | 34.16 | 8-111 | 12 | – | – |
| Hawkes, C.J. | 162 | 5 | 32.40 | 4-18 | – | – | – |
| Hayhurst, A.N. | 3918 | 86 | 45.55 | 4-27 | – | – | – |
| Haynes, D.L. | 201 | 7 | 28.71 | 1-2 | – | – | – |
| Haynes, G.R. | 210 | 0 | – | – | – | – | – |
| Headley, D.W. | 2516 | 60 | 41.93 | 5-46 | 2 | – | – |
| Hegg, W.K. | 7 | 0 | – | – | – | – | – |
| Hemmings, E.E. | 41461 | 1404 | 29.53 | 10-175 | 66 | 14 | – |
| Henderson, P.W. | 405 | 10 | 40.50 | 3-59 | – | – | – |
| Hepworth, P.N. | 902 | 19 | 47.47 | 3-51 | – | – | – |
| Hick, G.A. | 5575 | 142 | 39.26 | 5-37 | 4 | 1 | – |
| Hindson, J.E. | 74 | 8 | 9.25 | 5-42 | 1 | – | – |
| Hinks, S.G. | 381 | 8 | 47.62 | 2-18 | – | – | – |
| Hodgson, G.D. | 65 | 0 | – | – | – | – | – |
| Hoey, C.J. | 144 | 5 | 28.80 | 3-38 | – | – | – |
| Hooper, A.M. | 275 | 6 | 45.83 | 1-5 | – | – | – |
| Hooper, C.L. | 6039 | 181 | 33.36 | 5-33 | 5 | – | – |
| Hughes, J.G. | 450 | 7 | 64.28 | 3-56 | – | – | – |
| Hughes, S.P. | 14587 | 458 | 31.84 | 7-35 | 10 | – | – |

| | Runs | Wkts | Avge | Best | 5wI | 10wM | 100wS |
|---|---|---|---|---|---|---|---|
| Hussain, N. | 198 | 1 | 198.00 | 1-38 | – | – | – |
| Hutton, S. | 4 | 0 | – | – | – | – | – |
| Igglesden, A.P. | 9275 | 328 | 28.27 | 6-34 | 14 | 2 | – |
| Ijaz Ahmed | 533 | 20 | 26.65 | 4-50 | – | – | – |
| Illingworth, R.K. | 16749 | 525 | 31.90 | 7-50 | 19 | 4 | – |
| Ilott, M.C. | 3980 | 117 | 34.01 | 6-87 | 5 | – | – |
| Inzamam-ul-Haq | 1217 | 37 | 32.89 | 5-80 | 2 | – | – |
| Irani, R.C. | 292 | 5 | 58.40 | 2-21 | – | – | – |
| James, K.D. | 7228 | 219 | 33.00 | 6-22 | 7 | – | – |
| Jarvis, P.W. | 12571 | 457 | 27.50 | 7-55 | 18 | 3 | – |
| Javed Miandad | 6395 | 191 | 33.48 | 7-39 | 6 | – | – |
| Jean-Jacques, M. | 4091 | 115 | 35.57 | 8-77 | 2 | 1 | – |
| Jeh, M.P.W. | 846 | 17 | 49.76 | 3-44 | – | – | – |
| Jenkins, R.H.J. | 1610 | 24 | 67.08 | 5-100 | 1 | – | – |
| Johnson, P. | 510 | 5 | 102.00 | 1-9 | – | – | – |
| Johnson, R.L. | 71 | 1 | 71.00 | 1-25 | – | – | – |
| Johnson, S.W. | 1601 | 16 | 100.06 | 3-62 | – | – | – |
| Jones, A.N. | 13143 | 408 | 32.21 | 7-30 | 12 | 1 | – |
| Jones, D.M. | 966 | 15 | 64.40 | 1-0 | – | – | – |
| Keech, M. | 36 | 0 | – | – | – | – | – |
| Kellett, S.A. | 19 | 0 | – | – | – | – | – |
| Kemp, T.R. | 128 | 1 | 128.00 | 1-35 | – | – | – |
| Kendrick, N.M. | 3259 | 95 | 34.30 | 6-61 | 5 | 1 | – |
| Kirnon, S. | 21 | 1 | 21.00 | 1-14 | – | – | – |
| Knight, N.V. | 32 | 0 | – | – | – | – | – |
| Krikken, K.M. | 40 | 0 | – | – | – | – | – |
| Lamb, A.J. | 199 | 8 | 24.87 | 2-29 | – | – | – |
| Lampitt, S.R. | 5673 | 186 | 30.50 | 5-32 | 8 | – | – |
| Larkins, W. | 1858 | 42 | 44.23 | 5-59 | 1 | – | – |
| Lathwell, M.N. | 323 | 5 | 64.60 | 1-9 | – | – | – |
| Lawrence, D.V. | 16162 | 507 | 31.87 | 7-47 | 21 | 1 | – |
| Leatherdale, D.A. | 59 | 1 | 59.00 | 1-12 | – | – | – |
| Lefebvre, R.P. | 2945 | 74 | 39.79 | 6-53 | 2 | – | – |
| Lenham, N.J. | 1395 | 29 | 48.10 | 4-85 | – | – | – |
| Lewis, C.C. | 7757 | 271 | 28.62 | 6-22 | 13 | 3 | – |
| Lewis, D.A. | 232 | 4 | 58.00 | 2-39 | – | – | – |
| Llong, N.J. | 264 | 7 | 37.71 | 3-50 | – | – | – |
| Lloyd, G.D. | 186 | 1 | 186.00 | 1-57 | – | – | – |
| Lloyd, T.A. | 1682 | 23 | 73.13 | 3-7 | – | – | – |
| Lovell, G.B.T. | 141 | 1 | 141.00 | 1-13 | – | – | – |
| Lynch, M.A. | 1360 | 26 | 52.30 | 3-6 | – | – | – |
| McBrine, A. | 221 | 6 | 36.83 | 3-64 | – | – | – |
| McCague, M.J. | 2997 | 101 | 29.67 | 8-26 | 7 | 1 | – |
| McCrum, C. | 97 | 3 | 32.33 | 3-57 | – | – | – |
| McCrum, P. | 173 | 1 | 173.00 | 1-80 | – | – | – |
| MacDonald, R.H. | 645 | 15 | 43.00 | 3-66 | – | – | – |
| McEwan, S.M. | 4869 | 156 | 31.21 | 6-34 | 3 | – | – |
| MacLeay, K.H. | 9080 | 300 | 30.26 | 6-93 | 6 | – | – |
| Malcolm, D.E. | 12500 | 394 | 31.72 | 7-74 | 10 | 1 | – |
| Malik, H.S. | 88 | 0 | – | – | – | – | – |
| Mallender, N.A. | 22368 | 842 | 26.56 | 7-27 | 33 | 5 | – |
| Marsh, S.A. | 227 | 2 | 113.50 | 2-20 | – | – | – |
| Marshall, M.D. | 28511 | 1524 | 18.70 | 8-71 | 83 | 13 | 2 |
| Martin, P.J. | 3814 | 96 | 39.72 | 4-30 | – | – | – |
| Maru, R.J. | 15538 | 479 | 32.43 | 8-41 | 15 | 1 | – |

|  | Runs | Wkts | Avge | Best | 5wI | 10wM | 100wS |
|---|---|---|---|---|---|---|---|
| Maynard, M.P. | 566 | 5 | 113.20 | 3-21 | – | – | – |
| Mendis, G.D. | 158 | 1 | 158.00 | 1-65 | – | – | – |
| Metcalfe, A.A. | 316 | 4 | 79.00 | 2-18 | – | – | – |
| Metson, C.P. | 0 | 0 | – | – | – | – | – |
| Middleton, T.C. | 237 | 5 | 47.40 | 2-41 | – | – | – |
| Mike, G.W. | 684 | 14 | 48.85 | 3-48 | – | – | – |
| Milburn, S.M. | 115 | 1 | 115.00 | 1-54 | – | – | – |
| Millns, D.J. | 5227 | 195 | 26.80 | 9-37 | 11 | 2 | – |
| Moin Khan | 3 | 0 | – | – | – | – | – |
| Moles, A.J. | 1763 | 36 | 48.97 | 3-21 | – | – | – |
| Montgomerie, R.R. | 31 | 0 | – | – | – | – | – |
| Moody, T.M. | 2365 | 73 | 32.39 | 7-43 | 1 | 1 | – |
| Moores, P. | 16 | 0 | – | – | – | – | – |
| Morris, H. | 380 | 2 | 190.00 | 1-6 | – | – | – |
| Morris, J.E. | 753 | 5 | 150.60 | 1-13 | – | – | – |
| Morrison, D.K. | 8795 | 266 | 33.06 | 7-82 | 9 | – | – |
| Mortensen, O.H. | 9673 | 411 | 23.53 | 6-27 | 15 | 1 | – |
| Moxon, M.D. | 1474 | 28 | 52.64 | 3-24 | – | – | – |
| Mudassar Nazar | 5221 | 152 | 34.34 | 6-32 | 2 | – | – |
| Mullally, A.D. | 4701 | 119 | 39.50 | 5-119 | 1 | – | – |
| Munton, T.A. | 10839 | 392 | 27.65 | 8-89 | 15 | 3 | – |
| Murphy, A.J. | 6841 | 174 | 39.31 | 6-97 | 5 | – | – |
| Mushtaq Ahmed | 4896 | 197 | 24.85 | 9-93 | 11 | 2 | – |
| Naved Anjum | 6595 | 304 | 21.69 | 9-45 | 17 | 1 | – |
| Neale, P.A. | 369 | 2 | 184.50 | 1-15 | – | – | – |
| Newell, M. | 282 | 7 | 40.28 | 2-38 | – | – | – |
| Newport, P.J. | 15757 | 568 | 27.74 | 8-52 | 27 | 3 | – |
| Nicholas, M.C.J. | 3208 | 72 | 44.55 | 6-37 | 2 | – | – |
| North, J.A. | 1164 | 37 | 31.45 | 4-47 | – | – | – |
| O'Gorman, T.J.G. | 207 | 3 | 69.00 | 1-7 | – | – | – |
| Ostler, D.P. | 90 | 0 | – | – | – | – | – |
| Parker, P.W.G. | 699 | 11 | 63.54 | 2-21 | – | – | – |
| Parks, R.J. | 166 | 0 | – | – | – | – | – |
| Parsons, G.J. | 18436 | 606 | 30.42 | 9-72 | 18 | 1 | – |
| Patel, D.N. | 18111 | 534 | 33.91 | 7-46 | 19 | 2 | – |
| Patel, M.M. | 1328 | 34 | 39.05 | 6-57 | 2 | 1 | – |
| Patterson, T.J.T. | 96 | 3 | 32.00 | 2-54 | – | – | – |
| Payne, A. | 71 | 1 | 71.00 | 1-71 | – | – | – |
| Pearson, R.M. | 2369 | 35 | 67.68 | 5-108 | 1 | – | – |
| Penberthy, A.L. | 1909 | 50 | 38.18 | 4-91 | – | – | – |
| Penn, C. | 9493 | 283 | 33.54 | 7-70 | 12 | – | – |
| Pennett, D.B. | 981 | 26 | 37.73 | 4-58 | – | – | – |
| Penney, T.L. | 39 | 0 | – | – | – | – | – |
| Pick, R.A. | 11521 | 352 | 32.73 | 7-128 | 11 | 3 | – |
| Pickles, C.S. | 3638 | 83 | 43.83 | 4-40 | – | – | – |
| Pierson, A.R.K. | 3753 | 85 | 44.15 | 6-82 | 3 | – | – |
| Pigott, A.C.S. | 18426 | 600 | 30.71 | 7-74 | 23 | 1 | – |
| Piper, K.J. | 57 | 1 | 57.00 | 1-57 | – | – | – |
| Pitcher, C.M. | 453 | 3 | 151.00 | 1-35 | – | – | – |
| Pollard, P.R. | 113 | 1 | 113.00 | 1-46 | – | – | – |
| Pooley, J.C. | 11 | 0 | – | – | – | – | – |
| Potter, L. | 6121 | 153 | 40.00 | 4-52 | – | – | – |
| Prichard, P.J. | 409 | 1 | 409.00 | 1-28 | – | – | – |
| Pringle, C. | 3003 | 93 | 32.29 | 7-52 | 2 | 1 | – |
| Pringle, D.R. | 19189 | 732 | 26.21 | 7-18 | 25 | 3 | – |

| | Runs | Wkts | Avge | Best | 5wI | 10wM | 100wS |
|---|---|---|---|---|---|---|---|
| Radford, N.V. | 23469 | 900 | 26.07 | 9-70 | 45 | 7 | 2 |
| Ramiz Raja | 158 | 2 | 79.00 | 1-9 | – | – | – |
| Ramprakash, M.R. | 583 | 6 | 97.16 | 1-0 | – | – | – |
| Randall, D.W. | 413 | 13 | 31.76 | 3-15 | – | – | – |
| Rashid Latif | 37 | 3 | 12.33 | 2-17 | – | – | – |
| Ratcliffe, J.D. | 96 | 1 | 96.00 | 1-15 | – | – | – |
| Reeve, D.A. | 10424 | 373 | 27.94 | 7-37 | 6 | – | – |
| Remy, C.C. | 593 | 12 | 49.41 | 4-63 | – | – | – |
| Rhodes, S.J. | 30 | 0 | – | – | – | – | – |
| Richards, I.V.A. | 9835 | 219 | 44.90 | 5-88 | 1 | – | – |
| Richardson, A.W. | 38 | 2 | 19.00 | 2-38 | – | – | – |
| Richardson, M.S. | 64 | 2 | 32.00 | 2-49 | – | – | – |
| Richardson, R.B. | 204 | 5 | 40.80 | 5-40 | 1 | – | – |
| Ripley, D. | 103 | 2 | 51.50 | 2-89 | – | – | – |
| Roberts, A.R. | 2571 | 61 | 42.14 | 6-72 | 1 | – | – |
| Robinson, J.D. | 1152 | 28 | 41.14 | 3-22 | – | – | – |
| Robinson, M.A. | 7624 | 227 | 33.58 | 6-57 | 3 | 1 | – |
| Robinson, P.E. | 238 | 1 | 238.00 | 1-10 | – | – | – |
| Robinson, R.T. | 254 | 3 | 84.66 | 1-22 | – | – | – |
| Robson, A.G. | 508 | 9 | 56.44 | 4-37 | – | – | – |
| Rose, G.D. | 8340 | 264 | 31.59 | 6-41 | 4 | – | – |
| Roseberry, M.A. | 382 | 4 | 95.50 | 1-1 | – | – | – |
| Russell, A.B. | 98 | 3 | 32.66 | 2-27 | – | – | – |
| Russell, R.C. | 38 | 1 | 38.00 | 1-4 | – | – | – |
| Salim Jaffer | 5956 | 240 | 24.81 | 7-29 | 12 | 2 | – |
| Salim Malik | 1714 | 57 | 30.07 | 5-19 | 2 | – | – |
| Salisbury, I.D.K. | 8168 | 210 | 38.89 | 7-54 | 9 | 2 | – |
| Sargeant, N.F. | 88 | 1 | 88.00 | 1-88 | – | – | – |
| Saxelby, M. | 765 | 9 | 85.00 | 3-41 | – | – | – |
| Scott, C.W. | 10 | 0 | – | – | – | – | – |
| Scott, R.J. | 1830 | 40 | 45.75 | 3-43 | – | – | – |
| Seymour, A.C.H. | 27 | 0 | – | – | – | – | – |
| Shahid, N. | 947 | 24 | 39.45 | 3-91 | – | – | – |
| Sharp, M.A. | 21 | 1 | 21.00 | 1-21 | – | – | – |
| Sheridan, K.L.P. | 104 | 1 | 104.00 | 1-62 | – | – | – |
| Shine, K.J. | 3384 | 95 | 35.62 | 8-47 | 5 | 1 | – |
| Shoaib Mohammad | 616 | 12 | 51.33 | 2-8 | – | – | – |
| Simmons, P.V. | 1538 | 38 | 40.47 | 5-24 | 1 | – | – |
| Sladdin, R.W. | 2361 | 66 | 35.77 | 6-58 | 2 | – | – |
| Sleep, P.R. | 13380 | 341 | 39.23 | 8-133 | 8 | – | – |
| Small, G.C. | 21497 | 750 | 28.66 | 7-15 | 27 | 2 | – |
| Smith, A.M. | 1818 | 53 | 34.30 | 4-41 | – | – | – |
| Smith, B.F. | 91 | 1 | 91.00 | 1-5 | – | – | – |
| Smith, D.M. | 1574 | 30 | 52.46 | 3-40 | – | – | – |
| Smith, I. | 2692 | 60 | 44.86 | 3-48 | – | – | – |
| Smith, N.M.K. | 2763 | 57 | 48.47 | 5-61 | 1 | – | – |
| Smith, P.A. | 8768 | 243 | 36.08 | 6-91 | 7 | – | – |
| Smith, R.A. | 691 | 12 | 57.58 | 2-11 | – | – | – |
| Snape, J.N. | 62 | 1 | 62.00 | 1-20 | – | – | – |
| Snell, R.P. | 3401 | 124 | 27.42 | 6-58 | 5 | – | – |
| Speak, N.J. | 92 | 2 | 46.00 | 1-0 | – | – | – |
| Speight, M.P. | 32 | 2 | 16.00 | 1-2 | – | – | – |
| Stanley, N.A. | 19 | 0 | – | – | – | – | – |
| Stemp, R.D. | 1602 | 46 | 34.82 | 6-67 | 3 | 1 | – |
| Stephenson, F.D. | 12884 | 536 | 24.03 | 8-47 | 32 | 8 | 1 |

| | Runs | Wkts | Avge | Best | 5wI | 10wM | 100wS |
|---|---|---|---|---|---|---|---|
| Stephenson, J.P. | 2903 | 89 | 32.61 | 6-54 | 2 | – | – |
| Stewart, A.J. | 352 | 3 | 117.33 | 1-7 | – | – | – |
| Storie, A.C. | 199 | 2 | 99.50 | 1-17 | – | – | – |
| Such, P.M. | 9034 | 301 | 30.01 | 6-17 | 9 | – | – |
| Sylvester, S.A. | 320 | 4 | 80.00 | 2-34 | – | – | – |
| Tanvir Mehdi | 2268 | 101 | 22.45 | 7-74 | 6 | 1 | – |
| Tavaré, C.J. | 720 | 5 | 144.00 | 1-3 | – | – | – |
| Taylor, C.W. | 2044 | 59 | 34.64 | 5-33 | 1 | – | – |
| Taylor, J.P. | 3479 | 105 | 33.13 | 7-23 | 4 | 1 | – |
| Taylor, N.R. (H) | 131 | 4 | 32.75 | 3-44 | – | – | – |
| Taylor, N.R. (K) | 891 | 16 | 55.68 | 2-20 | – | – | – |
| Tendulkar, S.R. | 1172 | 16 | 73.25 | 3-60 | – | – | – |
| Tennant, L. | 503 | 15 | 33.53 | 4-54 | – | – | – |
| Terry, V.P. | 58 | 0 | – | – | – | – | – |
| Thomas, S.D. | 404 | 18 | 22.44 | 5-79 | 2 | – | – |
| Thomson, K. | 82 | 2 | 41.00 | 1-27 | – | – | – |
| Thorpe, G.P. | 738 | 13 | 56.76 | 2-31 | – | – | – |
| Thursfield, M.J. | 165 | 4 | 41.25 | 1-11 | – | – | – |
| Tolley, C.M. | 1641 | 42 | 39.07 | 4-69 | – | – | – |
| Topley, T.D. | 9473 | 351 | 26.98 | 7-75 | 15 | 2 | – |
| Trump, H.R.J. | 6038 | 158 | 38.21 | 7-52 | 6 | 1 | – |
| Tufnell, P.C.R. | 11975 | 377 | 31.76 | 7-47 | 19 | 2 | – |
| Turner, I.J. | 1628 | 46 | 35.39 | 5-81 | 1 | – | – |
| Turner, R.J. | 26 | 0 | – | – | – | – | – |
| Tutt, A. | 53 | 0 | – | – | – | – | – |
| Twose, R.G. | 1802 | 55 | 32.76 | 6-63 | 1 | – | – |
| Udal, S.D. | 3050 | 82 | 37.19 | 8-50 | 2 | – | – |
| Van Troost, A.P. | 1033 | 27 | 38.25 | 6-48 | 2 | – | – |
| Vaughan, J.T.C. | 1462 | 43 | 34.00 | 5-72 | 1 | – | – |
| Walker, A. | 6871 | 221 | 31.09 | 6-50 | 2 | – | – |
| Walsh, C.A. | 22244 | 989 | 22.49 | 9-72 | 55 | 11 | 1 |
| Waqar Younis | 7261 | 355 | 20.45 | 7-64 | 32 | 8 | 1 |
| Ward, D.M. | 113 | 2 | 56.50 | 2-66 | – | – | – |
| Ward, I.J. | 35 | 0 | – | – | – | – | – |
| Ward, T.R. | 535 | 6 | 89.16 | 2-48 | – | – | – |
| Warner, A.E. | 10591 | 326 | 32.48 | 5-27 | 2 | – | – |
| Wasim Akram | 10167 | 455 | 22.34 | 7-42 | 36 | 7 | – |
| Watkin, S.L. | 11532 | 374 | 30.83 | 8-59 | 16 | 3 | – |
| Watkinson, M. | 15486 | 460 | 33.66 | 7-25 | 21 | 1 | – |
| Waugh, M.E. | 3882 | 105 | 36.97 | 5-37 | 1 | – | – |
| Weekes, P.N. | 1047 | 23 | 45.52 | 3-57 | – | – | – |
| Wells, A.P. | 690 | 9 | 76.66 | 3-67 | – | – | – |
| Wells, C.M. | 13410 | 392 | 34.20 | 7-42 | 7 | – | – |
| Wells, V.J. | 1165 | 51 | 22.84 | 5-43 | 1 | – | – |
| Weston, M.J. | 3108 | 80 | 38.85 | 4-24 | – | – | – |
| Weston, W.P.C. | 237 | 2 | 118.50 | 2-39 | – | – | – |
| Whitaker, J.J. | 268 | 2 | 134.00 | 1-29 | – | – | – |
| White, C. | 700 | 15 | 46.66 | 5-74 | 1 | – | – |
| White, G.W. | 30 | 1 | 30.00 | 1-30 | – | – | – |
| Whitticase, P. | 7 | 0 | – | – | – | – | – |
| Whittington, J.M.S. | 44 | 0 | – | – | – | – | – |
| Wight, R.M. | 748 | 19 | 39.36 | 3-65 | – | – | – |
| Williams, N.F. | 15141 | 515 | 29.40 | 8-75 | 16 | 2 | – |
| Williams, R.C. | 381 | 6 | 63.50 | 3-44 | – | – | – |
| Williams, R.G. | 12722 | 376 | 33.83 | 7-73 | 9 | – | – |

193

| | Runs | Wkts | Avge | Best | 5wI | 10wM | 100wS |
|---|---|---|---|---|---|---|---|
| Wood, B.S. | 1017 | 16 | 63.56 | 2-24 | – | – | – |
| Wood, J. | 534 | 17 | 31.41 | 5-68 | 1 | – | – |
| Wood, J.R. | 38 | 1 | 38.00 | 1-5 | – | – | – |
| Wren, T.N. | 629 | 15 | 41.93 | 3-14 | – | – | – |
| Wright, A.J. | 68 | 1 | 68.00 | 1-16 | – | – | – |
| Yates, G. | 2334 | 39 | 59.84 | 4-94 | – | – | – |
| Zahid Fazal | 89 | 0 | – | – | – | – | – |

# LEADING CURRENT PLAYERS

The leading career records of players currently registered for first-class county cricket. All figures are to the end of the 1992 English season.

## BATTING
(Qualification: 100 innings)

| | Runs | Avge |
|---|---|---|
| G.A.Hick | 19083 | 59.08 |
| M.W.Gatting | 28512 | 50.10 |
| I.V.A.Richards | 34977 | 49.40 |
| A.J.Lamb | 28495 | 48.87 |
| Salim Malik | 11875 | 48.86 |
| G.A.Gooch | 36126 | 48.16 |
| D.L.Haynes | 21176 | 46.84 |
| M.A.Atherton | 8424 | 45.53 |
| R.A.Smith | 14227 | 44.18 |
| R.B.Richardson | 9863 | 43.25 |
| G.P.Thorpe | 5650 | 43.12 |
| N.Hussain | 5163 | 43.02 |
| R.T.Robinson | 20209 | 42.72 |
| M.P.Maynard | 11362 | 42.08 |
| N.H.Fairbrother | 12177 | 41.98 |
| R.J.Bailey | 13725 | 41.59 |
| C.L.Hooper | 6528 | 41.57 |
| T.S.Curtis | 15311 | 41.49 |
| M.R.Benson | 16035 | 41.32 |
| P.D.Bowler | 8256 | 41.07 |
| M.D.Moxon | 15234 | 40.84 |
| A.J.Moles | 10814 | 40.80 |
| A.Fordham | 6759 | 40.71 |
| N.R.Taylor | 15622 | 40.15 |
| D.I.Gower | 25203 | 40.00 |
| D.M.Ward | 6430 | 39.93 |
| G.D.Lloyd | 3478 | 39.52 |
| M.R.Ramprakash | 6327 | 39.29 |
| C.J.Tavaré | 24278 | 39.28 |
| A.J.Stewart | 12608 | 39.27 |

## BOWLING
(Qualification: 100 wickets)

| | Wkts | Avge |
|---|---|---|
| M.D.Marshall | 1524 | 18.70 |
| Waqar Younis | 355 | 20.45 |
| I.R.Bishop | 325 | 20.49 |
| C.E.L.Ambrose | 420 | 22.12 |
| C.A.Walsh | 989 | 22.49 |
| Wasim Akram | 455 | 22.34 |
| A.A.Donald | 546 | 23.05 |
| O.H.Mortensen | 411 | 23.53 |
| N.A.Foster | 896 | 23.96 |
| F.D.Stephenson | 536 | 24.03 |
| N.G.Cowans | 620 | 24.58 |
| J.R.Ayling | 131 | 24.83 |
| Mushtaq Ahmed | 197 | 24.85 |
| K.M.Curran | 409 | 25.88 |
| J.E.Emburey | 1366 | 26.06 |
| N.V.Radford | 900 | 26.07 |
| W.K.M.Benjamin | 343 | 26.08 |
| D.R.Pringle | 732 | 26.21 |
| A.R.C.Fraser | 355 | 26.41 |
| N.A.Mallender | 842 | 26.56 |
| D.J.Millns | 195 | 26.80 |
| M.P.Bicknell | 383 | 26.88 |
| T.D.Topley | 351 | 26.98 |
| I.T.Botham | 1159 | 27.08 |
| D.G.Cork | 115 | 27.26 |
| P.A.J.DeFreitas | 542 | 27.39 |
| P.W.Jarvis | 457 | 27.50 |
| S.J.Base | 323 | 27.60 |
| T.A.Munton | 392 | 27.65 |
| P.J.Newport | 568 | 27.74 |

## WICKET-KEEPING

| | Total | Ct | St |
|---|---|---|---|
| B.N.French | 867 | 772 | 95 |
| R.C.Russell | 651 | 567 | 84 |
| S.J.Rhodes | 566 | 504 | 62 |
| D.Ripley | 427 | 372 | 55 |
| C.P.Metson | 417 | 387 | 30 |
| S.A.Marsh | 399 | 368 | 31 |
| M.A.Garnham | 392 | 361 | 31 |

## FIELDING

| | Ct |
|---|---|
| G.A.Gooch | 478 |
| I.V.A.Richards | 447 |
| J.E.Emburey | 403 |
| C.J.Tavaré | 396 |
| M.W.Gatting | 376 |
| C.W.J.Athey | 369 |
| D.W.Randall | 355 |

# LIMITED-OVERS INTERNATIONALS
# CAREER RECORDS

These career records for players currently registered for first-class county cricket in 1993 are complete to the end of the 1992 season (excluding Sri Lanka v Australia 1992-93) and have been compiled by **Philip Bailey**.

## BATTING AND FIELDING

| | M | I | NO | HS | Runs | Avge | 100 | 50 | Ct/St |
|---|---|---|---|---|---|---|---|---|---|
| Ambrose, C.E.L. (WI) | 71 | 41 | 19 | 26* | 294 | 13.36 | – | – | 17 |
| Atherton, M.A. | 10 | 10 | 1 | 74 | 335 | 37.22 | – | 3 | 3 |
| Bailey, R.J. | 4 | 4 | 2 | 43* | 137 | 68.50 | – | – | 1 |
| Barnett, K.J. | 1 | 1 | – | 84 | 84 | 84.00 | – | 1 | – |
| Benjamin, W.K.M. (WI) | 60 | 36 | 7 | 31 | 190 | 6.55 | – | – | 11 |
| Benson, M.R. | 1 | 1 | – | 24 | 24 | 24.00 | – | – | – |
| Bicknell, M.P. | 7 | 6 | 2 | 31* | 96 | 24.00 | – | – | 2 |
| Bishop, I.R. (WI) | 35 | 16 | 8 | 33* | 148 | 18.50 | – | – | 8 |
| Blakey, R.J. | 1 | 1 | – | 25 | 25 | 25.00 | – | – | 1/1 |
| Botham, I.T. | 116 | 106 | 15 | 79 | 2113 | 23.21 | – | 9 | 36 |
| Broad, B.C. | 34 | 34 | – | 106 | 1361 | 40.02 | 1 | 11 | 10 |
| Cairns, C.L. (NZ) | 10 | 8 | 3 | 42 | 83 | 16.60 | – | – | 7 |
| Capel, D.J. | 23 | 19 | 2 | 50* | 327 | 19.23 | – | 1 | 6 |
| Cook, N.G.B. | 3 | – | – | – | – | – | – | – | 2 |
| Cork, D.G. | 1 | – | – | – | – | – | – | – | – |
| Cowans, N.G. | 23 | 8 | 3 | 4* | 13 | 2.60 | – | – | 5 |
| Cummins, A.C. (WI) | 19 | 9 | 4 | 24 | 62 | 12.40 | – | – | 1 |
| Curran, K.M. | 11 | 11 | – | 73 | 287 | 26.09 | – | 2 | 1 |
| DeFreitas, P.A.J. | 78 | 51 | 19 | 49* | 494 | 15.43 | – | – | 21 |
| Donald, A.A. (SA) | 14 | 3 | 1 | 5* | 8 | 4.00 | – | – | 1 |
| Ellison, R.M. | 14 | 12 | 4 | 24 | 86 | 10.75 | – | – | 2 |
| Emburey, J.E. | 58 | 43 | 10 | 34 | 471 | 14.27 | – | – | 19 |
| Fairbrother, N.H. | 29 | 27 | 6 | 113 | 860 | 40.95 | 1 | 7 | 13 |
| Foster, N.A. | 48 | 25 | 12 | 24 | 150 | 11.53 | – | – | 12 |
| Fowler, G. | 26 | 26 | 2 | 81* | 744 | 31.00 | – | 4 | 4/2 |
| Fraser, A.R.C. | 24 | 10 | 4 | 38* | 69 | 11.50 | – | – | 1 |
| French, B.N. | 13 | 8 | 3 | 9* | 34 | 6.80 | – | – | 13/3 |
| Gatting, M.W. | 85 | 82 | 17 | 115* | 2049 | 31.52 | 1 | 9 | 22 |
| Gooch, G.A. | 111 | 109 | 6 | 142 | 4071 | 39.52 | 8 | 23 | 38 |
| Gower, D.I. | 114 | 111 | 8 | 158 | 3170 | 30.77 | 7 | 12 | 44 |
| Haynes, D.L. (WI) | 203 | 202 | 25 | 152* | 7513 | 42.44 | 16 | 46 | 48 |
| Hemmings, E.E. | 33 | 12 | 6 | 8* | 30 | 5.00 | – | – | 5 |
| Hick, G.A. | 21 | 20 | 4 | 86* | 628 | 39.25 | – | 6 | 11 |
| Hooper, C.L. (WI) | 80 | 70 | 17 | 113* | 1511 | 28.50 | 1 | 6 | 33 |
| Hussain, N. | 2 | 2 | 1 | 15* | 17 | 17.00 | – | – | 1 |
| Illingworth, R.K. | 16 | 5 | 2 | 14 | 40 | 13.33 | – | – | 8 |
| Jarvis, P.W. | 5 | 2 | 1 | 5* | 5 | 5.00 | – | – | – |
| Lamb, A.J. | 122 | 118 | 16 | 118 | 4010 | 39.31 | 4 | 26 | 31 |
| Larkins, W. | 25 | 24 | – | 124 | 591 | 24.62 | 1 | – | 8 |
| Lawrence, D.V. | 1 | – | – | – | – | – | – | – | – |
| Lewis, C.C. | 30 | 19 | 4 | 33 | 135 | 9.00 | – | – | 12 |
| Lloyd, T.A. | 3 | 3 | – | 49 | 101 | 33.66 | – | – | – |
| Lynch, M.A. | 3 | 3 | – | 6 | 8 | 2.66 | – | – | 1 |
| Malcolm, D.E. | 4 | 2 | 1 | 4 | 7 | 7.00 | – | – | – |
| Marshall, M.D. (WI) | 136 | 83 | 19 | 66 | 955 | 14.92 | – | 2 | 15 |

| | M | I | NO | HS | Runs | Avge | 100 | 50 | Ct/St |
|---|---|---|---|---|---|---|---|---|---|
| Morris, J.E. | 8 | 8 | 1 | 63* | 167 | 23.85 | – | 1 | 2 |
| Moxon, M.D. | 8 | 8 | – | 70 | 174 | 21.75 | – | 1 | 5 |
| Mushtaq Ahmed (P) | 48 | 24 | 9 | 17* | 155 | 10.33 | – | – | 8 |
| Pringle, D.R. | 42 | 29 | 12 | 49* | 419 | 24.64 | – | – | 11 |
| Radford, N.V. | 6 | 3 | 2 | 0* | 0 | 0.00 | – | – | 2 |
| Ramprakash, M.R. | 2 | 2 | 2 | 6* | 6 | – | – | – | – |
| Randall, D.W. | 49 | 45 | 5 | 88 | 1067 | 26.67 | – | 5 | 25 |
| Reeve, D.A. | 15 | 8 | 6 | 31* | 118 | 59.00 | – | – | 6 |
| Rhodes, S.J. | 3 | 2 | 1 | 8 | 9 | 9.00 | – | – | 3 |
| Richards, I.V.A. (WI) | 187 | 167 | 24 | 189* | 6721 | 47.00 | 11 | 45 | 101 |
| Richardson, R.B. (WI) | 163 | 159 | 20 | 122 | 4883 | 35.12 | 5 | 37 | 56 |
| Robinson, R.T. | 26 | 26 | – | 83 | 597 | 22.96 | – | 3 | 6 |
| Russell, R.C. | 26 | 19 | 6 | 50 | 261 | 20.07 | – | 1 | 26/5 |
| Salim Malik (P) | 152 | 142 | 19 | 102 | 4038 | 32.82 | 5 | 23 | 43 |
| Small, G.C. | 53 | 24 | 9 | 18* | 98 | 6.53 | – | – | 7 |
| Smith, D.M. | 2 | 2 | 1 | 10* | 15 | 15.00 | – | – | – |
| Smith, R.A. | 47 | 46 | 7 | 128 | 1547 | 39.66 | 2 | 11 | 18 |
| Stewart, A.J. | 41 | 36 | 4 | 103 | 1007 | 31.46 | 1 | 6 | 28/3 |
| Tavaré, C.J. | 29 | 28 | 2 | 83* | 720 | 27.69 | – | 4 | 7 |
| Tufnell, P.C.R. | 15 | 7 | 6 | 5* | 13 | 13.00 | – | – | 3 |
| Walsh, C.A. (WI) | 97 | 34 | 14 | 29* | 166 | 8.30 | – | – | 13 |
| Waqar Younis (P) | 47 | 16 | 8 | 20* | 91 | 11.37 | – | – | 4 |
| Wasim Akram (P) | 126 | 94 | 19 | 86 | 1013 | 13.50 | – | 1 | 25 |
| Wells, C.M. | 2 | 2 | – | 17 | 22 | 11.00 | – | – | – |
| Whitaker, J.J. | 2 | 2 | 1 | 44* | 48 | 48.00 | – | – | 1 |

## BOWLING

| | Balls | Runs | Wkts | Avge | Best | 4w |
|---|---|---|---|---|---|---|
| Ambrose, C.E.L. | 3847 | 2263 | 111 | 20.38 | 5-17 | 7 |
| Bailey, R.J. | 36 | 25 | 0 | – | – | – |
| Benjamin, W.K.M. | 3237 | 2235 | 69 | 32.39 | 3-21 | – |
| Bicknell, M.P. | 413 | 347 | 13 | 26.69 | 3-55 | – |
| Bishop, I.R. | 1774 | 1199 | 59 | 20.32 | 5-27 | 5 |
| Botham, I.T. | 6271 | 4139 | 145 | 28.54 | 4-31 | 3 |
| Broad, B.C. | 6 | 6 | 0 | – | – | – |
| Cairns, C.L. | 367 | 362 | 11 | 32.90 | 4-55 | 1 |
| Capel, D.J. | 1038 | 805 | 17 | 47.35 | 3-38 | – |
| Cook, N.G.B. | 144 | 95 | 5 | 19.00 | 2-18 | – |
| Cork, D.G. | 66 | 37 | 1 | 37.00 | 1-37 | – |
| Cowans, N.G. | 1282 | 913 | 23 | 39.69 | 3-44 | – |
| Cummins, A.C. | 1011 | 690 | 29 | 23.79 | 5-31 | 2 |
| Curran, K.M. | 506 | 398 | 9 | 44.22 | 3-65 | – |
| DeFreitas, P.A.J. | 4417 | 2856 | 90 | 31.73 | 4-35 | 1 |
| Donald, A.A. | 742 | 545 | 24 | 22.70 | 5-29 | 1 |
| Ellison, R.M. | 696 | 510 | 12 | 42.50 | 3-42 | – |
| Emburey, J.E. | 3281 | 2226 | 75 | 29.68 | 4-37 | 2 |
| Fairbrother, N.H. | 6 | 9 | 0 | – | – | – |
| Foster, N.A. | 2627 | 1836 | 59 | 31.11 | 3-20 | – |
| Fraser, A.R.C. | 1336 | 797 | 23 | 34.65 | 3-22 | – |
| Gatting, M.W. | 386 | 334 | 10 | 33.40 | 3-32 | – |
| Gooch, G.A. | 1946 | 1423 | 36 | 39.52 | 3-19 | – |
| Gower, D.I. | 5 | 14 | 0 | – | – | – |
| Haynes, D.L. | 30 | 24 | 0 | – | – | – |
| Hemmings, E.E. | 1752 | 1294 | 37 | 34.97 | 4-52 | 1 |

| | Balls | Runs | Wkts | Avge | Best | 4w |
|---|---|---|---|---|---|---|
| Hick, G.A. | 148 | 114 | 4 | 28.50 | 2-7 | – |
| Hooper, C.L. | 3083 | 2255 | 69 | 32.68 | 4-34 | 1 |
| Illingworth, R.K. | 967 | 666 | 20 | 33.30 | 3-33 | – |
| Jarvis, P.W. | 287 | 187 | 6 | 31.16 | 4-33 | 1 |
| Lamb, A.J. | 6 | 3 | 0 | – | – | – |
| Larkins, W. | 15 | 22 | 0 | – | – | – |
| Lawrence, D.V. | 66 | 67 | 4 | 16.75 | 4-67 | 1 |
| Lewis, C.C. | 1366 | 1007 | 33 | 30.51 | 4-30 | 2 |
| Malcolm, D.E. | 234 | 171 | 6 | 28.50 | 2-19 | – |
| Marshall, M.D. | 7175 | 4233 | 157 | 26.96 | 4-18 | 6 |
| Mushtaq Ahmed | 2403 | 1850 | 62 | 29.83 | 3-14 | – |
| Pringle, D.R. | 2253 | 1578 | 43 | 36.69 | 4-42 | 1 |
| Radford, N.V. | 348 | 230 | 2 | 115.00 | 1-32 | – |
| Randall, D.W. | 2 | 2 | 1 | 2.00 | 1-2 | – |
| Reeve, D.A. | 538 | 322 | 15 | 21.46 | 3-20 | – |
| Richards, I.V.A. | 5644 | 4228 | 118 | 35.83 | 6-41 | 3 |
| Richardson, R.B. | 58 | 46 | 1 | 46.00 | 1-4 | – |
| Salim Malik | 584 | 510 | 14 | 36.42 | 5-35 | 1 |
| Small, G.C. | 2793 | 1942 | 58 | 33.48 | 4-31 | 1 |
| Tavaré, C.J. | 12 | 3 | 0 | – | – | – |
| Tufnell, P.C.R. | 774 | 528 | 12 | 44.00 | 3-40 | – |
| Walsh, C.A. | 5175 | 3374 | 108 | 31.24 | 5-1 | 5 |
| Waqar Younis | 2216 | 1581 | 86 | 18.38 | 6-26 | 10 |
| Wasim Akram | 6369 | 4097 | 171 | 23.95 | 5-21 | 6 |

# COUNTY BENEFITS/TESTIMONIALS
# AWARDED FOR 1993

| | |
|---|---|
| Derbyshire | – |
| Durham | – |
| Essex | N.A.Foster |
| Glamorgan | – |
| Gloucestershire | D.V.Lawrence |
| Hampshire | T.M.Tremlett (coach) |
| Kent | R.M.Ellison |
| Lancashire | G.D.Mendis |
| Leicestershire | J.J.Whitaker |
| Middlesex | N.G.Cowans |
| Northamptonshire | R.J.Bailey |
| Nottinghamshire | D.W.Randall |
| Somerset | – |
| Surrey | H.T.Brind (head groundsman) |
| Sussex | C.M.Wells |
| Warwickshire | – |
| Worcestershire | D.B.D'Oliveira and M.J.Weston |
| Yorkshire | M.D.Moxon |

# TEST CAREER RECORDS

These records are complete to the end of the 1992 season in England but exclude the three-match series between Sri Lanka and Australia which began on 17 August. They include every player who has appeared in Test cricket since 1989. Career records for all Tests prior to 1989-90 are published in *The Wisden Book of Test Cricket – Volume II*.

## AUSTRALIA
### BATTING AND FIELDING

|                | M    | I   | NO  | HS   | Runs | Avge  | 100 | 50  | Ct/St  |
|----------------|------|-----|-----|------|------|-------|-----|-----|--------|
| T.M.Alderman   | 41   | 53  | 22  | 26*  | 203  | 6.54  | –   | –   | 27     |
| D.C.Boon       | 63   | 115 | 12  | 200  | 4538 | 44.05 | 13  | 19  | 62     |
| A.R.Border     | 130  | 224 | 42  | 205  | 9532 | 52.37 | 23  | 55  | 135    |
| G.D.Campbell   | 4    | 4   | –   | 6    | 10   | 2.50  | –   | –   | 1      |
| I.A.Healy      | 36   | 52  | 2   | 69   | 1016 | 20.32 | –   | 4   | 108/2  |
| M.G.Hughes     | 37   | 49  | 5   | 72*  | 688  | 15.63 | –   | 2   | 17     |
| D.M.Jones      | 49   | 83  | 10  | 216  | 3355 | 45.95 | 10  | 12  | 32     |
| G.F.Lawson     | 46   | 68  | 12  | 74   | 894  | 15.96 | –   | 4   | 10     |
| C.J.McDermott  | 36   | 50  | 5   | 42*  | 501  | 11.13 | –   | –   | 9      |
| G.R.Marsh      | 50   | 93  | 7   | 138  | 2854 | 33.18 | 4   | 15  | 38     |
| G.R.J.Matthews | 28   | 44  | 8   | 130  | 1411 | 39.19 | 4   | 6   | 14     |
| T.M.Moody      | 5    | 8   | –   | 106  | 385  | 48.12 | 2   | 2   | 6      |
| W.N.Phillips   | 1    | 2   | –   | 14   | 22   | 11.00 | –   | –   | –      |
| C.G.Rackemann  | 12   | 14  | 4   | 15*  | 53   | 5.30  | –   | –   | 2      |
| B.A.Reid       | 26   | 32  | 13  | 13   | 91   | 4.78  | –   | –   | 5      |
| P.R.Reiffel    | 1    | 1   | –   | 9    | 9    | 9.00  | –   | –   | 1      |
| P.R.Sleep      | 14   | 21  | 1   | 90   | 483  | 24.15 | –   | 3   | 4      |
| M.A.Taylor     | 30   | 56  | 4   | 219  | 2694 | 51.80 | 8   | 17  | 38     |
| P.L.Taylor     | 13   | 19  | 3   | 87   | 431  | 26.93 | –   | 2   | 10     |
| M.R.J.Veletta  | 8    | 11  | –   | 39   | 207  | 18.81 | –   | –   | 12     |
| S.K.Warne      | 2    | 4   | 1   | 20   | 28   | 9.33  | –   | –   | 1      |
| M.E.Waugh      | 11   | 17  | 2   | 139* | 637  | 42.46 | 2   | 2   | 21     |
| S.R.Waugh      | 44   | 67  | 11  | 177* | 2097 | 37.44 | 3   | 13  | 32     |
| M.R.Whitney    | 9    | 14  | 7   | 12   | 31   | 4.42  | –   | –   | 1      |

### BOWLING

|                | O      | R    | W   | Avge   | Best  | 5wI | 10wM |
|----------------|--------|------|-----|--------|-------|-----|------|
| T.M.Alderman   | 1696.5 | 4616 | 170 | 27.15  | 6-47  | 14  | 1    |
| D.C.Boon       | 2      | 5    | 0   | –      | –     | –   | –    |
| A.R.Border     | 571.1  | 1339 | 37  | 36.18  | 7-46  | 2   | 1    |
| G.D.Campbell   | 158.3  | 503  | 13  | 38.69  | 3-79  | –   | –    |
| M.G.Hughes     | 1403.3 | 4154 | 144 | 28.84  | 8-87  | 5   | 1    |
| D.M.Jones      | 33     | 64   | 1   | 64.00  | 1-5   | –   | –    |
| G.F.Lawson     | 1853   | 5501 | 180 | 30.56  | 8-112 | 11  | 2    |
| C.J.McDermott  | 1392.4 | 4329 | 153 | 28.29  | 8-97  | 9   | 2    |
| G.R.J.Matthews | 826.1  | 2402 | 49  | 49.02  | 5-103 | 2   | 1    |
| T.M.Moody      | 41     | 68   | 1   | 68.00  | 1-23  | –   | –    |
| C.G.Rackemann  | 453.1  | 1137 | 39  | 29.15  | 6-86  | 3   | 1    |
| B.A.Reid       | 987.4  | 2633 | 106 | 24.84  | 7-51  | 4   | 2    |
| P.R.Reiffel    | 28     | 80   | 2   | 40.00  | 2-34  | –   | –    |
| P.R.Sleep      | 497    | 1397 | 31  | 45.06  | 5-72  | 1   | –    |
| P.L.Taylor     | 371.1  | 1068 | 27  | 39.55  | 6-78  | 1   | –    |
| S.K.Warne      | 68     | 228  | 1   | 228.00 | 1-150 | –   | –    |
| M.E.Waugh      | 108    | 298  | 9   | 33.11  | 4-80  | –   | –    |
| S.R.Waugh      | 679.2  | 1980 | 44  | 45.00  | 5-69  | 2   | –    |
| M.R.Whitney    | 364.2  | 1107 | 35  | 31.62  | 7-27  | 2   | 1    |

# ENGLAND

## BATTING AND FIELDING

|  | M | I | NO | HS | Runs | Avge | 100 | 50 | Ct/St |
|---|---|---|---|---|---|---|---|---|---|
| M.A.Atherton | 21 | 39 | 1 | 151 | 1311 | 34.50 | 3 | 9 | 20 |
| C.W.J.Athey | 23 | 41 | 1 | 123 | 919 | 22.97 | 1 | 4 | 13 |
| K.J.Barnett | 4 | 7 | – | 80 | 207 | 29.57 | – | 2 | 1 |
| M.R.Benson | 1 | 2 | – | 30 | 51 | 25.50 | – | – | – |
| I.T.Botham | 102 | 161 | 6 | 208 | 5200 | 33.54 | 14 | 22 | 120 |
| B.C.Broad | 25 | 44 | 2 | 162 | 1661 | 39.54 | 6 | 6 | 10 |
| D.J.Capel | 15 | 25 | 1 | 98 | 374 | 15.58 | – | 2 | 6 |
| J.H.Childs | 2 | 4 | 4 | 2* | 2 | – | – | – | 1 |
| N.G.B.Cook | 15 | 25 | 4 | 31 | 179 | 8.52 | – | – | 5 |
| N.G.Cowans | 19 | 29 | 7 | 36 | 175 | 7.95 | – | – | 9 |
| T.S.Curtis | 5 | 9 | – | 41 | 140 | 15.55 | – | – | 3 |
| P.A.J.DeFreitas | 31 | 46 | 4 | 55* | 527 | 12.54 | – | 1 | 6 |
| R.M.Ellison | 11 | 16 | 1 | 41 | 202 | 13.46 | – | – | 2 |
| J.E.Emburey | 60 | 89 | 18 | 75 | 1540 | 21.69 | – | 8 | 33 |
| N.H.Fairbrother | 7 | 9 | 1 | 33* | 64 | 8.00 | – | – | 4 |
| N.A.Foster | 28 | 43 | 7 | 39 | 410 | 11.38 | – | – | 7 |
| G.Fowler | 21 | 37 | – | 201 | 1307 | 35.32 | 3 | 8 | 10 |
| A.R.C.Fraser | 11 | 14 | 1 | 29 | 88 | 6.76 | – | – | 1 |
| B.N.French | 16 | 21 | 4 | 59 | 308 | 18.11 | – | 1 | 38/1 |
| M.W.Gatting | 68 | 117 | 14 | 207 | 3870 | 37.57 | 9 | 18 | 51 |
| G.A.Gooch | 99 | 179 | 6 | 333 | 7573 | 43.77 | 17 | 41 | 96 |
| D.I.Gower | 117 | 204 | 18 | 215 | 8231 | 44.25 | 18 | 39 | 74 |
| E.E.Hemmings | 16 | 21 | 4 | 95 | 383 | 22.52 | – | 2 | 5 |
| G.A.Hick | 11 | 17 | – | 51 | 307 | 18.05 | – | 1 | 22 |
| N.Hussain | 3 | 5 | – | 35 | 100 | 20.00 | – | – | 1 |
| A.P.Igglesden | 1 | 1 | 1 | 2* | 2 | – | – | – | 1 |
| R.K.Illingworth | 2 | 4 | 2 | 13 | 31 | 15.50 | – | – | 1 |
| P.W.Jarvis | 6 | 9 | 2 | 29* | 109 | 15.57 | – | – | – |
| A.J.Lamb | 79 | 139 | 10 | 142 | 4656 | 36.09 | 14 | 18 | 75 |
| W.Larkins | 13 | 25 | 1 | 64 | 493 | 20.54 | – | 3 | 8 |
| D.V.Lawrence | 5 | 6 | – | 34 | 60 | 10.00 | – | – | – |
| C.C.Lewis | 14 | 19 | 1 | 70 | 446 | 24.77 | – | 3 | 13 |
| D.E.Malcolm | 21 | 29 | 8 | 15* | 105 | 5.00 | – | – | 3 |
| N.A.Mallender | 2 | 3 | – | 4 | 8 | 2.66 | – | – | – |
| M.P.Maynard | 1 | 2 | – | 10 | 13 | 6.50 | – | – | – |
| H.Morris | 3 | 6 | – | 44 | 115 | 19.16 | – | – | 3 |
| J.E.Morris | 3 | 5 | 2 | 32 | 71 | 23.66 | – | – | 3 |
| M.D.Moxon | 10 | 17 | 1 | 99 | 455 | 28.43 | – | 3 | 10 |
| T.A.Munton | 2 | 2 | 1 | 25* | 25 | 25.00 | – | – | – |
| P.J.Newport | 3 | 5 | 1 | 40* | 110 | 27.50 | – | – | 1 |
| P.W.G.Parker | 1 | 2 | – | 13 | 13 | 6.50 | – | – | – |
| A.C.S.Pigott | 1 | 2 | 1 | 8* | 12 | 12.00 | – | – | 1 |
| D.R.Pringle | 30 | 50 | 4 | 63 | 695 | 15.10 | – | 1 | 10 |
| N.V.Radford | 3 | 4 | 1 | 12* | 21 | 7.00 | – | – | – |
| M.R.Ramprakash | 9 | 15 | 1 | 29 | 241 | 17.21 | – | – | 5 |
| D.W.Randall | 47 | 79 | 5 | 174 | 2470 | 33.37 | 7 | 12 | 31 |
| D.A.Reeve | 3 | 5 | – | 59 | 124 | 24.80 | – | 1 | 1 |
| R.T.Robinson | 29 | 49 | 5 | 175 | 1601 | 36.38 | 4 | 6 | 8 |
| R.C.Russell | 31 | 49 | 10 | 128* | 1060 | 27.17 | 1 | 3 | 80/8 |
| I.D.K.Salisbury | 2 | 3 | – | 50 | 66 | 22.00 | – | 1 | – |

# ENGLAND

## BATTING AND FIELDING (continued)

| | M | I | NO | HS | Runs | Avge | 100 | 50 | Ct/St |
|---|---|---|---|---|---|---|---|---|---|
| G.C.Small | 17 | 24 | 7 | 59 | 263 | 15.47 | – | 1 | 9 |
| D.M.Smith | 2 | 4 | – | 47 | 80 | 20.00 | – | – | – |
| R.A.Smith | 36 | 66 | 14 | 148* | 2645 | 50.86 | 7 | 18 | 26 |
| J.P.Stephenson | 1 | 2 | – | 25 | 36 | 18.00 | – | – | – |
| A.J.Stewart | 22 | 40 | 4 | 190 | 1493 | 41.47 | 4 | 6 | 27 |
| C.J.Tavaré | 31 | 56 | 2 | 149 | 1755 | 32.50 | 2 | 12 | 20 |
| V.P.Terry | 2 | 3 | – | 8 | 16 | 5.33 | – | – | 2 |
| P.C.R.Tufnell | 10 | 13 | 8 | 8 | 23 | 4.60 | – | – | 4 |
| S.L.Watkin | 2 | 3 | – | 6 | 8 | 2.66 | – | – | – |
| J.J.Whitaker | 1 | 1 | – | 11 | 11 | 11.00 | – | – | 1 |
| N.F.Williams | 1 | 1 | – | 38 | 38 | 38.00 | – | – | – |

## BOWLING

| | O | R | W | Avge | Best | 5wI | 10wM |
|---|---|---|---|---|---|---|---|
| M.A.Atherton | 61 | 282 | 1 | 282.00 | 1-60 | – | – |
| K.J.Barnett | 6 | 32 | 0 | – | – | – | – |
| I.T.Botham | 3635.5 | 10878 | 383 | 28.40 | 8-34 | 27 | 4 |
| B.C.Broad | 1 | 4 | 0 | – | – | – | – |
| D.J.Capel | 333.2 | 1064 | 21 | 50.66 | 3-88 | – | – |
| J.H.Childs | 86 | 183 | 3 | 61.00 | 1-13 | – | – |
| N.G.B.Cook | 695.4 | 1689 | 52 | 32.48 | 6-65 | 4 | 1 |
| N.G.Cowans | 575.2 | 2003 | 51 | 39.27 | 6-77 | 2 | – |
| T.S.Curtis | 3 | 7 | 0 | – | – | – | – |
| P.A.J.DeFreitas | 1104.4 | 3017 | 93 | 32.44 | 7-70 | 3 | – |
| R.M.Ellison | 337.2 | 1048 | 35 | 29.94 | 6-77 | 3 | 1 |
| J.E.Emburey | 2371.1 | 5105 | 138 | 36.99 | 7-78 | 6 | – |
| N.H.Fairbrother | 2 | 9 | 0 | – | – | – | – |
| N.A.Foster | 1013.3 | 2797 | 88 | 31.78 | 8-107 | 5 | 1 |
| G.Fowler | 3 | 11 | 0 | – | – | – | – |
| A.R.C.Fraser | 517.4 | 1255 | 47 | 26.70 | 6-82 | 4 | – |
| M.W.Gatting | 125.2 | 317 | 4 | 79.25 | 1-14 | – | – |
| G.A.Gooch | 382.3 | 894 | 22 | 40.63 | 3-39 | – | – |
| D.I.Gower | 6 | 20 | 1 | 20.00 | 1-1 | – | – |
| E.E.Hemmings | 739.3 | 1825 | 43 | 42.44 | 6-58 | 1 | – |
| G.A.Hick | 129 | 306 | 6 | 51.00 | 4-126 | – | – |
| A.P.Igglesden | 37 | 146 | 3 | 48.66 | 2-91 | – | – |
| R.K.Illingworth | 56.4 | 213 | 4 | 53.25 | 3-110 | – | – |
| P.W.Jarvis | 224.3 | 708 | 14 | 50.57 | 4-107 | – | – |
| A.J.Lamb | 5 | 23 | 1 | 23.00 | 1-6 | – | – |
| D.V.Lawrence | 181.3 | 676 | 18 | 37.55 | 5-106 | 1 | – |
| C.C.Lewis | 516 | 1520 | 42 | 36.19 | 6-111 | 2 | – |
| D.E.Malcolm | 803.3 | 2673 | 74 | 36.12 | 6-77 | 4 | 1 |
| N.A.Mallender | 74.5 | 215 | 10 | 21.50 | 5-50 | 1 | – |
| M.D.Moxon | 8 | 30 | 0 | – | – | – | – |
| T.A.Munton | 67.3 | 200 | 4 | 50.00 | 2-22 | – | – |
| P.J.Newport | 111.3 | 417 | 10 | 41.70 | 4-87 | – | – |
| A.C.S.Pigott | 17 | 75 | 2 | 37.50 | 2-75 | – | – |
| D.R.Pringle | 881.1 | 2518 | 70 | 35.97 | 5-95 | 3 | – |

# ENGLAND

## BOWLING (continued)

|  | O | R | W | Avge | Best | 5wI | 10wM |
|---|---|---|---|---|---|---|---|
| N.V.Radford | 113 | 351 | 4 | 87.75 | 2-131 | – | – |
| M.R.Ramprakash | 1.1 | 8 | 0 | – | – | – | – |
| D.W.Randall | 2.4 | 3 | 0 | – | – | – | – |
| D.A.Reeve | 24.5 | 60 | 2 | 30.00 | 1-4 | – | – |
| R.T.Robinson | 1 | 0 | 0 | – | – | – | – |
| I.D.K.Salisbury | 70.1 | 306 | 5 | 61.20 | 3-49 | – | – |
| G.C.Small | 654.3 | 1871 | 55 | 34.01 | 5-48 | 2 | – |
| R.A.Smith | 4 | 6 | 0 | – | – | – | – |
| C.J.Tavaré | 5 | 11 | 0 | – | – | – | – |
| P.C.R.Tufnell | 462.1 | 1091 | 38 | 28.71 | 7-47 | 4 | 1 |
| S.L.Watkin | 36 | 153 | 5 | 30.60 | 3-38 | – | – |
| N.F.Williams | 41 | 148 | 2 | 74.00 | 2-148 | – | – |

# SOUTH AFRICA

## BATTING AND FIELDING

|  | M | I | NO | HS | Runs | Avge | 100 | 50 | Ct/St |
|---|---|---|---|---|---|---|---|---|---|
| T.Bosch | 1 | 2 | 2 | 5* | 5 | – | – | – | – |
| W.J.Cronje | 1 | 2 | – | 5 | 7 | 3.50 | – | – | – |
| A.A.Donald | 1 | 2 | – | 0 | 0 | 0.00 | – | – | – |
| A.C.Hudson | 1 | 2 | – | 163 | 163 | 81.50 | 1 | – | 1 |
| P.N.Kirsten | 1 | 2 | – | 52 | 63 | 31.50 | – | 1 | 2 |
| A.P.Kuiper | 1 | 2 | – | 34 | 34 | 17.00 | – | – | 1 |
| M.W.Pringle | 1 | 2 | – | 15 | 19 | 9.50 | – | – | – |
| D.J.Richardson | 1 | 2 | – | 8 | 10 | 5.00 | – | – | 6 |
| M.W.Rushmere | 1 | 2 | – | 3 | 6 | 3.00 | – | – | – |
| R.P.Snell | 1 | 2 | – | 6 | 6 | 3.00 | – | – | – |
| K.C.Wessels | 1 | 2 | – | 74 | 133 | 66.50 | – | 2 | 1 |
| | | | | | | | | | |
| K.C.Wessels (A/SA) | 25 | 44 | 1 | 179 | 1894 | 44.04 | 4 | 11 | 19 |

## BOWLING

|  | O | R | W | Avge | Best | 5wI | 10wM |
|---|---|---|---|---|---|---|---|
| T.Bosch | 39.3 | 104 | 3 | 34.66 | 2-61 | – | – |
| A.A.Donald | 45 | 144 | 6 | 24.00 | 4-77 | – | – |
| M.W.Pringle | 34.4 | 104 | 2 | 52.00 | 2-61 | – | – |
| R.P.Snell | 34 | 158 | 8 | 19.75 | 4-74 | – | – |
| K.C.Wessels | – | | | | | | |
| | | | | | | | |
| K.C.Wessels (A/SA) | 15 | 42 | 0 | – | – | – | – |

# WEST INDIES

## BATTING AND FIELDING

|  | M | I | NO | HS | Runs | Avge | 100 | 50 | Ct/St |
|---|---|---|---|---|---|---|---|---|---|
| J.C.Adams | 1 | 2 | 1 | 79* | 90 | 90.00 | – | 1 | 2 |
| I.B.A.Allen | 2 | 2 | 2 | 4* | 5 | – | – | – | 1 |
| C.E.L.Ambrose | 34 | 51 | 9 | 53 | 513 | 12.21 | – | 1 | 7 |
| K.L.T.Arthurton | 6 | 10 | 2 | 59 | 186 | 23.25 | – | 1 | 2 |
| E.A.E.Baptiste | 10 | 11 | 1 | 87* | 233 | 23.30 | – | 1 | 2 |
| K.C.G.Benjamin | 1 | 2 | – | 7 | 8 | 4.00 | – | – | – |
| C.A.Best | 8 | 13 | 1 | 164 | 342 | 28.50 | 1 | 1 | 8 |
| I.R.Bishop | 11 | 17 | 7 | 30* | 156 | 15.60 | – | – | 1 |
| P.J.L.Dujon | 81 | 115 | 11 | 139 | 3322 | 31.94 | 5 | 16 | 267/5 |
| C.G.Greenidge | 108 | 185 | 16 | 226 | 7558 | 44.72 | 19 | 34 | 96 |
| D.L.Haynes | 103 | 180 | 21 | 184 | 6725 | 42.29 | 16 | 37 | 59 |
| C.L.Hooper | 32 | 54 | 4 | 134 | 1409 | 28.18 | 3 | 7 | 29 |
| C.B.Lambert | 1 | 2 | – | 39 | 53 | 26.50 | – | – | 2 |
| B.C.Lara | 2 | 4 | – | 64 | 130 | 32.50 | – | 1 | 6 |
| A.L.Logie | 52 | 78 | 9 | 130 | 2470 | 35.79 | 2 | 16 | 57 |
| M.D.Marshall | 81 | 107 | 11 | 92 | 1810 | 18.85 | – | 10 | 25 |
| E.A.Moseley | 2 | 4 | – | 26 | 35 | 8.75 | – | – | 1 |
| B.P.Patterson | 27 | 37 | 16 | 21* | 145 | 6.90 | – | – | 5 |
| I.V.A.Richards | 121 | 182 | 12 | 291 | 8540 | 50.23 | 24 | 45 | 122 |
| R.B.Richardson | 63 | 109 | 10 | 194 | 4693 | 47.40 | 14 | 18 | 70 |
| P.V.Simmons | 8 | 16 | – | 38 | 268 | 16.75 | – | – | 5 |
| C.A.Walsh | 51 | 69 | 22 | 30* | 456 | 9.70 | – | – | 7 |
| D.Williams | 1 | 2 | – | 5 | 6 | 3.00 | – | – | 4/1 |

## BOWLING

|  | O | R | W | Avge | Best | 5wI | 10wM |
|---|---|---|---|---|---|---|---|
| J.C.Adams | 26.4 | 59 | 4 | 14.75 | 4-43 | – | – |
| I.B.A.Allen | 47 | 180 | 5 | 36.00 | 2-69 | – | – |
| C.E.L.Ambrose | 1370 | 3320 | 148 | 22.43 | 8-45 | 6 | 1 |
| K.L.T.Arthurton | 17 | 46 | 0 | – | – | – | – |
| E.A.E.Baptiste | 227 | 563 | 16 | 35.18 | 3-31 | – | – |
| K.C.G.Benjamin | 34 | 108 | 2 | 54.00 | 2-87 | – | – |
| C.A.Best | 5 | 21 | 0 | – | – | – | – |
| I.R.Bishop | 405.1 | 1091 | 53 | 20.58 | 6-87 | 3 | – |
| C.G.Greenidge | 4.2 | 4 | 0 | – | – | – | – |
| D.L.Haynes | 3 | 8 | 1 | 8.00 | 1-2 | – | – |
| C.L.Hooper | 485.4 | 1247 | 15 | 83.13 | 2-28 | – | – |
| C.B.Lambert | 0.4 | 4 | 1 | 4.00 | 1-4 | – | – |
| A.L.Logie | 1.1 | 4 | 0 | – | – | – | – |
| M.D.Marshall | 2930.4 | 7876 | 376 | 20.94 | 7-22 | 22 | 4 |
| E.A.Moseley | 87 | 261 | 6 | 43.50 | 2-70 | – | – |
| B.P.Patterson | 778.5 | 2748 | 92 | 29.87 | 5-24 | 5 | – |
| I.V.A.Richards | 861.4 | 1964 | 32 | 61.37 | 2-17 | – | – |
| R.B.Richardson | 10 | 14 | 0 | – | – | – | – |
| P.V.Simmons | 8 | 20 | 0 | – | – | – | – |
| C.A.Walsh | 1686.5 | 4444 | 178 | 24.96 | 6-62 | 5 | 1 |

# NEW ZEALAND

## BATTING AND FIELDING

| | M | I | NO | HS | Runs | Avge | 100 | 50 | Ct/St |
|---|---|---|---|---|---|---|---|---|---|
| J.G.Bracewell | 41 | 60 | 11 | 110 | 1001 | 20.42 | 1 | 4 | 32 |
| G.E.Bradburn | 4 | 7 | 2 | 30* | 97 | 19.40 | – | – | 3 |
| C.L.Cairns | 5 | 8 | – | 61 | 165 | 20.62 | – | 1 | 4 |
| J.J.Crowe | 39 | 65 | 4 | 128 | 1601 | 26.24 | 3 | 6 | 41 |
| M.D.Crowe | 59 | 98 | 10 | 299 | 4205 | 47.78 | 13 | 14 | 58 |
| T.J.Franklin | 21 | 37 | 1 | 101 | 828 | 23.00 | 1 | 4 | 8 |
| M.J.Greatbatch | 20 | 33 | 5 | 146* | 1116 | 39.85 | 2 | 5 | 14 |
| Sir R.J.Hadlee | 86 | 134 | 19 | 151* | 3124 | 27.16 | 2 | 15 | 39 |
| B.R.Hartland | 3 | 6 | – | 45 | 88 | 14.66 | – | – | 1 |
| P.A.Horne | 4 | 7 | – | 27 | 71 | 10.14 | – | – | 3 |
| A.H.Jones | 23 | 42 | 5 | 186 | 1929 | 52.13 | 6 | 6 | 16 |
| R.T.Latham | 1 | 1 | – | 25 | 25 | 25.00 | – | – | 1 |
| D.K.Morrison | 25 | 35 | 10 | 27* | 146 | 5.84 | – | – | 7 |
| A.C.Parore | 2 | 4 | 1 | 20 | 47 | 15.66 | – | – | 10/1 |
| D.N.Patel | 16 | 31 | 2 | 99 | 598 | 20.62 | – | 2 | 3 |
| M.W.Priest | 1 | 1 | – | 26 | 26 | 26.00 | – | – | – |
| C.Pringle | 6 | 10 | 2 | 24* | 80 | 10.00 | – | – | – |
| K.R.Rutherford | 30 | 49 | 4 | 107* | 831 | 18.46 | 1 | 5 | 21 |
| I.D.S.Smith | 63 | 88 | 17 | 173 | 1815 | 25.56 | 2 | 6 | 168/8 |
| M.C.Snedden | 25 | 30 | 8 | 33* | 327 | 14.86 | – | – | 7 |
| M.L.Su'a | 2 | 3 | 2 | 36 | 56 | 56.00 | – | – | 1 |
| S.A.Thomson | 4 | 8 | 2 | 80* | 242 | 40.33 | – | 2 | 3 |
| R.H.Vance | 4 | 7 | – | 68 | 207 | 29.57 | – | 1 | – |
| W.Watson | 10 | 14 | 5 | 11 | 54 | 6.00 | – | – | 3 |
| D.J.White | 2 | 4 | – | 18 | 31 | 7.75 | – | – | – |
| J.G.Wright | 77 | 138 | 6 | 185 | 4964 | 37.60 | 12 | 21 | 36 |

## BOWLING

| | O | R | W | Avge | Best | 5wI | 10wM |
|---|---|---|---|---|---|---|---|
| J.G.Bracewell | 1400.3 | 3653 | 102 | 35.81 | 6-32 | 4 | 1 |
| G.E.Bradburn | 62 | 194 | 2 | 97.00 | 1-32 | – | – |
| C.L.Cairns | 188 | 700 | 20 | 35.00 | 6-52 | 2 | – |
| J.J.Crowe | 3 | 9 | 0 | – | – | – | – |
| M.D.Crowe | 223.3 | 651 | 14 | 46.50 | 2-25 | – | – |
| M.J.Greatbatch | 1 | 0 | 0 | – | – | – | – |
| Sir R.J.Hadlee | 3653 | 9611 | 431 | 22.29 | 9-52 | 36 | 9 |
| A.H.Jones | 36 | 126 | 1 | 126.00 | 1-40 | – | – |
| D.K.Morrison | 866 | 3011 | 78 | 38.60 | 5-69 | 5 | – |
| D.N.Patel | 348.4 | 961 | 15 | 64.06 | 4-87 | – | – |
| M.W.Priest | 12 | 26 | 1 | 26.00 | 1-26 | – | – |
| C.Pringle | 221 | 695 | 18 | 38.61 | 7-52 | 1 | 1 |
| K.R.Rutherford | 42.4 | 161 | 1 | 161.00 | 1-38 | – | – |
| I.D.S.Smith | 3 | 5 | 0 | – | – | – | – |
| M.C.Snedden | 795.5 | 2199 | 58 | 37.91 | 5-68 | 1 | – |
| M.L.Su'a | 100 | 236 | 8 | 29.50 | 3-87 | – | – |
| S.A.Thomson | 87.4 | 282 | 6 | 47.00 | 3-63 | – | – |
| W.Watson | 488 | 1100 | 30 | 36.66 | 6-78 | 1 | – |
| D.J.White | 0.3 | 5 | 0 | – | – | – | – |
| J.G.Wright | 5 | 5 | 0 | – | – | – | – |

# INDIA

## BATTING AND FIELDING

| | M | I | NO | HS | Runs | Avge | 100 | 50 | Ct/St |
|---|---|---|---|---|---|---|---|---|---|
| S.A.Ankola | 1 | 1 | – | 6 | 6 | 6.00 | – | – | – |
| Arshad Ayub | 13 | 19 | 4 | 57 | 257 | 17.13 | – | 1 | 2 |
| M.Azharuddin | 46 | 70 | 3 | 199 | 3168 | 47.28 | 11 | 10 | 35 |
| S.T.Banerjee | 1 | 1 | – | 3 | 3 | 3.00 | – | – | – |
| Gursharan Singh | 1 | 1 | – | 18 | 18 | 18.00 | – | – | 2 |
| N.D.Hirwani | 14 | 18 | 10 | 17 | 45 | 5.62 | – | – | 5 |
| Kapil Dev | 115 | 168 | 13 | 163 | 4690 | 30.25 | 7 | 24 | 58 |
| A.Kumble | 1 | 1 | – | 2 | 2 | 2.00 | – | – | – |
| Maninder Singh | 34 | 38 | 12 | 15 | 99 | 3.80 | – | – | 9 |
| S.V.Manjrekar | 21 | 34 | 2 | 218 | 1303 | 40.71 | 3 | 5 | 12 |
| K.S.More | 38 | 53 | 12 | 73 | 1104 | 26.92 | – | 6 | 82/16 |
| C.S.Pandit | 5 | 8 | 1 | 39 | 171 | 24.42 | – | – | 14/2 |
| M.Prabhakar | 18 | 30 | 7 | 95 | 876 | 38.08 | – | 6 | 6 |
| S.L.V.Raju | 7 | 12 | 3 | 31 | 151 | 16.77 | – | – | 3 |
| W.V.Raman | 6 | 10 | 1 | 96 | 303 | 33.66 | – | 3 | 3 |
| V.Razdan | 2 | 2 | 1 | 6* | 6 | 6.00 | – | – | – |
| G.Sharma | 5 | 4 | 1 | 10* | 11 | 3.66 | – | – | 1 |
| S.K.Sharma | 2 | 3 | 1 | 38 | 56 | 28.00 | – | – | 1 |
| R.J.Shastri | 76 | 115 | 14 | 206 | 3760 | 37.22 | 11 | 12 | 36 |
| N.S.Sidhu | 20 | 33 | 2 | 116 | 894 | 28.83 | 2 | 4 | 3 |
| K.Srikkanth | 43 | 72 | 3 | 123 | 2062 | 29.88 | 2 | 12 | 40 |
| J.Srinath | 5 | 9 | 4 | 21 | 78 | 15.60 | – | – | 1 |
| S.R.Tendulkar | 16 | 25 | 2 | 148* | 956 | 41.56 | 3 | 4 | 10 |
| D.B.Vengsarkar | 116 | 185 | 22 | 166 | 6868 | 42.13 | 17 | 35 | 78 |
| A.S.Wassan | 4 | 5 | 1 | 53 | 94 | 23.50 | – | 1 | 1 |

## BOWLING

| | O | R | W | Avge | Best | 5wI | 10wM |
|---|---|---|---|---|---|---|---|
| S.A.Ankola | 30 | 128 | 2 | 64.00 | 1-35 | – | – |
| Arshad Ayub | 610.3 | 1438 | 41 | 35.07 | 5-50 | 3 | – |
| M.Azharuddin | 1 | 8 | 0 | – | – | – | – |
| S.T.Banerjee | 18 | 47 | 3 | 15.66 | 3-47 | – | – |
| N.D.Hirwani | 645.2 | 1799 | 58 | 31.01 | 8-61 | 3 | 1 |
| Kapil Dev | 4161.1 | 11894 | 401 | 29.66 | 9-83 | 23 | 2 |
| A.Kumble | 60 | 170 | 3 | 56.66 | 3-105 | – | – |
| Maninder Singh | 1302.4 | 3143 | 81 | 38.80 | 7-27 | 3 | 2 |
| S.V.Manjrekar | 1.5 | 11 | 0 | – | – | – | – |
| K.S.More | 2 | 12 | 0 | – | – | – | – |
| M.Prabhakar | 762.2 | 2331 | 53 | 43.98 | 6-132 | 3 | – |
| S.L.V.Raju | 271.3 | 588 | 20 | 29.40 | 6-12 | 1 | – |
| W.V.Raman | 43 | 66 | 2 | 33.00 | 1-7 | – | – |
| V.Razdan | 40 | 141 | 5 | 28.20 | 5-79 | 1 | – |
| G.Sharma | 217.5 | 418 | 10 | 41.80 | 4-88 | – | – |
| S.K.Sharma | 69 | 247 | 6 | 41.16 | 3-37 | – | – |
| R.J.Shastri | 2565.1 | 6027 | 148 | 40.72 | 5-75 | 2 | – |
| N.S.Sidhu | 1 | 9 | 0 | – | – | – | – |
| K.Srikkanth | 36 | 114 | 0 | – | – | – | – |
| J.Srinath | 201.1 | 553 | 10 | 55.30 | 3-59 | – | – |
| S.R.Tendulkar | 41 | 119 | 3 | 39.66 | 2-10 | – | – |
| D.B.Vengsarkar | 7.5 | 36 | 0 | – | – | – | – |
| A.S.Wassan | 118.4 | 504 | 10 | 50.40 | 4-108 | – | – |

# PAKISTAN

## BATTING AND FIELDING

| | M | I | NO | HS | Runs | Avge | 100 | 50 | Ct/St |
|---|---|---|---|---|---|---|---|---|---|
| Aamer Malik | 13 | 17 | 3 | 117 | 489 | 34.92 | 2 | 2 | 15 |
| Aamir Sohail | 5 | 9 | 1 | 205 | 413 | 51.62 | 1 | 1 | 3 |
| Abdul Qadir | 67 | 77 | 11 | 61 | 1029 | 15.59 | – | 3 | 15 |
| Akram Raza | 3 | 2 | – | 5 | 5 | 2.50 | – | – | 4 |
| Aqib Javed | 13 | 10 | 3 | 10 | 26 | 3.71 | – | – | 1 |
| Asif Mujtaba | 8 | 13 | – | 59 | 292 | 22.46 | – | 3 | 7 |
| Ata-ur-Rehman | 1 | – | – | – | – | – | – | – | – |
| Ijaz Ahmed | 19 | 25 | – | 122 | 743 | 29.72 | 2 | 3 | 16 |
| Imran Khan | 88 | 126 | 25 | 136 | 3807 | 37.69 | 6 | 18 | 28 |
| Inzamam-ul-Haq | 4 | 6 | 1 | 26 | 66 | 13.20 | – | – | 4 |
| Javed Miandad | 117 | 177 | 21 | 280* | 8465 | 54.26 | 23 | 41 | 93/1 |
| Mansoor Akhtar | 19 | 29 | 3 | 111 | 655 | 25.19 | 1 | 3 | 9 |
| Masood Anwar | 1 | 2 | – | 37 | 39 | 19.50 | – | – | – |
| Moin Khan | 9 | 11 | 2 | 32 | 134 | 14.88 | – | – | 17/1 |
| Mushtaq Ahmed | 8 | 11 | 2 | 11 | 49 | 5.44 | – | – | 1 |
| Nadeem Abbasi | 3 | 2 | – | 36 | 46 | 23.00 | – | – | 6 |
| Nadeem Ghauri | 1 | 1 | – | 0 | 0 | 0.00 | – | – | – |
| Naved Anjum | 2 | 3 | – | 22 | 44 | 14.66 | – | – | – |
| Ramiz Raja | 44 | 71 | 5 | 122 | 2149 | 32.56 | 2 | 16 | 27 |
| Rashid Latif | 1 | 1 | – | 50 | 50 | 50.00 | – | 1 | 2/1 |
| Saeed Anwar | 1 | 2 | – | 0 | 0 | 0.00 | – | – | 1 |
| Salim Jaffer | 14 | 14 | 6 | 10* | 42 | 5.25 | – | – | 2 |
| Salim Malik | 71 | 101 | 18 | 165 | 3743 | 45.09 | 10 | 21 | 48 |
| Salim Yousuf | 32 | 44 | 5 | 91* | 1055 | 27.05 | – | 5 | 91/13 |
| Shahid Mahboob | 1 | – | – | – | – | – | – | – | – |
| Shahid Saeed | 1 | 1 | – | 12 | 12 | 12.00 | – | – | – |
| Shoaib Mohammad | 39 | 58 | 6 | 203* | 2443 | 46.98 | 7 | 10 | 20 |
| Tausif Ahmed | 33 | 37 | 19 | 35* | 297 | 16.50 | – | – | 9 |
| Waqar Younis | 19 | 21 | 5 | 20* | 127 | 7.93 | – | – | 1 |
| Wasim Akram | 44 | 56 | 9 | 123 | 971 | 20.66 | 1 | 4 | 12 |
| Zahid Fazal | 6 | 10 | – | 78 | 223 | 22.30 | – | 1 | 4 |
| Zakir Khan | 2 | 2 | 2 | 9* | 9 | – | – | – | 1 |

## BOWLING

| | O | R | W | Avge | Best | 5wI | 10wM |
|---|---|---|---|---|---|---|---|
| Aamer Malik | 21 | 73 | 1 | 73.00 | 1-0 | – | – |
| Aamir Sohail | 5 | 14 | 0 | – | – | – | – |
| Abdul Qadir | 2854.2 | 7742 | 236 | 32.80 | 9-56 | 15 | 5 |
| Akram Raza | 79.2 | 218 | 5 | 43.60 | 2-37 | – | – |
| Aqib Javed | 334 | 1013 | 25 | 40.52 | 4-100 | – | – |
| Asif Mujtaba | 16 | 32 | 1 | 32.00 | 1-0 | – | – |
| Ata-ur-Rehman | 18 | 69 | 3 | 23.00 | 3-69 | – | – |
| Ijaz Ahmed | 9 | 18 | 1 | 18.00 | 1-9 | – | – |
| Imran Khan | 3243 | 8258 | 362 | 22.81 | 8-58 | 23 | 6 |
| Javed Miandad | 245 | 682 | 17 | 40.11 | 3-74 | – | – |
| Masood Anwar | 26.5 | 102 | 3 | 34.00 | 2-59 | – | – |
| Mushtaq Ahmed | 264.4 | 716 | 19 | 37.68 | 3-32 | – | – |
| Nadeem Ghauri | 8 | 20 | 0 | – | – | – | – |
| Naved Anjum | 57 | 162 | 4 | 40.50 | 2-57 | – | – |
| Salim Jaffer | 421.5 | 1139 | 36 | 31.63 | 5-40 | 1 | – |

| | O | R | W | Avge | Best | 5wI | 10wM |
|---|---|---|---|---|---|---|---|
| Salim Malik | 45.2 | 118 | 5 | 23.60 | 1-3 | – | – |
| Shahid Mahboob | 49 | 131 | 2 | 65.50 | 2-131 | – | – |
| Shahid Saeed | 15 | 43 | 0 | – | – | – | – |
| Shoaib Mohammad | 42 | 113 | 5 | 22.60 | 2-8 | – | – |
| Tausif Ahmed | 1267.2 | 2888 | 93 | 31.05 | 6-45 | 3 | – |
| Waqar Younis | 624.1 | 1908 | 93 | 20.51 | 7-76 | 10 | 2 |
| Wasim Akram | 1608.1 | 4100 | 169 | 24.26 | 6-62 | 11 | 2 |
| Zakir Khan | 74 | 259 | 5 | 51.80 | 3-80 | – | – |

## SRI LANKA

### BATTING AND FIELDING

| | M | I | NO | HS | Runs | Avge | 100 | 50 | Ct/St |
|---|---|---|---|---|---|---|---|---|---|
| S.D.Anurasiri | 8 | 10 | 3 | 16 | 33 | 4.71 | – | – | 1 |
| M.S.Atapattu | 1 | 2 | – | 0 | 0 | 0.00 | – | – | – |
| E.A.R.De Silva | 10 | 16 | 4 | 50 | 185 | 15.41 | – | 1 | 4 |
| P.A.De Silva | 25 | 44 | 2 | 267 | 1639 | 39.02 | 5 | 4 | 16 |
| A.P.Gurusinha | 17 | 28 | 3 | 119 | 947 | 37.88 | 3 | 3 | 13 |
| U.C.Hathurusinghe | 6 | 10 | – | 81 | 375 | 37.50 | – | 3 | 1 |
| S.T.Jayasuriya | 6 | 9 | 2 | 81 | 380 | 54.28 | – | 3 | 2 |
| D.S.B.P.Kuruppu | 4 | 7 | 1 | 201* | 320 | 53.33 | 1 | – | 1 |
| G.F.Labrooy | 9 | 14 | 3 | 70* | 158 | 14.36 | – | 1 | 3 |
| A.W.R.Madurasinghe | 2 | 4 | – | 11 | 19 | 4.75 | – | – | – |
| R.S.Mahanama | 11 | 16 | – | 85 | 375 | 23.43 | – | 2 | 6 |
| C.P.H.Ramanayake | 10 | 15 | 5 | 34* | 100 | 10.00 | – | – | 3 |
| A.Ranatunga | 33 | 57 | 7 | 135* | 1830 | 33.88 | 2 | 13 | 15 |
| D.Ranatunga | 2 | 3 | – | 45 | 87 | 29.00 | – | – | – |
| R.J.Ratnayake | 23 | 36 | 6 | 56 | 433 | 14.43 | – | 2 | 9 |
| J.R.Ratnayeke | 22 | 38 | 6 | 93 | 807 | 25.21 | – | 5 | 1 |
| M.A.R.Samarasekera | 4 | 7 | – | 57 | 118 | 16.85 | – | 1 | 3 |
| C.P.Senanayake | 3 | 5 | – | 64 | 97 | 19.40 | – | 1 | 2 |
| H.P.Tillekeratne | 9 | 15 | 1 | 55 | 306 | 21.85 | – | 1 | 25 |
| K.P.J.Warnaweera | 3 | 5 | 1 | 3 | 6 | 1.50 | – | – | – |
| A.G.D.Wickremasinghe | 1 | 1 | – | 2 | 2 | 2.00 | – | – | 3 |
| G.P.Wickremasinghe | 3 | 3 | 1 | 1* | 1 | 0.50 | – | – | 1 |
| K.I.W.Wijegunawardene | 2 | 4 | 1 | 6* | 14 | 4.66 | – | – | – |

### BOWLING

| | O | R | W | Avge | Best | 5wI | 10wM |
|---|---|---|---|---|---|---|---|
| S.D.Anurasiri | 212.1 | 493 | 13 | 37.92 | 4-71 | – | – |
| E.A.R.De Silva | 388 | 1032 | 8 | 129.00 | 2-67 | – | – |
| P.A.De Silva | 53 | 220 | 3 | 73.33 | 2-65 | – | – |
| A.P.Gurusinha | 104.4 | 298 | 11 | 27.09 | 2-19 | – | – |
| U.C.Hathurusinghe | 24 | 68 | 1 | 68.00 | 1-40 | – | – |
| S.T.Jayasuriya | 7 | 19 | 0 | – | – | – | – |
| G.F.Labrooy | 359.4 | 1194 | 27 | 44.22 | 5-133 | 1 | – |
| A.W.R.Madurasinghe | 42 | 101 | 3 | 33.66 | 3-60 | – | – |
| R.S.Mahanama | 1 | 3 | 0 | – | – | – | – |
| C.P.H.Ramanayake | 348.2 | 1116 | 19 | 58.73 | 2-39 | – | – |
| A.Ranatunga | 308.2 | 811 | 14 | 57.92 | 2-17 | – | – |
| R.J.Ratnayake | 826.5 | 2563 | 73 | 35.11 | 6-66 | 5 | – |
| J.R.Ratnayeke | 638.5 | 1972 | 56 | 35.21 | 8-83 | 4 | – |
| M.A.R.Samarasekera | 32 | 104 | 3 | 34.66 | 2-38 | – | – |
| K.P.J.Warnaweera | 94.3 | 205 | 4 | 51.25 | 3-90 | – | – |
| G.P.Wickremasinghe | 92 | 273 | 8 | 34.12 | 5-73 | 1 | – |
| K.I.W.Wijegunawardene | 60.4 | 147 | 7 | 21.00 | 4-51 | – | – |

# FIRST-CLASS CRICKET RECORDS

## UPDATED TO THE END OF THE 1992 SEASON

### TEAM RECORDS

#### HIGHEST INNINGS TOTALS

| | | | |
|---|---|---|---|
| 1107 | Victoria v New South Wales | Melbourne | 1926-27 |
| 1059 | Victoria v Tasmania | Melbourne | 1922-23 |
| 951-7d | Sind v Baluchistan | Karachi | 1973-74 |
| 918 | New South Wales v South Australia | Sydney | 1900-01 |
| 912-8d | Holkar v Mysore | Indore | 1945-46 |
| 910-6d | Railways v Dera Ismail Khan | Lahore | 1964-65 |
| 903-7d | England v Australia | The Oval | 1938 |
| 887 | Yorkshire v Warwickshire | Birmingham | 1896 |
| 863 | Lancashire v Surrey | The Oval | 1990 |
| 860-6d | Tamil Nadu v Goa | Panjim | 1988-89 |

There have been 26 instances of a team scoring 800 runs or more in an innings, the most recent being by Bombay (855-6d, including 48 penalty runs) v Hyderabad at Bombay in 1990-91. Tamil Nadu's total of 860-6d was boosted to 912 by 52 penalty runs.

#### HIGHEST SECOND INNINGS TOTAL

| | | | |
|---|---|---|---|
| 770 | New South Wales v South Australia | Adelaide | 1920-21 |

#### HIGHEST FOURTH INNINGS TOTAL

| | | | |
|---|---|---|---|
| 654-5 | England v South Africa | Durban | 1938-39 |

#### HIGHEST MATCH AGGREGATE

| | | | |
|---|---|---|---|
| 2376 | Maharashtra v Bombay | Poona | 1948-49 |

#### RECORD MARGIN OF VICTORY

| | | |
|---|---|---|
| Innings and 851 runs: Railways v Dera Ismail Khan | Lahore | 1964-65 |

#### MOST RUNS IN A DAY

| | | | |
|---|---|---|---|
| 721 | Australians v Essex | Southend | 1948 |

#### MOST HUNDREDS IN AN INNINGS

| | | | |
|---|---|---|---|
| 6 | Holkar v Mysore | Indore | 1945-46 |

#### LOWEST INNINGS TOTALS

| | | | |
|---|---|---|---|
| 12 | † Oxford University v MCC and Ground | Oxford | 1877 |
| 12 | Northamptonshire v Gloucestershire | Gloucester | 1907 |
| 13 | Auckland v Canterbury | Auckland | 1877-78 |
| 13 | Nottinghamshire v Yorkshire | Nottingham | 1901 |

| 14 | Surrey v Essex | Chelmsford | 1983 |
| 15 | MCC v Surrey | Lord's | 1839 |
| 15 | † Victoria v MCC | Melbourne | 1903-04 |
| 15 | † Northamptonshire v Yorkshire | Northampton | 1908 |
| 15 | Hampshire v Warwickshire | Birmingham | 1922 |

† Batted one man short

There have been 26 instances of a team being dismissed for under 20, the most recent being by Surrey in 1983 (above).

## LOWEST MATCH AGGREGATE BY ONE TEAM

| 34 | (16 and 18) Border v Natal | East London | 1959-60 |

## LOWEST COMPLETED MATCH AGGREGATE BY BOTH TEAMS

| 105 | MCC v Australians | Lord's | 1878 |

## FEWEST RUNS IN AN UNINTERRUPTED DAY'S PLAY

| 95 | Australia (80) v Pakistan (15-2) | Karachi | 1956-57 |

## TIED MATCHES

Before 1948 a match was considered to be tied if the scores were level after the fourth innings, even if the side batting last had wickets in hand when play ended. Law 22 was amended in 1948 and since then a match has been tied only when the scores are level after the fourth innings has been completed. There have been 49 tied first-class matches, five of which would not have qualified under the current law. The most recent is:

| Kent (381/408-7d) v Sussex (353/436) | Hove | 1991 |

## BATTING RECORDS

### HIGHEST INDIVIDUAL INNINGS

| 499 | Hanif Mohammad | Karachi v Bahawalpur | Karachi | 1958-59 |
| 452* | D.G.Bradman | New South Wales v Queensland | Sydney | 1929-30 |
| 443* | B.B.Nimbalkar | Maharashtra v Kathiawar | Poona | 1948-49 |
| 437 | W.H.Ponsford | Victoria v Queensland | Melbourne | 1927-28 |
| 429 | W.H.Ponsford | Victoria v Tasmania | Melbourne | 1922-23 |
| 428 | Aftab Baloch | Sind v Baluchistan | Karachi | 1973-74 |
| 424 | A.C.MacLaren | Lancashire v Somerset | Taunton | 1895 |
| 405* | G.A.Hick | Worcestershire v Somerset | Taunton | 1988 |
| 385 | B.Sutcliffe | Otago v Canterbury | Christchurch | 1952-53 |
| 383 | C.W.Gregory | New South Wales v Queensland | Brisbane | 1906-07 |
| 377 | S.V.Manjrekar | Bombay v Hyderabad | Bombay | 1990-91 |
| 369 | D.G.Bradman | South Australia v Tasmania | Adelaide | 1935-36 |
| 366 | N.H.Fairbrother | Lancashire v Surrey | The Oval | 1990 |
| 365* | C.Hill | South Australia v NSW | Adelaide | 1900-01 |
| 365* | G.St A.Sobers | West Indies v Pakistan | Kingston | 1957-58 |
| 364 | L.Hutton | England v Australia | The Oval | 1938 |
| 359* | V.M.Merchant | Bombay v Maharashtra | Bombay | 1943-44 |
| 359 | R.B.Simpson | New South Wales v Queensland | Brisbane | 1963-64 |
| 357* | R.Abel | Surrey v Somerset | The Oval | 1899 |

| 357 | D.G.Bradman | South Australia v Victoria | Melbourne | 1935-36 |
| 356 | B.A.Richards | South Australia v W Australia | Perth | 1970-71 |
| 355* | G.R.Marsh | W Australia v S Australia | Perth | 1989-90 |
| 355 | B.Sutcliffe | Otago v Auckland | Dunedin | 1949-50 |
| 352 | W.H.Ponsford | Victoria v New South Wales | Melbourne | 1926-27 |
| 350 | Rashid Israr | Habib Bank v National Bank | Lahore | 1976-77 |

There have been 105 triple hundreds in first-class cricket, W.V.Raman (313) and Arjan Kripal Singh (302*) for Tamil Nadu v Goa at Panjim in 1988-89 providing the only instance of two batsmen scoring 300 in the same innings.

## MOST HUNDREDS IN SUCCESSIVE INNINGS

| 6 | C.B.Fry | Sussex and Rest of England | 1901 |
| 6 | D.G.Bradman | South Australia and D.G.Bradman's XI | 1938-39 |
| 6 | M.J.Procter | Rhodesia | 1970-71 |

## TWO DOUBLE HUNDREDS IN A MATCH

| 244 | 202* | A.E.Fagg | Kent v Essex | Colchester | 1938 |

## TRIPLE HUNDRED AND HUNDRED IN A MATCH

| 333 | 123 | G.A.Gooch | England v India | Lord's | 1990 |

## DOUBLE HUNDRED AND HUNDRED IN A MATCH MOST TIMES

| 4 | Zaheer Abbas | Gloucestershire | 1976-81 |

## TWO HUNDREDS IN A MATCH MOST TIMES

| 8 | Zaheer Abbas | Gloucestershire and PIA | 1976-82 |
| 7 | W.R.Hammond | Gloucestershire, England and MCC | 1927-45 |

## MOST HUNDREDS IN A SEASON

| 18 | D.C.S.Compton | 1947 | 16 | J.B.Hobbs | 1925 |

## MOST HUNDREDS IN A CAREER

|  | Total | | 100th Hundred | |
|  | Hundreds | Inns | Season | Inns |
| J.B.Hobbs | 197 | 1315 | 1923 | 821 |
| E.H.Hendren | 170 | 1300 | 1928-29 | 740 |
| W.R.Hammond | 167 | 1005 | 1935 | 679 |
| C.P.Mead | 153 | 1340 | 1927 | 892 |
| G.Boycott | 151 | 1014 | 1977 | 645 |
| H.Sutcliffe | 149 | 1088 | 1932 | 700 |
| F.E.Woolley | 145 | 1532 | 1929 | 1031 |
| L.Hutton | 129 | 814 | 1951 | 619 |
| W.G.Grace | 126 | 1493 | 1895 | 1113 |
| D.C.S.Compton | 123 | 839 | 1952 | 552 |
| T.W.Graveney | 122 | 1223 | 1964 | 940 |
| D.G.Bradman | 117 | 338 | 1947-48 | 295 |
| I.V.A.Richards | 112 | 764 | 1988-89 | 658 |
| Zaheer Abbas | 108 | 768 | 1982-83 | 658 |

|              |                    | Total    |      | 100th Hundred |      |
| ------------ | ------------------ | -------- | ---- | ------------- | ---- |
|              |                    | Hundreds | Inns | Season        | Inns |
| A.Sandham    |                    | 107      | 1000 | 1935          | 871  |
| M.C.Cowdrey  |                    | 107      | 1130 | 1973          | 1035 |
| T.W.Hayward  |                    | 104      | 1138 | 1913          | 1076 |
| J.H.Edrich   |                    | 103      | 979  | 1977          | 945  |
| G.M.Turner   |                    | 103      | 792  | 1982          | 779  |
| E.Tyldesley  |                    | 102      | 961  | 1934          | 919  |
| L.E.G.Ames   |                    | 102      | 951  | 1950          | 915  |
| D.L.Amiss    |                    | 102      | 1139 | 1986          | 1081 |

**Most 400s:**       2 – W.H.Ponsford

**Most 300s or more:**  6 – D.G.Bradman

**Most 200s or more:**  37 – D.G.Bradman; 36 – W.R.Hammond

## MOST RUNS IN A MONTH

1294     (avge 92.42)     L.Hutton     Yorkshire     June 1949

## MOST RUNS IN A SEASON

| Runs |              |           | I  | NO | HS   | Avge  | 100 | Season |
| ---- | ------------ | --------- | -- | -- | ---- | ----- | --- | ------ |
| 3816 | D.C.S.Compton | Middlesex | 50 | 8  | 246  | 90.85 | 18  | 1947   |
| 3539 | W.J.Edrich   | Middlesex | 52 | 8  | 267* | 80.43 | 12  | 1947   |
| 3518 | T.W.Hayward  | Surrey    | 61 | 8  | 219  | 66.37 | 13  | 1906   |

The feat of scoring 3000 runs in a season has been achieved on 28 occasions, the most recent instance being by W.E.Alley (3019) in 1961. The highest aggregate in a season since 1969, when the number of County Championship matches was substantially reduced, is 2755 by S.J.Cook in 1991.

## 1000 RUNS IN A SEASON MOST TIMES

28     W.G.Grace (Gloucestershire), F.E.Woolley (Kent)

## HIGHEST BATTING AVERAGE IN A SEASON

### (Qualification: 12 innings)

| Avge   |              |             | I  | NO | HS   | Runs | 100 | Season |
| ------ | ------------ | ----------- | -- | -- | ---- | ---- | --- | ------ |
| 115.66 | D.G.Bradman  | Australians | 26 | 5  | 278  | 2429 | 13  | 1938   |
| 102.53 | G.Boycott    | Yorkshire   | 20 | 5  | 175* | 1538 | 6   | 1979   |
| 102.00 | W.A.Johnston | Australians | 17 | 16 | 28*  | 102  | –   | 1953   |
| 101.70 | G.A.Gooch    | Essex       | 30 | 3  | 333  | 2746 | 12  | 1990   |
| 100.12 | G.Boycott    | Yorkshire   | 30 | 5  | 233  | 2503 | 13  | 1971   |

## FASTEST HUNDRED AGAINST GENUINE BOWLING

35 min  P.G.H.Fender     Surrey v Northamptonshire  Northampton    1920

## FASTEST DOUBLE HUNDRED

113 min  R.J.Shastri     Bombay v Baroda     Bombay    1984-85

## FASTEST TRIPLE HUNDRED

181 min  D.C.S.Compton     MCC v NE Transvaal     Benoni    1948-49

## MOST SIXES IN AN INNINGS

| 15 | J.R.Reid | Wellington v N Districts | Wellington | 1962-63 |
|----|----------|--------------------------|------------|---------|
| 14 | Shakti Singh | Himachal Pradesh v Haryana | Dharmsala | 1990-91 |
| 13 | Majid Khan | Pakistanis v Glamorgan | Swansea | 1967 |
| 13 | C.G.Greenidge | D.H.Robins' XI v Pakistanis | Eastbourne | 1974 |
| 13 | C.G.Greenidge | Hampshire v Sussex | Southampton | 1975 |
| 13 | G.W.Humpage | Warwickshire v Lancashire | Southport | 1982 |
| 13 | R.J.Shastri | Bombay v Baroda | Bombay | 1984-85 |

## MOST SIXES IN A MATCH

| 17 | W.J.Stewart | Warwickshire v Lancashire | Blackpool | 1959 |
|----|-------------|----------------------------|-----------|------|

## MOST SIXES IN A SEASON

| 80 | I.T.Botham | Somerset and England | 1985 |
|----|-----------|----------------------|------|

## MOST BOUNDARIES IN AN INNINGS

| 68 | P.A.Perrin | Essex v Derbyshire | Chesterfield | 1904 |
|----|-----------|--------------------|--------------|------|

## MOST RUNS OFF ONE OVER

| 36 | G.St A.Sobers | Nottinghamshire v Glamorgan | Swansea | 1968 |
|----|---------------|------------------------------|---------|------|
| 36 | R.J.Shastri | Bombay v Baroda | Bombay | 1984-85 |

Both batsmen hit all six balls in an over (bowled by M.A.Nash and Tilak Raj respectively) for six.

## MOST RUNS IN A DAY

| 345 | C.G.Macartney | Australians v Nottinghamshire | Nottingham | 1921 |
|-----|---------------|--------------------------------|------------|------|

There have been 18 instances of a batsman scoring 300 or more runs in a day, the most recent being by N.H.Fairbrother (311*) for Lancashire v Surrey at The Oval in 1990.

## HIGHEST PARTNERSHIPS

**First Wicket**

| 561 | Waheed Mirza/Mansoor Akhtar | Karachi W v Quetta | Karachi | 1976-77 |
|-----|------------------------------|---------------------|---------|---------|
| 555 | P.Holmes/H.Sutcliffe | Yorkshire v Essex | Leyton | 1932 |
| 554 | J.T.Brown/J.Tunnicliffe | Yorkshire v Derbys | Chesterfield | 1898 |

**Second Wicket**

| 475 | Zahir Alam/L.S.Rajput | Assam v Tripura | Gauhati | 1991-92 |
|-----|------------------------|------------------|---------|---------|
| 465* | J.A.Jameson/R.B.Kanhai | Warwickshire v Glos | Birmingham | 1974 |
| 455 | K.V.Bhandarkar/B.B.Nimbalkar | Maha'tra v Kathiawar | Poona | 1948-49 |

**Third Wicket**

| 467 | A.H.Jones/M.D.Crowe | N Zealand v Sri Lanka | Wellington | 1990-91 |
|-----|---------------------|------------------------|------------|---------|
| 456 | Khalid Jrtiza/Aslam Ali | United Bank v Multan | Karachi | 1975-76 |
| 451 | Mudassar Nazar/Javed Miandad | Pakistan v India | Hyderabad | 1982-83 |
| 445 | P.E.Whitelaw/W.N.Carson | Auckland v Otago | Dunedin | 1936-37 |

| 434 | J.B.Stollmeyer/G.E.Gomez | Trinidad v Br Guiana | Port-of-Spain | 1946-47 |
| 424* | W.J.Edrich/D.C.S.Compton | Middlesex v Somerset | Lord's | 1948 |

**Fourth Wicket**

| 577 | V.S.Hazare/Gul Mahomed | Baroda v Holkar | Baroda | 1946-47 |
| 574* | C.L.Walcott/F.M.M.Worrell | Barbados v Trinidad | Port-of-Spain | 1945-46 |
| 502* | F.M.M.Worrell/J.D.C.Goddard | Barbados v Trinidad | Bridgetown | 1943-44 |
| 470 | A.I.Kallicharran/G.W.Humpage | Warwickshire v Lancs | Southport | 1982 |

**Fifth Wicket**

| 464*† | M.E.Waugh/S.R.Waugh | NSW v W Australia | Perth | 1990-91 |
| 405 | S.G.Barnes/D.G.Bradman | Australia v England | Sydney | 1946-47 |
| 397 | W.Bardsley/C.Kelleway | NSW v S Australia | Sydney | 1920-21 |
| 393 | E.G.Arnold/W.B.Burns | Worcs v Warwickshire | Birmingham | 1909 |

†Includes 20 runs for no-balls under ACB experimental rule – worth only 7 under Laws of cricket.

**Sixth Wicket**

| 487* | G.A.Headley/C.C.Passailaigue | Jamaica v Tennyson's | Kingston | 1931-32 |
| 428 | W.W.Armstrong/M.A.Noble | Australians v Sussex | Hove | 1902 |
| 411 | R.M.Poore/E.G.Wynyard | Hampshire v Somerset | Taunton | 1899 |

**Seventh Wicket**

| 347 | D.St E.Atkinson/C.C.Depeiza | W Indies v Australia | Bridgetown | 1954-55 |
| 344 | K.S.Ranjitsinhji/W.Newham | Sussex v Essex | Leyton | 1902 |
| 340 | K.J.Key/H.Philipson | Oxford U v Middlesex | Chiswick Park | 1887 |

**Eighth Wicket**

| 433 | V.T.Trumper/A.Sims | Australians v C'bury | Christchurch | 1913-14 |
| 292 | R.Peel/Lord Hawke | Yorkshire v Warwicks | Birmingham | 1896 |
| 270 | V.T.Trumper/E.P.Barbour | NSW v Victoria | Sydney | 1912-13 |

**Ninth Wicket**

| 283 | J.Chapman/A.Warren | Derbys v Warwicks | Blackwell | 1910 |
| 251 | J.W.H.T.Douglas/S.N.Hare | Essex v Derbyshire | Leyton | 1921 |
| 245 | V.S.Hazare/N.D.Nagarwalla | Maharashtra v Baroda | Poona | 1939-40 |

**Tenth Wicket**

| 307 | A.F.Kippax/J.E.H.Hooker | NSW v Victoria | Melbourne | 1928-29 |
| 249 | C.T.Sarwate/S.N.Banerjee | Indians v Surrey | The Oval | 1946 |
| 235 | F.E.Woolley/A.Fielder | Kent v Worcs | Stourbridge | 1909 |

## MOST RUNS IN A CAREER

| | Career | I | NO | HS | Runs | Avge | 100 |
|---|---|---|---|---|---|---|---|
| J.B.Hobbs | 1905-34 | 1315 | 106 | 316* | 61237 | 50.65 | 197 |
| F.E.Woolley | 1906-38 | 1532 | 85 | 305* | 58969 | 40.75 | 145 |
| E.H.Hendren | 1907-38 | 1300 | 166 | 301* | 57611 | 50.80 | 170 |
| C.P.Mead | 1905-36 | 1340 | 185 | 280* | 55061 | 47.67 | 153 |
| W.G.Grace | 1865-1908 | 1493 | 105 | 344 | 54896 | 39.55 | 126 |
| W.R.Hammond | 1920-51 | 1005 | 104 | 336* | 50551 | 56.10 | 167 |
| H.Sutcliffe | 1919-45 | 1088 | 123 | 313 | 50138 | 51.95 | 149 |
| G.Boycott | 1962-86 | 1014 | 162 | 261* | 48426 | 56.83 | 151 |
| T.W.Graveney | 1948-71/72 | 1223 | 159 | 258 | 47793 | 44.91 | 122 |
| T.W.Hayward | 1893-1914 | 1138 | 96 | 315* | 43551 | 41.79 | 104 |
| D.L.Amiss | 1960-87 | 1139 | 126 | 262* | 43423 | 42.86 | 102 |

|  | Career | I | NO | HS | Runs | Avge | 100 |
|---|---|---|---|---|---|---|---|
| M.C.Cowdrey | 1950-76 | 1130 | 134 | 307 | **42719** | 42.89 | 107 |
| A.Sandham | 1911-1937/38 | 1000 | 79 | 325 | **41284** | 44.82 | 107 |
| L.Hutton | 1934-60 | 814 | 91 | 364 | **40140** | 55.51 | 129 |
| M.J.K.Smith | 1951-75 | 1091 | 139 | 204 | **39832** | 41.84 | 69 |
| W.Rhodes | 1898-1930 | 1528 | 237 | 267* | **39802** | 30.83 | 58 |
| J.H.Edrich | 1956-78 | 979 | 104 | 310* | **39790** | 45.47 | 103 |
| R.E.S.Wyatt | 1923-57 | 1141 | 157 | 232 | **39405** | 40.04 | 85 |
| D.C.S.Compton | 1936-64 | 839 | 88 | 300 | **38942** | 51.85 | 123 |
| G.E.Tyldesley | 1909-36 | 961 | 106 | 256* | **38874** | 45.46 | 102 |
| J.T.Tyldesley | 1895-1923 | 994 | 62 | 295* | **37897** | 40.60 | 86 |
| K.W.R.Fletcher | 1962-88 | 1167 | 170 | 228* | **37665** | 37.77 | 63 |
| C.G.Greenidge | 1970-92 | 889 | 75 | 273* | **37354** | 45.88 | 92 |
| J.W.Hearne | 1909-36 | 1025 | 116 | 285* | **37252** | 40.98 | 96 |
| L.E.G.Ames | 1926-51 | 951 | 95 | 295 | **37248** | 43.51 | 102 |
| D.Kenyon | 1946-67 | 1159 | 59 | 259 | **37002** | 33.63 | 74 |
| W.J.Edrich | 1934-58 | 964 | 92 | 267* | **36965** | 42.39 | 86 |
| J.M.Parks | 1949-76 | 1227 | 172 | 205* | **36673** | 34.76 | 51 |
| D.Denton | 1894-1920 | 1163 | 70 | 221 | **36479** | 33.37 | 69 |
| G.H.Hirst | 1891-1929 | 1215 | 151 | 341 | **36323** | 34.13 | 60 |
| G.A.Gooch | 1973-92 | 816 | 66 | 333 | **36126** | 48.16 | 99 |
| A.Jones | 1957-83 | 1168 | 72 | 204* | **36049** | 32.89 | 56 |
| W.G.Quaife | 1894-1928 | 1203 | 185 | 255* | **36012** | 35.37 | 72 |
| R.E.Marshall | 1945/46-72 | 1053 | 59 | 228* | **35725** | 35.94 | 68 |
| G.Gunn | 1902-32 | 1061 | 82 | 220 | **35208** | 35.96 | 62 |

## BOWLING RECORDS

### ALL TEN WICKETS IN AN INNINGS

This feat has been achieved on 73 occasions at first-class level.
**Three Times**: A.P.Freeman (1929, 1930, 1931)
**Twice**: V.E.Walker (1859, 1865); H.Verity (1931, 1932); J.C.Laker (1956)

**Instances since 1945**:

| W.E.Hollies | Warwickshire v Notts | Birmingham | 1946 |
|---|---|---|---|
| J.M.Sims | East v West | Kingston on T | 1948 |
| J.K.R.Graveney | Gloucestershire v Derbyshire | Chesterfield | 1949 |
| T.E.Bailey | Essex v Lancashire | Clacton | 1949 |
| R.Berry | Lancashire v Worcestershire | Blackpool | 1953 |
| S.P.Gupte | President's XI v Combined XI | Bombay | 1954-55 |
| J.C.Laker | Surrey v Australians | The Oval | 1956 |
| K.Smales | Nottinghamshire v Glos | Stroud | 1956 |
| G.A.R.Lock | Surrey v Kent | Blackheath | 1956 |
| J.C.Laker | England v Australia | Manchester | 1956 |
| P.M.Chatterjee | Bengal v Assam | Jorhat | 1956-57 |
| J.D.Bannister | Warwicks v Combined Services | Birmingham | 1959 |
| A.J.G.Pearson | Cambridge U v Leicestershire | Loughborough | 1961 |
| N.I.Thomson | Sussex v Warwickshire | Worthing | 1964 |
| P.J.Allan | Queensland v Victoria | Melbourne | 1965-66 |
| I.J.Brayshaw | Western Australia v Victoria | Perth | 1967-68 |
| Shahid Mahmood | Karachi Whites v Khairpur | Karachi | 1969-70 |
| E.E.Hemmings | International XI v W Indians | Kingston | 1982-83 |
| P.Sunderam | Rajasthan v Vidarbha | Jodhpur | 1985-86 |
| S.T.Jefferies | Western Province v OFS | Cape Town | 1987-88 |
| Imran Adil | Bahawalpur v Faisalabad | Faisalabad | 1989-90 |
| G.P.Wickremasinghe | Sinhalese SC v Kalutara | Colombo | 1991-92 |

## MOST WICKETS IN A MATCH

19   J.C.Laker        England v Australia              Manchester            1956

## MOST WICKETS IN A SEASON

| Wkts | | Season | Matches | Overs | Mdns | Runs | Avge |
|------|------|--------|---------|--------|------|------|-------|
| 304  | A.P.Freeman | 1928 | 37 | 1976.1 | 423 | 5489 | 18.05 |
| 298  | A.P.Freeman | 1933 | 33 | 2039 | 651 | 4549 | 15.26 |

The feat of taking 250 wickets in a season has been achieved on 12 occasions, the last instance being by A.P.Freeman in 1933. 200 or more wickets in a season have been taken on 59 occasions, the last being by G.A.R.Lock (212 wickets, average 12.02) in 1957.

The highest aggregates of wickets taken in a season since the reduction of County Championship matches in 1969 are as follows:

| Wkts | | Season | Matches | Overs | Mdns | Runs | Avge |
|------|------|--------|---------|--------|------|------|-------|
| 134  | M.D.Marshall | 1982 | 22 | 822 | 225 | 2108 | 15.73 |
| 131  | L.R.Gibbs | 1971 | 23 | 1024.1 | 295 | 2475 | 18.89 |
| 125  | F.D.Stephenson | 1988 | 22 | 819.1 | 196 | 2289 | 18.31 |
| 121  | R.D.Jackman | 1980 | 23 | 746.2 | 220 | 1864 | 15.40 |

Since 1969 there have been 46 instances of bowlers taking 100 wickets in a season.

## MOST HAT-TRICKS IN A CAREER

7  D.V.P.Wright
6  T.W.J.Goddard, C.W.L.Parker
5  S.Haigh, V.W.C.Jupp, A.E.G.Rhodes, F.A.Tarrant

## MOST WICKETS IN A CAREER

| | Career | Runs | Wkts | Avge | 100w |
|------|--------|------|------|------|------|
| W.Rhodes | 1898-1930 | 69993 | **4187** | 16.71 | 23 |
| A.P.Freeman | 1914-36 | 69577 | **3776** | 18.42 | 17 |
| C.W.L.Parker | 1903-35 | 63817 | **3278** | 19.46 | 16 |
| J.T.Hearne | 1888-1923 | 54352 | **3061** | 17.75 | 15 |
| T.W.J.Goddard | 1922-52 | 59116 | **2979** | 19.84 | 16 |
| W.G.Grace | 1865-1908 | 51545 | **2876** | 17.92 | 10 |
| A.S.Kennedy | 1907-36 | 61034 | **2874** | 21.23 | 15 |
| D.Shackleton | 1948-69 | 53303 | **2857** | 18.65 | 20 |
| G.A.R.Lock | 1946-70/71 | 54709 | **2844** | 19.23 | 14 |
| F.J.Titmus | 1949-82 | 63313 | **2830** | 22.37 | 16 |
| M.W.Tate | 1912-37 | 50571 | **2784** | 18.16 | 13+1 |
| G.H.Hirst | 1891-1929 | 51282 | **2739** | 18.72 | 15 |
| C.Blythe | 1899-1914 | 42136 | **2506** | 16.81 | 14 |
| D.L.Underwood | 1963-87 | 49993 | **2465** | 20.28 | 10 |
| W.E.Astill | 1906-39 | 57783 | **2431** | 23.76 | 9 |
| J.C.White | 1909-37 | 43759 | **2356** | 18.57 | 14 |
| W.E.Hollies | 1932-57 | 48656 | **2323** | 20.94 | 14 |
| F.S.Trueman | 1949-69 | 42154 | **2304** | 18.29 | 12 |
| J.B.Statham | 1950-68 | 36995 | **2260** | 16.36 | 13 |
| R.T.D.Perks | 1930-55 | 53770 | **2233** | 24.07 | 16 |
| J.Briggs | 1879-1900 | 35430 | **2221** | 15.95 | 12 |

| | Career | Runs | Wkts | Avge | 100w |
|---|---|---|---|---|---|
| D.J.Shepherd | 1950-72 | 47302 | **2218** | 21.32 | 12 |
| E.G.Dennett | 1903-26 | 42571 | **2147** | 19.82 | 12 |
| T.Richardson | 1892-1905 | 38794 | **2104** | 18.43 | 10 |
| T.E.Bailey | 1945-67 | 48170 | **2082** | 23.13 | 9 |
| R.Illingworth | 1951-83 | 42023 | **2072** | 20.28 | 10 |
| F.E.Woolley | 1906-38 | 41066 | **2068** | 19.85 | 8 |
| N.Gifford | 1960-88 | 48731 | **2068** | 23.56 | 4 |
| G.Geary | 1912-38 | 41339 | **2063** | 20.03 | 11 |
| D.V.P.Wright | 1932-57 | 49307 | **2056** | 23.98 | 10 |
| J.A.Newman | 1906-30 | 51111 | **2032** | 25.15 | 9 |
| A.Shaw | 1864-97 | 24579 | **2027**† | 12.12 | 9 |
| S.Haigh | 1895-1913 | 32091 | **2012** | 15.94 | 11 |

† Excluding one wicket for which no analysis is available.

## ALL-ROUND RECORDS

### THE 'DOUBLE'

**3000 runs and 100 wickets:** J.H.Parks (1937)
**2000 runs and 200 wickets:** G.H.Hirst (1906)
**2000 runs and 100 wickets:** F.E.Woolley (4), J.W.Hearne (3), W.G.Grace (2), G.H.Hirst (2), W.Rhodes (2), T.E.Bailey, D.E.Davies, G.L.Jessop, V.W.C.Jupp, James Langridge, F.A.Tarrant, C.L.Townsend, L.F.Townsend
**1000 runs and 200 wickets:** M.W.Tate (3), A.E.Trott (2), A.S.Kennedy

**Most Doubles:** W.Rhodes (16), G.H.Hirst (14), V.W.C.Jupp (10)

**Double in Debut Season:** D.B.Close (1949) – aged 18, he is the youngest to achieve this feat

The feat of scoring 1000 runs and taking 100 wickets in a season has been achieved on 305 occasions, R.J.Hadlee (1984) and F.D.Stephenson (1988) being the only players to complete the 'double' since the reduction of County Championship matches in 1969.

## WICKET-KEEPING RECORDS

### MOST DISMISSALS IN AN INNINGS

| 8 (8ct) | A.T.W.Grout | Queensland v W Australia | Brisbane | 1959-60 |
|---|---|---|---|---|
| 8 (8ct) | D.E.East | Essex v Somerset | Taunton | 1985 |
| 8 (8ct) | S.A.Marsh | Kent v Middlesex | Lord's | 1991 |

### MOST DISMISSALS IN A MATCH

| 12 (8ct, 4st) | E.Pooley | Surrey v Sussex | The Oval | 1868 |
|---|---|---|---|---|
| 12 (9ct, 3st) | D.Tallon | Queensland v NSW | Sydney | 1938-39 |
| 12 (9ct, 3st) | H.B.Taber | NSW v South Australia | Adelaide | 1968-69 |

### MOST CATCHES IN A MATCH

| 11 | A.Long | Surrey v Sussex | Hove | 1964 |
|---|---|---|---|---|
| 11 | R.W.Marsh | W Australia v Victoria | Perth | 1975-76 |
| 11 | D.L.Bairstow | Yorkshire v Derbyshire | Scarborough | 1982 |

| 11 | W.K.Hegg | Lancashire v Derbyshire | Chesterfield | 1989 |
| 11 | A.J.Stewart | Surrey v Leicestershire | Leicester | 1989 |
| 11 | E.J.Nielson | S Australia v W Australia | Perth | 1990-91 |

## MOST DISMISSALS IN A SEASON

128 (79ct, 49st)      L.E.G.Ames      1929

## MOST DISMISSALS IN A CAREER

|  | Career | Dismissals | Ct | St |
|---|---|---|---|---|
| R.W.Taylor | 1960-88 | **1649** | 1473 | 176 |
| J.T.Murray | 1952-75 | **1527** | 1270 | 257 |
| H.Strudwick | 1902-27 | **1497** | 1242 | 255 |
| A.P.E.Knott | 1964-85 | **1344** | 1211 | 133 |
| F.H.Huish | 1895-1914 | **1310** | 933 | 377 |
| B.Taylor | 1949-73 | **1294** | 1083 | 211 |
| D.Hunter | 1889-1909 | **1253** | 906 | 347 |
| H.R.Butt | 1890-1912 | **1228** | 953 | 275 |
| J.H.Board | 1891-1914/15 | **1207** | 852 | 355 |
| H.Elliott | 1920-47 | **1206** | 904 | 302 |
| J.M.Parks | 1949-76 | **1181** | 1088 | 93 |
| R.Booth | 1951-70 | **1126** | 948 | 178 |
| L.E.G.Ames | 1926-51 | **1121** | 703 | 418 |
| D.L.Bairstow | 1970-90 | **1099** | 961 | 138 |
| G.Duckworth | 1923-47 | **1096** | 753 | 343 |
| H.W.Stephenson | 1948-64 | **1082** | 748 | 334 |
| J.G.Binks | 1955-75 | **1071** | 895 | 176 |
| T.G.Evans | 1939-69 | **1066** | 816 | 250 |
| A.Long | 1960-80 | **1046** | 922 | 124 |
| G.O.Dawkes | 1937-61 | **1043** | 895 | 148 |
| R.W.Tolchard | 1965-83 | **1037** | 912 | 125 |
| W.L.Cornford | 1921-47 | **1017** | 675 | 342 |

## FIELDING RECORDS

## MOST CATCHES IN AN INNINGS

| 7 | M.J.Stewart | Surrey v Northamptonshire | Northampton | 1957 |
| 7 | A.S.Brown | Gloucestershire v Nottinghamshire | Nottingham | 1966 |

## MOST CATCHES IN A MATCH

| 10 | W.R.Hammond | Gloucestershire v Surrey | Cheltenham | 1928 |

## MOST CATCHES IN A SEASON

| 78 | W.R.Hammond | 1928 | 77 | M.J.Stewart | 1957 |

## MOST CATCHES IN A CAREER

| 1018 | F.E.Woolley | 1906-38 | 784 | J.G.Langridge | 1928-55 |
| 887 | W.G.Grace | 1865-1908 | 764 | W.Rhodes | 1898-1930 |
| 830 | G.A.R.Lock | 1946-70/71 | 758 | C.A.Milton | 1948-74 |
| 819 | W.R.Hammond | 1920-51 | 754 | E.H.Hendren | 1907-38 |
| 813 | D.B.Close | 1949-86 | | | |

# TEST CRICKET RECORDS

## (EXCLUDING 1992-93 SEASON)

### TEAM RECORDS

### HIGHEST INNINGS TOTALS

| 903-7d | England v Australia | The Oval | 1938 |
|--------|---------------------|----------|------|
| 849 | England v West Indies | Kingston | 1929-30 |
| 790-3d | West Indies v Pakistan | Kingston | 1957-58 |
| 758-8d | Australia v West Indies | Kingston | 1954-55 |
| 729-6d | Australia v England | Lord's | 1930 |
| 708 | Pakistan v England | The Oval | 1987 |
| 701 | Australia v England | The Oval | 1934 |
| 699-5 | Pakistan v India | Lahore | 1989-90 |
| 695 | Australia v England | The Oval | 1930 |
| 687-8d | West Indies v England | The Oval | 1976 |
| 681-8d | West Indies v England | Port-of-Spain | 1953-54 |
| 676-7 | India v Sri Lanka | Kanpur | 1986-87 |
| 674-6 | Pakistan v India | Faisalabad | 1984-85 |
| 674 | Australia v India | Adelaide | 1947-48 |
| 671-4 | New Zealand v Sri Lanka | Wellington | 1990-91 |
| 668 | Australia v West Indies | Bridgetown | 1954-55 |
| 659-8d | Australia v England | Sydney | 1946-47 |
| 658-8d | England v Australia | Nottingham | 1938 |
| 657-8d | Pakistan v West Indies | Bridgetown | 1957-58 |
| 656-8d | Australia v England | Manchester | 1964 |
| 654-5 | England v South Africa | Durban | 1938-39 |
| 653-4d | England v India | Lord's | 1990 |
| 652-7d | England v India | Madras | 1984-85 |
| 652-8d | West Indies v England | Lord's | 1973 |
| 652 | Pakistan v India | Faisalabad | 1982-83 |
| 650-6d | Australia v West Indies | Bridgetown | 1964-65 |

**The highest innings for South-Africa and Sri Lanka are:**

| 622-9d | South Africa v Australia | Durban | 1969-70 |
|--------|--------------------------|--------|---------|
| 497 | Sri Lanka v New Zealand | Wellington | 1990-91 |

### LOWEST INNINGS TOTALS

| 26 | New Zealand v England | Auckland | 1954-55 |
|----|------------------------|----------|---------|
| 30 | South Africa v England | Port Elizabeth | 1895-96 |
| 30 | South Africa v England | Birmingham | 1924 |
| 35 | South Africa v England | Cape Town | 1898-99 |
| 36 | Australia v England | Birmingham | 1902 |
| 36 | South Africa v Australia | Melbourne | 1931-32 |
| 42 | Australia v England | Sydney | 1887-88 |
| 42 | New Zealand v Australia | Wellington | 1945-46 |
| 42 | India v England | Lord's | 1974 |
| 43 | South Africa v England | Cape Town | 1888-89 |
| 44 | Australia v England | The Oval | 1896 |
| 45 | England v Australia | Sydney | 1886-87 |
| 45 | South Africa v Australia | Melbourne | 1931-32 |
| 47 | South Africa v England | Cape Town | 1888-89 |
| 47 | New Zealand v England | Lord's | 1958 |

| | | | |
|---|---|---|---|
| 53 | West Indies v Pakistan | Faisalabad | 1986-87 |
| 62 | Pakistan v Australia | Perth | 1981-82 |
| 82 | Sri Lanka v India | Chandigarh | 1990-91 |

## BATTING RECORDS

### HIGHEST INDIVIDUAL INNINGS

| | | | | |
|---|---|---|---|---|
| 365* | G.St A.Sobers | WI v P | Kingston | 1957-58 |
| 364 | L.Hutton | E v A | The Oval | 1938 |
| 337 | Hanif Mohammad | P v WI | Bridgetown | 1957-58 |
| 336* | W.R.Hammond | E v NZ | Auckland | 1932-33 |
| 334 | D.G.Bradman | A v E | Leeds | 1930 |
| 333 | G.A.Gooch | E v I | Lord's | 1990 |
| 325 | A.Sandham | E v WI | Kingston | 1929-30 |
| 311 | R.B.Simpson | A v E | Manchester | 1964 |
| 310* | J.H.Edrich | E v NZ | Leeds | 1965 |
| 307 | R.M.Cowper | A v E | Melbourne | 1965-66 |
| 304 | D.G.Bradman | A v E | Leeds | 1934 |
| 302 | L.G.Rowe | WI v E | Bridgetown | 1973-74 |
| 299* | D.G.Bradman | A v SA | Adelaide | 1931-32 |
| 299 | M.D.Crowe | NZ v SL | Wellington | 1990-91 |
| 291 | I.V.A.Richards | WI v E | The Oval | 1976 |
| 287 | R.E.Foster | E v A | Sydney | 1903-04 |
| 285* | P.B.H.May | E v WI | Birmingham | 1957 |
| 280* | Javed Miandad | P v I | Hyderabad | 1982-83 |
| 278 | D.C.S.Compton | E v P | Nottingham | 1954 |
| 274 | R.G.Pollock | SA v A | Durban | 1969-70 |
| 274 | Zaheer Abbas | P v E | Birmingham | 1971 |
| 271 | Javed Miandad | P v NZ | Auckland | 1988-89 |
| 270* | G.A.Headley | WI v E | Kingston | 1934-35 |
| 270 | D.G.Bradman | A v E | Melbourne | 1936-37 |
| 268 | G.N.Yallop | A v P | Melbourne | 1983-84 |
| 267 | P.A.De Silva | SL v NZ | Wellington | 1990-91 |
| 266 | W.H.Ponsford | A v E | The Oval | 1934 |
| 262* | D.L.Amiss | E v WI | Kingston | 1973-74 |
| 261 | F.M.M.Worrell | WI v E | Nottingham | 1950 |
| 260 | C.C.Hunte | WI v P | Kingston | 1957-58 |
| 260 | Javed Miandad | P v E | The Oval | 1987 |
| 259 | G.M.Turner | NZ v WI | Georgetown | 1971-72 |
| 258 | T.W.Graveney | E v WI | Nottingham | 1957 |
| 258 | S.M.Nurse | WI v NZ | Christchurch | 1968-69 |
| 256 | R.B.Kanhai | WI v I | Calcutta | 1958-59 |
| 256 | K.F.Barrington | E v A | Manchester | 1964 |
| 255* | D.J.McGlew | SA v NZ | Wellington | 1952-53 |
| 254 | D.G.Bradman | A v E | Lord's | 1930 |
| 251 | W.R.Hammond | E v A | Sydney | 1928-29 |
| 250 | K.D.Walters | A v NZ | Christchurch | 1976-77 |
| 250 | S.F.A.F.Bacchus | WI v I | Kanpur | 1978-79 |

### The highest individual innings for India is:

| | | | | |
|---|---|---|---|---|
| 236* | S.M.Gavaskar | I v WI | Madras | 1983-84 |

## MOST RUNS IN A SERIES

| Runs | | | Series | M | I | NO | HS | Avge | 100 | 50 |
|------|------|------|------|---|---|-----|------|--------|-----|-----|
| 974 | D.G.Bradman | A v E | 1930 | 5 | 7 | 0 | 334 | 139.14 | 4 | – |
| 905 | W.R.Hammond | E v A | 1928-29 | 5 | 9 | 1 | 251 | 113.12 | 4 | 1 |
| 839 | M.A.Taylor | A v E | 1989 | 6 | 11 | 1 | 219 | 83.90 | 2 | 5 |
| 834 | R.N.Harvey | A v SA | 1952-53 | 5 | 9 | 0 | 205 | 92.66 | 4 | 3 |
| 829 | I.V.A.Richards | WI v E | 1976 | 4 | 7 | 0 | 291 | 118.42 | 3 | 2 |
| 827 | C.L.Walcott | WI v A | 1954-55 | 5 | 10 | 0 | 155 | 82.70 | 5 | 2 |
| 824 | G.St A.Sobers | WI v P | 1957-58 | 5 | 8 | ·2 | 365* | 137.33 | 3 | 3 |
| ·810 | D.G.Bradman | A v E | 1936-37 | 5 | 9 | 0 | 270 | 90.00 | 3 | 1 |
| 806 | D.G.Bradman | A v SA | 1931-32 | 5 | 5 | 1 | 299* | 201.50 | 4 | – |
| 779 | E.de C.Weekes | WI v I | 1948-49 | 5 | 7 | 0 | 194 | 111.28 | 4 | 2 |
| 774 | S.M.Gavaskar | I v WI | 1970-71 | 4 | 8 | 3 | 220 | 154.80 | 4 | 3 |
| 761 | Mudassar Nazar | P v I | 1982-83 | 6 | 8 | 2 | 231 | 126.83 | 4 | 1 |
| 758 | D.G.Bradman | A v E | 1934 | 5 | 8 | 0 | 304 | 94.75 | 2 | 1 |
| 753 | D.C.S.Compton | E v SA | 1947 | 5 | 8 | 0 | 208 | 94.12 | 4 | 2 |
| 752 | G.A.Gooch | E v I | 1990 | 3 | 6 | 0 | 333 | 125.33 | 3 | 2 |

## HIGHEST PARTNERSHIP FOR EACH WICKET

| | | | | | |
|------|------|------|------|------|------|
| 1st | 413 | V.Mankad/Pankaj Roy | I v NZ | Madras | 1955-56 |
| 2nd | 451 | W.H.Ponsford/D.G.Bradman | A v E | The Oval | 1934 |
| 3rd | 467 | A.H.Jones/M.D.Crowe | NZ v SL | Wellington | 1990-91 |
| 4th | 411 | P.B.H.May/M.C Cowdrey | E v WI | Birmingham | 1957 |
| 5th | 405 | S.G.Barnes/D.G.Bradman | A v E | Sydney | 1946-47 |
| 6th | 346 | J.H.W.Fingleton/D.G.Bradman | A v E | Melbourne | 1936-37 |
| 7th | 347 | D.St E.Atkinson/C.C.Depeiza | WI v A | Bridgetown | 1954-55 |
| 8th | 246 | L.E.G.Ames/G.O.B.Allen | E v NZ | Lord's | 1931 |
| 9th | 190 | Asif Iqbal/Intikhab Alam | P v E | The Oval | 1967 |
| 10th | 151 | B.F.Hastings/R.O.Collinge | NZ v P | Auckland | 1972-73 |

## WICKET PARTNERSHIPS OF OVER 300

| | | | | | |
|------|------|------|------|------|------|
| 467 | 3rd | A.H.Jones/M.D.Crowe | NZ v SL | Wellington | 1990-91 |
| 451 | 2nd | W.H.Ponsford/D.G.Bradman | A v E | The Oval | 1934 |
| 451 | 3rd | Mudassar Nazar/Javed Miandad | P v I | Hyderabad | 1982-83 |
| 446 | 2nd | C.C.Hunte/G.St A.Sobers | WI v P | Kingston | 1957-58 |
| 413 | 1st | V.Mankad/Pankaj Roy | I v NZ | Madras | 1955-56 |
| 411 | 4th | P.B.H.May/M.C.Cowdrey | E v WI | Birmingham | 1957 |
| 405 | 5th | S.G.Barnes/D.G.Bradman | A v E | Sydney | 1946-47 |
| 399 | 4th | G.St A.Sobers/F.M.M.Worrell | WI v E | Bridgetown | 1959-60 |
| 397 | 4th | Qasim Omar/Javed Miandad | P v SL | Faisalabad | 1985-86 |
| 388 | 4th | W.H.Ponsford/D.G.Bradman | A v E | Leeds | 1934 |
| 387 | 1st | G.M.Turner/T.W.Jarvis | NZ v WI | Georgetown | 1971-72 |
| 382 | 2nd | L.Hutton/M.Leyland | E v A | The Oval | 1938 |
| 382 | 1st | W.M.Lawry/R.B.Simpson | A v WI | Bridgetown | 1964-65 |
| 370 | 3rd | W.J.Edrich/D.C.S.Compton | E v SA | Lord's | 1947 |
| 369 | 2nd | J.H.Edrich/K.F.Barrington | E v NZ | Leeds | 1965 |
| 359 | 1st | L.Hutton/C.Washbrook | E v SA | Jo'burg | 1948-49 |
| 351 | 2nd | G.A.Gooch/D.I.Gower | E v A | The Oval | 1985 |
| 350 | 4th | Mushtaq Mohammad/Asif Iqbal | P v NZ | Dunedin | 1972-73 |
| 347 | 7th | D.St E.Atkinson/C.C.Depeiza | WI v A | Bridgetown | 1954-55 |
| 346 | 6th | J.H.W.Fingleton/D.G.Bradman | A v E | Melbourne | 1936-37 |
| 344* | 2nd | S.M.Gavaskar/D.B.Vengsarkar | I v WI | Calcutta | 1978-79 |
| 341 | 3rd | E.J.Barlow/R.G.Pollock | SA v A | Adelaide | 1963-64 |

| | | | | | | | | |
|---|---|---|---|---|---|---|---|---|
| 338 | 3rd | E.de C.Weekes/F.M.M.Worrell | WI v E | Port-of-Spain | 1953-54 |
| 336 | 4th | W.M.Lawry/K.D.Walters | A v WI | Sydney | 1968-69 |
| 331 | 2nd | R.T.Robinson/D.I.Gower | E v A | Birmingham | 1985 |
| 329 | 1st | G.R.Marsh/M.A.Taylor | A v E | Nottingham | 1989 |
| 323 | 1st | J.B.Hobbs/W.Rhodes | E v A | Melbourne | 1911-12 |
| 322 | 4th | Javed Miandad/Salim Malik | P v E | Birmingham | 1992 |
| 319 | 3rd | A.Melville/A.D.Nourse | SA v E | Nottingham | 1947 |
| 316 † | 3rd | G.R.Viswanath/Yashpal Sharma | I v E | Madras | 1981-82 |
| 308 | 7th | Waqar Hassan/Imtiaz Ahmed | P v NZ | Lahore | 1955-56 |
| 308 | 3rd | R.B.Richardson/I.V.A.Richards | WI v A | St John's | 1983-84 |
| 308 | 3rd | G.A.Gooch/A.J.Lamb | E v I | Lord's | 1990 |
| 303 | 3rd | I.V.A.Richards/A.I.Kallicharran | WI v E | Nottingham | 1976 |
| 301 | 2nd | A.R.Morris/D.G.Bradman | A v E | Leeds | 1948 |

† 415 runs were added for this wicket in two separate partnerships. D.B.Vengsarkar retired hurt and was replaced by Yashpal Sharma after 99 runs had been added.

## 4000 RUNS IN TESTS

| Runs | | | M | I | NO | HS | Avge | 100 | 50 |
|---|---|---|---|---|---|---|---|---|---|
| 10122 | S.M.Gavaskar | I | 125 | 214 | 16 | 236* | 51.12 | 34 | 45 |
| 9532 | A.R.Border | A | 130 | 224 | 42 | 205 | 52.37 | 23 | 55 |
| 8540 | I.V.A.Richards | WI | 121 | 182 | 12 | 291 | 50.23 | 24 | 45 |
| 8465 | Javed Miandad | P | 117 | 177 | 21 | 280* | 54.26 | 23 | 41 |
| 8231 | D.I.Gower | E | 117 | 204 | 18 | 215 | 44.25 | 18 | 39 |
| 8114 | G.Boycott | E | 108 | 193 | 23 | 246* | 47.72 | 22 | 42 |
| 8032 | G.St A.Sobers | WI | 93 | 160 | 21 | 365* | 57.78 | 26 | 30 |
| 7624 | M.C.Cowdrey | E | 114 | 188 | 15 | 182 | 44.06 | 22 | 38 |
| 7573 | G.A.Gooch | E | 99 | 179 | 6 | 333 | 43.77 | 17 | 41 |
| 7558 | C.G.Greenidge | WI | 108 | 185 | 16 | 226 | 44.72 | 19 | 34 |
| 7515 | C.H.Lloyd | WI | 110 | 175 | 14 | 242* | 46.67 | 19 | 39 |
| 7249 | W.R.Hammond | E | 85 | 140 | 16 | 336* | 58.45 | 22 | 24 |
| 7110 | G.S.Chappell | A | 87 | 151 | 19 | 247* | 53.86 | 24 | 31 |
| 6996 | D.G.Bradman | A | 52 | 80 | 10 | 334 | 99.94 | 29 | 13 |
| 6971 | L.Hutton | E | 79 | 138 | 15 | 364 | 56.67 | 19 | 33 |
| 6868 | D.B.Vengsarkar | I | 116 | 185 | 22 | 166 | 42.13 | 17 | 35 |
| 6806 | K.F.Barrington | E | 82 | 131 | 15 | 256 | 58.67 | 20 | 35 |
| 6725 | D.L.Haynes | WI | 103 | 180 | 21 | 184 | 42.29 | 16 | 37 |
| 6227 | R.B.Kanhai | WI | 79 | 137 | 6 | 256 | 47.53 | 15 | 28 |
| 6149 | R.N.Harvey | A | 79 | 137 | 10 | 205 | 48.41 | 21 | 24 |
| 6080 | G.R.Viswanath | I | 91 | 155 | 10 | 222 | 41.93 | 14 | 35 |
| 5807 | D.C.S.Compton | E | 78 | 131 | 15 | 278 | 50.06 | 17 | 28 |
| 5410 | J.B.Hobbs | E | 61 | 102 | 7 | 211 | 56.94 | 15 | 28 |
| 5357 | K.D.Walters | A | 74 | 125 | 14 | 250 | 48.26 | 15 | 33 |
| 5345 | I.M.Chappell | A | 75 | 136 | 10 | 196 | 42.42 | 14 | 26 |
| 5234 | W.M.Lawry | A | 67 | 123 | 12 | 210 | 47.15 | 13 | 27 |
| 5200 | I.T.Botham | E | 102 | 161 | 6 | 208 | 33.54 | 14 | 22 |
| 5138 | J.H.Edrich | E | 77 | 127 | 9 | 310* | 43.54 | 12 | 24 |
| 5062 | Zaheer Abbas | P | 78 | 124 | 11 | 274 | 44.79 | 12 | 20 |
| 4964 | J.G.Wright | NZ | 77 | 138 | 6 | 185 | 37.60 | 12 | 21 |
| 4882 | T.W.Graveney | E | 79 | 123 | 13 | 258 | 44.38 | 11 | 20 |
| 4869 | R.B.Simpson | A | 62 | 111 | 7 | 311 | 46.81 | 10 | 27 |
| 4737 | I.R.Redpath | A | 66 | 120 | 11 | 171 | 43.45 | 8 | 31 |
| 4693 | R.B.Richardson | WI | 63 | 109 | 10 | 194 | 47.40 | 14 | 18 |
| 4690 | Kapil Dev | I | 115 | 168 | 13 | 163 | 30.25 | 7 | 24 |

| Runs | | | M | I | NO | HS | Avge | 100 | 50 |
|------|--------------------|----|----|-----|----|------|-------|-----|----|
| 4656 | A.J.Lamb | E | 79 | 139 | 10 | 142 | 36.09 | 14 | 18 |
| 4555 | H.Sutcliffe | E | 54 | 84 | 9 | 194 | 60.73 | 16 | 23 |
| 4538 | D.C.Boon | A | 63 | 115 | 12 | 200 | 44.05 | 13 | 19 |
| 4537 | P.B.H.May | E | 66 | 106 | 9 | 285* | 46.77 | 13 | 22 |
| 4502 | E.R.Dexter | E | 62 | 102 | 8 | 205 | 47.89 | 9 | 27 |
| 4455 | E.de C.Weekes | WI | 48 | 81 | 5 | 207 | 58.61 | 15 | 19 |
| 4415 | K.J.Hughes | A | 70 | 124 | 6 | 213 | 37.41 | 9 | 22 |
| 4399 | A.I.Kallicharran | WI | 66 | 109 | 10 | 187 | 44.43 | 12 | 21 |
| 4389 | A.P.E.Knott | E | 95 | 149 | 15 | 135 | 32.75 | 5 | 30 |
| 4378 | M.Amarnath | I | 69 | 113 | 10 | 138 | 42.50 | 11 | 24 |
| 4334 | R.C.Fredericks | WI | 59 | 109 | 7 | 169 | 42.49 | 8 | 26 |
| 4205 | M.D.Crowe | NZ | 59 | 98 | 10 | 299 | 47.78 | 13 | 14 |
| 4114 | Mudassar Nazar | P | 76 | 116 | 8 | 231 | 38.09 | 10 | 17 |

## MOST HUNDREDS

| | | | Inns | E | A | SA | Opponents WI | NZ | I | P | SL |
|----|----------------|----|------|----|----|----|----|----|----|----|----|
| 34 | S.M.Gavaskar | I | 214 | 4 | 8 | – | 13 | 2 | – | 5 | 2 |
| 29 | D.G.Bradman | A | 80 | 19 | – | 4 | 2 | – | 4 | – | – |
| 26 | G.St A.Sobers | WI | 160 | 10 | 4 | – | – | 1 | 8 | 3 | – |
| 24 | G.S.Chappell | A | 151 | 9 | – | – | 5 | 3 | 1 | 6 | 0 |
| 24 | I.V.A.Richards | WI | 182 | 8 | 5 | – | – | 1 | 8 | 2 | – |
| 23 | A.R.Border | A | 224 | 7 | – | – | 2 | 4 | 4 | 6 | 0 |
| 23 | Javed Miandad | P | 177 | 2 | 6 | – | 2 | 7 | 5 | – | 1 |
| 22 | G.Boycott | E | 193 | – | 7 | 1 | 5 | 2 | 4 | 3 | – |
| 22 | M.C.Cowdrey | E | 188 | – | 5 | 3 | 6 | 2 | 3 | 3 | – |
| 22 | W.R.Hammond | E | 140 | – | 9 | 6 | 1 | 4 | 2 | – | – |
| 21 | R.N.Harvey | A | 137 | 6 | – | 8 | 3 | – | 4 | 0 | – |
| 20 | K.F.Barrington | E | 131 | – | 5 | 2 | 3 | 3 | 3 | 4 | – |

## BOWLING RECORDS

### MOST WICKETS IN AN INNINGS

| 10-53 | J.C.Laker | E v A | Manchester | 1956 |
|-------|--------------|----------|----------------|---------|
| 9-28 | G.A.Lohmann | E v SA | Johannesburg | 1895-96 |
| 9-37 | J.C.Laker | E v A | Manchester | 1956 |
| 9-52 | R.J.Hadlee | NZ v A | Brisbane | 1985-86 |
| 9-56 | Abdul Qadir | P v E | Lahore | 1987-88 |
| 9-69 | J.M.Patel | I v A | Kanpur | 1959-60 |
| 9-83 | Kapil Dev | I v WI | Ahmedabad | 1983-84 |
| 9-86 | Sarfraz Nawaz | P v A | Melbourne | 1978-79 |
| 9-95 | J.M.Noreiga | WI v I | Port-of-Spain | 1970-71 |
| 9-102 | S.P.Gupte | I v WI | Kanpur | 1958-59 |
| 9-103 | S.F.Barnes | E v SA | Johannesburg | 1913-14 |
| 9-113 | H.J.Tayfield | SA v E | Johannesburg | 1956-57 |
| 9-121 | A.A.Mailey | A v E | Melbourne | 1920-21 |

## MOST WICKETS IN A TEST

| | | | | |
|---|---|---|---|---|
| 19-90 | J.C.Laker | E v A | Manchester | 1956 |
| 17-159 | S.F.Barnes | E v SA | Johannesburg | 1913-14 |
| 16-136 | N.D.Hirwani | I v WI | Madras | 1987-88 |
| 16-137 | R.A.L.Massie | A v E | Lord's | 1972 |
| 15-28 | J.Briggs | E v SA | Cape Town | 1888-89 |
| 15-45 | G.A.Lohmann | E v SA | Port Elizabeth | 1895-96 |
| 15-99 | C.Blythe | E v SA | Leeds | 1907 |
| 15-104 | H.Verity | E v A | Lord's | 1934 |
| 15-123 | R.J.Hadlee | NZ v A | Brisbane | 1985-86 |
| 15-124 | W.Rhodes | E v A | Melbourne | 1903-04 |

## MOST WICKETS IN A SERIES

| Wkts | | | Series | M | Balls | Runs | Avge | 5 wI | 10 wM |
|---|---|---|---|---|---|---|---|---|---|
| 49 | S.F.Barnes | E v SA | 1913-14 | 4 | 1356 | 536 | 10.93 | 7 | 3 |
| 46 | J.C.Laker | E v A | 1956 | 5 | 1703 | 442 | 9.60 | 4 | 2 |
| 44 | C.V.Grimmett | A v SA | 1935-36 | 5 | 2077 | 642 | 14.59 | 5 | 3 |
| 42 | T.M.Alderman | A v E | 1981 | 6 | 1950 | 893 | 21.26 | 4 | — |
| 41 | R.M.Hogg | A v E | 1978-79 | 6 | 1740 | 527 | 12.85 | 5 | 2 |
| 41 | T.M.Alderman | A v E | 1989 | 6 | 1616 | 712 | 17.36 | 6 | 1 |
| 40 | Imran Khan | P v I | 1982-83 | 6 | 1339 | 558 | 13.95 | 4 | 2 |
| 39 | A.V.Bedser | E v A | 1953 | 5 | 1591 | 682 | 17.48 | 5 | 1 |
| 39 | D.K.Lillee | A v E | 1981 | 6 | 1870 | 870 | 22.30 | 2 | 1 |
| 38 | M.W.Tate | E v A | 1924-25 | 5 | 2528 | 881 | 23.18 | 5 | 1 |
| 37 | W.J.Whitty | A v SA | 1910-11 | 5 | 1395 | 632 | 17.08 | 2 | — |
| 37 | H.J.Tayfield | SA v E | 1956-57 | 5 | 2280 | 636 | 17.18 | 4 | 1 |
| 36 | A.E.E.Vogler | SA v E | 1909-10 | 5 | 1349 | 783 | 21.75 | 4 | 1 |
| 36 | A.A.Mailey | A v E | 1920-21 | 5 | 1465 | 946 | 26.27 | 4 | 2 |
| 35 | G.A.Lohmann | E v SA | 1895-96 | 3 | 520 | 203 | 5.80 | 4 | 2 |
| 35 | B.S.Chandrasekhar | I v E | 1972-73 | 5 | 1747 | 662 | 18.91 | 4 | — |
| 35 | M.D.Marshall | WI v E | 1988 | 5 | 1219 | 443 | 12.65 | 3 | 1 |

## 200 WICKETS IN TESTS

| Wkts | | | M | Balls | Runs | Avge | 5 wI | 10 wM |
|---|---|---|---|---|---|---|---|---|
| 431 | Sir R.J.Hadlee | NZ | 86 | 21918 | 9611 | 22.29 | 36 | 9 |
| 401 | Kapil Dev | I | 115 | 24967 | 11894 | 29.66 | 23 | 2 |
| 383 | I.T.Botham | E | 102 | 21815 | 10878 | 28.40 | 27 | 4 |
| 376 | M.D.Marshall | WI | 81 | 17584 | 7876 | 20.94 | 22 | 4 |
| 362 | Imran Khan | P | 88 | 19458 | 8258 | 22.81 | 23 | 6 |
| 355 | D.K.Lillee | A | 70 | 18467 | 8493 | 23.92 | 23 | 7 |
| 325 | R.G.D.Willis | E | 90 | 17357 | 8190 | 25.20 | 16 | — |
| 309 | L.R.Gibbs | WI | 79 | 27115 | 8989 | 29.09 | 18 | 2 |
| 307 | F.S.Trueman | E | 67 | 15178 | 6625 | 21.57 | 17 | 3 |
| 297 | D.L.Underwood | E | 86 | 21862 | 7674 | 25.83 | 17 | 6 |
| 266 | B.S.Bedi | I | 67 | 21364 | 7637 | 28.71 | 14 | 1 |
| 259 | J.Garner | WI | 58 | 13169 | 5433 | 20.97 | 7 | — |
| 252 | J.B.Statham | E | 70 | 16056 | 6261 | 24.84 | 9 | 1 |
| 249 | M.A.Holding | WI | 60 | 12680 | 5898 | 23.68 | 13 | 2 |
| 248 | R.Benaud | A | 63 | 19108 | 6704 | 27.03 | 16 | 1 |
| 246 | G.D.McKenzie | A | 60 | 17681 | 7328 | 29.78 | 16 | 3 |
| 242 | B.S.Chandrasekhar | I | 58 | 15963 | 7199 | 29.74 | 16 | 2 |
| 236 | A.V.Bedser | E | 51 | 15918 | 5876 | 24.89 | 15 | 5 |
| 236 | Abdul Qadir | P | 67 | 17126 | 7742 | 32.80 | 15 | 5 |
| 235 | G.St A.Sobers | WI | 93 | 21599 | 7999 | 34.03 | 6 | — |
| 228 | R.R.Lindwall | A | 61 | 13650 | 5251 | 23.03 | 12 | — |

| Wkts | | | M | Balls | Runs | Avge | 5 wI | 10 wM |
|------|---|---|----|-------|------|-------|------|-------|
| 216 | C.V.Grimmett | A | 37 | 14513 | 5231 | 24.21 | 21 | 7 |
| 202 | A.M.E.Roberts | WI | 47 | 11136 | 5174 | 25.61 | 11 | 2 |
| 202 | J.A.Snow | E | 49 | 12021 | 5387 | 26.66 | 8 | 1 |
| 200 | J.R.Thomson | A | 51 | 10535 | 5601 | 28.00 | 8 | – |

### HAT-TRICKS

| | | | |
|---|---|---|---|
| F.R.Spofforth | Australia v England | Melbourne | 1878-79 |
| W.Bates | England v Australia | Melbourne | 1882-83 |
| J.Briggs | England v Australia | Sydney | 1891-92 |
| G.A.Lohmann | England v South Africa | Port Elizabeth | 1895-96 |
| J.T.Hearne | England v Australia | Leeds | 1899 |
| H.Trumble | Australia v England | Melbourne | 1901-02 |
| H.Trumble | Australia v England | Melbourne | 1903-04 |
| T.J.Matthews (2)* | Australia v South Africa | Manchester | 1912 |
| M.J.C.Allom † | England v New Zealand | Christchurch | 1929-30 |
| T.W.J.Goddard | England v South Africa | Johannesburg | 1938-39 |
| P.J.Loader | England v West Indies | Leeds | 1957 |
| L.F.Kline | Australia v South Africa | Cape Town | 1957-58 |
| W.W.Hall | West Indies v Pakistan | Lahore | 1958-59 |
| G.M.Griffin | South Africa v England | Lord's | 1960 |
| L.R.Gibbs | West Indies v Australia | Adelaide | 1960-61 |
| P.J.Petherick | New Zealand v Pakistan | Lahore | 1976-77 |
| C.A.Walsh ‡ | West Indies v Australia | Brisbane | 1988-89 |
| M.G.Hughes ‡ | Australia v West Indies | Perth | 1988-89 |

*Hat-trick in each innings † Four wickets in five balls
‡ Involving both innings

### WICKET-KEEPING RECORDS

#### MOST DISMISSALS IN AN INNINGS

| | | | | |
|---|---|---|---|---|
| 7 | Wasim Bari | Pakistan v New Zealand | Auckland | 1978-79 |
| 7 | R.W.Taylor | England v India | Bombay | 1979-80 |
| 7 | I.D.S.Smith | New Zealand v Sri Lanka | Hamilton | 1990-91 |
| 6 | A.T.W.Grout | Australia v South Africa | Johannesburg | 1957-58 |
| 6 | D.T.Lindsay | South Africa v Australia | Johannesburg | 1966-67 |
| 6 | J.T.Murray | England v India | Lord's | 1967 |
| 6 † | S.M.H.Kirmani | India v New Zealand | Christchurch | 1975-76 |
| 6 | R.W.Marsh | Australia v England | Brisbane | 1982-83 |
| 6 | S.A.R.Silva | Sri Lanka v India | Colombo (SSC) | 1985-86 |
| 6 | R.C.Russell | England v Australia | Melbourne | 1990-91 |

† Including one stumping

#### MOST STUMPINGS IN AN INNINGS

| | | | | |
|---|---|---|---|---|
| 5 | K.S.More | India v West Indies | Madras | 1987-88 |

#### MOST DISMISSALS IN A TEST

| | | | | |
|---|---|---|---|---|
| 10 | R.W.Taylor | England v India | Bombay | 1979-80 |
| 9 † | G.R.A.Langley | Australia v England | Lord's | 1956 |
| 9 | D.A.Murray | West Indies v Australia | Melbourne | 1981-82 |
| 9 | R.W.Marsh | Australia v England | Brisbane | 1982-83 |
| 9 | S.A.R.Silva | Sri Lanka v India | Colombo (SSC) | 1985-86 |
| 9 † | S.A.R.Silva | Sri Lanka v India | Colombo (PSS) | 1985-86 |

† Including one stumping

## MOST DISMISSALS IN A SERIES

| | | | |
|---|---|---|---|
| 28 | R.W.Marsh | Australia v England | 1982-83 |
| 26 (inc 3st) | J.H.B.Waite | South Africa v New Zealand | 1961-62 |
| 26 | R.W.Marsh | Australia v West Indies (6 Tests) | 1975-76 |
| 24 (inc 2st) | D.L.Murray | West Indies v England | 1963 |
| 24 | D.T.Lindsay | South Africa v Australia | 1966-67 |
| 24 (inc 3st) | A.P.E.Knott | England v Australia (6 Tests) | 1970-71 |
| 24 | I.A.Healy | Australia v England | 1990-91 |

## 100 DISMISSALS IN TESTS

| Total | | | Tests | Ct | St |
|---|---|---|---|---|---|
| 355 | R.W.Marsh | Australia | 96 | 343 | 12 |
| 272 † | P.J.L.Dujon | West Indies | 81 | 267 | 5 |
| 269 | A.P.E.Knott | England | 95 | 250 | 19 |
| 228 | Wasim Bari | Pakistan | 81 | 201 | 27 |
| 219 | T.G.Evans | England | 91 | 173 | 46 |
| 198 | S.M.H.Kirmani | India | 88 | 160 | 38 |
| 189 | D.L.Murray | West Indies | 62 | 181 | 8 |
| 187 | A.T.W.Grout | Australia | 51 | 163 | 24 |
| 176 | I.D.S.Smith | New Zealand | 63 | 168 | 8 |
| 174 | R.W.Taylor | England | 57 | 167 | 7 |
| 141 | J.H.B.Waite | South Africa | 50 | 124 | 17 |
| 130 | W.A.S.Oldfield | Australia | 54 | 78 | 52 |
| 114 † | J.M.Parks | England | 46 | 103 | 11 |
| 110 | I.A.Healy | Australia | 36 | 108 | 2 |
| 104 | Salim Yousuf | Pakistan | 32 | 91 | 13 |

† Including two catches taken in the field

## FIELDING RECORDS
(Excluding Wicket-Keepers)

## MOST CATCHES IN AN INNINGS

| | | | | |
|---|---|---|---|---|
| 5 | V.Y.Richardson | Australia v South Africa | Durban | 1935-36 |
| 5 | Yajurvindra Singh | India v England | Bangalore | 1976-77 |
| 5 | M.Azharuddin | India v Pakistan | Karachi | 1989-90 |
| 5 | K.Srikkanth | India v Australia | Perth | 1991-92 |

## MOST CATCHES IN A TEST

| | | | | |
|---|---|---|---|---|
| 7 | G.S.Chappell | Australia v England | Perth | 1974-75 |
| 7 | Yajurvindra Singh | India v England | Bangalore | 1976-77 |

## MOST CATCHES IN A SERIES

| | | | |
|---|---|---|---|
| 15 | J.M.Gregory | Australia v England | 1920-21 |

## 100 CATCHES IN TESTS

| Total | | | Tests |
|---|---|---|---|
| 135 | A.R.Border | Australia | 130 |
| 122 | G.S.Chappell | Australia | 87 |
| 122 | I.V.A.Richards | West Indies | 121 |
| 120 | I.T.Botham | England | 102 |
| 120 | M.C.Cowdrey | England | 114 |
| 110 | R.B.Simpson | Australia | 62 |
| 110 | W.R.Hammond | England | 85 |
| 109 | G.St A.Sobers | West Indies | 93 |
| 108 | S.M.Gavaskar | India | 125 |
| 105 | I.M.Chappell | Australia | 75 |

|  |  |  | E | A | SA | WI | NZ | I | P | SL |
|---|---|---|---|---|---|---|---|---|---|---|
|  |  |  |  |  |  | *Opponents* |  |  |  |  |
| England | 117 | D.I.Gower | – | 42 | – | 19 | 13 | 24 | 17 | 2 |
| Australia | 130 | A.R.Border | 41 | – | – | 26 | 17 | 20 | 22 | 4 |
| South Africa | 50 | J.H.B.Waite | 21 | 14 | – | – | 15 | – | – | – |
| West Indies | 121 | I.V.A.Richards | 36 | 34 | – | – | 7 | 28 | 16 | – |
| New Zealand | 86 | Sir R.J.Hadlee | 21 | 23 | – | 10 | – | 14 | 12 | 6 |
| India | 125 | S.M.Gavaskar | 38 | 20 | – | 27 | 9 | – | 24 | 7 |
| Pakistan | 117 | Javed Miandad | 22 | 25 | – | 13 | 17 | 28 | – | 12 |
| Sri Lanka | 33 | A.Ranatunga | 3 | 4 | – | – | 7 | 8 | 11 | – |

## MOST CONSECUTIVE TEST APPEARANCES

| 127 | A.R.Border | Australia | March 1979 to February 1992 |
|---|---|---|---|
| 106 | S.M.Gavaskar | India | January 1975 to February 1987 |

## MOST MATCHES BETWEEN APPEARANCES

| 104 | Younis Ahmed | Pakistan | November 1969 to February 1987 |
|---|---|---|---|
| 103 | D.Shackleton | England | November 1951 to June 1963 |

# SUMMARY OF ALL TEST MATCHES

### To 16 August 1992

|  | Opponents | Tests | E | A | SA | WI | NZ | I | P | SL | Tied | Drawn |
|---|---|---|---|---|---|---|---|---|---|---|---|---|
|  |  |  |  |  | *Won by* |  |  |  |  |  |  |  |
| England | Australia | 274 | 88 | 104 | – | – | – | – | – | – | – | 82 |
|  | South Africa | 102 | 46 | – | 18 | – | – | – | – | – | – | 38 |
|  | West Indies | 104 | 24 | – | – | 43 | – | – | – | – | – | 37 |
|  | New Zealand | 72 | 33 | – | – | – | 4 | – | – | – | – | 35 |
|  | India | 78 | 31 | – | – | – | – | 11 | – | – | – | 36 |
|  | Pakistan | 52 | 14 | – | – | – | – | – | 7 | – | – | 31 |
|  | Sri Lanka | 4 | 3 | – | – | – | – | – | – | 0 | – | 1 |
| Australia | South Africa | 53 | – | 29 | 11 | – | – | – | – | – | – | 13 |
|  | West Indies | 72 | – | 29 | – | 24 | – | – | – | – | 1 | 18 |
|  | New Zealand | 26 | – | 10 | – | – | 6 | – | – | – | – | 10 |
|  | India | 50 | – | 24 | – | – | – | 8 | – | – | 1 | 17 |
|  | Pakistan | 34 | – | 12 | – | – | – | – | 9 | – | – | 13 |
|  | Sri Lanka | 4 | – | 3 | – | – | – | – | – | 0 | – | 1 |
| South Africa | West Indies | 1 | – | – | 0 | 1 | – | – | – | – | – | – |
|  | New Zealand | 17 | – | – | 9 | – | 2 | – | – | – | – | 6 |
| West Indies | New Zealand | 24 | – | – | – | 8 | 4 | – | – | – | – | 12 |
|  | India | 62 | – | – | – | 26 | – | 6 | – | – | – | 30 |
|  | Pakistan | 28 | – | – | – | 10 | – | – | 7 | – | – | 11 |
| New Zealand | India | 31 | – | – | – | – | 6 | 12 | – | – | – | 13 |
|  | Pakistan | 32 | – | – | – | – | 3 | – | 13 | – | – | 16 |
|  | Sri Lanka | 9 | – | – | – | – | 4 | – | – | 0 | – | 5 |
| India | Pakistan | 44 | – | – | – | – | – | 4 | 7 | – | – | 33 |
|  | Sri Lanka | 8 | – | – | – | – | – | 3 | – | 1 | – | 4 |
| Pakistan | Sri Lanka | 12 | – | – | – | – | – | – | 6 | 1 | – | 5 |
|  |  | 1193 | 239 | 211 | 38 | 112 | 29 | 44 | 49 | 2 | 2 | 467 |

*(continued on p 247)*

# LIMITED-OVERS INTERNATIONALS
## SUMMARY OF RESULTS

To end of 1992 season in England
(Excluding Sri Lanka v Australia 1992-93)

| Opponents | | Matches | Won by | | | | | | | | | | | | Tied | NR |
|---|---|---|---|---|---|---|---|---|---|---|---|---|---|---|---|---|
| | | | E | A | I | NZ | P | SA | SL | WI | Z | B | C | EA | | |
| **England** | Australia | 52 | 25 | 25 | – | – | – | – | – | – | – | – | – | – | 1 | 1 |
| | India | 23 | 13 | – | 10 | – | – | – | – | – | – | – | – | – | – | – |
| | New Zealand | 40 | 20 | – | – | 17 | – | – | – | – | – | – | – | – | – | 3 |
| | Pakistan | 36 | 23 | – | – | – | 12 | – | – | – | – | – | – | – | – | 1 |
| | South Africa | 2 | 2 | – | – | – | – | 0 | – | – | – | – | – | – | – | – |
| | Sri Lanka | 9 | 8 | – | – | – | – | – | 1 | – | – | – | – | – | – | – |
| | West Indies | 43 | 18 | – | – | – | – | – | – | 23 | – | – | – | – | – | 2 |
| | Zimbabwe | 1 | 0 | – | – | – | – | – | – | – | 1 | – | – | – | – | – |
| | Canada | 1 | 1 | – | – | – | – | – | – | – | – | – | 0 | – | – | – |
| | East Africa | 1 | 1 | – | – | – | – | – | – | – | – | – | – | 0 | – | – |
| **Australia** | India | 40 | – | 24 | 13 | – | – | – | – | – | – | – | – | – | – | 3 |
| | New Zealand | 50 | – | 34 | – | 14 | – | – | – | – | – | – | – | – | – | 2 |
| | Pakistan | 34 | – | 15 | – | – | 17 | – | – | – | – | – | – | – | – | 2 |
| | South Africa | 1 | – | 0 | – | – | – | 1 | – | – | – | – | – | – | – | – |
| | Sri Lanka | 21 | – | 16 | – | – | – | – | 3 | – | – | – | – | – | – | 2 |
| | West Indies | 63 | – | 24 | – | – | – | – | – | 37 | – | – | – | – | 1 | 1 |
| | Zimbabwe | 5 | – | 4 | – | – | – | – | – | – | 1 | – | – | – | – | – |
| | Bangladesh | 1 | – | 1 | – | – | – | – | – | – | – | 0 | – | – | – | – |
| | Canada | 1 | – | 1 | – | – | – | – | – | – | – | – | 0 | – | – | – |
| **India** | New Zealand | 29 | – | – | 16 | 13 | – | – | – | – | – | – | – | – | – | – |
| | Pakistan | 38 | – | – | 12 | – | 24 | – | – | – | – | – | – | – | – | 2 |
| | South Africa | 4 | – | – | 2 | – | – | 2 | – | – | – | – | – | – | – | – |
| | Sri Lanka | 26 | – | – | 17 | – | – | – | 7 | – | – | – | – | – | – | 2 |
| | West Indies | 40 | – | – | 10 | – | – | – | – | 29 | – | – | – | – | 1 | – |
| | Zimbabwe | 5 | – | – | 5 | – | – | – | – | – | 0 | – | – | – | – | – |
| | Bangladesh | 2 | – | – | 2 | – | – | – | – | – | – | 0 | – | – | – | – |
| | East Africa | 1 | – | – | 1 | – | – | – | – | – | – | – | – | 0 | – | – |
| **N Zealand** | Pakistan | 25 | – | – | – | 11 | 13 | – | – | – | – | – | – | – | – | 1 |
| | South Africa | 1 | – | – | – | 1 | – | 0 | – | – | – | – | – | – | – | – |
| | Sri Lanka | 23 | – | – | – | 19 | – | – | 4 | – | – | – | – | – | – | – |
| | West Indies | 14 | – | – | – | 2 | – | – | – | 11 | – | – | – | – | – | 1 |
| | Zimbabwe | 3 | – | – | – | 3 | – | – | – | – | 0 | – | – | – | – | – |
| | Bangladesh | 1 | – | – | – | 1 | – | – | – | – | – | 0 | – | – | – | – |
| | East Africa | 1 | – | – | – | 1 | – | – | – | – | – | – | – | 0 | – | – |
| **Pakistan** | South Africa | 1 | – | – | – | – | 0 | 1 | – | – | – | – | – | – | – | – |
| | Sri Lanka | 36 | – | – | – | – | 28 | – | 7 | – | – | – | – | – | – | 1 |
| | West Indies | 57 | – | – | – | – | 17 | – | – | 39 | – | – | – | – | 1 | – |
| | Zimbabwe | 1 | – | – | – | – | 1 | – | – | – | 0 | – | – | – | – | – |
| | Bangladesh | 2 | – | – | – | – | 2 | – | – | – | – | 0 | – | – | – | – |
| | Canada | 1 | – | – | – | – | 1 | – | – | – | – | – | 0 | – | – | – |
| **S Africa** | Sri Lanka | 1 | – | – | – | – | – | 0 | 1 | – | – | – | – | – | – | – |
| | West Indies | 4 | – | – | – | – | – | 1 | – | 3 | – | – | – | – | – | – |
| | Zimbabwe | 1 | – | – | – | – | – | 1 | – | – | 0 | – | – | – | – | – |
| **Sri Lanka** | West Indies | 12 | – | – | – | – | – | – | 1 | 11 | – | – | – | – | – | – |
| | Zimbabwe | 1 | – | – | – | – | – | – | 1 | – | 0 | – | – | – | – | – |
| | Bangladesh | 3 | – | – | – | – | – | – | 3 | – | – | 0 | – | – | – | – |
| **W Indies** | Zimbabwe | 3 | – | – | – | – | – | – | – | 3 | 0 | – | – | – | – | – |
| | | 760 | 111 | 144 | 88 | 82 | 115 | 6 | 28 | 156 | 2 | 0 | 0 | 0 | 4 | 24 |

# 1992 WORLD CUP FINAL

## ENGLAND v PAKISTAN

**Played at Melbourne Cricket Ground, on 25 March.**
**Toss: Pakistan. Result: PAKISTAN won by 22 runs.**
Match Award: Wasim Akram.                                    Attendance: 87,182.

| PAKISTAN | Runs | Mins | Balls | 6s | 4s | Fall |
|---|---|---|---|---|---|---|
| Aamir Sohail c Stewart b Pringle | 4 | 20 | 19 | – | – | 1-20 |
| Ramiz Raja lbw b Pringle | 8 | 36 | 26 | – | 1 | 2-24 |
| *Imran Khan c Illingworth b Botham | 72 | 159 | 110 | 1 | 5 | 4-197 |
| Javed Miandad c Botham b Illingworth | 58 | 125 | 98 | – | 4 | 3-163 |
| Inzamam-ul-Haq b Pringle | 42 | 46 | 35 | – | 4 | 5-249 |
| Wasim Akram run out (Stewart) | 33 | 31 | 18 | – | 4 | 6-249 |
| Salim Malik not out | 0 | 1 | 1 | – | – |  |
| Ijaz Ahmed ⎫ |  |  |  |  |  |  |
| †Moin Khan ⎬ did not bat |  |  |  |  |  |  |
| Mushtaq Ahmed ⎪ |  |  |  |  |  |  |
| Aqib Javed ⎭ |  |  |  |  |  |  |
| Extras (LB19, W6, NB7) | 32 |  |  |  |  |  |

**Total (50 overs; 212 minutes)**      249-6 closed

| ENGLAND | Runs | Mins | Balls | 6s | 4s | Fall |
|---|---|---|---|---|---|---|
| *G.A.Gooch c Aqib b Mushtaq | 29 | 93 | 66 | – | 1 | 4-69 |
| I.T.Botham c Moin b Wasim | 0 | 12 | 6 | – | – | 1-6 |
| †A.J.Stewart c Moin b Aqib | 7 | 22 | 16 | – | 1 | 2-21 |
| G.A.Hick lbw b Mushtaq | 17 | 49 | 36 | – | 1 | 3-59 |
| N.H.Fairbrother c Moin b Aqib | 62 | 97 | 70 | – | 3 | 7-180 |
| A.J.Lamb b Wasim | 31 | 54 | 41 | – | 2 | 5-141 |
| C.C.Lewis b Wasim | 0 | 1 | 1 | – | – | 6-141 |
| D.A.Reeve c Ramiz b Mushtaq | 15 | 38 | 32 | – | 1 | 8-183 |
| D.R.Pringle not out | 18 | 29 | 16 | – | 1 | – |
| P.A.J.DeFreitas run out (Salim/Moin) | 10 | 13 | 8 | – | – | 9-208 |
| R.K.Illingworth c Ramiz b Imran | 14 | 9 | 10 | – | 2 | 10-227 |
| Extras (LB5, W13, NB6) | 24 |  |  |  |  |  |

**Total (49.2 overs; 213 minutes)**      227

| ENGLAND | O | M | R | W | PAKISTAN | O | M | R | W |
|---|---|---|---|---|---|---|---|---|---|
| Pringle | 10 | 2 | 22 | 3 | Wasim | 10 | 0 | 49 | 3 |
| Lewis | 10 | 2 | 52 | 0 | Aqib | 10 | 2 | 27 | 2 |
| Botham | 7 | 0 | 42 | 1 | Mushtaq | 10 | 1 | 41 | 3 |
| DeFreitas | 10 | 1 | 42 | 0 | Ijaz | 3 | 0 | 13 | 0 |
| Illingworth | 10 | 0 | 50 | 1 | Imran | 6.2 | 0 | 43 | 1 |
| Reeve | 3 | 0 | 22 | 0 | Aamir | 10 | 0 | 49 | 0 |

**Umpires: B.L.Aldridge and S.U.Bucknor.**

## WORLD CUP FINALS

| 1975 | WEST INDIES (291-8) beat Australia (274) by 17 runs | Lord's |
|---|---|---|
| 1979 | WEST INDIES (286-9) beat England (194) by 92 runs | Lord's |
| 1983 | INDIA (183) beat West Indies (140) by 43 runs | Lord's |
| 1987-88 | AUSTRALIA (253-5) beat England (246-8) by 7 runs | Calcutta |
| 1991-92 | PAKISTAN (249-6) beat England (227) by 22 runs | Melbourne |

# LIMITED-OVERS INTERNATIONALS RECORDS

Compiled by Philip Bailey (excluding 1992-93 season)

## TEAM RECORDS

### HIGHEST TOTALS BY EACH COUNTRY

| | | | |
|---|---|---|---|
| 363-7 (55 overs) | ENGLAND v Pakistan | Nottingham | 1992 |
| 360-4 (50 overs) | WEST INDIES v Sri Lanka | Karachi | 1987-88 |
| 338-4 (50 overs) | NEW ZEALAND v Bangladesh | Sharjah | 1989-90 |
| 338-5 (60 overs) | PAKISTAN v Sri Lanka | Swansea | 1983 |
| 332-3 (50 overs) | AUSTRALIA v Sri Lanka | Sharjah | 1989-90 |
| 313-7 (49.2 overs) | SRI LANKA v Zimbabwe | New Plymouth | 1991-92 |
| 312-4 (50 overs) | ZIMBABWE v Sri Lanka | New Plymouth | 1991-92 |
| 299-4 (40 overs) | INDIA v Sri Lanka | Bombay | 1986-87 |
| 288-2 (46.4 overs) | SOUTH AFRICA v India | Delhi | 1991-92 |

### HIGHEST TOTAL BATTING SECOND

| | | | |
|---|---|---|---|
| WINNING: | | | |
| 313-7 (49.2 overs) | Sri Lanka v Zimbabwe | New Plymouth | 1991-92 |
| LOSING: | | | |
| 289-7 (40 overs) | Sri Lanka v India | Bombay | 1986-87 |

### HIGHEST MATCH AGGREGATE

| | | | |
|---|---|---|---|
| 626-14 (120 overs) | Pakistan v Sri Lanka | Swansea | 1983 |

### LOWEST TOTALS BY EACH COUNTRY
*(Excluding abbreviated matches)*

| | | | |
|---|---|---|---|
| 45 (40.3 overs) | CANADA v England | Manchester | 1979 |
| 55 (28.3 overs) | SRI LANKA v West Indies | Sharjah | 1986-87 |
| 63 (25.5 overs) | INDIA v Australia | Sydney | 1980-81 |
| 64 (35.5 overs) | NEW ZEALAND v Pakistan | Sharjah | 1985-86 |
| 70 (25.2 overs) | AUSTRALIA v England | Birmingham | 1977 |
| 74 (40.2 overs) | PAKISTAN v England | Adelaide | 1991-92 |
| 93 (36.2 overs) | ENGLAND v Australia | Leeds | 1975 |
| 111 (41.4 overs) | WEST INDIES v Pakistan | Melbourne | 1983-84 |
| 134 (46.1 overs) | ZIMBABWE v England | Albury | 1991-92 |
| 152 (43.4 overs) | SOUTH AFRICA v West Indies | Port-of-Spain | 1991-92 |

### LOWEST MATCH AGGREGATE

| | | | |
|---|---|---|---|
| 91-12 (54.2 overs) | England v Canada | Manchester | 1979 |

### LARGEST MARGINS OF VICTORY

| | | | |
|---|---|---|---|
| 232 runs | Australia beat Sri Lanka | Adelaide | 1984-85 |
| 206 runs | New Zealand beat Australia | Adelaide | 1985-86 |
| 202 runs | England beat India | Lord's | 1975 |
| 10 wickets | Nine instances | | |

## TIED MATCHES

| | | | | | |
|---|---|---|---|---|---|
| Australia | 222-9 | West Indies | 222-5 | Melbourne | 1983-84 |
| England | 226-5 | Australia | 226-8 | Nottingham | 1989 |
| West Indies | 186-5 | Pakistan | 186-9 | Lahore | 1991-92 |
| India | 126 | West Indies | 126 | Perth | 1991-92 |

## BATTING RECORDS

### HIGHEST INDIVIDUAL SCORE FOR EACH COUNTRY

| | | | | |
|---|---|---|---|---|
| 189* | I.V.A.Richards | WEST INDIES v England | Manchester | 1984 |
| 175* | Kapil Dev | INDIA v Zimbabwe | Tunbridge Wells | 1983 |
| 171* | G.M.Turner | NEW ZEALAND v East Africa | Birmingham | 1975 |
| 158 | D.I.Gower | ENGLAND v New Zealand | Brisbane | 1982-83 |
| 145 | D.M.Jones | AUSTRALIA v England | Brisbane | 1990-91 |
| 142 | D.L.Houghton | ZIMBABWE v New Zealand | Hyderabad | 1987-88 |
| 126* | Shoaib Mohammad | PAKISTAN v New Zealand | Wellington | 1988-89 |
| 121 | R.L.Dias | SRI LANKA v India | Bangalore | 1982-83 |
| 90 | K.C.Wessels | SOUTH AFRICA v India | Delhi | 1991-92 |
| 90 | P.N.Kirsten | SOUTH AFRICA v New Zealand | Auckland | 1991-92 |

### HIGHEST PARTNERSHIP FOR EACH WICKET

| | | | | | |
|---|---|---|---|---|---|
| 1st | 212 | G.R.Marsh/D.C.Boon | A v I | Jaipur | 1986-87 |
| 2nd | 221 | C.G.Greenidge/I.V.A.Richards | WI v I | Jamshedpur | 1983-84 |
| 3rd | 224* | D.M.Jones/A.R.Border | A v SL | Adelaide | 1984-85 |
| 4th | 173 | D.M.Jones/S.R.Waugh | A v P | Perth | 1986-87 |
| 5th | 152 | I.V.A.Richards/C.H.Lloyd | WI v SL | Brisbane | 1984-85 |
| 6th | 154 | R.B.Richardson/P.J.L.Dujon | WI v P | Sharjah | 1991-92 |
| 7th | 115 | P.J.L.Dujon/M.D.Marshall | WI v P | Gujranwala | 1986-87 |
| 8th | 117 | D.L.Houghton/I.P.Butchart | Z v NZ | Hyderabad (Ind) | 1987-88 |
| 9th | 126* | Kapil Dev/S.M.H.Kirmani | I v Z | Tunbridge Wells | 1983 |
| 10th | 106* | I.V.A.Richards/M.A.Holding | WI v E | Manchester | 1984 |

### 4000 RUNS

| | | M | I | NO | HS | Runs | Avge | 100 | 50 |
|---|---|---|---|---|---|---|---|---|---|
| D.L.Haynes | WI | 203 | 202 | 25 | 152* | 7513 | 42.44 | 16 | 46 |
| I.V.A.Richards | WI | 187 | 167 | 24 | 189* | 6721 | 47.00 | 11 | 45 |
| Javed Miandad | P | 197 | 187 | 37 | 119* | 6550 | 43.66 | 7 | 46 |
| A.R.Border | A | 241 | 223 | 32 | 127* | 5900 | 30.89 | 3 | 37 |
| C.G.Greenidge | WI | 128 | 127 | 13 | 133* | 5134 | 45.03 | 11 | 31 |
| D.M.Jones | A | 132 | 129 | 23 | 145 | 5048 | 47.62 | 7 | 37 |
| R.B.Richardson | WI | 163 | 159 | 20 | 122 | 4883 | 35.12 | 5 | 37 |
| G.R.Marsh | A | 117 | 115 | 6 | 126* | 4357 | 39.97 | 9 | 22 |
| Ramiz Raja | P | 133 | 132 | 10 | 119* | 4176 | 34.22 | 7 | 24 |
| K.Srikkanth | I | 146 | 145 | 4 | 123 | 4092 | 29.02 | 4 | 27 |
| G.A.Gooch | E | 111 | 109 | 6 | 142 | 4071 | 39.52 | 8 | 23 |
| Salim Malik | P | 152 | 142 | 19 | 102 | 4038 | 32.82 | 5 | 20 |
| A.J.Lamb | E | 122 | 118 | 16 | 118 | 4010 | 39.31 | 4 | 26 |
| D.C.Boon | A | 122 | 118 | 9 | 122 | 4001 | 36.70 | 5 | 21 |

**Leading aggregates for other countries:**

| | | M | I | NO | HS | Runs | Avge | 100 | 50 |
|---|---|---|---|---|---|---|---|---|---|
| M.D.Crowe | NZ | 122 | 121 | 15 | 105* | 3950 | 37.26 | 3 | 28 |
| A.Ranatunga | SL | 107 | 103 | 20 | 88* | 2856 | 34.40 | – | 20 |
| K.C.Wessels | SA | 15 | 15 | 2 | 90 | 578 | 44.46 | – | 6 |
| D.L.Houghton | Z | 20 | 19 | – | 142 | 567 | 29.84 | 1 | 4 |

# BOWLING RECORDS

## BEST ANALYSIS FOR EACH COUNTRY

| 7-37 | Aqib Javed | PAKISTAN v India | Sharjah | 1991-92 |
|------|------------|------------------|---------|---------|
| 7-51 | W.W.Davis | WEST INDIES v Australia | Leeds | 1983 |
| 6-14 | G.J.Gilmour | AUSTRALIA v England | Leeds | 1975 |
| 5-15 | R.J.Shastri | INDIA v Australia | Perth | 1991-92 |
| 5-20 | V.J.Marks | ENGLAND v New Zealand | Wellington | 1983-84 |
| 5-23 | R.O.Collinge | NEW ZEALAND v India | Christchurch | 1975-76 |
| 5-26 | S.H.U.Karnain | SRI LANKA v N Zealand | Moratuwa | 1983-84 |
| 5-29 | A.A.Donald | SOUTH AFRICA v India | Calcutta | 1991-92 |
| 4-21 | E.A.Brandes | ZIMBABWE v England | Albury | 1991-92 |

## HAT-TRICKS

| Jalaluddin | Pakistan v Australia | Hyderabad | 1982-83 |
|------------|---------------------|-----------|---------|
| B.A.Reid | Australia v New Zealand | Sydney | 1985-86 |
| C.Sharma | India v New Zealand | Nagpur | 1987-88 |
| Wasim Akram | Pakistan v West Indies | Sharjah | 1989-90 |
| Wasim Akram | Pakistan v Australia | Sharjah | 1989-90 |
| Kapil Dev | India v Sri Lanka | Calcutta | 1990-91 |
| Aqib Javed | Pakistan v India | Sharjah | 1991-92 |

## 100 WICKETS

|  |  | M | Balls | Runs | Wkts | Avge | Best | 4w |
|--|--|---|-------|------|------|------|------|----|
| Kapil Dev | I | 189 | 9527 | 5933 | 226 | 26.25 | 5-43 | 4 |
| Imran Khan | P | 175 | 7461 | 4845 | 182 | 26.62 | 6-14 | 4 |
| Wasim Akram | P | 126 | 6369 | 4097 | 171 | 23.95 | 5-21 | 6 |
| Sir R.J.Hadlee | NZ | 115 | 6182 | 3407 | 158 | 21.56 | 5-25 | 6 |
| M.D.Marshall | WI | 136 | 7175 | 4233 | 157 | 26.96 | 4-18 | 6 |
| J.Garner | WI | 98 | 5330 | 2752 | 146 | 18.84 | 5-31 | 5 |
| I.T.Botham | E | 116 | 6271 | 4139 | 145 | 28.54 | 4-31 | 3 |
| M.A.Holding | WI | 102 | 5473 | 3034 | 142 | 21.36 | 5-26 | 6 |
| E.J.Chatfield | NZ | 114 | 6065 | 3621 | 140 | 25.86 | 5-34 | 4 |
| C.J.McDermott | A | 88 | 4769 | 3301 | 132 | 25.00 | 5-44 | 4 |
| Abdul Qadir | P | 102 | 4996 | 3364 | 131 | 25.67 | 5-44 | 6 |
| R.J.Shastri | I | 145 | 6415 | 4498 | 127 | 35.41 | 5-15 | 3 |
| S.R.Waugh | A | 129 | 5102 | 3772 | 124 | 30.41 | 4-33 | 2 |
| I.V.A.Richards | WI | 187 | 5644 | 4228 | 118 | 35.83 | 6-41 | 3 |
| M.C.Snedden | NZ | 93 | 4519 | 3235 | 114 | 28.37 | 4-34 | 1 |
| C.E.L.Ambrose | WI | 71 | 3847 | 2263 | 111 | 20.38 | 5-17 | 7 |
| Mudassar Nazar | P | 122 | 4855 | 3431 | 111 | 30.90 | 5-28 | 2 |
| S.P.O'Donnell | A | 87 | 4350 | 3102 | 108 | 28.72 | 5-13 | 6 |
| C.A.Walsh | WI | 97 | 5175 | 3374 | 108 | 31.24 | 5-1 | 5 |
| D.K.Lillee | A | 63 | 3593 | 2145 | 103 | 20.82 | 5-34 | 6 |

**Leading aggregates for other countries:**

|  |  | M | Balls | Runs | Wkts | Avge | Best | 4w |
|--|--|---|-------|------|------|------|------|----|
| J.R.Ratnayeke | SL | 78 | 3573 | 2865 | 85 | 33.70 | 4-23 | 1 |
| A.A.Donald | SA | 14 | 742 | 545 | 24 | 22.70 | 5-29 | 1 |
| E.A.Brandes | Z | 12 | 619 | 508 | 16 | 31.75 | 4-21 | 1 |
| A.J.Traicos | Z | 20 | 1128 | 673 | 16 | 42.06 | 3-35 | – |

## WICKET-KEEPING RECORDS
### MOST DISMISSALS IN AN INNINGS

| | | | | |
|---|---|---|---|---|
| 5 (5ct) | R.W.Marsh | Australia v England | Leeds | 1981 |
| 5 (5ct) | R.G.de Alwis | Sri Lanka v Australia | Colombo (PSS) | 1982-83 |
| 5 (5ct) | S.M.H.Kirmani | India v Zimbabwe | Leicester | 1983 |
| 5 (3ct, 2st) | S.Viswanath | India v England | Sydney | 1984-85 |
| 5 (3ct, 2st) | K.S.More | India v New Zealand | Sharjah | 1987-88 |
| 5 (5ct) | H.P.Tillekeratne | Sri Lanka v Pakistan | Sharjah | 1990-91 |

### MOST DISMISSALS IN A CAREER

204 (183ct, 21st) P.J.L.Dujon (West Indies) in 169 matches

## FIELDING RECORDS
### MOST CATCHES IN AN INNINGS

| | | | | |
|---|---|---|---|---|
| 4 | Salim Malik | Pakistan v New Zealand | Sialkot | 1984-85 |
| 4 | S.M.Gavaskar | India v Pakistan | Sharjah | 1984-85 |
| 4 | R.B.Richardson | West Indies v England | Birmingham | 1991 |
| 4 | K.C.Wessels | South Africa v West Indies | Kingston | 1991-92 |

### MOST CATCHES IN A CAREER

| | | |
|---|---|---|
| A.R.Border | Australia | 111 in 241 matches |
| I.V.A.Richards | West Indies | 101 in 187 matches |

## ALL-ROUND RECORDS
### 1000 RUNS AND 100 WICKETS

| | | M | R | W |
|---|---|---|---|---|
| I.T.Botham | England | 116 | 2113 | 145 |
| Sir R.J.Hadlee | New Zealand | 115 | 1749 | 158 |
| Imran Khan | Pakistan | 175 | 3709 | 182 |
| Kapil Dev | India | 189 | 3486 | 226 |
| Mudassar Nazar | Pakistan | 122 | 2624 | 111 |
| S.P.O'Donnell | Australia | 87 | 1242 | 108 |
| I.V.A.Richards | West Indies | 187 | 6721 | 118 |
| R.J.Shastri | India | 145 | 3037 | 127 |
| Wasim Akram | Pakistan | 126 | 1103 | 171 |
| S.R.Waugh | Australia | 129 | 2542 | 124 |

### 1000 RUNS AND 100 DISMISSALS

| | | M | R | Dis |
|---|---|---|---|---|
| P.J.L.Dujon | West Indies | 169 | 1945 | 204 |
| R.W.Marsh | Australia | 92 | 1225 | 124 |

## MOST APPEARANCES FOR EACH COUNTRY

| | | |
|---|---|---|
| Australia | 241 | A.R.Border |
| West Indies | 203 | D.L.Haynes |
| Pakistan | 197 | Javed Miandad |
| India | 189 | Kapil Dev |
| New Zealand | 147 | J.G.Wright |
| England | 122 | A.J.Lamb |
| Sri Lanka | 107 | A.Ranatunga |
| Zimbabwe | 20 | D.L.Houghton, A.J.Pycroft, A.J.Traicos |
| South Africa | 15 | A.P.Kuiper, D.J.Richardson, R.P.Snell, K.C.Wessels |

# ENGLAND v AUSTRALIA
## 1876-77 to 1990-91

### Captains

| Season | England | Australia | T | E | A | D |
|---|---|---|---|---|---|---|
| 1876-77 | James Lillywhite | D.W.Gregory | 2 | 1 | 1 | – |
| 1878-79 | Lord Harris | D.W.Gregory | 1 | – | 1 | – |
| 1880 | Lord Harris | W.L.Murdoch | 1 | 1 | – | – |
| 1881-82 | A.Shaw | W.L.Murdoch | 4 | – | 2 | 2 |
| 1882 | A.N.Hornby | W.L.Murdoch | 1 | – | 1 | – |
| 1882-83 | Hon. Ivo Bligh | W.L.Murdoch | 4 | 2 | 2 | – |
| 1884 | Lord Harris[1] | W.L.Murdoch | 3 | 1 | – | 2 |
| 1884-85 | A.Shrewsbury | T.Horan[2] | 5 | 3 | 2 | – |
| 1886 | A.G.Steel | H.J.H.Scott | 3 | 3 | – | – |
| 1886-87 | A.Shrewsbury | P.S.McDonnell | 2 | 2 | – | – |
| 1887-88 | W.W.Read | P.S.McDonnell | 1 | 1 | – | – |
| 1888 | W.G.Grace[3] | P.S.McDonnell | 3 | 2 | 1 | – |
| 1890 | W.G.Grace | W.L.Murdoch | 2 | 2 | – | – |
| 1891-92 | W.G.Grace | J.McC.Blackham | 3 | 1 | 2 | – |
| 1893 | W.G.Grace[4] | J.McC.Blackham | 3 | 1 | – | 2 |
| 1894-95 | A.E.Stoddart | G.Giffen[5] | 5 | 3 | 2 | – |
| 1896 | W.G.Grace | G.H.S.Trott | 3 | 2 | 1 | – |
| 1897-98 | A.E.Stoddart[6] | G.H.S.Trott | 5 | 1 | 4 | – |
| 1899 | A.C.MacLaren[7] | J.Darling | 5 | – | 1 | 4 |
| 1901-02 | A.C.MacLaren | J.Darling[8] | 5 | 1 | 4 | – |
| 1902 | A.C.MacLaren | J.Darling | 5 | 1 | 2 | 2 |
| 1903-04 | P.F.Warner | M.A.Noble | 5 | 3 | 2 | – |
| 1905 | Hon F.S.Jackson | J.Darling | 5 | 2 | – | 3 |
| 1907-08 | A.O.Jones[9] | M.A.Noble | 5 | 1 | 4 | – |
| 1909 | A.C.MacLaren | M.A.Noble | 5 | 1 | 2 | 2 |
| 1911-12 | J.W.H.T.Douglas | C.Hill | 5 | 4 | 1 | – |
| 1912 | C.B.Fry | S.E.Gregory | 3 | 1 | – | 2 |
| 1920-21 | J.W.H.T.Douglas | W.W.Armstrong | 5 | – | 5 | – |
| 1921 | Hon L.H.Tennyson[10] | W.W.Armstrong | 5 | – | 3 | 2 |
| 1924-25 | A.E.R.Gilligan | H.L.Collins | 5 | 1 | 4 | – |
| 1926 | A.W.Carr[11] | H.L.Collins[12] | 5 | 1 | – | 4 |
| 1928-29 | A.P.F.Chapman[13] | J.Ryder | 5 | 4 | 1 | – |
| 1930 | A.P.F.Chapman[14] | W.M.Woodfull | 5 | 1 | 2 | 2 |
| 1932-33 | D.R.Jardine | W.M.Woodfull | 5 | 4 | 1 | – |
| 1934 | R.E.S.Wyatt[15] | W.M.Woodfull | 5 | 1 | 2 | 2 |
| 1936-37 | G.O.B.Allen | D.G.Bradman | 5 | 2 | 3 | – |
| 1938 | W.R.Hammond | D.G.Bradman | 4 | 1 | 1 | 2 |
| 1946-47 | W.R.Hammond[16] | D.G.Bradman | 5 | – | 3 | 2 |
| 1948 | N.W.D.Yardley | D.G.Bradman | 5 | – | 4 | 1 |
| 1950-51 | F.R.Brown | A.L.Hassett | 5 | 1 | 4 | – |
| 1953 | L.Hutton | A.L.Hassett | 5 | 1 | – | 4 |
| 1954-55 | L.Hutton | I.W.Johnson[17] | 5 | 3 | 1 | 1 |
| 1956 | P.B.H.May | I.W.Johnson | 5 | 2 | 1 | 2 |
| 1958-59 | P.B.H.May | R.Benaud | 5 | – | 4 | 1 |
| 1961 | P.B.H.May[18] | R.Benaud[19] | 5 | 1 | 2 | 2 |
| 1962-63 | E.R.Dexter | R.Benaud | 5 | 1 | 1 | 3 |
| 1964 | E.R.Dexter | R.B.Simpson | 5 | – | 1 | 4 |
| 1965-66 | M.J.K.Smith | R.B.Simpson[20] | 5 | 1 | 1 | 3 |
| 1968 | M.C.Cowdrey[21] | W.M.Lawry[22] | 5 | 1 | 1 | 3 |

232

| Season | England | Australia | T | E | A | D |
|--------|---------|-----------|---|---|---|---|
| 1970-71 | R.Illingworth | W.M.Lawry[23] | 6 | 2 | – | 4 |
| 1972 | R.Illingworth | I.M.Chappell | 5 | 2 | 2 | 1 |
| 1974-75 | M.H.Denness[24] | I.M.Chappell | 6 | 1 | 4 | 1 |
| 1975 | A.W.Greig[25] | I.M.Chappell | 4 | – | 1 | 3 |
| 1976-77 | A.W.Greig | G.S.Chappell | 1 | – | 1 | – |
| 1977 | J.M.Brearley | G.S.Chappell | 5 | 3 | – | 2 |
| 1978-79 | J.M.Brearley | G.N.Yallop | 6 | 5 | 1 | – |
| 1979-80 | J.M.Brearley | G.S.Chappell | 3 | – | 3 | – |
| 1980 | I.T.Botham | G.S.Chappell | 1 | – | – | 1 |
| 1981 | J.M.Brearley[26] | K.J.Hughes | 6 | 3 | 1 | 2 |
| 1982-83 | R.G.D.Willis | G.S.Chappell | 5 | 1 | 2 | 2 |
| 1985 | D.I.Gower | A.R.Border | 6 | 3 | 1 | 2 |
| 1986-87 | M.W.Gatting | A.R.Border | 5 | 2 | 1 | 2 |
| 1987-88 | M.W.Gatting | A.R.Border | 1 | – | – | 1 |
| 1989 | D.I.Gower | A.R.Border | 6 | – | 4 | 2 |
| 1990-91 | G.A.Gooch[27] | A.R.Border | 5 | – | 3 | 2 |

|  |  | T | E | A | D |
|--|--|---|---|---|---|
| | The Oval | 30 | 13 | 5 | 12 |
| | Manchester | 25 | 7 | 5 | 13 |
| | Lord's | 29 | 5 | 11 | 13 |
| | Nottingham | 16 | 3 | 5 | 8 |
| | Leeds | 20 | 6 | 6 | 8 |
| | Birmingham | 8 | 3 | 1 | 4 |
| | Sheffield | 1 | – | 1 | – |
| | Melbourne | 49 | 18 | 24 | 7 |
| | Sydney | 49 | 20 | 23 | 6 |
| | Adelaide | 25 | 7 | 13 | 5 |
| | Brisbane | 15 | 5 | 7 | 3 |
| | Perth | 7 | 1 | 3 | 3 |
| | In England | 129 | 37 | 34 | 58 |
| | In Australia | 145 | 51 | 70 | 24 |
| | Totals | 274 | 88 | 104 | 82 |

The following deputised for the official captain or were appointed for only a minor proportion of the series:

[1] A.N.Hornby (1st). [2] W.L.Murdoch (1st), H.H.Massie (3rd), J.M.Blackham (4th). [3] A.G.Steel (1st). [4] A.E.Stoddart (1st). [5] J.M.Blackham (1st). [6] A.C. MacLaren (1st, 2nd, 5th). [7] W.G.Grace (1st). [8] H.Trumble (4th, 5th). [9] F.L.Fane (1st, 2nd, 3rd). [10] J.W.H.T.Douglas (1st, 2nd). [11] A.P.F.Chapman (5th). [12] W.Bardsley (3rd, 4th). [13] J.C.White (5th). [14] R.E.S.Wyatt (5th). [15] C.F.Walters (1st). [16] N.W.D.Yardley (5th). [17] A.R.Morris (2nd). [18] M.C.Cowdrey (1st, 2nd). [19] R.N.Harvey (2nd). [20] B.C.Booth (1st, 3rd). [21] T.W.Graveney (4th). [22] B.N. Jarman (4th). [23] I.M.Chappell (7th). [24] J.H.Edrich (4th). [25] M.H.Denness (1st). [26] I.T.Botham (1st, 2nd). [27] A.J.Lamb (1st).

## HIGHEST INNINGS TOTALS

| England | in England | 903-7d | The Oval | 1938 |
|---|---|---|---|---|
| | in Australia | 636 | Sydney | 1928-29 |
| Australia | in England | 729-6d | Lord's | 1930 |
| | in Australia | 659-8d | Sydney | 1946-47 |

## LOWEST INNINGS TOTALS

| England | in England | 52 | The Oval | 1948 |
|---|---|---|---|---|
| | in Australia | 45 | Sydney | 1886-87 |
| Australia | in England | 36 | Birmingham | 1902 |
| | in Australia | 42 | Sydney | 1887-88 |

## HIGHEST INDIVIDUAL INNINGS

| England | in England | 364 | L.Hutton | The Oval | 1938 |
|---|---|---|---|---|---|
| | in Australia | 287 | R.E.Foster | Sydney | 1903-04 |
| Australia | in England | 334 | D.G.Bradman | Leeds | 1930 |
| | in Australia | 307 | R.M.Cowper | Melbourne | 1965-66 |

## HIGHEST AGGREGATE OF RUNS IN A SERIES

| England | in England | 732 (av 81.33) D.I.Gower | 1985 |
|---|---|---|---|
| | in Australia | 905 (av 113.12) W.R.Hammond | 1928-29 |
| Australia | in England | 974 (av 139.14) D.G.Bradman | 1930 |
| | in Australia | 810 (av 90.00) D.G.Bradman | 1936-37 |

## RECORD WICKET PARTNERSHIPS – ENGLAND

| 1st | 323 | J.B.Hobbs (178), W.Rhodes (179) | Melbourne | 1911-12 |
|---|---|---|---|---|
| 2nd | 382 | L.Hutton (364), M.Leyland (187) | The Oval | 1938 |
| 3rd | 262 | W.R.Hammond (177), D.R.Jardine (98) | Adelaide | 1928-29 |
| 4th | 222 | W.R.Hammond (240), E.Paynter (99) | Lord's | 1938 |
| 5th | 206 | E.Paynter (216*), D.C.S.Compton (102) | Nottingham | 1938 |
| 6th | 215 | L.Hutton (364), J.Hardstaff, jr (169*) | The Oval | 1938 |
| | 215 | G.Boycott (107), A.P.E.Knott (135) | Nottingham | 1977 |
| 7th | 143 | F.E.Woolley (133*), J.Vine (36) | Sydney | 1911-12 |
| 8th | 124 | E.H.Hendren (169), H.Larwood (70) | Brisbane | 1928-29 |
| 9th | 151 | W.H.Scotton (90), W.W.Read (117) | The Oval | 1884 |
| 10th | 130 | R.E.Foster (287), W.Rhodes (40*) | Sydney | 1903-04 |

## RECORD WICKET PARTNERSHIPS – AUSTRALIA

| 1st | 329 | G.R.Marsh (138), M.A.Taylor (219) | Nottingham | 1989 |
|---|---|---|---|---|
| 2nd | 451 | W.H.Ponsford (266), D.G.Bradman (244) | The Oval | 1934 |
| 3rd | 276 | D.G.Bradman (187), A.L.Hassett (128) | Brisbane | 1946-47 |
| 4th | 388 | W.H.Ponsford (181), D.G.Bradman (304) | Leeds | 1934 |
| 5th | 405 | S.G.Barnes (234), D.G.Bradman (234) | Sydney | 1946-47 |
| 6th | 346 | J.H.W.Fingleton (136), D.G.Bradman (270) | Melbourne | 1936-37 |
| 7th | 165 | C.Hill (188), H.Trumble (46) | Melbourne | 1897-98 |
| 8th | 243 | R.J.Hartigan (113), C.Hill (160) | Adelaide | 1907-08 |
| 9th | 154 | S.E.Gregory (201), J.M.Blackham (74) | Sydney | 1894-95 |
| 10th | 127 | J.M.Taylor (108), A.A.Mailey (46*) | Sydney | 1924-25 |

## BEST INNINGS BOWLING ANALYSIS

| England | in England | 10-53 | J.C.Laker | Manchester | 1956 |
|---|---|---|---|---|---|
| | in Australia | 8-35 | G.A.Lohmann | Sydney | 1886-87 |
| Australia | in England | 8-31 | F.Laver | Manchester | 1909 |
| | in Australia | 9-121 | A.A.Mailey | Melbourne | 1920-21 |

## BEST MATCH BOWLING ANALYSIS

| England | in England | 19-90 | J.C.Laker | Manchester | 1956 |
|---|---|---|---|---|---|
| | in Australia | 15-124 | W.Rhodes | Melbourne | 1903-04 |
| Australia | in England | 16-137 | R.A.L.Massie | Lord's | 1972 |
| | in Australia | 13-77 | M.A.Noble | Melbourne | 1901-02 |

## HAT-TRICKS

| England | W.Bates | Melbourne | 1882-83 |
|---|---|---|---|
| | J.Briggs | Sydney | 1891-92 |
| | J.T.Hearne | Leeds | 1899 |
| Australia | F.R.Spofforth | Melbourne | 1878-79 |
| | H.Trumble | Melbourne | 1901-02 |
| | H.Trumble | Melbourne | 1903-04 |

## HIGHEST AGGREGATE OF WICKETS IN A SERIES

| England | in England | 46 (av 9.60) | J.C.Laker | | 1956 |
|---|---|---|---|---|---|
| | in Australia | 38 (av 23.18) | M.W.Tate | | 1924-25 |
| Australia | in England | 42 (av 21.26) | T.M.Alderman | | 1981 |
| | in Australia | 41 (av 12.85) | R.M.Hogg | | 1978-79 |

## MOST RUNS

| | Tests | I | NO | HS | Runs | Avge |
|---|---|---|---|---|---|---|
| D.G.Bradman (A) | 37 | 63 | 7 | 334 | 5028 | 89.78 |
| J.B.Hobbs (E) | 41 | 71 | 4 | 187 | 3636 | 54.26 |
| D.I.Gower (E) | 42 | 77 | 4 | 215 | 3269 | 44.78 |
| A.R.Border (A) | 41 | 73 | 18 | 196 | 3115 | 56.63 |
| G.Boycott (E) | 38 | 71 | 9 | 191 | 2945 | 47.50 |
| W.R.Hammond (E) | 33 | 58 | 3 | 251 | 2852 | 51.85 |
| H.Sutcliffe (E) | 27 | 46 | 5 | 194 | 2741 | 66.85 |
| C.Hill (A) | 41 | 76 | 1 | 188 | 2660 | 35.46 |
| J.H.Edrich (E) | 32 | 57 | 3 | 175 | 2644 | 48.96 |
| G.S.Chappell (A) | 35 | 65 | 8 | 144 | 2619 | 45.94 |
| M.C.Cowdrey (E) | 43 | 75 | 4 | 113 | 2433 | 34.26 |
| L.Hutton (E) | 27 | 49 | 6 | 364 | 2428 | 56.46 |
| R.N.Harvey (A) | 37 | 68 | 5 | 167 | 2416 | 38.34 |
| V.T.Trumper (A) | 40 | 74 | 5 | 185* | 2263 | 32.79 |
| W.M.Lawry (A) | 29 | 51 | 5 | 166 | 2233 | 48.54 |
| S.E.Gregory (A) | 52 | 92 | 7 | 201 | 2193 | 25.80 |
| W.W.Armstrong (A) | 42 | 71 | 9 | 158 | 2172 | 35.03 |
| I.M.Chappell (A) | 30 | 56 | 4 | 192 | 2138 | 41.11 |
| K.F.Barrington (E) | 23 | 39 | 6 | 256 | 2111 | 63.96 |
| A.R.Morris (A) | 24 | 43 | 2 | 206 | 2080 | 50.73 |

D.G.Bradman holds the unique record of scoring 2000 runs in both countries in this series (2674 runs in England and 2354 in Australia). J.B.Hobbs is the only other batsman to score 2000 runs in either country (2493 runs in Australia).

## MOST WICKETS

| | Tests | Balls | Runs | Wkts | BB | 5wI | Avge |
|---|---|---|---|---|---|---|---|
| D.K.Lillee (A) | 29 | 8516 | 3507 | 167 | 7-89 | 11 | 21.00 |
| I.T.Botham (E) | 36 | 8479 | 4093 | 148 | 6-78 | 9 | 27.65 |
| H.Trumble (A) | 31 | 7895 | 2945 | 141 | 8-65 | 9 | 20.88 |
| R.G.D.Willis (E) | 35 | 7294 | 3346 | 128 | 8-43 | 7 | 26.14 |
| M.A.Noble (A) | 39 | 6845 | 2860 | 115 | 7-17 | 9 | 24.86 |
| R.R.Lindwall (A) | 29 | 6728 | 2559 | 114 | 7-63 | 6 | 22.44 |
| W.Rhodes (E) | 41 | 5791 | 2616 | 109 | 8-68 | 6 | 24.00 |
| S.F.Barnes (E) | 20 | 5749 | 2288 | 106 | 7-60 | 12 | 21.58 |
| C.V.Grimmett (A) | 22 | 9224 | 3439 | 106 | 6-37 | 11 | 32.44 |
| D.L.Underwood (E) | 29 | 8000 | 2770 | 105 | 7-50 | 4 | 26.38 |
| A.V.Bedser (E) | 21 | 7065 | 2859 | 104 | 7-44 | 7 | 27.49 |
| G.Giffen (A) | 31 | 6457 | 2791 | 103 | 7-117 | 7 | 27.09 |
| W.J.O'Reilly (A) | 19 | 7864 | 2587 | 102 | 7-54 | 8 | 25.36 |
| R.Peel (E) | 20 | 5216 | 1715 | 101 | 7-31 | 5 | 16.98 |
| C.T.B.Turner (A) | 17 | 5195 | 1670 | 101 | 7-43 | 11 | 16.53 |
| T.M.Alderman (A) | 17 | 4717 | 2117 | 100 | 6-47 | 11 | 21.17 |
| J.R.Thomson (A) | 21 | 4951 | 2418 | 100 | 6-46 | 5 | 24.18 |

## MOST WICKET-KEEPING DISMISSALS

| | Tests | Ct | St | Total |
|---|---|---|---|---|
| R.W.Marsh (A) | 42 | 141 | 7 | 148 |
| A.P.E.Knott (E) | 34 | 97 | 8 | 105 |
| W.A.S.Oldfield (A) | 38 | 59 | 31 | 90 |
| A.F.A.Lilley (E) | 32 | 65 | 19 | 84 |
| A.T.W.Grout (A) | 22 | 69 | 7 | 76 |
| T.G.Evans (E) | 31 | 63 | 12 | 75 |

# YOUNG CRICKETER OF THE YEAR

This annual award, made by The Cricket Writers' Club (founded in 1946), is currently restricted to England-qualified cricketers under the age of 23 on 1st April. In 1986 their ballot resulted in a dead heat. Only five of their selections have ended their first-class careers without playing Test cricket.

| | | | |
|---|---|---|---|
| 1950 | R.Tattersall | 1972 | D.R.Owen-Thomas |
| 1951 | P.B.H.May | 1973 | M.Hendrick |
| 1952 | F.S.Trueman | 1974 | P.H.Edmonds |
| 1953 | M.C.Cowdrey | 1975 | A.Kennedy |
| 1954 | P.J.Loader | 1976 | G.Miller |
| 1955 | K.F.Barrington | 1977 | I.T.Botham |
| 1956 | B.Taylor | 1978 | D.I.Gower |
| 1957 | M.J.Stewart | 1979 | P.W.G.Parker |
| 1958 | A.C.D.Ingleby-Mackenzie | 1980 | G.R.Dilley |
| 1959 | G.Pullar | 1981 | M.W.Gatting |
| 1960 | D.A.Allen | 1982 | N.G.Cowans |
| 1961 | P.H.Parfitt | 1983 | N.A.Foster |
| 1962 | P.J.Sharpe | 1984 | R.J.Bailey |
| 1963 | G.Boycott | 1985 | D.V.Lawrence |
| 1964 | J.M.Brearley | 1986 { | A.A.Metcalfe |
| 1965 | A.P.E.Knott | | J.J.Whitaker |
| 1966 | D.L.Underwood | 1987 | R.J.Blakey |
| 1967 | A.W.Greig | 1988 | M.P.Maynard |
| 1968 | R.M.H.Cottam | 1989 | N.Hussain |
| 1969 | A.Ward | 1990 | M.A.Atherton |
| 1970 | C.M.Old | 1991 | M.R.Ramprakash |
| 1971 | J.Whitehouse | 1992 | I.D.K.Salisbury |

# FIRST-CLASS UMPIRES 1993

**BALDERSTONE**, John **Christopher** (Paddock Council S, Huddersfield), b Longwood, Huddersfield, Yorks 16 Nov 1940. RHB, SLA. Yorkshire 1961-69. Leicestershire 1971-86 (cap 1973; testimonial 1984). **Tests:** 2 (1976); HS 35 v WI (Leeds) 1976; BB 1-80. Tour: Z 1980-81 (Le). 1000 runs (11); most – 1482 (1982). Hattrick 1976. HS 181* Le v Glos (Leicester) 1984. BB 6-25 Le v Hants (Southampton) 1978. F-c career: 390 matches; 19034 runs @ 34.11, 32 hundreds; 310 wickets @ 26.32; 210 ct. Soccer for Huddersfield Town, Carlisle United, Doncaster Rovers and Queen of the South. Appointed 1988.

**\*BIRD**, Harold Dennis (**'Dickie'**) (Raley SM, Barnsley), b Barnsley, Yorks 19 Apr 1933. RHB, RM. Yorkshire 1956-59. Leicestershire 1960-64 (cap 1960). MBE 1986. 1000 runs (1): 1028 (1960). HS 181* Y v Glam (Bradford) 1959. F-c career: 93 matches; 3314 runs @ 20.71, 2 hundreds. Appointed 1970. Umpired 47 Tests (1973 to 1992) and passed F.Chester's record (48) in Zimbabwe 1992-93. Officiated in 62 LOI (1973 to 1992), including 1975, 1979, 1983 and 1987-88 World Cup Finals, 1985-86 Asia Cup and 6 Sharjah tournaments.

**BOND**, John David (**'Jack'**) (Bolton S), b Kearsley, Lancs 6 May 1932. RHB, LB. Lancashire 1955-72 (cap 1955; captain 1968-72; coach 1973; manager 1980-86; benefit 1970). Nottinghamshire 1974 (captain/coach 1974). 1000 runs (2); most – 2125 (1963). HS 157 La v Hants (Manchester) 1962. Test selector 1988. F-c career: 362 matches; 12125 runs @ 25.90, 14 hundreds; 222 ct. Appointed 1988.

**BURGESS**, **Graham** Iefvion (Millfield S), b Glastonbury, Somerset 5 May 1943. RHB, RM. Somerset 1966-79 (cap 1968; testimonial 1977). HS 129 v Glos (Taunton) 1973. BB 7-43 (13-75 match) v OU (Oxford) 1975. F-c career: 252 matches; 7129 runs @ 18.90, 2 hundreds; 474 wickets @ 28.57. Appointed 1991.

**CONSTANT**, **David** John, b Bradford-on-Avon, Wilts 9 Nov 1941. LHB, SLA. Kent 1961-63. Leicestershire 1965-68. HS 80 Le v Glos (Bristol) 1966. F-c career: 61 matches; 1517 runs @ 19.20; 1 wicket @ 36.00. Appointed 1969. Umpired 36 Tests (1971 to 1988) and 29 LOI (1972 to 1990). Represented Gloucestershire at bowls 1984-86.

**DUDLESTON**, **Barry** (Stockport S), b Bebington, Cheshire 16 Jul 1945. RHB, SLA. Leicestershire 1966-80 (cap 1969; benefit 1980). Gloucestershire 1981-83. Rhodesia 1976-80. 1000 runs (8); most –1374 (1970). HS 202 Le v Derbys (Leicester) 1979. BB 4-6 Le v Surrey (Leicester) 1972. F-c career: 295 matches; 14747 runs @ 32.48, 32 hundreds; 47 wickets @ 29.04. Appointed 1984. Umpired 2 Tests (1991 to 1992) and 1 LOI (1992).

**\*HAMPSHIRE**, **John** Harry (Oakwood THS, Rotherham), b Thurnscoe, Yorks 10 Feb 1941. RHB, LB. Son of J. (Yorks 1937); brother of A.W. (Yorks 1975). Yorkshire 1961-81 (cap 1963; benefit 1976; captain 1979-80). Derbyshire 1982-84 (cap 1982). Tasmania 1967-69, 1977-79. **Tests:** 8 (1969 to 1975); 403 runs @ 26.86, HS 107 v WI (Lord's) 1969 on debut (only England player to score hundred at Lord's on debut in Tests). Tours: Aus 1970-71; SA 1972-73 (DHR), 1974-75 (DHR); WI 1964-65 (Cav); NZ 1970-71; Pak 1967-68 (Cwlth XI); SL 1969-70; Z 1980-81 (Le XI). 1000 runs (15); most – 1596 (1978). HS 183* Y v Sussex (Hove) 1971. BB 7-52 Y v Glam (Cardiff) 1963. F-c career: 577 matches; 28059 runs @ 34.55, 43 hundreds; 30 wickets @ 54.56; 445 ct. Appointed 1985. Umpired 10 Tests (1989 to 1992), including 4 in Pakistan 1989-90, and 5 LOI (1989 to 1992).

**HARRIS**, **John** Henry, b Taunton, Somerset 13 Feb 1936. LHB, RFM. Somerset 1952-59. Suffolk 1960-62. Devon 1975. HS 41 v Worcs (Taunton) 1957. BB 3-29 v Worcs (Bristol) 1959. F-c career: 15 matches; 154 runs @ 11.00; 19 wickets @ 32.57. Appointed 1983.

**HOLDER, John** Wakefield (Combermere S, Barbados), b St George, Barbados 19 Mar 1945. RHB, RFM. Hampshire 1968-72. Hat-trick 1972. HS 33 v Sussex (Hove) 1971. BB 7-79 v Glos (Gloucester) 1972. F-c career: 47 matches; 374 runs @ 10.68; 139 wickets @ 24.56. Appointed 1983. Umpired 10 Tests (1988 to 1991), including 4 in Pakistan 1989-90, and 8 LOI (1988 to 1990) including 1989-90 Nehru Cup.

**HOLDER, Vanburn** Alonza (Richmond SM, Barbados), b Bridgetown, Barbados 8 Oct 1945. RHB, RFM. Barbados 1966-78. Worcestershire 1968-80 (cap 1970; benefit 1979). Shropshire 1981. **Tests** (WI): 40 (1969 to 1978-79); HS 42 v NZ (P-o-S) 1971-72; BB 6-28 v A (P-o-S) 1977-78. LOI: 12. Tests (WI): E 1969, 1973, 1976; A 1975-76; I 1974-75, 1978-79; P 1973-74 (RW), 1974-75; SL 1974-75, 1978-79. HS 122 Barbados v Trinidad (Bridgetown) 1973-74. Wo HS 52 v Glos (Dudley) 1970. BB 7-40 v Glam (Cardiff) 1974. F-c career: 311 matches; 3559 runs @ 13.03, 1 hundred; 947 wickets @ 24.48. Appointed 1992.

**JONES, Allan** Arthur (St John's C, Horsham), b Horley, Surrey 9 Dec 1947. RHB, RFM. Sussex 1966-69. Somerset 1970-75 (cap 1972). Northern Transvaal 1972-73. Middlesex 1976-79 (cap 1976). Orange Free State 1976-77. Glamorgan 1980-81. HS 33 M v Kent (Canterbury) 1978. BB 9-51 Sm v Sussex (Hove) 1972. F-c career: 214 matches; 799 runs @ 5.39; 549 wickets @ 28.07. Appointed 1985.

**JULIAN, Raymond** (Wigston SM), b Cosby, Leics 23 Aug 1936. RHB, WK. Leicestershire 1953-71 (cap 1961). HS 51 v Worcs (Worcester) 1962. F-c career: 192 matches; 2581 runs @ 9.73; 421 dismissals (382 ct, 39 st). Appointed 1972.

**\*KITCHEN, Mervyn** John (Backwell SM, Nailsea), b Nailsea, Somerset 1 Aug 1940. LHB, RM. Somerset 1960-79 (cap 1966; testimonial 1973). Tour: Rhodesia 1972-73 (Int W). 1000 runs (7); most – 1730 (1968). HS 189 v Pakistanis (Taunton) 1967. BB 1-4. F-c career: 354 matches; 15230 runs @ 26.25, 17 hundreds; 2 wickets @ 54.50. Appointed 1982. Umpired 5 Tests (1990 to 1992) and 9 LOI (1983 to 1992).

**LEADBEATER, Barrie** (Harehills SS), b Harehills, Leeds, Yorks 14 Aug 1943. RHB, RM. Yorkshire 1966-79 (cap 1969; joint benefit with G.A.Cope 1980). Tour: WI 1969-70 (DN). HS 140\* v Hants (Portsmouth) 1976. F-c career: 147 matches; 5373 runs @ 25.34, 1 hundred; 1 wicket @ 5.00. Appointed 1981. Umpired 4 LOI (1983).

**\*MEYER, Barrie** John (Boscombe SS), b Bournemouth, Hants 21 Aug 1932. RHB, WK. Gloucestershire 1957-71 (cap 1958; benefit 1971). HS 63 v Indians (Cheltenham) 1959, v OU (Bristol) 1962, and v Sussex (Bristol) 1964. F-c career: 406 matches; 5367 runs @ 14.16; 826 dismissals (707 ct, 119 st). Soccer for Bristol Rovers, Plymouth Argyle, Newport County and Bristol City. Appointed 1973. Umpired 24 Tests (1978 to 1992) and 22 LOI (1977 to 1992), including 1979 and 1983 World Cup Finals.

**OSLEAR, Donald** Osmund, b Cleethorpes, Lincs 3 Mar 1929. No first-class appearances. Appointed 1975. Umpired 5 Tests (1980 to 1984) and 8 LOI (1980 to 1984).

**\*PALMER, Kenneth** Ernest (Southbroom SM, Devizes), b Winchester, Hants 22 Apr 1937. RHB, RFM. Brother of R. (below) and father of G.V. (Somerset 1982-88). Somerset 1955-69 (cap 1958; testimonial 1968). Tours: WI 1963-64 (Cav); P 1963-64 (Cwlth XI). **Tests:** 1 (1964-65; while coaching in South Africa); 10 runs; 1 wicket. 1000 runs (1): 1036 (1961). 100 wickets (4); most – 139 (1963). HS 125\* v Northants (Northampton) 1961. BB 9-57 v Notts (Nottingham) 1963. F-c career: 314 matches; 7761 runs @ 20.64, 2 hundreds; 866 wickets @ 21.34. Appointed 1972. Umpired 20 Tests (1978 to 1992) and 17 LOI (1977 to 1992).

**\*PALMER, Roy** (Southbroom SM), b Devizes, Wilts 12 Jul 1942. RHB, RFM. Brother of K.E. (above). Somerset 1965-70. HS 84 v Leics (Taunton) 1967. BB 6-45 v Middx (Lord's) 1967. F-c career: 74 matches; 1037 runs @ 13.29; 172 wickets @ 31.62. Appointed 1980. Umpired 1 Test (1992) and 5 LOI (1983 and 1992).

**\*PLEWS, Nigel** Trevor, b Nottingham 5 Sep 1934. Former policeman (Fraud Squad). No first-class appearances. Appointed 1982. Umpired 5 Tests (1988 to 1990) and 4 LOI (1986 to 1990).

**SHARP, George** (Elwick Road SS, Hartlepool), b West Hartlepool, Co Durham 12 Mar 1950. RHB, WK, occ LM. Northamptonshire 1968-85 (cap 1973; benefit 1982). HS 98 v Yorks (Northampton) 1983. BB 1-47. F-c career: 306 matches; 6254 runs @ 19.85; 1 wicket @ 70.00; 655 dismissals (565 ct, 90 st). Appointed 1992.

**\*SHEPHERD, David** Robert (Barnstaple GS; St Luke's C, Exeter), b Bideford, Devon 27 Dec 1940. RHB, RM. Gloucestershire 1965-79 (cap 1969; joint benefit with J.Davey 1978). Scored 108 on debut (v OU). Devon 1959-64. 1000 runs (2); most – 1079 (1970). HS 153 v Middlesex (Bristol) 1968. F-c career: 282 matches; 10672 runs @ 24.47, 12 hundreds; 2 wickets @ 53.00. Appointed 1981. Umpired 15 Tests (1985 to 1992) and 50 LOI (1983 to 1992), including 1987-88 and 1991-92 World Cups, 1985-86 Asia Cup and 4 Sharjah tournaments.

**STICKLEY, Gerald** Albert (Holly Lodge GS, Smethwick), b St Chad's Hospital, Birmingham 24 Sep 1938. No first-class appearances. Appointed 1992.

**WHITE, Robert** Arthur (Chiswick GS), b Fulham, London 6 Oct 1936. LHB, OB. Middlesex 1958-65 (cap 1963). Nottinghamshire 1966-80 (cap 1966; benefit 1974). 1000 runs (1): 1355 (1963). HS 116* Nt v Surrey (Oval) 1967. BB 7-41 Nt v Derbys (Ilkeston) 1971. F-c career: 413 matches; 12452 runs @ 23.18, 5 hundreds; 693 wickets @ 30.50. Appointed 1983.

**WHITEHEAD, Alan** Geoffrey Thomas, b Butleigh, Somerset 28 Oct 1940. LHB, SLA. Somerset 1957-61. HS 15 v Hants (Southampton) 1959 and v Leics (Leicester) 1960. BB 6-74 v Sussex (Eastbourne) 1959. F-c career: 38 matches; 137 runs @ 5.70; 67 wickets @ 34.41. Appointed 1970. Umpired 7 Tests (1982 to 1987) and 12 LOI (1979 to 1987).

**WIGHT, Peter** Bernard, b Georgetown, British Guiana 25 Jun 1930. RHB, OB. Brother of G.L. (West Indies 1949-53), H.A. and N. (all British Guiana). British Guiana 1950-51. Somerset 1953-65 (cap 1954; benefit 1963). Canterbury 1963-64. 1000 runs (10); most – 2375 (1960). HS 222* v Kent (Taunton) 1959. BB 6-29 v Derbys (Chesterfield) 1957. F-c career: 333 matches; 17773 runs @ 33.09, 28 hundreds; 68 wickets @ 33.26. Appointed 1966.

**WILLEY, Peter** (Seaham SS), b Sedgefield, Co Durham 6 Dec 1949. RHB, OB. Northamptonshire 1966-83 (cap 1971; benefit 1981). Leicestershire 1984-91 (cap 1984; captain 1987). E Province 1982-85. **Tests:** 26 (1976 to 1986); 1184 runs @ 26.90, HS 102* v WI (St John's) 1980-81; 7 wkts @ 65.14, BB 2-73 v WI (Lord's) 1980. LOI: 26. Tours: A 1979-80; SA 1972-73 (DHR), 1981-82 (SAB); WI 1980-81, 1985-86; I 1979-80; SL 1977-78 (DHR). 1000 runs (10); most – 1783 (1982). HS 227 Nh v Somerset (Northampton) 1976 sharing record Northants 4th wkt stand of 370 with R.T.Virgin. 50 wkts (3); most – 52 (1979). BB 7-37 Nh v OU (Oxford) 1975. F-c career: 559 matches; 24361 runs @ 30.56, 44 hundreds; 756 wickets @ 30.95. Appointed 1993.

## RESERVE LIST

P.ADAMS, A.CLARKSON, M.J.HARRIS, T.E.JESTY, M.K.REED.

\* On Test Match and Texaco Trophy Panel for 1993.

See page 64 for key to abbreviations.

# PRINCIPAL FIXTURES 1993

* *Includes Sunday play*

† *Reserve day Sunday*

### Wednesday 14 April

Fenner's: Cambridge U v Derbys
The Parks: Oxford U v Durham

### Saturday 17 April

*Fenner's: Cambridge U v Yorks
The Parks: Oxford U v Lancs

### Tuesday 20 April

The Oval: Rapid Cricketline
  Champions (Surrey 2nd XI) v
  England Under-19 (Four days)

### Wednesday 21 April

Fenner's: Cambridge U v Kent
The Parks: Oxford U v Glam
*Tetley Bitter Shield*
*Chelmsford: Britannic Assurance
  Champions (Essex) v England 'A'
  (Four days)

### Saturday 24 April

Fenner's: Combined Us v Middx
  (One day)

### Sunday 25 April

Fenner's: Combined Us v Northants
  (One day)

### Tuesday 27 April

*Benson and Hedges Cup*
Preliminary Round
Hartlepool: Durham v Minor Cos
Bristol: Glos v Derbys
Southampton: Hants v Combined Us
Canterbury: Kent v Glam
Forfar: Scotland v Essex

### Thursday 29 April

*Britannic Assurance Championship*
*Cardiff: Glam v Sussex
*Bristol: Glos v Middx
*Southampton: Hants v Somerset
*Leicester: Leics v Surrey
*Trent Bridge: Notts v Worcs
*Edgbaston: Warwicks v Northants

*Other Match*
Headingley: Yorks v Lancs (Four days)

### Friday 30 April

*Tourist Match*
Radlett: England Amateur XI v
  Australians (One day)

### Saturday 1 May

*Fenner's: Cambridge U v Essex

### Sunday 2 May

*Tourist Match*
Arundel: Lavinia, Duchess of Norfolk's
  XI v Australians (One day)

### Monday 3 May

*Tourist Match*
Lord's: Middx v Australians (One day)

### Wednesday 5 May

*Tetley Bitter Challenge*
Worcester: Worcs v Australians
*Other Matches*
Fenner's: Cambridge U v Glam
The Parks: Oxford U v Hants

### Thursday 6 May

*Britannic Assurance Championship*
Chelmsford: Essex v Yorks
Old Trafford: Lancs v Durham
Leicester: Leics v Notts
Lord's: Middx v Kent
Northampton: Northants v Glos
Hove: Sussex v Surrey
Edgbaston: Warwicks v Derbys

### Saturday 8 May

*Tetley Bitter Challenge*
*Taunton: Somerset v Australians

### Sunday 9 May

*AXA Equity & Law League*
Chelmsford: Essex v Yorks
Old Trafford: Lancs v Durham
Leicester: Leics v Notts

Lord's: Middx v Kent
Northampton: Northants v Glos
Hove: Sussex v Surrey
Edgbaston: Warwicks v Derbys

## Tuesday 11 May

*Benson and Hedges Cup*
First Round
Stockton or Jesmond: Durham or
  Minor Cos v Hants or Combined Us
Bristol or Derby: Glos or Derbys v
  Middx
Canterbury or Cardiff: Kent or Glam v
  Sussex
Leicester: Leics v Warwicks
Trent Bridge: Notts v Somerset
The Oval: Surrey v Lancs
Worcester: Worcs v Scotland or Essex
Headingley: Yorks v Northants

## Thursday 13 May

*Britannic Assurance Championship*
Derby: Derbys v Glam
Stockton: Durham v Hants
Canterbury: Kent v Warwicks
Lord's: Middx v Notts
Taunton: Somerset v Lancs
The Oval: Surrey v Essex
Bradford: Yorks v Worcs
*Tetley Bitter Challenge*
*Hove: Sussex v Australians

## Saturday 15 May

*Fenner's: Cambridge U v Leics
The Parks: Oxford U v Northants

## Sunday 16 May

*AXA Equity & Law League*
Derby: Derbys v Glam
Stockton: Durham v Hants
Canterbury: Kent v Warwicks
Lord's: Middx v Notts
Taunton: Somerset v Lancs
The Oval: Surrey v Essex
Headingley: Yorks v Worcs
*Tourist Match*
Northampton: Northants v Australians
  (One day)

## Wednesday 19 May

TEXACO TROPHY
Old Trafford: ENGLAND v

AUSTRALIA
(First One-day International)
*Other Matches*
Fenner's: Cambridge U v Lancs
The Parks: Oxford U v Middx

## Thursday 20 May

*Britannic Assurance Championship*
Chelmsford: Essex v Derbys
Swansea: Glam v Northants
Bristol: Glos v Durham
Southampton: Hants v Yorks
Trent Bridge: Notts v Kent
Horsham: Sussex v Leics
Worcester: Worcs v Somerset

## Friday 21 May

TEXACO TROPHY
Edgbaston: ENGLAND v AUSTRALIA
(Second One-day International)

## Sunday 23 May

TEXACO TROPHY
Lord's: ENGLAND v AUSTRALIA
(Third One-day International)
*AXA Equity & Law League*
Chelmsford: Essex v Derbys
Pentrych: Glam v Northants
Bristol: Glos v Durham
Southampton: Hants v Yorks
Trent Bridge: Notts v Kent
Horsham: Sussex v Leics
Worcester: Worcs v Somerset

## Tuesday 25 May

*Benson and Hedges Cup*
Quarter-Finals
*Tetley Bitter Challenge*
‡The Oval or Headingley: Surrey or
  Yorks v Australians

‡Either Northants or Notts to play
Australia if both Surrey and Yorks are
involved in B&H Quarter-Finals.

## Thursday 27 May

*Britannic Assurance Championship*
Derby: Derbys v Hants
Darlington: Durham v Kent
tba: Glos v Worcs

Liverpool: Lancs v Warwicks
Lord's: Middx v Sussex
Taunton: Somerset v Glam

## Saturday 29 May

*Tetley Bitter Challenge*
*Leicester: Leics v Australians
*Other Match*
The Parks: Oxford U v Notts

## Sunday 30 May

*AXA Equity & Law League*
Checkley: Derbys v Hants
Darlington: Durham v Kent
tba: Glos v Worcs
Old Trafford: Lancs v Warwicks
Lord's: Middx v Sussex
Taunton: Somerset v Glam

## Thursday 3 June

FIRST CORNHILL INSURANCE
TEST MATCH
*Old Trafford: ENGLAND v AUSTRALIA
*Britannic Assurance Championship*
Chelmsford: Essex v Somerset
Tunbridge Wells: Kent v Glos
Leicester: Leics v Durham
Lord's: Middx v Derbys
Northampton: Northants v Worcs
Trent Bridge: Notts v Hants
The Oval: Surrey v Lancs
Edgbaston: Warwicks v Sussex
Middlesbrough: Yorks v Glam

## Sunday 6 June

*AXA Equity & Law League*
Chelmsford: Essex v Somerset
Tunbridge Wells: Kent v Glos
Leicester: Leics v Durham
Lord's: Middx v Derbys
Northampton: Northants v Worcs
Trent Bridge: Notts v Hants
The Oval: Surrey v Lancs
Edgbaston: Warwicks v Sussex
Middlesbrough: Yorks v Glam

## Tuesday 8 June

*Benson and Hedges Cup*
Semi-Finals

## Wednesday 9 June

*Tetley Bitter Challenge*
‡Edgbaston or Trent Bridge: Warwicks
or Notts v Australians

‡Somerset to play Australia if both
Warwicks and Notts are involved in
B&H Semi-Finals.

## Thursday 10 June

*Britannic Assurance Championship*
Chesterfield: Derbys v Yorks
Gateshead Fell: Durham v Middx
Basingstoke: Hants v Kent
Old Trafford: Lancs v Essex
The Oval: Surrey v Glam
Hove: Sussex v Northants
Worcester: Worcs v Leics

## Saturday 12 June

*Tetley Bitter Challenge*
*Bristol: Glos v Australians
*Other Matches*
*Fenner's: Cambridge U v Notts
The Parks: Oxford U v Warwicks
*Eglinton: Ireland v Scotland
(Three days)

## Sunday 13 June

*AXA Equity & Law League*
Chesterfield: Derbys v Yorks
Gateshead Fell: Durham v Middx
Basingstoke: Hants v Kent
Old Trafford: Lancs v Essex
The Oval: Surrey v Glam
Hove: Sussex v Northants
Worcester: Worcs v Leics

## Thursday 17 June

SECOND CORNHILL INSURANCE
TEST MATCH
*Lord's: ENGLAND v AUSTRALIA
*Britannic Assurance Championship*
Colwyn Bay: Glam v Durham
Canterbury: Kent v Derbys
Old Trafford: Lancs v Sussex
Northampton: Northants v Hants
Trent Bridge: Notts v Essex
Bath: Somerset v Middx
Edgbaston: Warwicks v Surrey
Sheffield: Yorks v Glos

**Friday 18 June**

*Worcester: Worcs v Oxford U

**Sunday 20 June**

*AXA Equity & Law League*
Colwyn Bay: Glam v Durham
Canterbury: Kent v Derbys
Old Trafford: Lancs v Sussex
Northampton: Northants v Hants
Trent Bridge: Notts v Essex
Bath: Somerset v Middx
Edgbaston: Warwicks v Surrey
Sheffield: Yorks v Glos

**Tuesday 22 June**

*NatWest Trophy*
First Round
Marlow: Bucks v Leics
Warrington: Cheshire v Notts
Exmouth: Devon v Derbys
Swansea: Glam v Oxon
Bristol: Glos v Herts
Canterbury: Kent v Middx
Lakenham: Norfolk v Warwicks
Northampton: Northants v Lancs
Edinburgh (Myreside): Scotland v
  Worcs
Telford (St Georges): Shrops v
  Somerset
Stone: Staffs v Hants
Bury St Edmunds: Suffolk v Essex
The Oval: Surrey v Dorset
Hove: Sussex v Minor Cos Wales
Trowbridge: Wilts v Durham
Headingley: Yorks v Ireland

**Wednesday 23 June**

*Tourist Match*
The Parks: Combined Us v Australians
  (Three days)

**Thursday 24 June**

*Britannic Assurance Championship*
Derby: Derbys v Lancs
Stockton: Durham v Worcs
Ilford: Essex v Warwicks
Swansea: Glam v Notts
Leicester: Leics v Glos
Lord's: Middx v Surrey
Luton: Northants v Somerset
Headingley: Yorks v Kent

**Saturday 26 June**

*Tetley Bitter Challenge*
*Southampton: Hants v Australians
*Other Match*
*Hove: Sussex v Cambridge U

**Sunday 27 June**

*AXA Equity & Law League*
Derby: Derbys v Lancs
Stockton: Durham v Worcs
Ilford: Essex v Warwicks
Swansea: Glam v Notts
Leicester: Leics v Glos
Lord's: Middx v Surrey
Luton: Northants v Somerset
Headingley: Yorks v Kent

**Wednesday 30 June**

*Varsity Match*
Lord's: Oxford U v Cambridge U

**Thursday 1 July**

**THIRD CORNHILL INSURANCE
TEST MATCH**
Trent Bridge: ENGLAND v AUSTRALIA
*Britannic Assurance Championship*
Cardiff: Glam v Middx
Bristol: Glos v Hants
Maidstone: Kent v Essex
Leicester: Leics v Lancs
Northampton: Northants v Notts
Taunton: Somerset v Sussex
The Oval: Surrey v Durham
Edgbaston: Warwicks v Yorks
Kidderminster: Worcs v Derbys

**Sunday 4 July**

*AXA Equity & Law League*
Cardiff: Glam v Middx
Bristol: Glos v Hants
Maidstone: Kent v Essex
Leicester: Leics v Lancs
Northampton: Northants v Notts
Taunton: Somerset v Sussex
The Oval: Surrey v Durham
Edgbaston: Warwicks v Yorks
Worcester: Worcs v Derbys

**Wednesday 7 July**

*NatWest Trophy*
Second Round
Marlow or Leicester: Bucks or Leics v
  Surrey or Dorset

Warrington or Trent Bridge: Cheshire
or Notts v Shrops or Somerset
Cardiff or Oxford (Christ Church):
Glam or Oxon v Wilts or Durham
Bristol or Hitchin: Glos or Herts v
Yorks or Ireland
Lakenham or Edgbaston: Norfolk or
Warwicks v Kent or Middx
Glasgow (Titwood) or Worcester:
Scotland or Worcs v Devon or
Derbys
Bury St Edmunds or Chelmsford:
Suffolk or Essex v Northants or Lancs
Hove or Colwyn Bay: Sussex or Minor
Cos Wales v Staffs or Hants

## Thursday 8 July

*Tourist Match*
Stone: Minor Cos v Australians
(One day)

## Saturday 10 July

Lord's: *#Benson & Hedges Cup Final*
*Tourist Match*
Dublin (Clontarf): Ireland v
Australians (One day)

#Reserve days Sunday and Monday.

## Sunday 11 July

‡*AXA Equity & Law League*
Llanelli: Glam v Sussex
Moreton-in-Marsh: Glos v Middx
Southampton: Hants v Somerset
Leicester: Leics v Surrey
Trent Bridge: Notts v Worcs
Edgbaston: Warwicks v Northants

‡Matches involving B&H Cup Finalists
to be played on Tuesday 13 July.

## Monday 12 July

Harrogate: Tilcon Trophy (Three days)

## Tuesday 13 July

*Tetley Bitter Challenge*
Derby: Derbys v Australians
*Other Match*
Jesmond: England XI v Rest of the
World XI (One day)

## Wednesday 14 July

Jesmond: England XI v Rest of the
World XI (One day)
*Seeboard Trophy*
Canterbury: Kent v Surrey (One day)

## Thursday 15 July

*Britannic Assurance Championship*
Southend: Essex v Leics
Portsmouth: Hants v Worcs
Old Trafford: Lancs v Glam
Trent Bridge: Notts v Somerset
Guildford: Surrey v Glos
Arundel: Sussex v Kent
Edgbaston: Warwicks v Middx
Harrogate: Yorks v Northants

## Saturday 17 July

*Tetley Bitter Challenge*
*Durham University: Durham v
Australians

## Sunday 18 July

*AXA Equity & Law League*
Southend: Essex v Leics
Portsmouth: Hants v Worcs
Old Trafford: Lancs v Glam
Trent Bridge: Notts v Somerset
Guildford: Surrey v Glos
Hove: Sussex v Kent
Edgbaston: Warwicks v Middx
Headingley: Yorks v Northants

## Thursday 22 July

**FOURTH CORNHILL INSURANCE
TEST MATCH**
*Headingley: ENGLAND v AUSTRALIA
*Britannic Assurance Championship*
Derby: Derbys v Sussex
Chelmsford: Essex v Durham
Old Trafford: Lancs v Notts
Leicester: Leics v Warwicks
Lord's: Middx v Hants
Northampton: Northants v Surrey
Taunton: Somerset v Kent
Worcester: Worcs v Glam

## Sunday 25 July

*AXA Equity & Law League*
Derby: Derbys v Sussex

Chelmsford: Essex v Durham
Old Trafford: Lancs v Notts
Leicester: Leics v Warwicks
Lord's: Middx v Hants
Northampton: Northants v Surrey
Taunton: Somerset v Kent
Worcester: Worcs v Glam

## Tuesday 27 July

*NatWest Trophy*
Quarter-Finals

## Wednesday 28 July

*Tetley Bitter Challenge*
‡Northampton or Old Trafford:
    Northants or Lancs v Australians

‡Depends on outcome of NatWest
    Trophy First Round.

## Thursday 29 July

*Britannic Assurance Championship*
Durham University: Durham v Sussex
Chelmsford: Essex v Worcs
Cheltenham: Glos v Derbys
Southampton: Hants v Warwicks
Canterbury: Kent v Leics
Taunton: Somerset v Yorks
The Oval: Surrey v Notts

## Saturday 31 July

*Tetley Bitter Challenge*
*Neath: Glam v Australians

## Sunday 1 August

*AXA Equity and Law League*
Durham University: Durham v Sussex
Chelmsford: Essex v Worcs
Cheltenham: Glos v Derbys
Southampton: Hants v Warwicks
Canterbury: Kent v Leics
Taunton: Somerset v Yorks
The Oval: Surrey v Notts
*Other Match*
Lord's: Women's World Cup Final
    (One day)

## Wednesday 4 August

*Seeboard Trophy*
Hove: Sussex v Kent or Surrey
    (One day)

## Thursday 5 August

### FIFTH CORNHILL INSURANCE TEST MATCH
*Edgbaston: ENGLAND v AUSTRALIA
*Britannic Assurance Championship*
Durham University: Durham v Derbys
Cardiff: Glam v Warwicks
Cheltenham: Glos v Lancs
Canterbury: Kent v Surrey
Lord's: Middx v Leics
Northampton: Northants v Essex
Trent Bridge: Notts v Yorks
Hove: Sussex v Worcs
*Other Match*
Leicester: England Under-19 v West
    Indies Under-19 (First Youth
    One-day International)

## Saturday 7 August

Chelmsford: England Under-19 v West
    Indies Under-19 (Second Youth
    One-day International)

## Sunday 8 August

*AXA Equity & Law League*
Durham University: Durham v Derbys
Neath: Glam v Warwicks
Cheltenham: Glos v Lancs
Canterbury: Kent v Surrey
Lord's: Middx v Leics
Northampton: Northants v Essex
Trent Bridge: Notts v Yorks
Hove: Sussex v Worcs

## Tuesday 10 August

*NatWest Trophy*
Semi-Finals

## Wednesday 11 August

*Tetley Bitter Challenge*
‡Canterbury: Kent v Australians

‡Will be played as a one-day game on
    Friday 13 August if Kent involved in
    NWT Semi-Finals.

## Thursday 12 August

*Britannic Assurance Championship*
Derby: Derbys v Somerset
Southampton: Hants v Lancs
Leicester: Leics v Glam

Northampton: Northants v Durham
Eastbourne: Sussex v Notts
Edgbaston: Warwicks v Glos
Worcester: Worcs v Surrey
Scarborough; Yorks v Middx
*Other Match*
*Trent Bridge: England Under-19 v
West Indies Under-19 (First Youth
Test Match) (Four days)

## Saturday 14 August

*Tetley Bitter Challenge*
*Chelmsford: Essex v Australians

## Sunday 15 August

*AXA Equity & Law League*
Derby: Derbys v Somerset
Southampton: Hants v Lancs
Leicester: Leics v Glam
Northampton: Northants v Durham
Eastbourne: Sussex v Notts
Edgbaston: Warwicks v Glos
Worcester: Worcs v Surrey
Scarborough: Yorks v Middx

## Monday 16 or Tuesday 17 August

*Bain Clarkson Trophy*
Semi-Finals (One day)

## Thursday 19 August

### SIXTH CORNHILL INSURANCE TEST MATCH
*The Oval: ENGLAND v AUSTRALIA
*Britannic Assurance Championship*
Ilkeston: Derbys v Surrey
Darlington: Durham v Warwicks
Swansea: Glam v Hants
Bristol: Glos v Essex
Old Trafford: Lancs v Yorks
Lord's: Middx v Northants
Weston-super-Mare: Somerset v Leics
Worcester: Worcs v Kent

## Sunday 22 August

*AXA Equity & Law League*
Ilkeston: Derbys v Surrey
Darlington: Durham v Warwicks
Swansea: Glam v Hants
Bristol: Glos v Essex
Old Trafford: Lancs v Yorks
Lord's: Middx v Northants

Weston-super-Mare: Somerset v Leics
Worcester: Worcs v Kent

## Thursday 26 August

*Britannic Assurance Championship*
Colchester: Essex v Middx
Abergavenny: Glam v Glos
Portsmouth: Hants v Sussex
Lytham: Lancs v Kent
Northampton: Northants v Leics
Trent Bridge: Notts v Derbys
The Oval: Surrey v Somerset
Edgbaston: Warwicks v Worcs
Headingley: Yorks v Durham
*Other Match*
*Hove: England Under-19 v West Indies
Under-19 (Second Youth Test
Match) (Four days)

## Sunday 29 August

*AXA Equity & Law League*
Colchester: Essex v Middx
Ebbw Vale: Glam v Glos
Portsmouth: Hants v Sussex
Old Trafford: Lancs v Kent
Northampton: Northants v Leics
Trent Bridge: Notts v Derbys
The Oval: Surrey v Somerset
Edgbaston: Warwicks v Worcs
Headingley: Yorks v Durham

## Tuesday 31 August

*Britannic Assurance Championship*
Chester-le-Street: Durham v Notts
Canterbury: Kent v Northants
Leicester: Leics v Yorks
Taunton: Somerset v Glos
The Oval: Surrey v Hants
Hove: Sussex v Essex
Worcester: Worcs v Lancs

## Saturday 4 September

Lord's: *NatWest Trophy Final*
(*Reserve days Sunday and Monday.*)

## Sunday 5 September

*AXA Equity & Law League*
Chester-le-Street: Durham v Notts

Canterbury: Kent v Northants
Leicester: Leics v Yorks
Taunton: Somerset v Glos
The Oval: Surry v Hants
Hove: Sussex v Essex
Worcester: Worcs v Lancs
*Other Match*
TBC: Glamorgan v Zimbabwe
(One day)
*Matches involving NWT Finalists to be
played on Tuesday 7 September.*

### Monday 6 September

*Bain Clarkson Trophy Final (One day)*
Scarborough: Joshua Tetley Festival
Trophy (Three days)

### Tuesday 7 September

Edgbaston: Warwicks v Zimbabwe
(One day)

### Wednesday 8 September

The Oval: Surrey v Zimbabwe
(Three days)

### Thursday 9 September

*Britannic Assurance Championship*
Derby: Derbys v Northants
Cardiff: Glam v Essex
Bristol: Glos v Notts
Southampton: Hants v Leics
Lord's: Middx v Lancs
Edgbaston: Warwicks v Somerset
Scarborough: Yorks v Sussex

### Friday 10 September

*Old Trafford: England Under-19 v
West Indies Under-19 (Third Youth
Test Match) (Four days)

### Saturday 11 September

Canterbury: Kent v Zimbabwe
(Three days)

### Sunday 12 September

*AXA Equity & Law League*
Derby: Derbys v Northants
Cardiff: Glam v Essex
Bristol: Glos v Notts
Southampton: Hants v Leics
Lord's: Middx v Lancs
Edgbaston: Warwicks v Somerset
Scarborough: Yorks v Sussex

### Thursday 16 September

*Britannic Assurance Championship*
Hartlepool: Durham v Somerset
Chelmsford: Essex v Hants
Canterbury: Kent v Glam
Old Trafford: Lancs v Northants
Leicester: Leics v Derbys
Trent Bridge: Notts v Warwicks
The Oval: Surrey v Yorks
Hove: Sussex v Glos
Worcester: Worcs v Middx

### Sunday 19 September

*AXA Equity & Law League*
Hartlepool: Durham v Somerset
Chelmsford: Essex v Hants
Canterbury: Kent v Glam
Old Trafford: Lancs v Northants
Leicester: Leics v Derbys
Trent Bridge: Notts v Warwicks
The Oval: Surrey v Yorks
Hove: Sussex v Glos
Worcester: Worcs v Middx

## RESULTS SUMMARY OF ALL TEST MATCHES
*continued from p 225:*

|  | Tests | Won | Lost | Drawn | Tied | Toss Won |
|---|---|---|---|---|---|---|
| England | 686 | 239 | 187 | 260 | – | 339 |
| Australia | 513 | 211 | 146 | 154 | 2 | 259 |
| South Africa | 173 | 38 | 78 | 57 | – | 81 |
| West Indies | 291 | 112 | 70 | 108 | 1 | 151 |
| New Zealand | 211 | 29 | 85 | 97 | – | 105 |
| India | 273 | 44 | 95 | 133 | 1 | 136 |
| Pakistan | 202 | 49 | 44 | 109 | – | 103 |
| Sri Lanka | 37 | 2 | 19 | 16 | – | 19 |

# SECOND XI FIXTURES 1993

Abbreviations:  (R)  Rapid Cricketline Championship (Three days)
                (BC) Bain Clarkson Trophy (One day)

**APRIL**

| Tue 20 | | The Oval | Surrey v England Under-19 (Four days) |
|---|---|---|---|
| Wed 28 | (R) | Derby | Derbyshire v Hampshire |
| | (R) | Old Trafford | Lancashire v Surrey |
| | (R) | Uxbridge | Middlesex v Gloucestershire |
| | (R) | Hove | Sussex v Durham |
| | (R) | Coventry & N Warwicks | Warwickshire v Nottinghamshire |
| | (R) | Worcester | Worcestershire v Leicestershire |

**MAY**

| Sun 2 | (R) | Bath | Somerset v Gloucestershire |
|---|---|---|---|
| Mon 3 | (R) | The Oval | Surrey v Kent |
| | (BC) | Edgbaston | Warwickshire v Northamptonshire |
| Tue 4 | (BC) | Ilkeston (Rutland Rec Ground) | Derbyshire v Leicestershire |
| | (BC) | Harrow | Middlesex v Sussex |
| | (BC) | Bingley | Yorkshire v Nottinghamshire |
| Wed 5 | (BC) | Ilkeston (Rutland Rec Ground) | Derbyshire v Warwickshire |
| | (R) | Cardiff | Glamorgan v Northamptonshire |
| | (R) | Bristol | Gloucestershire v Surrey |
| | (R) | Oakham | Leicestershire v Kent |
| | (R) | Harrow | Middlesex v Sussex |
| | (R) | Trent Bridge | Nottinghamshire v Worcestershire |
| | (R) | Headingley | Yorkshire v Essex |
| Mon 10 | (BC) | Bristol | Gloucestershire v Worcestershire |
| | (BC) | Southport | Lancashire v Yorkshire |
| | (BC) | Hinckley | Leicestershire v Durham |
| | (BC) | Southgate | MCC YCs v Middlesex |
| Tue 11 | (BC) | Chesterfield | Derbyshire v Durham |
| | (BC) | Newbury Park | Essex v Sussex |
| | (BC) | Southampton | Hampshire v Gloucestershire |
| | (BC) | Old Trafford | Lancashire v Somerset |
| | (BC) | Edgbaston | Warwickshire v Somerset |
| Wed 12 | (R) | Chesterfield | Derbyshire v Durham |
| | (R) | Chelmsford | Essex v Sussex |
| | (R) | Ammanford | Glamorgan v Nottinghamshire |
| | (R) | Southampton | Hampshire v Gloucestershire |
| | (R) | Maidstone | Kent v Warwickshire |
| | (R) | Old Trafford | Lancashire v Leicestershire |
| | (R) | Harrow | Middlesex v Northamptonshire |
| | (R) | Old Hill | Worcestershire v Somerset |
| Mon 17 | (BC) | Bristol | Gloucestershire v Somerset |
| | (BC) | Leicester | Leicestershire v Derbyshire |
| | (BC) | Lensbury | Middlesex v MCC YCs |
| | (BC) | Hove | Sussex v Kent |
| Tue 18 | (BC) | Cardiff | Glamorgan v Hampshire |
| | (BC) | Bristol | Gloucestershire v Warwickshire |
| | (BC) | Canterbury | Kent v Essex |
| | (BC) | Crosby (Northern) | Lancashire v Durham |
| | (BC) | Leicester | Leicestershire v Nottinghamshire |
| | (BC) | Northampton | Northamptonshire v Somerset |

| Wed 19 | (R) | Cardiff | Glamorgan v Hampshire |
|---|---|---|---|
| | (R) | Canterbury | Kent v Essex |
| | (R) | Leicester | Leicestershire v Nottinghamshire |
| | (R) | Northampton | Northamptonshire v Somerset |
| | (R) | Kidderminster | Worcestershire v Lancashire |
| | (R) | Headingley | Yorkshire v Middlesex |
| | | Stratford-on-Avon | Warwickshire v England Under-19 |
| | | | (Three days) |
| Mon 24 | (BC) | Portsmouth | Hampshire v Glamorgan |
| | (BC) | Farnsfield | Nottinghamshire v Derbyshire |
| | (BC) | Taunton | Somerset v Worcestershire |
| | (BC) | Solihull | Warwickshire v Gloucestershire |
| Tue 25 | (BC) | Chesterfield | Derbyshire v Yorkshire |
| | (BC) | Newbury Park | Essex v Middlesex |
| | (BC) | Bridgend | Glamorgan v Warwickshire |
| | (BC) | Eastbourne | Sussex v MCC YCs |
| Wed 26 | (R) | Heanor | Derbyshire v Leicestershire |
| | (R) | Colchester | Essex v Somerset |
| | (R) | Swansea | Glamorgan v Kent |
| | (R) | Portsmouth | Hampshire v Yorkshire |
| | (R) | Lensbury | Middlesex v Durham |
| | (R) | Oundle School | Northamptonshire v Worcestershire |
| | (R) | Walmley | Warwickshire v Lancashire |

**JUNE**

| Tue 1 | (BC) | Southampton | Hampshire v Worcestershire |
|---|---|---|---|
| | (BC) | Tunbridge Wells | Kent v Middlesex |
| | (BC) | Leicester | Leicestershire v Lancashire |
| | (BC) | Taunton | Somerset v Gloucestershire |
| Wed 2 | (R) | Felling | Durham v Surrey |
| | (R) | Swansea | Glamorgan v Yorkshire |
| | (R) | Harrow | Middlesex v Leicestershire |
| | (R) | Worthington Simpson | Nottinghamshire v Derbyshire |
| | (R) | Taunton | Somerset v Lancashire |
| | (R) | Hove | Sussex v Warwickshire |
| | | Canterbury | Kent v England Under-19 |
| | | | (Three days) |
| Mon 7 | (BC) | Durham City CC | Durham v Derbyshire |
| | (BC) | Shenley | Middlesex v Kent |
| | (BC) | Taunton | Somerset v Hampshire |
| Tue 8 | (BC) | Southend | Essex v Surrey |
| | (BC) | Finchampstead | Hampshire v Warwickshire |
| | (BC) | Sittingbourne (Gore Court) | Kent v Sussex |
| | (BC) | Bradford (Park Avenue) | Yorkshire v Derbyshire |
| Wed 9 | (R) | Southend | Essex v Warwickshire |
| | (R) | Pontymister | Glamorgan v Surrey |
| | (R) | Cheltenham (Dowty Arle Ct) | Gloucestershire v Worcestershire |
| | (R) | Sittingbourne (Gore Court) | Kent v Sussex |
| | (R) | Southport | Lancashire v Durham |
| | (R) | Leicester | Leicestershire v Hampshire |
| | (R) | Old Northamptonians | Northamptonshire v Nottinghamshire |
| | (R) | Harrogate | Yorkshire v Derbyshire |
| Mon 14 | (BC) | Merthyr Tydfil | Glamorgan v Northamptonshire |
| | (BC) | Maidstone | Kent v Surrey |
| | (BC) | Southgate | MCC YCs v Sussex |

| Tue 15 | (BC) Norton CC | Durham v Nottinghamshire |
| | (BC) Bristol | Gloucestershire v Northamptonshire |
| | (BC) Lewes Priory | Sussex v Essex |
| | (BC) Worcester | Worcestershire v Somerset |
| Wed 16 | (R) Shildon | Durham v Nottinghamshire |
| | (R) Chelmsford | Essex v Leicestershire |
| | (R) Bristol | Gloucestershire v Northamptonshire |
| | (R) Southampton | Hampshire v Kent |
| | (R) Uxbridge (RAF Vine Lane) | Middlesex v Glamorgan |
| | (R) The Oval | Surrey v Warwickshire |
| Mon 21 | (BC) Southampton | Hampshire v Northamptonshire |
| | (BC) Blackpool | Lancashire v Derbyshire |
| | (BC) Collingham | Nottinghamshire v Leicestershire |
| | (BC) Taunton | Somerset v Glamorgan |
| | (BC) Worcester | Worcestershire v Gloucestershire |
| Tue 22 | (BC) Southampton | Hampshire v Somerset |
| | (BC) Worksop College | Nottinghamshire v Yorkshire |
| | (BC) Oxted | Surrey v Essex |
| | (BC) Edgbaston | Warwickshire v Worcestershire |
| Wed 23 | (R) Abbotsholme S, Rocester | Derbyshire v Glamorgan |
| | (R) Old Trafford | Lancashire v Kent |
| | (R) Worksop CC | Nottinghamshire v Yorkshire |
| | (R) Taunton | Somerset v Durham |
| | (R) Oxted | Surrey v Essex |
| | (R) Worcester | Worcestershire v Sussex |
| Mon 28 | (BC) Worthington Simpson | Nottinghamshire v Durham |
| | (BC) Taunton | Somerset v Northamptonshire |
| | (BC) The Oval | Surrey v MCC YCs |
| | (BC) Worcester | Worcestershire v Warwickshire |
| Tue 29 | (BC) Knypersley | Derbyshire v Nottinghamshire |
| | (BC) Philadelphia CC | Durham v Leicestershire |
| | (BC) Wickford | Essex v MCC YCs |
| | (BC) Tring | Northamptonshire v Gloucestershire |
| | (BC) Hove | Sussex v Surrey |
| | (BC) Worcester | Worcestershire v Glamorgan |
| Wed 30 | (R) Derby | Derbyshire v Somerset |
| | (R) Chester-le-Street | Durham v Leicestershire |
| | (R) Old Trafford | Lancashire v Glamorgan |
| | (R) Uxbridge | Middlesex v Hampshire |
| | (R) Luton Town CC | Northamptonshire v Kent |
| | (R) Hove | Sussex v Surrey |
| | (R) Sheffield (Abbeydale Park) | Yorkshire v Warwickshire |

**JULY**

| Sat 3 | (R) Southampton | Hampshire v Nottinghamshire |
| Mon 5 | (BC) Durham School | Durham v Lancashire |
| | (BC) Bridgend | Glamorgan v Somerset |
| | (BC) Canterbury | Kent v MCC YCs |
| | (BC) Harrow | Middlesex v Essex |
| Tue 6 | (BC) Northampton | Northamptonshire v Hampshire |
| | (BC) Taunton | Somerset v Warwickshire |
| | (BC) Bingley | Yorkshire v Lancashire |
| Wed 7 | (R) Boldon CC | Durham v Glamorgan |
| | (R) Dartford | Kent v Worcestershire |
| | (R) Southgate | Middlesex v Nottinghamshire |
| | (R) Northampton | Northamptonshire v Essex |
| | (R) Taunton | Somerset v Sussex |

|          |      |                            |                                      |
|----------|------|----------------------------|--------------------------------------|
|          | (R)  | The Oval                   | Surrey v Derbyshire                  |
|          | (R)  | Todmorden                  | Yorkshire v Lancashire               |
| Fri 9    | (BC) | Bristol                    | Gloucestershire v Hampshire          |
| Sun 11   | (R)  | Taunton                    | Somerset v Hampshire                 |
| Mon 12   | (BC) | Wickford                   | Essex v Kent                         |
|          | (BC) | Cardiff                    | Glamorgan v Gloucestershire          |
|          | (BC) | Northampton                | Northamptonshire v Worcestershire    |
|          | (BC) | Trent Bridge               | Nottinghamshire v Lancashire         |
|          | (BC) | The Oval                   | Surrey v Sussex                      |
| Tue 13   | (BC) | Gloucester (King's School) | Gloucestershire v Glamorgan          |
|          | (BC) | Leicester                  | Leicestershire v Yorkshire           |
|          | (BC) | Southgate                  | MCC YCs v Essex                       |
|          | (BC) | Northampton                | Northamptonshire v Warwickshire      |
| Wed 14   | (R)  | Gloucester (King's School) | Gloucestershire v Kent               |
|          | (R)  | Leicester                  | Leicestershire v Glamorgan           |
|          | (R)  | Bedford School             | Northamptonshire v Derbyshire        |
|          | (R)  | The Oval                   | Surrey v Somerset                    |
|          | (R)  | Hove                       | Sussex v Hampshire                   |
|          | (R)  | Old Edwardians             | Warwickshire v Middlesex             |
|          | (R)  | Halesowen                  | Worcestershire v Essex               |
| Mon 19   | (BC) | Slough                     | MCC YCs v Surrey                      |
|          | (BC) | Hove                       | Sussex v Middlesex                   |
|          | (BC) | Coventry & N Warwicks      | Warwickshire v Glamorgan             |
|          | (BC) | Worcester                  | Worcestershire v Northamptonshire    |
|          | (BC) | Bradford (Park Avenue)     | Yorkshire v Leicestershire           |
| Tue 20   | (BC) | Leek                       | Derbyshire v Lancashire              |
|          | (BC) | Banbury CC                 | Northamptonshire v Glamorgan         |
|          | (BC) | Guildford                  | Surrey v Middlesex                   |
| Wed 21   | (R)  | Chesterfield               | Derbyshire v Lancashire              |
|          | (R)  | Seaton Carew               | Durham v Kent                        |
|          | (R)  | Bristol                    | Gloucestershire v Essex              |
|          | (R)  | Southampton                | Hampshire v Worcestershire           |
|          | (R)  | Wellingborough School      | Northamptonshire v Yorkshire         |
|          | (R)  | Trent Bridge               | Nottinghamshire v Somerset           |
|          | (R)  | The Oval                   | Surrey v Middlesex                   |
|          | (R)  | Nuneaton (Griff & Coton)   | Warwickshire v Leicestershire        |
| Mon 26   | (BC) | Bishop Auckland            | Durham v Yorkshire                   |
|          | (BC) | Slough                     | MCC YCs v Kent                        |
|          | (BC) | Harrow                     | Middlesex v Surrey                   |
|          | (BC) | Ombersley                  | Worcestershire v Hampshire           |
| Tue 27   | (BC) | Panteg                     | Glamorgan v Worcestershire           |
|          | (BC) | Wigan                      | Lancashire v Nottinghamshire         |
|          | (BC) | Knowle & Dorridge          | Warwickshire v Hampshire             |
|          | (BC) | Marske-by-Sea              | Yorkshire v Durham                   |
| Wed 28   | (R)  | Cardiff                    | Glamorgan v Gloucestershire          |
|          | (R)  | Folkestone                 | Kent v Derbyshire                    |
|          | (R)  | Leicester                  | Leicestershire v Surrey              |
|          | (R)  | Shireoaks (Steetley)       | Nottinghamshire v Essex              |
|          | (R)  | Horsham                    | Sussex v Northamptonshire            |
|          | (R)  | Leamington Spa             | Warwickshire v Hampshire             |
|          | (R)  | Worcester                  | Worcestershire v Middlesex           |
|          | (R)  | Marske-by-Sea              | Yorkshire v Durham                   |

**AUGUST**

|          |      |             |                                      |
|----------|------|-------------|--------------------------------------|
| Tue 3    | (R)  | Southampton | Hampshire v Northamptonshire         |
|          |      | Hove        | Sussex v England Under-19            |
|          |      |             | (One day)                            |

| Wed 4 | (R) | Chelmsford | Essex v Middlesex |
| | (R) | Bristol | Gloucestershire v Derbyshire |
| | (R) | Maidstone | Kent v Somerset |
| | (R) | Old Trafford | Lancashire v Nottinghamshire |
| | (R) | The Oval | Surrey v Yorkshire |
| | (R) | Horsham | Sussex v Leicestershire |
| | (R) | Moseley | Warwickshire v Glamorgan |
| | (R) | Barnt Green | Worcestershire v Durham |
| Wed 11 | (R) | Sunderland CC | Durham v Northamptonshire |
| | (R) | Southend | Essex v Derbyshire |
| | (R) | Usk | Glamorgan v Worcestershire |
| | (R) | Blackpool | Lancashire v Hampshire |
| | (R) | Worksop College | Nottinghamshire v Surrey |
| | (R) | Clevedon | Somerset v Leicestershire |
| | (R) | Studley | Warwickshire v Gloucestershire |
| | (R) | Elland | Yorkshire v Sussex |
| Sun 15 | (R) | South Shields | Durham v Gloucestershire |
| Mon 16 | (BC) | | Bain Clarkson Trophy Semi-Finals |
| or Tue 17 | | | |
| Wed 18 | (R) | Chelmsford | Essex v Lancashire |
| | (R) | Hinckley | Leicestershire v Gloucestershire |
| | (R) | Northampton | Northamptonshire v Surrey |
| | (R) | Trent Bridge | Nottinghamshire v Kent |
| | (R) | Taunton | Somerset v Middlesex |
| | (R) | Hove | Sussex v Glamorgan |
| | (R) | Edgbaston | Warwickshire v Durham |
| | (R) | York | Yorkshire v Worcestershire |
| Wed 25 | (R) | Derby | Derbyshire v Middlesex |
| | (R) | Bristol | Gloucestershire v Nottinghamshire |
| | (R) | Southampton | Hampshire v Essex |
| | (R) | Folkestone | Kent v Yorkshire |
| | (R) | Kibworth | Leicestershire v Northamptonshire |
| | (R) | Taunton | Somerset v Glamorgan |
| | (R) | Eastbourne | Sussex v Lancashire |
| | (R) | Worcester | Worcestershire v Warwickshire |

**SEPTEMBER**

| Wed 1 | (R) | Colchester | Essex v Durham |
| | (R) | Basingstoke | Hampshire v Surrey |
| | (R) | Eltham (British Gas plc) | Kent v Middlesex |
| | (R) | Old Trafford | Lancashire v Gloucestershire |
| | (R) | Trent Bridge | Nottinghamshire v Sussex |
| | (R) | Edgbaston | Warwickshire v Northamptonshire |
| | (R) | Bradford (Park Avenue) | Yorkshire v Somerset |
| Mon 6 | (BC) | | Bain Clarkson Trophy Final |
| | | | (Reserve Day Tuesday 7) |
| Wed 8 | (R) | Boldon CC | Durham v Hampshire |
| | (R) | Chelmsford | Essex v Glamorgan |
| | (R) | Leicester | Leicestershire v Yorkshire |
| | (R) | Uxbridge (RAF Vine Lane) | Middlesex v Lancashire |
| | (R) | Taunton | Somerset v Warwickshire |
| | (R) | Banstead | Surrey v Kent |
| | (R) | Hove | Sussex v Gloucestershire |
| | (R) | Worcester | Worcestershire v Derbyshire |
| Wed 15 | (R) | Chesterfield | Derbyshire v Sussex |
| | (R) | Bristol | Gloucestershire v Yorkshire |
| | (R) | Crosby (Northern) | Lancashire v Northamptonshire |
| | (R) | Banstead | Surrey v Worcestershire |

# MINOR COUNTIES FIXTURES 1993

**APRIL**

| | | |
|---|---|---|
| | | *Benson & Hedges Cup* |
| Tue 27 | Hartlepool | Durham v Minor Counties |

**MAY**

| | | |
|---|---|---|
| Tue 11 | Jesmond | Hampshire or Combined Universities v Minor Counties |
| | | *Holt Cup Preliminary Round* |
| Sun 23 | Lakenham | Norfolk v Bedfordshire |
| | Bury St Edmunds | Suffolk v Cambridgeshire |
| | Bishop's Stortford | Hertfordshire v Berkshire |
| | Chesham | Buckinghamshire v Oxfordshire |
| | | *Championship* |
| Sun 30 | Sleaford | (E) Lincolnshire v Hertfordshire |
| | Jesmond | (E) Northumberland v Bedfordshire |
| | Pressed Steel | (W) Oxfordshire v Shropshire |
| | Ebbw Vale | (W) Wales v Herefordshire |
| | Westbury | (W) Wiltshire v Devon |

**JUNE**

| | | |
|---|---|---|
| Tue 1 | Kidmore End | (W) Berkshire v Shropshire |
| | Aylesbury | (E) Buckinghamshire v Staffordshire |
| | Barrow | (E) Cumberland v Bedfordshire |
| | framlingham | (E) Suffolk v Hertfordshire |
| Wed 2 | Wisbech | (E) Cambridgeshire v Norfolk |
| | | *Holt Cup First Round* |
| Sun 6 | Lakenham | Norfolk or Bedfordshire |
| | or Bedford School | v Suffolk or Cambridgeshire |
| | Shenley Park | Hertfordshire or Berkshire |
| | or Maidenhead & Bray | v Buckinghamshire or Oxfordshire |
| | Hereford City | Herefordshire v Staffordshire |
| | Usk | Wales v Shropshire |
| | Sherborne | Dorset v Devon |
| | Trowbridge | Wiltshire v Cornwall |
| | Jesmond | Northumberland v Lincolnshire |
| | Warrington | Cheshire v Cumberland |
| | | *Friendly Match* |
| Wed 9 | Marlow | NAYC v Minor Counties XI |
| | | *Championship* |
| Sun 13 | Henlow | (E) Bedfordshire v Suffolk |
| | Carlisle | (E) Cumberland v Lincolnshire |
| | Sherborne | (W) Dorset v Wales |
| | St Albans | (E) Hertfordshire v Northumberland |
| | Christ Church | (W) Oxfordshire v Berkshire |
| Mon 14 | Stalybridge | (W) Cheshire v Cornwall |
| Tue 15 | Beaconsfield | (E) Buckinghamshire v Northumberland |
| | Brewood | (E) Staffordshire v Cambridgeshire |
| Wed 16 | Bridgnorth | (W) Shropshire v Cornwall |
| Thu 17 | Weymouth | (W) Dorset v Herefordshire |
| Sun 20 | | *Holt Cup Quarter-Finals* |
| | | *Championship* |
| Sun 27 | Leighton Buzzard | (E) Bedfordshire v Buckinghamshire |
| | Dorchester | (W) Dorset v Devon |
| | Jesmond | (E) Northumberland v Lincolnshire |

| | | |
|---|---|---|
| Sun 27 | Challow & Chidrey | (W) Oxfordshire v Wiltshire |
| | Wellington | (W) Shropshire v Cheshire |
| | Pontardulais | (W) Wales v Berkshire |
| Mon 28 | Radlett | (E) Hertfordshire v Staffordshire |
| Tue 29 | Colwall | (W) Herefordshire v Cheshire |
| Wed 30 | Ransome's | (E) Suffolk v Cambridgeshire |

**JULY**

| | | |
|---|---|---|
| Sun 4 | | *Holt Cup Semi-Finals* |
| | | *Championship* |
| Sun 4 | Burghley Park | *(E) Lincolnshire v Buckinghamshire |
| Mon 5 | Lakenham | (E) Norfolk v Cumberland |
| Wed 7 | Bury St Edmunds | (E) Suffolk v Cumberland |
| | | *Representative Match* |
| Thu 8 | Stone | Minor Counties v Australians (One day) |
| | | *Championship* |
| Thu 8 | Marlborough | (W) Wiltshire v Herefordshire |
| Sun 11 | Bedford Town | (E) Bedfordshire v Lincolnshire |
| | Canford | (W) Dorset v Cornwall |
| | Hereford City | (W) Herefordshire v Oxfordshire |
| | Colwyn Bay | (W) Wales v Cheshire |
| Mon 12 | Fenner's | (E) Cambridgeshire v Hertfordshire |
| Tue 13 | Wolverhampton | (E) Staffordshire v Northumberland |
| | Trowbridge | (W) Wiltshire v Cornwall |
| Sun 18 | Falmouth | (W) Cornwall v Wales |
| | Hertford | (E) Hertfordshire v Cumberland |
| | Cleethorpes | (E) Lincolnshire v Norfolk |
| | St Edward's School | (W) Oxfordshire v Dorset |
| | Shifnal | (W) Shropshire v Devon |
| Tue 20 | Luton | (E) Bedfordshire v Staffordshire |
| | Marlow | (E) Buckinghamshire v Cumberland |
| | Bowdon | (W) Cheshire v Devon |
| | Jesmond | (E) Northumberland v Norfolk |
| Sun 25 | Truro | (W) Cornwall v Berkshire |
| | Leominster | (W) Herefordshire v Shropshire |
| | Jesmond | (E) Northumberland v Cambridgeshire |
| | Meir Heath | (E) Staffordshire v Lincolnshire |
| | Copdock C.C. | (E) Suffolk v Buckinghamshire |
| Tue 27 | Netherfield | (E) Cumberland v Cambridgeshire |
| | Torquay | (W) Devon v Berkshire |
| | Lakenham | (E) Norfolk v Buckinghamshire |
| | Trowbridge | (W) Wiltshire v Shropshire |
| Thu 29 | Lakenham | (E) Norfolk v Suffolk |

**AUGUST**

| | | |
|---|---|---|
| Sun 1 | Millom | (E) Cumberland v Northumberland |
| | St Albans | (E) Hertfordshire v Bedfordshire |
| | Banbury C.C. | (W) Oxfordshire v Cheshire |
| | Swansea | (W) Wales v Wiltshire |
| Mon 2 | Lakenham | (E) Norfolk v Staffordshire |
| Tue 3 | Reading | (W) Berkshire v Cheshire |
| Wed 4 | March | (E) Cambridgeshire v Lincolnshire |
| | Mildenhall | (E) Suffolk v Staffordshire |
| Thu 5 | Lakenham | (E) Norfolk v Bedfordshire |
| Sun 8 | Finchampstead | (W) Berkshire v Wiltshire |
| | Slough | (E) Buckinghamshire v Cambridgeshire |

| | | |
|---|---|---|
| Sun 8 | Shrewsbury | (W) Shropshire v Dorset |
| | Northop Hall | (W) Wales v Oxfordshire |
| Tue 10 | Boughton Hall | (W) Cheshire v Dorset |
| Sun 15 | Falkland C.C. | (W) Berkshire v Dorset |
| | St Austell | (W) Cornwall v Oxfordshire |
| | Exmouth | (W) Devon v Herefordshire |
| | Lincoln Lindum | (E) Lincolnshire v Suffolk |
| | Leek | (E) Staffordshire v Cumberland |
| Mon 16 | Hertford | (E) Hertfordshire v Norfolk |
| Tue 17 | Camborne | (W) Cornwall v Herefordshire |
| | Bovey Tracey | (W) Devon v Oxfordshire |
| | Jesmond | (E) Northumberland v Suffolk |
| Wed 18 | Fenner's | (E) Cambridgeshire v Bedfordshire |
| Sun 22 | Neston | (W) Cheshire v Wiltshire |
| | Sidmouth | (W) Devon v Cornwall |
| | Oswestry | (W) Shropshire v Wales |
| Wed 25 | Lord's | *Holt Cup Final* |
| | | (Reserve day Thu 26 August) |
| | | *Championship* |
| Sun 29 | Amersham | (E) Buckinghamshire v Hertfordshire |
| | Instow | (W) Devon v Wales |
| | Weymouth | (W) Dorset v Wiltshire |
| | Brockhampton | (W) Herefordshire v Berkshire |

**SEPTEMBER**

| | | |
|---|---|---|
| Sun 12 | Worcester | *Championship Final* |

\* *Indicates possible clash with Holt Cup Round.*

# ICC TOURS PROGRAMME

(Full Member Countries)

**1992-93**
Mar/May  Pakistan to West Indies

**1993**
May/Aug  Australia to England

**1993-94**
Jul/Aug  India to Sri Lanka
Aug/Sep  South Africa to Sri Lanka
Oct/Nov  West Indies to Sri Lanka\*
Nov  South Africa/Sri Lanka to India
Nov/Jan  New Zealand to Australia
Nov/Feb  South Africa to Australia
Nov/Jan  India to Pakistan
Feb/Apr  England to West Indies
Feb/Mar  Australia to South Africa
Feb/Mar  India to Sri Lanka
Feb/Mar  Pakistan to New Zealand
Mar/Apr  Australia to Pakistan\*

**1994**
May/Jul  New Zealand to England
Jun/Aug  South Africa to England

**1994-95**
Jul/Aug  Pakistan to Sri Lanka
Oct/Feb  England to Australia
Nov/Dec  West Indies to India
Nov/Dec  New Zealand to South Africa
Jan/Feb  South Africa to India\*
Jan/Mar  Pakistan to India\*
Feb/Mar  West Indies to New Zealand

\*Unconfirmed

Typeset by
J&L Composition Ltd, Filey, North Yorkshire

Printed and bound in Great Britain by
HarperCollins Manufacturing, Glasgow

HEADLINE BOOK PUBLISHING PLC
Headline House
79 Great Titchfield Street
London W1P 7FN